FROM JUBILEE TO HIP HOP

Readings in African American Music

FROM JUBILEE TO HIP HOP

Readings in African American Music

Kip Lornell, Editor
The George Washington University

LONDON AND NEW YORK

First published 2010 by Pearson Education, Inc.

Published 2016 by Routledge
2 Park Square, Milton Park, Abingdon, Oxon OX14 4RN
711 Third Avenue, New York, NY 10017, USA

Routledge is an imprint of the Taylor & Francis Group, an informa business

Copyright © 2010 Taylor & Francis. All rights reserved.

All rights reserved. No part of this book may be reprinted or reproduced or utilised in any form or by any electronic, mechanical, or other means, now known or hereafter invented, including photocopying and recording, or in any information storage or retrieval system, without permission in writing from the publishers.

Notice:
Product or corporate names may be trademarks or registered trademarks, and are used only for identification and explanation without intent to infringe.

Credits and acknowledgments borrowed from other sources and reproduced, with permission, in this textbook appear on appropriate page within text.

ISBN: 9780136013228 (pbk)

Cover Design: Bruce Kenselaar

Library of Congress Cataloging-in-Publication Data
From jubilee to hip hop : readings in African American music / Kip Lornell, editor.
   p. cm.
 Includes bibliographical references and index.
 ISBN 0-13-601322-8
1. African Americans—Music—History and criticism. 2. Blues (Music)—History and criticism. 3. Jazz—History and criticism. I. Lornell, Kip
  ML3479.F76 2010
  780.89'96073—dc22

2009019083

CONTENTS

Preface vii

Introduction ix

Black American Music Since Reconstruction: An Overview xix

1. Adrift on Stormy Seas 1
   J. B. T. Marsh
2. Richards and Pringle's Original Georgia Minstrels and Billy Kersands, 1889–1895 6
   Lynn Abbott and Doug Seroff
3. The Virginia Jubilee Singers in Bourke, Australia 13
   Anonymous
4. African Banjo Echoes in Appalachia: A Conclusion 15
   Cecelia Conway
5. War on Ragtime and Suppression of "Ragtime" 23
   Anonymous
6. Of the Sorrow Songs 26
   W. E. B. Du Bois
7. The Nineteenth-Century Origins of Jazz 33
   Lawrence Gushee
8. Marshall Lullaby 51
   Kip Lornell and Charles Wolfe
9. The Scene and the Players in New York 63
   Thomas Riis
10. Jelly Roll Blues 75
    Jelly Roll Morton with Alan Lomax
11. William Marion Cook 80
    Cary B. Lewis
12. Ma Rainey and the Traveling Minstrels 85
    Charles Edward Smith
13. Black Sacred Harp Singing from Southeast Alabama 90
    Henry Willett
14. A Negro Explains "Jazz" 95
    Anonymous
15. Paul Robeson, Musician 98
    Doris Evans McGinty and Wayne Shirley
16. Conflict and Resolution in the Life of Thomas Andrew Dorsey 106
    Michael W. Harris
17. Fats Waller (Comedy Tonight) 123
    Gary Giddins

18 "Dean of Afro-American Composers" or "Harlem Renaissance Man": The New Negro and the Musical Poetics of William Grant Still   129
   Gayle Murchison

19 Easter Sunday   148
   Marian Anderson

20 Caldonia   154
   John Chilton

21 Elder Beck's Temple   166
   William Russell

22 T-Bone Blues: T-Bone Walker's Story in His Own Words   169
   T-Bone Walker

23 The Impact of Gospel Music on the Secular Music Industry   173
   Portia K. Maultsby

24 Singing in the Streets of Raleigh, 1963: Some Recollections   188
   Clyde R. Appleton

25 Motown Calls "The Rock & Roll Kid"   194
   Dennis Coffey

26 Respect: 1964–1965   201
   Rob Bowman

27 Clifton Chenier: "They Call Me the King"   221
   Ben Sandmel

28 The Art of the Muscle: Miles Davis as American Knight and American Knave   237
   Gerald Early

29 Evaluating Ellington   255
   Mark Tucker

30 The P-Funk Empire: Tear the Roof Off the Sucker   260
   Rickey Vincent

31 Hip-Hop, Puerto Ricans, and Ethnoracial Identities in New York   276
   Raquel Z. Rivera

32 Daughters of the Blues: Women, Race, and Class Representation in Rap Music Performance   297
   Cheryl L. Keyes

33 Media Interventions   314
   Maureen Mahon

34 Black Artistic Invisibility: A Black Composer Talking 'bout Taking Care of the Souls of Black Folks While Losing Much Ground Fast   333
   William Banfield

35 Stepping Out an African Heritage   342
   Elizabeth Fine

36 Rhythm and Bullshit? The Slow Decline of R&B   357
   Mark Anthony Neal

Credits   373

Index   376

PREFACE

Assembling a single-volume anthology of writings about the music created by African Americans since 1865 for an adult audience (ranging from the casual fan to college students taking an introductory American music course) is a daunting task, which is no doubt why none existed until now. I decided to take on this quixotic—some would argue impossibly ambitious—task despite the nearly 150 year time frame, the large number of important genres, the varied personalities, and the sheer complexity of African American musical culture.

Despite the fact that I limited my search to items published in English, the sheer number of books, articles, essays, liner notes, newspaper articles, and other writings on these topics remains truly overwhelming. *From Jubilee to Hip Hop: Readings in African American Music* includes 36 items that address topics ranging from the expected (gospel and hip hop) to the largely unknown (shape note singing and zydeco). Although none of these articles contain musically technical language or layers of academic jargon, articles by scholars such as Gerald Early or Portia Maultsby will no doubt challenge some readers who I think will ultimately benefit from the experience.

This book could not have reached its final form without the help of many people. Foremost is my understanding and sympathetic family: Kim, Cady, and Max, who gave me the space and time to complete this task. Several other folks, most notably Courtney Fitch, Graham Norwood, Maribeth Payne assisted greatly in moving this project forward through two earlier iterations. I also wish to thank Richard Carlin of Prentice Hall, who very quickly saw the need for this book and ultimately brought it to his house. I also wish to thank those who reviewed earlier versions of the manuscript for this book, some of whom commented on this project at several junctures, whose suggestions and criticisms improved this book at every step of the way. They challenged me to rethink some of my choices, asked me to expand the "Introduction," recommended articles that I had overlooked (several of which I ultimately used), and helped to shape this book in many subtle and significant ways. Those reviewers include Jerry Zolten, Penn State University, Altoona; Peter Loewen, Rice University; Frederick J. Taylor, Georgia State University; Yvonne P. Johnson, Delaware State University; Darhyl Ramsey, University of North Texas; Timothy Holley, North Carolina Central University; Daniel Avorgbedor, Ohio State University; Prudence Layne, Elon University; Peter Hollerbach, The City University of New York; Gerald H. Tolson, University of Louisville.

Finally, I am compelled to thank the musicians who have inspired me and so many others to listen to, research and write about twentieth-century black American music. Some of them, such as Sonny Boy Williamson, Lead Belly, Robert Johnson, and John Coltrane, have been with me for about 35 years while others, like D.C. go-go bands, such as Trouble Funk, E.U., and Rare Essence, have come to me more recently. Ultimately, *From Jubilee to Hip Hop: Readings in African American Music* would not exist without the music created by these innovative and talented musicians.

Kip Lornell
Department of Music
The George Washington University

INTRODUCTION

Lift Every Voice and Sing

Lift every voice and sing
Till earth and heaven ring,
Ring with the harmonies of Liberty;
Let our rejoicing rise
High as the listening skies,
Let it resound loud as the rolling sea.
Sing a song full of the faith that the dark past has taught us,
Sing a song full of the hope that the present has brought us,
Facing the rising sun of our new day begun
Let us march on till victory is won.

JAMES WELDON JOHNSON (ca. 1920)

This verse from poet, novelist, songwriter, and essayist James Weldon Johnson's famous song about hope, struggle, and community—sometimes referred to as the "Negro National Anthem"—underscores some of the themes that initially appeared in nineteenth-century spirituals and that can still be found in the songs of black Americans in the twenty-first century. These themes include perseverance and persistence in light of overwhelming odds as well as the importance of spirituality and the power of communal action.

Nonetheless, struggle is arguably the most fundamental theme in African American culture. For more than two centuries African Americans have struggled for freedom, for economic equality, for dignity, for respect, and for self-determination. Music of many types provides the most righteous, public, forceful, and potent voices (ranging from unknown slaves in the antebellum South to Kanye West's pointed comments about race and Hurricane Katrina in 2005) that speak both to other black Americans and to an increasing number of people across the entire globe.

The struggles of African Americans represent a core musical theme when black expressive culture began slowly emerging from the South in the decades following the Revolutionary War and that became more central to American culture with the close of the Civil War. If the Civil War significantly altered the soundscape of the Old South, emancipation utterly shattered it. Emancipation not only brought freedom (of a sort), it also slowly drew African American expressive culture into the mainstream. Music and popular culture in the United States have been utterly transformed as a result of this complex, sustained, and ongoing process.

Within five years after the first classes were held at Fisk University in Nashville, Tennessee, on January 9, 1866, its Jubilee Singers began bringing the music of former slaves to larger, increasingly multiracial audiences. At first, jubilee singers performed only in the United States, but by the 1890s they had brought their message of freedom and music to audiences as far afield as Australia. Jumping ahead to the first decade of the twenty-first century, it is clear that the myriad forms of hip hop have emerged as the planet's single most influential musical voice.

Johnson's inspirational words resonated when they were first written, especially with those black Americans with first-hand experience with slavery. They helped to carry men, women, and children through the less racially progressive period prior to the modern Civil Rights Movement that began in the mid-1950s and continue to hold meaning early in the twenty-first century. Many people—myself included—believe that more battles lie before us and that this struggle slowly and inexorably moves us toward becoming a country that truly offers equal opportunities for all its citizens.

WHAT IS AFRICAN AMERICAN MUSIC?

This seemingly simple question is critical because of the underlying issues that it implies and that are raised in this collection. Black American music not only encompasses genres like ragtime and gospel and important figures such as Ma Rainey and Miles Davis, it also includes notions of racial identity as well as cultural ownership and theft. In the twenty-first century, for example, relevant questions include: Who should be included in the history of hip-hop culture and who has the right to define its current boundaries? Because of the United States' particular history, these questions carry profound cultural, economic, social, and political baggage.

Moreover, the answer to "What is African American music" depends upon whom you ask and when you ask the question. Two greatly admired twentieth-century black American musical performers, born within two years of one another in North Carolina, would respond differently: The answer given by the eccentric funk genius George Clinton would certainly only at times intersect with that of gospel great Shirley Caesar. I am quite certain that a Puerto Rican American living in New York City today would have very different perspectives on the nature of African American music than my own cousins living in New Ulm, Minnesota. Similarly, the response to this question offered by a twenty-first-century college student would clearly differ greatly from that of her or his counterpart in the 1940s.

African American music is an overarching term given to a wide range of music and musical practices that emerged from or were influenced by the culture of black Americans who were originally brought to North America (largely from West and Sub-Saharan Africa) to work as slaves. The majority of enslaved blacks settled in the South, where they typically worked in agrarian situations ranging from large cotton plantations in the Mississippi Delta to small farms in the Carolina Piedmont. Once in the United States, they were gradually exposed to a wide range of European or European-derived musical genres. This contact and exposure resulted in the development of a wide range of musical genres ranging from nineteenth-century spirituals to contemporary jazz that combine African and European musical sensibilities.

The extent of African contributions to African American musical culture raises a long-standing debate, which was eloquently addressed by Melville Herskovits as long ago as the early 1940s in *The Myth of the Negro Past*. One realm of belief (now largely dismissed) is that the musical culture developed by black Americans was nothing more than poorly constructed attempts to imitate European-derived culture. Because they felt that it would break down resistance on the part of enslaved black Americans, white slave owners generally tried to destroy all traces of African culture as quickly as possible. Despite the efforts of slave owners, African-derived folk culture, religion, language, and musical culture remained an integral part of the lives of black Americans and were usually passed along by way of oral tradition and other informal means.

The first schools of higher education for black Americans were established immediately after Emancipation. Most of the first schools, such as Fisk University in Nashville and Hampton Institution (now Hampton University) in Tidewater Virginia, were located in the South. These schools eventually numbered over 100 and several dozen—including Kentucky State University, North Carolina Central University, and Prairie View A&M University in Texas—began with state support.

Such schools constituted the intellectual life for most black Americans seeking higher education well into the twentieth century as most "white" colleges didn't truly integrate until after the Civil Rights Movement. Historically black colleges and universities (HBCUs) usually offered students their initial exposure to the ideas and writings of W. E. B. DuBois or the music of a black composer such as Nathaniel Dett. Vernacular musical culture was also sometimes maintained through such formal organizations as "jubilee" singing groups or gospel "quartets" that often represented their school off-campus.

In the highly politically charged atmosphere of the decade beginning in the middle 1960s, members of the Black Power Movement and the Black Arts Movement built upon the works of John Hope Franklin, Melville Herskovits, and other scholars who carefully revisited and reshaped our thoughts on the importance and impact of African American cultural history. These younger scholars took a more militant Afro-centric perspective, theorizing and pronouncing that African American culture formed the most important basis for *all* contemporary American culture. This philosophy reflected not only the radical edge of the times, but also the sense of black nationalism that helped to propel writers/thinkers/ intellectuals such as Kwame Ture (Stokely Carmichael) and Arimi Biraka (Leroi Jones) into the public spotlight.

These movements helped to establish programs and departments of Black Studies or African American Studies in dozens of colleges and universities in the United States. By the 1970s the novels, short stories, and poems of African American writers had finally found their way into the curriculum of hundreds of English departments throughout the United States. Such changes in the typically staid world of scholars helped to establish the possibility that Latino Studies and Women's Studies also deserved a place at the academic table.

Another view, which generally holds sway today and seems most sensible to me, is that African American music and culture resulted from a decades-long process of acculturation and the synthesis of ideas and practices. In other words, African American culture blends African and European cultures, though not always in equal parts. Chris Waterman's fascinating essay, published in *Music and the Racial Imagination*, carefully examines the complex relationships among black songster Bo Chatman (née Carter), the song "Corinna, Corinna," the early record industry, and the racial reception/perception of this late-nineteenth-century American ballad. Jazz historians continue to wrestle with racial issues when, for example, they access the contributions of important white musicians such as Bix Beiderbecke, Benny Goodman, or Gil Evans. Even more significantly, American popular culture erupted in the middle 1950s when white and black musical worlds merged and rock 'n' roll emerged. In many subtle and broad ways these blends have resulted in contributions that are not only singular, but that have become central to many aspects of American expressive culture as well.

Since Reconstruction, almost all vernacular musics (from southern gospel to rock) that have developed in the United States contain some elements of African American performance practices, such as movement on stage and the use of call and response, which are underpinned by complex, syncopated rhythms. Rock 'n' roll and the subsequent rock-based genres that have emerged since the mid-1960s provide a shining example of these influences, but other earlier genres, such as western swing in the late 1930s, also bear the clear influence of African American music. More recently, the influence of music of the Carribean (most notably reggae and reggaeton) and the influx of new African immigrants, often from Mali or other west African countries, have reinvigorated and further complicated the ways that African American music has itself been impacted by other forms of black "world" music.

Contemporary black American music's influence is worldwide and profound. Within twenty-five years after Emancipation, jubilee singing groups had already toured the world. As early as the 1920s jazz musicians such as the New Orleans-bred reed man Sidney Bechet had found a more congenial home in Paris, where he entertained and influenced a generation of Europeans fascinated by this new music. During the three decades following World War II, rhythm and blues, soul, and Motown captured the imagination of music consumers across the United States and eventually throughout our increasingly shrinking world. The 1950s saw the first European tours by blues men like Big Bill (Broonzy) and Muddy Waters. Jazz artists as diverse as Duke Ellington and Louis Armstrong broadened their touring and were booked from Cairo to Tokyo, sometimes under the auspices of the United States Department of State. Since the early 1980s, hip hop has become a critical and influential part of the language of popular music not only from Portland, Maine, to Portland, Oregon, but also throughout the world.

Because African American music has became a worldwide phenomenon, contemporary black American vernacular music comes closest to being a musical global lingua franca. From blues to gospel to jazz to Motown to hip hop, music performed by Bessie Smith, Mahalia Jackson, John Coltrane, the Supremes, and Cam'ron is just as likely to be heard over an Internet radio station based in Seattle, Washington, as in a bar in Paris, France, or in a home in Tokyo, Japan. This trend has been a long time coming as the impact of African American music increased slowly throughout the twentieth century, but much more dramatically and rapidly since the 1960s.

As the number of writers exploring African American music has expanded, the musical genres and the musicians about which they write have also expanded. Magazine writers for both general and specialized audiences have covered a wide range of topics related to black American music since the twentieth century began. Today *VIBE* and *JazzTimes* are two of the scores of general-interest (nonscholarly) magazines devoted to African American musical culture that have found audiences not only in the United States, but across the globe as well. Plenty of writing and information about African American music can also be found online, but little of it approaches the depth and length found in magazines and books.

Academic scholars, however, generally took up the mantle much more slowly. Beginning with jazz in the 1930s, academic scholars have written theses, dissertations, brochure notes for sound recordings, journal articles, and books about African American music. Stalwart resistance to the serious study of American music in most colleges and universities persisted throughout the 1950s and very slowly began to melt in the 1960s as the academic world (primarily music departments) gradually opened its doors to a wider range of topics related to American and African American music. Since the 1970s, thankfully, the number of scholars paying serious attention to black music and musicians—though still relatively small—has increased dramatically.

Refreshingly, African American women have often taken a lead role in writing about black music. Eileen Southern's seminal *Music of Black Americans* first appeared in 1971 and reached a third edition before Professor Southern's death in 2002. Portia Maultsby's numerous studies of black popular music from World War II into the twenty-first century have been disseminated via many book chapters, journal articles, documentary radio series, and, most recently, a book (coedited with Indiana University colleague Melonee Burnim), *The Music of Black Americans: A History*. Before her untimely death, Irene V. Jackson edited an important volume, *More Than Dancing: Essays on Afro-American Music and Musicians*, which contained essays on varied sacred and secular topics rooted in the twentieth century by scholars including Horace Boyer, Doris McGinty, and Portia Maultsby.

The opportunities to publish well-researched, serious, and in-depth books about African American music have also dramatically increased over the past forty years. The lists of series such as *Music in American Life* (University of Illinois Press) and *American Made Music* (University Press of Mississippi) include dozens of books devoted to black music or musicians. Academically oriented journals such as *Black Perspectives in Music* (1973–1990) and *Black Music Research Journal* (1980–present) have devoted their pages to articles and reviews by both academic and nonacademic scholars.

This expansion naturally leads to a greater understanding about the depth, scope, diversity, and importance of African American music. Because of the long-standing interest in jazz, many books have been published about topics ranging from the development of bebop to the life of avant-garde futurist Sun Ra. Duke Ellington, widely acknowledged as one of the twentieth century's most important composers, has been the subject of a half-dozen biographies and thousands of newspaper and magazine articles. Since the mid-1920s, Ellington's music has been available on formats ranging from 78-rpm records to compact discs. Ellington's music inspired the formation of the Duke Ellington Society, which has been devoted to studying his life and music since 1955.

In strong contrast to the works on Duke Ellington (and jazz generally) over many years, a far smaller number of articles and books have been written about more regional musical genres such as zydeco—an Afro-French form of creolized musical culture that pervades the small towns and rural areas of southwestern Louisiana and southeastern Texas. Efforts to document and promote zydeco music mean that anyone interested in the musical culture that spawned Amédé Ardoin, Buckwheat Zydeco, Rockin' Dupsee, and Clifton Chenier can now explore this music by way of films, and records and in print. The music itself is increasingly accessible to more people than the folks living in the swamps and prairies that lie between Lafayette, Louisiana, and Houston, Texas, by way of zydeco music festivals and music clubs booking zydeco bands that have sprung up throughout the United States.

Part of this book's purpose is to expose more people to the diversity of post–Civil War African American music. Those expecting to find articles about jazz and jazz musicians will not be disappointed; writings about hip hop and gospel are also part of this anthology. But I have also included more obscure genres, such as sacred harp singing, and steppin', in order to familiarize more people with the diversity of African American music that is often misunderstood or all but overlooked by the mainstream media.

"R-E-S-P-E-C-T": AFRICAN AMERICAN MUSIC'S IMPACT IN THE TWENTY-FIRST CENTURY

Although everyday folks have appreciated and consumed African American music for decades, some of our most powerful educational, corporate, and governmental officials are finally stepping forward to acknowledge the power and influence of African American music in interesting and unprecedented ways. Three recent examples not only provide "official" recognition of black American music's importance; they also hold powerful symbolic value. Suddenly, it would seem, African American music is not only acceptable, but also downright respectable! With hip hop so firmly entrenched in popular culture, perhaps leading institutions are finally following the will of the people.

Perhaps most surprising is Harvard University, which had little, if anything, to do with any type of twentieth-century American music prior to the 1990s. But on April 13, 2000, a Harvard University press release declared

> Afro-American Studies Department Chair Henry Louis Gates Jr. announced Friday the creation of the first endowed professorship in African-American music at Harvard and possibly in the nation. The chair, created with a $3 million gift from media giant Time Warner Inc., is named for celebrated African merican jazz performer, actor, and producer Quincy Delight Jones Jr. The chair's official name is the "Quincy Jones Professorship of African-American Music, Supported by the Time Warner Endowment." . . . At a news conference before the dinner where the new professorship was announced, [Jones] added that he believed the giants of African American music, such as jazz great Louis Armstrong, would one day be counted alongside such giants of classical music as Brahms, Beethoven, and Bach. "Blues, jazz, spiritual, gospel . . . will be the classical music of this country," Jones said.

This Harvard chair is currently held by Professor Ingrid Monson, a specialist in jazz, African American music, and music of the African diaspora. She adds greatly to the diversity of the university's once entirely Euro-centric department of music.

Because the commodification of African American music has so handsomely rewarded a multinational corporation such as Time Warner, its public support of these musics is understandable and, in many ways, appropriate. But corporate America doesn't always get it right. The Miller Brewing Company had to furiously backpeddle in August 2004 when its commemorative can series honoring the first half-century of rock 'n' roll failed to include any African American artists. Their August 28, 2004, press release states, in part,

> Miller Brewing Company sincerely apologizes to the African-American community, to music fans and to our valued consumers for this occurrence. African Americans obviously have played a formative role in the development of rock 'n' roll, and despite our efforts, we did not manage this component of the promotion appropriately. The commemorative cans promotion was one part of a multi-pronged campaign, executed in partnership with *Rolling Stone* magazine, which includes several events and promotional activities that prominently and proudly feature African-American music artists. . . . By making the public fully aware of the breadth of our plan, which does include tributes to black music artists, Miller Brewing Company reaffirms its ongoing commitment to the contributions of African-Americans to American culture.

Virgis Colbert, Miller's executive vice president of worldwide operations, further stated: "We took a hard look at the situation and realize where we fell short. You can count on Miller to step up."

Ironically, even the White House (the nexus of the "Terrordome" that Public Enemy had decried a mere decade before) publicly recognized the power and importance of African American music. In a carefully worded, generally accurate, and direct statement, President George W. Bush declared June 2002 to be "Black Music Month." I view it as a well-meaning, somewhat gratuitous (albeit welcome) gesture. Even though I teach at a university located a mere six blocks from the White House and consider myself to be acutely attuned to important events related to contemporary African American music, I noticed that this proclamation didn't cause a ripple on the streets of Washington, D.C.

May 31, 2002
By the President of the United States of America
A Proclamation

America's diverse and extraordinary musical heritage reflects the remarkable cultural and artistic history of our Nation. From gospel, blues, and jazz to rock and roll, rap, and hip-hop, our Nation's musical landscape offers an astounding array of uniquely American styles. During Black Music Month, we celebrate a critically important part of this heritage by highlighting the enduring legacy of African American musicians, singers, and composers, and urging every American to appreciate and enjoy the fabulous achievements of this highly creative community.

Early forms of black American music developed out of the work song, which had its roots in African tribal chants. Through this music, slaves shared stories, preserved history, and established a sense of community. As many African slaves in early America became Christians, they adapted their music into the songs and life of the church. These spirituals eventually evolved into a genre that remains vibrant and very meaningful today—gospel music. This great musical tradition developed under the leadership of people like Thomas Dorsey, who was known as the Father of Gospel Music. He composed many great gospel songs that have become standards, and he established the tradition of the gospel music concert.

Following emancipation, African Americans enjoyed unprecedented opportunities but also faced many new and frequently oppressive challenges. Frustrations from these struggles for freedom and equality found expression in a style of music that came to be known as the blues. Innovative musical geniuses like W. C. Handy, Robert Johnson, the Reverend Gary Davis, and Mamie Smith were among the legendary pioneers of blues music.

As blacks migrated throughout the United States in the early 1900s, they tapped into their collective experience and creativity to develop new expressions of music. New Orleans became the center for a particularly American form of music—jazz. This novel genre combined unique rhythms and melodies with the sounds of stringed, brass, and woodwind instruments. Jazz captured the interest of 20th century America, making household names of great African American artists like Louis Armstrong, Charlie Parker, Ella Fitzgerald, and Miles Davis. The unparalleled brilliance of these and other great jazz musicians had an extraordinary effect upon the American musical tradition, while bringing great pleasure to millions of fans.

In the 1940s, rhythm and blues emerged, synthesizing elements from gospel, blues, and jazz; and from these styles came the birth of rock and roll. A fabulous array of artists helped to pioneer this modem musical transformation, including Chuck Berry, Ray Charles, Marvin Gaye, Aretha Franklin, and Stevie Wonder.

As we reflect on the rich and distinctive history of so many talented artists, we celebrate the incredible contributions that black musicians have made to the history of American music and their influence on countless forms of music around the world.

Now, Therefore, I, George W. Bush, President of the United States of America, by virtue of the authority vested in me by the Constitution and laws of the United States, do hereby proclaim June 2002 as Black Music Month. I call on Americans of all backgrounds to learn more about the rich heritage of black music and how it has shaped our culture and our way of life, and urge them to take the opportunity to enjoy the great musical experiences available through the contributions of African American music.

In Witness Whereof, I have hereunto set my hand this thirty-first day of May, in the year of our Lord two thousand two, and of the Independence of the United States of America the two hundred and twenty-sixth.

George W. Bush
Filed with the Office of the Federal Register, 8:45 a.m., June 4, 2002

SCOPE AND ALLIED WORKS

From Jubilee to Hip Hop: Readings in African American Music consists of 36 selections that underscore the breath and variety of African American musical culture. Whether it is Marian Anderson's recollection of the legendary 1939 Daughters of the American Revolution (D.A.R.) Constitution Hall debacle or John Chilton's story of the impact of Louis Jordan's song "Caldonia," each of these selections relates something notable and interesting about the African American musical culture since Emancipation.

In many important, though sometimes subtle, regards, the selections included in this anthology underscore the surprising continuity and sense of the past that inform the various post-Reconstruction black American musical genres. In my class about black American music at the George Washington University—"Musical Cultures of Black Americans"—I emphasize the musical, historical, and cultural relationships between hip hop and other black traditions, in particular Pentecostal church services. Students are usually blasé and even quite skeptical when I initially suggest these relationships exist.

However, through a combination of readings, such as "The Impact of Gospel Music on the Secular Music Industry" by Portia Maultsby, students rethink their own experiences while consuming hip hop, as well as directed listening and video material and gradually understand the strong ties between seemingly unrelated musical cultures. I further emphasize how the use of call and response, the blurring of lines between performer and audience, and a strong sense of community are performance practices found not only in Pentecostal church services and hip hop concerts, but also at a local go-go performance in Washington, D.C., as well as a contemporary fife and drum band picnic in rural northeastern Mississippi.

The fifth piece in *From Jubilee to Hip Hop*, "War on Ragtime" (from the *American Musician*, July 1901), discusses the controversies surrounding a genre of music that had developed during the 1890s and whose popularity was viewed with alarm by some musicians who decried its lack of redeeming content. The author quotes the president of the American Federation of Musicians: "The ragtime craze has lowered the standard of American music as compared with other countries. We have duty as well as business to look after, and we will not give way to a popular demand that is degrading." Similar sentiments resonated throughout the twentieth century and similar comments have been applied most recently to rap when it developed in the late 1970s and then blossomed into hip hop during the following twenty years.

Black American music has often found itself in the midst of controversy. Whether it is ragtime's "senseless jumble of words and notes" at the turn of the century or Kanye West's infamous "George Bush doesn't care about black people" nationally televised comment during a benefit concert for Hurricane Katrina relief on NBC, black American music has often found itself in the middle of a struggle for recognition and understanding. The world that influenced and produced black American music changed so profoundly during the twentieth century that one can only imagine what ragtime pioneer Scott Joplin would think about Talib Kweli, Dilated Peoples, or Ludacris.

The inclusion of articles and essays about the regionalized, less commercially viable genres reflects my own fascination with music that exists (and sometimes flourishes) outside of the national electronic and print media's spotlight. I believe that most people will be unfamiliar with the African American shape note singing tradition, which can be heard only in the Deep South, most notably in east Texas and south central Alabama. Hank Willett's article focuses on the tradition in Alabama in the late twentieth century. One can only draw the conclusion that black shape note singing is not thriving and is likely to soon disappear from our musical landscape.

On the other hand, the funky swamp sounds of the Louisiana-based zydeco music will almost certainly garner adherents as more people hear it. Zydeco has slowly gained nationwide interest since the

1970s following its "discovering" by an increasingly large multiracial mix of dancers and music fans. Ben Sandmel's article about Clifton Chenier is included because of both Chenier's stature as the founder of modern zydeco and the author's engaging and sensitive portrait of the music and the man.

Inevitably and regrettably, I was unable to use all the articles that I would have liked. Aside from being limited to one large volume, the control of some desirable pieces, especially from small, defunct presses, proved to be impossible to pin down. A small number of topical essays or book chapters were excluded simply because they were unobtainable due to cost. Other solid and interesting articles have already been reprinted recently and on numerous occasions. For example, "Puerto Rocks: New York Ricans State Their Claim," a study that examines the relationships between Puerto Rican and African American musical cultures in the early development of hip hop by sociologist Juan Flores, is presently in print (in one form or another) in three different books.

In another instance, Timothy Brooks and I went around in circles for several months strategizing the various ways to pare down his landmark piece about George Johnson, the first black American recording artist. This lengthy article was initially part of *Lost Sounds* (University of Illinois Press 2004), Brooks's important book about the pioneering black recording artists of the late nineteenth and early twentieth centuries. In the end, neither of us could think of what could be excised and still relate this complex and compelling story, so we gave up. Had "George W. Johnson, the First Black Recording Artist" been included, this article alone would have taken up approximately one-fourth of the entire book!

Like all other scholars of African American music, I am deeply indebted to the pioneering work of Eileen Southern. In 1987, she published *Readings in Black American Music* as an adjunct to her highly regarded *The Music of Black Americans: A History*. Because Southern emphasizes the eighteenth and nineteenth centuries and I focus on the post–Civil War era (primarily the twentieth century), these two readers, taken together, provide an overview of nearly three centuries of African American music history.

Since 2000, the publication of American music readers of all types has proliferated. These readers encompass a wide range of topics, but most of them examine popular and folk-based music. Some focus on an individual—*The Bill Monroe Reader*, edited by Tom Ewing (University of Illinois Press, 2000)—or a specific group—*The Grateful Dead Reader*, edited by David Dodd and Diana Spaulding (Oxford University Press, 2000). Others take on a single genre, *The Sound and the Fury: 40 Years of Classic Rock Journalism: A Rock's Backpages Reader*, edited by Barney Hoskyns (Bloomsbury USA, 2003), while *The Pop, Rock, and Soul Reader: Histories and Debates*, edited by David Brackett (Oxford University Press, 2004) cuts a very wide swath, but inevitably includes a large African American component.

Thankfully, well-organized readers devoted to individual genres of black music or individual black artists are becoming more widespread. Jazz is particularly well served by readers. Mark Tucker's *The Duke Ellington Reader* (Oxford University Press, 1993), Rob Walser's *Keeping Time: Readings in Jazz History* (Oxford University Press, 1999), Rob van der Blick's *The Thelonious Monk Reader* (Oxford University Press, 2001), and *Riffs & Choruses: A New Jazz Anthology*, edited by Andrew Clark (Continuum, 2001) are all highly recommended. The blues is the focus of *Write Me a Few of Your Lines: A Blues Reader*, edited by Steve Tracy (University of Massachusetts Press, 2000) and *Ramblin' on My Mind: New Perspectives on the Blues*, edited by David Evans (University of Illinois Press, 2008). Hip hop, not surprisingly has spawned several well-crafted readers, most notably *That's the Joint: The Hip-Hop Studies Reader*, edited by Murray Forman and Mark Anthony Neal (Routledge, 2004) and Raquel Capeda's *And It Don't Stop: The Best American Hip-Hop Journalism of the Last 25 Years* (Faber & Faber, 2004). Religious music finally has its first reader, *Readings in African American Church Music and Worship*, edited by James Abbington (GIA Publications 2002).

ORGANIZATION

The organization of a reader is always a critical issue and I have eschewed the approach of grouping these pieces by genre, a form which comes with its own set of problems and contradictions, or a rigid "decade-by-decade" scheme. I considered a thematic approach and dropped that form, too. While each of these approaches has its virtues, they are in many ways too problematic, overly programmatic, and simply do not work well in light of the complexities of twentieth-century African American music. For example, should an article about Fats Waller be classified in a section entitled "Jazz," "Composers," or the "1930s"? What about the problems inherent as pigeonholing an artist as eclectic as Clifton Chenier? He's clearly not a blues, jazz, gospel, or hip hop artist, and except for zydeco, what easy tag does one attribute to Mr. Chenier?

Instead, I arranged these selections in roughly chronological order. They unfold in the same way that most college courses devoted to African American music are structured. The range of articles also invites *From Jubilee to Hip Hop* readers not only to revisit their favorite genre or artist but also to explore an unfamiliar topic.

The opening piece, a chapter from the first book about the Fisk University Jubilee Singers that was initially published in 1881, underscores the fact that African American music slowly began to reach a wider, multiracial audience soon after 1865. Near the end of the book, the selection about the steppin' tradition underscores the worldwide implications for black American musical culture in the early twenty-first century. In addition to these pieces are 34 writings that initially appeared in scholarly books and journals, a weekly newspaper, a newsletter, and newspapers. The topics, which range from the role of black composers in the late twentieth century, the recollections of jazz pioneer Jelly Roll Morton, music and the Civil Rights Movement, to the importance of Louis Jordan's "Caldonia," are equally varied. These articles, most of which were written by music journalists and academics, further underscore the complexities—as well as the variety—of music that come under the ever-expanding "African American music" rubric.

Kip Lornell

BLACK AMERICAN MUSIC SINCE RECONSTRUCTION: AN OVERVIEW

INTRODUCTION

The twelve years immediately following the end of the War Between the States (the Civil War) are often referred to as the era of Reconstruction, during which the United States sought to resolve the complicated and onerous issues revolving around the end of slavery and the defeat of the Confederacy. Reconstruction brought not only some basic legal rights for black Americans, which they hoped would eventually lead to more social justice and economic progress, it also began the process of melding an African-based culture with the largely European dominate culture. Although a significant minority of white Americans were exposed to black American expressive culture through their own first-hand experience of living in the South or by traveling minstrel shows, Reconstruction marks the initial, tentative emergence of African American musical forms that are powerfully important, highly influential, and seemingly ubiquitous in the twenty-first century.

The evolution of African American music is very complicated and "Black American Music Since Reconstruction" should not be construed as comprehensive. Instead, this compact introductory essay outlines the complex history and development of African American music from the late nineteenth century when the modern gospel, jazz, and blues traditions were emerging to twenty-first century hip hop. It is designed to help you to better understand the essays, liner notes, newspaper articles, and other writings reprinted in this book by placing them in a larger cultural and historical context.

This overview addresses the emergence and importance of the most significant genres, such as blues and hip hop, as well as important musicians, including Ma Rainey, William Grant Still, Louis Jordan, and Duke Ellington, whose contributions to twentieth-century American music are discussed by Mark Tucker in "Evaluating Ellington." Because of the extended time frame and complexity of the issues, this essay is divided into six very broad chronological "eras." The first era focuses on the musical cultures that developed during the first several decades following the end of the Civil War. The notoriously repressive "Jim Crow" period that began in the 1890s and that reverberated well into the twentieth century forms the core of the second era, a time during which gospel, blues, and jazz emerged. Era number three begins in the 1920s, when phonograph records began to document and more widely disseminate "race music" to a broader, increasingly multiracial, and international audience. The close of the Second World War, when small, scrappy, independent companies recorded a wide range of talent including the newly minted R&B and early rock 'n' roll artists, opens the fourth era. The early 1960s, when Motown became the first record company (actually a brand) that truly brought black American music into the popular mainstream, marks the beginning of the fifth era. This overview closes with an examination of the period that began in the late 1970s and continues to the present time, when rap and now hip hop have become worldwide forms of expressive culture.

"MAKE ME A WORLD" (1865–1890)

When General Robert E. Lee surrendered his Army of Northern Virginia on April 9, 1865, at Appomattox Court House, Virginia, black Americans suddenly lived in a country that banned legalized slavery. The twelve years of Reconstruction (1865–1877) dealt not only with the legal status of newly freed Negroes, but also the reuniting of the northern states with the secessionist southern states to form a stronger, long-lasting union. During this initial transitional period, black Americans began creating a new world celebrating the hope of freedom that was based on their past with strong ties to West Africa and southern slave plantations.

We know the most about sacred music during this era, which is generally associated with "Negro spirituals." The historically significantly "Jubilee" singing movement pioneered by students from Fisk University (who often performed antebellum spirituals in a more formalized setting) represents the first highly public display of African American music. Fisk University, located in Nashville, Tennessee, opened its doors in 1866 and immediately found itself in a desperate financial struggle. By 1871, the first of many groups bearing the "Fisk Jubilee Singers" name went on the road in order to raise money to support the college. "Adrift on Stormy Seas" by J. B. T. Marsh discusses the struggles faced by this jubilee singing group, while "The Virginia Jubilee Singers" (published in the noted black newspaper *Indianapolis Freeman*) provides an account of a touring jubilee singing group that was active some twenty years after the Fisk University Singers initially left Nashville.

Most sacred music, which ranged from spirituals to composed hymns, was performed in less formal settings. Black Americans often sang religious songs at home in the evening or on weekends as well as in small churches associated with Methodist or Baptist sects that were formed and built by freed slaves and soon dotted the southern landscape. Some of these churches, most notably in the Sea Islands of Georgia and South Carolina, retained close ties with West African expressive culture such as movement (that would look like dancing to our modern eyes) and the extensive use of call and response, known more formally as antiphony. Portia Maultsby's essay "The Impact of Gospel Music on the Secular Music Industry" describes musical worship practices, such as the importance of movement and highly rhythmic accompaniment to their singing, that remain essential elements of contemporary secular black music and continue to inform the worship services in Pentecostal Churches, such as the Church of God in Christ.

In addition to personal contact, nineteenth-century black music also reached a large, multiracial audience by way of traveling minstrel shows. Minstrel shows began in the 1830s, presenting white and black performers (not together, but in segregated, separate troupes) in a mélange of solo singing, comedy skits, recitations, quartet singing, dramatic sketches, and banjo singing. The typical minstrel performance generally followed a three-act structure that began with the entire troupe dancing onto the stage while exchanging jokes and singing. The second part featured a variety show followed by a final act that almost always included a play. Minstrel songs and sketches featured several stock, essentially stereotypical, black characters, most popularly the slave and the well-heeled dandy, as well as a mammy and a wise old man, which reverberate to this day.

Minstrel performers, both black and white, asserted that their songs and dances were authentically black, a claim that remains highly debatable at best. Spirituals and banjo-accompanied songs were incorporated into minstrel performances during the antebellum period and remained a musical staple until such shows dwindled in popularity in the early twentieth century when vaudeville and traveling tent shows began to gain favor. Small minstrel shows, however, remained on the road, mostly in rural areas, until the 1950s. "Richards and Pringle's Original Georgia Minstrels and Billy Kersands, 1889–1895," by Lynn Abbott and Doug Seroff discusses one of the more important traveling black minstrel shows along with one of its most dynamic performers during a period when the popularity of minstrel shows was beginning to wane.

Only a small amount of late-nineteenth-century African American music was presented as publicly as the jubilee singing groups or the performers who appeared on the stages of minstrel shows. Black music was largely performed for black audiences, most of whom lived in the rural South, often on or near the farms or plantations on which they were born and now worked. Music provided relief from their everyday life of tedious and difficult manual labor. The work was eased by singing solo work songs, also known as arhoolies, or by group work songs that coordinated labor like lining track.

Black Americans during this period also sometimes played homemade instruments ranging from fifes crafted from cane to mouth-bows fashioned from a small tree limb and twine, to banjos. These instruments were often played informally at home or for small community gatherings. Sometimes musicians performed together, playing in small ensembles such as the fife and drum bands heard at picnics held in the hill country of northern Mississippi.

Elsewhere in the South, these groups frequently consisted of string players. In Virginia and North Carolina small string bands often performed at rural gatherings, such as a corn shuckings that were held on weekends late in the fall. Entertainment was also provided during holidays, such as the week between Christmas and New Year's Day. Until guitars became more widely available in the early twentieth century, these southern string bands featured fiddles and banjos as their core instruments.

The five-string banjo, most closely associated today with contemporary white country music and bluegrass, actually has its origins in West Africa. Its prototype was sometimes called a banjar or a bantar and often had four strings. These homemade instruments were brought to this country by slaves who continued playing them in America well into the late twentieth century as detailed in Ce Ce Conway's article. The fifth string was not added until the mid–nineteenth century and the instrument we know today as a banjo didn't become more standardized in style and size until manufacturers—such as Buckbee, Gibson, and Vega—began marketing them to a larger audience in the 1880s and 1890s.

"JUMP JIM CROW" (1890–1910)

Because Reconstruction offered the promise of major cultural, social, economic, and legal reforms following the end of decades of slavery, black Americans slowly began building their own new world based on the premise of freedom. But by the late 1870s some of the gains made by black Americans, particularly in the legal realm, began to reverse. Their legal ability to own land, run for political office, or operate a business became increasingly difficult. By the early 1890s most of the rights gained during the heady decades following the end of the Civil War quickly faded into memory as the country, and the South in particular, entered the era known as "Jim Crow." The most important laws passed during the 1880s and 1890s required that public schools, public places, and public transportation, like trains and buses, maintain separate facilities for whites and blacks. The Jim Crow era represented a major step backward in civil rights in the United States.

These restrictions entitled the two races to receive the same services (schools, hospitals, water fountains, bathrooms) and resulted in the curious "separate but equal" doctrine mandating different facilities for the two groups. Although such separate facilities were almost never equal, the legitimacy of such laws was upheld by the U.S. Supreme Court in the notorious 1896 case of *Plessy* v. *Ferguson* (163 U.S. 537). These laws resulted in a legal resegregation of black Americans, which was in place and enforced by the time the twentieth century began. Resegregation led not only to the creation of "colored" water fountains and bathrooms in public institutions, it also sparked a new burst of energy in African American expressive culture and music. W. E. B. Du Bois reflected this exceptionally difficult period in black American history in his classic essay *The Souls of Black Folk*. "Of the Sorrow Songs," the Du Bois assessment of spirituals and sacred song, is one chapter from this extended essay.

New Orleans and the "creoles of color" provide an interesting and unique case study of how these laws affected local musical culture. Prior to the 1890s, the mixed-race "creoles of color" occupied a singular position between black and white cultures in New Orleans and were treated differently than either race. They developed their own education system, helped to support the local opera halls, and thrived as local businessmen and merchants. But the Jim Crow laws legally altered their status, placing them for the first time as black Americans, not as a separate entity. Suddenly they were thrown together with other black citizens of New Orleans, most of whom did not enjoy the same level of education, often didn't thrive economically, and carried different musical sensibilities to the mix. The music that we now call jazz resulted from this uneasy and unwelcome juncture, a complex tale that is clearly dissected in "The Nineteenth-Century Origins of Jazz" by Lawrence Gushee.

Even more significantly, the three essential and now well-known genres of African American music that informed the entire twentieth century—jazz, blues, and gospel—emerged during the Jim Crow era. Not surprisingly, they are also rooted in the South, which is where the majority of black American citizens resided prior to the Great Migrations that began in the early 1900s. While jazz developed in a very specific geographic location (New Orleans), early blues and gospel music enjoyed a wider initial distribution across the South before diffusing throughout the United States and eventually the world.

It is difficult to pinpoint the geographical origins of blues and gospel music because their emergence, unlike that of hip hop from the Bronx in the late 1970s, was neither highly public nor properly documented at the time. Furthermore, their development was gradual, more evolution than revolution.

For these reasons, it is impossible to state exactly when and where black Americans began performing blues and singing gospel songs. But as scholars have become more interested in these genres, their research has clarified that blues and gospel music were part of our musical vernacular by the first decade of the twentieth century.

One of the earliest scholarly articles about blues, "The 'Blues' as Folk-Songs" by Dorothy Scarborough, was published by the *Journal of American Folklore* in 1916, but for the most part the blues, gospel, and jazz traditions emerged all but unnoticed by contemporary scholars. Of course these genres gained some press, most often a brief newspaper article about a performance by a musician or group coming to town or an advertisement of a traveling minstrel or tent show. "Ma Rainey and the Traveling Minstrels" by Charles Edward Smith underscores the importance of these traveling shows in bringing the blues to a more geographically diverse audience.

What might seem like quaint, old-fashioned conservative music to us now was not always viewed that way at the turn of the twentieth century. Around 1900, blues and jazz, in particular, were as new, fresh and controversial as disco some seventy-five years later. "War on Ragtime" and "Suppression of 'Ragtime'" (two brief essays published in *American Musician* in 1901 that conflate the terms ragtime and jazz, which were synonymous at the time) underscore the contentious nature of these new genres.

Controversy is one of the underlying themes associated with black American music, one that began long before the early 1990s with gangsta rap or even before the early 1950s when an increasing number of white teenagers listened to rhythm and blues music in anticipation of the rock and roll explosion sparked by Elvis Presley in 1955. Ever since minstrel shows promoted African American musical culture in the 1830s and continued into the ragtime era of the 1890s, African American music has often been associated with controversy.

Blues developed first in the Deep South, perhaps in the lower Mississippi River delta, before spreading to other parts of the country, first by way of traveling musicians and eventually via sheet music and phonograph records. "Marshall Lullaby" by Kip Lornell and Charles Wolfe describes the early life, times, and blues-based music of Huddie "Lead Belly" Ledbetter while growing up in rural northwestern Louisiana near the beginning of the twentieth century—some three decades before he moved to New York City and became famous.

Shaped from the field hollers, work songs, spirituals, and country dance tunes that preceded them, these early blues was often loosely based on the twelve-bar form so familiar today. Liberties were taken with the AAB verse form that became more standardized by the 1920s. Contrary to popular belief, blues lyrics are not always sad and they address a wide range of topics, ranging from the relationships between men and women, natural disasters such as floods, and politics.

Modern gospel music is performed by solo singers, mass choirs, quartets featuring four-part harmony, and family or community-based groups singing material from a variety of sources including nineteenth-century spirituals, camp meeting songs, biblical texts, and newly composed songs. Gospel is often associated with the mainstream protestant churches, most notably Baptists and Methodists, but the influence of the Pentecostal movement on gospel and secular music is profound.

But not all forms of black sacred music from this era reached a wide audience, nor did it influence other forms of secular music. This is particularly true of interesting styles that are restricted to a particular geographical section of the South, such as "shape note" singing that is now all but extinct. "Black Sacred Harp Singing in Southeast Alabama" by Hank Willett discusses the cultural and musical history of this distinctive form of a cappella singing with roots in the nineteenth century and that is more often associated with southern white American sacred music.

"CRAZY BLUES" (1910–1945)

Geographical movement and wider recognition mark this era of African American music. During the 1910s and into the 1920s, hundreds of thousands of black Americans moved from the rural South to larger southern cities such as Atlanta, Dallas, and Memphis in search of cultural and economic opportunities. Many of them found a new home in these cities, but tens of thousands of blacks joined their rural counterparts who moved directly from the rural South to northern cities. If you lived in northern Mississippi, for example, you were most likely to move to Chicago. If you lived on a small farm on the eastern shore of Maryland, then Philadelphia probably called out to you.

Over a period of several decades the Great Migrations helped to swell the urban population of black Americans, further disseminating their musical culture. "Jelly Roll Blues" by Jelly Roll Morton with Alan Lomax underscores the fact that musicians not only traveled extensively, but also that the southern base of support for Morton's blues and jazz mix remained vitally important. Just as black Americans brought their cuisine and language with them, their musical tastes migrated, too.

During this era New York City and Chicago emerged as the most significant urban centers for African American culture. New York City developed a thriving vaudeville and theatrical scene featuring talented black artists such as Bert Williams. "The Scene and the Players in New York" by Tom Riis describes the development of black musical theater in the early twentieth century. Similarly, Cary B. Lewis's "William Marion Cook" details the life and works of this important violinist and composer, whose career spanned the 1890s well into the 1930s.

But migration was not the only reason why black American music spread across the United States during this thirty-five-year period. Sheet music featuring jazz-like and ragtime tunes began to circulate at the turn of the century, followed by blues songs in the first two decades of the twentieth century. The sales of sheet music in general rose throughout the first three decades of the twentieth century, though jazz and blues songs constituted only a small minority of all sheet music published in the United States. Gospel music also circulated in print, occasionally on sheet music, but more often by way of gospel songbooks, the most famous of which was the *Gospel Pearls* series from the 1920s.

Every since KDKA (the country's first commercial radio station) signed on the air in Pittsburgh, Pennsylvania, in 1920, the radio also helped disseminate black vernacular music across the United States. These pioneering AM radio stations operated in a largely unregulated atmosphere and featured a wide range of local musicians as diverse as organ soloists, hillbilly bands, and small chamber orchestras who performed live in the studio in block programs of fifteen or thirty minutes. Radio caught on quickly and by the onset of the Great Depression, hundreds of radio stations had sprung up throughout the United States.

Black American music, especially in larger cities, became a small, but important, component of radio during the 1920s and 1930s. Although down-home rural blues singers rarely appeared on the radio during this period, a few of the better-known female vaudeville performers, most notably Bessie Smith, occasionally gave radio performances. Many more jazz performers graced the airways during this time. The list is headed by such popular performers as Fletcher Henderson and Fats Waller, an appreciation of whom is found in "Fats Waller—Comedy Tonight" by Gary Giddins. Radio was important because it instantly brought black music to an eager and inquisitive audience and by the late 1920s the fledgling radio networks were able to bring the music of Duke Ellington to radios across the United States.

In 1920 the OKeh Record Company issued "Crazy Blues" by Mamie Smith, a black female singer who was working the vaudeville circuit. Although record companies began recording black artists as early as about 1891, the success of "Crazy Blues" spurred them to record and market jazz, blues, and gospel talents more aggressively. Much of the early talent came through the professional ranks as artists like Louis Armstrong, Bessie Smith, Butterbeans and Susie, and Lonnie Johnson transferred their talents from the stage to the studio. The record industry ultimately proved vastly more important than radio in bringing "race" talent to the record-buying public.

By the mid-1920s, companies such as RCA Victor, Paramount, and Columbia were scouting musical talent more widely. They eventually recorded artists such as Bob Coleman, Sugar Underwood, Tom Dickson, the Zach White Orchestra, and Blind Benny Paris, who made a few selections and faded back into obscurity. Other black artists, including the Rev. J. M. Gates, Blind Lemon Jefferson, and Duke Ellington's Orchestra, enjoyed more success and returned to the studios for multiple sessions. Eventually these companies issued thousands of "race" records that helped disseminate black vernacular music across the country.

Although they benefited from the sales of blues, jazz, and gospel records by black artists, the executives operating these companies remained largely white. Mayo "Ink" Williams was one of a handful of black Americans employed by companies to deal with talent, though he did not work in the corporate offices. Harry Pace co-founded Black Swan Records in 1921, which is generally cited as the first black-owned record company in the United States that enjoyed wide general distribution.

Few record companies, however, paid special attention to classical genres and music composed by black Americans. As Gayle Murchison points out in "Dean of Afro-American Composers or 'Harlem Renaissance Man,'" William Grant Still began his distinguished career writing symphonic works, movie scores, and operas in the late 1920s. Contralto Marian Anderson debuted with the New York Philharmonic on August 26, 1925, and scored an immediate critical and popular success. Three years later she sang for the first time at Carnegie Hall, which solidified her place as one of the country's premier opera singers. "Easter Sunday" by Marian Anderson describes her groundbreaking 1939 performance before a multiracial audience at the outdoor Lincoln Memorial, which occurred because her race prevented Anderson from appearing at nearby D.A.R. Constitution Hall.

The multitalented Paul Robeson also rose to prominence as a performer in the 1920s following an All-American gridiron career at Rutgers University and a law degree from Columbia University. He appeared in eleven films between 1925 and 1942 as well as several well-received stage productions in New York City. He is perhaps best known for his version of "Ole Man River" from the 1936 film version of *Showboat.* "Paul Robeson, Musician" by Doris McGinty and Wayne Shirley documents his musical talents.

Inspired by turn-of-the-century writers like the Rev. C. A. Tindley of Philadelphia, gospel composers wrote an increasing number of gospel songs that reached eager churchgoers during the 1920s. Modern gospel music, however, largely emerged from Chicago in the early 1930s and the Rev. Thomas A. Dorsey—a former blues singer then known as Georgia Tom—is largely responsible for this movement. Dorsey, who wrote dozens of gospel songs (the best known of which is "Precious Lord, Take My Hand"), helped to organize gospel choirs and choruses and championed this new and controversial music that blended secular music practices with a religious message. "Conflict and Resolution in the Life of Thomas Andrew Dorsey" by Michael Harris carefully details Dorsey's personal, professional, and religious life that continued for many decades until his death in 1993.

This new gospel music proved so popular that within a decade professional gospel groups began touring the country. By 1940 at least two gospel quartets—the Famous Blue Jay Singers (Birmingham, Alabama) and the Soul Stirrers (Houston, Texas)—gained enough of a following to chisel out a full-time living singing gospel music. Mahalia Jackson and Sister Rosetta Tharpe, two women with strong ties to Chicago, moved in the same direction. With the support of a network of churches providing them performance venues, some radio broadcasts, and a few recordings, these pioneering professionals paved the "gospel highway" that became a more well-traveled road following the close of World War II.

The African American jazz tradition that began in New Orleans and eventually moved to Chicago and New York City by the early 1920s crossed over to become popular music in the mid-1930s. Swing, as it was called then, was inspired by the jazz orchestras of Duke Ellington, Bennie Moten, Don Redman, and Cab Calloway. Talented white big band leaders Benny Goodman, Artie Shaw, and Tommy Dorsey, among others, made a handsome living playing swing music across the land. One of the most highly respected black jazz orchestra leaders and arrangers, Fletcher Henderson, was hired by Benny Goodman in 1939. Goodman's band thrived with Henderson's assistance. In turn, Henderson's association with Goodman only solidified the clarinetist's position as the most popular musician in the United States for a decade beginning in the mid-1930s.

Swing was the predominant form of popular music for nearly twenty years until rock 'n' roll developed in the middle 1950s. Recordings by jazz-oriented bands and singers as diverse as Frank Sinatra and Ella Fitzgerald topped the charts and the phenomenal popularity of swing helped to heighten the awareness of black jazz orchestras. Although Goodman and Shaw produced many very popular and some artistically successful recordings, they were hard-pressed to equal the exciting work of Count Basie and his "All American Rhythm Section" (Jo Jones on drums, Walter Page on drums, with Basie at the piano). The saxophonists who worked with Basie during the late 1930s and early 1940s—Lester Young, Hershel Evans, and Eddie "Lockjaw" Davis—included some of the best in jazz. Basie's band also featured first Jimmy Rushing and later Joe Williams, two of the most influential big band blues shouters. Two of his small group recordings from this era ("Sent for You Yesterday" and "Going to Chicago") clearly presage the rhythm 'n' blues (R&B) genre that blossomed after World War II.

World War II marked a significant period, not just in world history, but also in the development of black American music. The war effort necessitated recycling shellac from which 78-rpm records were pressed, causing a shortage of material. Late in 1942 a dispute between the musicians' union and the major recording companies that lasted for nearly two years further curtailed recording activities. Furthermore, the rationing of gas and a shortage of rubber to manufacture tires made travel costly and difficult. This combination of factors effectively postponed the nascent professional gospel industry as well as the pioneering jump blues artists from spreading across the country as quickly as they might have. The end of the war in the summer of 1945 not only brought jubilation to the world, it also signaled a new era in the development and dissemination of black American music.

"THE RISE OF RHYTHM 'N' BLUES" (1945–1962)

The magnetic tape recorder, developed by Germans during World War II, revolutionized the recording industry because it was more portable, less expensive, and more versatile than the technology that preceded it. Prior to its introduction in the United States late in 1948, virtually all commercial recording was done in radio stations, in permanent recording studios located in major cities, or in portable studios set up for several days to a week (often in a hotel) that required the use of large, cumbersome machines that usually cut direct to a master disc. These modern reel-to-reel machines soon offered relative portability at a price that an increasing number of people could afford.

These factors, along with the availability of shellac to once again press records, led more people to venture into the record industry. Literally hundreds of regional and local independent record companies sprang up across the United States in the decade following the close of World War II and the beginning of rock 'n' roll. Most of them were small, ephemeral outfits. But a few companies, most notably Chess (based in Chicago) and Atlantic (located in New York City), began as labels with a local and then regional impact that eventually morphed into companies with national impact.

Independent record companies often filled the niches left untouched or underserved by the major record companies. They recorded an astonishing array of music, including older ethnic traditions, blues, sacred music of all sorts, and the newly emerging genre of bluegrass. While the major companies, most notably Columbia and Victor, continued to be full-service labels that recorded a wide variety of genres from classical to country, smaller labels often focused on a particular niche, frequently one of personal or regional interest. Hundreds of black artists and groups found recording opportunities for the first time with such well-known artists as Chicago blues man Muddy Waters (Aristocrat—later renamed Chess) and bebop jazz legend Charlie Parker (Savoy) who were making their commercial record debuts as band leaders. But as John Chilton describes in "Caldonia," Louis Jordan stands out as the best-selling black artist in the decade after WWII, with a score of hits on the Decca label.

Jordan, a versatile entertainer with a bent for broad comedy who would have felt at home on a vaudeville stage, pioneered a type of music known often called rhythm and blues (R&B). Perhaps best described as blues played by a stripped down swing band, R&B was the most popular form of black music in the late 1940s well into the 1950s, and men like Big Joe Turner, Roy Milton, and Roy Brown shouted the blues in a style that Count Basie vocalist Jimmy Rushing pioneered in the late 1930s. Jordan was not only a widely sought-after performer for live performances, he also recorded extensively and appeared on two-to-three minute jukebox films called "soundies." Songs such as "Five Guys Named Moe," "Buzz Me," and, especially his 1945 hit "Caldonia" were heard on jukeboxes and record players across the entire United States.

Gospel music, particularly that sung by quartets, was also very influential during the decade after the close of the war during a period that is often characterized as "The Golden Age of Gospel Music." Groups such as the Spirit of Memphis, the Dixie Hummingbirds, and the Harmonizing Four of Richmond brought the sound of four-part harmony singing to eager audiences. Although they started off featuring four voices, these quartets evolved to include instrumental accompaniment, often starting with a guitar and then adding a more compete rhythm section, and eventually featuring lead singers who sometimes became as well known as the groups themselves.

The Soul Stirrers, for example, formed in Texas in the late 1920s, became one of the first fully professional quartets some ten years later and emerged as one of gospel's premier groups after World War II. Today they are generally well known for the flowing lead singing of Sam Cooke, who joined the group in 1951. Cooke's success with the group began almost immediately with his stunning recording of "Jesus Gave Me Water" and was capped by his emotional rendering of "Touch the Hem of His Garment," recorded in February 1956. Cooke left the Soul Stirrers (and gospel music) in the summer of 1957 in order to pursue a solo pop singing career.

As Portia Maultsby points out in her essay "The Impact of Gospel Music on the Secular Music Industry," the music of black churches served as a breeding ground for soul singers who—like Sam Cooke—came of age during the 1950s and 1960s. Lou Rawls, James Brown, and Aretha Franklin are among the hundreds of soul artists who came up singing in church groups. Franklin's father, the Rev. C. L. Franklin, stands out as an important leader in the Baptist Church, first in Memphis and later in Detroit, where he often hosted important Civil Rights leaders like Martin Luther King, Jr. The relationship between religious music and this struggle for social, economic, and racial justice is explored in "Singing in the Streets of Raleigh, 1963: Some Recollections" by Clyde Appleton.

Gospel music consisted of more than quartet singing, of course. Solo performers like Brother Joe May, Mahalia Jackson, Sister Rosetta Tharpe, each of whom had close ties to Pentecostal churches, appealed to a wide audience that by the early 1950s was beginning to cross over to include more white listeners. "Elder Beck's Temple" by William Russell describes the musical culture of a small Pittsburgh Pentecostal church and represents the type of neighborhood church that spawned Tharpe, Jackson, and others. Far better known than Elder Beck, Mahalia Jackson was launched on a career that reached a commercial zenith beginning in the mid-1950s when she signed with Columbia Records. Other female gospel ensembles, including the Caravans and the Ward Singers, also attracted a large and loyal fan base. In fact, fans of all types of gospel music flocked to churches and community centers, purchased the latest record, or heard them on the radio.

African American performers had appeared as performers and announcers on radio since the early 1920s, but full-time black-oriented radio broadcasting didn't begin until June 1947 when WDIA began broadcasting in Memphis. WDIA initially reached black Americans only in the greater Memphis region but became a powerful force in the Mid-South when their transmitter was authorized to broadcast at 50,000 watts in June 1954. With "block programming" that consisted of fifteen- and thirty-minute shows, the station brought a wide range of black musical talent, including future blues superstar B. B. King (whose career was launched by his radio work), the vaudeville-inspired work of Rufus Thomas, and the Spirit of Memphis into homes across the Mid-South. WDIA was the first station in the nation to be programmed for and by black Americans. Within several years, stations in New York City, Chicago, Atlanta, and other larger urban areas had followed suit.

"T-Bone Walker in His Own Words" touches upon the development of the urban, electrified blues that developed across the country beginning in the late 1940s and formed the basis for rock 'n' roll. Walker's oral history provides a colorful account of his fascinating life, including the critical postwar period. His life story sets the context into which black proto-rockers, most notably Little Richard and Chuck Berry (whose music bridged the gap between R&B and pop music and rock 'n' roll), emerged in the mid-1950s.

The 1950s also saw the rise to prominence not only of vocal gospel quartets, but also secular groups, which are usually called "doo-wop" or "vocal harmony" groups. These vocal groups are sometimes referred to as "bird groups" because of the proliferation of names such as "The Robins," "The Ravens," "The Crows," and "The Wrens." A variety of bluesy and slow ballads, bawdy up-tempo selections, and songs about teen angst and romance constituted their repertoire. Smokey Robinson, who sang with the Miracles and then attracted attention in the middle 1960s as a Motown artist, and funk master George Clinton (as a member of Parliament), whose career truly flowered beginning in the middle 1970s, represent two of the most famous alumni of vocal groups.

"DANCING IN THE STREETS" (1962–1980)

During this era black popular music moved closer to the commercial mainstream and in the case of Motown soul and funk, it became American pop music. Simultaneously several older forms of black music, most notably down-home blues, were finding a new white audience. Perhaps just as significant, somewhat more obscure regional styles thrived with continued community support.

For example, southwestern Louisiana provided a solid home for zydeco music, which featured the button accordion, fiddle, triangle, and songs performed in creolized French in a style that began developing in the late nineteenth century. Ben Sandmel points out in "Clifton Chenier: 'They Call Me the King'" that the 1950s zydeco merged with R&B into a more popular, often electrified gumbo native to this section of the United States. Significantly modern zydeco remains very popular in its home territories.

The white interest in blues, which was slowly falling out of favor with its core black audience during this era, began in the late 1950s as more white teens began to hear the music of Little Richard and Chuck Berry. While Muddy Waters, T-Bone Walker, and Bobby "Blue" Bland almost always performed for all black audiences throughout the 1950s, their audiences became increasingly integrated and within twenty years became predominately white.

The so-called "folk revival" kicked off in 1958 when the Kingston Trio hit the pop charts with "Tom Dooley." In addition to a renewed interest in southern grassroots genres like bluegrass and old-time string bands, a small group of enthusiasts and budding academics also began investigating the rural down-home blues tradition that began to be documented on records in the early 1920s. By the late 1960s magazines such as *Blue Unlimited* and Paul Oliver (both residing in the United Kingdom) focused on the blues. Folk festivals in the United States, began featuring older acoustic blues players, most notably Mississippi John Hurt, Bukka White, and Son House, each of whom had first recorded in the late 1920s and early 1930s. The audience and interest in this music from the 1960s to the present have been almost entirely white.

The "blues revival" propelled a handful of scholars to research related forms of rural African American music. In the years following the folk revival's peak, folklorists and ethnomusicologists sought out and documented some of the lesser-known forms of black folk music. The black banjo tradition, which is the subject of Cecelia Conway's "Conclusion" to her book *African Banjo Echoes in Appalachia: A Story of Folk Traditions* provides one example. Increasingly, books and articles on topics ranging from work songs to the sacred "play shout" tradition in coastal Georgia appeared with sound recordings and documentary films.

Although the "crossover" from black to white musical culture slowly began with minstrelsy in the 1840s, the Motown phenomenon represents the most dramatic, widespread, and wide-ranging postmodern example. In retrospect, we can better understand why Motown blossomed at the beginning of major social and cultural upheavals in the early 1960s. The Civil Rights Movement was gaining momentum, with attention focused on joint black and white voting rights efforts in the deep South. Stories about Vietnam, once an obscure southeast Asian country, began appearing in newspapers and an increasing number of people started to question the values associated with what became known as the military–industrial complex. Black-oriented radio stations now hit the airwaves in every major city—and many smaller ones—in the United States, bringing the sounds of James Brown, Sam Cooke, and Chubby Checker to an increasingly racially integrated audience. And an increasing number of artists heard on the radio were from Detroit, most of which were either on the Tamla or the Motown label, both of which were owned and operated by a former steel worker named Barry Gordy.

By 1962 Gordy released well-crafted pop records, marketed as "The Sound of Young America," that were heard on black and white radio stations across the United States. Millions of young men and women tuned their radios to the local "Top-40" AM radio station, which kept "You've Really Got a Hold of Me" by Smokey Robinson and the Miracles, Mary Wells's "You Beat Me to the Punch," Marvin Gaye's "Hitch Hike," and the Contour's stompin' "Do You Love Me?" on their regular rotation. These and scores of other well-crafted pop records by Little Stevie Wonder, Martha and the Vandellas, the Temptations, Mary Wells, and the Supremes emerged from the company's unassuming "Hitsville USA" studios. "Motown Calls 'The Rock & Roll Kid'" by Dennis Coffey presents an informal, amusing, insider view of this multiracial group of in-house musicians, collectively known as the "Funk Brothers," who helped turn Motown into a color-blind, money-making juggernaut and established Gordon as a nationally recognized tastemaker.

Although Motown emerged as the most successful record company during the 1960s, it was not the only Afro-centric record company bringing hit sounds to eager young listeners. "Respect: 1964–1965" by Rob Bowman chronicles the impact of the more soulful, southern sounds of Stax during a two-year period when records by Booker T and the MG's, Carla Thomas, and, especially, Otis Redding began to appear on the pop music charts. This Memphis-based record company (founded as Satellite Records in 1957) featured more emotionally charged singing and a greater degree of soulful improvisation than their counterparts in Detroit.

Despite such early hits that began with "Please, Please, Please" in 1956, the soul-drenched sounds of James Brown didn't gain widespread recognition until the early 1960s. His 1963 album "Live at the Apollo" is generally considered to be a masterpiece of the soul genre and with the Famous Flames he virtually set the template for the funk music that became the most popular black music in the early 1970s. Two of Brown's signature tunes, "Papa's Got a Brand New Bag" and "I Got You (I Feel Good)," both from 1965, became his first Top-10 pop hits and number-1 R&B hits.

By this time Brown, well known as a harsh and unforgiving taskmaster on stage, became the first major selling black artist to exercise complete control of his sound in the studio. Smash Records now released his recordings and between 1967 and 1969, he helped redefine the role of rhythm and percussion in black popular music. With an extended drum break and a harmony that was reduced to a single chord change, his 1967 recording of "Cold Sweat" is often cited by musicians and critics alike as the first funk record. "Give It Up or Turnit a Loose," "Licking Stick-Licking Stick" (1968), and "Funky Drummer" (1969) refined and further developed Brown's mid-1960s style. The well-rehearsed horn section, guitars, bass, and drums produced intricate rhythmic patterns based on multiple interlocking riffs, somewhat reminiscent of the juju music that developed in West Africa during the 1950s.

By the late 1960s Brown's vocals—rhythmic declarations, somewhere between singing and speaking with hints of pitch and melody—sounded increasingly like a Pentecostal preacher, overtaken by the spirit and preaching to his flock. This vocal style, often electronically "sampled" beginning in the 1980s, influenced what was to be called rapping, one of the foundations of the hip hop revolution.

Clearly one of the most soulful, funkiest, and most influential black musicians to emerge since World War II, James Brown strongly impacted George Clinton, a one-time street corner doo-wop vocalist who in the late 1960s became enamored with rock and the mind-altering drugs that influenced Clinton and his group Parliament-Funkadelic and their music. Along with Sly and the Family Stone; Earth, Wind, and Fire; and the Meters, the collective group of musicians known as P-Funk (aka Pure Funk or, most commonly, Parliament-Funkadelic) impacted the world of black popular music for a decade beginning around 1970.

Their music, generally called funk, was earthy and sexy and was underpinned by wickedly syncopated bass and drums. Once again the spirit of James Brown informed funk. Bootsy Collins (the innovative, creative, and wild bass player) played with Brown in 1970 before joining the P-Funk mob. The arrangements heard on P-Funk records and live performances were also heavily influenced by the Famous Flames and the JB's (Brown's bands of the late 1960s and early 1970s), which were organized and arranged by trombonist Fred Wesley and reed player Maceo Parker. Early Funkadelic albums, most notably *Free Your Mind* and *Maggot Brain* (both from 1971), contained a heavy dose of Hendrix-influenced guitar by Eddie Hazel along with the funk. This group proved beyond any doubt that black groups could play rock music. "Media Interventions" by Maureen Mahon investigates the media's reaction to the overlooked and misunderstood "black rock" movement that developed in the 1970s but flowered in New York City in the mid-1980s.

In the mid-1970s live P-Funk performances were wild affairs that went on nonstop for many hours. A typical performance featured long instrumental jams that provided plenty of solo space as well as extended call-and-response sections between the band and audience. The outrageous costumes (consider Bootsy Collins's appearance on stage garbed in a diaper), the layers of makeup, and George

Clinton's over-the-top, multicolored 'fro were all informed by a message of love (sexual and otherwise) and togetherness. The performances began with Clinton emerging from The Mothership, a spacecraft worthy of (and inspired by) jazz visionary Sun Ra. For a more lengthy examination of this unique presentation, please read "The P-Funk Empire: Tear the Roof Off the Sucker" by Rickey Vincent and listen to "One Nation Under a Groove," (1978), arguably the strongest studio work issued by P-Funk.

That black music had become very big business by now is indisputable. Motown kicked off the trend in the mid-1960s with Jimi Hendrix, Sly and the Family Stone, James Brown, and so many others selling millions of singles and albums to a wide, multiracial audience in the United States and increasingly across the world. The increased corporatization of the black music business only accelerated during the 1970s. Even jazz, the audience for which dramatically dropped off in the late 1960s, made a larger commercial splash in the 1970s.

Motown briefly flirted with jazz with its Jazz Workshop label (1962–1964) but dropped the effort due to poor sales. Perhaps they gave up too soon because jazz reached a larger audience in the 1970s by way of the fusion of jazz, rock, and funk pioneered by Miles Davis in the late 1960s. Known as jazz-rock, jazz-funk, or, most often, fusion jazz, Miles Davis's 1969 *Bitches Brew* helped launch a genre that brought jazz from a niche market closer to the pop mainstream.

Prior to *Bitches Brew,* much of the most creative jazz from the early to middle 1960s—most notably by John Coltrane, Bill Evans, Ornette Coleman, and their peers—reached a relatively small audience. Ironically, some of the most innovative music from the mid-1960s came from Miles Davis's group in the years between 1963 and 1968 when he employed superb musicians such as pianist Herbie Hancock, sax player Wayne Shorter, bassist Ron Carter, and drummer Tony Williams. During the prefusion era the more adventurous jazz musicians moved into new rhythmic realms that explored new ideas of "swing" as well as new concepts of harmony.

Fusion jazz also took advantage of new technology built on the move from tube to electronic equipment. Keyboard players often switched from acoustic pianos to electric models or to the even more versatile synthesizers, which helped move Chick Corea, Herbie Hancock, and Joseph Zawinul (all veterans of various Miles Davis groups) into the public spotlight. Recordings by Hancock's Headhunters group sold exceptionally well as did Chick Corea's Return to Forever and Weather Report, formed in 1970 by Zawinul and Wayne Shorter.

Jazz fans complained that fusion jazz wandered too far from its creative roots and was really popular music. Miles Davis, in particular, was the target of much of this criticism. "The Art of the Muscle: Miles Davis as American Knight and American Knave" by Gerald Early insightfully places Davis within the context of his nearly five decades as a highly influential jazz artist. Despite all the critical press, the fusion movements nudged jazz into territory that it had abandoned some thirty years previously when swing music was popular music.

"HIP HOP AMERICA" (1980–2009)

While the roots of hip hop can be found in African American, West African, Jamaican, and Puerto Rican expressive culture, New York City, which has long enjoyed a particular place as our largest and perhaps our most culturally diverse urban center, provided its geographic center. Innovation often occurred in such circumstances, especially in the twentieth century, so it is not surprising that hip hop began in New York. What may surprise some, however, are its multiethnic roots.

Hip hop today is almost always associated with black Americans, but "Hip-Hop, Puerto Ricans, and Ethnoracial Identities in New York" by Raquel Rivera underscores the importance of Puerto Ricans in hip hop's early days—specifically in its nascent period in the mid- to late 1970s. By the beginning of the 1980s, hip hop culture (initially consisting of break dancing, graffiti, DJing, and rapping) began percolating outside of the Bronx and Brooklyn neighborhoods that provided its initial support. Today DJing and rapping are the two aspects of hip hop culture that remain paramount.

Hip hop emerged in New York City in the mid-1970s when DJs began isolating the percussion break from funk or disco songs during marathon dance sessions. They began playing these records using two turntables, resulting in a new creation often referred to a remix. Just as the pulsating music heard at discos provided a nonstop dance event, these new mixes provided the nascent hip hop crowd with funky beats that lasted for many hours. DJs demonstrated their creativity not only by way of what (and when and how) they selected to mix together, but also by adding special affects like "scratching."

At hip hop events an emcee (MC) introduced the DJ and the music and hyped the audience. The MCs would speak between songs, often recognizing those who "represented" specific parts of town or even neighborhoods, as well as telling jokes and stories. A good DJ would also exhort the party people to dance. Early hip hop MCs fulfilled a role much like that of their Jamaican "dub" counterparts, who worked the crowds using sound systems that enabled them to be heard over the din of indoor dance halls found in Kingston and other urban areas during the 1960s. It is not coincidental that one of the most widely acknowledged "godfathers" of hip hop, DJ Kool Herc, came from the Jamaican immigrant community in New York City.

By the close of the 1970s, MCing emerged as an essential element of hip hop and no party in the Bronx was successful if the DJ and MC didn't work well together. MCing also became more stylized, and eventually became known as rapping. In fact, the term hip hop was not widely used until the mid-1990s and was of the musical culture that was simply referred to as "rap." Rap quickly became a commercially recorded music genre and entered the American mainstream by way of recordings such as "The Breaks" by Kurtis Blow and "Rapper's Delight" by the Sugarhill Gang. Both of these 1980 singles received extensive airplay across the United Sates and for many these records served as their introduction to hip hop.

Hip hop culture was not limited to New York City, of course, and both the Los Angeles and the San Francisco metro regions spawned their own hip hop culture as early as the late 1970s. But West Coast hip hop did not flower until the early 1980s. The emerging West Coast sound was a bit different. "Electro hop"—a hybrid of rap and dance music that featured a very bass-heavy sound—came from the studios of Mix Master Spade, DJ Unkown, and World Class Wreckin' Cru during this initial wave.

Crack was becoming epidemic, which resulted not only in a major spike in drug problems but also in increase in criminal activity. By the time that hip hop blossomed, the "gangsta" element became apparent in early West Coast rap artists and it brought notoriety to a small cadre of artists by end of the 1980s. Ice-T's "6 in the Mornin'" (1986) received some airplay, but his 1987 recording of "Rhyme Pays" proved to be a watershed and can be considered one of the first gangsta rap albums.

Soon, Ice-T's gold record "N.W.A." ("Niggaz With Attitude") emerged on the scene, it proved to be the first truly nationally influential West Coast rap group. Eazy-E, Ice Cube, Dr. Dre, DJ Yella, and MC Ren constituted N.W.A. and "Straight Outta Compton" (1988) shot them to the top of the charts and into a national controversy. Influenced by sounds as varied as hard-core punk, 1970s soul music, and P-funk as well as rap, these blunt and direct sounds were criticized for promoting violence, hedonism, misogyny, and a criminal lifestyle. Following "Straight Outta Compton," the individual members of N.W.A. thrived. Dr. Dre produced Eazy-E and released his commercially successful debut album *Eazy-Duz-It* while Ice Cube released two platinum and widely acclaimed albums—*AmeriKKKa's Most Wanted* (1990), followed one year later by *Death Certificate*.

Throughout the 1980s, hip hop culture spread from its urban core, but it wasn't until late in the decade that the first pop-rap artist emerged in the form of a former Oakland Athletics' bat boy. Stanley Kirk Burrell, best known as MC Hammer, initially hit the scene in 1988 with an independent release, "Let's Get It Started." In the fall of 1988 a video of "Pump It Up" premiered or reaired on the premiere season of *Yo! MTV Raps*, and the album *Let's Get It Started* (now released by Capitol Records) eventually went triple-platinum. Three other songs, "Turn This Mutha Out" (the album's biggest hit), "Feel My Power," and "They Put Me in the Mix," saw heavy radio station airplay for about six months into early 1989. In the 1990s, MC Hammer's second album, *Please Hammer Don't Hurt 'Em*, included the smash single "U Can't Touch This," which sampled Rick James's 1981 hit "Super Freak." Decried as too clean and not creative enough, MC Hammer's rap career lasted three years, but he did bring the genre into millions of living rooms across the country.

As in most forms of post-Reconstruction black popular music, women play a secondary role in hip hop. Women rarely ascend the hip hop business ladder and the sight of female DJing or rapping is uncommon. They are not entirely absent, of course. In fact, a handful of women, most notably the Real Roxanne and Salt-n-Pepa, gained notoriety as early rap artists. "Daughters of the Blues: Women, Race, and Class Representation in Rap Music Performance" by Cheryl Keyes explores the issues related to gender and class in hip hop during the 1980s and 1990s.

Hip hop has also emerged as a popular music form across the globe. In the Caribbean and South America, elements of hip hop became fused with numerous styles of music, including reggae, cumbia, and samba, for example. Because of the importance of beats and rhythm in our increasingly technological digital world, it is not surprising that the Senegalese mbalax rhythm, for example, has became a component of hip hop. In the United Kingdom and Belgium, hip hop artists have explored a wide variety of electronic music fusions of hip hop, most notably British trip hop.

Since the 1990s, hip hop has also matured and diversified. Most important has been the rise of Southern rap artists, starting with OutKast and Goodie Mob (Soul Food), based in Atlanta. In New Orleans, Master P (Ghetto D) built up an impressive roster of popular artists (the No Limit posse). The wacked-out crunk sound developed first in Atlanta with other proponents, later finding a home in Houston. The Atlanta-based Lil Jon and the Eastside Boyz have several albums with crunk in the title, such as *Kings of Crunk, Crunk Juice, Get Crunk, We Still Crunk,* and *Crunk Rock.*

Not all hip hop is so oriented toward huge record sales and extensive radio airplay. Genres such as "alternative rap," "conscious rap," or "alternative hip hop" have developed during the past twenty years. These less commercially oriented genres are less concerned with drugs, sex, and money than with systemic social or political change or monetary gain. A handful of such groups—most notably a Tribe Called Quest—and artists like Mos Def, Common, Kanye West, and Nas have attained commercial and critical success, but most continue to labor in the underground.

Since its inception, hip hop has successfully challenged rock and rock-based music as the predominant form of American popular music. It has also resulted in some interesting crossovers. As early as the late 1980s, white artists such as the Beastie Boys, Vanilla Ice, and 3rd Bass enjoyed some popular success and gained at least some critical acceptance as rappers from the hip hop community. Eminem's success, beginning in 1999 with the triple platinum album *The Slim Shady,* came straight out of Detroit and placed him as a (white) hip hop superstar. Like most other successful hip hop artists since the late 1980s, Eminem came to be criticized for alleged glorification of violence, misogyny, and drug abuse, as well as homophobia and albums laced with constant profanity. Rapcore (a fusion of hip hop and heavy metal) became popular among mainstream white audiences. Rage Against the Machine, Linkin Park, and Limp Bizkit were among the most popular rapcore bands.

In February 2008, African American artists were routinely among the top-selling artists on the popular music singles and album charts. Many, but not all, of them are hip hop denizens. Keyshia Cole and Jill Scott are clearly influenced by hip hop, while Kanye West and Soulja Boy (though strikingly different) fit under the hip hop umbrella. The predominance of hip hop has caused some concern and consternation about other pop music genres. This is the subject of "Rhythm and Bullshit? The Slow Decline of R&B" by Mark Anthony Neal.

Toward the close of the first decade of the twenty first century, the varieties of black American music remain quite diverse, though most people are aware only of the trends in popular music. Other genres of African American music, however, remain largely underground, unknown to most people. For example, "Black Artistic Invisibility: A Black Composer Talking 'bout Taking Care of the Souls of Black Folks While Losing Much Ground Fast" by William Banfield decries the lack of interest and understanding of music composed by contemporary black Americans.

Nonetheless, a regional genre-like go-go continues to thrive in and around Washington, D.C., supported by a fierce local audience that attends weekly live performances by Back Yard Band, Natural Causes Band, Chuck Brown, and Lissen; listens to WKYS's Sunday evening go-go programming; submits new and old go-go videos to youtube.com; and checks out tmottgogo.com for the latest news. Washington, D.C., also supports a wide range of churches, where music also commands great respect, admiration, and participation. In a scene echoed in thousands of black churches across the United States, the choir at Bibleway Baptist Church (located within sight of the Capitol) sways and rocks several thousand people every Sunday. About one mile away, Howard University's fraternities and sororities participate in step shows, the background of which are described in "Steppin' Out an African Heritage" by Elizabeth Fine. Step shows combine precise movement with body percussion, music, and chanting in a competition that is the highlight of the October homecoming and the grand intercollegiate Saturday night show held at the National Guard Armory that always sells out.

These Washington, D.C., examples echo throughout the United States, from the contemporary zydeco scene in Southwestern Louisiana to trombone choirs heard in dozens of United House of Prayer for All People churches from North Carolina to New England. They underscore that fact that not all black American music is touched by hip hop or is entirely consumed by corporate entities. And the steppin' tradition, which can be found at every HBCU in the United States, simply confirms that contemporary black American music continues to draw upon many sources of inspiration and that its African roots (transformed and translated as they might be) are perhaps not as distant as people might believe.

Selected Further Reading

Lynn Abbott and Doug Seroff. *Out of Sight: The Rise of African American Popular Music, 1889–1895* (Jackson: University Press of Mississippi, 2002).

Gwen Ansell. *Soweto Blues: Jazz, Popular Music, and Politics in South Africa* (New York: Continuum International Publishing Group, 2004).

Imamu Amiri Baraka. *Black Music* (New York: Da Capo Press, 1999).

Horace Boyer. *How Sweet the Sound: The Golden Age of Gospel Music* (Urbana: University of Illinois Press, 2000).

Melonee Burnim and Portia Maultsby. *The Music of Black Americans: A History* (New York: Routledge Press, 2005).

William T. Dargan. *Lining Out the Word: Dr. Watts Hymn Singing in the Music of Black Americans* (Berkeley: University of California Press, 2006).

Samuel Floyd. *The Power of Black Music: Interpreting Its History from Africa to the United States* (New York: Oxford University Press, 1996).

Murray Foreman. *The 'Hood Comes First: Race, Space, and Place in Rap and Hip-Hop* (Middletown, CT: Wesleyan University Press, 2002).

Nelson George. *The Death of Rhythm & Blues* (New York: Pantheon Books, 1988).

Michael W. Harris. *The Rise of Gospel Blues—The Music of Thomas Andrew Dorsey in the Urban Church* (New York: Oxford University Press, 1992).

Melville Herskovits. *The Myth of the Negro Past* (Boston: Beacon Hill Press, 1990).

Irene V. Jackson. *More Than Dancing: Essays on Afro-American Music and Musicians* (Lanham, MD: Greenwood Press, 1985).

Leroi Jones. *Blues People: Negro Music in White America* (New York: Harper Perennial, 1990).

Robin D. G. Kelly and Earl Lewis. *To Make Our World Anew: Volume II: A History of African Americans Since 1880* (New York: Oxford University Press, 2005).

Kip Lornell. *"Happy in the Service of the Lord:" African American Sacred Vocal Harmony Quartets in Memphis, Tennessee* (Knoxville: University Press of Tennessee, 1995).

Kip Lornell and Charles Stephenson, *The Beat! Go Go Music from Washington D.C.*, 2nd edition (Jackson: University Press of Mississippi, 2009).

Sidney W. Mintz and Richard Price. *The Birth of African-American Culture: An Anthropological Perspective* (Boston: Beacon Hill Press, 1992).

Mark Anthony Neal. *What the Music Said: Black Popular Music and Black Public Culture* (New York: Routledge, 1998).

Eric Porter. *What Is This Thing Called Jazz? African American Musicians as Artists, Critics, and Activists* (Berkeley: University of California Press, 2002).

Eithne Quinn. *Nuthin' but a "G" Thang: The Culture and Commerce of Gangsta Rap* (New York: Columbia University Press, 2004).

Ronald Radano and Phillip Bohlman. *Music and the Racial Imagination* (Chicago: University of Chicago Press, 2000).

Ronald Radano. *Lying Up a Nation: Race and Black Music* (Chicago: University of Chicago Press, 2003).

Guy Ramsey. *Race Music: Black Cultures from Bebop to Hip-Hop* (Berkeley: University of California Press, 2004).

Arnold Shaw. *Honkers and Shouters: The Golden Years of Rhythm & Blues* (New York: Macmillan, 1978).

Suzanne Smith. *Dancing in the Streets: Motown and the Culture Politics of Detroit* (Cambridge: Harvard University Press, 1999).

Eileen Southern. *The Music of Black Americans: A History,* 3rd ed. (New York: W. W. Norton, 1997).

Craig Werner. *A Change Is Gonna Come: Music, Race, and the Soul of America* (New York: Plume, 1999).

1

Adrift on Stormy Seas

J. B. T. MARSH

Following the close of the War Between the States in 1865, black Americans finally gained rights previously denied to them during slavery. One of the most important rights related to education and in 1866 former slaves—aided by the abolitionist American Missionary Association—started the Fisk Free Colored School. This pioneering institution was named after the local Freedman's Bureau commander General Clinton Bowen Fisk, who turned a large number of former Union army hospital barracks over to the school's founders.

For its first few years the school was operated by literate freed slaves whose ranks were augmented by a small number of northerners, most of whom held strong Protestant views. George Leonard White, a veteran of Gettysburg, took on the difficult task of treasurer. His main job was to collect enough money from impoverished Fisk students to keep the doors open. White's true love was music. A choirmaster prior to his military service, he had served as a band sergeant during the war. In addition to serving as Fisk's treasurer, White taught contemporary choral and European classical vocal works to the most talented of the school's singers.

As freed slaves, Fisk students had grown up with spirituals but refrained from singing them in public because of their negative associations with slavery. Nonetheless, George White occasionally overheard his assistant, Ella Sheppard, quietly sing "Swing Low, Sweet Chariot" and "I Been in the Storm So Long" and he came to truly appreciate spirituals. Over the next five years, White reduced scores of these spirituals to sheet music both for the purpose of preservation as well as performance.

When the school faced financial disaster in 1871, White convinced Fisk's president, Adam Knight Spence, that he should take the singers on the road in order to raise money to keep the school afloat. On October 6, George White and the Fisk Jubilee Singers boarded a train for Cincinnati to begin a tour of small towns and cities along the former Underground Railroad. This bold, innovative idea met with quiet success at first, but within two years proved to be so successful that the Jubilee Singers had enriched the school's coffers by tens of thousands of dollars and the group had embarked on its first overseas tour to England. "Adrift on Stormy Seas" is a chapter from J. B. T. Marsh's 1892 book about the Jubilee Singers—The Story of the Jubilee Singers; with Their Songs—that describes the group's initial and difficult tour.

The company as it left Nashville, October 6, 1871, followed by the good wishes, prayers, misgivings, and anxieties of the whole University, numbered thirteen persons. These were Mr. White, who was at the same time the captain, supercargo, pilot, steward, and crew of the ship; Miss Wells, the Principal of an American Missionary Association school at Athens, Alabama, who took the oversight of the girls of the party; and eleven students—Ella Sheppard, Maggie L. Porter, Jennie Jackson, Minnie Tate, Eliza Walker, Phœbe J. Anderson, Thomas Rutling, Benjamin M. Holmes, Greene Evans, Isaac P. Dickerson, and George Wells.

The day after reaching Cincinnati the Singers met with the Rev. Messrs. Halley and Moore, the pastors of the two leading Congregational churches of the city, who were so delighted with their songs that they immediately arranged to hold praise meetings in their churches on Sunday, the next day, that their people might have the pleasure of hearing them. Full audiences greeted them in both services. On Monday a free concert was given and a collection taken at the close. The audience was large but the contribution small.

It was on this Sunday and Monday, so well remembered all over the world, that the great Chicago fire swept away the houses of one hundred thousand people and property to the value of $200,000,000. In Ohio, as everywhere else, people could scarcely think or talk about anything else, much less give money to any other object.

There had not been for ten years a week that would have been, to all appearances, such an unfavorable time for the Singers to commence their work. Out of money and in debt as they were, they donated the entire proceeds of their first paid concert, which amounted to something less than $50, to the Chicago relief fund. This was given in Chillicothe, and called out a card from the Mayor and leading citizens cordially commending to public patronage the two concerts that followed.

Here at Chillicothe they met with an indignity which was often repeated in the next year's experience. Applying at one of the principal hotels for entertainment, they were refused admittance because of their color. Treated in the same way at a second, they only secured shelter at a third by the landlord's giving up his own bedroom to them to use as a parlor, and furnishing them their meals before the usual hour, that his other guests might not leave the house. This odious and cruel caste-spirit it was to be a part of their mission—little as it was in their plans and painful as it was in experience—to break down. It was owing not a little to their triumphant success as singers, and to the story of the distinguished attentions they received from the people of highest rank and culture both in America and Great Britain, that the prejudice against color, the hateful heritage of slavery, which was so prevalent and powerful as to make those insults common in their first year's work, was so broken down that they were quite unfrequent in their travels three years afterwards. People who would not sit in the same church-pew with a negro, under the magic of their song were able to get new light on questions of social equality.

Returning to Cincinnati to fill engagements for the Sabbath, they found a dense audience gathered at Mr. Moore's church, in spite of rainy and unpleasant weather. It was hoped that the increasing enthusiasm manifested in connection with these praise services would insure a good audience at the paid concert which had been appointed at Mozart Hall for Tuesday evening; for hotel and traveling bills were already assuming serious proportions. But the receipts were barely sufficient to defray the local expenses of the concert.

However, it was not altogether lost labor. "It was," said one of the dailies, "probably the first concert ever given by a colored troupe in this temple, which has resounded with the notes of the best vocalists of the land. The sweetness of the voices, the accuracy of the execution, and the precision of the time, carried the mind back to the early concerts of the Hutchinsons, the Gibsons, and other famous families, who years ago delighted audiences and taught them with

Columbia *New Process* Records

FISK UNIVERSITY JUBILEE SINGERS
Famous Since 1871

THIS celebrated organization of Race artists dates back to 1871 when its members toured America and Europe and sang the Race spirituals before the crowned heads of Europe. Of their many remarkable Columbia recordings, "Shout All Over God's Heaven," on the same record with "Keep a' Inchin' Along," is a notable example.

The Fisk University Singers are Exclusive Columbia Artists

EZEKIEL SAW THE WHEEL LITTLE DAVID	818-D	75c
SHOUT ALL OVER GOD'S HEAVEN KEEP A' INCHIN' ALONG	658-D	75c
STEAL AWAY TO JESUS EVERY TIME I FEEL THE SPIRIT	562-D	75c
HOPE I'LL JOIN THE BAND YOU BETTER GET SOMEBODY ON YOUR BOND	163-D	75c

Viva-tonal Recording. The Records without Scratch [25]

This 1926 Columbia Record Company catalogue lists the most recent recordings by the Fisk University Jubilee Singers, who began recording for Columbia in 1915.

Credit: Catalogue from the collection of Kip Lornell.

sentiment while they pleased them with melody." Jennie Jackson's rendering of the "Old Folks at Home," as an encore, was received with rapturous applause. Mr. Dickerson sang the "Temperance Medley" here for the first time, and the class trembled for him, as he stood there with his knees beating a tattoo against each other, in a rusty coat that was as much too long for the fashion as his trousers were too short for neighborly acquaintance with his low shoes. But confidence came with the sound of his own voice, and the audience forgot the appearance of the singer in their enjoyment of his song.

Journeying next to Springfield, to fill an appointment for a concert at Black's Opera-house, they found less than twenty people gathered to hear them, and with heavy hearts they announced that they would postpone the entertainment.

A Synod of Presbyterian ministers was in session here, and Mr. White obtained permission for the Singers to appear before them. Assigned a half-hour in which to sing, and state their cause, it was a full hour before the Synod would release them. And not only did they testify their delight "in a vociferous, heartfelt, and decidedly unclerical manner, with hands, feet, and voice," but they passed a resolution "heartily commending them to the favor of the Christian community," and emphasized it by taking up a collection for their benefit of $105.

Working their way in a zig-zag path northward, they gave a concert at Yellow Springs, where the colored Baptist church was kindly placed at their disposal. At Xenia two concerts yielded them $84, and afforded the colored students of Wilberforce University a stimulus that was worth, in another way, quite as much more. For those were days in which anything well done by a colored man was an inspiration to all the rest of his race to whose knowledge it came.

At London, their singing in Springfield before the Synod bore fruit in the active efforts of the Presbyterian pastor in their behalf. The Sabbath was spent in Columbus, the Singers taking the place of the choir at one of the churches, and singing at a Sunday-school concert which is remembered as an occasion of special interest.

At Worthington they met a hearty welcome from Professor Ogden and his wife, their old instructors at Fisk, who had done work of lasting value in laying its foundation, but were now in charge of the Ohio State Normal School at that place. There they remained several days for much-needed rest, giving a concert meanwhile which, thanks specially to the active efforts of these two old friends, yielded $60. At Delaware their concert paid still better, and, for the first time on their trip, they were permitted to sit in the same parlors and at the same tables in the hotel as white people. Three concerts at Wellington netted them little more than enough money to take them on to Cleveland; where they sang on Sunday at the First Presbyterian and Plymouth Congregational churches, with the satisfaction that their unique praise services invariably gave.

All this time they were living, as the old phrase has it, from hand to mouth,—depending on the proceeds of one concert to pay the next morning's hotel charges and buy their railway-tickets to the next appointment. Any special collapse in an evening's receipts left them helpless till some friend stepped forward—as there was almost always some friend in such an emergency who did—and paid hall and hotel bills.

But the great trial was that no light had dawned on their mission. They would have done better to stay at home if they were to make nothing above expenses. So scantily clad were they that Miss Sheppard was obliged to travel one rainy day with no protection for her feet but cloth slippers. It was not until some time after the biting weather of the Northern winter, to whose severity they were quite unused, had fully set in that Mr. White was able, by borrowing $5 that had been given to Minnie Tate, and picking up $19 in other ways, to purchase overcoats for two of the young men, who had really been suffering for want of them.

In one way and another a comfortable outfit had been secured for the young women; but such were the varieties of style represented that it was not uncommon for Ella Sheppard to be asked if Minnie Tate was her daughter,—the former being twenty and the latter fourteen. And Jennie Jackson, who was nineteen, was sometimes taken to be the mother of Eliza Walker, who was fourteen.

The coolness, amounting often to indifference and sometimes to suspicion, with which even many of the warmest friends and supporters of the American Missionary Association looked upon this new agency for raising funds for its work, was one of the specially discouraging and trying features of the enterprise. Ministers were often loth, and not unnaturally, to let the Singers into their choirs; and if they gave them the use of their churches for a praise meeting, they sometimes showed a strong inclination to take their own seats among the audience and near the door!

But Mr. White's grip upon his purpose was not easily loosened, and he learned to let none of those things move him, knowing that the enthusiasm of these doubting friends after the service was almost sure to be in about an inverse ratio to their expectations before it.

During these days of experiment and trial Mr. White was loaded down with the work of at least four men. In other enterprises of this sort—and the same plan was afterwards found to be essential to the largest success of the Jubilee Singers—it is considered necessary to have a business manager, who lays out the route, visits or corresponds with editors and public men, and arranges the general plan of the campaign. Then an advance agent goes forward and puts these plans in operation, while his alternate accompanies the troupe to take up the tickets, pay the bills, and look after the details of the evening's management. A musical director arranges the programme, drills the singers, and answers the rattling volley of questions from curious and admiring friends. And where school-girls are in the company, and especially those hitherto unused to self-care and the demands of cultivated society, a governess is needed to look after their health and deportment.

In those early days the duties of general manager, advance agent, musical director, ticket-seller, and porter all fell to Mr. White. When the Singers halted somewhere for rest, he pushed ahead to lay out a new route; sometimes, when but a few appointments remained, he left Miss Wells and Miss Sheppard, the pianist, to attend to them while he went off to make new ones. The Singers he kept in drill the best he could. A rehearsal of some piece on their evening's programme was often the first course when they gathered about the dinner-table.

With all this work on his hands, there lay on his heart the burden of increasing debt and the consciousness that, while the business affairs of the University were needing his presence, the fact that he was earning no money and sending them no encouragement was adding to the uneasiness and anxiety of his associates at home. Many a time their last dollar was paid out for provisions; and he and they found frequent occasions to adopt the prayer of the old slave-song,—

"O Lord, O my Lord, O my good Lord!
    Keep me from sinking down."

But with a steadfast Christian faith, that seemed little less than obstinacy to those who could not read the Divine leadings, he held on.

2

Richards and Pringle's Original Georgia Minstrels and Billy Kersands, 1889–1895

LYNN ABBOTT AND DOUG SEROFF

Although minstrels initially brought the African American expressive culture to a wider audience as early as the 1830s, this trend increased dramatically during Reconstruction with the end of legal slavery. Minstrel shows were segregated—troupes were either black or white—and so were the audiences. Nonetheless minstrels provided entertainment for patrons of all colors well into the twentieth century. The entertainment offered by these traveling shows was quite varied but typically included comedy skits, a dramatic scene, novelty acts, and music.

Minstrel shows paved the road for vaudeville early in the twentieth century and, later, for pioneering television variety shows hosted by Milton Berle, Ed Sullivan, and others. Minstrel shows also provided the basic format for late-night talk shows hosted by Jack Paar, Johnny Carson, Jay Leno, and David Letterman. These men harken back to the minstrel show interlocutor, who served as the master of ceremonies, telling jokes, introducing the other entertainers, and generally overseeing the on-stage flow. The entertainment frequently played on the themes of black southern culture, often utilizing stereotypical "Mammy" and "Dandy" characters and music from the slave days.

In the late nineteenth century, long before television or radio, minstrel shows provided everyday people with entertainment. During their height of popularity in the 1890s Richards and Pringle's Original Georgia Minstrels arguably included the most talented performers on the minstrel circuit. This African American touring group gained a loyal, mostly black, audience by crisscrossing the South, performing in cities as large as Memphis and as small as McComb. Mississippi. Richards and Pringle's Original Georgia Minstrels proved so popular that they brought their show to larger northern cities such as Chicago and Detroit.

The African American minstrel troupe that captured the largest and most loyal black southern following during the 1890s was Richards and Pringle's Georgia Minstrels. When they played the Avenue Theater in New Orleans in 1887, the *Daily Picayune* noted, "Colored people are turned away nightly. There would be millions in it if the manager could give up the biggest part of his house to the colored people instead of the smallest, when the genuine Georgia Minstrels play their engagements."[1] At Memphis in the fall of 1896 the *Freeman* noted, "Richards & Pringle's Georgia Minstrels succeeded in drawing . . . in the neighborhood of 5,000 people—4,000 Negroes and 1,000 whites, the largest indoor paid audience ever known in that city."[2] By the turn of the century Richards and Pringle's *Freeman* correspondent could claim with certain conviction, "The Georgias reign supreme in the South."

Black turn-of-the-century community musical organizations treated members of Richards and Pringle's Georgia Minstrels like visiting royalty. While playing New Orleans in 1898, the "Georgias" were feted by Prof. W. J. Nickerson and his Student Orchestra, which included Nickerson's daughter Camille, piano; T. V. Baquet, cornet; and Baquet's son George, clarinet.[3] At Sedalia, Missouri, on March 25, 1899, they were banqueted by "Messrs. Williams and McCallahan, managers of the '400' club"[4] Later that year at Pensacola, Florida, they were "entertained most royally by the celebrated Utopia Club" with its "Pensacola orchestra of color . . . Prof. Ed Wyer, clarionet, Wm. Wyer double bass, Wm. Pontz cornet, Miss Flo Wyer piano and Ed Wyer Jr. 1st violin."[5]

The troupe's white proprietors, O. E. Richards and C. W. Pringle, attached themselves to an agglomerated history that claimed direct descent from the Georgia Minstrels of the 1860s. The credibility of this claim was largely fastened to their perennial star comedian, Billy Kersands, who first toured with a troupe of "Georgias" in 1871, under Charles B. Hicks's management. Kersands's unflagging charisma was an essential factor in Richards and Pringle's southern triumphs. When they showed at Houston, Texas, on January 8, 1901, representatives of the black community in Galveston arranged to "run a special excursion from Galveston to Houston, over the S.P.R.R., and carried nearly 400 people to see Billy Kersands and the big show. Long live Billy. He will ever be appreciated in this section of the country."[6]

Widely heralded during the 1890s and thereafter as an "unconscious," "nature-gifted" performer, Billy Kersands was one of the original architects of African American minstrelsy's "ancient oddities." According to a retrospective sketch in the *Freeman*, he was born in 1842 in Baton Rouge, Louisiana, then "went to New York and engaged in the boot black trade."[7] However, a later sketch in the same paper insists he was actually born on Hester Street in New York City.[8]

Charles B. Hicks recalled having first seen Kersands perform in 1870 "at Jake Berry's Cellar Music Hall, Broadway and Prince street, New York, billed as 'Cudjoe the Wonder,' admission ten cents, doing the 'essence of old Virginny' . . . I was then enroute to England with the 'Georgias,' but it had a lasting impression on me, so much so, that, upon my return in 1871, I hunted him up . . . Then it was that he commenced a career that placed him in the front ranks of minstrelsy. His 'Old Aunt Jemima' became a household word."[9]

Kersands's "Essence of Virginny" was a vernacular dance that required a nimble "combination of knee work and head buttoning to keep time with the music."[10] His song "Old Aunt Jemima" was, in effect, a vehicle for stringing together traditional floating verses. The connecting rod was a repeatedly chanted vocal refrain—"Old Aunt Jemima, oh, oh, oh." A different group of verses is given for "Old Aunt Jemima" in each of three different Georgia Minstrels songbooks.[11] The version in *Willie E. Lyle's Great Georgia Minstrels Song Book* (1875) includes these two:

> *My old missus promised me*
>   *Old Aunt Jemima, oh, oh, oh,*
> *When she died she'd set me free,*
>   *Old Aunt Jemima, oh, oh, oh,*
> *She lived so long her head got bald,*
>   *Old Aunt Jemima, oh, oh, oh,*
> *She swore she would not die at all,*
>   *Old Aunt Jemima, oh, oh, oh.*
>
> *I went to the hen-house on my knees,*
>   *Old Aunt Jemima, oh, oh, oh,*
> *I thought I heard a chicken sneeze,*
>   *Old Aunt Jemima, oh, oh, oh,*

*'Twas nothing but a rooster saying his
prayers,*
    Old Aunt Jemima, oh, oh, oh,
*He gave out the hymn, "Such a gittin' up
stairs,"*
    Old Aunt Jemima, oh, oh, oh.

"Old Aunt Jemima" was commercially recorded at least one time, in 1947, by an excellent white male quartet known as the Singing Sentinels.[12] The "my old missus" verse was in the air by 1845, when this variation was cited in a mainstream magazine:

Massa and Misse promised me
When they died they'd set me free;
Massa and Misse dead an' gone,
Here's old Sambo hillin'-up corn![13]

Highly suggestive of "authentic slave humor," the "my old missus" verse turned up during the 1920s in published collections of Negro folksongs[14] and on early "Race" and "Hillbilly" recordings by black vocal quartets and white southern string bands.[15]

The ubiquitous "hen house" verse takes off on "Down in the valley on my knees, asked my Lord, 'Have mercy, please,'" from the jubilee song "Every Time I Feel the Spirit." It is preserved, in subtle variations, on early race recordings, including the 1931 recording of "Who Stole the Lock (from the Henhouse Door)" by one of Birmingham, Alabama's greatest black community quartets, the Dunham Jubilee Singers.[16]

In 1880 Billy Kersands introduced "Mary's Gone Wid a Coon," a forerunner of the "coon song" phenomenon that soon came to dominate the repertoire of black and white minstrels. While keeping pace with trends in minstrel song and humor during the 1889–1895 period, Kersands was not expected to be an innovator; Billy Kersands made his way into the twentieth century as a living treasure of African American minstrelsy, "the old wagon that never broke down."[17]

Some particular accounts of the 1889–1895 activities of Richards and Pringle's Georgia Minstrels and their star comedian are preserved in the *New York Clipper* and various African American weeklies.

- JUNE 1, 1889: "The Stage," "Richards and Pringles, colored Georgia Minstrels, headed by the famous Billy Kersands closed their season last Saturday night, in Chicago. Colored talent in all lines of the business are wanted for next season" (*Indianapolis Freeman*).
- OCTOBER 21, 1889: "The following from McComb, Miss., dated Oct. 5, comes from Richards & Pringle's Minstrels: 'Billy Kersand and Miss J. A. Watts, and Billy Farrell and Miss W. Gauze were married here today. They received many presents from the company, and have the best wishes of their many friends" (*New York Clipper*).

Note: This was obviously intended as a joke, since Gauze and Watts were both female impersonators. That it originated from McComb, Mississippi, in the fall of the year suggests that Richards and Pringle were already coordinating their troupe's southern tours to follow the harvest season. During the 1890s and early 1900s, autumns in the Mississippi Delta were increasingly congested with African American minstrel shows.

- APRIL 12, 1890: "The old reliable Richards & Pringle's Famous Georgia Minstrels, Silver Cornet Band and Classic orchestra, just closed a successful season of 37 weeks. The man in white perambulated every Sunday. Now reorganizing for the season of 1890–1891 . . . and

This photograph (ca. 1936) documents that minstrel shows toured throughout the South well into the 1930s.
Credit: Collections of the Library of Congress.

will be headed by the only and original Billy Kersands, the man with many imitators, but no equals. Wanted, Colored talent in all branches . . . Richards & Pringle, care National Printing Co., 119 Monroe Street, Chicago, Ill." (*New York Clipper*).

Note: Such phrases as "The man in white perambulated," or "The ghost makes his usual weekly visits" are variations of the popular showbusiness expression, "The ghost walks," which signified that paydays were being regularly met.[18]

- **DECEMBER 27, 1890:** "Notes from Richard & Pringle's Georgia Minstrels," "We are now in the twentieth week of our present season, and everything is sailing smoothly with O. E. Richards as captain and C. W. Pringle as our pilot. There has not been any dissention in the ranks since we started out. Charles Walker is at present on the sick list. Chas. Wallace, Will Eldridge, Tom Brown and Frank Mallory have of late been investing in precious stones. W. O. Terry was presented lately with a beautiful diamond pin by Will Gauze. The presentation took place on the stage . . . Afterwards there was a popping of corks. Jim Gilliam is at present leader of the band, this being his fifth season as the occupant of that position. The Vestibule Car Porters and Continental Guards' Drill emanated from the Mallory Bros. (Frank and Ed), and is under the personal supervision of Frank Mallory. Billy Johnson joined us some time ago, and as an aged negro delineator he is 'way up.' Dennis B. Rice has purchased a home at Clarksville, Tenn. The ghost makes his usual weekly visits" (*New York Clipper*).

- *MAY 22, 1891 (DETROIT, MICHIGAN):* "Mr. Wm. Gauze, the famous male soprano of Detroit has just closed a season of 40 weeks with the Richard and Pringle minstrels and can be seen shaking hands with his many friends" (*Detroit Plaindealer*).
- *MAY 23, 1891:* "Since our arrival at Chicago most of the company have departed for other climes. Billy Kersands has gone to Louisville. Thomas Brown opened at the Buckingham Theatre May 18. Wm. Johnson is visiting his parents at Charleston, S.C. Wm. Eldridge is with his mother at St. Louis. Prof. Charles Johnson, leader of orchestra, is traveling with Thearle's 'U.T.C.' Co. W. O. Terry is at his home, Charleston, W. Va., and Dennis B. Rice is located at Clarksville, Tenn., with his wife and little daughter. John H. Grant is doing the swell at New Orleans. James Lacey has the leadership of an orchestra at Kansas City. Chas. Wallace is kept quite busy arranging music for several Chicago firms. Frank Mallory is on his way to his home at Jacksonville, Ill. . . . His brother, Ed., is spending his vacation with his parents, his wife and child having joined him, from Galveston, Tex. Ed. is having a brand new cornet manufactured for his express use . . . James Gilliam remains in the Windy City. Will Gauze will play several weeks through the West, after a brief visit to his home, Windsor, Ont. Managers Richards & Pringle are at Chicago, making big preparations for next season" (*New York Clipper*).
- *JUNE 27, 1891:* "Manager O. E. Richards has returned to Chicago, from his recent trip to the Hawkeye State, where he visited his relatives and numerous friends . . . C. W. Pringle remains at his post of duty . . . Jno. H. Grant has returned to Chicago from New Orleans, the climate of the latter place having proved disasterous to his health . . . Chas. Walker . . . with the others of his quartet will commence an engagement at the Olympic June 29. Chas. Johnson, leader of orchestra, has completed his Summer engagement with Thearle's 'U.T.C.,' and is now on his way to his home at Lawrence, Kas." (*New York Clipper*).
- *OCTOBER 18, 1891:* "Stage Notes," "Richard and Pringle's minstrels report a good success through the South with old time favorite Billy Kersands" (*Topeka Weekly Call*).
- *OCTOBER 24, 1891:* "Ed. Mallory, of the Mallory Bros., with Richards & Pringle's Minstrels, was presented by his wife with a handsome cluster diamond pin, at Galveston, Tex., on Oct. 2. The Venetian Mandolin Drill, as produced by them, is said to be a pleasing success" (*New York Clipper*).
- *OCTOBER 31, 1891:* "Our Musical People," "Richard's & Sprigle's [sic] Minstrels are now doing the Southern States. They appeared in Columbus, Miss. last week" (*Indianapolis Freeman*).
- *JANUARY 3, 1892: (TOPEKA, KANSAS):* "The grand minstrel performance at Crawford's opera house on the 22nd, headed by Billy Kersands, the emperor of comedians, was one of the finest we have had for years" (*Topeka Weekly Call*).
- *MARCH 12, 1892:* "Stage," "The original Georgia Minstrels with Billy Kersands are in California" (*Indianapolis Freeman*).
- *AUGUST 5, 1893:* "Richards & Pringle's Georgia Minstrels open their seventeenth regular season at Valparaiso, Ind., Aug. 12, with the following roster: Billy Kersands, Tom Brown, Ganzer [sic], Jas. White, Hillman and Vernon, C. A. Walker, J. A. Howard, Hi Wooten, J. A. Watts, Prof. C. F. Alexander, Jas. Y. Gilliam, Jas. Lacey, Jas. Moore, D. B. Rice, W. O. Terry, Walter Mitchell, H. Woodley, Sargeant Reims and his twelve Dohamy [sic] cadets. O. E. Richards is the sole owner and manager; R. A. Rusco, agent, and Geo. Gurgen, assistant agent" (*New York Clipper*).
- *NOVEMBER 11, 1893:* "Tom Brown's original production of 'A Game of Craps' and his 'Old Fashion Cake Walk' are meeting with success through the Southern States" (*New York Clipper*).

- *OCTOBER 20, 1894:* "Notes from Richards & Pringle's Minstrels," "We played in Charleston, W. Va., Oct. 8, and as it is the home of W. O. Terry, who is connected with the company, a large audience assembled. There are ten Knights of Pythias with the show, and after the performance Capital City Lodge, Knights of Pythias, gave them an enjoyable reception. Sir Knight Jones delivered an address of welcome to the visiting Knights and was responded to by W. O. Terry. Then all sat down to a bounteous feast. During the evening the minstrel orchestra discoursed delightful music. Billy Kersands, James White and James Moore did their share toward making the occasion lively" (*New York Clipper*).
- *JANUARY 18, 1895:* "At Donaldsonville, La., on the 6th inst Billy Kersands, the noted colored minstrel at the head of Richards & Pringle's Georgia Minstrels, was married to Widow Armstrong [sic], one of the best known colored residents of Donaldsonville and who is reputed to be quite wealthy. The ceremony was to have taken place on the stage of Phoenix Opera House during the performance of the Georgians, but owing to the opposition of the Strong family who are devout Catholics, the project was abandoned and the couple were united by the parochial priest, Very Rev. Father Dubernard" ("Brotherhood," *Kansas City American Citizen*).

Note: Kersands's new wife, Louise, also became his regular stage partner. Her maiden name may have been Fernandez. An article in the December 23, 1905, edition of the *Freeman* identified her as "the Widow Strong . . . a Louisiana girl, born and reared in the town of Donaldsonville, sixty-four miles west of New Orleans, on the Texas and Pacific Railroad, where she is recognized by both races as one of the most estimable women in the community. Until her marriage to Mr. Kersands, she was proprietress of the best kept restaurant in the town of Donaldsonville."

- *MAY 18, 1895:* "Notes from Richards & Pringle's Minstrels," "We closed May 11, at Fargo, N.D., our twenty-fourth season on the road . . . A number of the old folks have signed for next season, including Billy Kersands, which makes his eleventh year with the show. We will open about Aug. 1" (*New York Clipper*).
- *JULY 13, 1895:* "The following have signed with Richards & Pringle's for next season: Billy Kersands, Eugene Hillman, Robt. Vernon, Neil Moore, Bobby Kemp, Marsh Craig Jalvan, Pickaninny Quartet, Reese Bros., Brown and Thomas, Jas. Lacy, W. O. Terry, D. B. Rice, John Easson, S. B. Foster, Wm. Lacy, Jas. F. Leitch, Crescent City Quartet (Watts, Collins, Becker and Wooten), W. C. Tiede, John Terry, Oscar Hodge . . . O. E. Richards, sole proprietor. Their season opens at the Alhambra, Chicago, Aug. 11. They travel in their private car, Georgia" (*New York Clipper*).

In 1903 the Georgia Minstrels and Bil Kersands finally parted ways, and Kersands went out under his own name. In Texas during the fall of 1906, his ancient powers were reconfirmed: "At Texarkana we were compelled to deputize thirty police to keep order, so large were the crowds eager to pay homage to the exalted ruler of Negro minstrelsy, the one man who, through wind and tide, has proved himself a minstrel king, true and noble, pure and simple—a singer natural as the changes of nature . . . Billy Kersands—a man whose gestures and every character of stage deportment has been copied and imitated for many years but never equalled, the real beacon light of genuine minstrelsy."[19]

Billy Kersands "took his final curtain call" on June 30, 1915, at a theater in Artesia, New Mexico, where he suffered a fatal heart attack after his second performance of the evening. He was seventy-three.[20] *Freeman* columnist and fellow performer Salem Tutt Whitney eulogized him as the "best known and best beloved minstrel America has known, regardless of color.

Billy's name was a byword for minstrelsy the country over."[21] Another eulogist spoke of "OUR BILLY . . . Possessed with no college education, but owner of the greatest asset 'Mother Wit,' he vied with the best in educating mankind."[22]

Notes

1. *Daily Picayune*, September 28, 1887.
2. "The Stage," *Freeman*, October 24, 1896.
3. "The Stage," *Freeman*, December 31, 1898.
4. "The Stage," *Freeman*, April 8, 1899. For an historical account of the 400 Club and Scott Joplin's relationship to it, see Edward A. Berlin, *King of Ragtime: Scott Joplin and His Era* (New York: Oxford University Press, 1994), pp. 34–44.
5. *Freeman*, December 30, 1899. Ed Wyer, Jr. and his younger brother J. Paul Wyer were later associated with W. C. Handy's Memphis Blues Band.
6. "Stage," *Freeman*, January 26, 1901.
7. "Stage Gossip," *Freeman*, July 10, 1915.
8. *Freeman*, November 11, 1916.
9. Letter from Charles B. Hicks, June 17, 1902, in "Stage," *Freeman*, September 6, 1902.
10. "Gossip of the Stage," *Freeman*, February 8, 1913.
11. See Toll, *Blacking Up*, pp. 259–60.
12. The Singing Sentinels, "Old Aunt Jemima," Sonora 1137, included in 78rpm "Album Set" no. 483, "American Ballads," c. 1947.
13. James K. Kennard, Jr., "Who Are Our National Poets?" *Knickerbocker Magazine* (1845), reproduced in Eileen Southern, "Black Musicians and Early Ethiopian Minstrelsy," in Annemarie Bean, James V. Hatch, and Brooks McNamara, eds., *Inside the Minstrel Mask: Readings in Nineteenth-Century Blackface Minstrelsy* (Hanover: University Press of New England, 1996), pp. 43–63.
14. Toll cites Tally, *Negro Folk Rhymes*, 1922; and Scarborough, *On the Trail of Negro Folksongs*, 1925.
15. "Raise R-U-K-U-S Tonight," Norfolk Jazz Quartette, Paramount 12032, 1923, reissued on Document DOCD-5382; "Gonna Raise Rukus Tonight," Riley Puckett, Columbia 15455, 1928; "Gonna Have Lasses in the Morning," Golden Melody Boys, Paramount 3087, 1928; "Raise a Rukus To-Night," Birmingham Jubilee Singers, Columbia 14263, 1927, reissued on Document DOCD-5346; "Poor Mourner," Four Dusty Travelers, Columbia 14477, 1929, reissued on Document DOCD-5538; "Come Along Little Children," Picaninny Jug Band, Champion 16654, 1932, reissued on RST BDCD-6002. In the latter three renditions the final line is given in variations of "She got out of the notion of dying at all."
16. Columbia 14609-D, 1931, reissued on Document DOCD-5498. Also: Bryant's Jubilee Quartet, "Who Stole De Lock," Banner 32173, 1931, reissued on Document DOCD-5437; and The Blue Chips, "Oh! Monah," ARC 6–09–55, 1936, reissued on Document DOCD-5488.
17. "The Stage," *Freeman*, June 23, 1900.
18. For different explanations of the origin of the term see "The Stage," *Freeman*, January 4, 1908; and Henry T. Sampson, *The Ghost Walks* (Metuchen: The Scarecrow Press, 1988), pp. vii–viii.
19. "The Stage," *Freeman*, October 27, 1906.
20. "Stage Gossip," *Freeman*, July 10, 1915.
21. Salem Tutt Whitney, "Seen and Heard While Passing," *Freeman*, July 17, 1915.
22. "Our Billy Kersands, Pioneer in the Profession, Valued for His Long Record," *Freeman*, July 24, 1915.

3 The Virginia Jubilee Singers in Bourke, Australia

ANONYMOUS

Orpheus McAdoo is a fascinating and important figure in black American music during Reconstruction. Not simply an entrepreneur satisfied with touring the United States, McAdoo was one of the first to introduce the rest of the world to the forms of African American music that emerged in the late nineteenth century. South Africans, for instance, had their first formal contact with African Americans and African American music on June 19, 1890, when the minstrel troupe operated by Orpheus Myron McAdoo, the Virginia Jubilee Singers from Hampton, Virginia, presented a series of concerts in Cape Town.

Born in 1858 in Greensboro, North Carolina, McAdoo attended the Hampton Institute in Hampton, Virginia, where he studied and graduated as a teacher in 1876. Before turning to music as a professional career in 1886, he taught school in Virginia for ten years. In 1886 he left his career as a teacher and toured Europe, Australia, New Zealand, and the Far East as a member of a Fisk Jubilee Singers group.

Smitten by the prospect of singing abroad, McAdoo returned to the United States around 1888 and formed his own company by recruiting some ex-students and graduates from Hampton, including his future wife, Mattie Allen, and his brother, Eugene. With a newly formed troupe consisting of six women and four men, McAdoo set sail on a European tour in 1888. Two years later they arrived in Cape Town, South Africa, as McAdoo's Virginia Concert Company and Jubilee Singers.

McAdoo's minstrels stayed and toured throughout South Africa for eighteen months, visiting places in the province of the Eastern Cape such as Grahamstown, King Williamstown, and Alice, where they performed at Lovedale College, the black South African equivalent of Tuskegee University in the United States. Musical history indicates that their impact and influence upon the old Zulu and Xhosa choral traditions were quite significant, as their music introduced innovative new harmonic concepts and structures. It is ironic that this genre of African American minstrelsy, spiritual music, should return across the Atlantic Ocean to inform indigenous music in South Africa.

This brief newspaper review of a September 1892 performance in Bourke, Australia, which initially appeared in a New South Wales Australian newspaper, was reproduced several weeks later in the Indianapolis Freeman, *arguably the leading black-oriented newspaper in the Midwest in the late nineteenth century [and more recently reprinted in Abbott and Seroff (2002), p. 125]. The review underscores the variety of songs in the Singers's repertoire, the mixture of solo and group performances, and its balance of sacred and secular music. It doesn't,*

> *unfortunately, clearly relate the audience's reaction to this exotic group. Even though jubilee groups were commonplace by the 1890s, the fact that the Virginia Jubilee Singers, among others, were touring the world presages the global importance of African American music a century later.*

On Wednesday evening the Virginia Concert Company, or the Jubilee Singers—the name by which they are more familiarly known—made their first appearance in Bourke . . . , and Albert hall was well filled. There is very little pretension about the company, all of whom are American natives, an organ, a piano and several chairs being the only furniture required by them on the stage. But all the effect of stage scenery so necessary to other performers would not make the soul-stirring melodies of the Jubilee Singers one whit more beautiful. Each and every one has a magnificent voice of its own peculiar class and range. The programme was a mixed one, containing both sacred and secular selections. The opening chorus was followed by the singing of "The Lord's Prayer." "Get you ready, there's a meeting here tonight," was sung most vociferously, and was very descriptive of the calling of a meeting of slaves. Mr. O. McAdoo then sang the bass solo, "A hundred fathoms deep." He has really a wonderful voice, and one would imagine that his lowest note, the four-barred G, which is fully and fairly taken, comes from the soles of his boots. An encore could only be expected, when Mr. McAdoo sang "Old Black Joe," the rest of the singers, who had retired to the back of the stage behind a screen, joined in the chorus. The effect was astonishing . . . The chorus, "The Band of Gideon" was well given, and then Miss Laura A. Carr won an encore for her soprano solo, "When the swallows come again." This singer is as black as the ace of spades, but when you hear her sing, a lover of music feels that she must have a soul as white as the driven snow. The chorus "Ring Those Chiming Bells," was followed by a quartette, "Josephus and Bohuncas," by Messrs. Collins, Hodges, and J. and O. McAdoo. This was very funny, and "The bulldog on the bank, and bullfrog in the pool" was given as an encore. This caused considerable merriment. The first part of the program was concluded by the chorus, "Good News, The Chariot's Coming." After an intermission of ten minutes for the manipulation of "ice water," as suggested by Mr. McAdoo, the second part was commenced by the rendition of a sweet pretty medley of English, Irish, Scotch and American songs. Unfortunately, Miss Mattie Allen was indisposed, and had to be excused from singing "Mona," and Miss Belle Gibbons filled the vacancy by singing "The song that reached my heart." . . . Miss Julia C. Wormley gave a recitation, which told a beautiful story about an old choir singer, the effect being considerably added to by the company softly singing "Rock of Ages." Miss Wormley, in reply to vociferous applause, gave "The Hindoo's Paradise," the funniest item of the evening. The song and chorus "Mother, is Massa Going to Sell me Tomorrow," was nicely sung by R. H. Collins and the company . . . M. Hamilton Hodges then charmed the audience with a fine baritone song, entitled "Only the sound of a voice." . . . A duet, "Good-night beyond," was given by Messrs. Collins and Julius [sic] McAdoo. The glee, "Good-night, gentle folks," brought the concert to a close.

4 African Banjo Echoes in Appalachia: A Conclusion

CECELIA CONWAY

Most people in the twenty-first century closely associate the banjo with country music, most specifically with bluegrass. The banjo is, in fact, at the core of bluegrass ensembles as well as its precursor, "old-time" string bands that developed in the late nineteenth century and displayed extreme regional variations. Well into the twentieth century these old-time string bands provided music for black as well as white music gatherings, such as corn shuckings and community dances. The fact is that the lineage of the banjo can be traced to the vast West Africa savannahs, along with many of the slaves, who brought three- or four-string instruments with names like bantar or bandora with them to the New World. Although slaves were dispersed throughout the South, hundreds of thousands of them ended up living in the Piedmont of the East Coast from Georgia into Maryland, which is where the black American banjo tradition persisted the longest.

This final chapter from African Banjo Echoes in Appalachia: A Story of Folk Traditions in many ways sums up not only the book's important points but also raises several issues that are critical to understanding black American vernacular music since Reconstruction and that recur throughout From Jubilee to Hip-Hop. Foremost, perhaps, is the ongoing interchange between white and black musical culture, interactions that began almost as soon as slaves were brought to this country by European settlers. It is a dialogue that continues to inform our musical culture today. The impact and significance of minstrelsy in shaping twentieth-century American music also inform Conway's "Conclusion" as it does some of the previous chapters in this collection—most directly the Abbott and Seroff excerpt. I would argue that the ways in which hip-hop artists present themselves on stage can, in some ways, be traced back to stereotypical characters, such as the Dandy, found on minstrel stages.

The fact that Dink Roberts, in particular, carried on with the banjo "songster" tradition in Piedmont North Carolina into the 1970s suggests a deep-seated cultural importance. The fact that he played nineteenth-century songs, such as "Cindy Gal," "Old Joe Clark," and "Love Somebody" that came from the white tradition as well as "Roustabout" and "Old Reuben," which appear to be black in origin, underscores both the depth and length of the racial interchange. Musical persistence in light of immense changes, which helps to solidity a strong sense of community and tradition, was important not only to Dink Roberts, but also to his peers singing sacred music in southern Alabama. (Sacred music singers are discussed in Chapter 13.)

> You can tromp down the flowers all around my grave
> But they'll rise and bloom again,
> Yes, they'll rise and bloom again.
>
> —Tommy Jarrell, "Rylan Spenser,"
> learned from African American Jim Rawley

The banjo has long signified at the crossroads of the South and today remains a symbol of the mountain musician. The twentieth-century folk banjo tradition, indeed, has persisted most strongly among southern mountain whites who continue to play on homemade banjos. Importantly, this living tradition is the complex result of more than a century and a half of exchange between African Americans and others. But the early written records prove that, even a century before this exchange began, blacks had brought the banjo with them from Africa. The banjo remained in the sole stewardship of African Americans until about 1830, and some still play today. Although blacks have played banjos for more than two centuries, researchers have located, interviewed, and recorded very few in this century. Thus, the North Carolina musicians—Dink Roberts, John Snipes, and Odell Thompson—are historically crucial, for, like the African griots [a West African term for a wandering poet, storyteller, or singer considered to be a repository of oral tradition], they have been the "praise singers" and have carried on "some of the most important aspects of traditional culture: genealogy, rites of passage (personal identity), healing, and divining."[1] Their traditions and practices have provided a means for reaching beyond the written records to an understanding of a continuous strand of African-American musical culture, its impact upon white tradition, especially in the Southeast and in Appalachia, and its contribution to American folk music. What once sounded like "mumbling" to whites has for a long time now been heard as "solemn," "resonant," "brilliant' and has been taken up, preserved, and modified.

When I began to visit these black banjo players, I suddenly began to realize that the white mountain music traditions that were so familiar to me were only part of this old-time music story. Next I began to see everything in terms of black influence. Finally, I hope to have come to a place that seems more carefully informed by history and appreciative of the significance of different cultural roles at different historical moments.

With a homemade banjo, driving rhythms, and sliding notes, the distinctive aesthetic of African-American musicians shaped the playing styles and song forms of their identifiable repertory and influenced white musicians. For the first century after their arrivals in the 1740s, blacks accompanied their songs and dances in this country with the banjo patterned after the gourd instrument brought from Africa. Like griots, these men contributed to crucial aspects of traditional culture: they offered personal expression and communication among the community, social rituals enacted through song and dance, celebrations of the past, clarifications of hardship, of challenges, and of identity, and they performed affecting mediations and eased social pain.

By the early 1800s, the African-American banjo tradition was well established in New Orleans and along the Mississippi River Valley and in its earlier stronghold in the Upland South. From the earliest days, the banjo-drum ensemble dominated the Louisiana area, playing for large groups of dancers. The banjo accompanied by clapping or percussion instruments thumped and echoed across the country. But in the Upland South, a tradition of banjo lead and sometimes solo performance persisted tenaciously, especially after drumming was curtailed near the end of the eighteenth century. The banjo player often sang and played for individual buck dancing and small sets of dancers. The early transplanted Wolof [a West

Joe Thompson (fiddle) and Odell Thompson (banjo), two cousins from Orange County, North Carolina, carried the African American string band tradition into the 1990s.

Credit: Photograph by Kip Lornell

African ethnic group found largely in Senegal, The Gambia, and Mauritania] and more widespread savannah griot practices influenced banjo tradition and interacted with diverse African backgrounds to influence regional preferences for solo (or banjo lead) playing in contrast to the extensive percussive ensemble playing of the Deep South. But local legislation, social sanctions, and close contact with whites were also pressing factors in the early divergence of the instrumental traditions of the two long-standing centers of the banjo tradition. The unique ensemble of the banjo and fiddle did emerge in the Upland South before the Civil War, but the continuing associations of the banjo with song, dance, and entertainment were more pertinent reasons for the persistence of the African instrument. The African-American banjo tradition that remained vigorous throughout the nineteenth century resulted from an African instrument in the care of an enslaved people in a foreign land. The banjo stood at the crossroads as a symbol of African-American identity, cultural continuity, and a cooperative community.

Before the middle of the nineteenth century, southern whites became fascinated with black banjo tradition. By the early 1840s, whites across the country had begun to imitate slave dance and song, as well as banjo playing, and to incorporate these imitations into stage performances—the minstrel shows. The majority of first generation minstrels were folk musicians themselves and acquired their African-American traditions traveling or living in the South. The influence of southerners Ferguson and the Sweeneys alone was extensive among early minstrels who became famous. The minstrels accompanied their banjo performances with percussion instruments, an ensemble long standing in black tradition. Although we may never know who introduced the fiddle-banjo combination, there is evidence that the minstrels popularized this ensemble—one of the first intricate, creative mergings of Celtic-American and African-American tradition. Late in the century, minstrel performances, which all too often had included distasteful stereotyped caricatures of blacks, lost touch with their early folk roots and faded from public interest.

Far from the minstrel stage, the African-American banjo tradition, however, had begun to take hold with the mountain folk about two decades before the time of the Civil War. By the beginning of the nineteenth century, black banjo players had reached the mountain frontier, and whites in these regions had also had contact with African-American musical traditions in the southern Piedmont and on the river routes to New Orleans—well before the advent of minstrelsy. The white musicians, Ferguson of Western Virginia and the Sweeneys of Virginia, all played by the early 1840s.

Furthermore, in the early decades of the twentieth century, black banjo players, whose ancestors had arrived before the Civil War, lived, for example, in the Blue Ridge Mountains of northwestern North Carolina. A number of accomplished white downstroke banjo players also lived in these areas, all of whom had long-standing contact with black musicians. There is every likelihood that Piedmont blacks carried downstroking into the mountains and that local whites acquired their banjo playing directly from African Americans.

The banjo itself underwent a number of changes during its cross-cultural transmission in the nineteenth century. The gourd banjo, present from the earliest days, gave way to wooden-rim banjos. These sturdier banjos soon had five strings and became popular enough to replace the instruments of three and four strings. But some characteristics persisted and suggest the playing styles used by blacks before they passed them on to whites. The persistence of the African-American thumb string and the smooth fingerboard suggests that the driving rhythms of the drone-string playing styles and the twists and bends of left-hand slide techniques that characterize white mountain and black Piedmont banjo playing today existed well before the acquisition of the banjo by whites. This likelihood is supported by the pictures and descriptions of slave playing and is confirmed by early minstrel instruction manuals, which document downstroking as the only style used by the first generation of minstrels and hence the initial style acquired from African Americans. Reports from elderly white mountain players confirm that downstroking, or "thumping," was the early and favored way of playing in Appalachia.

Present-day mountain whites share many basic techniques used by the minstrels and some of their tunings. These correspondences have given rise to the claim that minstrels initially transmitted this style to mountain musicians. But the fact that black banjo players today use these same techniques and tunings makes it more likely that their ancestors directly influenced mountain whites, just as they did the minstrels. Several facts support my claim. First, mountain whites had more frequent and direct access to the blacks than to the early minstrels. Before 1865, for example, minstrel shows either seldom traveled in the South or were comprised primarily of southern folk musicians. Second, after that time, the increasingly commercially oriented minstrels were losing interest in downstroking, for they were growing fascinated with the picking styles of banjo playing. Furthermore, present-day southern blacks and whites share certain special tunings and techniques that are not described or emphasized by the early minstrel banjo instruction books. Minstrels, then, seem to have had little or no impact upon the formation of mountain banjo playing and provided limited influence upon the continuous evolution of this southern folk tradition beyond specific repertory items and settings.

The ancestors of the southern blacks and whites who have continued to play banjo had strong musical traditions. They were highly influential, inquisitive, and open to musical exchange. But they remained more conservative and subtle than the popular and commercial entertainers that the minstrels became. In the mountains, the newly acquired thumping or downstroke banjo tradition flourished among whites and resulted in fashioning and refashioning of banjo songs and in the complex interweave of fiddle-banjo music often played for dancing.

In the first decade of the twentieth century, black banjo tradition began to decline soon after inexpensive guitars became readily available and after urbanization and industrialization heightened social pressures in the South. The guitars echoed the banjo techniques, supported the vocal and increasingly assertive expression of singers, consolidated the new blues genre, and traveled from house parties and juke joints into bars from Chicago to Harlem and elsewhere. No longer common today, the African-American banjo tradition has been left largely to white southern (usually mountain) musicians. In Appalachia, thumping survived minstrelsy and even the African-American banjo tradition that was its source. But eventually, like the minstrels in the 1870s and the blacks at the end of the nineteenth century, southern whites began to turn to new picking styles and other instruments. By the 1930s they had added the guitar to the fiddle-banjo combination to form old-time string bands that played (and sometimes sang) all together at the same time and reflected the democratic ideals of self-sufficiency and cooperative agrarian life. By the 1940s they had created bluegrass banjo music, played on larger, louder, and even more durable banjos. The new bluegrass music continues to thrive, evolve, mirror its changing and industrialized cultural context, and, like old-time banjo playing, to reflect its African-American and Celtic-American roots.

But while downstroke banjo playing was still a tradition strongly shared by blacks and whites, the complex exchanges between southern black and white folk musicians gave rise to a distinct genre of American folk music—the banjo song. The banjo-song genre is the culmination of the influence of the African banjo, a playing style, and an aesthetic upon white tradition. Although initially and predominantly influenced by African-American tastes, the exchange of more than 150 years led to a complex and interesting group of songs that reflect the identity and vitality of both traditions.

Accurately characterizing the banjo-song genre and identifying its constituents is not a simple matter. It is the interplay of an appropriate banjo-song textual structure or model with two other elements—the banjo performance and the vocal line—that characterizes the genre. In an effort to discover the nature of this genre, I turned especially to the music of Dink Roberts, whose banjo performances seem to illustrate characteristics of the early black banjo tradition. The description of Roberts's banjo-song performances has to be slightly broadened to accommodate Celtic-American inclinations in defining the genre, but five musical features are common to performances in both traditions: 1) rhythmic banjo playing throughout the performance, especially when singing; 2) compressed vocal lines of two or more syllables per beat; 3) elaborated instrumental interludes; 4) occasional and irregular interruptions of the stanza by instrumental interludes; and 5) varied repetition of instrumental elements. Banjo songs by both blacks and whites reflect African-American delight with improvisation, percussion, rhythmic variety, and (vocal) call and (instrumental) response.

The texts of Dink's banjo songs also show distinctive traits. Like his playing style, his repertory is largely of pre-blues origin. He acquired his repertory at the beginning of this century before the advent and influence of radio and sound recordings, a time when downstroke banjo playing was at the peak of its shared development. Although Dink's repertory covers a number of themes, including love, liquor, food, work, and the symbolic antics of animals, I chose for analysis several texts about man against the law. Comparison of these texts with other variants has revealed basic characteristics shared by both black and white texts: 1) lyricism effected by the presence of a participant persona who speaks direct address lines; 2) a tone sympathetic with the central character; and 3) a paratactic form for a song core comprised of a dramatic (often threatening) antithesis and a resolution. Direct address is the response device that characterizes the resolution of the song and permits personal or ethnic variation within the pattern of the genre. The response line may express personal idiosyncrasies, black feelings, white actions, or whatever. The persona may announce how he feels as easily as what he has done: "What's gonna 'come of me?" or "I shot 'em in the head with my .44." This lyric song pattern is embodied in a wide group of songs and, especially in combination with the banjo and the man-against-the-law theme, is an African-American song model.

The banjo-song model also provides a convenient means for comparing the themes and lyricism of different texts. In these and other African-American banjo songs on other themes, the central character does not fully control his own destiny. The very fact that a threat is built into the song structure characterizes the persona as vulnerable. He is threatened in some vague though terrifying way, often by the law of the dominant society. (Earlier threatened by the system of slavery rather than the law, the slaves in their songs encouraged the listeners to protect themselves and to "Run, Nigger, Run.") In these songs about the system of another man's law, the persona fears capture, confinement, or death, and his response to this threat is foremost a verbal expression of emotion, often addressed to a particular member of his own community. Although he may "lay low" or move away from his adversary, the ironic distance and understatement of his response define his self-contained dignity. Dink's question is the one that needs to be answered: "What's gonna 'come of me?"

On this theme, other more complex songs about semilegendary figures, such as "Garfield," reflect the community values that surround the common man's conflict with the law of the dominant society. Whatever the legal consequences, the song continues to support the speaker, who has moved into action against the authority figures of the dominant culture. The conversational structure, extensions, and complexities of these songs emphasize support for the speaker from his friends and relations and an understanding of his need to take violent action. These are songs for every man; their lyric, dreamlike images and mythic resonances express the point of view of the particular singer and of the folk community that listens to them.

The music of Roberts and the other black songsters contributes to our understanding of banjo repertory. Some of the tunes are fiddle instrumentals with words, and many, like "Love Somebody," "Alabama [Buffalo] Gals," "Cindy Gal," and "Old Joe Clark," are apparently acquired and modified from white tradition. Others are banjo songs with special tunings, like "Old Reuben," "Tough Luck," "Coo Coo," "John Lover's Gone," "Fox Chase," and "Roustabout," and some, like "Punkin Pie" and "Old Corn Liquor," seem especially characteristic of the melodic simplicity and rhythmic emphasis of early African-American tradition. These songs contribute to our understanding of the overlapping banjo repertories of blacks and whites. Other songs shared by blacks and whites include "Bile Dem Cabbage Down," "Hook and Line," "Molly Hare," "Molly Put the Kettle On," "Black-Eyed Daisy," "Georgia Buck," "Shortening Bread," "Going Down Town (to carry my 'bacca round)," "Going Down the Road Feeling Bad," "Little Brown Jug," "Mountain Dew," and "Ain't Gonna Rain No More." Some are about important figures or challengers: "High Sheriff," "Garfield," "John Henry," and "John Hardy." Most of these songs are played at a fast, dance-clip pace.

In form, the black repertory draws upon slave songs and earlier African music, material common during minstrelsy (some created by whites, some modified from white tradition, and much borrowed and adapted from black tradition), and fiddle repertory, including many dance instrumentals of particular rhythmic interest. These jump-up songs and dance songs are often improvisatory rather than delivering a fixed musical or verbal text, and they are more lyrical than narrative. Some banjo titles, like "Soldier's Joy," may suggest the differences between traditions, for the piece is also known in white tradition as "Pay Day in the Army" but is usually called "Love Somebody" in black tradition. But the overlapping banjo repertory is full of songs, and their titles, phrases, and evocative images characterize what matters most to southern men (both black and white) about country life: food, liquor, women, work, being on the move, and being free and independent.

These men sing banjo songs with a lyrical, dream-image aesthetic quite different from the story-telling emphasis of white narrative ballad singing. Their playing method, lyric song genre, and intricate interweaving of instrumental and vocal performance are highly complex, improvisational, and, like their instrument and aesthetic, the result of decades of musical exchange. The tradition is one that reflects directly upon the southern experience of cultural exchange and its creations and reflects the democratic opportunity and experience ideally at the heart of American cultural identity and integrity.

The songs and performances of contemporary African-American banjo players, together with historical documents and the banjos themselves, have provided us with a view of a continuous tradition that reaches back to the arrival of the blacks in this country and even beyond to the homes of the griots in the savannah grasslands and steppes of Africa. African Americans have a distinctive instrument; its aesthetic, playing styles, and song forms have influenced white musicians continuously. The black musicians brought or made three- and four-string fretless banjos in the new land. For more than a century, they accompanied their song, dance, and sometimes drumming with the African short-string gourd instrument. They improvised African songs and Celtic fiddle tunes; they began to sing new songs in their new language. They entertained whites. They sang from the heart for their own community and asserted their identity in a new land among strangers by expressing their traditions.

Before the middle of the nineteenth century, the African-American tradition of banjo playing began to influence whites. White musicians became intrigued with the black traditions; their interest and interaction with black traditions resulted in minstrelsy, the five-string, wooden-rim banjo, and the popularization of the fiddle-banjo ensemble. Away from the popular stage in the southern mountains, the old downstroking style of playing flourished among whites, accompanied dances, produced a variety of intricate banjo songs, interacted with the fiddle, nourished the string bands, and persisted sturdily into the twentieth century.

For an intense period of time from the Civil War to the end of the century, at least in the still rural and agrarian South, the black and white folk traditions grew very close together. But with the availability of inexpensive guitars and in response to the imposition of fierce Jim Crow laws and lynchings, southern black songsters and musicianers left their banjo songs and began to express their past and their American citizenship in the new assertive songs of the genre of the blues. They became bluesmen at the crossroads and on the go.

Today, despite a century of complex musical exchange between the long-standing black and white traditions, the echo of the old banjo lead or solo African-American banjo tradition is still audible. Thumping (in the downstroking style) on fretless, short drone-string banjos, variant tunings, and lyric banjo songs persist among southern whites and blacks. Although community frolics are less common nowadays in the North Carolina Piedmont than they were at the beginning of this century, some African Americans (perhaps still committed to the democratic and interactive ideals of self-sufficiency and cooperative agrarian life) continue to play the banjo and sing for the dancing, cheer, consolation, and staunchness of family and friends just as their griot ancestors did for communities more than two centuries ago here and in African villages. But now banjo music also echoes along the ridges of Appalachia. Are mountaineers today less oppressed by the dominant culture? Do the musicianers still feel remote enough to express their independent values safely and aggressively? Whatever the case may be, the mountain musicians play a music brought by blacks, and they share a music that in the fiddle-banjo combination and the banjo-song genre symbolizes an intense historical moment built upon long-standing exchange and cooperation. In the mountain hollows, the echo is strong; the banjo songs now express southerners, both black and white. Some southerners have achieved a new independent yet ethnically rooted and regionally broadened pattern of call and response.

Note

1. Michael T. Coolen, "Senegambia Archetypes for the American Folk Banjo," *Western Folklore* 43(2), April 1984, pg. 131.

5 War on Ragtime and Suppression of "Ragtime"

ANONYMOUS

Although it may seem astonishing now, brief derogatory pieces like these appeared in the popular press during the infancy of ragtime. The controversies surrounding the emergence and popularity of ragtime between 1895 and 1900 have echoes throughout the twentieth century. In the late 1940s, for example, enthusiasts of classic New Orleans jazz viewed be-bop as "anti-music." The highly regarded and popular bandleader Cab Calloway famously characterized be-bop as "Chinese music." Similar derogatory remarks were made of the avant-guard "free" jazz performed by Ornette Coleman, John Coltrane, and Cecil Taylor in the early 1960s.

Hip hop (rap in particular) has also garnered its share of criticism. This has been particularly true of so-called gangster rap groups, such as NWA or Public Enemy because of their glorification of violence. In the early twenty-first century, popular hip hop artists like Usher and 50 Cent have been taken to task for their "negative" messages, which often demean women and extol the importance of wealth over social progress and spiritual enlightenment.

Therefore, comments about the lack of "real music" in ragtime or the observation that the "ragtime craze has lowered the standard of American music . . . and we will not give way to a popular demand that is degrading" ("War on Ragtime") will sound familiar to hip hop fans. In a statement somehow reminiscent of "Disco Demolition Night" at Comiskey Park on July 12, 1979, the anonymous author of 'Suppression of Ragtime'" states that "Last week a national association of musicians, in convention at Denver solemnly swore to play no ragtime, and to do all in their power to counteract the pernicious influence exerted by 'Mr. Johnson,' 'My Ragtime Lady,' and others of the Negro school."

Ragtime has passed the zenith of its popularity, musicians say, and they are now anxious to lay out the corpse. The edict has gone forth from the convention hall of the American Federation of Musicians. Ragtime must go.

"That does not mean," said the emergency President of the A. F. of M., "that we are to play nothing but Beethoven's symphonies to park Sunday crowds, but it does mean that, we will substitute music of some real merit for ragtime trash, and show the people the difference. We don't have to play classics to play good music. We intend to play popular airs instead of a senseless jumble of words and notes. The musicians know what is good, and if the people don't, we will have to teach them.

"Why, some bands have almost forgotten how to play real music, and publishers won't think of taking any compositions that are really meritorious. But just see how they snatch at *Ragtime Skedaddle*, and other ridiculous and, in some cases, obscure songs.

"The ragtime craze has lowered the standard of American music as compared with other countries. We have duty as well as business to look after, and we will not give way to a popular demand that is degrading."

John C. Weber, the popular and well known leader, has ideas of his own on the subject. At the Eden Park concert Sunday he played a ragtime medley. "It's like this," said he, "suppose you are a grocer. You don't like Limburger cheese. But some other people do. When they ask for it, you sell it to them, although you can't see how they can eat it. That's the way with us about ragtime. If the people want it, why let them have it. One thing is certain when ragtime is called for I'll have it played and won't worry about whims or dislike from any of my performers. I shall always endeavor to please those who pay the fiddler."

A resolution, adopted by the members of the American Federation of Musicians, to do everything in their power to suppress "ragtime" tunes, is the subject of much discussion. A writer in the *New York Sun* has grown sarcastic about it. He says:

"It is possible to be too high and mighty in regard to music as in regard to literature. It is your duty, many essayists and lecturers say, to read only the best books and the greatest. We have a theory that these excellent advisers read 'Ouida's' novels. We have heard a great purist in music—one of those fellows who order you to stick to Bach and Handel and the other immortals—such a faultless being have we heard whistling 'coon songs.' So difficult it is to be on stilts all the time. The safe rule is to like what you please, and if you like 'ragtime' music, like it, and bid those who would interfere with you go hang. It is better to be tolerant than to be learned. But ragtime strains are delightful all the same. We doubt if the man who haughtily turns his ears upon them can really appreciate either Bach or Handel. The great composers had their moments of ragtime. Shall not the little composers have leave to frolic, too?"

The Cincinnati Post adds

Leave us our *Coal Black Lady*.
"If you hear music and like it, be sure that somebody will explain to you that it was popular and therefore immoral; that it lacked soul and technique and verve, and some more tommyrot that has very little to do with the music lovers, who do not want to be uplifted, and who do want to enjoy themselves."

Last week a national association of musicians, in convention at Denver solemnly swore to play no ragtime, and to do all in their power to counteract the pernicious influence exerted by *Mr. Johnson, My Ragtime Lady* and others of the Negro school.

To most people music is not a serious matter. It is amusement and relaxation. It drives away the blues, and makes happy thrills run all over our system. It is refining and has a natural tendency to elevate mankind.

But the people do not want to be educated all the time. They have not asked anybody to change their natures. They know what they want. Their great desire with music is to be pleased—to forget for a time that there is anything in this world but sunshine and laughter, and birds and flowers and purling brooks.

And they find all those things in the homely and catchy pieces that quicken the heart-beats and make the nerves tingle with delight; yes, in ragtime, bubbling, frothing, sparkling; as light as a summer breeze and as sweet as woman's kiss.

Ragtime is here to stay. It's the people's music. It's the children's delight. The musicians who play what the people want are wise, and the self-summoned martyrs who would take away a pleasure that is wholly innocent will have themselves to thank when jobs are few.

6
Of the Sorrow Songs
W. E. B. DU BOIS

Born in 1868 in Great Barrington, Massachusetts, William Edward Burghardt Du Bois developed into a noted scholar, editor, and African American activist. Du Bois was a founding member in 1909 of the National Association for the Advancement of Colored People (NAACP), the largest and oldest civil rights organization in America. Throughout his life Du Bois fought discrimination and racism through his significant contributions to debates about race, politics, and history in the United States in the first half of the twentieth century, primarily through his varied writings and often highly impassioned speeches on race relations. Du Bois also served as editor of The Crisis magazine and published several scholarly works on race and African American history. At the time of his death he had written seventeen books, edited four journals, and played a key role in reshaping black-white relations in America. Ironically, Du Bois died on the eve of the historic march on Washington in 1963. Actor and playwright Ossie Davis read an announcement of his death to the 250,000 people gathered the next day at the Washington Monument.

Since its initial publication in 1903, The Souls of Black Folk, which consists of fourteen essays on topics ranging from education to music, has been widely praised and remains one of the seminal books about African American cultural history and sociology. Many of these essays had already appeared in altered—usually shortened—form in Atlantic Monthly, The World's Work, The Dial, The New World, and the Annals of the American Academy of Political and Social Science. Du Bois refers to "Of the Sorrow Songs" (Chapter XIV) as "a chapter of song" in his opening to The Souls of Black Folk, "The Forethought." Like the rest of these essays, "Of the Sorrow Songs" draws from Du Bois's personal experiences and passionately describes his feelings about the slave spirituals and related songs that found a larger audience during Reconstruction, first through the work of George White and the Fisk Jubilee Singers and later through the efforts of similar groups, to become an important part of the American musical vernacular.

I walk through the churchyard
To lay this body down;
I know moon-rise, I know star-rise;
I walk in the moonlight, I walk in the starlight;
I'll lie in the grave and stretch out my arms,
I'll go to judgment in the evening of the day,
And my soul and thy soul shall meet that day,
When I lay this body down.

NEGRO SONG.

They that walked in darkness sang songs in the olden days—Sorrow Songs—for they were weary at heart. And so before each thought that I have written in this book I have set a phrase, a haunting echo of these weird old songs in which the soul of the black slave spoke to men. Ever since I was a child these songs have stirred me strangely. They came out of the South unknown to me, one by one, and yet at once I knew them as of me and of mine. Then in after years when I came to Nashville I saw the great temple builded of these songs towering over the pale city. To me Jubilee Hall seemed ever made of the songs themselves, and its bricks were red with the blood and dust of toil. Out of them rose for me morning, noon, and night, bursts of wonderful melody, full of the voices of my brothers and sisters, full of the voices of the past.

Little of beauty has America given the world save the rude grandeur God himself stamped on her bosom; the human spirit in this new world has expressed itself in vigor and ingenuity rather than in beauty. And so by fateful chance the Negro folk-song—the rhythmic cry of the slave—stands today not simply as the sole American music, but as the most beautiful expression of human experience born this side the seas. It has been neglected, it has been, and is, half despised, and above all it has been persistently mistaken and misunderstood; but notwithstanding, it still remains as the singular spiritual heritage of the nation and the greatest gift of the Negro people.

Away back in the thirties the melody of these slave songs stirred the nation, but the songs were soon half forgotten. Some, like "Near the lake where drooped the willow," passed into current airs and their source was forgotten; others were caricatured on the "minstrel" stage and their memory died away. Then in war-time came the singular Port Royal experiment after the capture of Hilton Head, and perhaps for the first time the North met the Southern slave face to face and heart to heart with no third witness. The Sea Islands of the Carolinas, where they met, were filled with a black folk of primitive type, touched and moulded less by the world about them than any others outside the Black Belt. Their appearance was uncouth, their language funny, but their hearts were human and their singing stirred men with a mighty power. Thomas Wentworth Higginson hastened to tell of these songs, and Miss McKim and others urged upon the world their rare beauty. But the world listened only half credulously until the Fisk Jubilee Singers sang the slave songs so deeply into the world's heart that it can never wholly forget them again.

There was once a blacksmith's son born at Cadiz, New York, who in the changes of time taught school in Ohio and helped defend Cincinnati from Kirby Smith. Then he fought at Chancellorsville and Gettysburg and finally served in the Freedmen's Bureau at Nashville. Here he formed a Sunday-school class of black children in 1866, and sang with them and taught them to sing. And then they taught him to sing, and when once the glory of the Jubilee songs passed into the soul of George L. White, he knew his life-work was to let those Negroes sing to the world as they had sung to him. So in 1871 the pilgrimage of the Fisk Jubilee Singers began. North to Cincinnati they rode,—four half-clothed black boys and five girl-women,—led by a man with a cause and a purpose. They stopped at Wilberforce, the oldest of Negro schools, where a black bishop blessed them. Then they went, fighting cold and starvation, shut out of hotels, and cheerfully sneered at, ever northward; and ever the magic of their song kept thrilling hearts, until a burst of applause in the Congregational Council at Oberlin revealed them to the world. They came to New York and Henry Ward Beecher dared to welcome them, even though the metropolitan dailies sneered at his "Nigger Minstrels." So their songs conquered till they sang across the land and across the sea, before Queen and Kaiser, in Scotland and Ireland, Holland and Switzerland. Seven years they sang, and brought back a hundred and fifty thousand dollars to found Fisk University.

Since their day they have been imitated—sometimes well, by the singers of Hampton and Atlanta, sometimes ill, by straggling quartettes. Caricature has sought again to spoil the quaint beauty of the music, and has filled the air with many debased melodies which vulgar ears scarce know from the real. But the true Negro folk-song still lives in the hearts of those who have heard them truly sung and in the hearts of the Negro people.

What are these songs, and what do they mean? I know little of music and can say nothing in technical phrase, but I know something of men, and knowing them, I know that these songs are the articulate message of the slave to the world. They tell us in these eager days that life was joyous to the black slave, careless and happy. I can easily believe this of some, of many. But not all the past South, though it rose from the dead, can gainsay the heart-touching witness of these songs. They are the music of an unhappy people, of the children of disappointment; they tell of death and suffering and unvoiced longing toward a truer world, of misty wanderings and hidden ways.

The songs are indeed the siftings of centuries; the music is far more ancient than the words, and in it we can trace here and there signs of development. My grandfather's grandmother was seized by an evil Dutch trader two centuries ago; and coming to the valleys of the Hudson and Housatonic, black, little, and lithe, she shivered and shrank in the harsh north winds, looked longingly at the hills, and often crooned a heathen melody to the child between her knees, thus:

> Do ba-na co-ba, ge-ne me, ge-ne me!
> Do ba-na co-ba, ge-ne me, ge-ne me!
> Ben d' nu-li, nu-li, nu-li, ben d' le.

The child sang it to his children and they to their children's children, and so two hundred years it has travelled down to us and we sing it to our children, knowing as little as our fathers what its words may mean, but knowing well the meaning of its music.

This was primitive African music; it may be seen in larger form in the strange chant which heralds "The Coming of John":

> "You may bury me in the East,
> You may bury me in the West,
> But I'll hear the trumpet sound in that morning,"

—the voice of exile.

Ten master songs, more or less, one may pluck from the forest of melody-songs of undoubted Negro origin and wide popular currency, and songs peculiarly characteristic of the slave. One of these I have just mentioned. Another ... is "Nobody knows the trouble I've seen."

When, struck with a sudden poverty, the United States refused to fulfill its promises of land to the freedmen, a brigadier-general went down to the Sea Islands to carry the news. An old woman on the outskirts of the throng began singing this song; all the mass joined with her, swaying. And the soldier wept.

The third song is the cradle-song of death which all men know,—"Swing low, sweet chariot,"—whose bars begin the life story of "Alexander Crummell." Then there is the song of many waters, "Roll, Jordan, roll," a mighty chorus with minor cadences. There were many songs of the fugitive like that which opens "The Wings of Atalanta," and the more familiar "Been a-listening." The seventh is the song of the End and the Beginning—"My Lord, what a mourning! when the stars begin to fall"; a strain of this is placed before "The Dawn of Freedom." The song of groping—"My way's cloudy"—begins "The Meaning of Progress"; the ninth is the song of this chapter—"Wrestlin' Jacob, the day is a-breaking,"—a paean of hopeful strife. The last master song is the song of songs—"Steal away,"—sprung from "The Faith of the Fathers."

There are many others of the Negro folk-songs as striking and characteristic as these . . . ; and others I am sure could easily make a selection on more scientific principles. There are, too, songs that seem to be a step removed from the more primitive types: there is the maze-like medley, "Bright sparkles," one phrase of which heads "The Black Belt"; the Easter carol, "Dust, dust and ashes"; the dirge, "My mother's took her flight and gone home"; and that burst of melody hovering over "The Passing of the First-Born"—"I hope my mother will be there in that beautiful world on high."

These represent a third step in the development of the slave song, of which "You may bury me in the East" is the first, and songs like "March on" . . . and "Steal away" are the second. The first is African music, the second Afro-American, while the third is a blending of Negro music with the music heard in the foster land. The result is still distinctively Negro and the method of blending original, but the elements are both Negro and Caucasian. One might go further and find a fourth step in this development, where the songs of white America have been distinctively influenced by the slave songs or have incorporated whole phrases of Negro melody, as "Swanee River" and "Old Black Joe." Side by side, too, with the growth has gone the debasements and imitations—the Negro "minstrel" songs, many of the "gospel" hymns, and some of the contemporary "coon" songs,—a mass of music in which the novice may easily lose himself and never find the real Negro melodies.

In these songs, I have said, the slave spoke to the world. Such a message is naturally veiled and half articulate. Words and music have lost each other and new and cant phrases of a dimly understood theology have displaced the older sentiment. Once in a while we catch a strange word of an unknown tongue, as the "Mighty Myo," which figures as a river of death; more often slight words or mere doggerel are joined to music of singular sweetness. Purely secular songs are few in number, partly because many of them were turned into hymns by a change of words, partly because the frolics were seldom heard by the stranger, and the music less often caught. Of nearly all the songs, however, the music is distinctly sorrowful. The ten master songs I have mentioned tell in word and music of trouble and exile, of strife and hiding; they grope toward some unseen power and sigh for rest in the End.

The words that are left to us are not without interest, and, cleared of evident dross, they conceal much of real poetry and meaning beneath conventional theology and unmeaning rhapsody. Like all primitive folk, the slave stood near to Nature's heart. Life was a "rough and rolling sea" like the brown Atlantic of the Sea Islands; the "Wilderness" was the home of God, and the "lonesome valley" led to the way of life. "Winter'll soon be over," was the picture of life and death to a tropical imagination. The sudden wild thunderstorms of the South awed and impressed the Negroes,—at times the rumbling seemed to them "mournful," at times imperious:

> "My Lord calls me,
> He calls me by the thunder,
> The trumpet sounds it in my soul."

The monotonous toil and exposure is painted in many words. One sees the ploughmen in the hot, moist furrow, singing:

> "Dere's no rain to wet you,
> Dere's no sun to burn you,
> Oh, push along, believer,
> I want to go home."

The bowed and bent old man cries, with thrice-repeated wail:

> "O Lord, keep me from sinking down,"

and he rebukes the devil of doubt who can whisper:

> "Jesus is dead and God's gone away."

Yet the soul-hunger is there, the restlessness of the savage, the wail of the wanderer, and the plaint is put in one little phrase:

> My soul wants something that's new, that's new

Over the inner thoughts of the slaves and their relations one with another the shadow of fear ever hung, so that we get but glimpses here and there, and also with them, eloquent omissions and silences. Mother and child are sung, but seldom father; fugitive and weary wanderer call for pity and affection, but there is little of wooing and wedding; the rocks and the mountains are well known, but home is unknown. Strange blending of love and helplessness sings through the refrain:

> "Yonder's my ole mudder,
> Been waggin' at de hill so long;
> 'Bout time she cross over,
> Git home bime-by."

Elsewhere comes the cry of the "motherless" and the "Farewell, farewell, my only child."
Love-songs are scarce and fall into two categories—the frivolous and light, and the sad. Of deep successful love there is ominous silence, and in one of the oldest of these songs there is a depth of history and meaning:

> Poor Ro-sy, poor gal; Poor Ro-sy,
> poor gal; Ro-sy break my poor heart,
> Heav'n shall-a-be my home.

A black woman said of the song, "It can't be sung without a full heart and a troubled sperrit." The same voice sings here that sings in the German folk-song:

> "Jetz Geh i' an's brunele, trink' aber net."

Of death the Negro showed little fear, but talked of it familiarly and even fondly as simply a crossing of the waters, perhaps—who knows?—back to his ancient forests again. Later days transfigured his fatalism, and amid the dust and dirt the toiler sang:

> "Dust, dust and ashes, fly over my grave,
> But the Lord shall bear my spirit home."

The things evidently borrowed from the surrounding world undergo characteristic change when they enter the mouth of the slave. Especially is this true of Bible phrases. "Weep, O captive daughter of Zion," is quaintly turned into "Zion, weep-a-low," and the wheels of Ezekiel are turned every way in the mystic dreaming of the slave, till he says:

> "There's a little wheel a-turnin' in-a-my heart."

As in olden time, the words of these hymns were improvised by some leading minstrel of the religious band. The circumstances of the gathering, however, the rhythm of the songs, and the limitations of allowable thought, confined the poetry for the most part to single or double lines, and they seldom were expanded to quatrains or longer tales, although there are some few examples of sustained efforts, chiefly paraphrases of the Bible. Three short series of verses have always attracted me,—the one that heads this chapter, of one line of which Thomas Wentworth Higginson has fittingly said, "Never, it seems to me, since man first lived and suffered was his infinite longing for peace uttered more plaintively." The second and third are descriptions of the Last Judgment,—the one a late improvisation, with some traces of outside influence:

> "Oh, the stars in the elements are falling,
> And the moon drips away into blood,
> And the ransomed of the Lord are returning unto God,
> Blessed be the name of the Lord."

And the other earlier and homelier picture from the low coast lands:

> "Michael, haul the boat ashore,
> Then you'll hear the horn they blow,
> Then you'll hear the trumpet sound,
> Trumpet sound the world around,
> Trumpet sound for rich and poor,
> Trumpet sound the Jubilee,
> Trumpet sound for you and me."

Through all the sorrow of the Sorrow Songs there breathes a hope—a faith in the ultimate justice of things. The minor cadences of despair change often to triumph and calm confidence. Sometimes it is faith in life, sometimes a faith in death, sometimes assurance of boundless justice in some fair world beyond. But whichever it is, the meaning is always clear: that sometime, somewhere, men will judge men by their souls and not by their skins. Is such a hope justified? Do the Sorrow Songs sing true?

The silently growing assumption of this age is that the probation of races is past, and that the backward races of today are of proven inefficiency and not worth the saving. Such an assumption is the arrogance of peoples irreverent toward Time and ignorant of the deeds of men. A thousand years ago such an assumption, easily possible, would have made it difficult for the Teuton to prove his right to life. Two thousand years ago such dogmatism, readily welcome, would have scouted the idea of blond races ever leading civilization. So wofully unorganized is sociological knowledge that the meaning of progress, the meaning of "swift" and "slow" in human doing, and the limits of human perfectability, are veiled, unanswered sphinxes on the shores of science. Why should Æschylus have sung two thousand years before Shakespeare was born? Why has civilization flourished in Europe, and flickered, flamed, and died in Africa? So long as the world stands meekly dumb before such questions, shall this nation proclaim its ignorance and unhallowed prejudices by denying freedom of opportunity to those who brought the Sorrow Songs to the Seats of the Mighty?

Your country? How came it yours? Before the Pilgrims landed we were here. Here we have brought our three gifts and mingled them with yours: a gift of story and song—soft, stirring melody in an ill-harmonized and unmelodious land; the gift of sweat and brawn to beat back the wilderness, conquer the soil, and lay the foundations of this vast economic empire two hundred years earlier than your weak hands could have done it; the third, a gift of the Spirit. Around us the history of the land has centred for thrice a hundred years; out of the nation's heart we have called all that was best to throttle and subdue all that was worst; fire and blood, prayer and sacrifice, have billowed over this people, and they have found peace only in the altars of the God of Right. Nor has our gift of the Spirit been merely passive. Actively we have woven ourselves with the very warp and woof of this nation,—we fought their battles, shared their sorrow, mingled our blood with theirs, and generation after generation have pleaded with a headstrong, careless people to despise not Justice, Mercy, and Truth, lest the nation be smitten with a curse. Our song, our toil, our cheer, and warning have been given to this nation in blood-brotherhood. Are not these gifts worth the giving? Is not this work and striving? Would America have been America without her Negro people?

Even so is the hope that sang in the songs of my fathers well sung. If somewhere in this whirl and chaos of things there dwells Eternal Good, pitiful yet masterful, then anon in His good time America shall rend the Veil and the prisoned shall go free. Free, free as the sunshine trickling down the morning into these high windows of mine, free as yonder fresh young voices welling up to me from the caverns of brick and mortar below—swelling with song, instinct with life, tremulous treble and darkening bass. My children, my little children, are singing to the sunshine, and thus they sing:

> Let us cheer the wea-ry trav-el-ler,
> Cheer the wea-ry trav-el-ler, Let us
> cheer the wea-ry trav-el-ler
> Along the heav-en-ly way.

And the traveller girds himself, and sets his face toward the Morning, and goes his way.

THE AFTERTHOUGHT

Hear my cry, O God the Reader; vouchsafe that this my book fall not still-born into the world wilderness. Let there spring, Gentle One, from out its leaves vigor of thought and thoughtful deed to reap the harvest wonderful. Let the ears of a guilty people tingle with truth, and seventy millions sigh for the righteousness which exalteth nations, in this drear day when human brotherhood is mockery and a snare. Thus in Thy good time may infinite reason turn the tangle straight, and these crooked marks on a fragile leaf be not indeed

THE END

7 The Nineteenth-Century Origins of Jazz

LAWRENCE GUSHEE

An emeritus professor of music at the University of Illinois, Dr. Lawrence Gushee has long balanced his interests in medieval music with a passion for early jazz and ragtime. Among his jazz writings are articles and books about Jelly Roll Morton, King Oliver's Original Creole Jazz Band, and Louis Armstrong. This article carefully explores the immediate antecedents to jazz, which, Gushee argues, emerged by the end of the first decade of the twentieth century.

The author's look at the development of jazz focuses most directly on New Orleans in the period between 1880 and the early 1900s. In order to understand how musicians and the musical culture in New Orleans contributed to the birth of jazz, the author reviews a wide variety of sources including the impact of the Supreme Court's 1896 Plessy v. Ferguson *decision that created the "separate but equal" concept; census records; the role played by local bandleader Basile Barès; and the importance dances such as the Turkey Trot played in shaping the sounds of New Orleans proto-jazz music in the late nineteenth century. He concludes by suggesting that two of the more important ingredients in this story—the Original Dixieland Jazz Band and the "roustabouts who made the New Orleans levee one of the wonders of nineteenth-century America"—were critical factors in shaping the music that Gushee suggests could be called jazz around 1914.*

The question of the origins of jazz has, one might well imagine, received many answers in the seventy-five years since the music burst like a rocket over the American musical landscape. The least palatable perhaps is that offered by reactionary champions of the musical originality of the Original Dixieland Jazz Band (ODJB), for example, Horst Lange. Much of his evidence is easy to dismiss, but one point at least makes us pause and think. He writes:

> It was always a riddle for the serious friend of jazz, why the fabulous and legendary New Orleans jazz hadn't already been discovered around 1900 or 1910 in the city itself, since not only was it full of home-grown talent and musical professionals, but also received a constant stream of visitors and tourists. Shouldn't there have been someone, among all these people surely interested in music, who was struck by this novel music, which was later designated "jazz"? (Lange 1991, 28; my translation)

In fact, there's no question that the particular instrumentation, manner of playing, and repertory of the Original Dixieland Jazz Band, decisively assisted by the superb recording technique of the Victor Talking Machine Company, were copied by hundreds of young musicians, many of whom never had visited and never would visit New Orleans.

Someone who came close to fitting Lange's music-loving visitor to New Orleans was J. Russell Robinson (1892–1963), a pianist and songwriter who had worked in that city around 1910 and was eventually to become a member of the ODJB. Many years later he recalled his reaction to these recordings: first, it was a new, interesting, and exciting sound, a bit blood-curdling; second, the musicians were recognizable as nonreaders; third, jazz was nothing but ragtime, played by ear (Robinson 1955, 13). Thus the sound, while strikingly novel and surely deserving of the acclaim of Lange, was recognized by an experienced professional as being but one species of the genus, ragtime played by ear by "fakers," to use the usual term of the day.[1]

Even at the time, however, New Orleans colleagues and competitors of the ODJB fully acknowledged the debt all of them owed to African Americans. For example, Walter Kingsley reported the views of clarinetist Alcide "Yellow" Nunez:

> In 1916 Brown's Band from Dixieland came to Chicago direct from New Orleans, and with it came Tutor Spriccio. They knew all the old negro melodies with the variations taught by Spriccio. . . . This bunch from New Orleans played by ear entirely. (Kingsley 1918, 867)

Then after a discussion of the "Livery Stable Blues" and the break routines for which Nunez claimed credit: "All this, however, was derived from the New Orleans blacks and John Spriccio" (867).

These statements are offered not only to refute Lange's revisionism, but as one more illustration—Is one needed?—of the pervasive bias that constantly obscures investigation of the contributions of African Americans. Spriccio has a name, but not the "old negroes" or the "New Orleans blacks."

As is often the case, things look different from the other side of the color line. It is interesting to go back to what seems to have been the first published attempt by an African-American native of New Orleans to plumb the mystery of the origin of jazz. The year was 1933, the author E. Belfield Spriggins, social editor of the *Lousiana Weekly*. He wrote, under the title "Excavating Local Jazz":

> For quite some years now there has been an unusual amount of discussion concerning the popular form of music commonly called "jazz." . . . Many years ago jazz tunes in their original terms were heard in the Crescent City. Probably one of the earliest heard was one played by King Bolden's Band. . . . The rendition of this number became an over night sensation and the reputation of Bolden's hand became a household word with the patrons of the Odd Fellows Hall, Lincoln and Johnson Parks, and several other popular dance halls around the city. (Spriggins 1933, 6)

The tune in question was "Funky Butt"—the unexpurgated text of which Spriggins was unwilling to print. More widely known as "Buddy Bolden's Blues," as copyrighted by Jelly Roll Morton, this was a descendant or a cousin of the second strain of the 1904 rag "St. Louis Tickle," which, though designated a rag, is clearly a different species from Scott Joplin's compositions.

Be that as it may, Spriggins makes no unqualified claim for the priority of Buddy Bolden, hedging his remarks with a caution that was to be lost in succeeding years, as in the designation of Bolden as "First Man of Jazz" (Marquis 1978). Still, there seems to be no question that his band made an unforgettable impression, not always to the good, on many of those who heard it around 1905.

Other expert witnesses would come up with different candidates for the position of giant of early jazz. Guitarist Johnny St. Cyr (1890–1966) remembered toward the end of his life that

> Every band had their specialties that they played hot, one out of every five or six selections.... But the Golden Rule band played everything hot,... they were the original hot band that I knew.... [Bolden was] not hot, just ordinary, but he had a little hot lick he used. To me he was not as hot as the Golden Rule Band. (St. Cyr 1966, 6)

Cross-examination of the witnesses being out of the question, there is ample room for the free play of preconceptions and foregone conclusions in preferring one bit of evidence over another. But there seems to be no reason to doubt that at least by 1905 some bands, whether Bolden's, the Golden Rule, or some other, were playing a music that we might consider an ancestor of jazz. To be sure, St. Cyr was not of an age to testify to bands, events, and sounds much earlier than that.

Stymied by the mortality of our informants, we might well consider another strategy: instead of carrying things backwards as far as we can, perhaps we might begin early in the nineteenth century and advance toward 1900, thus cornering the elusive quarry.

This was the intention of Henry Kmen, a historian whose pioneering work on music and musical life in New Orleans up to 1841 has contributed much to the field. But until I reread his book in preparation for this discussion, the degree to which he thought of his own work as a prelude to the history of jazz had escaped me.

Although he could find comparatively little evidence for music making by African Americans, in his final chapter Kmen was able to cite an impressive list of activities which provided him justification for a startling and provocative concluding paragraph.

> Is it not here, ... in the whole overpowering atmosphere of music in New Orleans that the Negro began to shape the music that would eventually be Jazz? Certainly all these strands were a part of his life, and if to the weaving of them he brought something of his own, it was as an American rather than as an African. Or so it seems to this writer. (Kmen 1966, 245; note capital "J")

From this point of view, every musical activity of the African American in antebellum as well as postbellum New Orleans could be considered part of the prehistory of jazz. This seems to fit David Fischer's description of the "fallacy of indiscriminate pluralism":

> It appears in causal explanations where the number of causal components is not defined, or their relative weight is not determined or both.... [It is] an occupational hazard of academic historians, who are taught to tell comprehensive truths. (Fischer 1970, 175–176)

There is also a categorical problem, namely that a variety of social activities involving music are seen as ancestors of a distinctive kind of music, something Kmen seems to recognize:

"The method used is that of the social historian. Which is to say, the book is not concerned with the structure and development of the music itself—that is left for the musicologist" (Kmen 1966, viii).

No small challenge, particularly given the inadequacy of notated music in indicating the distinctive features of music of the oral tradition. To be sure, thanks to Dena Epstein (1977) one can consult hundreds of verbal descriptions of antebellum African-American musical practices in the United States generally, most of them from the Southern states. But these are often too vague for us to imaginatively reconstruct the sounds the writer heard; none of the thirty-odd references to New Orleans or Louisiana appear to describe specific practices that might be related to the hot or ratty[2] ragtime played around 1900.

Likewise for the few instances of local practice reflected in musical notation: the "Creole songs" that Louis Moreau Gottschalk used for some of his piano pieces presumably are a sampling of music he heard in the New Orleans of the 1830s. Charming and historically important, but no more nor less an ancestor of jazz than some of the raggy banjo pieces transcribed or collected by Dan Emmett (Nathan 1962, 340–348).

On the other hand, the rhythms notated in the seven songs in Creole dialect which conclude Allen, Ware, and Garrison's pioneering (1867–1951) collection of slave songs sound to me more pertinent. They seem distinctively West Indian in their various ways of singing five notes in the time of four. In strong contrast to the rest of the collection, the songs are also all secular, and a case can be made for the "urban" character of three or four of them, despite their having been collected on Good Hope Plantation in St. Charles Parish—or rather because of having been collected there, a half-day's journey or less from the metropolis. Also of great interest is the fact that the first four of the songs, those which, in fact, could be said to have West Indian rhythms, were danced to "a simple dance, a sort of minuet, called the *Coon jai*; the name and the dance are probably both of African origin" (113).

We know, of course, that at the outset and for decades to follow jazz was functionally music for dancing. Nothing was more clear to Henry Kmen than this, and surely it was the reason why he began his work with chapters on dancing. But he conveys virtually no details concerning the participation of African-American musicians in what, after all, would have been the bread and butter of the professional musician.

Kmen terminated his history at 1841, a fact all the more regrettable because of the great shift in social dance style—and its accompanying music—which took place in the 1840s and 1850s all over urban Europe and America, North and South. The change was not only a shift from the quadrille, cotillion, and contradance to the closed couple dances of waltz, polka, and the other new dances to follow in their wake (mazurka, redowa, etc.), but also of social meaning, well described by Jean-Michel Guilcher:

> It's true that dancing remained a pleasure. But the nature of the pleasure has changed. Under the Consulate and the Empire, any personal expression, whatever amplitude it may take, was within the social forms inherited from the past. After 1840, the closed couple dance took over. Although other periods had already given much room to the expression of the couple, none allowed it to take on the character it was now to assume. The series of courantes and minuets had expressed at the same time both solidarity and hierarchy. . . . The waltz and the polka made no pretense at expressing anything whatever. Closed in on itself, the couple dances for itself alone, . . . the ball no longer manifested unanimous agreement; it juxtaposed solitudes. (Guilcher 1969, 173–174; my translation)

This new configuration of dances was to last until the century's end. Already challenged by the two-step circa 1895, it was definitively replaced by a cluster of new dances around 1910. Of this, more below.

There is clearly much work to be done in continuing the story of music in New Orleans after 1841. My own research into music for dancing begins some twenty years later, with a few tentative forays into the massive city archives held by the New Orleans Public Library. As an example of what can be learned, one might cite a ledger of permits issued in 1864 by the acting military mayor, which included some 150 licenses for balls, private parties, and soirées between January 1 and March 12. Included are the names of the licensees, the locations of the events, whether wines were permitted, the ending time, whether the event was masked or not, and whether it was "colored." A good many of the balls are so designated, but more important, perhaps, a number of entrepreneurs are African American, still designated "free persons of color" as the Thirteenth Amendment was not to take effect for nearly two more years. These entrepreneurs were A. J. Brooks, Paul Porée, Eugene Joseph, and John Hall; those often sponsoring "colored" balls were Emile Segura, Madame Charles (patroness of the quadroon balls), Benjamin Graham, Aaron Allen, Benjamin Colburn, J. J. Bouseau, Josephine Brown, and John Reed. It appears that similar documents have not been saved, except for several after 1900.

We do not need these data to show that New Orleans was a dancing city—a long-established fact—but the fact that African Americans were so much involved in the *business* end is most interesting. Did such entrepreneurship entail substantial employment for African-American musicians? Did it continue following Reconstruction in a city increasingly repressive of its African-American population?

Another kind of documentation to consider is offered by the five extant post–Civil War censuses, 1870 to 1910. One assumes that the majority of African Americans calling themselves musicians were earning most of their money playing dance music.[3]

Of the 222 musicians, teachers of music, and practitioners of the music trades enumerated in the 1870 census, 44 percent were of German, Austrian, or Swiss birth, 15 percent French, 10 percent Italian; in all, including some smaller groups, a staggering 80 percent were of foreign birth and only 20 percent were born in the United States. Of this small fraction three were black, seven mulatto, and one is listed as white, but is known to be African American. The African-American musicians then, although making a poor showing overall—that is, about 5 percent—make up about a quarter of this native-born contingent.

The passage of one decade from 1870 to 1880 made a great difference. There is a substantial overall increase in the number of musicians, but also a drastic shift in favor of the native-born. The total of all foreign-born musicians is at this point a mere 45 percent, now overtaken by the 55 percent born on North American soil. (It is interesting that only 4 percent of the 55 percent were *not* from the South.) Much of this change is accounted for by the fact that somewhere between fifty and sixty individual musicians or music teachers were African American, a number that remains more or less constant for the next twenty years, although the overall total of musicians increases by 25 percent.[4]

The 1910 census marked a dramatic change from those of 1890 and 1900. While the overall total of male musicians and music teachers increased by a striking 33 percent, the number of African Americans doubled, thus forming 30 percent of the total. Perhaps the ragtime craze was good for the African-American musician.

The story of musical opportunity told by the census—or rather, the story it allows us to tell—is amply confirmed by the complaint of a New Orleans correspondent to the trade magazine *Metronome* at the end of 1888: "We have here some twenty to twenty-five bands averaging twelve men apiece. The colored race monopolize the procession music to a great extent as they are not regular workers at any trade, as are most of the white players, no musical merit in any of these." It would be easy to assume that the writer meant this derogatory remark to apply to the "colored" bands, but it is possible that he means it to apply to the twenty to twenty-five bands, as he goes on to say: "We have only one really fine military band, that is the one at West End" (*Metronome* December 1888, 14).

It is, to be sure, only too common for African Americans to be treated as a stereotyped group by the nineteenth-century press. While we are beginning to remedy this by painstaking sifting of city directories, census returns, license registers, and other primary source materials, such names are, as it were, "faceless" and otherwise unremarkable.

Someone who is far from faceless is Basile Barés (1845–1902), bandleader to New Orleans society of the 1870s and perhaps later. Disappointingly, his nearly thirty dance compositions lack—to my ears—any of those novel and vigorous rhythms beginning to show up in music published in Cuba or Brazil. No pre-rag, no proto-habanera; just excellently crafted dance music or *morceaux de salon*.

There is no necessity, of course, that such exotic traits appear only or principally in works by African Americans. It was not the free persons of color who embodied "characteristic" rhythms in their antebellum works for the piano, but Louis Moreau Gottschalk. One also fails to find "characteristic" traits in the early works of the African-American Lawrence Dubuclet (1866–1909) who, in a manner of speaking, takes the torch from Barés, still writing waltzes, polkas, and mazurkas in the 1880s, then adapting to changing fashion and writing cakewalks, marches, and two-steps in the 1890s,[5] and finally moving to Chicago after 1900 to pursue a more cosmopolitan career than was feasible in his native city.

What are we looking for, after all, in written music? Think for a moment of the several ways in which the new idiom of blues made tentative appearances in popular song and piano music for at least fifteen years before the minor blues explosion of 1912. Blues traits, however, stick out like the proverbial sore thumb in certain idiosyncratic harmonic progressions, phrase structures, and melodic turns. For that matter, the syncopations that characterize cakewalks and rags are equally obvious. Here too, there is a long period of preparation in which what we might call "proto-ragtime" syncopation pops up, often together with pentatonic melody, both of them no doubt going back to the minstrel shows of 1840—and of course before that in oral tradition. But jazz lacks such easily transcribable and readily recognized distinctive features. We surely need to keep looking; it would be a great help if we had an authoritative bibliography of New Orleans music imprints before 1900.[6]

Surely, to ask Lange's question again with a change of venue, if there had been some kind of striking African-American music in New Orleans in these postbellum years, some visitor would have attempted a description in a diary, a letter home, a travel book, or some other means that would make up for the lack of traces in published music. One immediately thinks of the extraordinary Greek-born Lafcadio Hearn (1850–1904), who during his stint as a reporter in Cincinnati in the late 1870s wrote exceptionally detailed descriptions of roustabout songs and dancing in Ryan's dance-house, a riverfront dive (Hearn 1924, 161–164).

Hearn moved to New Orleans in 1877, where he remained for some ten years. One could hardly ask for a better observer: Hearn, a European, was enthralled by folklore and sympathetic to people of color; not only that, his dear friend was the critic and musicologist Henry Krehbiel, who published the first book on African-American folksong in 1913. In response to his friend, who was even then fascinated with the folk music of black Americans, Hearn wrote a number of letters reporting what he heard in New Orleans.

One observation in particular has been widely cited. Hearn wrote in a letter of 1881: "Did you ever hear negroes play the piano by ear? There are several curiosities here, Creole negroes. Sometimes we pay them a bottle of wine to come here and play for us. They use the piano exactly like a banjo. It is good banjo-playing, but no piano-playing" (quoted in Bisland 1906, 232).[7]

And then there is what must be the most evasive will o' the wisp to investigators of the prehistory of jazz. Walter Kingsley (1876–1929), a press agent for the Palace Theatre in New York City, was quick to discuss the jazz phenomenon which had taken the metropolis by storm, contributing an article to the *New York Sun*, August 5, 1917, headlined "Whence Comes Jass? Facts from the Great Authority on the Subject." His fateful words were:

> In his studies of the creole patois and idiom in New Orleans Lafcadio Hearn reported that the word "jaz," meaning to speed things up, to make excitement, was common among the blacks of the South and had been adopted by the Creoles as a term to be applied to music of a rudimentary syncopated type.

You can imagine how many hours have been spent by how many people, plowing through the voluminous published writings of Hearn in an attempt to nail down this earth-shattering remark—with nothing to show for it, alas. Although it seems that the remark might be found in Hearn's (1885) dictionary of creole proverbs, "*Gombo Zhèbes*," it is not there.[8] It is possible, however, that Hearn conveyed such information to Krehbiel in a letter, or even in conversation, the few times that he was in New York. And it is possible that Kingsley knew Krehbiel.[9]

But one of the lessons we have finally learned from jazz history is that New Orleans musicians did not know that their music was called "jazz" until they went north. Certainly many of them said so; here and there, however, in the interviews collected by Russell and Allen, now held in the William Ransom Hogan Jazz Archive at Tulane University, the contrary is stated. For example, Eddie Dawson—a professional musician from about 1905 on—asserts that the term was first used in bands around the time he began and was only applied to music (Dawson 1959).[10] Similarly, Tom Albert, a violinist born in 1877, maintained that "in the real old days they called it jazz and ragtime.... There wasn't any real difference between ragtime bands and the jazz bands.... Jazz was [the term] used mostly though" (Albert 1959, reel 2 digest, p. 6).

To return to Hearn after this substantial digression, one might hope that someone with such broad and unfettered tastes as his, and with such a musically knowledgeable and curious friend as Krehbiel, would tell us something about how African-American musicians played dance music in New Orleans in the 1880s. In the first place, Hearn seems not to have been much of a partygoer. Second, and far more consequential, he was not, I think, fond of Creole music that he perceived as strongly Europeanized. For example, in a letter written to Krehbiel just before he left Martinique after a first brief trip in 1887, Hearn states:

> My inquiries about the marimba and other instruments have produced no result except the discovery that our negroes play the guitar, the flute, the flageolet, the cornet-à-piston. Some play very well; all the orchestras and bands are coloured. But the civilized instrument has killed the native manufacture of aboriginalities. The only hope would be in the small islands, or where slavery still exists, as in Cuba. (quoted in Bisland 1906, 411)

Still, we can not rule out the possibility that African or West Indian rhythms were largely absent from the New Orleans dance music of the 1880s. One remark, from an 1887 letter to Krehbiel, seems to support this: "My friend Matas has returned. He tells me delightful things about Spanish music, and plays for me. He also tells me much concerning Cuban and Mexican music. He says these have been very strongly affected by African influence—full of contretemps" (quoted in Bisland 1906, 380). What an opportunity for Hearn to add, "just like I've heard here in New Orleans"! Or for that matter, such a comment might have come from Rudolph Matas (1860–1957), himself a New Orleans native. No such confirmation occurs, however, despite the fad for Mexican music, which was at the time in full swing after having been triggered by the appearance of various groups of Mexican musicians at the Cotton Exposition of 1884–1885 (Stewart 1991). Alas, when Hearn wrote his essays—well over 100,000 words—about his eighteen-month stay in Martinique, he made but one solitary reference to New Orleans, that having to do with architecture (Hearn 1890, 36).

Nevertheless, there is an inherent plausibility to the notion that New Orleans was receptive to all kinds of "Latin" music, perhaps because of geographical proximity as much as traditional ethnic preferences. The New Orleans composer W. T. Francis, visiting New York City in 1889 and commenting on the differing musical tastes in the United States, had this to say:

> It does not seem to be a matter of states or divisions of the land, but rather of particular localities. New York, Boston, Chicago, New Orleans, Brooklyn, Philadelphia and Baltimore are the best music centers of the east; San Francisco and Denver in the west. . . . Among the cities named, there is a great difference in their preferences regarding the style of music they will patronize. The two most widely differing cities in this regard are Boston and New Orleans. In the former, everything runs to classical music. . . . In New Orleans, the most popular music is that which is marked by melody. As a result, every new song and dance which appears in Paris, Madrid, Florence, Vienna, or Berlin appears in [New Orleans] anywhere from six months to two years before it is heard in [Boston]. Another interesting result is that you can listen in New Orleans to the melodic music of the Spanish nations. . . . It would seem as if the love of melody decreases as you come north from the gulf of Mexico and reaches its smallest development when it encounters the northern tier of the states of the union.

Francis here suggests two favorite themes in discussions of the nineteenth century origins of jazz. I will call one the "French Opera hypothesis" and the other the "Spanish tinge hypothesis," both of them accounting for a love of lyrical expressiveness in music, but the second specifically accounting for the presence in New Orleans of Caribbean or Mexican rhythms.

This is not all Francis had to say in the New York interview. He goes on to state a seductive theory that can account for much of what has taken place in the development of American vernacular music since 1890, not just New Orleans music or jazz:

> The rewards of music are far larger in the north than in the south. In the latter, they are regarded as a necessity and paid for, as most necessities are, in small amounts of money. In the north they are classed with luxuries, and are paid for in accordance. Business principles alone will, therefore, soon compel the production of southern music in the north, if merely for the sake of testing its commercial value. When once heard, I am certain that the northern public will want it a second time. ("New Orleans Taste in Music" 1890)

To be sure, this is no theory of origin. But at least it is conceivable that there never would have been such a thing as jazz without the economic force that brought it to the ears of the wider American public.

We may eventually find another musician, not necessarily or perhaps not even preferably an American, who describes specific musical practices which we can reasonably see as like or leading to jazz. In 1917 the Music Teachers' National Association held its thirty-ninth annual meeting in New Orleans. Among the speakers was Walter Goldstein, a music teacher at Newcomb College who was born in New York in 1882 and graduated from Tulane in 1903. His contribution was entitled "The Natural Harmonic and Rhythmic Sense of the Negro." It had been Goldstein's intention to illustrate some of his points with "the singing of a quartet of Negroes. . . . [B]ut the unreliability of our dark brother in the matter of keeping an appointment has made this impossible." Accordingly, he had recourse to Victor record 16448 by the Fisk University Quartet (Goldstein 1918, 38–39). The author's opening words are poignant:

> It is only a desire to "do my bit," rather than any special fitness for the task, that has led me to accept the appointment to make an investigation into the harmonic and rhythmic talent of the Negro as I find him here in his natural environment. . . . It is not very easy, as I have learned in the last two months, to get very near to the primitive Negro, in a large city like this, but the attempt has been something of a lark, and I have run the gamut all the way from being the unexpected orator at a Sunday service of the most aristocratic Negro congregation in the city, to being ordered off the public docks as a German spy with incendiary motives. (29)

He did get around a bit—for example, to the biweekly sacrament service of the Gretna Colored Baptist Church as well as to St. James AME Church—and had a few interesting things to say, particularly in describing ragtime—but not a whisper about jazz. The situation of being surrounded by a vibrant new music and not hearing it is in hindsight almost inconceivable to us; on reflection, though, it is just one more testimony to the power of received categories to mold our perceptions, unless, of course, the usual run of dance music was not anything special, and the unusual—that is, hot ragtime and blues with a local accent—rather rare. Perhaps this is another instance of what we could call the "Lange problem."

Bringing ragtime into the picture may seem to offer clarification to the beginnings of jazz, inasmuch as we know when ragtime began. But actually we know nothing of the sort; all we know is when ragtime sheet music in its various forms began being published in Chicago and New York and, consequently, everywhere in the country, not to speak of Western Europe. But just as the origins of jazz become fuzzy once we begin looking for jazz *before* jazz, so it is with ragtime. A couple of explanations offered by knowledgeable African-American musicians close to the events may illustrate the complexities of the question.

First, Will Foster, writing in the *Indianapolis Freeman* in 1911 under the pseudonym of Juli Jones Jr., contributed a fascinating article on the "great colored song writers":

> The success of the Mobile buck found its way to the river cities on the Ohio and Mississippi rivers, when steamboats held sway in this country. . . . Sometime along in the early eighties a triple combination of song, walk and dance by the name of "Coon Jine, Baby, Coon Jine," sprang up among the roustabouts on the many boats and spread like wildfire. The song and dance found its way into the levee resorts, where all prosperous houses had old hand-me-down square pianos with a half dozen broken keys; yet these instruments were considered jewels in those days, as it only required a few keys to play the "Coon Jine." This is where the original ragtime started from—the quick action of the right-hand fingers playing the "Coon Jine." (Jones 1911)

While this kind of single-origin theory is obviously inadequate to explain a multifaceted phenomenon like ragtime in general, it nonetheless singles out a particular dance song with a complex history that may, in fact involve New Orleans (see, e.g., Krehbiel 1962, 116, 121, 138). One imagines that Hearn's "Creole Negroes" who played the piano like the banjo had "Coon Jine" in their repertory.

Another witness to his time, the eminent composer Will Marion Cook (1869–1944), contributed a brief overview, "Negro Music," to the *New York Age* seven years later. He singled out the period 1875–1888 as one of stagnation because the Negro had been taught too well by whites that he was inferior. "About 1888 [1898 is what was printed] marked the starting and quick growth of the so-called 'rag-time.' As far back as 1875 Negroes in questionable resorts along the Mississippi had commenced to evolve this musical figure, but at the World's Fair in Chicago, 'ragtime' got a running start and swept the Americas, next Europe, and today the craze has not diminished" (Cook 1918).[11]

Actually, Cook had expounded his views on the matter some twenty years earlier, with a rather different slant. His article was intended as a refutation of the proposition that Negro music, as exemplified by such "ephemeral clap-trap compositions as 'The New Bully,' 'A Hot Time in the Old Town,' 'All Coons Look Alike to Me,' was degenerate, when compared with the soul-stirring slave melodies." He says:

> One special characteristic of these songs is the much advertised "rag" accompaniment, the origin and character of which will be discussed later on in this article. . . . This kind of movement, which was unknown until about fifteen years ago, grew out of the visits of Negro sailors to Asiatic ports, and particularly to those of Turkey, when the odd rhythms of the *dance du ventre* soon forced itself upon them; and in trying to reproduce this they have worked out the "rag."
>
> During the World's Columbian Exposition at Chicago, the "Midway Plaisance" was well filled with places of amusement where the peculiar music of the "muscle dance" was continually heard, and it is worthy of note that after that time the popularity of the "rag" grew with astonishing rapidity and became general among Negro pianists. (Cook 1898)[12]

One wonders whether this bit of history was cooked up by the author or taken from another source. To us it seems fanciful; perhaps it was the obtrusiveness of the drum rhythms traditionally accompanying belly dancing that caught Cook's ear.[13]

Neither Foster nor Cook mentions New Orleans, except by implication, the city being the southern terminus of what might be called levee lowlife culture.[14] We must look further for early evidence specifically linking New Orleans to ragtime or proto-ragtime. Although they are not extensively trained musicians like Francis and Goldstein, nor articulate in the manner of Hearn, one might well think that the "old-timers" interviewed principally by Bill Russell and Dick Allen for the Hogan Jazz Archives would tell us a lot about the hot or ratty ragtime of their youth. Certainly the interviewers asked a lot of the right questions: What kind of band did you play in when you began? What were some of the tunes you played early on? When did you first hear the blues? and so on. The biggest limitation in using this testimony as evidence for the beginning of jazz is that, by the time the project was funded and under way, very few musicians born around 1880 or before, those whose professional careers had begun before the turn of the century, were available to bear witness to the early days.

Be that as it may, certain particulars are heard over and over again: the oldest interviewees quite frequently first played in or were impressed by three- or four-piece string bands—such as violin, guitar, and string bass, or mandolin, guitar, and bass—with or without one wind instrument. Accordingly, their first instrument was often mandolin or guitar. Drums started to be used in larger dance orchestras only around 1900. Pianos entered the picture as orchestra instruments even later. The oldest interviewees were accustomed to playing polkas, mazurkas, schottisches, lancers, and varieties (these last two set dances were subspecies of the quadrille). The first blues came in around 1905, with, for example, "Make Me a Pallet on the Floor." Finally, there was a notable generation gap between the older musicians, who would not tolerate playing by ear or deviating from the notes as written, and the young turks of 1900. To the older, conservative generation belonged such musicians as cornetist George Moret, who was remembered with praise by Louis Armstrong, and the two fraternal clarinetists, Luis Tio and Lorenzo Tio Sr.[15]

There remains little doubt that important changes in instrumentation and repertory took place around 1900, give or take some number of years. This conclusion is amply supported by changes in clarinet performing style between, say, Alphonse Picou, born in 1879, and "Big Eye" Louis Delille Nelson, born sometime between 1880 and 1885. Or between that of George Baquet, born in 1881, and his younger brother Achille, born in 1885. Remarkably, all four men left recordings that surely speak louder than any verbal statements. For research purposes, the interviewers found Picou difficult to reach and an "unproductive" source; Big Eye was long on anecdotes, but short on information; George Baquet, potentially an exceptionally rich source of data and musical insight, had died in 1949; and his brother, approached in Los Angeles in the late 1930s, rebuffed his would-be interviewer.[16]

Given the weak representation of survivors from the turn of the century in the Tulane archive, it becomes very important to locate and interpret any earlier interviews if we are to have any hope of gaining insight into music before 1900. Particularly important are those by Russell conducted outside of the Tulane project and still untapped in any systematic way, as well as those conducted by the Belgian poet Robert Goffin. Perhaps there are others we may find if we search concertedly.

In some ways the most intriguing and frustrating of all of these earlier testimonies is a brief interview with trombonist George Filhe that was conducted for *They All Played Ragtime* (Janis and Blesh 1971). The relevant extracts are as follows:

> It was a style just natural to them, and whenever I can remember, it was jazz.
>
> * * * * *
>
> Percy Wenrich came to N.O. (between 1908 and 1909). We played it straight and the 2nd time we'd improvise. He came running up the steps: "That was my intentions and my ideas but I could not get them out!"
>
> * * * * *
>
> In 1892—played [solo cornet] with Cousto & Desdunes, Cousto solo cornet, O'Neill cornet, Desdunes, violin & baritone. Played jazz, would always swing the music, that was their novelty. Solo B cornet came in then and replaced the old rotary valve E-flat cornet. They played quadrilles, schottisches, straight. Onward Brass Band. Younger musicians about 1892 began to "swing." Older men used lots of Mexican music. (Filhe 1949)[17]

Filhe was born in 1872, a youngster compared to Sylvester Coustaut, born in 1863, but a near contemporary of Dan Desdunes, born about 1870. What did he mean by "swing" and "older musicians," and how literally should we take the date 1892? In any event, what is really interesting here is the identification of a drastic shift, from Mexican music to a new kind that, by contrast, swung. To be sure, this is both good news and bad news for those who think that some kind of "Spanish tinge" was essential in producing the New Orleans manner of playing ragtime. It is also extremely interesting to learn of Percy Wenrich's reaction. Wenrich, an excellent and very successful ragtime composer from Missouri, can be taken as another witness from the outside, testifying to the existence of a distinctive New Orleans way of playing ragtime before 1910.

Another early interview that speaks of an abrupt change comes from the highly respected and often cited cornetist, Manuel Perez, to whom Robert Goffin spoke (in French) probably in 1944, or possibly on the occasion of an earlier visit in 1941. This interview, published in French in 1946, has been unduly neglected, first because it has never been translated and second because of the creative embroidery to which Coffin was prone. Caution is clearly required.

In any event Perez was born in 1881 on Urquhart Street in the Seventh Ward. Just as he was beginning to learn trumpet, at age twelve, there was a

> syncopated evolution. Vocal groups composed of young creoles, or even of whites, such as those of the spasmband, retained the rhythmic aspect of all the badly digested music.... At this time, his teacher, a certain Constant ["Coustaut"] who lived on St. Philip Street had nothing but contempt and mockery for the "fakers" who went around from street to street. Two musicians were popular among the creoles and had a great influence on the young generation: Lorenzo Tio and Doublet. Perez remembers that after 1895, even though they usually played polkas and schottisches, they [i.e., Tio and Doublet] let themselves be tempted by the infatuation of the audiences and went along with the new music. They constituted the link ... between popular music and ragtime. (Goffin 1946, 69–70)

There's a lot more in this interview, but I have singled out this passage because of Perez's emphatic focus on the brief period 1893–1895 and on two specific musicians of the older school, Lorenzo Tio and Doublet.

Both Lorenzo Tio Sr. and Charles Doublet were born in 1867 and were in fact cousins through the Hazeur family (Kinzer 1993). They appear to have begun operating under the name of Big Four String Band in 1887, although they soon were being advertised as "Tio & Doublet's Orchestra or String Band." Their last known advertisement comes from February 23, 1895, among the precious fragments of the *Crusader* so meticulously reassembled and dated by Lester Sullivan and held in Special Collections, Xavier University. On that Saturday night just before Mardi Gras, they played for a grand masquerade ball at Francs-Amis Hall on North Robertson Street.

It was gratifying to learn of the survival of some documents of the Société des Jeunes Amis, a benevolent society similar to the Francs-Amis, particularly in that the membership consisted significantly of persons descended from the old caste of free people of color. In the report of the finance committee for 1890, there is a payment of $30.00, dated September 8, 1890, to Fabregas for music, then a similar payment three months later of $28.00. It seems likely that "Fabregas" is the Frequito Fabregas, enumerated in the 1880 census as a nineteen-year-old white musician born in Louisiana of Spanish parents.

It is at least worth suggesting that the Jeunes Amis were thus demonstrating their taste in music, of a sort which, according to Filhe (1949), was soon to be replaced. There is no way to know, of course, whether Fabregas and his musicians—the orchestra must have been relatively large to judge from the payment—played Latin music. It is also worth noting that among their membership of over two hundred, the society included a number of eminent musicians, most notably William Nickerson and Daniel Desdunes (Société des Jeunes Amis Collection, Box 25-6).

Of course, what we would like to have, for the Jeunes Amis or for any organization giving a dance, are programs or dance cards listing the types of dances or perhaps even the specific pieces. In fact, any New Orleans-centered collection of such ephemera would be welcome, whatever the source. My steps in this direction have just begun, but some of the results are worth reporting. A typical, if rather grand, sequence of dances is that from the program of the Pickwick Club's ball, February 25, 1889: ouverture, waltz, polka, mazurka, lancers, waltz, polka, schottische, varieties, and so on for thirty dances, concluding with, predictably, "Home Sweet Home." This is not that different from the Installation and Hop given at Turner's Hall on December 8, 1894, by the Ramblers Club, which offered grand march, waltz, polka, mazurka, varieties, waltz, polka, schottische, lancers, and so forth.

At this point it should be recalled that the most important social dance innovation of the 1890s was the two-step. In the limited number of New Orleans dance programs I have seen there is a near series (1896, 1897, 1899) from the Carnival balls of the Twelfth Night Revelers. In 1896, we find a not unusual succession of waltz, lanciers, waltz, polka, waltz, and in seventh position a deux temps, at this time another name for the two-step. In the remainder of the program of thirty dances, there are two more deux temps, along with two other innovations, the glide and the York. The 1897 ball begins with a royal march and a lancers, whereupon an unbroken alternation of waltz and two-step takes over. Gone are the polkas, mazurkas, varieties, galops, and raquets of yesteryear. This alternating pattern is quite standard for the first years of the twentieth century until probably around 1912, at which point the newly fashioned one-step would begin to overtake the two-step.[18]

What I have not been able to find yet are any programs from African-American organizations. Finally, whatever we learn about these more formal events with printed dance cards may well be quite misleading with respect to rougher venues with unstructured or differently structured programs. It is nonetheless interesting to see that the date mentioned by Manuel Perez as the year in which Tio and Doublet allowed themselves to be enticed away from the polka and schottische is bracketed by the 1894 and 1896 programs above.

The two-step, although it was often associated at the outset with 6/8 time, as in Sousa's march "The Washington Post," had become by the end of the decade the dance to which ragtime was played. To judge from the few programs I have seen, the adoption of the two-step in the Crescent City was a couple of years late, but perhaps that is to be expected. So far as rougher, rattier dancing is concerned, there is not a great deal of evidence. That kind of dancing surely existed, and it was fairly common for the oldtimers of the Tulane interviews to talk about a drastic change in the character of the music and the dancing after midnight, when the more sedate folk went home to bed. But there do exist at least a couple of intriguing references, both of which give much food for thought and hints for further investigation.

The first of these is a type of news story frequently encountered all over the country during the reform years before World War I. It comes from the somewhat scruffy *New Orleans Item* of January 15, 1908, headlined "The Moral Wave Strikes New Orleans Dancing Schools":

No More Turkey Trot, a Dance Which Was Developed Into Its Highest State of Efficiency at Milneburg and Bucktown.

Signs Up "No Turkey Trotting Allowed"; "No Applause is Necessary"; "No Dancing With Hat in Hand"; "No Ungentlemanly Conduct Will Be Tolerated." At Washington Artillery Hall last evening, hundreds of couples arrived to do the turkey trot.

Brookhoven's band played "Walk Right In and Walk Right Out Again."[19]

This is really rather startling, since every source claims that the turkey trot was a product of San Francisco's Barbary Coast dance halls and that it made the trip East only at the beginning of 1911.

Indeed it was at that time that *Variety*'s New Orleans correspondent—then and for a number of years to come, O. M. Samuels—sent in an item that, if at all accurate, turns the spotlight again on 1895 or 1896, albeit not in conjunction with the two-step.[20] Samuels wrote:

> Now that a siege of erotic dances has started in New York, it may be as well to place New Orleans on record as the home of "the Grizzly Bear," "Turkey Trot," "Texas Tommy," and "Todolo" dances. San Francisco has been receiving the questionable honor.
>
> Fifteen years ago, at Customhouse and Franklin streets, in the heart of New Orleans' "Tenderloin," these dances were first given, at an old negro dance hall. The accompanying music was played by a colored band, which has never been duplicated. The band often repeated the same selection, but never played it the same way twice.
>
> Dances popular in the lower strata of New Orleans society just now are the "Te-na-na," and "Bucktown Slow Drag." They, too, may find their way to the stage—authorities permitting. (Samuels 1911)

The corner of Customhouse and Franklin is certainly a noteworthy address in the New Orleans dance hall directory. Between 1900 and 1915, three of its four corners were occupied, respectively, by Shoto's Honky Tonk, the 101 Ranch, and the Pig Ankle tonk; this is according to the highly knowledgeable (if sometimes erroneous) map drawn for the Esquire Jazz Book (Miller 1945).

It is interesting that the downtown river corner of the intersection is occupied on the map by a joint called both the "101 Ranch" and "28." The former is the more recent of the two appellations; I assume that "28" was the old street number—analogous to the Big 25, also on Franklin Street but a bit closer to Canal Street. It is asserted that "28" was a haunt of Buddy Bolden's band (Rose and Souchon 1967, 220), and there is a couple of typically picturesque paragraphs in Bill Russell's essay in *Jazzmen* (Ramsey and Smith 1939, 34).

Samuels's stylistic observation is more than interesting, since so much of the earliest jazz on phonograph records is so little improvised. It gains credibility to the extent that it is quite unmotivated by the main point of a brief item, that is, that New Orleans had priority over San Francisco so far as the modern "erotic" dances are concerned.

These two references to the turkey trot clarify the lyrics to Ernest Hogan's famous song of 1895, "La Pas Ma La," which mentions, in addition to the title dance, the Bumbisha, the Saint Louis Pass, the Chicago Salute, and finally, "to the world's fair and do the Turkey Trot."[21]

Samuels broke another lance for the honor of New Orleans five years later, when jazz was on its way to becoming a national mania. In so doing, he gave support to the notion that the music called "jazz" could not be exchanged for all New Orleans ragtime, but was a new phase of it. His dispatch appeared under the "Cabaret" rubric in the November 3, 1916, issue of *Variety*:

> Chicago's claim to originating "Jazz Bands" and "Balling the Jack" are as groundless, according to VARIETY's New Orleans correspondent, as "Frisco"'s assumption to be the locale for the first "Todolo" and "Turkey Trot" dances. Little negro tots were "Bailin' the Jack" in New Orleans over ten years ago, and negro roustabouts were "Turkey Trotting" and doing the "Todolo" in New Orleans as far

back as 1890, he says. "Jazz Bands" have been popular there for over two years, and Chicago cabaret owners brought entertainers from that city to introduce the idea. New Orleans' "Brown Skin" dance is also to be instituted in the Windy City shortly, is the claim. (Samuels 1916)

And so we are back where we started, both to the Original Dixieland Jazz Band and to the roustabouts who made the New Orleans levee one of the wonders of nineteenth-century America. Except that there is the perplexing remark, "over two years," which would take us back so far as jazz is concerned to early 1914, a date that may correspond to stylish New Orleans's somewhat tardy embrace of a turkey trot (and similar dances) that had managed to rise above their humble origins in Bucktown or in the unnamed dance hall at Customhouse and Franklin.

I have suggested that the *onmium-gatherum* approach of the esteemed Henry Kmen and others in his footsteps is too indiscriminate. I have suggested that, while it is obvious that what the country came to know as jazz in 1917 came out of ragtime dance music as it was played in New Orleans in the first years of the century, it was the abandonment of the nexus of social dances first imported from Paris in the 1840s—the polka, mazurka, schottische, quadrille, and their relatives—in the course of the 1890s (although older dancers undoubtedly still kept on asking for them even twenty years later) that was the sine qua non for later developments. What replaced them was a simple walking and sliding dance—the two-step—ideally suited for ragtime, but also some new sexy dances, not yet quite fit for public consumption, of which the turkey trot and its sundry relatives and variations were eventually to emerge between 1911 and 1914 to define a new era of social dance, for which jazz was the accompaniment of choice.

Such a view leaves out any consideration of the astonishing expressiveness with which New Orleans African-American musicians (and the European-American musicians they inspired) imbued their run-of-the-mill dance music. In this, indeed, the local predilection for melody, as defined by W. T. Francis above, could well have played a role. But surely in the city of *Plessy v Ferguson* there was a need somehow to speak out, in whatever way one could—even in an arena, such as social dance music, that is by definition ephemeral and frivolous but by historical circumstance endowed with imagination and eloquence.

Notes

1. Or *routiniers,* to use the somewhat less derogatory and more descriptive French term. The fact that orchestral ragtime was undoubtedly played by ear in many parts of the country accounts for many musicians' rejection of New Orleans's claim to originating jazz.
2. The slang term "ratty" is commonly used to describe "hot" music or the older ragtime style or a kind of "strutting walk" (see Russell 1978, 7+; Rose 1974, 177; Merriam-Webster 1986, 1871).
3. There is, to be sure, a difficulty involved in using census data as evidence for the practice of music. Some of those who are enumerated as musicians may have frequently practiced another trade, depending on the season of the year and the state of the economy.
4. The overall total of musicians and music teachers increased by leaps and bounds between 1880 and 1910: this was largely due to the increase in the number of female music teachers, very few of whom were known as professional musicians. For the complete list of African-American musicians in the 1880 census as well as a provisional comparative table of decennial census numbers, see Gushee (1991, 61–62). The publication of this essay was unauthorized; additional research conducted between the original submission and eventual publication could have corrected or

augmented much of the biographical data presented, as well as the census statistics presented.

5. I compare his probable first composition, the self-published waltz "Bettina" of 1886 (dedicated "to my professor signor Giovani Luciani"), followed by his op. 2 of the same year, "Les yeux doux" (also self-published), with his op. 7, the "World's Fair March" of 1893, and the march and two-step "The Belle of the Carnival" (1897).

6. We ought not limit ourselves to published music, per se. G. F. Patton's exhaustive *A Practical Guide to the Arrangement of Band Music* (1875) can surely he seen as reflecting the best New Orleans practice, as the author acknowledges the professional assistance of New Orleanians Robert Meyer, John Eckert, and Charles Bothe. Also, Patton cites as an example of an interpolated passage in another key, the "Washington Artillery Polka," "a well known *Polka Quickstep* played by all the New Orleans bands" (Patton 1875, 29). Patton further devotes some forty pages to the various genres of dance music, if we needed any convincing that brass bands counted playing for dances among their manifold functions; and the comprehensive discussion of the functions of the second cornet part might almost have been written with Louis Armstrong in mind. There are no references, however, to African Americans.

7. Surely these "curiosities," whom Hearn had taken the trouble to ask to leave their normal place of business for the purpose of demonstrating their art, had names.

8. Hearn states in his introduction that he was "wholly indebted" to Professor William Henry, principal of the Jefferson Academy of New Orleans, for the Louisiana proverbs included, as well as a number of explanatory notes and examples of the local patois.

9. It is unfortunate that Krehbiel's books and papers, in principle preserved after his death in 1923, seem to have been dispersed. Some are at the New York Public Library; but no such statement by Hearn has yet been found in those documents that are available. In addition, despite the many books and essays that have been devoted to Hearn and his voluminous correspondence, some letters are still unpublished and others have reached print in censored form.

10. Manuel Marietta, also present at the interview and a professional who began at about the same time as Dawson, averred that older bands from uptown were called "ragtime" bands and were later called "Dixieland" bands.

11. Much of the content of the *New York Age* article had already been printed in Cary B. Lewis's column in the *Chicago Defender* of May 1, 1915. The latter source gives 1888 instead of 1898, clearly erroneous in view of the other dates mentioned.

12. The article was evidently reprinted from *The Prospect*, an Afro-American monthly of sixty-four pages, published in New York City, the first and perhaps last issue of which appeared in April 1898. No copy is extant; more's the pity, as the original article appears to have had musical examples that are missing in the Springfield newspaper.

13. That Cook was not the only musician to be struck by such a connection is shown in the piano medley "Pasquila" by W. J. Voges. (It is easily available in Baron 1980). While somewhat tame by the standards for rhythmic complexity established by Joplin and others from 1898 onward, it nonetheless is noteworthy for the insistence and variety of its cakewalk rhythms and for the inscriptions over the several sections: "Hot Stuff. "Good Thing, Push It Along." The strain entitled "Koochie-Koochie Dance" is indeed a version of the ubiquitous melody and makes prominent use of . . . syncopation (in meter).

14. Interesting in this regard is the 1906 song "Don't Go Way Nobody," often mentioned as part of the repertory of Buddy Bolden's band. The crudely drawn cover depicts a levee scene in the background, in accordance with Percy Cahill's lyrics: "I've worked out on the levee front,/Right in the broiling sun;/I've worked on every steamboat too. That ever dare to run./Worked at the docks, from morn 'till night./And burnt out lots of men;/When the whistle blew to knock off,/The boss would yell out then: Don't go way nobody, don't nobody leave."

15. The greatest lack in the collection is of interviews from older white musicians, as well as from musicians who have little or no

identification with jazz. On some points, indeed, the latter might be helpful witnesses, being less inclined to take ragtime, blues, and jazz for granted.

16. One should no doubt add Alcide Nunez (1884–1934) to this list, although his early death meant that he was never interviewed (unless, one wants to count the Kingsley [1918] article that seems clearly based on an interview). Remarkably, for the clarinet, biography, recordings, and musical compositions (all tour individuals mentioned have some to their credit) form a continuity against which change in musical style clearly stands out.

17. O'Neill is perhaps the father of the rather obscure violinist O'Neill Levasseur, mentioned from time to time in the Tulane interviews but also in the 1910 census as a white "musician—dancing hall" at 1558 Bienville Street.

18. One relatively late program, that of the "New Orleanser Quartett Club" at Odd Fellows' Hall on March 9, 1909, gives two-step, polka, and mazurka nearly equal representation. It warns us to be on the lookout for variations depending on ethnicity and social level.

19. Jack Stewart was kind enough to send me this article, which had been collected by Russell Levy in his line-by-line reading of the *Item* some years ago; I had in fact seen, copied, and forgotten it about ten years ago, at a time when the last thing on my mind was the turkey trot.

20. My thanks to Bruce Vermazen who, knowing of my passionate interest in the turkey trot, called the article to my attention. Oscar Monte Samuels was born in 1885 and died in 1945 after a long career as building contractor and house-wrecker. His obituary (New Orleans *Times Picayune*, March 12, 1945, 2) states that he was recognized as an authority on the theater.

21. Hogan's piece was preceded in print by Irving Jones's "Possumala Dance or My Honey" (1894), which has quite different lyrics and melody. It does in fact, bear a startling likeness to some of Ben Harney's songs, which were soon to become extremely popular. There is one point of perhaps far-fetched resemblance. Whereas Irving Jones's song repeats the rhythm in the voice part no fewer than eleven times in succession, Hogan's piece has in virtually every measure of the accompaniment, verse and chorus alike, the rhythm. There are other pieces in the orbit of Hogan's and Jones's work, e.g., New Orleans composer Sidney Perrin's "The Jennie Cooler Dance" (1898); Paul Rubens's "Rag Time Pasmala (Characteristique Two Step)" (1898); Theo H. Northrup's "Louisiana Rag Two-Step (Pas Ma La)," with the additional title-page inscription "Description of Louisiana Niggers Dancing (The Pas Ma La Rag)" (1897). No doubt there are others.

References

Albert, Tom. 1959. Interview with William Russell and Ralph Collins, September 25. William Ransom Hogan Jazz Archive, Tulane University, New Orleans, Louisiana.

Allen, William Francis, Charles Pickard Ware, and Lucy McKim Garrison. [1867] 1951. *Slave songs of the United States.* New York: Peter Smith.

Baron, John H. 1980. *Piano music from New Orleans 1851–1898.* New York: Da Capo.

Bisland, Elizabeth. 1906. *The life and letters of Lafcadio Hearn.* Vol. 1. London: Archibald Constable.

Cook, Will Marion. 1898. Music of the Negro. [Illinois] *Record* May 14: 1, 4.

———. 1918. Negro Music. *New York Age* September 9: 6.

Dawson, Eddie. 1959. Interview by William Russell and Ralph Collins, August 11. William Ransom Hogan Jazz Archive, Tulane University, New Orleans, Louisiana.

Epstein, Dena J. 1977. *Sinful tunes and spirituals: Black folk music to the Civil War.* Urbana: University of Illinois Press.

Filhe, George. 1949. Typescript of an interview by Harriet Janis and Rudi Blesh. Held in the author's personal collection.

Fischer, David Hackett. 1970. *Historians' fallacies: Toward a logic of historical thought.* New York: Harper & Row.

Garner, Fradley, and Alan Merriam. 1960. The word jazz. *The Jazz Review* 3, no. 3: 39–40; no. 4: 40–42; no. 5: 40; no. 6: 40–41; no. 7: 36–37.

Goffin, Robert. 1946. *La Nouvelle-Orleans, capitale du jazz.* New York: Editions de la Maison Française.

Goldstein, Walter. 1918. The natural harmonic and rhythmic sense of the Negro. In *Studies in musical education: History and aesthetics.* Papers and proceedings of the Music Teachers National Association (MTNA) at its 39th Annual Meeting. New Orleans, December 27–29, 1917. Hartford. Conn.: MTNA.

Guilcher, Jean-Michel. 1969. *La Contredanse et les renouvellements de la danse française.* Paris: Mouton.

Gushee, Lawrence. 1991. Black professional musicians in New Orleans c. 1880. *Inter-American Music Review* 11: 53–63.

Hearn, Lafcadio. 1885. *"Gombo Zhèbes." Little dictionary of Creole proverbs.* New York: Will Coleman.

———. 1890. *Two years in the French West Indies.* New York: Harper.

———. 1924. *Miscellanies: Articles and stories now first collected by Albert Mordell.* Vol. 1. London: William Heinemann.

Janis, Harriet, and Rudi Blesh. 1971. *They all played ragtime.* New York: Oak.

Jones, Juli, Jr. 1911. Great colored song writers and their songs. [Indianapolis] *Freeman* December 23: 6.

Kingsley. Walter. 1917. Whence comes jass? Facts from the great authority on the subject. *New York Sun* August 5: sect. 3, 3.

———. 1918. Vaudville volley. *Dramatic Mirror* December 14.

Kinzer, Samuel. 1993. The Tio family: Four generations of New Orleans musicians, 1814–1933. Ph.D. diss., Louisiana State University.

Kmen, Henry A. 1966. *Music in New Orleans: The formative years, 1791–1841.* Baton Rouge: Louisiana State University Press.

Krehbiel, Henry Edward. 1962. *Afro-American folksongs: A study in racial and national music.* 1913; New York: Frederick Ungar.

Lange, Horst. 1991. *Als der jazz begann. 1916–1923.* Berlin: Colloquium Verlag.

Marquis, Donald M. 1978. *In search of Buddy Bolden, first man of jazz.* Baton Rouge: Louisiana State University Press.

Merriam-Webster. 1986. *Webster's third international dictionary.* Springfield, Mass.: Merriam-Webster.

Miller, Paul Eduard. 1945. *Esquire's 1945 jazz book.* New York: A.S. Barnes.

The moral wave strikes New Orleans dancing schools. 1908. *New Orleans Item* January 15.

Nathan, Hans. 1962. *Dan Emmett and the rise of early Negro minstrelsy.* Norman: University of Oklahoma Press.

New Orleans taste in music. 1890. *New Orleans Daily Picayune* January 2: 3.

Patton, G. F. 1875. *A practical guide to the arrangement of band music.* Leipzig: John F. Stratton.

Ramsey, Frederic, Jr., with Charles Edward Smith. 1939. *Jazzmen.* New York: Harcourt, Brace.

Robinson, J. Russell. 1955. The story of J. Russell Robinson. *The Second Line* 6, no. 9/10: 13–15, 30.

Rose, Al. 1974. *Storyville, New Orleans, being an authentic, illustrated account of the notorious red-light district.* University: University of Alabama Press.

Rose, Al, and Edmond Souchon. 1967. *New Orleans jazz: A family album.* Baton Rouge: Louisiana State University Press.

Russell, William. 1978. Albert Nicholas talks about Jelly Roll: Part II of an interview. *The Second Line* 30 (Spring): 3–10.

[Samuels, Oscar Monte]. 1911. New Orleans makes a claim. *Variety* July 1.

———. 1916. Cabaret. *Variety* November 3.

Spriggins, E. Belfield. 1933. Excavating local jazz. *Louisiana Weekly* April 22.

St. Cyr, Johnny. 1966. Jazz as I remember it. *Jazz Journal* September: 6–9.

Stewart, Jack. 1991. The Mexican band legend. *Jazz Archivist* 6: 2.

8

Marshall Lullaby

KIP LORNELL AND CHARLES WOLFE

"Lead Belly," born Huddie William Ledbetter on Jeter Plantation in Mooringsport, Louisiana, ca. January 29, 1885, became one of the most influential and widely recognized black folk artists of the twentieth century. Taught to play accordion and the rudiments of guitar by his uncle, Terrell Ledbetter, he soon employed his talents at local "sukey-jump" parties. This chapter from Lornell and Wolfe's award-winning biography discusses the complex and rich musical culture to which Huddie was exposed during his East Texas youth.

Huddie left home around 1903 to became, by turns, an itinerant musician and a farm laborer, working between Dallas and Shreveport. During this peripatetic period Ledbetter married his first wife, "Lethe" Henderson (July 8, 1908), and about four years later met and spent about eight months playing with the legendary blues singer Blind Lemon Jefferson and acquired the first of his signature twelve-string guitars.

Huddie's initial brush with the law occurred in 1915, when he was jailed for assault in Harrison County, Texas. He spent much of the next nineteen years incarcerated for a variety of crimes ranging from simple assault to "assaulting to kill." In a curious turn of events, "Lead Belly" (as he was now known) was granted a full pardon in 1925 by Texas governor Pat Neff, who heard him perform at the Sugarland Prison, located near Houston.

While imprisoned in Louisiana's notorious Angola Penitentiary in the early 1930s, Huddie Ledbetter's life changed forever when he met John Lomax and his son, Alan, who were collecting African American folk songs for the Library of Congress in the summer of 1933. Lomax recorded Lead Belly and returned the next summer with improved equipment. This time Lead Belly reworked his pardon song, addressing it to Louisiana governor O. K. Allen, as well as recording (what would become) his trademark song "Goodnight Irene."

Hopeful of finding a new audience and wishing to escape from the racist South following his prison release in August 1934, Lead Belly proved a sensation upon his arrival in New York City on December 31, 1934. Newspapers printing lurid descriptions of his convict past helped. John Lomax quickly negotiated a contract with Macmillan to write Negro Folk Songs as Sung by Leadbelly (1936) and persuaded the March of Time's newsreel to film Huddie. Lead Belly sent to Louisiana for Martha Promise, with whom he had taken up after being released from Angola; he married her in Wilton, CT, on January 21, 1935.

In addition to more recordings for the Library of Congress, John Lomax also arranged a recording contract with The American Record Company (now CBS/Sony). The records sold poorly; however, progressive, white urban intellectuals found him fascinating. For the rest of his life, Huddie Ledbetter would record for and entertain virtually all-white audiences.

> The Ledbetters survived largely on musical jobs and welfare. Always ready to adapt to his environment, Lead Belly added "topical" and "protest" songs about segregation and natural disasters to his repertoire. These musical and social impulses led him to keep company with "urban folk" musicians such as Woody Guthrie, Sonny Terry, Brownie McGhee, Pete Seeger, The Golden Gate Quartet, and Burl Ives. In addition to performing, Huddie eventually recorded dozens of selections for Capital, RCA, Musicraft, and Asch/Folkways. While in Paris late in 1948, persistent muscle problems led to a diagnosis of Lou Gehrig's disease—amyotrophic lateral sclerosis. Six months later, on December 6, 1949, he succumbed to the disorder. Ironically, one year later, his trademark song "Goodnight Irene," which he had learned from his uncle Bob Ledbetter, became a nationwide number-one hit for the Weavers.

In later years, Huddie Ledbetter would always talk about the blues and how much it contributed to his own musical background. But in the complex rural black culture of Harrison County, Texas, in the waning years of the nineteenth century, there were many other musical forms and styles. Some styles—blues and gospel songs—became part of the stereotyped image that whites had of black folk music, while ballads, string band music, hollers, topical broadsides, and others almost vanished from later black folk music. All, however, were part of the musical mélange young Huddie was exposed to in the years from 1888 to 1900 and contributed to one of the most wonderfully diverse repertoires in folk music history.

Huddie apparently began trying to make music when he was as young as two years old. Irene Campbell recalled stories her grandmother told her about Huddie picking up a twig, hollowing it out, whittling holes, and creating his own primitive fife. It is quite possible that he saw older men doing something like this with larger, heavier cane, the source of fifes still played by some older black musicians in north-central Mississippi. But Huddie also was drawn to other more formal instruments as well. Again drawing on her grandmother's stories, Irene Campbell said, "He would sit in his little rocking chair. His feet could not touch the ground, but he could play tunes on the accordion and the mandolin."

When no instrument was around, Huddie used his voice—the most basic of all instruments. He vividly recalled how he would get up in the morning to go to school and race out into the yard to give a "getting-up" holler to his friends. "When I was a little boy, going to a country school, the little boys, we was living in the woods about three and four miles apart from each other. First little boy [that] gets up in the morning, he wanted to let the others know he was up, wanted to see which one beat up. They had a little echo, call it 'Ho-day,' and the first one to get up, he'd run outside and start hollering." The other boys would eventually echo this greeting.

Huddie was quick to point out that these hollers were different from the field hollers later used in picking cotton or working in the fields. These were purely celebratory hollers, ways to let your friends know that you were up and all right—or that you had managed to beat them in getting up. In an age before telephones, such communication was quite common between neighbors in the backwoods South. Some hollers became quite elaborate, and in some communities an entire repertoire of hollers developed: from distress hollers requesting help to good-morning hollers designed to celebrate a new day. Certain people became acknowledged experts at complex hollers that could be heard for long distances. Huddie and his friends even knew hollers that verged on becoming little songs, replete with blueslike lyrics:

> One dollar bill, baby, won't buy you no shoes.
> One dollar bill, baby, won't buy you no shoes.
>
> Dollar bill, baby, won't buy you no shoes.

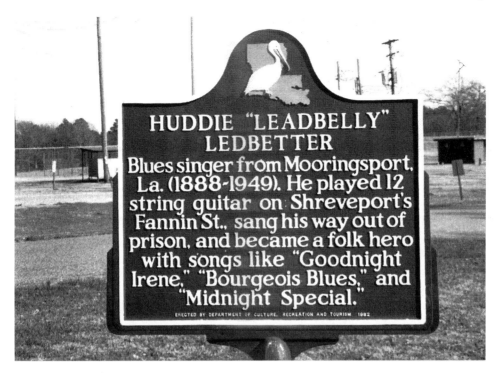

In 1982 the State of Louisiana's Department of Culture, Recreation, and Tourism placed this historical marker in Lead Belly's hometown of Mooringsport, Louisiana.

Credit: Photograph by Kip Lornell.

School itself even offered different types of music to a young boy fascinated with sounds and rhymes. During recess most of the boys played ball while the girls would organize "play-parties" or "ring" games. Sometimes the boys would join these activities that combined actions and songs into an infectious game, which could be expanded to fit a specific length of time. Such games fascinated young Huddie and gave him one of his first opportunities to actually sing about some part of his life. The "play" that he best remembered was one that later became one of his favorite musical pieces, "Ha, Ha Thisaway." Though he later recorded numerous different verses of the song, one of the most cogent was:

> I'm gonna tell you, tell you, tell you,
> I'm gonna tell you, to save my soul.
> Teacher's gonna fail you, fail you, fail you,
> Teacher's gonna fail you, so I was told.

There was also, at the Lake Chapel School about 1900, a teacher with a strong interest in music named George Summers. He organized a little band among the students there. Karnack native Mary Patterson, who was about the same age as Huddie, recalls how Summers taught Huddie some of the rudiments: "He had me playing a little old string instrument, a mandolin. There was three or four of us in that little band. Huddie played the guitar." Nobody knows exactly what kind of repertoire the "little band" played, but it was probably full of dance music and waltzes. Summers's instruction, probably the only formal teaching in music ever received by Huddie, most likely concentrated on tuning, keeping time, and chord positions. A few of the songs that Huddie recalled in later years, such as the vaudeville piece "Lindy Lou," were known to have been in the repertoires of black string bands from the Deep South.

At home Huddie's interest in music pleased both parents. Though he was not a singer, Wes Ledbetter certainly liked music and apparently could even play a little on the guitar. Sallie, whose fine voice often led the choir at the Shiloh Baptist Church, sang lullabies and spirituals to her young son. But the real role models for music making came from his two uncles, Bob and Terrell. Both lived nearby (though Terrell eventually settled in, ironically, a town named Terrell, Texas) and worked full-time chopping cotton and plowing. They also enjoyed local reputations as guitarists and vocalists of the kind Huddie later referred to as "songster." This term denoted a person who was a noted singer, played a stringed instrument, and possessed a wide repertoire of sacred and secular music. Songsters like Uncle Terrell sometimes roamed about, picking up songs from traveling minstrels and vaudeville stages as well as from their peers. He eventually taught Huddie the work song "Looky Yonder Where the Sun Done Gone" and the pan-Southern drug classic "Take a Whiff on Me," which was equally popular in both black and white circles. The latter song was about cocaine—still a legal drug at the turn of the century—and warned, "Cocaine's for horses and not for men,/ the doctor say it kill you, but he won't say when." Uncle Bob stayed closer to home, mostly around Oil City. John Lomax recorded him for the Library of Congress in 1940, including the "Cleveland Campaign Song" about the election of Grover Cleveland in 1884. Bob's son, Edmond, became a songster and he would often play with Huddie when they were both teenagers. Margaret Coleman wrote that "through all this there was an unfinished duty he looked forward to, so he talked it over with his parents to get him some kind of an instrument so he could learn music." When Huddie was seven this dream came true when Uncle Terrell dropped by the house, returning by mule from Mooringsport. A "windjammer" (a small button accordion) hung from his saddle and he gave it to his excited nephew. Huddie worked on it all evening and into the night, trying to find the proper combination of rhythm and buttons to make a tune. His experimentation wore down Sallie and Wes's patience, but they understood his enthusiasm. By morning Huddie had mastered a rough version of "There's No Cornbread Here." A few days later his mother taught him an old jig called "Dinah's Got a Wooden Leg." Soon she was adding to his repertoire some of the lullabies and spirituals she sang in church and Huddie was learning that the windjammer could be as much at home in the church as at the local square dance.

During the next several years, Huddie began to find out that he had a special talent for remembering the words and melodies to the songs he heard in his community. They were not only the church songs and simple jigs and reels he had started with, but the whole range of contemporary southern black folk music. Though he was later called a bluesman, at this date blues were just emerging as a musical genre separate from others such as ragtime, work songs, and dance tunes.

Other instruments came his way and Huddie displayed an aptitude for them all: harmonica, piano, Jew's harp, and even the old reed organ at the Shiloh Church. Soon he was being asked to come to the country dances to play his accordion. Huddie would mount his pony, hook the windjammer to the saddle horn, and ride far into the countryside. By 1903, he had become a fixture at the sukey jumps, which paid him fifty cents a night. Huddie gradually grew more fascinated with stringed instruments, especially with the drive and rhythm he could generate with them. His early experience with the mandolin and guitar in the Lake Chapel School had only whetted his appetite. "He loved music," Mary Patterson said, "but he liked string music even better."

In addition to learning from his uncles, Huddie learned some music from two local boys, Bud Coleman and Jim Fagin, who played for country dances. One played the guitar, the other the mandolin, and Huddie soon followed them to every dance at which they performed. He begged his father to buy him a guitar, and after a day during which Huddie was particularly persuasive, Wes relented. As with the accordion, Huddie stayed up the entire first night trying to pick out the tunes he'd heard Coleman and Fagin perform: "Green Corn" was the first tune he learned. It was an old dance song often played by white fiddlers at square dances—the "green corn" of the title refers to newly run moonshine whiskey carried in a "jimmy-john"—and Huddie would keep it in his repertoire the rest of his life. From Jim Fagin he learned "Po' Howard," a song about a legendary black fiddler from the early Emancipation days.

Huddie probably got his guitar around 1903, about the time the instrument was experiencing a real surge of popularity in the rural South. Throughout much of the previous century, the guitar was known as a genteel parlor instrument, suitable for strumming by the lady of the house or the unmarried daughter wanting to entertain a suitor. President Andrew Jackson's wife Rachael owned a guitar and in the 1870s and 1880s music publishers issued dozens of books and sheet music pieces that made the guitar resemble the staid, classical instrument it once was in European culture. There are a few scattered instances, though, of the instruments falling into the hands of folk musicians: a foot soldier in the Civil War, a black entertainer in a band in a St. Louis tavern at the turn of the century, a cowboy accompanying himself in a ballad in the New Mexico territory. Generally, though, it was not a favorite instrument with nineteenth century blacks. In a survey of musical instruments mentioned in interviews with former slaves done by the Works Progress Administration in the 1930s, the guitar was seldom mentioned in comparison with the fiddle and the banjo. While 205 ex-slaves mentioned fiddles and 106 recalled the banjo, only 15 talked about guitars. Suddenly, at the end of the century, all this began to change when companies like Gibson and the new mail-order house of Sears, Roebuck began to manufacture inexpensive guitars.

Huddie lacked neither mentors nor partners with whom to pick. His first cousin, Edmond Ledbetter, Uncle Bob's son, remembered the kind of music he and Huddie used to make. "We were kids together, used to make music. Sometimes he played a mandolin and I'd second him with a guitar and sometimes we played the guitar together. Used to play all 'round here, up to Mooringsport, over to Leigh [Texas], and back to the Jeter Plantation." The two boys were so close that people often thought that they were brothers. Often they were joined by Starling Myers, another part-time songster who also worked as a local guide for Caddo Lake fishermen.

Huddie demonstrated an immediate aptitude not only for learning music but for learning it quickly and skillfully. Though he was good at school, Huddie was even better with music. Soon he was out in the country playing music for parties and dances, but he always came home in time for work and school. But there was a lot yet to come—new songs, emerging styles of music, new ways to sell himself to an audience. Huddie was starting to emerge as a brash and self-confident teenager who was beginning to sense some of the possibilities for his music.

Most of the parties and dances that Margaret Coleman talked about were held in rural houses miles from the nearest town and often miles from the nearest white homestead. "They called them sukey jumps," Huddie recollected many years later. *Sukey*, or *sookie*, was apparently a Deep South slang term dating from the 1820s and referring to a servant or slave. A sukey jump, therefore, was once a dance or party in slave quarters. Huddie himself once explained the term by saying, "Because they dance so fast, the music was so fast and the people had to jump, so they called them sooky jumps." *Sookie*, Huddie thought, was derived from the field term for cow and was used to call a cow, too. Whatever the case, these late nineteenth century country dances gave Leadbelly the first public platform for his music.

Often the dances were held in private homes, which the owners had prepared by moving most of the furniture outside or up against the wall. By dusk, a big bonfire would be started out front, both to help cook the food and to alert people about the exact location for the dance. Zora Neale Hurston, the famed writer and folklorist who later came to know Leadbelly in New York, described such a dance in the book *Mules and Men*:

> You can tell the dances are to be held by the fires. Huge bonfires of faulty logs and slabs are lit outside the house in which the dances are held. The refreshments are parched peanuts, fried rabbit, fish, chicken, and chitterlings. The only music is guitar music and the only dance is the ole square dance.

In another account, she noted that many times the only music was performed on a guitar, and while "one guitar was enough for a dance, to have two was considered excellent. Where two were playing one man played the lead and the other seconded him. The first player was 'picking' and the second 'framing,' that is, playing chords while the lead carried the melody by dexterous finger-work."

Mance Lipscomb, the Texas songster and bluesman who was some ten years Huddie's junior, also spent an apprenticeship at rural house parties, mostly along the Brazos River in Texas. As a youth, he went to the dances in order to learn new material. "I wasn't out there for nothin'; I was catchin' them songs," he recalled. Later he began to play his guitar for the dances, sometimes with three different sets of musicians who were set up in shifts so that the dance could go on all night without interruption. Lipscomb remembered:

> The first crew was eight o'clock. I played an hour with them. They had everything in bloom. Long about twelve o'clock, here come another crew in there. Fresh crew! I fan them out. Played all night till four o'clock, in the morning, sometimes eleven o'clock on a Sunday. Setting right in one chair. And they had me settin' up there, and wasn't no electric lights. Had old lamp lights. No electricity. No fan. And I'd get down there an'set by that window to get a little air. Lots of nights I played all night long, didn't have nothin' on but my pants. No shirt at all. Just sweaty as I could be. Trying to stay cool. And long about twelve or one o'clock, you'd hear a gun somewhere, in the house or out the house. "Boom!" Somebody died.

The earliest dances that Huddie remembered featured music played on the fiddle or accordion, or windjammer. Years later he could still play some of the old dance tunes on his accordion, pieces such as "Sukey Jump" and the minstrel show song "Jawbone." Like so many of the old fiddle tunes, they were primarily instrumental, with a few vocal choruses thrown in for variety's sake.

Jawbone eat and Jawbone talk,
Jawbone eat with a knife and fork.

But the most interesting description of a late nineteenth century sukey jump comes from Chris Franklin, an ex-slave from Caddo Parish interviewed about his musical activities in 1937:

> De white folk low dem [allow them] to have de frolic with de fiddle or banjo or windjammer. Dey dance out on de grass, forty or fifty niggers, and dem big girls nineteen years old git out dere barefoot as de goose. It jes' de habit of de times, 'cause dey all have shoes. Sometimes dey call de jig dance and some of dem sho' dance it, too. De prompter call "All git ready." Den de holler, "All balance," and den he sing out "Swing your pardner," and dey does it. Den he say "All promenade," and dey goes in de circle. One thing dey calls, "Bird in de Cage." Three join hands round de gal in de middle, and dance around her, and den she git out and her pardner git in the center and dey dance awhile.

One old fiddle song—one borrowed from the African American fiddle tradition, not necessarily from whites—was Leadbelly's version of the familiar "Give the Fiddler a Dram," which he called "Gwine Dig a Hole to Put the Devil In." This hard-driven breakdown with simple, expandable verses could easily be drawn out to a fifteen- or twenty-minute set. Whites had often sung about giving the fiddler a dram of liquor; the line among black performers dealt with the concept of digging a hole for the devil. Huddie explained that "long years ago that was when they see the boss comin', you know, and the boys would see the boss comin', well, they didn't like him, you know, but they'd be together, nothing but Negroes, all piled-up there together. When they see him comin' they say 'Well, we gonna dig a hole to put the Devil in, boy they 'started to jumpin'."

These turn-of-the-century gatherings featured a number of different styles of dancing. The older people preferred the classic Texas square dance, which had been developed from the French cotillion and contra dance decades earlier. "They called the sets all the time when they danced," said Huddie. "They called 'Shoo Fly,' uses 'shoo fly' mean square dance." It worked this way: a couple would get on the dance floor and, on cue from the caller, begin to circle to the right. And then, said Huddie,

> when you get back to your home [starting place], grab your partner, the first man on the head "shoo fly." When they begin to "shoo fly" then they holler:
>
> Shoo fly, shoo fly,
> Shoo fly, shoo fly,
>
> Then they commence hollering:
>
> One dollar bill baby, won't buy you no shoes,
> One dollar bill baby, won't buy you no shoes,
> One dollar bill baby, won't buy you no shoes.

Then the next man would "head shoo fly": get his partner and circle around. This continued until each couple of them had circled to home; they then would make a ring and circle again, find their partners, and began to "dance on ahead and dance toward the candy stand."

Younger partners preferred a faster beat and a faster tune, and did a complex set of dance steps that Huddie later referred to as "breakdowns" or "the old buck and wing": "You got to do it real fast. And when you breakdown you ain't tapping, you just working your legs. Now a long time ago my grandfather, great grandfather, say you ain't dancing 'til you cross you legs." The Baptist church tried to discourage African religious practices among slaves. It forbade not only drumming, but any kind of dancing—with dancing defined as movement that involved crossing the legs. Thus these rural dances were not just an incidental part of Huddie's growing up; they were deep-rooted links to his African American heritage and a vital part of the rich musical culture that was nourishing him.

Another account from the turn of the twentieth century describes a dance called the Dog Scratch being done by two individuals surrounded by a circle of men who shouted encouragement, and clapped and eventually joined in. Mance Lipscomb recalled seeing two dancers engaged in "cutting contests . . . seein' who could outdance the other one. You ever see two roosters flappin' up alongside on another? It was like that." Leadbelly also recalled a step called "Knockin' a Pigeon-Wing," which he asserted went well with a song like "You Can't Losa-Me Cholly." The Pigeon Wing was, in fact, one of the most enduring of these old dance steps; dancers scraped and shaked one foot, then another, fluttering their arms like an awkward bird trying to fly. Then there was the Eagle Rock, which Huddie later celebrated in a barrelhouse piano solo for Capitol Records. This was yet another "bird" dance, descended from an even earlier plantation dance called the Buzzard Lope. (Mance Lipscomb remembered dancers doing this step at some of his parties, but it pretty much died out by the 1930s.) In the Eagle Rock, the dancer rocked his body from side to side while making preening, wing-like movements with his arms. This dance made it into the dance halls and bordellos of urban areas in the region; veteran New Orleans cornet player Charlie Love recalled that he and his friends danced the Eagle Rock to the music of Buddy Bolden, the legendary cornet player who laid the groundwork for New Orleans jazz.

All of these things young Huddie took in, and the hours he spent watching dancers in all manner of dusty cabins and tin-roofed farmhouses were not lost. He, in fact, became a dancer himself, and his early reputation was built as much on his dancing as on his singing or guitar playing. He did the old buck dances and square dances and he could "cut" the Pigeon Wing along with the Short Dog along with the best of them. But the dance that he really specialized in was a newer dance derived from these old steps, the tap dance. His niece, Irene Campbell, recalled some of the Saturday night get-togethers the family or the community would have, and how Huddie would be the center of attention: "He did tap dancing. He was the first person that I ever saw do tap dancing. It was very much like they have today. It was entertainment, sometimes just for the family. You know that we would come by. They would have competitions to see who could 'cut it,' called it 'Cut the Pigeon Wing.'"

In later years, Huddie recorded a sample of the kind of dancing he did for such affairs, under the title "Leadbelly's Dance." It was fast and complex, involving the feet, the hands, and slapping "hambone" on the body. Parts of it combined storytelling with dance. For one sequence, he explains, "My mama used to make flapjacks and here's the way she's make em up"; for another, Leadbelly says, "I used to walk down to the levee with my gal and here's the way she'd walk."

In fact, Leadbelly seems to have done what most dance historians call a "soft shoe," the older forerunner of tap-dancing that was done without the actual metal taps. This kind of dance probably came from a merging of English-Irish jigs and clog dances with African American solo dances. An ex-slave named James W. Smith described "jigging contests" held on plantations about the time of the Civil War in Texas, where one of the dancers could "make his feet go like triphammers and sound like the snaredrum." Early minstrel show dancers soon began to make distinctions between the clog and the soft shoe, and during the days following the Civil War, black minstrel stars like Billy Kersands began to feature a version of the soft shoe he called Essence of Old Virginia. Influential later dancers such as George Primrose popularized "leather soles" even more, and traveling circuses, tent shows, and vaudeville revues took these innovations deep into the hinterlands. In a sense, they returned them to the folk tradition.

Huddie probably learned from what he had seen of the soft-shoe dance on stage and copied it. A few years later, when young Huddie spent time with the blind bluesman and songster Blind Lemon Jefferson, one of his jobs was to do a soft-shoe tap dance while Jefferson played a guitar instrumental such as the ragtime-styled "Hot Dog" (which he later recorded for Paramount Records). Dancing was clearly intrinsic to Huddie's music.

Huddie always worked during the week, and Saturday night was the night to really kick back and let off steam. But there was another side to that coin on Sunday morning. The Ledbetters attended the local Shiloh Baptist Church. "He used to be a secretary, . . ." Huddie said of his father years later. "And my mother used to lead prayer meetings and my father, too, they always worked their hymns out, the Baptists do." The old Shiloh Baptist Church is just south of the Jeter Plantation, where Huddie was born, and it was at this church he heard the old hymns and spirituals. "Death is slow but death is sure, Hallelu, Hallelu," he would sing as a lad, listening to his father "line out" the songs, call out the words line by line before the congregation sang it. This was a stark but evocative body of songs, rich in imagery and strong in melody, and it took its place in young Huddie's imagination, alongside the old folk ballads, reels, and field hollers. During the first years of Huddie's popularity in the middle 1930s, most of his fans and admirers overlooked this aspect of his music, but in later years Huddie made up for the oversight by recording dozens of religious songs and including them in his programs.

Huddie grew up in the church, although he did not actually join a congregation until he was around twenty. He became thoroughly familiar with the different styles of prayer meetings, revivals, Sunday services, singing styles, and even the techniques for preaching a sermon. Huddie became adept at imitating the singsong, emotional chants of the old preachers and in 1943 he recorded such a parody for a New York record company:

> There's a lot of pretty girls up in Heaven—
> That's going to make everybody want to go to Heaven—
> Going up there to see the pretty girls—
> There's a big stream of molasses,
> run right down through heaven—
> It may sound funny, it don't cost money—
> But there's a big stream of honey
> running down through Heaven—
> And there's lots of flapjacks
> and a lot of good butter—
> And a good sharp knife sittin' on each side—

Huddie also learned the essential elements of song leading, how to "line out" a song, and how to understand the age-old types of poetic meter used in the songs, such as "common meter," "long meter," and "short meter." Such metrical schemes referred not to the musical notation but simply to the number of syllables in each individual line of a song. Leadbelly explained that "Must I Be Carried to the Sky on Flowered Beds of Ease" was "the long meter.

You see, I didn't cut that off at all ... [in] common meter you cut off between them two verses. You got to always cut off between the verses to make it common. And to make it long, you sing two verses right at once on the long time."

As Huddie's reputation as a singer grew, he began to find himself more in demand to sing in church. One of the big events in the church year was the "tracted meeting," annual revival services that lasted for several days. The meetings were almost a form of folk theater, in which the congregation participated as much as the preacher, improvising with passion, blurring the boundary lines between singing, preaching, praying, and testifying. Huddie once described such a prayer meeting on a recording for the Library of Congress:

> Now, they sing that first song at the beginning of the prayer meeting, [then] they'd get down to prayer. Now, they open up but they keep on all night. They call on one brother or one sister to pray and when they call on some of the sisters to pray they just shakes, you know, some of 'em be so nervous, you know, they can't hardly pray trembling in their voice. Well, some men be like that. Now, that's the way they carry on their meeting down South, at my home.

After the first round of prayers, they would sing again—"they'll sing, they goin' around to the mourners, everybody goin' get around the mourners and start singing for a while and then the preacher going [to] preach." Later, when the men were done praying, the "Amen corner" sisters started out:

> The Amen corner sisters, the ones who do this moanin', starts out, the whole church can help 'em. But they starts out, and when the preacher, and when the men is prayin', to give 'em some spirit, they'd moan behind 'em and that would make 'em pray and the sisters would holler "C'mon and mon there Sister Sally."

Of course, the same kind of talent and fame that helped him fill the collection plate through his singing eventually brought him into the bad graces of some of the older church members. As his reputation as a "rounder" and a party-goer grew, some of the women got a little nervous. Sallie Hooks, a long-time resident of Mooringsport and cousin of Martha Promise (later to be Huddie's wife), saw Huddie in church as a child and thought of him as a "worldly man":

> He could play church songs. I remember when we first got our organ at church. I was a little girl back then and he played the organ. We didn't have nobody else could play and lots of old folks liked to have had a spell because he didn't belong to the church. My daddy and all got around the old sisters wouldn't let them bother him.

Although the image of the young, strapping teenager being protected from a posse of "older sisters" seems a bit odd, the story of Huddie playing the first organ at his church remains a familiar legend in western Caddo Parish. Huddie's niece Pinkie Williams agrees with the story, but views it from a slightly different angle. She recalls that Wes Ledbetter was a "secretary" for the church and that the entire family was active in the church. "The whole family was in the church. Huddie was the first organist at the Shiloh Baptist Church; his name is on the church record. He could play just about anything."

Wes and Sallie undoubtedly pressured their son to go to church, to join the church, and to become a Christian. Huddie, however, never did actually join until after he left home. His interests seem to have been in the music, rather than the spiritual message. "I never led no prayer," he remarked. "I just used to lead singing. They never would call on me to pray. Of course, I could do it all right . . . I can pray and preach, too. I can *sure* pray."

How much of the church Huddie truly believed in and how much of it he viewed as mere theater is debatable. His two nieces Viola and Irene Campbell both feel that he was more serious about his beliefs than many thought. "He had a deep-down . . . belief in religion. Because if someone would come in and they would be cursing and using profanity, wrong language, Huddie would say 'Look, you don't do that here. These are my nieces and you don't do that here!' And usually when he would speak like that, people would move."

But gradually Huddie began to slide away from the church. By his mid-teens, Huddie Ledbetter had become, in the eyes of some church members, a "backslider." "That was when somebody done belong to the church and done turned back," remarked Huddie. At revivals and prayer meetings, the members would sing, "Backslider, fare you well, I will meet you on kingdom's shore." Yet Huddie himself never really felt any dramatic isolation from his church, or from his religion. He later said, "I believe I got as good a religion as I ever had before but I just liked music and singing, you know, and dancing. I just went on back and started doing it."

And years later, hundreds of miles from the Shiloh Church and Mooringsport, he could vividly recall and sing the songs he learned there: "Get on Board," "Let It Shine on Me," "Must I Be Carried to the Sky on Flowered Beds of Ease?," "Down in the Valley to Pray," "Run Sinners," "Ride On," "The Blood Done Signed Your Name," and others. It was a music as rich as that he heard at the sukey jumps, as steeped in tradition, as passionate, as memorable; it was a ballast that would help him through the stormy seas ahead.

Notes

Marshall Lullaby

The background about Huddie's early musical activity and Campbell's quote are from Sandra Cuson, "A Marshall Lullaby," Shreveport *Times*, August 3, 1975.

"When I was a little boy . . ." from an interview released on Playboy LP 119.

"One dollar bill, baby . . ." is described more fully in *Negro Folk Songs of Lead Belly* (New York: Macmillan, 1936), p. 115.

HA, HA THISAWAY. New words and new music arragement by Huddie Ledbetter. Collected and adapted by John A. Lomax and Alan Lomax, TRO- ©Copyright 1936 (Renewed) Folkways Music Publishers, Inc New York, NY and Global Jukebox Publishing (BMI).

"He had me playing . . ." from Moore's 1972 interview.

"through all this . . ." from Library of Congress "Leadbelly" files letter, Margaret Coleman's letter reveals some information about Huddie's first accordion and his early repertoire. John Reynolds also comments upon this in personal conversations with the authors.

"He loved . . ." from Wyatt Moore's 1972 interview with Mary Patterson.

Larry Cohn talks more about "Po' Howard" in his notes to the Elektra box set, ELK 3C1/302.

The information about the WPA slave narratives and musical instruments is summarized by Bob Winans in a chart that accompanies an unpublished manuscript in the possession of the authors.

By 1908, Sears, Rocbuck was offering a standard-sized "starter" guitar for only $1.98. This low price, combined with guitars American soldiers brought back from the Spanish-American war, made the guitar a favorite with rural musicians.

"We were kids together . . ." from Wyatt Moore's interview with Edmond Ledbetter, Longwood, LA, 1971.

Eric Partridge, *Dictionary of Slang and Unconventional English*, 7th ed. (New York: Macmillan, 1970) discusses the etymology of sukey.

"They called them sukey jumps . . ." and his next quote from the notes to the Elektra box set.

This quote from Zora Neale Hurston from *Mules and Men* (New York: Harper Collins, 1990; orig. pub. 1935), p. 61. Her next quote comes from Paul Oliver, *The Story of the Blues* (Radnor, PA: Chilton, 1969), p. 42

These quotes from Mance Lipscomb are from an unpublished manuscript prepared by A. Glen Myers, pp. 35–37. This manuscript is housed at the Barker History Center, University of Texas at Austin.

"De White folks . . ." from George Rawick, ed., *The American Slave: A Composite Autobiography*, vol. 1 (Westport, CT: Greenwood Press, 1972). p. 55.

"long ago that was . . ." from a performance issued on the Elektra box set.

The descriptions of the "Shoo Fly" square dance and the "buck and wing" come from the notes to the Elektra box set and from the Mance Lipscomb manuscript, pp. 38–39.

Marshall and Jean Stearns, *Jazz Dance* (New York: Macmillan, 1968), pp. 26–50, is our source for these and the later descriptions of black vernacular dance.

"He did tap dancing . . ." from Moore's 1972 interview.

"My mama used to make . . ." from the notes to Stinson LP #48.

"He used to be a secretary . . ." from Huddie's recorded comments in "Backslider, Fare You Well," AAFS 4470 B-2, originally recorded for the Library of Congress, August 1940, and transcribed to the notes to the Elektra box set, p. 14.

"Now, they sing . . ." was originally recorded in 1940 for the LC, AAFS 4470, B-4 ("Must I Be Carried to the Sky on Flowered Beds of Ease").

"There's a lot of pretty girls . . ." from Stinson LP #19.

Huddie's explanation of meters and description of services from the notes to the Elektra box set, pp. 14–16.

Hooks's description appears in J. L. Wilson's article, "Kinfolk Remember their 'Leadbelly,'" Shreveport *Times Sunday Magazine,* undated clipping in the Special Collections, Louisiana State University, Shreveport.

"The whole family . . ." Phil Martin "Ties to Huddie," Shreveport *Journal,* September 25, 1985, p. 1.

"I never led no prayer . . ." from a Library of Congress interview with Alan Lomax, AFS 4472A-3.

"He had a deep down . . ." from Moore's 1972 interview.

Quotes about backsliding appear in the Elektra set, pp. 14–15.

TALKING, PREACHING (GOOD GOOD GOOD) Words and Music by Huddie Ledbetter. Tro- Copyright 1963 (Renewed) 1965 (Renewed) Folkways Music Publishers, Inc., New York, NY. International Copyright Secured Made in U.S.A. All rights reserved including public performance for profit. Used by Permission.

ONE DOLLAR BILL, BABY. Words and Music by Huddie Ledbetter. Collected and adapted by John A. Lomax and Alan Lomax. TRO-© Copyright 1936 (Renewed) 1959 (Renewed) Folkways Music Publishers, Inc. New York And Global Jukebox Publishing, Marshall, TX. International Copyright Secured Made in U.S.A. All rights reserved including public performance for profit. Used by Permission.

9 The Scene and the Players in New York

THOMAS RIIS

New York City, thriving, bustling, modern magnet at the dawn of the twentieth century, attracted immigrants not only from around the United States but also from across the world. Its skyline bristled with newly built skyscrapers and the Brooklyn Bridge was being hailed as the height of structural modernity. This chapter from Just Before Jazz: Black Musical Theater in New York, 1890–1915, *explores the involvement of black Americans in the musical theater.*

New York City also sported world-class entertainment, from opera to vaudeville. Theaters ranging from the magnificent Casino Theater to small, second-rate vaudeville venues dotted the landscape from Broadway to Union Square. "African Broadway" (lower Seventh Avenue) not only catered to black patrons eager to see "race" productions such as Bob Cole's A Trip to Coontown *(1897) or Williams's and Walker's* In Dahomey *(1902), it also attracted black actors, writers, and choreographers who had found a home in the theater and wanted to work there.*

Riis surveys New York City and the players who developed the nascent black musical theater in an era when the majority of African American's still lived in the rural South. He focuses on the period between 1898 and 1911 when shows, written and staged by Ernest Hogan, Bert Williams and George Walker, and James Cole and Rosamond Johnson featuring all-black casts, were the rage on African Broadway. These shows underscored the importance of variety in the theater by incorporating elements of minstrelsy, comedy, song and dance, farce, and operetta. But the music featured in shows as diverse as Hogan's Rufus Rastus *(1905) and Will Marion Cook's* Clorindy *(1909) emerged as its single most important element. These composers drew upon the musical vernacular of the day, including ragtime and jubilee songs.*

New York at the turn of the century was characterized by its citizens and visitors, its boosters and detractors alike, as a city of expansiveness, industry, pleasure, and above all, wealth. It was "a cosmopolis, a world city," as Moses King explained, "the peer of any city, ancient or modern. In great lofty structures; in commercial activity; in financial affairs; in notable scientific achievements; in colossal individual aggrandizements; in mammoth corporate wealth; in maritime commerce; in absolute freedom of her citizens; and in the aggregation of civil, social, philanthropic and religious associations New York stands unsurpassed anywhere on the globe." Theodore Dreiser recalled, "The splendor of the, to me, new dynamic, new-world metropolis! Its romance, its enthusiasm, its illusions, its difficulties! The immense crowds everywhere. . . ." Even its critics were awed. "Remarkable, unspeakable New York!" exclaimed Henry James, who was simultaneously amazed and offended by this "perpendicular" city and its brilliant variety, its "aliens," its wealth, and its prodigality.[1]

New York, a city of inspiring skyscrapers and the newly completed Brooklyn Bridge, of widespread electrification and coal-powered elevated trains, was also frenetic, noisy, and dirty. It was "the shiftless outcome of squalid barbarism and reckless extravagance," scoffed tourist Rudyard Kipling.[2] New York's 1870 population of 1.5 million had nearly doubled by 1900. Manhattan, already a city of enormous ethnic diversity, was getting crowded. In 1900 nearly one-third of the residents of New York were foreign born. Germans constituted the largest ethnic group with over 300,000 people. There were approximately 275,000 Irish, 150,000 Russians, and 145,000 Italians.[3] Of the 60,000 black citizens of New York in 1900, three-quarters of those employed were common laborers or servants, and only about 1,000 people (less than three percent of the total employed) held professional or clerical jobs.[4] The young sociologist W. E. B. DuBois estimated that some 15,000 black people in New York constituted the unemployed, "struggling, unsuccessful sub-stratum . . . 'God's poor, the devil's poor and the poor devils,' and also the vicious and criminal classes."[5] Members of all economic groups were clustered in crowded, poorly ventilated tenements in districts between Twentieth and Fortieth Streets on the West Side, an area frequently referred to as the Tenderloin.[6] The neighborhoods gradually expanded north into the mid-Sixties, a zone which became known as San Juan Hill.

New York's black population, despite its generally low social estate and overcrowded condition, was not entirely isolated from the spirit of verve and optimism of the city as a whole. In his last novel, *The Sport of the Gods*, Paul Laurence Dunbar captures the excited dream of his provincial black heroes when they decide to go to New York: "They had heard of New York as a place vague and far away, a city that, like Heaven, to them had existed by faith alone. All the days of their lives they had heard of it, and it seemed to them the centre of all the glory, all the wealth, and all the freedom of the world. New York. It had an alluring sound. Who would know them there? Who would look down upon them?"[7]

The reality was a mixture of good and bad. Housing and sanitation for the very poor were deplorable, and discrimination and a lack of professional training programs limited blacks' job opportunities, yet a socially active black middle class did thrive. Jacob Riis observed a "neat and orderly" community in Harlem different from the "black and tan slums of the lower city," and there were well-to-do blacks in Brooklyn. A few black entertainers prospered; black sportsmen, particularly jockeys, emerged as heroes of the day; several black businesses thrived, and the number of black professionals gradually increased.[8]

New York also provided commercial entertainment for all of its people. Two dozen first-class theaters existed in 1879, and the number had nearly doubled by 1890. The glamorous Casino Theatre, its novel roof garden a boon on sultry summer nights, opened its doors in 1882, and the Metropolitan Opera House replaced the aging Academy of Music as the locus of cultivated taste in the following year. Broadway, the distinctive main artery of Manhattan, was the center of stage entertainment, although the theater district was located nearer to Union Square than Times Square. New York theaters in 1900 offered entertainments in diverse genres and languages, everything from vaudeville to opera, from Gilbert and Sullivan to Shakespeare.[9]

Segregation was a persistent problem in the large downtown theaters, but Seventh Avenue from the Twenties to the Forties became known as the African Broadway, an area fashionable blacks patronized for shopping and entertainment.[10] The Marshall and Maceo Hotels on West Fifty-third Street between Sixth and Seventh also became social settings, and the Marshall emerged as a site of considerable artistic activity and intellectual discussion. James Weldon Johnson, who achieved renown as a writer and diplomat, and his brother J. Rosamond Johnson moved into the hotel. Bob Cole lived two doors away but came there to work. Bert Williams, a rising young comedian and singer, eventually took up residence there.[11] The Marshall hosted virtually all of the major black entertainers in the decade following 1900. Several white entertainers and socialites visited there as well. James Weldon Johnson observed, "In time, the Marshall came to be one of the sights of New York. But it was more than a 'sight;' its importance as the radiant point of the forces that cleared the way for the Negro on the New York stage cannot be overestimated."[12]

The overriding importance of New York as a center for theater is confirmed by statistics, aside from the many first-person accounts of the period. In 1890, national census figures showed 1,490 "actors and professional showmen" and 1,881 "musicians and teachers of music" among the "colored" population of the United States.[13] Virtually all of the actors were occupied in either minstrelsy or vaudeville, as were many of the musicians. For the city of New York the figures are incomplete; seventy-three black men and women claimed to be employed as musicians or teachers of music; the number of actors and showpeople is not given. However, in 1900 musicians and actors constituted the two largest professional employment categories for blacks nationwide, after clergymen and teachers. In New York (and Chicago as well) musicians and actors outnumbered all other professional groups by a considerable margin (see Figure 1). By 1910 the number of black actors had nearly doubled over the 1890 statistic, perhaps as much because of the large number of traveling musical comedies using New York actors as because of the general increase in population.

Fig. 1 Blacks employed in "professional service" in New York and Chicago in 1900 (U.S. Census data)

	New York			Chicago		
	Male	Female	Total	Male	Female	Total
Actors and professional showmen	254	75	329	150	51	201
Musicians and teachers of music	195	73	268	207	49	256
Teachers and professors in colleges, etc.	32	96	128	20	38	58
Clergymen/women	90	6	96	63	6	69
Physicians and surgeons	32	10	42	45	15	60
Artists and teachers of art	22	8	30	7	7	14
Lawyers	26	0	26	46	0	46
Dentists	25	0	25	8	0	8
Electricians	18	0	18	15	0	15
Engineers and surveyors	7	0	7	2	0	2

The census figures, while providing an index of people who considered themselves "professional" musicians, do not account for all the music making that was going on or all the people involved in it. Black New York enjoyed a rich musical life with dance orchestras led by Miss Hallie Anderson and Mr. Walter Craig, to cite only two well-advertised examples, in the thick of many large social functions. Brass bands, informal ensembles, church choirs, and individual amateur performers all were widespread.[14]

Amidst many small schools of music, New York also boasted the National Conservatory of Music, which from its inception in 1885 opened its doors to blacks. Conceived by the idealistic and magnanimous Jeannette Meyers Thurber and incorporated by an act of Congress in 1891, the Conservatory was a bold experiment. Mrs. Thurber obtained the services of a distinguished faculty and an internationally known director, Antonin Dvořák; at the end of its first decade it claimed 57 teachers and 631 pupils.[15] Among the many black musicians who attended the Conservatory were Will Marion Cook and J. Tim Brymn, known for their popular songs; Harry T. Burleigh, singer and art-song composer; and Melville Charlton, composer and organist at St. Philips Episcopal Church and the Temple Emanu-E1.[16]

In summary, cosmopolitan New York provided the financial base and the educational apparatus for the creation of black musical comedies, as well as the social networks and diverse audiences that made them viable on the New York stage. By the end of the 1890s several black men and women of talent had congregated in New York, and it is to them that we now turn.

BOB COLE AND THE JOHNSON BROTHERS

Bob Cole was at the right place at the right time. He was working in an environment that had been dominated by the European operetta in the decade following the tremendous success of Gilbert and Sullivan's *H. M. S. Pinafore* (1879). The showy but dramatically unsubstantive extravaganzas temporarily were driven from the boards. At the same time the farce comedy, the direct progenitor of the musical comedy, was attracting more and more viewers. In pieces such as *Patchwork* (1875), *The Brook* (1879), and *Greenroom Fun* (1882), these first modest efforts placed a handful of characters in a familiar scene—at a museum, a street corner, or a country outing, for example—that provided a slim pretext for a string of songs and dances loosely connected by dialogue. The expansion of these sketches to full-evening entertainments turned the corner to musical comedy proper, pieces like *A Trip to Coontown* (1897).

After *A Trip to Coontown* closed, Cole dissolved his partnership with Billy Johnson because of Johnson's excessive drinking.[17] In the summer of 1899 Cole made the acquaintance in New York of J. Rosamond Johnson, who soon became a close friend and musical collaborator. Rosamond and his brother James Weldon immediately took a liking to Cole. During their first summer in New York, where the Johnsons had come to produce their own musical show, the three published and sold their first group effort; May Irwin paid them fifty dollars for the tune, "Louisiana Lize."[18] The song marked the beginning of the most successful songwriting partnership of the decade. Between 1900 and 1910 Cole and Rosamond Johnson, frequently assisted by James Weldon, wrote over 150 songs for more than a dozen shows, including their own shows for all-black casts, *The Shoo-Fly Regiment* (1906) and *The Red Moon* (1908).

Like Cole, Johnson came from a family that encouraged his musical talent. As a boy he took music lessons from his mother and was later sent north to attend the New England Conservatory to study singing, piano, organ, and composition. He pursued his theatrical interest by touring with John Isham's *Oriental America* (1896); after a year on the road he returned to Jacksonville, Florida, his home town, to teach music. He and his brother wrote an operetta,

Toloso, whose studio presentation was praised by musical leaders in Jacksonville, emboldening the Johnsons to take it to New York. *Toloso* was never produced, although many of its songs later were used in other shows. But together with some letters of introduction, *Toloso* served, in James Weldon Johnson's words, "to introduce us to practically all the important stars and producers of comic operas and musical plays in New York," including Harry B. Smith, Reginald De Koven, Oscar Hammerstein, Williams and Walker, the publisher Witmark, Harry T. Burleigh, Will Marion Cook, Ernest Hogan, the poet Paul Laurence Dunbar, and most importantly, Bob Cole. Rosamond moved to New York permanently in 1900, and the partnership was launched.[19]

Cole and Johnson presented most of their early songs in a vaudeville act in which they appeared in evening clothes. They entered the stage conversing about a party where they were to entertain. Johnson played the Paderewski *Minuet*, sang a German art song, and then both men moved to more modern material, their own original songs. White silk handkerchief in hand, Cole provided soft-shoe dancing "to the choruses played almost pianissimo." The act, described by James Weldon Johnson as "quiet, finished, and artistic to the minutest detail," worked well, and the team played in the top vaudeville houses in the United States as well as the Palace Theatre in London during a 1906 tour. Reportedly, the act was widely imitated.[20]

Publishers and producers pursued Cole and Johnson. They signed a contract with Joseph Stern in 1901, and after a call from Abe Erlanger they agreed to join the production staff of Klaw and Erlanger at the peak of their power. They composed all or nearly all the music for *The Belle of Bridgeport* (1900), a May Irwin vehicle; *Humpty Dumpty* (1904), a Drury Lane spectacle remade in America for the Christmas season; and *In Newport* (1904), a dramatic flop that closed after a week at the newly opened Liberty Theatre. Many of their most popular tunes, such as "Under the Bamboo Tree," "The Congo Love Song," "The Maiden with the Dreamy Eyes," and "Run, Brudder Possum, Run," were interpolated into *The Little Duchess* (1900), *The Rogers Brothers in Central Park* (1900), *Sally in Our Alley* (1902), *Sleeping Beauty and the Beast* (1902), *A Girl from Dixie* (1903), *Mr. Blackbeard* (1903), *Nancy Brown* (1903), *Mother Goose* (1903), and *An English Daisy* (1904), and probably into other smaller shows for which no credit was given.... In 1905 Cole and Johnson began to plan their own large show, to be called *The Shoo-Fly Regiment*. The time seemed ripe to capitalize on the success of their songs and the popularity of their vaudeville act. Both *The Shoo-Fly Regiment* and *The Red Moon* met with moderate audience and critical favor, but they also cost the stars a considerable amount of money. In 1910, at the close of the *Red Moon* road tour, Cole and Johnson returned to the vaudeville stage. Cole's collapse in April, 1911, and his subsequent death in a drowning accident (possibly a suicidal response to the onset of tertiary syphilis) marked the end of a phase in the life of J. Rosamond Johnson. It also closed a chapter in the history of black musicals.

Johnson returned to vaudeville but never again took out such a large show on his own. In 1912 he assumed the musical directorship of the Hammerstein Opera House in London. He returned to New York in 1914 and continued to be involved in a wide variety of musical projects: he published and arranged spirituals, headed the Music School Settlement for the Colored People of New York, and continued to act and compose from time to time. He died in 1954.

ERNEST HOGAN

Another member of the Black Patti Troubadours company who later carved out an independent career and starred in his own shows was Ernest Hogan. Like Cole and Johnson, Hogan was close to the center of the New York musical show activity in the 1890s and early 1900s. He was a protegé of Sam Lucas and Billy McClain, and his younger colleagues remembered him fondly "as the greatest of all colored showmen." Eubie Blake, Flournoy Miller, and Luckey Roberts all agreed that he was a superior performer.[21] In *Black Manhattan*, James Weldon Johnson described him as

> a veteran minstrel and a very funny, natural-blackface comedian.... Hogan was a notable exception among blackfaced comedians; his comic effects did not depend upon the caricature created by the use of cork and a mouth exaggerated by paint. His mobile face was capable of laughter-provoking expressions that were irresistible, notwithstanding the fact that he was a very good looking man. Some critics ranked him higher than Bert Williams.[22]

Hogan, born Reuben Crowdus in 1865 in Bowling Green, Kentucky, received his earliest training by acting in summer tent shows and minstrel shows.[23] Little else is known of his early years. He first became prominent as a writer of songs during the 1890s; in 1895 he composed his best-known tune, "All Coons Look Alike to Me." He went to his last years apologizing for the offense given by the title, although the rest of the lyrics are quite innocent of racist suggestion. The song succeeded in fueling a fad for "coon" songs, but Hogan rationalized the negative impact of his song by insisting that the vogue for such pieces provided money and jobs for many other composers. He told Tom Fletcher, "With the publication of that song a new musical rhythm was given to the people. Its popularity grew and sold like wildfire all over the United States and abroad.... That one song opened the way for a lot of colored and white song writers." Whether or not one takes Hogan's claims at face value, the coon-song fad was certainly prodigious, producing by one estimate some 600 songs from 1895 to 1900.[24]

Hogan toured with minstrel companies and played successfully in stock on the West Coast. He met Bert Williams and George Walker and helped them find performing opportunities. He returned to the East about 1895 and was eventually hired by the Black Patti Troubadours, remaining with it for two seasons. Will Marion Cook chose Hogan to train and appear with the dancers in his entertainment called *Clorindy, or the Origin of the Cakewalk*. In 1899 Hogan advertised his own forthcoming musical, but it did not materialize; he journeyed to Hawaii, Australia, and New Zealand in May 1899 with a minstrel company he had gathered.[25] By the following summer Hogan was back in the United States and was slated to appear in Will Marion Cook's *Jes Lak White Fo'ks*, a playlet with libretto, lyrics, and music all by Cook. This work, probably no more than forty-five minutes long and with a half-dozen songs, was Cook's least successful show, probably because it lacked catchy lyrics and had a somewhat incoherent plot.[26] Cook never again attempted such a one-man effort, but Hogan, undaunted, joined a traveling company called the Smart Set and then returned to vaudeville. In 1905 Hogan was featured with a group of twenty professional players—mandolinists, guitarists, banjoists, and cellists—calling themselves the Memphis Students (none were students or hailed from Memphis). The ensemble toured Europe successfully as the Tennessee Students—changing its name, according to Tom Fletcher, because the names of American states were more familiar than cities to Europeans—and appeared in Hammerstein's Victoria Theatre, the Olympia in Paris, the Palace in London, and the Schumann Circus in Berlin.

Hogan's own show *Rufus Rastus*, for which he wrote much of the book, music, and lyrics and played the starring role, was produced in 1905. During its sequel in which he also starred, *The Oyster Man*, Hogan contracted tuberculosis. He retired to Lakewood, New Jersey, for a cure but he never recovered, dying on May 20, 1909.[27]

A man in command of both pathos and humor, Hogan was renowned for the versatility of his "natural-blackface act." Although he was one of the few famous performers of this era with little or no formal education, like Billy McClain and George Walker he possessed a business shrewdness and combativeness that enabled him to become "the highest-priced single colored vaudeville performer in the business." He was a compulsive worker, constantly composing, staging, or organizing new acts. His infectious and crusading spirit, talent, and generosity were celebrated by Lester Walton in a *New York Age* obituary:

> That the stage loses one of its greatest colored comedians in the death of Ernest Hogan is admitted by all. But aside from the loss of one whose talents as an actor are well known, the colored members of the theatrical profession also lose one who might be termed in many respects, a "Moses" of the colored theatrical profession....
>
> Just how far the colored theatrical profession, in fact, the entire profession, is set back by the death of Ernest Hogan the writer will not attempt to even surmise; but it has sustained a great loss, for there is no one at this time to take his place.[28]

WILL MARION COOK

At the other end of the spectrum from Ernest Hogan in formal education and bearing, yet a person equally involved in the New York scene as well as Hogan's great friend, was the composer and conductor Will Marion Cook. Bob Cole, J. Rosamond Johnson, Williams and Walker, and most other performers of musical theater regarded Cook as a catalytic figure of the era. His training had been extensive, his instruction was inspiring, and his musicianship and conducting skills complemented the stage and business talents of Cole and Hogan. Alain Locke named Cook as one of the most important conductors of the period, and he was consistently cited by his contemporaries as a leader of black musical life.[29] Remarkably, although much of Cook's music is available and biographical material is accessible to scholarly research, scholars generally have overlooked his contribution.[30]

Cook was born on January 27, 1869, in a converted Army barracks behind Howard University in Washington, D.C. He was christened William Mercer Cook, changing his name during his college years. The son of college-educated parents—both Belle Lewis and John Cook had graduated from Oberlin College, and his father was the first dean of the Howard University Law School—Cook probably was expected after college to settle in the large and comparatively wealthy Washington, D.C., black community. But from the beginning Will was a feisty and spirited child, and when his father died from tuberculosis in 1879, Will became difficult. In 1881 he was sent to Chattanooga, Tennessee, where his mother hoped that the masculine and restraining influence of his grandfather William Cook would discourage Will's fighting. It did not. However, in Chattanooga he heard genuine black folk music for the first time and, like many before him, was enthralled.

Encouraged by his grandfather, who played the violin and clarinet, Will began to study violin, and about 1884 his mother sent him to the Oberlin preparatory school as a prelude to his entering Oberlin College. Cook eventually entered the College about 1886; his name is recorded on a few recital programs of that time. He studied violin with Amos Doolittle, who was impressed with the young man's progress. Feeling that a period of European study would improve his chances for a professional career, Doolittle encouraged Cook to audition for the famous German violinist Joachim, who was then teaching at the Hochschule für Musik in Berlin. The major obstacle to a European sojourn was, of course, lack of money. But with the assistance of Frederick Douglass, whose grandson was also an aspiring violinist, a benefit concert was arranged in the First Congregational Church in Washington for the young Cook.[31] He was featured in a recital that included the Mendelssohn Violin Concerto and the Wieniawski *Polonaise*, and the crowd—probably friends and wellwishers—was most generous. Nearly $2,000 was raised, quite enough to allow Cook to set out for Europe.

In his autobiography, Cook reports that despite a shaky audition Joachim recognized some spark of talent and accepted him for study. He remained in Europe for three years studying piano, harmony, counterpoint, and violin. He later continued his study of counterpoint with John White at the National Conservatory in New York. Cook returned to the United States apparently fit for a concert and orchestral career. He met with discrimination and frustration, and finally, during the 1890s, despite years of study Cook, to use James Weldon Johnson's phrase, "threw all these European standards over"[32] and began to pursue a career in popular music. He found his calling in teaching young show performers and stage managing, as well as accompanying at the keyboard and composing. He worked with Bob Cole and the All-Star Stock Company and briefly directed a band in Chicago,[33] but his major entrance into the public arena came with his summer entertainment, *Clorindy, or the Origin of the Cakewalk*, offered as one of a series of late-evening presentations by Edward Rice on the roof garden stage of the Casino Theatre. The success of *Clorindy* gave Cook some encouragement after months of setbacks. For the next fifteen years he worked at writing music for other all-black shows, as well as an occasional libretto or set of lyrics. He assisted the famous Williams and Walker team on *Abyssinia* (1906), *Bandanna Land* (1907), and their greatest success, *In Dahomey* (1902). He supplied songs to many other shows—May Irwin sang Cook songs in *The Casino Girl* (1900) and *The Wild Rose* (1902); conducted and rehearsed many choral groups; and accompanied his wife, Abbie Mitchell, in solo song recitals. Cook also formed a publishing partnership with R. C. McPherson, the Gotham-Attucks Publishing Company. In 1904 Cook wrote the music for a large show with a racially mixed cast, entitled *The Southerners*. He had no great ability to manage money—his shows, like many others, frequently went into the red—and he possessed an easily ignited temper, but Cook was universally admired for his musicianship. He was involved in rehearsing virtually every large New York black show until 1915. In that year he contracted tuberculosis, the disease that had fatally stricken his father in middle age.[34] His activity declined, of course, but by 1918 he had organized his most successful project since the international tour of *In Dahomey* in 1903, the Southern Syncopated Orchestra, which toured in the United States and Europe until 1920.[35] Cook remained active after 1920 but never was so prominent as he had been in the early years. He continued to perform with Abbie Mitchell and in 1926 collaborated as lyricist with Vincent Youmans for *I'm Comin' Virginia*. He died in New York on July 19, 1944.

Will Marion Cook is perhaps the least recognized among the dominant figures of the era, and in view of his estimable musical accomplishments it is curious that he was so entirely eclipsed long before his death. The answer seems to lie substantially with Cook's personality, specifically his undisguised impatience, his fiery temper, and his occasionally overweening personal vanity. As bitterly as other black public figures may have complained in private about racial discrimination, most managed to achieve stolid and nonthreatening façades that helped them reach their goals in a white society threatened by the prospect of aggressive blacks. Cook developed no such façade. He had received cultured and humane treatment in Europe and refused to tolerate anything less in America. Faced with American prejudice and the normal frustrations and competitions of the professional music world, Cook became ever more suspicious of people's motives and more ill tempered. Cook was not a loner by nature, but he tended to isolate himself, often moving quickly to insult or call into question others' motives. He was bound to run into trouble in a business that relied heavily on personal contacts, friendship, and mutual trust. His experience with his first publisher, Isidore Witmark (as contrasted with Cole and Johnson's long, harmonious relationship with Marks and Stern), says much. Without evidence in hand he accused the publisher of cheating him of royalties for the songs in *Clorindy* after receiving less than he believed he was entitled to; the result was to alienate Witmark permanently.[36] He was not universally popular in his own black world because he assumed a superior mien that many Americans associated with alien European attitudes. Such a posture could work only with equally educated and cultured members of black society. But Cook's refusal to maintain a quiet, dignified, low profile did little to endear him to such high-caste blacks. In short, he catered and kowtowed to no one; hence no one went out of the way to boost him, although his talent was never denied nor credit withheld when credit was due. He succeeded because his talent was unimpeachable, even if he was regarded as eccentric. As the highly diplomatic James Weldon Johnson put it in a confidential letter, "he has many of those personal peculiarities and eccentricities which we, no doubt, ought to expect and excuse in original geniuses."[37] To Cook's credit he consistently encouraged young talent, and Eva Jessye (the choral director of Virgil Thomson's *Four Saints in Three Acts* and Gershwin's *Porgy and Bess*) and Duke Ellington, among others, fondly remembered their instruction in his company.[38]

WILLIAMS AND WALKER

The most famous black comedy team at the beginning of the twentieth century was that of Bert Williams and George Walker. In their heyday, from 1898 to 1908, and for years after, they were the standard against which other comedy acts were compared, and they inspired many imitators. Their success lay close to the heart of black musical theater because they sang and danced as well as acted and joked. Many full-length musical comedies were built around Williams and Walker by the talented team of Alex Rogers as lyricist, Jesse Shipp as stage director, and Will Marion Cook as composer.

Williams was born in Nassau, the West Indies, in November of 1874.[39] His family moved to Riverside, California, in 1885. Williams graduated from Riverside High School and briefly attended Stanford University. In order to raise money for college he tried his luck as an entertainer but never returned to school after the first year. Working in San Francisco in 1893 he met George Walker, a native of Lawrence, Kansas, who had worked his way west with a medicine show. The pair decided to join forces, with Walker doing the comedy and Williams acting as straight man and ballad singer. At that time they worked in street clothes without blackface makeup.[40] They remained in California for over two years and then gradually worked their way east, changed their act somewhat, and made the acquaintance of show producer Thomas Canary, who offered them work in a New York show. The team appeared in Victor Herbert's short-lived *Gold Bug* (1896), which led to a contract to play at Koster and Bial's Music Hall. Williams and Walker developed a popular cakewalk act, capitalizing on the great dance fad of the time, which garnered them sustained runs at the best New York halls. The cakewalk, a duple-time dance with simple syncopations, had appeared in the Harrigan and Hart shows, and it may have been performed in public even earlier. Billy McClain, for example, claimed that he had been "the first to put a cakewalk on stage, with the Hyers Sisters [in the 1870s?].

Then I called it a 'walk around.'" The roots of the cakewalk go back to plantation life, when slave couples competed for a cake or other prizes by performing high-stepping dances. But this dance was not to achieve widespread popularity until the early 1890s, when the dance team of Charles Johnson and Dora Dean thrilled audiences coast to coast and introduced it on Broadway in 1895 (or so Johnson claimed)—three years before Williams and Walker appeared at Koster and Bial's Music Hall with their version of the dance.[41]

In the autumn of 1898 Williams and Walker were invited to assume Ernest Hogan's starring role in the Eastern tour of Cook's *Clorindy*. The cast was expanded to include some sixty people, and the entire presentation was billed as the Senegambian Carnival.[42] The show failed and folded quickly, but the team's fortunes improved under the management of Hurtig and Seamon with a variety show entitled *A Lucky Coon* and more ambitious undertakings that included fuller plots, such as *The Policy Players* (1899), *The Sons of Ham* (1900), and *In Dahomey* (1902), their greatest success. Other later productions included *Abyssinia* (1906) and *Bandanna Land* (1907). Walker fell ill during the tour of *Bandanna Land* and left show business. Williams continued without him in *Mr. Lode of Koal* (1909) and then signed to appear with Florenz Ziegfeld's *Follies of 1910*, the only black member of the cast. Walker's death in 1911 ended any speculation about a revived partnership. Williams remained with the *Follies* until 1919, appeared with Eddie Cantor in *Broadway Brevities* in 1920, and opened in his last show, a Shubert production called *Under the Bamboo Tree*, in 1922. While on tour he contracted a cold that developed into pneumonia and, probably because he insisted on staying with the show rather than taking a proper rest, he collapsed onstage. He returned to New York by train and died on March 4, 1922.[43]

Williams was the most famous black performer, perhaps even the most famous black person after Booker T. Washington, of his day. His comic timing and mimic artistry were widely admired, and the accolades before and after his death consistently resorted to superlatives. It is only fair to note, however, that his fame was guaranteed partly because he elected to appear as the only black star in an all-white revue, a decision for which he received a certain amount of criticism in the black community. He was indisputably a superior performer, but blacks who knew the entire picture of black theater did not always place his talents above those of Ernest Hogan, the minstrel comedian Billy Kersands, or Bob Cole. George Walker's contributions to the musical comedies they did together should also not be underestimated. Walker was the idea man of the team. He devised the plots, and it was his scenic conceptions that were realized (in the case of *Abyssinia* quite extravagantly) onstage.[44] Williams and Walker truly were a team. Following Walker's death and the mixed success of *Mr. Lode of Koal*, Williams was forced to find a new direction, and Ziegfeld provided the best opportunity.

The shows of Williams and Walker, Cole and Johnson, and Hogan constitute the principal, although not the only, contributions to black American musical theater from 1898 to 1911. They were created in an urban environment that had supported a variety of earlier forms of entertainment catering to diverse audiences: minstrel shows, extravaganzas, farce comedies, and operettas. Shows multiplied rapidly, stimulated by a large pool of young black talent that found receptive managers like William McConnell and John Isham and strong leaders like Bob Cole and George Walker. Onstage, however, it was finally the music that put the shows over. The successive vogues for music related to blacks—jubilee songs, coon songs, cakewalks, and ragtime—fueled the success of black stage entertainments. Conservatory-trained composers Will Marion Cook and J. Rosamond Johnson picked up where the earlier minstrel and rag composers had left off. Moreover, from the 1890s on, the growing industry of Tin Pan Alley imitated and reproduced black-composed music in ever-increasing quantity.

Given the critical role of music in black shows, it is necessary to examine a little more closely the repertoire of stage songs before considering the individual shows in which they appeared.

Notes

1. Moses King, *New York: The American Cosmopolis* (Boston: Moses King, 1893), p. 2; Theodore Dreiser, *The Color of a Great City* (New York: Boni and Liveright, 1923), p. vii; Henry James, *The American Scene* (1905; reprint ed., Bloomington: Indiana University Press, 1968), pp. 117–19, 186–87, 208.
2. Bayrd Still, *Mirror for Gotham* (New York: Washington Square Press, 1956), p. 250.
3. Ibid., p. 213.
4. Seth Scheiner, *Negro Mecca: A History of the Negro in New York City, 1865–1920* (New York: New York University Press, 1965), pp. 224–25.
5. W. E. B. DuBois, *The Black North in 1901: A Social Study* (New York: Arno Press, 1969), p. 11. This collection is a series of articles originally published in the *New York Times*, November–December 1901.
6. Ibid.; Scheiner, *Negro Mecca*, pp. 17–19; Jervis Anderson, *This Was Harlem* (New York: Farrar, Straus, Giroux, 1982), pp. 8–9.
7. Paul Laurence Dunbar, *The Sport of the Gods* (New York: Dodd, Mead and Company, 1902), pp. 77–78.
8. Still, *Mirror*, p. 217; Scheiner, *Negro Mecca*, pp. 45–61; Roi Ottley and William Weatherby, eds., *The Negro in New York* (Dobbs Ferry, NY: New York Public Library, 1967), pp. 146–47; Anderson, *This Was Harlem*, pp. 13–20, 92–98, 339–46.
9. Marv Henderson, *The City and the Theatre* (Clifton, NJ: James T. White and Co., 1973), pp. 123–24, 168–70, 219. An excellent overview of the variety of New York theatrical life can be found in *AMT*. George C. D. Odell, *Annals of the New York Stage* (New York: Columbia University Press, 1927–1941), 15 vols., is an indispensable compendium of periodical notes. Studies of the New York stage that concentrate on specific national contributions include Hamilton Mason, *The French Theatre in New York* (New York: Columbia University Press, 1946), and Fred A. H. Leuchs, *Early German Theatre in New York* (New York: Columbia University Press, 1928).
10. Anderson, *This Was Harlem*, pp. 8–9.
11. James Weldon Johnson, *Along This Way* (New York: Viking Press, 1933), p. 171.
12. Ibid., p. 177.
13. The census figures were extracted from the *Eleventh United States Census*, vol. 3 (Washington, DC: Government Printing Office, 1897), p. 452; *Twelfth United States Census Special Reports: Occupations*, vol. 2 (Washington, DC: Government Printing Office, 1904), p. 650. "Colored," as defined by the 1890 census, means "persons of negro descent, Chinese, Japanese, and civilized Indian." The statistics for Negroes alone were separated from other "colored" in 1900.
14. Samuel Charters and Leonard Kunstadt, *Jazz: The New York Scene* (Garden City, NY: Doubleday, 1962), pp. 13–22.
15. *New York Herald*, October 29, 1895; *New York Evening Post*, October 7, 1897; *New York Daily Tribune*, January 24, 1898. See also Dena Epstein, "Jeannette Meyers Thurber," in *Notable American Women 1607–1950*, vol. 2, ed. Edward T. James (Cambridge, MA: Belknap Press of the Harvard University Press, 1971), pp. 458–59.
16. *MOBA*, pp. 266, 268, 282.
17. Plummer biography, Cobb papers.
18. Johnson, *Along This Way*, pp. 152–53.
19. Ibid., pp. 149–50.
20. Ibid., p. 187.
21. *JD*, pp. 120, 117–24.
22. James Weldon Johnson, *Black Manhattan* (New York: Alfred A. Knopf, 1930), p. 102.
23. *Age*, May 27, 1909.
24. Tom Fletcher, *The Tom Fletcher Story: 100 Years of the Negro in Show Business* (New York: Burdge and Co., 1954), pp. 139, 141; Paul Oliver, *Songsters and Saints* (Cambridge: Cambridge University Press, 1984), p. 49.

25. *Age,* May 27, 1909: *DM,* February 25, 1909.
26. Charters, *Nobody,* p. 50. An eight-page libretto of *Jes Lak White Fo'ks* survives at the Music Division, Library of Congress, Washington, DC.
27. *Age,* May 29, 1909, p. 6.
28. Ibid.
29. Alain Locke, *The Negro and His Music* (1936; reprint ed., New York: Arno Press, 1969), pp. 65–66.
30. Marva Griffin Carter at the University of Illinois has completed a dissertation devoted to the life and work of Cook. The Cook biographical information contained here is based largely on accounts found in general music histories, such as *MOBA,* supplemented by an unpublished autobiography in the papers of Will Marion Cook's son, Dr. Mercer Cook; an interview with Dr. Cook; and supplementary correspondence.
31. Unfortunately, the church records do not cover activities not directly sponsored by the church. The church historian could not confirm this information received from Dr. Cook.
32. Johnson, *Along This Way,* p. 172.
33. Ike Simond, *Old Slack's Reminiscence and Pocket History of the Colored Profession from 1865 to 1891* (1891; reprint ed., Bowling Green, OH: Popular Press, 1974), p. 23.
34. *Crisis* 10, no. 2 (June 1815): 63.
35. *MOBA,* p. 354. This group was first known as the New York Syncopated Orchestra and later as the American Syncopated Orchestra before its European tour.
36. We have only Witmark's side of the story in Isidore Witmark and Isaac Goldberg, *From Ragtime to Swingtime* (1939; reprinted., New York: Da Capo Press, 1976), pp. 196–97, but it appears that Cook's own lawyer thought that he was in the wrong and that his accusation was at least abrupt.
37. Letter to Mr. William C. Graves, March 2, 1919, James Weldon Johnson Memorial Collection of American Literature, Beinecke Rare Book and Manuscript Library, Yale University.
38. Duke Ellington, *Music Is My Mistress* (Garden City, NY: Doubleday, 1973), pp. 95–97; Eileen Southern, *Music of Black Americans* (New York: Norton, 1971), pp. 432–33.
39. *AMT,* p. 191.
40. *Age,* January 12, 1911, p. 6; Charters, *Nobody,* p. 25.
41. *Freeman,* April 23, 1910, p. 6; *see also* Brooke Baldwin, "The Cakewalk: A Study in Stereotype and Reality," *Journal of Social History* 15 (1981): 205–18.
42. *Freeman,* January 14, 1911, p. 5.
43. Charters, *Nobody,* pp. 144–47; *AMT,* p. 354.
44. Charters, *Nobody,* pp. 69, 83.

10 Jelly Roll Blues

JELLY ROLL MORTON WITH ALAN LOMAX

Ferdinand "Jelly Roll" Morton claims to have "invented" jazz in New Orleans early in the twentieth century. Morton, who grew up in New Orleans, began playing the piano at the age of ten. As a young teen he was performing in the bordellos of Storyville (New Orleans's red light district), playing ragtime, French quadrilles, and other popular dances and songs. Always a colorful and peripatetic figure, Morton embarked on a career as an itinerant pianist (as well as a gambler and pool hall hustler), working in many cities in Louisiana, Mississippi, Alabama, and Florida.

Morton eventually spanned the country from New York City (where stride piano legend James P. Johnson heard Morton play his Jelly Roll Blues in 1911) to Los Angeles by 1917. He enjoyed Los Angeles and remained there for five years. His next move was to Chicago, home to many transplanted New Orleans musicians and the new center of jazz activity. Morton's recording debut occurred there in 1923, the first of a series of recordings for labels large and small that would continue until his death in 1941. His late 1920s Victor Red Hot Pepper recordings of "Grandpa's Spells," "Black Bottom Stomp," and "The Pearls" are clearly masterpieces of New Orleans style jazz.

Morton relocated to New York in 1928. Although jazz was evolving (pushed along by the compositions of Duke Ellington and the arrangements of Fletcher Henderson), he remained committed to the New Orleans style of collective improvisation. Ironically, his "King Porter Stomp" became a hit for Benny Goodman in the mid-1930s and helped to set the way for the swing era.

During the early years of the Great Depression, the older style of New Orleans jazz fell into disfavor and Morton was often judged as passé by a new generation of jazz listeners. He eventually found his way to Washington, D.C., where he managed a jazz club and occasionally performed. In 1938, the folklorist Alan Lomax invited him to come to the Library of Congress in order to record a lengthy series of interviews. In this fascinating oral history, Morton recalled his life story and played many musical examples to illustrate the musical changes that had occurred during his career. This memoir is taken from the oral histories that Morton recorded for the Library of Congress recordings and edited by Alan Lomax. They focus on the period of 1909–1910 when he traveled in the Deep South and composed "Jelly Roll Blues." The Library of Congress oral histories (which have been commercially available in several formats since they were first issued in 1948) and the publicity they generated helped to refocus the public's attention on Morton. But his declining health and death soon after only briefly revived the career of this seminal and colorful musician.

It was along about that time that the first hot arrangements came into existence. Up until then, everything had been in the heads of the men who played jazz out of New Orleans. Nowadays they talk about these jam sessions. Well, that is something I never permitted. Most guys, they improvise and they'll go wrong. Most of the so-called jazz musicians still don't know how to play jazz until this day; they don't understand the principles of jazz music. In all my recording sessions and in all my band work, I always wrote out the arrangements in advance. When it was a New Orleans man, that wasn't so much trouble, because those boys knew a lot of my breaks; but in traveling from place to place I found other musicians had to be taught. So around 1912 I began to write down this peculiar form of mathematics and harmonics that was strange to all the world.

For a time I had been working with McCabe's Minstrel Show and, when that folded in St. Louis, I began looking around for a job. My goodness, the snow was piled up till you couldn't see the streetcars. I was afraid that I'd meet some piano player that could top me a whole lot, so I wouldn't admit that I could play. I claimed that I was a singer. At that time I kinda figured I was a pretty good singer, which was way out of the way, but I figured it anyhow. Well, I was hired at the Democratic Club where they had a piano player named George Randalls. He was a bricklayer trying to play piano. He couldn't even read music. In fact, none of the boys couldn't read much and so it was very tough for them to get those tough tunes. They bought sheet music just to learn the words of the songs.

This George Reynolds, that couldn't read, played for me while I sang. Of course, George was a little bit chesty, because all the girls around were making eyes at him (he was a fairly nice-looking fellow); but I thought, if this guy's the best, the other piano players must be very, very terrible. So I asked George to play me one of the numbers I was going to sing. He played it, although he didn't seem very particular about doing it. I told him, "One of these parts here you don't play right. I'd like a little more pep in it." I forget what tune it was, some popular number of that time.

"Well," he said, not knowing I could play, "If you don't like the way I'm playing, you do better."

"Okay," I said, "If you don't play my tunes right, I can play them myself." So I sat down and showed him his mistakes.

Immediately he had a great big broad smile on his face. Seeing that I was superior to him, he wanted to make friends with me. I didn't object and we gotten to be friends right away. He asked me did I read music. I told him a little bit. So he put different difficult numbers on the piano—he thought they were difficult, but they were all simple to me. I knew them all. By that time he started getting in touch with the different musicians around town that was supposed to be good and they started bringing me different tunes. They brought me all Scott Joplin's tunes—he was the great St. Louis ragtime composer—and I knew them all by heart and played them right off. They brought me James Scott's tunes and Louis Chauvin's and I knew them all. Then Audie Mathews (the best reader in the whole bunch) brought me his *Pastimes* and I played it. So he decided to find out whether I could really read and play piano and he brought me different light operas like *Humoresque*, the *Overture from Martha*, the *Miserery from Ill Travadore* and, of course, I knowed them all.

Finally they brought me the *Poet and the Peasant*. It seems like in St. Louis, if you was able to play this piece correctly, you was really considered the tops. The man that brought it was the best musician in town and he hadn't been able to master this piece. Well, I had played this thing in recitals for years, but I started looking at it like I hadn't ever seen it before. Then

The sheet music for this widely circulated Spencer Williams and Clarence Williams song, which had previously circulated in oral tradition, suggests why Ferdinand Morton choose the nickname, "Jelly Roll."

Credit: Sheet Music from the collection of Kip Lornell.

I started in. I got to a very fast passage where I also had to turn the page over. I couldn't turn the page, due to the fact I had to manipulate this passage so fast. I went right on. Audie Mathews grabbed the tune from in front of me and said, "Hell, don't be messing with this guy. This guy is a shark!" I told them, "Boys, I been kidding you all along. I knew all these tunes anyhow. Just listen." Then I swung the *Miserery* and combined it with the *Anvil Chorus*.

You find, though, that people act very savage in this world. From then on it was George Reynolds' object to try to crush me. He couldn't do this, but he made things so unpleasant that I finally took a job out in the German section of town. The manager wanted a band, so I got some men together, although there wasn't many to pick from—clarinet, trumpet, mandolin, drums, and myself. These were not hot men, but they were Negroes and they could read. They didn't play to suit me, but I told them if they played what I put down on paper, they would be playing exactly as I wanted. Then I arranged all the popular tunes of that time—I even made a jazz arrangement of *Schnitzelbank*—and we made some pretty fair jazz for St. Louis in 1912.

St. Louis had been a great town for ragtime for years because Stark and Company specialized in publishing Negro music. Among the composers the Starks published were: Scott Joplin (the greatest ragtime writer who ever lived and composer of *Maple Leaf Rag*), Tom Turpin, Louis Chauvín, Audie Mathews, and James Scott. But St. Louis wasn't like New Orleans; it was prejudiced. I moved on to Kansas City and found it was like St. Louis, except it did not have one decent pianist and didn't want any. That was why I went on to Chicago. In Chicago at that time you could go anywhere you wanted regardless of creed or color. So Chicago came to be one of the earliest places that jazz arrived, because of nice treatment—and we folks from New Orleans were used to nice treatment.

Up to this time the published arrangements of hot music were simply a matter of writing down the ragtime tunes played by some theatre band. Then *Jelly Roll Blues* became so popular with the people of Chicago that I decided to name it in honor of the Windy City. I was the only one at the time that could play this tune, *The Chicago Blues*. In fact, I had a hard time trying to find anyone who could take it down. I went to Henri Klickman (author of the *Hysterics Rag* and arranger for the Will Rossiter publishing house), but he didn't know enough. So, finally, I wrote the score out myself. Dave Payton and several more said what I had put down was "wrong," but, when I said, "Correct me then," they couldn't do it. We argued for days and days, but they couldn't find no holes in my tune. Finally, Klickman made an arrangement from my score and the song was published. Immediately brass bands all over the country took it over and it was considered the hottest band arrangement anywhere....

The old original Elite at 3445 State Street was the most beautiful place on the South Side and the most famous place in the history of America's cabaret land. The trade was of the finest class—millionaires and good livers. When Teenan Jones, the owner, put his partner in charge of the Elite Number Two, corner 31st and State, this man, Art Cardozier, ran the place right into the deep blue sea. It was an A-No.-1 failure even with space enough to get Barnum and Bailey's Circus in every night, because they used operatic and symphonic musicians, which was considered obsolete in the city of Chicago since the invasion of Tony Jackson and Jelly Roll Morton.

Then Teenan Jones begged me to accept the manager's job. I explained that the only way I could bring his place to fame was if he would turn the cabaret department over to me with no contradictions. Mr. Jones agreed and I accepted the job as manager.

The first thing was done was to fire all the waiters. Next I fired all the musicians and entertainers, including "Give-a-Damn" Jones, Teenan's brother, who was cashier at the bar. "Give-a-Damn" got his name through an argument, when he stated that he would go to Paris just to buy a drink—which he did, because he didn't give a damn. I came near getting shot, when I fired him, because he was known to be a pistol man.

The first sign was put out Thursday. On Sunday there was two policemen holding the crowd back. The entertainers were highclass, and the band, the second Dixieland combination in the country, was in my name—*Jelly Roll Morton and His Incomparables*. It consisted of myself on piano, Menns on drums, Henry Massingill on trombone, Horace George on clarinet and John Armstrong on trumpet. We were the hottest thing in Chicago those days. In fact I got the offer to go with Vernon and Irene Castle, the great ballroom dancers, on their European tour, but I turned it down because I felt that I was very permanent at the Elite (I have since learned there is nothing permanent in the entertainment business), and I was making $50 a week when everyone else was making about $17. Anyhow, Jim Reece Europe [*sic**] went on that tour, took my clarinet player, and they featured my *Jelly Roll Blues* all across the continent.... (Isn't whiskey a wonderful thing at times!)

To show you how that job had me tied down, one night a very beautiful woman offered to take me to California and backed her proposition by filling my hat with money. I said I was very sorry; it looked like all the money in the world to me, but I liked Chicago. Then some history fell on me that caused me to change my mind. It was all through relatives.

My brother-in-law, Bill Johnson had gone into Freddie Keppard's Tuxedo Band to play bass fiddle, and, as Bill was a very, very good-looking boy in those days and all the girls taken to him and those bad chords on his bass fiddle and that song he sung ...

> Let me be your salty dog,
> I don't want to be your man at all ...

he taken over the Tuxedo Band. So Bill heard about California from me and he wrote my wife† and she financed a trip for the five pieces plus guitar and bass. On entering Los Angeles, the Tuxedo Band made such a tremendous success that the Pantages Circuit signed them immediately. They toured the country as The Original Creole Band over what was the largest circuit in the world at that time, finally landing at the Palace Theatre in New York. This was in 1913, long before the so-called Original Dixieland Band was thought of.

It was known that no act played the Palace Theatre in New York for more than one week, but the Original Creoles played for weeks to standing-room-only.

Later at the Grand Theatre in Chicago they took the town over and caused John Armstrong, my trumpet player, to quit.

Armstrong came from Louisville. I had tried to teach him New Orleans style, but he was stubborn. Well, when he heard Freddie Keppard, hitting those high C's, F's and G's as clean as a whistle, he got ashamed and refused to play anymore.

There was no limit to how Freddie could go. Louis Armstrong has never been in his class. Among trumpets I would rate Freddie first, Buddy Petit second, King Oliver third, and then comes Armstrong, all very great men. Freddie would agree with me. He was a real Creole, about my color, Creole accent, a good spender, wore plenty nice clothes, had women hanging around all day long, liked to drink a lot (all the band drank up everything they could find), and he talked so big that people misunderstood and thought he was egotistical. This caused the break-up of this great band in the end.

They were always in an argument on account of Freddie's big talk. He would arrive at rehearsal an hour late and say, "Let them wait for me. The band can't play till I get there." Morgan Prince, the comedian with the band, was not a Creole and he took Freddie seriously. In one argument he hit Keppard across the head with a cane and that started the breaking up of the band. I don't know when it happened but I understand that was the beginning of the end.

Anyhow Keppard certainly finished *me* at the Elite. Business went to the bad and as I did not wish to stay on and not satisfy everybody, I hit the road again.

---

*"James Reese Europe" is the correct spelling.
†Anita Gonzales, Bill Johnson's sister.

11 William Marion Cook

CARY B. LEWIS

Born in the District of Columbia on January 27, 1869, William Marion Cook was an established musician and composer when he was profiled by Cary B. Lewis in the May 1, 1915 edition of the Chicago Defender. Cook's proud and sometimes irascible nature did not always endear him to critics and journalists, but the public enjoyed his songs such as "Swing Along," "My Lady," and "Darktown Is Out Tonight." By the time of this profile, which appeared in one of the nation's premier black newspapers, he had collaborated with poet Paul Lawrence Dunbar on a series of theatrical skits entitled Clorindy (or The Origin of the Cakewalk).

Cook had begun composing in 1893 following a brief stint studying with Czech-born composer Antonin Dvořák, who was teaching at the National Conservatory of Music. Within two years Clorindy, with a caste featuring veteran singer, actor, and song writer Ernest Hogan, made its triumphant debut off-Broadway. "Who Dat Say Chicken in Dis Crowd" became an immediate hit, helping to propel Cook into the public limelight. Following the success of Clorindy, Cook composed more songs and revues, such as Uncle Eph's Christmas (1901) and The Southerners (1904), which drew upon his experience as an African American.

But Cook also wanted to be recognized as a "serious" composer and longed for the day when quality and creativity would trump the fact that he was black. In his Chicago Defender piece, Lewis quotes Cook as stating that "A school must, and will, be established, perhaps at Washington, D.C. To head this school, an eminent European composer and teacher secured (preferably a Russian) who, unhindered by prejudice, will understand, appreciate, and foster the peculiar musical genius of the Afro-American child." This profile is rife with long quotes from Cook in which he discusses his views on the origins of ragtime, the relationship between race and music in the United States, the importance of individual creativity, and the importance of Harry Burleigh (an important black composer who often looked to spirituals for his inspiration).

Cook's musical career continued until his death on July 19, 1944. He composed but made a more steady living performing music. In the late teens he formed The Southern Syncopaters, also known as The New York Syncopated Orchestra, which toured the United States and Europe. Soprano saxophone wizard Sidney Bechet was among the members of this orchestra. After he returned from Europe, Cook led an orchestra associated with the famed Clef Club that included Paul Robeson as a vocalist. But, despite his long and varied musical career, Will Marion Cook died feeling that he never received the proper recognition that he deserved.

Will Marion Cook, the greatest champion of the race in folklore songs, was in the city last week and stopped at the Wabash Y.M.C.A. This noted genius was to have appeared at the "All Colored Concert" at Orchestra Hall but owing to a physical breakdown had to return to his mother at Washington, D.C., the city of his birth. For a number of years Mr. Cook has lived in New York City and here he has labored in the musical world. His songs, for the most part racial, have been sung up and down Broadway with wonderful success. He has put more talented members of the race on the road than any of our musicians, namely; Holland Hayes, Abbie Mitchell, Harry Burleigh, Melville Chalton, and others of this character. Mr. Cook's forte is chorus directing. [He became] famous by directing the world-renowned Williams and Walker Company.

His genius, however, is [expressed in] his folklore compositions. Musical critics here and abroad claim that Mr. Cook has outclassed all other composers of this character. Some of his biggest songs are *Springtime, My Lady, Love's Lane, My Love Is in de Sky Mid de Moon, Exhortation, Rain Song, Swing Along, My Lady's Lips*. These are the numbers that stamped his individuality and ranked him as the champion of racial composers. A score of his compositions are among the incidental music in the shows of the race that have appeared in the past twenty-five years.

All the great singers of the race who have become successful used compositions from Will Marion Cook. His success as a director and composer of both the orchestra and the chorus and in developing of talented individuals is widely known both in this country and abroad. Chicagoans greatly regretted to learn of his serious illness last Thursday and hope he will be able soon to be at his desk to carry on the work which he has so nobly and ably begun. Speaking of "Afro-American music and musicians," he said:

"The songs of sorrow, of joy, of humor, and of sentiment, were the natural growth of a race, musically inclined, in Africa, and whose melodious outpourings were intensified by the conditions of slavery.

"1850–1865—Minstrel songs full of character, but less lofty of sentiment, and less true of real Negro aspiration and inspiration. (See songs of Jim Bland and others.)

"1870—Advent of jubilee singers—an artistic triumph.

"1875–1888—No further development in Negro music. Cause: The Afro-American had been so thoroughly taught by the white man that his color, condition and accomplishment were inferior, that the younger generation at once threw aside all tradition. Any reference to the past became a disgrace. Except in a few schools of the South, to sing jubilee melodies to an Afro-American audience would be an insult, and would lead to the dismissal of teacher urging them. The Moody and Sankey hymns were used exclusively in our churches and schools—the glorious old slave hymns and spirituals frowned upon as 'reminding us of a past full of shame and misery.' (This is quoted from the protest of a prominent music teacher twenty years ago in the city of Washington.) Talented Negroes sought in their musical study to eradicate all traces of that individual character that had attracted the attention of the world. Result, milk and water imitations of inferior white musicians."

BEGINNING OF RAGTIME

"About 1888. The starting and quick growth of so-called 'ragtime.' As far back as 1875, Negroes in the questionable resorts along the Mississippi had commenced to evolve this musical figure, but at the World's Fair, Chicago, 'ragtime' got a running start, swept the Americas, then

This rather obscure 1907 composition was introduced to the public as part of a George Walker and Bert Williams' show "Bandana Land."

Credit: Sheet Music from the collection of Kip Lornell.

Europe, and today the craze has not diminished. Cause of Success: The public was tired of the sing song, same, monotonous, mother, sister, father, sentimental, songs. Ragtime offered unique rhythms, curious groupings of words, and melodies that gave the zest of unexpectedness. Many Negroes, Irving Jones, Will Accoe, Bob Cole, Johnson Brothers, Gussie L. Davis, Sid Perrin, Ernest Hogan, Williams and Walker and others wrote some of the most celebrated rag songs of the day. In other instances white actors and song writers would hear in St. Louis such melodies as *New Bully, Hot Time*, etc., would change the words (often unprintable) and publish them as their own creations. At this time came Dvořák. He saw that from this people, even though their material had been debased, must come a great school of music—not necessarily national—but rather new and characteristic. The renaissance in Negro music. A few earnest Negro music students felt as did Dvořák. They studied the man—so broad, genial, and human—carefully and thoroughly."

HARRY BURLEIGH'S WORK

"Some Negroes of real musical accomplishment: Harry T. Burleigh, a pupil of Dvořák, is baritone soloist at St. George's Church, New York City, . . . George W. Walker, the late lamented partner of Bert Williams. His has been the greatest influence in the development of modern Negro music. At 28 he could not read a note and could hardly write his name, yet day and night he talked Negro music to his people, urged and compelled his writers to give something characteristic. Each year he wanted bigger, better things. He engaged the best Negro voices in the United States, and their success in ensemble singing was as great in London, Paris and Berlin as in New York, Boston and Chicago. (See criticisms of *In Dahomay, Bandanna Lond, Abyssinia.*) Dvořák would have been proud to have known such a man. In all reverence—Dvořák—George Walker. They had high ideals and they showed the way. Perhaps in a vast hereafter these two men may meet. The rough, uncouth, but genial Bohemian master; the uneducated but highly polished, ebony-hued African, with the gleaming ivory mouth. Do you doubt that with one impulse their hands will join, and the mastiff smile of the Bohemian will match the lazy grin of the American 'Zulu' as they both whisper one word: 'brother.'"

RACE MUSIC IN AMERICA

"Today. Developed Negro music has just begun in America. The Afro-American is finding himself. He has thrown aside puerile imitation of the white man. He has learned that a thorough study of the masters gives the knowledge of what is good and how to create. From the Russian, he has learned to get his inspiration from within; that his inexhaustible wealth of folklore legends and songs furnish him with material for compositions that will establish a great school of music and enrich musical literature.

"The Menace. The Afro-American wants results quickly. He does not believe in making haste slowly. He quickly turns to false white and colored friends, who wish to exploit him for ulterior motives. The political 'carpet bagger' of '68 and '72 has his prototype in the musical 'carpet bagger' of 1915. Dvořák, Safonoff, Hirsh and other great European directors and composers; De Bachman, D'Albert, Paderewski, as well as many great singers, have told of the coming glory of the Negro musician. It is becoming a fad.

"In some of the large cities of the country, New York in particular, well meaning but ill advised white people are gathering together large choruses of poorly trained singers, without education either musical or general, and, in conjunction with unschooled instrumentalists, are giving widely advertised concerts, claiming to represent the accomplishment of an entire race. They promise much—fulfill little. Let them rather show what their particular school is doing and, with success or failure, no harm is done.

"There is still an element of doubt in the mind of the cultured American. He says: 'We concede the Negro's talent for music; we doubt his capacity for thorough development.'"

"The right way. What the Afro-American has thus far accomplished is only a promise—an expectation; the realization belongs to the future. A school must, and will, be established, perhaps at Washington D.C. To head this school, an eminent European composer and teacher secured (preferably a Russian) who, unhindered by prejudice, will understand, appreciate, and foster the peculiar musical genius of the Afro-American child. While giving the child the same grasp upon the science of composition as was Beethoven's he will also show that strength of character and profound knowledge of his people, as well as technical skill that made Beethoven the master."

INDIVIDUALITY, AND THEN MORE INDIVIDUALITY

"Such a school will require money. It will not be forthcoming if, as soon as a few Negroes have learned the first principles of breathing, or being able to play the scale of G one or two octaves without serious offense to tonality, they are at once exploited in some temple of music, where, may be, the Boston Symphony Orchestra had just finished a concert, perfect in every detail.

"The Negro composer (and there are a few in the United States who are receiving serious consideration) should mainly find his inspiration in the imperishable melodies of his enslaved ancestors. When he shall have developed works worthy of rendition he will find both Negroes and Whites ready and willing to offer them. All through the South, Southwest and West there are Negroes with beautiful voices. What is known, because of the home life of these people they are gaining real culture, They are laying aside their shame of the past, and are beginning to glory in their unmatched heritage folklore and folk songs. The 'Afro-American Folk Singers,' Washington, D.C., the chorus at Howard University, and others, are ready to do justice to the choral works of a Negro Beethoven, should he appear. . . . To them we look for results, by them would we be judged. New York and other large cities of the North are neither seeking nor finding 'the right way.'"

Continuing, he said: "I do not mention Hampton, where they sing the primitive slave melodies so beautifully, for this reason: To sing works of development to which the composer gave thought and culture requires thought and culture. It you, admitting an inferior condition, fail to give to the child opportunity for breadth, which only come from comprehensive development, just so far you have hindered his understanding, appreciation and rendition of all masterpieces."

12 Ma Rainey and the Traveling Minstrels

CHARLES EDWARD SMITH

Gertrude "Ma" Rainey, along with Bessie Smith and Ida Cox, was the one of the most influential and popular of the classic vaudeville blues singers. Born in Columbus, Georgia, in 1886, Rainey began her career as a professional singer (and as a dancer for the first few years) around 1900 and continued to perform until her death on December 22, 1939. In addition to thousands of live performances over nearly four decades, Rainey recorded some 120 songs for the Paramount record label, often in the company of highly regarded jazz musicians.

Charles Edward Smith—a frequent contributor to The Record Changer *and co-author (with Frederick Ramsey) of the first book about jazz,* The Jazzmen *(1937), to be published in the United States—largely recounts the early career of "The Mother of the Blues." He emphasizes the importance of tent shows, such as the Florida Cotton Blossoms and The Smart Set, and Rainey's Paramount records in disseminating this music. Stage show entertainer Artiebelle McGinty is at the core of this short piece, which appeared in* The Record Changer *in 1953.*

At the age of twelve, McGinty began her career as a singer, dancer, and comedian with a traveling show, The Smart Set, at a time when Rainey headlined the show. Smith's quotes from his interview with McGinty add a new dimension to Ma Rainey's well-known life story, which is characterized by a larger-than-life stage show that included flamboyant costumes and outsized jewelry. At one point in her career she stepped out on stage from the inside of a huge wind-up phonograph. McGinty's recollections help to humanize a woman who was a star within the black American community and among a handful of record collectors, blues enthusiasts, and music scholars.

"We never went north of Virginia." Miss Artiebelle McGinty, veteran American Negro actress and comedienne, recalled the days when she trouped with Ma Rainey, and her words encompassed an historic and as yet unchronicled epoch in American music. Though Gertrude "Ma" Rainey later went north to play the theatres of the old T.O.B.A. (vaudeville) circuit and to Chicago to record for Paramount, she was essentially a singer of the South, a singer who in her person represented the fusion of rural and urban elements, the banjo, the jug and the hot muted cornet.

Squat and ugly, the star of the Rabbit's Foot Minstrels was warmly human. She was "Ma" to the sprawling black belt of the South and backstage mother to the troupes in the tent shows she sparked with her talent for three decades.

Pa and Ma Rainey worked with many shows but during almost the entire period of her professional career she was the featured star. In the early days, "Pa" Rainey did a comic turn and he and his wife worked as a song and dance team. An idea of her material may be gleaned from her records, though these (the records) might not indicate the large amount of topical and novelty songs in her repertoire. It was truly prodigious for, wherever she went, she was the articulate voice of her listeners, singing their homely country novelty songs (derived from folk music) and moaning the blues in a sensitive, somewhat small voice of unusual timbre and infinite pathos.

She taught this repertoire to a young girl from Memphis, Bessie Smith, and instilled in her the blues style and technique, the vocal style that was at the same time the basis for instrumental jazz. In New Orleans, Miss McGinty and others recalled, the members of the tent shows met the men who were later to be celebrated as jazz greats—King Oliver, Louis Armstrong, Sidney Bechet, Pops Foster and many others—early associations that must have been enriching to both the great blues singer and the early jazzmen.

In tents, sometimes playing with a regular stage arrangement, the footlights at one end of the tent, and at other times playing in the round, with four groups of dancers to face the four quadrants of the audience, they saw the days of gasoline mantle lanterns (for footlights) give way to portable electric power plants of the crude and not always trustworthy kind they had thirty years ago. They traveled in an age of steam and the first Diesels bypassed the winding iron roads that took them to the small cities and towns of the South. They traveled with Silas Green from New Orleans, with Al Gaines (of the Gaines Brothers), with Tolliver and C. W. Parks. The bands that backed up Ma's singing were pretty much the type of accompaniment one hears on many of her records, the playing with hot jazz pioneers a unique feature that the public seldom heard except on records. She got to know the jazzmen and sang with them, however, at parties, "She was always ready for a ball," a musician told me, "She was full of life . . . Ma Rainey and good old Bessie . . . they don't make 'em like that any more!"

Although Ma Rainey made only about 60 records, comprising some 120 titles, a weighty thesis could be written about them, assuming one had a few months to spare for the research indicated. There are, as might be expected, a preponderance of blues but these alone, if subjected to the scholarly scrutiny that has been accorded many spirituals, would provide richly rewarding sidelights on the cultural genesis of the Negro as an American. Indeed, these blues would interest, among others, the musicologist, the anthropologist and the social historian. Many of the blues melodies (in the classic twelve-bar form) would be traceable to African sources, others would undoubtedly contain elements relating to the heritage from the British Isles. *Boweavil Blues* (like the famous *John Henry*) is probably a fusion of both lines of influence. Ma had her own version of this folk saga of the redoubtable enemy of King Cotton, and of that other "standard" of Southern folk music, *C. C. Rider* (which Paramount titled *See See Rider*, apparently unaware that the initials stood for a railroad line). In her recorded repertoire you'll also find that archetype of riverboat gamblers, *Stack o'Lee*, a Levee camp moan, a Georgia cake-walk, a Louisiana hoodoo, a paean to the black bottom, and 16-bar blues that are not really blues at all but Tin Pan Alley tunes capitalizing on the idea. For back there on the Paramount label—a *race* label that packaged its product for Negro listeners—were songs for sale, songs that had survived through centuries of change but were still linked to the past, songs about booze and bad luck and evil men, songs of double meaning and songs strident

An artist's rendering of Ma Rainey appears on this rare and colorful Paramount Record Company label released in 1924.

Credit: Record label from the collection of Kip Lornell.

and harsh that sing of cruelty and frustration beyond belief. And, of course, the gusto and humor that are as much a part of the blues and Southern singing as are the bluer blues, the ones that are muted in sadness, poignant, nostalgic, evocative. If more of the novelty and topical songs had been recorded we would have an even better idea of this facet of Ma's talent. As it is, the listeners accustomed to the semantics of folksong will find much that is humor—sly, earthy, biting, sometimes grim, and occasionally humor that is manifestly out-of-date and that writers will sooner or later describe as archaic.

On her record dates will be found many illustrious jazzmen. Louis Armstrong is on *See See Rider* and *Jelly Bean Blues*, along with an unnamed master of that Afro-American instrument of the rural country-side, the five-string banjo. Another "Georgia" band (probably put together in Chicago) included "Cow Cow" Davenport, a blues and boogie woogie pianist from Alabama and Johnny Dodds, one of the great masters of New Orleans clarinet! On others you'll hear jugs, washboards and the guitar of an itinerant folk artist called "Tampa Red." Though "Madame Rainey" (as she was sometimes billed) did not usually have a jazz band to back her up, more jazz musicians than is generally believed have played accompaniments for her in various engagements. As far back as the history of jazz has been traced we find a two-way pattern at work—musicians coming into New Orleans from the country districts and from other cities and New Orleans musicians branching out into neighboring states to play dances, garden parties, theatre dates, and so forth. If you look for jazz pioneers only in jazz bands you have a woefully inadequate picture of what went on. (A somewhat analogous situation obtained in New York during the 1920's where there was no ready audience for the superior talents of Benny Goodman, Jack Teagarden, George Wettling and many others. In fact, most of the jazz greats of today have played in pit bands and in the night clubs of the Prohibition era.) But, generally speaking, in the tent show days there were usually only two musicians who bordered on "hot," the drummer and a pianist who had to be proficient in rags and blues.

The names of the shows Ma was in are almost legendary now, though some have been revived more recently—the Rabbit's Foot Minstrels, Florida Cotton Blossoms, The Smarter Set.

This last-named show is a clue to the relationship of the tent shows to show music generally. There was, as enthusiasts of show business are aware, a show called The Smart Set. This was a spoof of high society, as the magazine The Smart Set, was in some respects a spoof of both literary and social pretensions. (The nature of The Smarter Set might be suggested both by songs from Ma Rainey's repertoire and by a New Orleans period represented by such titles as *Cake Walkin' Babies From Home*.) The tent shows were often called minstrels but were often made up of elements from minstrels and from more modern urban forms, such as vaudeville. The Gaines Brothers put on a trapeze act and did a slack wire act as well. There were comic acts supplied by such veterans as Pa Rainey and by the then-young Artiebelle McGinty. (These comics who came right out of the Negro minstrels and into vaudeville, were a feature of all stage shows in the days when jazz fans went up to the Lafayette in Harlem to hear Louis, Bessie or Bechet for the first time. They were as memorable, in their field, as the great comics of burlesque, and their acts were often integrated with the music offered, so that the resulting entertainment was less in the nature of vaudeville than of a revue.)

In 1915, Artiebelle McGinty, barely out of grade school, did a singing, dancing and comedy act with The Smarter Set. (Later, still working the same shows as her friend Ma, it was a team, Legg & McGinty.) She said that then Ma was getting on in years (but of course Miss McGinty was just getting over being a gawky lanky kid and any age beyond thirty seemed old). They traveled in coaches, with special baggage cars for the show's paraphernalia, slept on lumpy seats and, with windows open or closed, breathed in the acrid, permeable smell of smoke and cinders. They were one big family, not always a perfectly happy one but a family just the same, with a Ma to mother them. They even had family jokes. The piano player was called "Peg" because of his wooden legs. He played a raggedy piano (nickelodeon syndrome) and liked the blues and when a stranger bumped into him accidentally he would wince and say, "Ouch, you done stepped on my toes!"

In the tent show days Negro centers of Southern cities were not as "urbanized," generally speaking, as their counterparts in the north where there was a trend (happily knocked for a loop by jazz, among other things) that regarded everything "down home" as countrified. So whether Ma sang at a crossroads or in a city the material was the same and its reception was assured. She was the voice of the South, singing of the South, to the South. In the big towns of the North she had only one part of her audience and that only part way. Her novelty songs were already a little out of date, old fashioned and crudely contrived, once they passed the Mason-Dixon. So Paramount did not encourage her to record further, when she made her last recordings and it is one of the tragic byproducts of the hiatus in blues and jazz appreciation (the decade of the mid-twenties to the mid-thirties, particularly when jazz and blues belonged to the *aficianados*) that no other record company cared to promote her talent. Ma Rainey belonged to an epoch and it was her tragedy to try to adjust herself to a world in which that epoch already belonged to the past.

Perhaps if you had talked with her in her later years, when her ugly-featured face became a chip on her shoulder and her pride had withered to an arrogance that seemed pretentious, you would have found a loneliness and a longing for the tent shows, when everyone knew Ma, and a hunger for the days when the pennies and nickels of the people were not enough for the tribute they felt, they gave their hearts. You might even find her romanticizing it a bit here and there, as old people do, making a bright patchwork of the good pieces. But somehow this would have been very close to the truth because almost everyone with whom this writer spoke, told of Ma's deep sincerity, of her honest love for people and her honest zest for life. In the words of Artiebelle McGinty, "She had a heart as big as this house."

Of course every jazz fan knows about Ma Rainey's necklace of gold coins, graduated in size from the small $2.50 discs that matched her earpendants to the large twenty-dollar gold-piece. This was the focal point of her somewhat flamboyant stage costume and she wore it offstage where otherwise her manner of dress was quite modest. She even slept with it on. One night on a train trip from one location to another she fell asleep as usual, on the lumpy coach seat, and didn't awaken until the morning. While still half caught up in stupor of sleep her hand went to her throat, as though she felt not fully dressed. She let out the most unlikely screech that side of Maynard Ferguson, jumped up on the frayed seat cushion, and gave a mighty tug at the emergency cord. The train jerked to a stop, knocking passengers about as the couplings clanked and the engine snorted. The conductor came into the car, seeking the source of the emergency (a sneak thief) and found Ma Rainey waiting for him. She put her hand to her throat again, where the glittering bright bangles had been and said, "They've been stolen."

"We never went north of Virginia," Miss McGinty had said, and the words stayed with me, took root in memories alongside the verses of a poem Sterling Brown had written about her. She was a star, with a star's top place in the billing, but she was also warm and close, with dark deep eyes and a greatness of voice that was her own special transmutation, ugly duckling to swan. Her listeners knew the format, as they knew the woman, and, already excited, so that it seemed no great enthusiasm was possible, nevertheless warmed up more and more to the performance with that palpable fervor that creates a tingling sensation both sides of the footlights, so that singer and audience were one as both approached the anticipated climax. There were novelty and topical songs, the latest paper "ballits" (as song sheets from the city were called) and then, as Miss McGinty expressed it, "When her last number came everybody would be waiting for that and it would be a blues."

13 Black Sacred Harp Singing from Southeast Alabama

HENRY WILLETT

Many important, though underrecognized, regional forms of African American music have developed across the United States. Modern zydeco, for example, has gained recognition outside the creolized bayous and prairies of southwest Louisiana and southeast Texas, where it was born shortly after the end of World War II. A handful, such as jazz and hip hop, began as very focused regional music but have developed into worldwide phenomena. The tradition among black Americans of singing from the Sacred Harp books, however, remains largely confined to southern Alabama, far from the spotlight that occasionally shines on American vernacular music.

The term "sacred harp" refers the 1844 hymnbook of the same name, initially published in Philadelphia by B. F. White and E. J. King. This book, and others like it, employed a notation that used different shapes to aid singers not familiar with standard Western notation to read music. Such books became popular in the South among black and white singers in the mid–nineteenth century and various editions of three of them remain in use today.

Shape-note singing remains relatively widespread among whites, particularly in Mississippi and Georgia. Black sacred harp singing, on the other hand, was never as widespread and was strongest in the area between Selma, Alabama, and Pensacola, Florida, especially in Dale and Ozark Counties in Alabama. This strength is underscored by the 1934 publication of The Colored Sacred Harp, compiled and published by Judge Jackson, the only book dedicated to compositions by African American sacred harp singers.

In the twenty-first century, Alabama's African American sacred harp singing is largely the domain of elderly men and women who grew up in the tradition. These monthly (usually between March and November) day-long events are social and religious gatherings as well as musical events. Singers trade off leading their favorite songs, standing in the center of a square surrounded on all four sides by alto, bass, soprano, and tenor singers—most of whom know their parts by heart. They usually take a break for dinner around 1:00 PM and continue until they quit around 6:00 PM in order to get home before dark. The singing is framed by an opening and closing prayer and is interrupted only by dinner and perhaps a tribute to a singer who is ill or has died.

These liner notes first accompanied a documentary long-play record issued by the Alabama Folklife Program in 1982. Willett served as the head of the program for several decades until health issues forced him to resign from this position in 2002. This version of the notes represents some rethinking and revising on the author's part as he reflected on more than twenty-five years of involvement with this important form of sacred singing.

"Sometimes an old Sacred Harp song will get on your mind in the middle of the night while you're lying in bed, and you'll just have to sing it over and over again in your head before you can go to sleep." To this octogenarian from Ozark, Alabama, Sacred Harp singing is more than a diversion—it is a way of life. On almost every Sunday between March and October, Dewey Williams joins with fellow singers at the County Line Church in Slocomb, or at the Mount Sinai Church in Henry County, or at any one of a dozen or so churches in Southeast Alabama, to form the "square" and sing "fa-sol-la" just as many southeast Alabamians have been doing for over 100 years.

Mr. Williams' grandparents were slaves from Barbour County, Alabama, and he remembers that they, too, sang from the *Sacred Harp*. A singing tradition characteristically associated with white culture in the Deep South, Southeast Alabama has enjoyed a vibrant, if rare, black Sacred Harp tradition for over a century. The black Henry County, Alabama, Singing Convention celebrated its one-hundredth anniversary in 1980.

During a typical singing, the participants arrange themselves in a square according to voice part, the basses facing the trebles, and the tenors facing the altos. A song leader stands in the middle of the square leading the singers first through the notes to the songs and then through the lyrics, a practice emanating from the traditional singing school classes, where singers are taught to sing the notes and then the words.

The singing style takes its name from the hymnbook *The Sacred Harp*, first published in Philadelphia by B. F. White and E. J. King. The musical style, however, predates the publication of the book. The itinerant singing-school master was a common phenomenon in colonial New England, and various masters competed in their efforts to devise an instructional system where congregations could be taught to sing "by note." By the mid-eighteenth century, religious songbooks were commonly employing shape-notes to indicate the sounds on the European musical scale of fa sol la fa sol la mi. From the fuguing tunes of William Billings to the popular melodies of Jeremiah Ingalls, religious songs found widespread circulation in hymnbooks such as William Walker's *Southern Harmony*, which was popular throughout the South in the early nineteenth century.

The important innovation introduced into the singing school tradition in the "Second Great Awakening" years of the early nineteenth century was the idea, first utilized by New Englander William Law, of assigning different shaped note-heads corresponding to the fa sol la and mi syllables. As the singing school tradition declined in New England, the new shape-note songbooks such as Kentucky Harmony, Virginia Harmony, Union Harmony, and Southern Harmony gained widespread popularity in the South. It was in this setting that the Sacred Harp made its initial appearance in Georgia in 1844. Despite the rapid decline of four-shaped tune books in the latter half of the nineteenth century, the Sacred Harp, in its various revisions, has maintained a popularity and currency in the South unequalled by any of the other shape-note songsters.

There are three major revisions of the Sacred Harp that enjoy current usage. The White revision, published in 1911 by J. L. White, is now used only in a few isolated areas of north Georgia. The most recent revision, the Denson revision, published in 1935, is by far the most widely used of the Sacred Harp revisions. It is found at most Sacred Harp singings throughout Georgia, in North Alabama, and in parts of Mississippi and Tennessee.

It is the Cooper revision of the Sacred Harp, first published in 1902, that is used by both white and black singers in South Alabama. W. M. Cooper, from Dothan, Alabama, prefaced his edition with the statement "the selections are from the old Sacred Harp, remodeled and revised, together with additions from the most eminent authors, including new music."

Chapter 13

For nearly 70 years Dewey Williams participated in and organized sacred harp singing near or in his Ozark, Dale County, Alabama, birthplace.

Credit: Photo courtesy of the Ralph Rinzler Folklife Archives and Collections, Smithsonian Institution

The "remodeling" he referred to was the transposing of a number of songs into a lower, more easily sung, key. The "revising" was the standardization of the alto part in all selections, a practice followed by the later revisers. Many of the melodies are adopted from traditional tunes including Celtic jigs and dance tunes. Typical of folk tunes, they are often in the Ionian and Aeolian modes, and occasionally the Mixolydian and Dorian. The song texts are taken mostly from the verses of the popular eighteenth century hymnists, most notably Isaac Watts and Charles Worley. The "additions" were a number of gospel songs and camp-meeting selections. The Cooper revision was again copyrighted in 1907, 1909, 1927, 1949 and 1960, and is currently published by the Sacred Harp Book Co., Inc., of Samson, Alabama.

In 1934 a most interesting Sacred Harp variant was published in Ozark, Alabama. *The Colored Sacred Harp* contains seventy-seven songs, all but one composed by black singers from southeast Alabama and northwestern Florida. Judge Jackson (1883–1958) is listed as the book's author and publisher. Jackson had first heard shape-note singing while a teenager in Montgomery County, Alabama, and was composing tunes of his own by his twenty-first birthday. In the 1920s Jackson had several of his compositions printed on broadsheets that he gave and sold to friends and acquaintances in Ozark and Dale County. In the 1930s a committee of the Dale County Colored Musical Institute and the Alabama and Florida Union State Convention offered the following recommendations:

> First: That we will have a musical book.
>
> Second: That the name of the book will be *The Colored Sacred Harp*.
>
> Third: That four shaped notes will be used.
>
> Fourth: That Bro. J. Jackson be author of the book.
>
> We hope this little book may prove a great blessing and be the means of saving souls.

The committee report was signed by fifteen members, many representing families still prominent in the black Sacred Harp tradition.

In the Depression year of 1934, Jackson himself was forced to subsidize the publication in collaboration with Bishop J. B. Walker. Jackson's son Japheth (currently president of the Alabama-Florida Union State Convention) remembers accompanying his father in a mule-drawn wagon to pick up the one thousand paperback songbooks at the Ozark train station.

The original edition contained, in addition to its seventy-seven songs, the Committee Report, pictures of Jackson and Walker, and a request:

> *We ask your cooperation, both White and Colored, to help us place this book in every home. That we may learn thousands of people, especially the youth, how to praise God in singing.*

The book, much to the frustration of Jackson, was not quickly adopted by the black shape-note singing community of southeast Alabama. It is not entirely clear why the book was not accepted, although the cause lies partly in the other county conventions' jealousy of the Dale County Convention, partly in Depression economics, and probably largely in the fact that the Sacred Harp tradition is conservative and only slowly adopts any innovations or new material.

Several songs, however, did catch the fancy of the singers. Among them are "Florida Storm," "My Mother's Gone," "Prosperity," and "The Signs of Judgement," which are all sung with regularity at black Sacred Harp singings. As might be expected, more songs from *The Colored Sacred Harp* are sung with regularity at the Jackson Memorial Singing, which occurs annually on the third Sunday in April.

By 1970, most singers were singing selections from *The Colored Sacred Harp* by memory as many of the original paperback copies had not withstood the more than thirty-five years of use. In 1973, *The Colored Sacred Harp* was reprinted in a hardcover edition with assistance from the National Endowment for the Arts and the Alabama State Council on the Arts and Humanities.

On the day of a typical black Sacred Harp singing, the singers casually arrive in the late morning, seat themselves in the square according to voice part, and begin to sing and socialize. The dinner break occurs in the early afternoon, and the singers enjoy a covered dish "dinner-on-the-grounds" (or in the church basement) prepared by the women singers. The most intense and emotional singing usually occurs after the dinner break. Each singer takes turn leading a song of his choice. He comes to the middle of the square, calls out his page number, and waits for the tuner to key the song. Singers are discouraged by the other singers from repeating a song that has already been sung or "used." This proscription is often dispensed with, however, if the singer is particularly young, particularly old, or if the song has special significance to the individual song leader (perhaps the favorite song of a recently deceased relative).

Every singer is given an opportunity to lead a song if he chooses to do so. Often, older or infirm singers will request a younger singer to lead their song. The motions of the song leader are highly stylistic, and are generally more emotional and pronounced than the motions of white Sacred Harp song leaders. Young children are taught in singing school to mark time with their right arm while holding the book in their left.

Typically, a young singer will stand in place at the center of the square while leading the note singing. When he begins to lead the lyrics portion of the song he will often begin to "walk time," rhythmically pacing from one side of the square to the other, being careful never to turn his back to the tenor section. As the singer grows older and more confident he develops his own distinctive leading style. During fuging songs, in particular, he may gesture to each section of the square as its part joins in. Skilled song leaders often elicit applause or other emotional responses from the group. Occasionally, a singer might reach an emotional pitch to the point of "getting happy." These episodes might include a personal testimony from the "happy" person followed by a repeat of the last verse or refrain from the previous song. The singers usually break up at around 5:00 P.M. in time to go home and prepare supper.

With the exception of the annual state convention, which includes reading of minutes and committee reports, most singings are interrupted only by an opening prayer, dinner, and a closing prayer, and perhaps a special tribute speech if it is a singing in someone's honor. Most singings are of one day's duration (almost always a Sunday), except in the cases of the state convention and larger county conventions that cover an entire weekend. Most singings occur between the months of March and October—months which are more conducive to travel and outdoor "dinners-on-the-grounds."

14 A Negro Explains "Jazz"

ANONYMOUS

The title of this April 26, 1919, Literary Digest article disguises the fact that it focuses on Lieutenant James Reese Europe's opinions and views about the state of jazz and syncopated hot dance in 1919. Europe, born on February 22, 1880, in Mobile, Alabama, displayed talent on the piano as a boy. In 1899 his family moved to Washington D. C., where he continued private music lessons. The family remained there for four years before relocating to New York City, where Europe's musical career truly blossomed. By 1905 he worked with Ernest Hogan in performances of musical comedy and soon began directing orchestras and choruses for musical shows, such as S. H. Dudley's Smart Set, featuring all-black casts.

In 1910, Europe helped to found the Clef Club, which served as a meeting ground for musicians as well as a nexus for booking musical engagements. Within two years, Europe felt Clef Club musicians were ready for a Carnegie Hall performance, and on May 2, 1912, various Clef Club acts performed for a sold-out house. Within a few years he returned to Carnegie Hall, leading musicians for annual concerts of the Negro Symphony Orchestra.

Europe enjoyed even greater commercial success and public recognition through his work with husband and wife dancing team and vaudeville veterans Vernon and Irene Castle. Before long the Castles and Europe's musicians were hired for private parties, featuring music by Europe's exclusive Society Orchestra band and dancing by the Castles. This successful collaboration encouraged the Castles to open a dance school called Castle House and a night club, both of which featured musicians associated with Europe and/or the Clef Club.

These associations helped move Europe into New York's high society and by late 1913 Europe was so successful that he formed his own Tempo Club. Over the next four years Europe was the toast of New York City's popular (black and white) dance music crowds. His sheet music sold well and his Society Orchestra recorded eight selections for the Victor Talking Machine Company, making him the first African American to lead his own band for a major company.

The declaration of war changed his plans for a tour of England and France. On September 18, 1916, Europe enlisted in the 15th New York Infantry and he was soon invited to organize a brass band as part of the 15th Infantry Regiment. In 1917, they were sent to France where they not only entertained numerous soldiers, officers, and French civilians but also earned the nickname "Hellfighters" after proving themselves in battle. After the Armistice, Europe and his men eventually returned to the United States and an eager public. They quickly returned to the recording studio and in March 1919 recorded a session for the Pathé company that solidified Europe's position as a transitional figure between syncopated ragtime dance music and jazz.

> Europe suffered a fatal stabbing two days after his band recorded another six titles for Pathé on May 7, approximately two weeks following the publication of this article. He was stabbed to death by a band member, Herbert Wright, following an altercation regarding the drummer's unprofessional behavior. Europe did not live long enough to see the flowering of jazz. This Literary Digest piece not only explores Europe's views on the origins and development of jazz but also discusses his perceptions about the reception of his music overseas as well as the importance of contemporary black American composers such as Will Marion Cook and Harry Burleigh.

The latest international word seems to be "jazz." It is used almost exclusively in British papers to describe the kind of music and dancing—particularly dancing—imported from America, thereby arousing discussions, in which bishops do not disdain to participate, to fill all the papers. While society once "ragged," they now "jazz." In this country, tho we have been tolerably familiar with the word for two years or more, we still try to pursue its mysterious origins. Lieut. James Reese Europe, late of the Machine-Gun Battalion of the 15th Regiment, tells Mr. Grenville Vernon, of the *New York Tribune*, that the word comes from Mr. Razz, who led a band in New Orleans some fifteen years ago and whose fame is perpetuated in a somewhat modified form. . . . Lieutenant Europe says:

"I believe that the term 'jazz' originated with a band of four pieces which was found about fifteen years ago in New Orleans, and which was known as 'Razz's Band.' This band was of truly extraordinary composition. It consisted of a baritone horn, a trombone, a cornet, and an instrument made out of the chinaberry-tree. This instrument is something like a clarinet, and is made by the southern Negroes themselves. Strange to say, it can be used only while the sap is in the wood, and after a few weeks' use has to be thrown away. It produces a beautiful sound and is worthy of inclusion in any band or orchestra. I myself intend to employ it soon in my band. The four musicians of Razz's Band had no idea at all of what they were playing; they improvised as they went along, but such was their innate sense of rhythm that they produced something which was very taking. From the small cafes of New Orleans they graduated to the St. Charles Hotel, and after a time to the Winter Garden, in New York, where they appeared, however, only a few days, the individual musicians being grabbed up by various orchestras in the city. Somehow in the passage of time Razz's Band got changed into 'Jazz Band,' and from this corruption arose the term 'jazz.'

"The Negro loves anything that is peculiar in music, and this 'jazzing' appeals to him strongly. It is accomplished in several ways. With the brass instruments we put in mutes and make a whirling motion with the tongue, at the same time blowing full pressure. With wind instruments we pinch the mouthpiece and blow hard. This produces the peculiar sound which you all know. To us it is not discordant, as we play the music as it is written, only that we accent strongly in this manner the notes which originally would be without accent. It is natural for us to do this; it is, indeed, a racial musical characteristic. I have to call a daily rehearsal of my band to prevent the musicians from adding to their music more than I wish them to. Whenever possible they all embroider their parts in order to produce new, peculiar sounds. Some of these effects are excellent and some are not, and I have to be continually on the lookout to cut out the results of my musicians' originality."

The news from Paris is so filled with weightier matters and the French papers are so much less loquacious than our Anglo-Saxon ones on the lighter sides of life that, until the lieutenant speaks, we haven't heard of the impression jazz has made on the French:

"I recall one incident in particular. From last February to last August I had been in the trenches, in command of my machine-gun squad. I had been through the terrific general attack in Champagne when General Gouraud annihilated the enemy by his strategy and finally put an end to their hopes of victory, and I had been through many a smaller engagement. I can tell you that music was one of the things furthest from my mind when one day, just before the Allied Conference in Paris, on August 18, Colonel Hayward came to me and said:

"'Lieutenant Europe, I want you to go back to your band and give a single concert in Paris.'

"I protested, telling him that I hadn't led the band since February, but he insisted. Well, I went back to my band, and with it I went to Paris. What was to be our only concert was in the Theatre des Champs-Elysees. Before we had played two numbers the audience went wild. We had conquered Paris. General Bliss and French high officers who had heard us insisted that we should stay in Paris, and there we stayed for eight weeks. Everywhere we gave a concert it was a riot, but the supreme moment came in the Tuileries Gardens when we gave a concert in conjunction with the greatest bands in the world, the British Grenadiers' Band, the band of the Garde Republicain, and the Royal Italian Band. My band, of course, could not compare with any of these, yet the crowd, and it was such a crowd as I never saw anywhere else in the world, deserted them for us. We played to 50,000 people at least, and, had we wished it, we might be playing yet.

"After the concert was over the leader of the band of the Garde Republicain came over and asked me for the score of one of the jazz compositions we had played. He said he wanted his band to play it. I gave it to him, and the next day he again came to see me. He explained that he couldn't seem to get the effects I got, and asked me to go to a rehearsal. I went with him. The great band played the composition superbly, but he was right; the jazz effects were missing. I took an instrument and showed him how it could be done, and he told me that his own musicians felt sure that my band had used special instruments. Indeed, some of them, afterward attending one of my rehearsals, did not believe what I had said until after they had examined the instruments used by my men."

It is the feeling of this musician, who, indeed, before the war supplied most of the music in New York dancing circles, that a higher plane in music may be attained by Negroes if they stick to their own form. He concludes:

"I have come back from France more firmly convinced than ever that Negroes should write Negro music. We have our own racial feeling and if we try to copy whites we will make bad copies. I noticed that the Morocco Negro bands played music which had an affinity to ours. One piece, *In Zanzibar,* I took for my band, and the white audiences seem to find it too discordant. I found it most sympathetic. We won France by playing music which was ours and not a pale imitation of others, and if we are to develop in America we must develop along our own lines. Our musicians do their best work when using Negro material. Will Marion Cook, William Tires, even Harry Burleigh and Coleridge-Taylor are not truly themselves in the music which expresses their race. [*sic*] Mr. Tires, for instance, writes charming waltzes; but the best of these have in them Negro influences. The music of our race springs from the soil, and this is true today with no other race, except possibly the Russians, and it is because of this that I and all my musicians have come to love Russian music. Indeed, as far as I am concerned, it is the only music I care for outside of Negro."

The Lieutenant then tells how he formed his band:

"When war broke out I enlisted as a private in Colonel Hayward's regiment, and I had just passed my officer's examination when the Colonel asked me to form a band. I told him that it would be impossible, as the Negro musicians of New York were paid too well to have them give up their jobs to go to war. However, Colonel Hayward raised $10,000 and told me to get the musicians wherever I could get them. The reed-players I got in Puerto Rico, the rest from all over the country. I had only one New York Negro in the band—my solo cornetist. These are the men who now compose the band, and they are all fighters as well as musicians, for all have seen service in the trenches."

15 Paul Robeson, Musician

DORIS EVANS MCGINTY AND WAYNE SHIRLEY

Born in Princeton, New Jersey, on April 9, 1898, Paul Robeson was the son of the Rev. William Robeson, who began his life in slavery. A true renaissance man, Paul Robeson made his mark as an athlete, an activist, and an actor as well as a singer. Following his graduation from nearby Somerville High School, where he excelled in sports, drama, singing, academics, and debating, Robeson was awarded a four-year academic scholarship to Rutgers University in 1915, becoming only the third black student in the school's history He was not only twice named to the All-American Football, Robeson was also a twelve-letter athlete, excelling in baseball, basketball, football, and track. He was recognized as a Phi Beta Kappa scholar, belonged to the Cap & Skull Honor Society, and graduated valedictorian of his class in 1919. Four years later he received a law degree from Columbia but left the law after a white secretary refused to take dictation from him.

At this point in his life Paul returned to his childhood love of drama and singing. He starred in Eugene O'Neill's All God's Chillun Got Wings *in 1924, followed by the lead in another racially themed O'Neill original,* Emperor Jones. *His eleven films included* Body and Soul, Jericho, *and* Proud Valley. *As McGinty and Shirley document in this essay, originally published in* Paul Robeson: Artist and Citizen, *Robeson's extensive performances included Negro spirituals, opera, and musical theater. His singing took Robeson around the world—from New York to Vienna, Prague, Budapest, Germany, Paris, Holland, London, and Moscow to Nairobi. In 1947, he was named by the House Committee on Un-American Activities, and the State Department denied him a passport until 1958. Events such as these, along with a negative public response, eventually led to the demise of his public career. Paul Robeson died on January 23, 1976, in Philadelphia, Pennsylvania, after living in seclusion for ten years.*

Of the several aspects of a life filled with outstanding achievements, none is so impressive as that of Paul Robeson, musician. In an early stage of his career as a singer, he performed a historical concert on April 19, 1925, at the Greenwich Village Theatre in New York with Lawrence Brown, an African American, as piano accompanist. The concert was historic not only because it garnered pivotal critical approval for Robeson, but also because it drew attention to the solo vocal program built exclusively around music reflecting black culture. Although Robeson had given a concert devoted to music by African Americans at Boston's Copley Plaza Hotel on November 2, 1924, the program was not exclusively vocal: a lengthy piano solo performance by his accompanist was included. Both concerts were well received. Critics writing for the *Boston Transcript* and the *Boston Post* were highly enthusiastic, but it was probably the overwhelming praise from the New York critics that brought wide attention to Robeson, the musician. He was acclaimed in the *New York Evening Post*, the *New York Times*, and the *New York News*: in the last, Edgar G. Brown called Robeson the "Embodiment of the New Negro and the next Caruso." This was the beginning of a lucrative and highly successful career as a concert singer.

From Robeson's point of view, embarking on a concert singing career was a leap into a new area of performance. By 1925, he was an established actor, with performances in New York and London to his credit. As a concert singer, however, he was practically a novice: prior to the Boston concert, which developed as a result of encouragement from his wife, Eslanda, and friends—especially Carl Van Vechten—Robeson had sung relatively little in public. Yet he accomplished the transition from theater to concert stage with apparent ease. His extraordinary vocal endowment was, of course, the major factor, but there were others. His experience on the dramatic stage, which included moments of singing, must have been helpful, and it is likely that his singular rapport with the music that he chose to sing was of great importance. He had a deep understanding of and great affection for the Negro spirituals and secular songs which he heard in church and community during his childhood, and he considered them integral to his being. The Greenwich Village Theatre audience overwhelmingly approved the experiment, and Robeson went on to repeat his triumph throughout the United States and in many other parts of the world. Lionized on both sides of the Atlantic, he sang to sold-out houses in the most eminent concert auditoriums such as Carnegie Hall in New York, the Royal Albert Hall in London, and Tchaikovsky Hall in Moscow. He was welcomed just as eagerly in African American churches—large and small—meeting halls of labor unions, and outdoor stadiums where his audiences sometimes numbered in the tens of thousands.[1] Robeson's contribution to rekindling interest in the spiritual, if judged solely by the number of persons who heard him sing, was enormous.

When Robeson sang Negro spirituals on his history-making programs, it was not the first time that the folk song had appeared in concert dress. The world had been awakened to the beauty and appeal of this music by the Fisk Jubilee Singers in their travels across the United States, England, and Europe in the 1870s. Setting out—with the purpose of aiding financially beleaguered Fisk University, the singers succeeded in raising over $150,000 for the school. In their performances the Fisk Jubilee Singers modified the folk songs which had been handed down by oral tradition from pre–Civil War days and created the tradition of the concert spiritual. European harmonies were added, and as a result some of the melodic inflections and rhythmic flexibility involved in the original performance practices were inhibited or eliminated. Moreover, the concert hall environment was less hospitable to the freedom and spontaneity that characterized the folk-style performance. The folk tradition did not die out, however, but continued to flourish in communities such as that in which Robeson spent his childhood. In the meantime, choral groups, including professional jubilee groups and choirs of historically black colleges and universities, performed in the concert tradition, often using arrangements supplied by African American composers.

In 1916, composer and baritone Harry T. Burleigh (1866–1949) published a version of the spiritual "Deep River" arranged for solo voice. Burleigh was the first recognized African American composer of art songs, the "high art" vocal compositions, mostly by European composers, that were used on programs of classical music. With "Deep River" Burleigh created a new format, sometimes known as the art song spiritual, and opened the door for the inclusion of the spiritual on vocal solo recitals. Several noted singers, including Marian Anderson and Roland Hayes and white singers John McCormack, Mary Jordan, and Oscar Seagle, soon began to include one or several Negro spirituals on their programs, although they continued the well-established custom of building their programs around German art songs and other standard European vocal literature and introducing non-standard songs in the final group. Against this backdrop, the pioneering aspect of Robeson's demonstration that the spiritual could be given a central place on the vocal recital designed for concertgoers accustomed to classical music can be viewed in its proper perspective.

The sixteen selections on the Greenwich Village Theatre program of April 19, 1925, included four spirituals arranged by Burleigh and eight arranged by Lawrence Brown, Robeson's friend and, for thirty-five years, his accompanist and vocal collaborator. Robeson used Brown's simple arrangements more often than any others, although Burleigh's "Deep River" and especially his "Go Down, Moses," both unpretentious arrangements, also came to be associated with Robeson's name. While he used many others, Robeson retained the original twelve spirituals in his repertory throughout his career, and he drew on them at dramatic moments such as when he sang "Go Down, Moses" ("Let my people go") during the turmoil of the Peekskill concert. In the last concert that he gave in the United States, held at Mother A.M.E. Zion Church in Harlem, where his brother Ben was pastor, Robeson concluded with a spiritual that was not in the original group but which he used often in his later career. After he announced that, with the partial restoring of his traveling privileges, his career had been reestablished and thanked the church, which he described as the place of his beginnings, he invited the audience to join him in singing "We Are Climbing Jacob's Ladder."

Even though he availed himself of concert arrangements of the spiritual, Robeson consciously emphasized folk elements in his performance, with more than a little assistance from Lawrence Brown, whose background, like that of Robeson, was saturated with the sounds of religious and secular African American folk music. Brown's participation with Robeson in call and response and occasional harmonizing in thirds—which arose spontaneously during one of their rehearsals—became a regular feature of their concerts, one which audiences enjoyed and came to expect. Robeson sometimes exercised a prerogative of folk song practice by adding verses or making changes in the words which underlined his struggle for liberation of the oppressed. For example, in "We Are Climbing Jacob's Ladder," the line "Soldiers of the cross" could become "Soldiers in the fight," or the line "Freedom, we must have" could appear in "No More Auction Block for Me."

It did not suit Robeson's aims to study voice extensively as would be expected of a concert artist devoted to classical music. However, in 1926, he worked with vocal coach Frantz Proschowskya and studied voice with Teresa Armitage, a high-school teacher, with an eye toward improving his vocal skills and learning to preserve his voice. When in the early 1930s he studied with Jerry Swinford, well-known vocal coach, we may conclude that his purpose was to extend his range as a musician as he expanded his repertoire, an expansion that will be described later in this essay. In 1934, Robeson clearly expressed his artistic aspirations: "I am not an artist in the sense in which they [music critics] want me to be an artist and of which they could approve. I have no desire to interpret the vocal genius of half a dozen cultures which are really alien cultures to me. I have a far more important task to perform."[2]

On the whole Robeson fared well at the hands of music critics who actually faced a challenge when writing about his concerts. Finding it difficult to review a non-traditional recital in the traditional manner, critics often relied upon descriptions of Robeson's stage presence, his dignity, his facial expressions, the affectionate delight he showed in his singing.

Almost unfailingly, they were moved by the power of the voice. Robeson's voice, marked by the deep resonance in the lower register that is associated with the true bass voice (although Robeson's was more frequently designated a bass-baritone), sent critics scrambling for adjectives like "mellow," "velvety," "luscious," "smooth," and "rich," and phrases such as "a voice in which deep bells ring," and "deep and rolling bass." Glenn Dillard Gunn of the *Chicago Herald Examiner* pronounced Robeson's voice "one of the most beautiful in the world" (February 1, 1926). Above all, critics responded to an undeniable authenticity in Robeson's rendition of the African American spiritual.

It was inevitable that music journalists would compare Robeson with Roland Hayes, the African American singer who had been acclaimed for his masterful singing of spirituals. At first, critics tended, generally, to prefer the Robeson style, pointing out his naturalness and expressing pleasure in the absence of the effects of formal training. Some, however, found the Robeson recitals lacking in artistry. And while, more often than not, critics expressed surprise that programs of spirituals could provide sufficient variety to sustain interest, a few writers were critical of what they conceived of as monotony in his programs. Appearances on programs with other musicians—violinist Wolfi, pianists Vitya Vronsky, Ania Dorfman, and Solomon, thereminist Clara Rockmore, the Brahms [string] Quartette, to name a few—might have served to answer the criticism of monotony. On one of the occasions when Robeson sang a concert using orchestral accompaniment for the spirituals instead of the piano, a change which might have been thought to create variety, another objection was raised, for critics found his Paris concert with Pierre Monteaux and orchestra somewhat artificial.

From time to time, reviews, even though laudatory, were somewhat condescending in tone, introducing such stereotypical concepts as the naiveté or childlike enthusiasm of the colored race. Even the frequent mentions of Robeson's naturalness, though apparently accurate when applied to Robeson's stage presence, smacked a bit of the oft-repeated notion that African Americans achieved artistic success not through the application of intellect or industry but only as a result of God-given talent.

The addition to his programs of art songs and operatic selections typical of the classical vocal recital seemed to be an obvious next step for Robeson, if he was to grow as a musician, let alone answer his critics. But, as if to emphasize his conviction regarding the value of and the contribution made by the music of black culture, he continued for five years to devote entire programs to Negro spirituals and secular folk songs. He was disappointed that audiences in some African American communities seemed to prefer programs of classical European content; yet he was not deterred from his mission. He stated it thus: "Now, if I can teach my audiences who know almost nothing about the Negro, to know him through my songs and through my roles . . . then I will feel that I am an artist, and that I am using my art for myself, for my race, and for the world."[3] Few, if any, other musicians of Paul Robeson's stature have been able to conduct a career in which the artist's philosophy and mission were reflected so clearly in the content of the music performed.

From 1929 onward, Robeson began to inject more frequent and lengthier comments between songs, discussing the meanings of the spirituals and highlighting their relationship to the universal sufferings of mankind. He also began to incorporate recitations from his famous roles in the theater. By the 1930s, the Negro spiritual was no longer the driving factor in his performances. In fact, neither of the two pieces now most closely associated with Robeson—"Ol' Man River" and *Ballad for Americans*—is a spiritual. We shall come back to these two at the end; first we shall take a general look at Robeson's repertory other than the spirituals.

For most of us the knowledge of Robeson's singing, and of his repertory, comes through his recordings. The late recordings, representing concert appearances, are accurate reflections of his repertory of the time. But we should look at the earlier Robeson discography with a certain skepticism. Concert audiences love to hear what a singer does best: thus the repertory of a touring singer changes slowly, and many works remain on the program from season to season. But recordings require constant new repertory: there's no point in rerecording something already on disc. Thus recordings often represent material gotten up for the session and then discarded. For Robeson this is particularly true for the pre-1940 recordings made for the English company Gramophone. Later recordings, done first for Columbia Records and then for a variety of labels including Robeson's own company Othello Records, tend to represent repertory he was committed to.

Among the Gramophone recordings, those with Lawrence Brown represent material Robeson did in concert; those with orchestra are more likely to be material gotten up for recording only. Some of the just-for-recording repertory is fairly routine: beloved hymns ("Nearer, My God, to Thee") and sentimental favorites ("Trees"). Other repertory is more puzzling to those seeking to understand Robeson. This is especially true of the fairly large number of Dear-Old-Southland numbers he recorded—"Dear Old Southland" itself; "Carry Me Back to Green Pastures," even "That's Why Darkies Were Born." Robeson sings these songs stunningly, but they were not part of his active repertory.

Nor, save for an occasional "St. Louis Blues," were the various blues and jazz numbers he recorded. These recordings are usually seen in the light of Count Basie's statement, "It certainly is an honor to be working with Mr. Robeson, but the man certainly can't sing the blues." Judged by less exacting standards, many of them are worth listening to: certainly they can hold their own against present-day Classical Crossover recordings.

Robeson's film songs are another example of special repertoire. One song Robeson learned for a film—Mendelssohn's "Lord God of Abraham," sung in *Proud Valley*—became a staple of his repertory; but of songs written especially for films, only "I Still Suits Me," written for the film version of *Show Boat*, was much performed by Robeson. Other film songs were duly released on recording—and therefore remain audible to this day—but were not sung by Robeson in concert. Thus for many years we could hear Robeson singing the faintly hilarious "Killing Song" from *Sanders of the River*, but not "O Isis and Osiris."[4]

As we have seen, Robeson's concert programs of the 1920s often contained one set described as "Negro folk-songs." This group would contain secular folk songs—notably "Water Boy"; it would often contain also one or two songs by the pre–World War I generation of African American composers. Robeson continued his loyalty to these composers through the 1930s, regularly performing such songs as J. Rosamond Johnson's "Li'l Gal" and Will Marion Cook's "Down de Lovah's Lane." Later Robeson assayed an occasional song in "Li'l Gal" style by a white composer: Clutsam's "Ma Curly-Headed Baby" remained in Robeson's repertory to the end, and Lily Strickland's "Mah Lindy Lou" was sung fairly often in the 1930s. (Perhaps it was these songs that caused Gramophone to suggest the Dear-Old-Southland numbers: if he sang J. Rosamond Johnson's "Dis Little Pickaninny's Gone to Sleep," why shouldn't he sing "Got the South in My Soul"?)

Late in 1930 Robeson began expanding his concert repertory beyond the spirituals and black secular numbers. In 1931 this expansion took the form of a direct onslaught on the central repertory of the classic Lieder singer: his 1931 programs often started with a group consisting of Beethoven's "Die Ehre Gottes aus der Natur," "O Isis und Osiris" from *The Magic Flute*, "Passing By" by Edward Purcell, and a Schumann song—sometimes "Die beiden Grenadiere," sometimes "Ich grolle nicht." (A second set would lead, by way of two Russian songs, to Robeson's black repertory, usually starting with "Water Boy.")

"Die Ehre Gottes" and "O Isis und Osiris" continue appearing, though not in tandem, on those recitals for which Robeson wanted a majestic opening number, until the early 1940s, when they are replaced by "Lord God of Abraham." But after 1931 he avoided performing an entire group weighted toward the Germanic repertory. During the early 1930s English recital songs—Roger Quilter's "Now Sleeps the Crimson Petal," John Ireland's "Sea Fever"—occasionally took up the slack. But by the late 1930s he tended, for concerts requiring a group from the standard concert-singer repertory, to do a Russian group, sometimes all-Moussorgsky. This allowed Robeson to sing in his beloved Russian: it also tantalized audiences with excerpts from *Boris Godunov*, causing many to wonder whether Robeson might take on the role on the operatic stage.

In 1934 Robeson began including a general folk-song group in his concerts. English audiences had long been accustomed to such a group; here the audience's expectation and Robeson's interest were one. Early folk-song groups are heavy on folk songs of the British islands—including Cecil Sharp's arrangement of "Oh No, John," which Robeson continued to program throughout his career. In later years he added folk songs of other lands. As his political commitment became stronger these songs were increasingly chosen from radical sources: "Chee Lai," "The Peat-Bog Soldiers." Along with these came more militant African American folk songs—songs from Lawrence Gellert's classic 1936 collection *Negro Songs of Protest* and militant early spirituals such as "No More Auction Block for Me."

In the early 1940s, with the release of his first song album for Columbia Records (his first Columbia album had been *Othello*), Robeson found a phrase for the music he was most interested in performing—*Songs of Free Men*. He explained in the notes to the album:

> The particular songs in this album have . . . folk quality and show in no uncertain way the common humanity of man. Beyond this, they issue from the present common struggle for a decent world, a struggle, in which the artist must also play his part.
>
> These songs are a very important part of my concert programs, expressing much of what I deeply feel and believe.

In fact the album included both folk songs—"The Four Insurgent Generals"; "The Peat-Bog Soldiers"—and songs in folk and popular styles such as Earl Robinson's "Joe Hill" and Marc Blitzstein's "The Purest Kind of a Guy." For the remainder of Robeson's career the "Songs of Free Men" were to be as important as the spirituals: this repertory is, finally, as important to understanding Robeson as musician as are the spirituals.

We rightly see this repertory in terms of Robeson the activist, but it also revitalized him as a musician. And his championing of the repertoire was finally important for the repertoire itself: In a world where status was granted to a piece by its appearance on concert programs, it was more significant that Robeson sang "The House I Live In" than that Sinatra sang it; it was the fact that Robeson sang "Joe Hill" that made it the well-known song it is today.

Suddenly, in mid-1935, "Ol' Man River," which had shown up on almost every Robeson program for several years previous, disappeared from his printed programs. It had not dropped out of Robeson's repertory, it had just become so inevitable as an encore that it lost its place on the regular program. (Its place as a formal ender was taken by "Joshua" or—for lighter programs—"Shortnin' Bread.")

It was Robeson's voice that suggested "Ol' Man River" to Jerome Kern and Oscar Hammerstein II, and Robeson's association with the song is so thorough that we must be reminded from time to time that he was not the first person to sing the song. The part of Joe, who sings "Ol' Man River," was sung in the original (1927) production of *Show Boat* by Julius ("Jules") Bledsoe. Robeson first sang the role in the 1928 London production. "Ol' Man River" first appeared on his concert programs in 1931; by then he had already recorded it three times.

In later life Robeson found his association with "Ol' Man River" something of a problem: how could he preach the need for action when people would not go home until he had sung this song, with its outer message of human powerlessness? Robeson, who was no stranger to the changing of words (he recorded Foster's "Old Black Joe" as "Poor Old Joe"; in his Carnegie Hall recording of Othello's final monologue "the circumcisèd dog" becomes "the damnèd heathen dog") solved this problem by altering the lyrics to make it a song of determination:

> But I keeps laughin'
> Instead of cryin';
> I must keep fightin'
> Until I'm dyin'...

This was a necessary change for Robeson (the alternative was to refuse to sing "Ol' Man River" at all), though it makes for a much more negative version of the song: the river, despite all that determination, just keeps rolling along. The original "Ol' Man River," in fact, carries the powerful subtext that it is Joe, as well as the river, that endures, but Robeson hoped not to endure but to prevail.

If Robeson reshaped one of the two pieces he is most identified with, he was part of the initial shaping of the other. When Earl Robinson rewrote his *Ballad of Uncle Sam* (originally written for a Federal Theater Project revue), for radio as *Ballad for Americans*, he did it in collaboration with Robeson, who made sure that the solos were in keys that could be sung in his person-to-person voice, without the mechanics of "classical" voice-projection, which the microphone had made unnecessary. During 1939–1940 the *Ballad for Americans* swept through America: it was even chosen to be the principal musical work at the 1940 Republican National Convention. (The Republicans hoped for Robeson, but he was elsewhere in New York that night, performing the *Ballad for Americans* in a program that also included the premiere of William Grant Still's *And They Lynched Him on a Tree*.[5]) Through the recording made in 1940 with the People's Chorus it continues to preach its doctrine that America was all Americans.

The *Ballad for Americans* suggests that you need not be of a particular ethnic group to speak for America. But in fact what you had to be to speak for America through *Ballad for Americans* was Paul Robeson. Other well-known baritones essayed the piece (they were wise enough not to record it), but it was only Robeson, who had earlier renounced the career of a strictly classical recital singer, who could do this piece without the artificiality that the classical baritone must impose on his material. Robeson could wear the mantle of classical baritone when he chose—many of us would give a good deal for a record of Robeson singing "Die Ehre Gottes aus der Natur," or for an adequate recording of "Lord God of Abraham." But to speak for all America it required someone who could shed the distancing of the concert artist and summon up instead—both in speech and in song—a seemingly casual but profound personal rapport with the listener—not a recitalist but a *mensch*. Many people will find some other aspect of Robeson's musical activity of more significance than *Ballad for Americans*, yet it does mark a moment when he did in fact do what he always hoped to do: speak for all America.

Notes

1. In the 1940s, at the peak of his career, Robeson drew crowds of 20,000 at Lewisohn Stadium in New York (1943 concert); 30,000 at the Hollywood Bowl; 160,000 at Grant Park in Chicago; and 22,000 at a Watergate Sunset Series concert in Washington, D.C. See Gloria Francis Dunn, "Paul Robeson's Career as a Musician: Implications for Music Education" (Ph.D. Dissertation, University of Michigan, 1987), 92. In 1952, during the time that Robeson's passport was denied to him, 30,000 Canadians heard him at Peace Arch Park on the border between British Columbia and the State of Washington. See Paul Robeson, *Here I Stand* (Boston: Beacon Press, 1971), 55.
2. *Chicago Defender*, May 19, 1934, 10.
3. Eslanda Goode Robeson, *Paul Robeson, Negro* (New York: Harper & Brothers, 1930), 97.
4. In 1992 Paul Robeson, Jr., produced a CD (Omega Classics OCD 3007) containing, with other material, a private recording of "O Isis und Osiris," made in the 1950s.
5. Robeson was not involved in *And They Lynched Him on a Tree*, although he did offer to coach the hapless narrator.

16 Conflict and Resolution in the Life of Thomas Andrew Dorsey

MICHAEL W. HARRIS

The development, dissemination, and popularization of twentieth-century African American gospel music are inextricably linked with one-time blues singer Thomas A. Dorsey. Much has been made of Dorsey's early career (mid- to late-1920s) as a blues pianist with Gertrude "Ma" Rainey and his commercially successful partnership with Tampa Red. But Dorsey's most important work comes during the 1930s when he championed gospel, a new form of religious music. Ethnomusicologist and historian Michael Harris's book The Rise of Gospel Blues—The Music of Thomas Andrew Dorsey in the Urban Church *not only details Dorsey's life but also relates the development of the early years of modern gospel music.*

In this essay, taken from the anthology We'll Understand It By and By, *Harris argues that Dorsey's marriage of blues and sacred music represents a unique synthesis that eventually persuaded even the most old-line churches that this hybrid deserved a place in their Sunday worship service. Harris focuses on the period in the late 1920s when modern gospel music was developing, but he also delves into Dorsey's earlier life to understand how a series of tensions—between the secular and sacred worlds, the duality of African American identity, lower- and middle-class values, and the rural South and the urban North—helped to shape his worldview and this new music.*

A biographical sketch of a person serves little purpose if it consists only of a narrative of life events. The life of Thomas Andrew Dorsey, the individual most often associated with the rise of gospel blues in Black Protestant churches during the early 1930s, is no exception to this rule. From his early years in rural Georgia and then Atlanta, to his career as a blues musician in Chicago, and finally to his troublesome metamorphosis into a gospel songwriter, Dorsey looms larger than the aggregate of incidents in his life. This essay portrays both the Dorsey who progresses from event to event and the Dorsey who is greater than the sum of those events. The latter Dorsey typifies African American society at various points in its history between the 1870s when post-Emancipation Black culture began to crystallize and the 1930s when gospel blues emerged in Protestant Black churches.

This essay is mosaic in structure. Its design consists of carefully selected events that show how Dorsey became the so-called father of gospel blues. These events have been gathered into thematic images that, when viewed as a whole or pieced together, illustrate how Dorsey did not evolve in some easily perceived line, the end of which was gospel blues. Instead, they show that Dorsey was shaped by three distinct periods of personal development, the last of which yielded the Dorsey who wrote gospel blues. The three periods can be thought of as exposure, conflict, and resolution.

There are two conflictive concepts that help make the link between these periods more obvious than Dorsey as the common subject. These concepts are overarching, social and cultural in their effect. The first of these is the notion of African American duality, as described by W. E. B. Du Bois—the quest for both racial and national identities, "two strivings in one dark body" (Du Bois [1903] 1961, 17). This idea of African American duality comprises an integral part of individuals' lives. As Dorsey evolved from his period of exposure through the other periods, he never escaped this struggle of twoness; he merely became aware of it again and again in the changing context of each period. In more ways than not, this same process mirrored the development of African American society as a whole, which is why Dorsey's life may be considered so representative of that whole.

The second conflictive concept is the idea of the sacred and secular in his life. In the African American society in which Dorsey evolved, the sacred and secular were not separated into distinct spheres, each with its own recognizable ethos. The sacred and secular instead seemed almost to be opportunistic intrusions. They appeared and reappeared, most often disguised as music—sometimes even as the same music.

The Thomas A. Dorsey who emerged in the 1930s as one of the principal figures in the gospel song movement was both an individual of personal dimensions and an individual of African American dimensions. His gospels are unmistakably renderings of the two. In essence, this essay will argue how the man became his music and, to the extent that African Americanness can be individualized, how Dorsey's gospels might be said to have become the man.

The period of exposure begins with Dorsey's childhood in Villa Rica, Georgia, a town about thirty miles west of Atlanta. There, Dorsey heard two contrasting types of sacred music. The first of these was something he called *moaning*. He remembers hearing his mother, father, and old people singing this style of music on the porch at night or in church: "I've heard my mother and other folk get together, get around and get to talking and then start moaning." At church, Dorsey would hear the congregation sing a hymn or spiritual and "then they [would] moan it out." It was mysterious to him as a child how moaning evoked shouts: "There's something to it that nobody knows . . ." (Harris 1976).

The other style of sacred music to which young Dorsey was exposed was known as shape-note singing. In this music, different degrees of the scale correspond to a specific shape; for example, the tonic, or first degree of the scale, *do,* is represented by a diamond note. Dorsey first heard this music at Mount Prospect Baptist Church, where his parents worshiped from time to time. Its presence there gives us a clue to the degree this music contrasted so greatly with moaning. Shape-note singing originated in New England in the early 1700s as part of a movement to improve singing in Puritan churches. Singing masters established singing schools to train illiterate people to read not only music but words, since students had to be able to read the texts of the songs too. By 1815, the singing teachers had migrated into the South. The most well known of these instructors was Ananias Davisson, whose tune book, the *Sacred Harp*, supplied the name of the movement by which it is known to this day. As

Between 1928 and 1932, when Thomas Dorsey turned exclusively to sacred music, Tampa Red and Georgia Tom (Dorsey) recorded dozens of blues sides for the Vocalion Record Company.

Credit: Advertisement from the collection of Kip Lornell.

shape-note singing had been an instrument of literacy in early New England, so it was in Villa Rica among unschooled, former slaves in the last quarter of the nineteenth century. Dorsey's uncle, Corrie Hindsman, was the person who brought the music to the church; he was also the teacher at the local Black school.

Dorsey found this music fascinating. The congregation up to that time had mostly sung spirituals spontaneously—moaning being one example: "the people sang from their very hearts." This new music, however, had a different sound to it: "The shape of the note gave you the tune and the pitch. And I mean every man and every woman knew their place. It was beautiful singing. You wouldn't hear any better singing now than those folks did in those days" (Harris 1976).

The difference between soulful and book-learned music is more than the music itself: it is a difference of cultures. In one, music is a spontaneous creation—a heartfelt act—first from the individual then shared by the community. In the other, it is a communal act of learning first to read, then to sing, and then, perhaps, to feel. Its origins reach into the Puritan experience and a need to rein in expressive spirituality. The other extends back to slavery and a compelling desire for both personal and group expression. That we find both of these disparate forms present in the life of young Thomas Andrew Dorsey attests to the twoness on which this first period is so precariously balanced. African Americans in the post-Emancipation period often faced choosing between indigenous and exogenous—virtually mutually exclusive—forms of expression. To choose the former meant to align oneself with the still-vibrant and appealing slave culture and its provision for communal inspiration. It also meant not assimilating into the dominant European American culture in which African American forms of expression—especially those rooted in enslavement—were profoundly alien. To choose one meant to forsake the other, except in Dorsey's childhood setting. That the antithetical could co-reside there is a testament to a breadth of cultural exposure in Dorsey's youth that sets him apart from much of rural southern Black American culture of the time. As well, this cross-cultural awareness would mark his approach to music making throughout his life.

Religion came to Dorsey in a kind of bifurcated unity as well, except it did not imply the cross-cultural twoness Du Bois wrote about. Instead, it concerned a polarity of feelings about the place of religion in one's life. On one end is an intensely private and deeply pietistic experience; this was his mother's, Etta Plant Dorsey. Writing about the role of motherhood in the formation of religious values in a child, Dorsey makes clear his belief that maternal and religious nurturing are one: "Mother in her office holds the key of the soul, and she it is who stamps the coin of character and makes the being, who would be a savage but for her gentle cares, a Christian man" (Dorsey 1935, 59–60). Dorsey's memories of his mother's religious life make it clear that he had her in mind when he wrote this passage. Etta ran the family Bible readings and devotionals. She made it a point to feed hobos and others in need who passed by their home. Taken together, these almost inconsequential acts bespeak Etta's deep commitment to piety and to being a model of religious devotion in her family.

On the other end of the polarity stood his father's religious experience. As one of the first generation of children of former slaves and as a graduate of Atlanta Baptist College (later Morehouse College) with a Bachelor of Divinity degree, Thomas Madison Dorsey was poised to continue down this path as one of a select group of educated Blacks in the post-Emancipation period. Things seemed to work differently for him, however. For example, he never pastored a church. He spent most of his career as a guest—sometimes even itinerant—preacher: "He was known by his preaching. He was kind of an itinerant preacher. He didn't want to pastor. . . . I don't think he wanted a church. He was known all over" (Harris 1976).

The preponderance of Thomas Madison's preaching as opposed to pastoring provided an image of religion for the young Dorsey that contrasted sharply with his mother's. One of Dorsey's most poignant memories of the impact of his father's religion concerns the way he, as a four- or five-year-old, would imitate his father's preaching: "I had a church under our front porch. The porch was high and under there was my church. [My mother and father] had bought me some kind of little cane; my father had a cane too. And [I'd] go down under the house and hang my cane up and then I'd start talking to what would be my audience as if they were there. [I'd] go in and I'd hang my cane up just like he'd go in and hang his cane up" (Harris 1976). Dorsey's mimicry even included props, a sure sign of the degree to which this kind of religious behavior, in the form of pulpitry, deeply impressed him.

So stark is the disparity between these polar-opposite images that it is hard to conceive of religion to young Dorsey as being something other than a dualized entity. The meldramatics of a cane-wielding pulpiteer and the quiet piety of a gentle believer, even if they were not antithetical in young Dorsey's mind, surely supplied him with a broad range of religious sensibilities. That he acted out the former and passively "drank in" the latter would seem to indicate how he resolved whatever conflicts he saw between them. Dorsey's acceptance of polar-opposite religious attitudes, however, would not last much beyond his childhood.

Unlike religion, the sacred and secular emerge during this period with less of the conflictive character they would have in Dorsey's later years. Sacred and secular, however, are abstractions; hence, Dorsey never recalls being aware of a sacred–secular continuum in his early years. His account of his Uncle Phil's (his mother's brother) blues guitar playing can be construed, however, as his introduction to the secular dimension of African American culture. Dorsey clearly discerned a difference, particularly with respect to the individual connected to this music. Phil Plant was not the most wholesome of Dorsey's relatives. Often he was gone, roaming about mostly as a hobo. When he stayed in Villa Rica, he engaged heavily in the bootlegging business. In fact, he would enlist his young nephew to deliver the illegal liquor to his customers. Dorsey recalls well his uncle playing. "He could really play it [the guitar]" (Harris 1976). More significantly, he remembers his uncle's popularity from being a good blues guitarist: "He was king 'round up in there" (Harris 1976). Just the setting of his uncle's performance would cause little Dorsey to associate this music—indeed, the guitar itself—with something opposite from the church settings of the other musical forms he heard. The unpredictability of his Uncle Phil's presence, the illicitness of his booze, the twanging of his guitar, and perhaps the not too savory character of his fans combined to make his uncle's music the opposite of the moaning and the shape-note singing Dorsey was accustomed to. No label was necessary.

More so than in his period of exposure, Dorsey's life during the second period—conflict—was affected by larger societal forces. Villa Rica was an isolated rural community in which the Dorseys were part of the Black elite class because Thomas Madison Dorsey was a preacher and a part-time schoolteacher. Even though neither of these careers was lucrative, Thomas Madison Dorsey still enjoyed an amount of community prestige that carried over to his family. Just being "the pastor's son," Dorsey recalls, caused people to "make over" him (Harris 1976).

This pleasant, insulated world was ruptured by some financial setbacks. In 1903, Dorsey's mother was forced to mortgage some of her land in order to pay for farming expenses. Borrowing against one's property in order to finance the coming crops was quite risky in the last decades of the nineteenth century, but it was even more since cotton and other staple commodity prices in the region had dropped precipitously. Thus, even though figures in the county land and tax records show that the actual aggregate value of Etta's land increased between 1903 and 1907, Thomas Madison Dorsey was forced to become a sharecropper for a white farmer. Even this arrangement only brought the family's income to subsistence level: "the land would not yield anything but peas and sweet potatoes," mostly for family consumption. The marketable crop. cotton, equaled yearly "just about one wagon load" (Dorsey 1961, 10). This development forced the Dorseys, along with thousands of other rural African Americans, to give up farming and to seek a better opportunity in the city. In 1908, the Dorsey family moved to Atlanta.

Contrary to their expectations, the Dorseys soon discovered that living in Atlanta actually brought about not only a further decline in their financial fortunes but a concomitant loss in their social prestige as well. Indeed, it is this sudden disorientation of his family in an urban environment that brought Dorsey face to face with many of the forces for change in African American culture and, therefore, into conflict with much of the world as he had known it up to then. Right away Thomas and Etta had to make drastic changes. Preaching became at most a sideline for Thomas. For the years 1909 through 1915, Thomas was listed in the *Atlanta City Directory* either as a porter or a laborer. Etta, who had never worked after she was married, became, according to the *Directory*, a laundress. Dorsey remembers that she worked, "taking in washing and ironing" (*Atlanta City Directory* 1909–15, 880, 716, 708, 674, 747, 823, 832).

For Dorsey the move was profoundly shocking. The family's first Christmas celebration in Atlanta almost failed to take place because Etta was sick and Thomas was only intermittently employed. The family became so desperate for food that Thomas was forced to sell the milk cow, Lily. Dorsey, who had responsibility to take care of Lily and had even walked her from Villa Rica to Atlanta, was given the task of driving her to the slaughter house: "There I saw her killed. I never got over that" (Harris 1976; Dorsey 1961, 14). Such incidents paled in significance when Dorsey began to encounter social ostracism from his schoolmates. He was barefooted, which meant that he "was looked upon as one of the common class" (Dorsey 1961). Contrary to his days in the country where he was "made over" because he was the pastor's son, he now began to confront a virtual caste system among Atlanta Blacks: "During that time when we were about the age of ten, the boys and girls would have their birthday parties. They didn't invite me, even though they knew me very well. I guess I was not good enough, they thought, to mingle with their friends. I used to stand outside and look through the windows" (Dorsey 1961). Dorsey's immediate response to such outright rejection was to quit school. And from this time on (he was approximately eleven years old), he never had any more formal education. With his family in abject poverty and regarded as "common" people. Dorsey now felt the need to earn money and to gain self-esteem. It was the pursuit of these two ends that brought him into Atlanta's music world.

If there was any microcosm of Black America during the first decades of the twentieth century, it was Atlanta. It had its upper economic classes and its intellectual elites living in the neighborhood surrounding Morehouse, Atlanta University, Spelman, and other Black institutions of higher education. It also had its poor and uneducated classes. The sizes of the latter groups so exceeded the former that W. E. B. Du Bois worried that "the increase of the race" would come from "the hovels of the alleys" instead of the "better class homes" (Du Bois 1902, 1).

Atlanta's Black music world mirrored this larger society. Moreover, these sharp class divisions brought out the inherent conflicts in the music and religion to which Dorsey was exposed in his early life. Dorsey was first introduced to music in the 81 Theater, a nickelodeon movie house in which he was a "butch boy" selling soft drinks and popcorn during intermissions. The pianist who accompanied the film, Ed Butler, taught him a few songs on an informal basis. The movie theater can be thought of as the center point of the Atlanta music world, a place where all Black classes could converge. The presence of racial segregation and the novelty of film entertainment together guaranteed that Blacks would ignore social barriers to attend the 81 Theater. Dorsey's first exposure to the piano thus was relatively uneventful, in that while he could address one of his twin personal pursuits—the need for money—he was in no way confronting the social divisiveness of the community.

This was not to be the case when he ventured into other domains of the Atlanta Black music world, especially when he seemed so desirous of personal prestige. Sensing that formal lessons would help his cause, Dorsey began taking piano from a Mrs. Graves, who had a music studio near Morehouse and who was affiliated with the college. There he learned music in a way totally different from his sporadic sessions with Butler: he had to learn to read, and he had to learn piano technique, "how to use your fingers" (Harris 1976). This kind of fingering technique, required for Western European classical music, was strange to a young boy accustomed to learning by rote. Even more strange, however, was the westside environment into which he walked in order to visit Mrs. Graves's studio. Here was Dorsey's indoctrination into Atlanta's Black upper-class tastes, ones that had little tolerance for the more indigenous ways of Blacks on his side of town. This encounter with musical literacy should have been the analogue of the shape-note singing he heard as a child. But Dorsey was not as impressed, mostly because the rote playing he had been exposed to at the 81 Theater seemed more directly to serve his purposes: "she wasn't a jazz musician. She taught around Morehouse. The music most the folk were playing was by ear" (Harris 1976).*

This reordering of Dorsey's tastes continued as he more aggressively sought personal prestige. He quit taking piano from Mrs. Graves—"I knew about as much as I needed to know"—and began to learn the movie pianist's art in earnest. His training with Mrs. Graves did help in one aspect of picture-show accompaniment: he could read and, in a quite rudimentary sense, write music. His notational skills were useful because the theater at times booked live performances, during which the pianist would not only have to play original songs written by the entertainers but at times would have to make arrangements of music. Dorsey steadily grew into this playing, so much so that Ed Butler allowed him to substitute for him. But Butler's position was too lucrative for him to give Dorsey any more than sporadic opportunities to play. After a little over a year, Dorsey realized that he was learning a lot but not gaining a reputation or professional advancement. "I didn't have a professional job and I wasn't called professional. You see a professional, you got to be doing something up there that will at least advertise the profession. I could do all of this, but you've got to have a place to do it and you've got to have somebody to hear it. [I] could read the music" (Harris 1976).

His disillusionment with the theater pianist's world, along with his growing need for self-importance, led him to make a sharp turn toward the most exotic of Atlanta's Black music settings: bordellos and rent parties. Opportunities to perform at these sites were gained only by one's reputation; and, of course, Dorsey wanted to build a good reputation, at almost any cost. There was one aspect of making a name in these places that directly affected Dorsey's

---

*Dorsey uses the word *jazz* here in a figurative sense. He probably meant blues or popular music, since he would readily admit that he did not even know the word *jazz* (or *jass*) until he moved to Chicago.

playing style: both places were under constant threat of "the law." The bordello housed prostitution and sold bootleg liquor (Atlanta was "dry" at that time): the rent party could get too noisy, and illegal alcohol flowed there, too. Thus the possibility of arrest was imminent:

> Down there in Atlanta, it's warm weather most of the time. You had to throw the windows open. You could hear the piano playing a block away almost, and when the folk get in there and they get noisy, the neighbor called the law and the law come in there. Sometimes they didn't bother anybody: see what's going on. But if it was one of those places, you know, where they handle bootleg liquor, anytime they'd come, they'd pull around the wagon down there and run them in. (Harris 1976)

For Dorsey to achieve notoriety in these settings, therefore, he had to become quite pragmatic in his approach to playing. Dorsey perfected a blues style that was soft, so that the piano did not disturb the peace; melodic, so that the listener could hum or sing along; and intensely rhythmic, through a liberal use of syncopation, so that his music could be danced to easily. No other player seems to have mastered this combination of stylistic elements to the degree that Dorsey did. His party blues so carefully balanced the seemingly competing ends of being utilitarian and aesthetically pleasing that he was considered the "No. 1" party pianist in Atlanta by 1915 or 1916: "they liked my style. Some of the fellows, you know, bump, beat, you know, they played loud and folk get loud and [somebody] called the law. But I played soft and easy; you could drag it out and hug the woman at the same time. Let the lights down low and they'd have to give attention to hear the piano" (Harris 1976).

Ironically, once Dorsey achieved his long-sought success, he simultaneously arrived at a full inversion of the music preferences he had cultivated from his early years. The shape-note singing he had once listened to in awe, with its four-part harmony and strange contrast with moaning, he now rejected because of his formal piano training and the westside Atlanta milieu in which he received it. The tawdriness of Uncle Phil's blues guitar and the adulation of his listeners, fueled very likely by the alcohol little Dorsey had fetched for them, were no less present in the brothels and sweaty get-togethers attended by Dorsey's now admiring, slow-dragging listeners whose consumption of illegal liquor he musically guarded. This metamorphosis occurred in less than seven years, the years of transition from Dorsey's childhood to early adolescence. He was scarcely aware of these inversions or their scale, but they represented the prelude to his later conflicts. This fundamental change took place against the backdrop of the increasing social stratification of Black America and the effect of that on Dorsey's family. Which is the cause and which the effect are not readily ascertainable; their interrelatedness, however, is undeniable.

The first of these conflicts arose in 1921 in Chicago. Dorsey had moved there in 1916 in search of better professional opportunities and, as in Atlanta, a name for himself. He had little luck: his down-home, soft and easy blues found an audience only among recent migrants from the South like himself. He and that crowd congregated in small, out-of-the-way bars, far from the glittery nightclubs where established musicians were just beginning to thrill their listeners with the faster, up-tempo blues they called *jass*. The same intraracial social divisions that plagued Dorsey in Atlanta were present in no less virulent forms in Chicago, the bourgeois appeal and setting of jass being a typical example. Indeed, the major difference between the two social settings was that the lower economic groups in Chicago tended to be Southern migrants who had arrived after the first World War. When Dorsey saw his career advancement stymied by the condescension shown his blues, he became quite stressed. This plus the general disorientation associated with his move led to a period of depression and finally a nervous breakdown. In October 1920 he returned to Atlanta and spent the winter recuperating there.

This period of sickness set the stage for his first serious conflict. In Atlanta, his changes in tastes had concerned only music. Now religion became a factor, first through his mother's admonition that he needed to "serve the Lord, serve the Lord" (Harris 1977a). She had stood by somewhat helplessly as he, lured into Atlanta's music underworld, drifted farther away from the religious values she had taught him. Her cautioning, moreover, was more and more compromised by the financial support Dorsey provided the family—now four children—from his ever-mounting earnings as a party pianist. Now with her son in her care and his success an ever-distant memory, Etta once again to "stamp the coin of character," to shape him into a Christian as she had so roundly in his childhood (Harris 1977a; Dorsey 1935, 59).

Even with his mother's words ringing in his ears, Dorsey ventured back to Chicago the following summer eager to return to the blues world: "I was in the . . . blues business; I *wanted* to be. I [wasn't] a member of anybody's church—there, my father's, nobody's. Didn't want to be a member" (Harris 1977a). But at the invitation of his uncle Joshua, a Chicago druggist, Dorsey attended a session of the forty-first annual meeting of the National Baptist Convention that was meeting in the city between September 7 and 12. That night Dorsey's religious emotions were rekindled by the singing of "I Do Don't You?" by the well-known evangelist W. M. Nix: "My inner being was thrilled. My soul was a deluge of divine rapture; my emotions were aroused; my heart was inspired to become a great singer and worker in the Kingdom of the Lord—and impress people just as this great singer did that Sunday morning" (Dorsey 1941, 19–20).

Shortly after this meeting, Dorsey joined New Hope Baptist Church and began to work as its director of music. A year later he registered his first sacred composition, "If I Don't Get There," with the U.S. Copyright Office. This song appeared in the following edition of *Gospel Pearls* (published in 1921), the newest songbook of the Convention (published in 1921). Soon after, he wrote "We Will Meet Him in the Sweet By and By," which appeared in *The Baptist Standard Hymnal* in one of its early editions (Townsend 1924).

This flurry of religious activities was destined to end. Within months of joining New Hope, Dorsey quit to accept an offer to join Will Walker's group, the Whispering Syncopators. The promise of forty dollars every week compared to sporadic donations was more than enough to dampen his newly found religious fervor. But something lurked more deeply in his psyche to guarantee that his religious rededication would be short-lived. He had been persuaded to become religious not by the content of Nix's song, but by the fact that Nix could impress so many people through his singing. Dorsey's religious sensibility was awakened by a musical version of the pulpitry that had so deeply impressed him as a child, when he stood under the porch imitating his father's preaching. He was convicted by the idea of becoming a great singer, not by a need for new religious consciousness. Missing was the complement of such religious histrionics: deep religious devotion of the sort he had seen in his mother. With his quest for recognition obstructed by his quaint blues playing and his emotional state in the fragile first stages of recovery from his breakdown, Dorsey was in position to be swept away by almost anything that promised to unify two of his most powerful urgings. Once he became aware that such a unity was for now illusory—that his need for personal and professional self-esteem was as dead-ended in New Hope Baptist as it was in the second-class, migrant bars—he was fated to drop religion and begin the search elsewhere.

Ironically, Dorsey's choice of the Whispering Syncopators as his next professional step set the stage for the second conflict. That Dorsey was invited to travel with the band already indicates that he was setting his career path on a nontraditional blues trajectory. The Syncopators, one of the established bands, played jass, ragtime, vaudeville, and other popular styles in the clubs, theaters, and dance halls in Chicago and in other major cities in which Blacks owned these types of establishments and could afford to book traveling groups. This position indicates one other significant advancement for Dorsey: to be a member of a stage band, he had to have been accepted in the Musicians' Protective Union. Dorsey had tried in vain to join the Union. Just playing a few bar jobs, however, left him unqualified for membership. Now he belonged to the Union, and his salary at forty dollars per week exceeded the pay scale for theater musicians, who earned thirty to thirty-three dollars per week (*Chicago Defender* 1920; Dorsey 1961, 46).

Dorsey's sudden move into the popular music establishment obviously followed some attendant change in his performance habits. Earlier he had rejected "jass" because it was too demanding: "No, jazz is a new name on the scene. Your execution was a little faster. All the piano boys were trying to get those extra keyboard frizzles and nimbling in their fingers to make [their music] sound jassy. That's why I didn't bother much with it—took too much energy. You couldn't last an evening. Too much bamstomping. You bump, beat, be wore out" (Harris 1976, 1977a). Also, his listeners, mostly newcomers from the South, found jazz disconcerting; jazz was "pep or hot—blues was slow." "You say the name jazz in some folk['s] house, 'We don't want that; don't come in here with stuff, jazz'" (Harris 1976, 1977a).

As is usual in accounting for changes in Dorsey's career path, the answer to his switch from blatant dismissal to professional endorsement of jazz lies at least in part in developments outside of his life. The major trend prompting Dorsey to turn away from his older blues was the recording industry. Beginning in 1920 with Mamie Smith's recording of two blues songs for OKeh Record Company, blues—much like Dorsey—began to develop a split identity. Smith, a vaudeville Black singer, sang her blues in a vaudeville rather than a more down-home style. White musicians accompanied her. Her blues songs were, in essence, a creation of the white entertainment industry rather than the indigenous blues of African Americans. Even so, Black Americans, so eager for records of their music—even if the music was not genuine—bought Smith's records with pronounced enthusiasm: during the first month, over ten thousand copies were purchased. One music shop in Harlem sold over two thousand copies in the first two weeks following the record's release (Godrich and Dixon 1982, 641; Dixon and Godrich 1970, 7–8; Bradford 1965, 48–49, 118–19, 121, 123–24). Record promoters conflated the concepts of vaudeville blues and jazz by having Smith record her next disk singing "Harlem Blues" (actually recorded as "Crazy Blues"), the hit song from the blues musical *Made in Harlem*, with the accompaniment of her own group of Black musicians, Mamie Smith's Jazz Hounds (Bradford 1965, 119, 122).

Blues-jazz, jazz, vaudeville blues, whatever the terminology, became a new industry overnight. Smith made her second record on August 14, 1920, a little over a year before Dorsey attended the National Baptist Convention (Godrich and Dixon 1982, 641). Well before he had joined the Whispering Syncopators, then, Dorsey had good reason to begin "nimbling" his fingers: he was on his way to obsolescence because of jazz.

Even more telling about Dorsey's response to the newer popular Black music is the appearance of his first copyrighted blues, "If You Don't Believe I'm Leaving, You Can Count the Days I'm Gone," on October 9, 1920. For years Dorsey had played blues that he had composed or borrowed. The older blues style, being highly improvisatory and non-notated for most of its life, lent itself to a kind of public-domain, shared existence: "All blues, we didn't put them nowhere. Blues was blues. All the blues belong to you. What you gonna steal? Nothin' you could do with it if you steal it ... all blues sounded alike for a while anyway, so we never bothered about the other fellow" (Harris 1977a).

The success of Smith's records drastically altered this attitude toward collective ownership. Someone could become rich off of a communal song. Dorsey, enjoying one benefit from his aborted formal study of music, was able to claim ownership of his songs and, for a fee, help others do the same for theirs because he could write music. By the end of 1923, he had copyrighted seven songs. As clearly as he had switched to commercialized performance practices of blues, he had as forthrightly adopted its notational conventions.

Dorsey had no reason to feel that he had made a wrong turn. By the end of 1923 he had become one of the major blues artists in the publishing and recording industries. The well-known Jack Mills music publishers put out a fox-trot arrangement of his "I Just Want a Daddy I Can Call My Own." Monette Moore, one of the leading vaudeville blues singers, recorded the song that same year. Undoubtedly his greatest popular success of that year came with Joe "King" Oliver's recording of "Riverside Blues" (Godrich and Dixon 1982, 515; Rust 1962, 467).

On the surface, such marked achievement in less than two years would indicate that this period of his life could hardly be characterized as one of conflict. But to make this steep ascent in such a short time, Dorsey sidestepped inner religious turmoil, pushed aside the blues style he preferred, and, perhaps the greatest sacrilege, took his spontaneous music and froze it in a notation not even designed to capture much of the blues player's art. If Dorsey's ego lay at the root of his drive. Dorsey also was prompted, as he had been earlier in Atlanta, by a sea of social change swirling around him. Migration, the rise of Black participation in vaudeville, the advent of the phonograph, the ever-sharpening lines between classes of African Americans all served as a tide that at some times could bring him rewards and at others could erode his most deeply held allegiances. At the end of this period of conflict Dorsey confronted blues once again, initially with devastating effects on his career, but it was the first of the resolutions he needed to make between competing musics.

Dorsey's confrontation with blues was already in the making in the beginning of 1923 as he was enjoying the first fruits of his success because of Bessie Smith's first recordings from Columbia Records. Smith sang in the older blues style instead of the vaudeville style prevalent in the recording industry. The purpose behind making her records was not to revert to the old style. Rather, it was a symptom of the increased competition among record companies to find new voices for the growing market. Indeed, Smith had been rejected by OKeh Records, the very company for which Mamie Smith had recorded. The standard was so alien to downhome singing that a voice like Smith's was considered "too rough." Her ultimate failure came when Black Swan Records, the only Black-owned company at that time, refused to invest in her. Columbia was obviously forced to gamble on a "tall and fat and scared" singer in order to keep pace with the industry. The payoff was unimaginable: within months, over 780,000 copies of Smith's first record had been sold. By the end of 1923, sales of her record approached 20 percent of all the "race" records bought that year (Albertson 1972, 27–65; Dixon and Godrich 1970, 20–22, 41, 59–60).

Without doubt, much of Smith's success was rooted in her talent. But the style through which she routed her ability was as much a factor. Black Americans, voting with their purchases of her "rough" sounding records, had given overwhelming approval to the down-home style as opposed to its "classic" counterpart crooned by the industry's ruling "queens." (For a description of classic versus down-home singers, see Titon 1977, xv–xvi.) Even more convincing proof followed Smith when Paramount Records, pressed to find not only another blues singer but one who sang like Smith, contracted with one of the most experienced of the older, original singers, Gertrude "Ma" Rainey. A veteran of years of touring throughout the South in minstrel shows. Rainey was the undisputed "Mother of the Blues" (*Chicago Defender* 1924). Rainey's popularity, though not as great as Smith's, if measured in record sales, was widespread.

To Dorsey, this sudden shift of blues preferences was perplexing: the very blues style he had found obsolete for his career goals was now popular. The most direct effect, however, concerned his role as a blues composer. Dorsey, who had copyrighted eight blues compositions in 1923 alone, no longer registered any of his music until 1928. The recording industry had little use for Tin Pan Alley blues of the sort that had given him fame. Ironically, Smith and Rainey had undercut Dorsey's career advancement with the music that Dorsey thought no longer mattered.

Dorsey's transition between his periods of conflict and resolution was not readily apparent to him. Unlike his sudden shift between the first and second periods, caused by his family's move to Atlanta and the problems attendant to urban living, this one was virtually in the making before Dorsey realized it. It was a time of fits and starts, of opportunities appearing nearby only to fade away as he tried to take advantage of them. The first concerned his attempt to ride the crest of the Smith/Rainey craze.

Although one cannot know how personally wrenching the resurgence of the older style of blues was to Dorsey, it is known that he recovered enough to return to his earlier style of music and to enjoy what would seem to him even greater success. In 1924, Ma Rainey hired Dorsey to be her accompanist because he was one of the best pianists who could play in the older style: "She was impressed with my playing and hired me as her accompanist. . . ." This joining with Rainey offered Dorsey a sense of resolution. Even more extraordinary and more indicative was his being able to compose and arrange vaudeville music for her tours in addition to accompanying her with the more traditional blues. To perform the show music, Rainey had Dorsey organize and direct her Wildcats Jazz Band (Dorsey 1961, 48).

To build his reputation with one of the most widely known down-home blues singers, not only with "lowdown" blues but with vaudeville ones too, should have been rewarding. But this apparently was not the deep musical unity Dorsey needed. Even with his playing such a major role in boosting Rainey's fame, even with his happy marriage to Nettie Harper—a woman he deeply loved—in August 1925, and even with his making an increasing number of recordings, Dorsey still fell into a deep depression similar to the one he suffered through in 1921. This one was worse, lasting over two years. During this sickness, Dorsey was unable to play piano; he spent large numbers of days in a state of profound melancholia and more than once contemplated suicide.

The clearest indication of the cause of this depression comes from what Dorsey believes to have been its cure: a religious conversion. As Dorsey describes it, he attended a church service one Sunday morning in 1928, after which he had a consultation with the minister, a Bishop H. H. Haley. Haley told Dorsey that the Lord had too "much work" for him to do to let him die. Then Haley pulled a "live serpent" out of Dorsey's throat. From that moment on, Dorsey announced that he suffered no more and pledged: "Lord, I am ready to do your work" (Dorsey 1961, 61; Harris 1977a). Shortly after this, a friend of his died after being ill for one day, leaving Dorsey to wonder why after two years of illness he was alive and his friend was dead after twenty-four hours of sickness.

This event, coming on the heels of his encounter with Haley, prompted Dorsey to make the pivotal turn toward his path to resolution. He could no longer deny that the simple pursuit of a career as a blues musician was unsatisfactory; he had only to consider his depression after beginning to work for Rainey. Even the blues he now played—the style he most ardently professed—sounded with the hollowness of his earlier jassy blues songs. Thus, by itself, musical change was a less than ample preventative against self-deprecation. Added to this reality were his brushes with religious surrealism and with the capriciousness of death. These were haunting experiences because they stirred his concern about abandoning the pious religion with which his mother had "stamped" his character in early childhood, a piety reasserted through her repeated admonition to "Serve the Lord, serve the Lord" during his 1921 bout with depression. He was utterly confounded, in essence, by the fundamental incongruities between the various musics and between the different practices of religion he had known since his childhood. This melange of indigenous and exogenous music, of pulpitry and piety, of careers made by craftily dodging one tendency to artfully exploit the other, now stood between him and his need to live a normal life.

Torn by this musical and religious fragmentation, Dorsey had every reason to seek a path that would invite the least resistance among these warring compulsions. Using his secular blues to serve the Lord—that is, composing gospel blues songs by writing sacred texts to blues songs—certainly seemed to him the logical route to some semblance of inner unity. By the evening of that long day in 1928, Dorsey had penned his first gospel song, "If You See My Savior, Tell Him That You Saw Me." Within a short time he followed this song with "How about You?"

Dorsey's personal growth had been shaped by social forces. Now firmly in the resolution period, the last of the three, Dorsey was about to feel these forces as he never had. His budding gospel career was destined to be even more formed by these forces because of a rather sudden turn in the history of African American Protestant churches in the urban North: they began to undergo changes that were similar to the ones that had so recently wracked Dorsey's life. Until these changes were completely made, however, Dorsey's new songs would cause considerable controversy.

During the late 1920s, Chicago's old-line Black Protestant churches stood as virtual mirrors of their white counterparts in terms of the worship aesthetic. No part of the Sunday morning liturgy was more illustrative of this than the music. At churches such as Olivet and Pilgrim Baptist, two of the largest congregations in Black Chicago, choirs sang the Western European-style anthems and sacred compositions of composers such as Mendelssohn, Mozart, Beethoven, Bach, and Rossini. Ministers in these churches carefully designed worship to control congregational participation, especially its more spontaneous aspects. This meant that they had to avoid the music associated with traditional Black worship. Black sacred song could be heard only in its Anglicized version, known as the concert or arranged Negro spiritual. More seriously, these ministers had to control their preaching so as not to stir emotions to the point that the congregation would erupt into the jubilation and demonstrativeness of the classic Black church. The effect of these standards of worship was to alter profoundly the ethos of upper-crust Black churches to the point that they can be considered Black only in terms of the racial, certainly not the cultural, makeup of their congregations.

These alien criteria had lengthy historic precedents. As early as the 1870s, Bishop Daniel Alexander Payne of the African Methodist Episcopal (AME) Church had tried to curtail such traditional practices as the ring shout and the singing of slave spirituals. He strongly criticized the adherents of these traditions: "Such persons are usually so because they are non-progressive, and, being illiterate, are consequently very narrow in views of men and things. A strong religious feeling coupled with a narrow range of knowledge often makes one a bigot" (Payne [1891] 198, 457).

The effort to obliterate indigenous worship music grew through the late nineteenth century with the compositions of Negro spirituals by noted Black composers such a Harry T. Burleigh and John Work. Work was explicit about his concern that the salve spiritual if not Anglicized, would serve as an impediment to racial progress: "In truth, the general adaptability of this music to a high degree of development is its hope of gaining artistic recognition. It deserves to be put into a finished form; it lends itself admirably to such a purpose; and those who would keep it as it was first reduced to writing in their mistaken zeal would doom it to stagnation and to the contempt of highly musical people" (Work 1915, 90–99). This trend was so pronounced by the 1920s—especially among the Black elite and therefore in their churches, such as Olivet and Pilgrim Baptist in Chicago—that one exasperated observer, C. W. Hyne, labeled the music "denatured spirituals." The attempt, he said, was to "dress them up." The whole process reminded him "of the attempt of one race to remove the curl from the hair and of the other to put it in" (Johnson 1930, v–vi).

At this point the ultimate effect of this religious development on Dorsey's newly conceived career plans is clear. The old-line churches into which a self-reconstituted Thomas A. Dorsey carried his new gospel songs in 1928 comprised a virtual monolith of anti-traditionalism, especially toward indigenous Black sacred song. Dorsey, driven to the depths of inner turmoil in part for having spurned classic down-home blues, was now rededicated not only to the song style itself as a tradition worth saving but to the cause to make it the major musical medium for the gospel message in Black Protestant churches.

This vast gulf that lay between the churches' and Dorsey's goals became a virtual prison for him between 1928 and 1932. What might appear, therefore, as a time of resolution for a man consumed by inner turmoil in fact became one of frustration and vacillation. On some occasions, Dorsey "was thrown out of some of the best churches" when he performed his sacred blues. On other occasions, he was simply ignored:

> I shall never forget the embarrassment I suffered one Sunday morning when I had made arrangements with a minister to sing and introduce one of my songs in the morning service in one of the largest churches in the city. I arrived that morning about thirty minutes before service time with my singer Rebecca Talbot. The minister greeted us and gave us a seat on the front row of pews and said, "I will call for you to sing just after the morning message."
>
> Was I beaming over with joy to know my song would be sung in this church which had over two thousand people worshiping that morning! But something happened or there was a change of mind. The choir marched in, the minister preached, extended the invitation for members, lifted the offering, dismissed the congregation, and left me and my singer sitting on the front row seats without a word of explanation. (Dorsey ca. 1961, 63–64; Harris 1977a)

He mailed free copies to over one thousand ministers and had to wait for over two years before he got a reply. Even then he only received a few orders, "not enough to make a market trend or even to reimburse me for expenses" (Harris 1977a).

By August 1928, Dorsey was convinced that his blues would find no church home. It is at this point that he began to waft on his commitment. For the first time in five years he registered a new popular song at the Copyright Office on August 2, 1928, called "When You're in Love." Around the same time he began arranging music for the Brunswick Recording Company, one of the top five record companies in the peak years of the industry (Dixon and Godrich 1970, 42; Godrich and Dixon 1982, 20; Dorsey 1961, 65).

While these instances of turning back to secular blues clearly compromised Dorsey's renewed religious dedication, they did not really amount to a rejection of his faith. They were, instead, desperate attempts at remaining financially solvent and at having a sense that he was still making progress as a songwriter/performer. But he wrote and recorded one other blues song in September 1928. This piece so clearly differed from any other he had composed that one would have to conclude that Dorsey had all but abandoned his new religious growth. This piece was called "It's Tight Like That." A guitarist friend, Hudson Whitaker, wrote the lyrics, which were full of sexual innuendo. Together, Dorsey and Whitaker recorded this song as the team of Georgia Tom and Tampa Red. Not only did Dorsey seem to have departed significantly from his gospel blues but, as fate would have it, he was rewarded for doing so: his first royalty check, the highest amount in his career, was written for $2,400.19. By December, the song was so popular that he and Whitaker recorded two more versions of it. The two became so notorious for their cunningly erotic blues that they coined a word for the style (*hokum*) and went on to name their duo after it, the Famous Hokum Boys. By 1932, they would make over sixty recordings of Dorsey's songs, appropriately titled, for example, "Pat That Bread" and "Somebody's Been Using That Thing" (Dorsey 1961, 36–37; Dixon and Godrich 1970, 62–63; Godrich and Dixon 1982, 199–200, 224–25, 344, 352, 574, 683–84, 748).

Just as Dorsey was basking in this fame, the kind for which he had craved during most of his career, his gospel songs seemed to attract new attention as well. A young woman sang "If You See My Savior" during the August 23, 1930, morning session of the annual meeting of the National Baptist Convention in Chicago. It was a decided hit, with "every man, woman and child ... singing or humming the tune" (Dorsey 1961, 70; Harris 1976). This is the event that Dorsey marks as the beginning of his success as a gospel songwriter: "[I've] been in the music business ever since.... That was the big moment right there." Having sold over four thousand copies at that Convention, Dorsey certainly had reason to feel that he had reached the level of acceptance for which he had labored for two years (Dorsey 1961, 69–70; Harris 1976, 1977a).

This point also may be considered the final resolution of the inner conflicts that had dogged him since 1926. Even though he had decided to dedicate himself to a Christian life and his music talents to sacred music, Dorsey had to fight against the cultural obstinacy of the big churches and the economic draw of his old career. Dorsey had tried to keep his gospel music going in a small church; even that was little consolation: "I wasn't giving all my time to the church, see. I was kind of straddling the fence—making money out there on the outside, you know, in the band business and then going to church Sunday morning helping what I could do for them for they wasn't able to pay nothing. I could make money out there" (Harris 1976).

A resolution of the same sort was about to bring Chicago's major Black churches to a more inclusive worship ritual. At Ebenezer Baptist Church, where the European orientation of the worship music matched or exceeded that at Pilgrim and Olivet, the desire for a more traditional mode of worship was fueled by the call of its pastor, J. H. L. Smith, one Sunday morning in the fall of 1931, for a new group to sing the older music. As recalled by June Levell, the historian of the Ebenezer Gospel Chorus, the pastor declaimed, "I have a vision of a group singing the good old fashion songs that were born in the hearts of our forefathers down in the Southland. I want those songs that my old forefathers and mothers sing down in, way down in the Southland" (Harris 1977b).

Smith, who had assumed the Ebenezer pastorate in August of that year, had found his first months in one of the most acculturated of Chicago's Black old-line churches discomforting. Having arrived in Chicago from Birmingham, Alabama, Smith had a pronounced preference for the very Southern worship style that these Chicago old-line churches were dedicated virtually to eradicating. He was, moreover, greatly encouraged to call for such a drastic change because the congregation had been split over the sudden (and suspicious) departure of the previous pastor. Ebenezer, therefore, was demoralized; its worship, uninspiring.

Not even one so convinced of the appropriateness of the traditional African American worship ritual as Smith could have anticipated the surge to affirm his call for the older music. On the second Sunday in January 1932, a chorus of over one hundred members made its debut at Ebenezer with Dorsey as pianist and Theodore Frye as director. At the root of this surprising development was more than Smith's call for down-home, musical therapy. Most of the one hundred choristers were recent migrants from the rural South. Since the beginning of World War I, their numbers had been growing steadily. Nowhere was this increase more evident than in the large, old-line churches. The new arrivals were drawn to the large churches because these institutions had social programs that included aid for settling in Chicago and for finding employment. To a great extent, however, the newcomers' presence had little effect on operations and virtually none on worship standards, since those churches served almost exclusively as the domains of Chicago's Black old settlers, residents, in many cases, for several generations. This group was most closely tied to the effort to guide the old-line churches into their mimicry of white Protestant worship norms. If this group had a visual and auditory locus in old-line churches, it was the choir. Thus the new migrants, large in number but weak in influence, sat passively, Sunday after Sunday, listening to their counterparts espouse the virtues of white middle-class culture through the Western European choral anthem:

> A lot of people here who remembered what singing was like down home, liked Smith, Lord, yes. The music the Senior Choir was singing was not what Reverend Smith nor the congregation was used to. And then them old songs that they had been used to hearing, like "This Rock I'm Standing On" or "By and By," see, the Senior Choir didn't sing them then. They sang ooh, ah, ooh, way up high and [they sang] the anthems. (Harris 1977b)

What had seemed an inexorable movement toward alien religious norms was now about to be brought to a halt by Smith's deliberate parrying of the migrants' musical sentiments off those of the old settlers: "And when he came here, of course, he'd been used to that old time singing down there and he wanted the same thing at Ebenezer" (Harris 1977b). Thus, at Smith's initiative, migrants gained a literal voice in the Sunday morning worship hour and, through them, traditional African American religious culture regained a place in old-line Protestantism.

This development is significant in that it represents the same resolution of a conflict between original and assimilated cultural experiences that Dorsey underwent. Dorsey's stumble back into down-home blues provided the correction for his earlier long slide into the commercial, Tin Pan Alley blues of his time of professional assimilation. Ebenezer's turn back to religious songs of the Southland likewise provided a counterforce to its long slide into religious assimilation. There is also a similarity to Dorsey's religious resolution: just as Dorsey experienced unrest by not being as sincere in his religious outlook as he felt he should, based on his mother's piety, so was Ebenezer deeply troubled by its attempt to separate Black Christianity from its cultural roots. In this instance the parallel situations are found in Dorsey's nervous breakdown and Ebenezer's demoralization at the loss of its preacher. In both cases, a spiritual rejuvenation was inextricably bound to music in a contextualized African American setting.

The point is more than coincidental: it portrays a delicate symbiosis between Dorsey's life and the emergence of gospel blues—indeed, between Black culture, Dorsey as an archetype of that culture, and the middle-class Black church as an institutionalization of that culture. Dorsey as an African American and the church as African American religion have complete histories only as subsets of African American culture. From the perspective of this interdependency, Dorsey's role as the "father" of gospel blues was limited in the sense of his being able to lay claim to its genesis. There was an asymmetry of old and new cultures—manifested as rural Southern and urban Northern—in Black churches. Dorsey happened to be there with an urbanized version of the rural culture's music that was powerful enough to counter the Beethoven and Mozart of the Northern culture and that was authentic enough to give status to the former Southerners. Thus, Dorsey conceived of "gospel blues," but its purpose and ultimate shape were not his to determine.

If there is a cause–effect factor in this tripartite symbiosis of (1) secular and sacred, (2) lower class and middle class, and (3) rural Southern and urban Northern, it has to be the notion of duality and its pervasiveness not just in Dorsey's life but in African American culture and religion. The similarities among exposure, conflict, and resolution between Dorsey's life and the church and the culture are traceable to the twoness that is central to the African American experience.

References

Albertson, Chris. 1972. *Bessie.* New York: Stein and Day.

Atlanta City Directory: Listings for 1909–15.

Bradford, Perry. 1965. *Born with the Blues: Perry Bradford's Own Story: The True Story of the Pioneering Blues Singers and Musicians in the Early Days of Jazz.* New York: Oak Publications.

Chicago Defender. 1920, 1923, 1924 (Feb. 2), and 1932.

Dixon, Robert M. W., and John Godrich. 1970. *Recording the Blues.* New York: Stein and Day.

Dorsey, Thomas A. 1935. *Inspirational Thoughts.* Chicago: Thomas A. Dorsey.

———. 1941. *Songs with a Message: With My Ups and Downs.* Chicago: Thomas A. Dorsey.

———. ca. 1961. "The Thomas Andrew Dorsey Story: From Blues-Jazz to Gospel Song." Unpublished typescript, Dorsey collection.

Du Bois, William E. B. 1902. "The Work of Negro Women in Society." *The Spelman Messenger* (Feb.): 1–3.

Godrich, John, and Robert M. W. Dixon, comp. 1982. *Blues and Gospel Records: 1902–1942.* London: Storyville Publications and Co.

Harris, Michael W. 1976, 1977a. Interviews with Thomas A. Dorsey, Chicago.

———. 1977b. Interview with June Levell, Chicago, Dec. 8.

Johnson. J. Rosamond, transc. 1930. *Utica Jubilee Singers Spirituals: As Sung at the Utica Normal and Industrial Institute of Mississippi.* Boston: Oliver Ditson Company.

Payne, Bishop Daniel E. [1891] 1968. *History of the African Methodist Episcopal Church.* Edited by C. S. Smith. Reprint. New York: Johnson Reprint Corporation.

Rust, Brian, comp. 1978. *Jazz Records: A–Z: 1897–1942,* 4th ed. 2 vols. New Rochelle, N.Y.: Arlington House.

Townsend, A. M., ed. 1924. *The Baptist Standard Hymnal with Responsive Readings: A New Book for All Services.* Nashville: Sunday School Publishing Board, National Baptist Convention, U.S.A.

Work, John. 1915. *Folk Songs of the American Negro.* Reprint. New York: Negro Universities Press, 1969.

17 Fats Waller (Comedy Tonight)

GARY GIDDINS

This brief appreciation first appeared in Gary Giddins's Visions of Jazz. *One of the finest contemporary writers focusing on jazz, Giddins is less interested in the biographical facts than he is in Waller's place in cultural history, his recorded legacy, and its impact on subsequent musicians. Giddens portraits this multitalented (musician, entertainer, and songwriter, often in collaboration with lyricist Andy Razaf) keyboardist as a larger-than-life figure whose on-stage "mask" consisted of "a rakishly tilted derby, one size too small, an Edwardian mustache . . . and eyebrows as thick as paint and pliable as curtains."*

But, as the author observes, Waller was more than an immensely large and talented keyboard player. He came out of the Harlem stride piano school and helped to bring the James P. Johnson, Lucky Roberts, and Willie "The Lion" Smith's legacy to a wider audience in the 1930s. Waller also brought his broad comedic sense—sharpened by his expressive face and wicked sense of timing—to a wide audience in the 1930s by his live appearances and his short films that played in theaters across the United States.

Waller also triumphed over the often dreadful tunes and songs that Victor A & R (Artist & Repertoire) men often saddled him with in the studio. Thus, his creative powers allowed him to soar over and above such drivel as "The Curse of an Aching Heart" and "It's a Sin to Tell a Lie," transforming them into songs that invited you back for repeated listens rather than to turn away in dismay. Fortunately, RCA Victor also permitted him to record his own compositions, such as "A Handful of Keys," "Keepin' Out of Mischief Now," and "Ain't Misbehavin'," which remain fresh classics in the twenty-first century.

Fats Waller, one of the most enduringly popular figures in American music, is a state of mind. Jazz has always claimed him (what idiom *wouldn't* claim him?) and yet he spent most of his abbreviated career cavorting through, and contributing to, the Tin Pan Alley canon—applying a determined jazz accent, perhaps, but with the sui generis detachment of a free-floating institution. He wasn't witty, if that word is taken to imply a kind of humor too subtle to engender belly laughs—he was funny. He was also bigger than life, Rabelaisian in intake, energy, and output. His greatest joy was playing Bach on the organ, but he buttered his bread as a clown, complete with a mask as fixed as that of Bert Williams or Spike Jones. It consisted of a rakishly tilted derby, one size too small, an Edwardian mustache that fringed his upper lip, eyebrows as thick as paint and pliable as curtains, flirtatious eyes, a mouth alternately pursed or widened in a dimpled smile, and immense girth, draped in the expensive suits and ties of a dandy.

A ripe sense of humor is indigenous in jazz. It's a music quick to enlist whatever barbs can best deflate pomposity and artificiality. But jazz has not always been rich in humorists, though one can point to a few in any given period. Those in the postwar era include Dizzy Gillespie, Clark Terry, James Moody, Jon Hendricks, Jaki Byard, Lester Bowie, Willem Breuker, the Jazz Passengers, and Waller's druggy disciple, Harry "The Hipster" Gibson. Humor was more extensive in the '20s and '30s, when Prohibition, the Depression, and the insularity of a new and predominantly black music conspired to create an undercurrent of protective irreverence. Accustomed to a place on the outside looking in, jazz took pleasure in skewering anything that made the mainstream feel safe and smug. It was a time when Fats Waller could count on a laugh by interrupting a particularly suave solo with the rumination, "Hmm, I wonder what the poor people are doing tonight."

Musicians, singers, and other entertainers created countless songs about bathtub gin, drugs, sex (of every variety), and other subjects unsuitable for Judge Hardy and his family, and invented slang—a new kind of signifying—to get it over. As late as the mid-'60s, Cab Calloway could cheerfully invite Ed Sullivan's audience to hi-de-ho with him on the joys of cocaine. Jazz recordings offered euphemisms so arcane (example, women's genitals: barbecue, paswonky, the boy in the boat) that no postgraduate course in ebonics could have brought them all to light. They slipped through broadcasting codes and around censors. The real measure of jazz grit in those years, however, was the way it stood up to the conventions of pop culture. Encumbered with the dreariest products of the songwriting factory, the stuff Alec Wilder *didn't* write about, musicians were obliged to transcend or annihilate the material. Waller did both with dog tunes Victor forced on him at one session after another; but his comic ebullience also informed his serious side, girding his exacting piano pieces and peerlessly swinging ensembles.

Waller's primary influence was James P. Johnson, the songwriter and grandmaster of the Harlem school of stride piano. The term "stride" is descriptive and refers to the movement of the pianist's left hand, which upholds the rhythm while swinging side to side, from distant bass notes, played on the first and third beats of the measure, to close chords in the octave below middle C, played on the second and fourth beats. Stride was a social music, powerful enough to surmount the din of a rent party and vigorous enough to encourage dancing. It was also a competitive music, a specialist's art. The best players were fine composers, but stride was malleable: they could stride pop songs or classical themes, just as an earlier generation of pianists could rag them. Stride per se never had a large audience. It was bypassed during the boogie-woogie rage and overlooked by all but a few in the years of bop. Of its key practitioners, only Waller achieved real commercial success, and then only because of his wisecracks. Had he done nothing but pursue his art as a pianist, he might be no better known than Johnson, Luckey Roberts, Willie "The Lion" Smith, Donald Lambert, Willie Gant, or other Harlem-based keyboard professors, who took themselves pretty seriously. The complaint aimed at Waller is that he didn't take himself seriously enough.

He was perversely inspired by kitsch, for example, the 1913 saloon tearjerker, "The Curse of an Aching Heart," which Fats leaps upon at breakneck tempo, with all the fake operatic bravado he can muster, somehow ending up with a splendid vehicle. Billie Holiday, who was also held in chancery by song pluggers, could transform the maudlin horror "It's a Sin to Tell a Lie" into an arresting and winsome love song—shaping the phrase, "I love you, yes I do, I love you," with a plaintive candor that turns frivolity into urgent revelation. For Waller, the song is simply ludicrous and must be skewered, shaken, and swung, especially that "I love you" line. An outsider like Spike Jones could make fun of rhythm itself, but not Waller. Pop was his cross, swing his salvation.

A local celebrity while still in his teens, Waller died unconscionably at thirty-nine, spurring the long debate as to how his genius might have been better realized had he lived to compose, perform, and record in more salubrious circumstances. But how much poorer we would be without the comic legacy, by far the predominant part of his more than 500 recordings. The idea that the full breadth of his gift was heard only in private after-hours settings or before a pipe organ doesn't quite comport with his boisterous personality. In the decades following his death, he was exhaustively acclaimed as a songwriter, in tribute albums by Louis Armstrong and Dinah Washington, among others, as well as the revue *Ain't Misbehavin'*. He was, indeed, after Ellington, the most successful songwriter to emerge from the heart of jazz. Supremely confident of his capabilities, he was known to trade songs (including a few that became standards) for hamburgers. He wrote them in minutes and improvised an entire instrumental suite in less than an hour. Yet only in the records, especially when he debunks other people's songs, are we encouraged to partake of the saucy leer, the fey hand movements, the metronomic time, the offhanded virtuosity, and nasal pitch-perfect voice.

Waller divides his vocal range for effect: middle octave for straight swinging variations, lower notes for rude asides, higher ones for feminine mockery and cries of encouragement to the band. Yet the miraculous thing about his comedy is that it is never an end in itself (unlike, for example, recordings of Jimmy Durante, who used his raggy piano chops purely as an adjunct to his clowning). Humor enabled Waller to sweep up the musical debris of the day, but also allowed him to inflect it with his own exuberance. Jazz in the swing era was frequently an alchemical art. Waller's musicianship complements his most abusive remarks. Significantly, he neglected to record some of his own best songs.

As the only stride pianist to achieve true stardom, Waller influenced generations of pianists drawn to the ideal articulation of his lateral left hand and the delicate refinement of his right. Duke Ellington's piano style was grounded in stride and so were many of his best compositions. Art Tatum once observed, "Fats, that's where I come from," and it is probably true that Waller's early blues instrumentals, notably "Blue Black Bottom" and "Numb Fumblin'," represent the most imperious blues technique in jazz piano until Tatum. Teddy Wilson expanded on Waller's broken tenths, and Count Basie began as a Waller-mimic and then edited his style down to its essentials. Thelonious Monk and Bud Powell occasionally employed Wallerian mannerisms, and most postmodernist pianists who turned to stride as a means of levitating their performances (Jaki Byard, Muhal Richard Abrams, Dave Burrell, Stanley Cowell, Hilton Ruiz) chose Waller as their point of departure. James P. Johnson demonstrated more imagination in his bass figures and greater concern with developing stride as a basis for large-scale composition, but Waller's rhythmic gait, matchless clarity, and joie de vivre were irresistable.

Waller's instrumental compositions are as rewarding as his songs, among them "Stealin' Apples" (a staple of jam sessions), "Whiteman Stomp," "A Handful of Keys," "Clothes Line Ballet," "Viper's Drag," "Smashing Thirds," "Fractious Fingering," "Alligator's Drag," and the largely improvised *London Suite*. A couple of them were orchestrated for big bands; the rest are charming piano pieces. His more famous songs include the endlessly recast "Honeysuckle Rose" and the abiding "Ain't Misbehavin'," as well as "Squeeze Me," "(What Did I Do to Be So) Black and Blue," "I've Got a Feeling I'm Falling," "Blue Turning Gray Over You," "I'm Crazy 'Bout My Baby," "Keepin' Out of Mischief Now," and "Ain'tcha Glad." He was fortunate in his stellar lyricist, Andy Razaf, a master of double entendre and original imagery, and in his insuperable interpreter and faithful advocate, Louis Armstrong. Waller himself was a gifted leader of small ensembles, able to whip musicians into a frenzy with shouts of encouragement and the rhythmic brawn of his piano.

Thomas Wright Waller was born in New York in 1904, the son of a clergyman. His mother played piano and organ and supervised his musical education. At fifteen, shortly before her death, Waller began playing professionally; he could always find work accompanying silent movies, a discipline that spurred him to cultivate the standard devices of melodrama. Those wary tremolos, ominous bass walks, and "Spring Song" epiphanies were later employed by Waller in his commentaries on pop songs. Sometimes, as in "Russian Fantasy," they *are* the song. At eighteen, he recorded his first piano pieces, "Muscle Shoals Blues" and "Birmingham Blues," both heavily indebted to James P. Johnson. For the next few years, he worked in various theaters, backing singers as well as movies, absorbing the latest fancies in Broadway musicals (he adored Gershwin), and assimilating the teachings of Johnson and, at Gershwin's urging, Leopold Godowski. As Johnson's heir apparent, he was in constant demand for all kinds of recording sessions—vaudevillian Juanita Stinette Chappelle, the Elkins Negro Ensemble, Porter Grainger, and a would-be singer (and nephew to the queen of Madagascar) who changed his name from Andreamenentania Paul Razafinkeriefo to Andy Razaf. But Waller was more at home with blues divas, among them Alberta Hunter, Rosa Henderson, Sara Martin, Hazel Myers, Maude Mills, and, though he never recorded with her, Bessie Smith.

By the 1926–27 season, Waller had made important contacts on Broadway and in jazz, and his career forged ahead. He took over the piano chair when Fletcher Henderson recorded his "Henderson Stomp" and "Whiteman Stomp," a pointed reference to the kings of a racially divided music; completed twenty-three piano rolls; and recorded a dozen pipe organ solos. At a session by the Louisiana Sugar Babes, his pipe organ was combined with James P. Johnson's piano. The payoff came in 1929, when he wrote three solid hits for the revue *Hot Chocolates*: "Black and Blue," "Sweet Savannah Sue," and the showstopper that secured Armstrong's reputation in New York, "Ain't Misbehavin'." That same year, RCA invited Waller to record several of his works for piano. At twenty-five, he was widely respected as a major young talent. Few could have imagined the strange turn his career was about to take.

The Depression slowed him down for three and a half years, during which he recorded very little, though memorably with Jack Teagarden, Pee Wee Russell, and vaudeville headliner Ted Lewis. But he kept busy. He played with several bands, collaborated with Spencer Williams on a show at Connie's Inn, accompanied Williams to France for a few weeks, accepted a great deal of radio work, including a long residency as staff pianist for a station in Cincinnati, and made occasional performance tours. In 1931, he recorded two solo numbers for OKeh, "Draggin' My Heart Around" and "I'm Crazy 'Bout My Baby," that suggest something of his bubbling potential as an entertainer. Yet three years would pass before he had another session under his own name. This time, in May 1934, he was under exclusive contract to Victor and at the helm of a sextet billed as Fats Waller and His Rhythm. In the first seconds of the farcical "A Porter's Love Song to a Chambermaid" (written, apparently with him in mind, by Johnson and Razaf), a new Fats was born—in J. R. Taylor's words, "the gargoyle Fats, spouting pianistic filigree while regarding the world through a mocking mask of bowed lips and swooping eyebrows." His success was immediate, but it should be noted that almost all his best songs were composed before his incarnation as court jester.

Waller's hundreds of Rhythm sides present a problem for the listener, especially when they are issued in complete and sequential boxes rather than sensibly edited anthologies.

Although the songs range from top-of-the-line to mind-shattering swill, the delivery tends to follow a pattern and the vocal asides ("my, my," "well, alright then," "one never knows, do one?") wear thin over too large a helping. Yet the energy level rarely flags. Waller is always center stage, exhorting soloists when they dally and charging the rhythm section with his thumping left hand. He is surrounded by a crew of talented, eager second-tier musicians. Trumpeter Herman Autrey (a skillful Armstrong man), saxophonist Gene Sedrick (merry if a bit wheezy), and trombonist Floyd O'Brian (melodic and slick) are almost always pleasing. On two sessions, Fats is availed of Bill Coleman's bright, masterful trumpet, and guitarist Al Casey is almost always around to beef up the rhythm. On those first dates, Waller's piano sparkles on "I Wish I Were Twins," "Do Me a Favor," "Have a Little Dream on Me," and "I Ain't Got Nobody."

Within a year, the material started to get really gruesome. That Waller can get as much as he does from "My Very Good Friend the Milkman" is miraculous; even he is stopped cold by "You're the Cutest One." He's ebullient on "Lulu's Back in Town" (hear him crank the engine during Autrey's solo); seductive on "Sweet and Slow"; stately on the straight rendition of "I'm Gonna Sit Right Down and Write Myself a Letter," one of his most admired recordings; irascible on "There'll Be Some Changes Made"; and suitably disrespectful on "Brother Seek and Ye Shall Find." He has his share of good period pieces ("Dinah," "Truckin"), but none of them are Waller originals. He recorded far too often to sustain his creativity, but the gems are luminous: "I Can't Give You Anything But Love" (with Una Mae Carlisle as straight woman), "Until the Real Thing Comes Along," "Hold Tight" (a lyric of Joycean complexity having to do with sex or constipation or both), "If I Were You," "Beat It Out," "Blue Turning Gray Over You" (one of his prettiest originals), "Christopher Columbus" ("the crew was making merry," he sings, then mutters "so Mary went home"), "Don't Let it Bother You" (ah, if only he could have had a shot at the '80s' similarly constituted "Don't Worry, Be Happy"), the remake of "I'm Crazy 'Bout My Baby," and dozens more. On a 1937 session, he uses steel guitar and sends up the "Sweet Leilani" craze with "Neglected," yet is maddeningly respectful of "Why Do Hawaiians Sing Aloha?"

Recording alone at the piano, he could betray frustration and a perfunctory attitude, even to the point of clumsy execution, as on the plodding blues "My Feelings Are Hurt." But such instances are rare. He was a born pianist with a distinctive attack and usually imperturbable. "Handful of Keys" is based on little more than a scale, but it is the embodiment of Harlem stride and boasts what is probably the single most imitated lick in the entire idiom. "I've Got a Feeling I'm Falling" is a lesson in voice leading with the left hand. "Numb Fumblin'" is a blues of exquisite finesse. "Valentine Stomp" and "Smashing Thirds" perfectly embody his clean, strutting, virtuoso control, varied bass lines, deft variations, and compositional imagination. All of these performances date from 1929; some that followed are more impressive: "African Ripples" deals playfully with Gershwin harmonies, "Clothes Line Ballet" wittily alternates between impressionism and stride, "E Flat Blues" is paced with the certainty of a metronome and the solicitude of a prayer.

Waller learned to heighten popular songs with an emotional texture rare in stride, yet devoid of the sentimentality that intrudes in the music of other stride pianists, for example that of Willie "The Lion" Smith. In addition to reharmonizing chords, he employs an eight-to-the-bar boogie framework to make the rhythms edgier. "Georgia on My Mind" is perhaps the peak example of his transfigurative powers, closely followed by "Tea for Two" (with shades of mock-classicism, boogie, and stride), "Basin Street Blues," "Keepin' Out of Mischief Now," "I Ain't Got Nobody," and a startling, sinuous "Ring Dem Bells." He recorded a fastidious if compressed version of James P. Johnson's "Carolina Shout" and a parodistic survey of

"Honeysuckle Rose" ("a la Bach-Beethoven-Brahms-Waller"). Some of his most intriguing solo work was recorded not for Victor, but at 1939 radio broadcasts that found him performing nineteenth-century spirituals and minstrel songs with a combination of nostalgic relish and blustery impatience—he takes the melodies seriously, but not the words, which he whimsically attacks as though telling outrageous stories.

During his European tour of 1938–39, he recorded spirituals on organ, popular songs with an English edition of his ensemble, stodgy duets with Adelaide Hall, and the six movements of *London Suite*, which is stiff in parts ("Bond Street," "Limehouse"), but also unforced ("Piccadilly"), lovely ("Chelsea"), stately ("Soho"), and even grand ("Whitechapel"). He was hugely successful everywhere and was soon summoned to Hollywood, where he appeared in three features. Yet for all his renown, Waller had a difficult time of it. A vindictive ex-wife was always trying to put him in jail (sometimes successfully) for unpaid alimony. The movie parts were patronizing and unrewarding, and his attempt to organize a big band in 1942 failed. Despite the money he made for Victor and others, he was stymied in his aspirations as organist and composer, constrained by the buffoonery that made him famous. In June 1943, however, he enjoyed a Broadway hit in *Early to Bed* (lyrics by George Marion, Jr.)—not his best work, but his song "The Ladies Who Sing with the Band" stopped the show nightly and it stayed the season. Waller died the following December, on a train en route from Hollywood to New York. With his last words, he unknowingly played one final joke on the gulf between black vernacular and white inference. The train had departed Chicago for Kansas, when Waller's manager, Ed Kirkeby, said, "Jesus, it's cold in here!" Fats agreed, "Yeah, hawkins is sure blowin' out there tonight," using a term common among black midwesterners for a bitter winter wind. In his biography of Waller, Kirkeby created the widely repeated legend that Fats went out contemplating Coleman Hawkins.

18 "Dean of Afro-American Composers" or "Harlem Renaissance Man":

The New Negro and the Musical Poetics of William Grant Still

GAYLE MURCHISON

William Grant Still (May 11, 1895–December 3, 1978) was a groundbreaking African American classical composer who wrote nearly 200 compositions. He was the first African American to conduct a major American orchestra, the first to have an opera performed by a major opera company, and the first to have an opera performed on national television. Although a native of Mississippi and raised in Arkansas, Still chose Ohio for college, attending Wilberforce College and Oberlin College. But he soon forsook his premedical school training, moved to New York City, first playing with and arranging for W. C. Handy and eventually writing longer musical forms. An important figure in the Harlem Renaissance, Still studied with Edgard Varèse and George Chadwick and his Afro-American Symphony was performed by the Rochester Philharmonic Orchestra in 1931.

In this carefully notated article, musicologist Gayle Murchison, who currently teaches at the College of William & Mary, explores Still's life and works, focusing on his most fruitful period. Murchison forcefully argues that Still was more than merely a first-rate composer: "Like Du Bois and Locke . . . he was a Race Man, advocating progress of the Race and progress in race relations so as to fully realize the democratic a ideals of the nation." As a Race Man, Still not only left an important and impressive legacy of composed music, he also helped "create a style of music that was expressive of America" based on African American musical concepts such as complex syncopation and the blues form.

Often referred to as the "Dean of Afro-American Composers," William Grant Still has been credited with pioneering the way and establishing a place for the African American composer of twentieth-century art music. Despite the recent increase of publications on Still and the issuance of numerous new recordings and re-releases of his music, there is still a need for critical study of his career and musical works. Still remains in many ways an enigma, both musically, as the figure he represents in African American art music, and historically, as an individual who lived during sweeping changes in American social history. The title "Dean of Afro-American Composers" is Still's due. Yet it does not aptly describe his accomplishments or the artistic and aesthetic ideals he pursued in his work. Such a title is easily bestowed on Still, who crossed many racial barriers during a period in American history when the achievements of African Americans were measured by *firsts* as a marker of racial progress and improvement in race relations. But to see him in this way is to accord him a place in American music history largely on the basis of his race and to consider only one facet of his accomplishments.

A more complete understanding of Still and his music results from situating him in music history and intellectual history based on other criteria. He participated in three musical trends in art music during the first half of the twentieth century. One of these was American musical modernism. During the period between the two world wars, young American composers, like their European counterparts, sought independence from the aesthetics and conventions of nineteenth-century German romanticism and explored new musical styles and modes of expression.[1] The second trend reflected American musical nationalism; American composers were engaged in a self-conscious attempt to create an art music that would be of an artistic quality equal to that of Europe and also reflective of American culture. The third was the cultural movement known as the Harlem Renaissance, which engaged a number of African American artists and intellectuals. The Harlem Renaissance, or New Negro movement, took place during a period of self-conscious African American culture definition lasting from approximately 1919 to 1934 and found expression in literature, art, music, theater, and the performing and plastic arts.

A deeper understanding of Still's position in American art music history begins by considering his position in African American art music history. Still should be viewed as a composer who reached artistic maturity in New York during the Harlem Renaissance. He can be deemed appropriately a Harlem Renaissance composer: throughout his career, his musical works and professional activities reified the visions of the leaders of the movement; his aesthetics, as voiced through his writings, amplified the mission of the figures associated with the Harlem Renaissance.

THE HARLEM RENAISSANCE

The Harlem Renaissance is conventionally perceived primarily as a literary movement, one that began toward the end of World War I and flourished during the 1920s and 1930s.[2] *The New Negro*, a collection of essays, poetry, and graphic art edited by Alain Locke, a professor of philosophy at Howard University, in 1925, served as a cultural manifesto, expressing the aspirations and visions of the movement. Locke identified New York's Harlem as a cultural and social mecca for African Americans, or the race capital. Attracting blacks from throughout the world, Harlem represented a place where "Negro life [was] seizing upon its first chances for group expression and self-determination."[3] Thus it symbolized the progress made by blacks from slavery through the mid-1920s. In his foreword, Locke described his efforts as presenting the "first fruits of the Negro Renaissance."[4] As such his book provides an important piece of the literary and philosophical background against which Still's work may be viewed. It contains poems by Countee Cullen, Claude McKay, Jean Toomer, James Weldon Johnson, and Arna Bontemps; short fiction by Zora Neale Hurston, Jean Toomer, and Richard Bruce (Nugent); essays on African American visual and graphic art, literature, legitimate and musical theater, and comedies; and a play by Willis Richardson. Music figured prominently in *The New Negro*. Locke contributed an essay, "The Negro Spirituals," and J. A. Rogers wrote "Jazz at Home." The book surveyed more than the arts. There were also essays on the life and culture of the African American in general, ranging from E. Franklin Frazier's "Durham: Capital of the Black Middle Class" to essays by Walter White and Melville Herskovitz on the new urban culture of the African American as reflected by Harlem.

The works of numerous writers—novels, poems, plays—were produced and published during this period, as were journals, newspapers, and magazines. These literary products served as vehicles for the ideas and aspirations of the exponents of the movement. Foremost among the writers who expressed the visions of the Harlem Renaissance were Locke, Johnson, Hurston, Cullen, W. E. B. Du Bois, Sterling Brown, and Langston Hughes. However, the movement was not confined to literature, for the artistic life of Harlem outside of literature was very rich. African Americans found opportunities in other arts such as painting, sculpture, and legitimate theater. Black vernacular music—jazz, blues, and musical theater—thrived. The all-black musical *Shuffle Along* (1921) sparked an interest in African American culture among white Americans. The music of artists such as Duke Ellington and Bessie Smith reached beyond the African American community and emerged on the local New York cultural scene, and into American popular culture. The decade of the 1920s was the heyday of black revues at Harlem theaters such as the Apollo and the Lafayette.[5]

Recently there has been a move toward a more inclusive conceptualization of the Harlem Renaissance, broadening its scope to view it as an intellectual and cultural movement as well as a literary movement. Although it was not specifically political, there were political dimensions to its vision. The chronology has been extended beyond the 1920s and 1930s. Samuel A. Floyd, Jr., considers the Harlem Renaissance as beginning before the end of World I and extends the movement even beyond the location of Harlem itself, viewing it not as an isolated period in African American literary history but as part of a continuum. Reviving Locke's term and referring to it as the Negro Renaissance, Floyd locates its origins in towns and cities across the country before the turn of the century and links it to changes in African American life and intellectual history. He links the Negro Renaissance to the trends of nineteenth-century African American nationalism, the movement of African Americans "from slavery to freedom" and their migration from "rural to city living."[6]

Not only was the Harlem Renaissance concerned with literature and popular music, but art music was a significant part of Harlem musical culture during the 1920s and 1930s. The watershed in art music and the Harlem Renaissance, according to David Levering Lewis, was tenor Roland Hayes's December 1923 Town Hall concert, where he performed both lieder and spirituals. Hayes, and other concert artists such as Marian Anderson and Paul Robeson, demonstrated that African American musical artists were more than capable of performing the classical repertoire. By performing spirituals on the same programs with Italian arias and German lieder, these soloists elevated the African American spiritual to the same artistic level.[7] Performers were not the only figures in African American art music who gained prominence: composers created a body of large- and small-scale works—symphonies, operas, solo and chamber music—many of which were programmed and performed by leading figures and musical institutions in American music.

STILL AND THE HARLEM RENAISSANCE

The biography of William Grant Still allows us to situate him *chronologically* within the framework of the Harlem Renaissance. Still was born in 1895 in Woodville, Mississippi, was raised in Little Rock, and came to maturity during the early years of the Harlem Renaissance. Still was also *geographically* in the midst of the Harlem Renaissance. Eileen Southern first drew attention to the fact that Still's move to New York coincided with the traditionally understood start of the Harlem Renaissance.[8]

Not only was Still in New York during this period, he also participated in the musical life of Harlem. Throughout his residence in New York, Still took part in myriad musical activities that ranged from jazz and popular music to art music to musical theater. During the earliest stages of his career, he was involved in popular music as a performing musician on oboe and cello and as an arranger. He was first drawn to New York by W. C. Handy with an offer in 1919 to work in the Pace & Handy Publishing Company, one of the earliest black-owned and operated publishing companies, and to play in Handy's band. After leaving Handy's band in 1920, he performed with numerous Harlem jazz and popular music ensembles such as the Clef Club orchestras.[9] In 1921 still was involved in the black musical revue *Shuffle Along*, in which he played the oboe and did several of the show's orchestrations. Later he worked for the Pace Recording Company (the Black Swan label), the first black-owned and operated record company, whose recordings included concert music. Still also performed art music, playing oboe in the Harlem Orchestra, a classical music organization. Following his departure from Pace Recording Company, Still turned more and more to orchestrating and arranging professionally, spending the second half of the twenties working not as a performing musician but as an arranger for several musical shows, such as *Rain or Shine* (1928), *Earl Carroll's Vanities of 1926*, and the black revue, *Dixie to Broadway* (1924).[10]

Still's involvement in the Harlem Renaissance extended beyond merely "being in the right place at the right time." He maintained close personal and professional relationships with several prominent novelists, poets, and playwrights. In his most publicized and documented collaboration, he composed the opera *Troubled Island*, a setting of Langston Hughes's libretto of his play *Drums of Haiti*, which was based on the story of Haiti's first emperor, Jean-Jacques Dessalines. Still wrote the opera between 1937 and 1939, completing it five years after his move to Los Angeles (Verna Arvey made minor changes to the libretto in 1941).[11] His collaborations with Harlem Renaissance literary figures began much earlier in New York. During the late twenties Still, desiring to write an opera, had approached several Harlem Renaissance writers and requested librettos from them, including in addition to Langston Hughes, Arna Bontemps and Countee Cullen.[12]

In late 1927 Cullen began to collaborate with Still on an opera originally entitled "Roshana" (later changed to "Rashana"). Cullen was enlisted to provide poetry for Grace Bundy Still's outline. In 1928 Cullen received a Guggenheim Fellowship and in June set sail for France. With Cullen less than enthusiastic about the project, their collaboration came to an end.[13] Another collaboration with a Harlem Renaissance artist during the thirties produced a completed work. A short story by the playwright and actor Carlton Moss provided the basis for the opera *Blue Steel*, and Harold Bruce Forsythe, a Los Angeles writer and musician . . . , supplied the libretto.[14]

Still was an artistic collaborator with Alain Locke. Locke first became aware of Still in the twenties and heard at least two of Still's early works.[15] Taking an interest in Still's career, Locke listed his compositions in the "Bibliography of Negro Music" in *The New Negro*. He brought several texts to Still's attention, one of which would serve as the basis for a major theater work. In 1927 Locke sent Still Richard Bruce's brief fiction, "Sahdji," which had appeared in *The New Negro*, suggesting it as the basis for an African ballet: "Frankly I would like to see you try your hand at this. Will you? Does it interest you?"[16] Locke was persuasive, and contributed to the final version of the scenario. Following the failure of the Still-Cullen collaboration on

"Rashana," Locke suggested to Still that he should write an opera with Bruce as librettist. Though the proposed project ("Atlantis") never materialized, Locke remained interested in Still's career, attending performances of his music and corresponding with him.[17]

Locke recognized Still's importance as one of the few African American art music composers and as someone who could contribute to his program for the promotion of African American culture and race relations. Following the first performance of Still's second symphony, on December 20, 1937, Locke wrote to Still encouraging him to continue his work of composition. Seeking to dispel the sting of negative reviews of the *Symphony in G Minor*, Locke offered his views on the future forms and styles of African American art music. Locke supported Still's musical ideas—his departures from conventional musical forms and musical language—and urged him to continue in the same direction. In addition, Locke expressed concern about the lack of interest among many African American musicians in art music: "It is so strange that nowhere among Negro musicians do you find any really intellectual interest in new works and experimenting."[18]

Thus Still may be situated within the context of the Harlem Renaissance on the basis of chronology, location, and his association with prominent artists and intellectuals. However, Still's involvement with the movement and its influence on his thinking and musical style is much more extensive. The depth of Still's participation in the Harlem Renaissance can be measured by first considering Locke's purpose in publishing *The New Negro*. Examining Still's own writings and his musical works reveals not only how they accord with those of Locke on aesthetic and philosophic points but also how they reflect the visions set forth by Locke and speak the voice of the Harlem Renaissance art music composer.

First appearing in an issue of the *Survey Graphic* dedicated to Harlem, Locke's cultural manifesto was expanded to become a book. In the foreword Locke described the purpose of the book: "to document the New Negro culturally and socially,—to register the transformations of the inner and outer life of the Negro in America that have so significantly taken place in the last few years."[19] Recognizing progressive changes in African American life such as the migrations from the rural South to the urban North and Midwest, Locke constructed the metaphor of the "New Negro." The "New Negro" of 1925 embodied the progress made by blacks since slavery and Reconstruction. These northward migrations produced not only a change in the geography of the black population, or outer life, but also a new psychological outlook and sense of self-awareness, or inner life, which awakened racial identity and racial pride. Locke also sought to show the progress that African Americans had made since the appearance of an earlier work that *The New Negro* evokes, Du Bois's *The Souls of Black Folk*.

In his book, Du Bois laid the intellectual foundation for Locke's volume and Still's intellectual aspirations. Examining the African American condition in 1903, almost a half century after Emancipation, and discussing problems facing the United States, Du Bois defined racism as *the* problem of the twentieth century and addressed issues of social, economic, and political inequality of African Americans. In the opening essay of his book, "Of Our Spiritual Strivings," Du Bois directly refers to the "Race problem" with the question, "how does it feel to be a problem?"[20] Denied the opportunity to speak for themselves and viewing themselves through the eyes of others, blacks lacked a "true self-consciousness."[21] Rather, they possessed a "double-consciousness," which arose from the complex of knowledge of the racial self and knowledge of the American self. The tensions between American democratic ideals, which declared all men equal, and American racism, which denied individuals social, political, and economic parity, resulted in the irony of being both American and black.

Du Bois wrote about racial progress or uplift in "Of the Strivings of Men," which dealt with the black man's striving to merge his two selves. Advancement could be achieved partly through education, artistic culture, and the efforts of the best members of the Race, which he called the "Talented Tenth." In the essay "The Training of Black Men," Du Bois discusses the role higher education could play in the economic progress of the Race by giving blacks the "key to knowledge" and a chance to become professionals rather than laborers or tradesmen.[22] Educated, cultured black individuals could contribute to advancement through the education of other blacks, to their social regeneration by teaching them about life, and to the solution of the race problem through contact and cooperation with whites.[23] These educated individuals would be the new leaders of their communities and would play a role in the future development of the South in improving race relations by promoting racial understanding and working to empower blacks.

In Du Bois's view, music and the arts played an important role in race progress and race relations. In the first essay, where Du Bois speaks of the African American as being handicapped, he wrote about the double bind of the black who desired to compose music. Du Bois described the artistic aspirations of blacks who, wanting "to be a co-worker in the kingdom of culture, to escape both death and isolation, to husband and use his best power and his latent genius," had lacked the opportunity to realize this potential. Speaking of music, he said that though black music was appreciated by blacks, if a black musician composed or performed black music, it was scorned by the "larger audience" outside the race. Without extensive musical training, a black artist had no chance to express his musical art in the concert hall; the black artists of the past "could not articulate the message of another people."[24] In "Of the Sorrow Songs," he described the gift and beauty of black music, specifically the spirituals, noting that they had long been "neglected, . . . half despised, . . . persistently mistaken and misunderstood." These songs were more than just music; they were the voice of the slave through which he spoke of his experience, through which he expressed the conditions of his life and messages of hope.[25] Du Bois considered them the "singular spiritual heritage of the nation and the greatest gift of the Negro people."[26] These "sorrow songs" were also part of America's musical heritage and were America's true cultural gift to the world.[27] For Du Bois, in achieving full participation in American culture, African Americans should be allowed to develop and create their own artistic forms.

Du Bois believed education, the arts, and the Talented Tenth would not only achieve progress in the life and condition of the lives of blacks; together they would also be factors in promoting racial understanding. Locke continued the same themes in his 1925 volume. He described a new generation in his own contribution, "The New Negro."[28] The New Negro was the Young Negro—urban, educated, with poetry, art, and a new outlook that promised a new leadership after fifty years of freedom.[29] The northward migrations then under way were a marker of two types of progress, one economic and the other of ethnic identity. "In the very process of being transplanted," he wrote, "the Negro is being transformed." The changes in African American culture and psychology that accompanied the migration resulted in the development of a new outlook, or a new consciousness. The most important change in the life of African Americans, as represented by the New Negro, was, in Locke's terms, "spiritual emancipation."[30]

Music was central to Locke's beliefs about the cultural strivings of the New Negro. Locke concurred with Du Bois that the spirituals were truly American, the gift of the Negro to American music, and were expressive of African American life, culture, history, and condition. In addition to their beauty and special position as a folk form to be treasured and preserved, the spirituals contained "the richest undeveloped musical resources anywhere available."[31] Thus, in Locke's view, the spirituals held promise for contemporary art music—a potential that had only been touched on by composers such as Dvořák. For Locke, it would not suffice to merely preserve the spirituals; they must also be cultivated.[32] Although Locke acknowledged that the masses were on the vanguard of change in African American life (e.g., migrations, vernacular music such as folk traditions, jazz and blues, and other vernacular culture), it was not folk or popular music that would be redemptive in his vision of artistic culture. Rather, it was a genius, or a member of the Talented Tenth, who should use the spirituals and other black vernacular musical idioms as a resource to create the foundation for an African American art music. Locke cast Still in this role.[33]

Referring to the "voluminous literature" written by others about the Negro, Locke intended to encourage blacks to represent themselves and to view themselves not as a "problem in common" but as a "life in common." In this respect, the arts had more than entertainment, religious, or creative purposes. By allowing the New Negro to speak in his or her own voice, the arts could serve a social purpose beyond individual creative self-expression: the arts were redemptive, serving the strivings of African Americans to develop an ethnic identity. The arts were useful in achieving the Negro's inner objectives as he or she attempted to repair a damaged group psychology and reshape a warped social perspective. By writing about themselves, these New Negroes were "shedding the old chrysalis of the Negro Problem."[34] Through their writings, paintings, poems, plays, ballets, and music—through the creation of a body of artistic works that were expressive of African American thought, history, and contemporary life—African Americans were actively forging a new self-image and ethnic identity other than that of the slave past or of socioeconomic despair. The arts also had a place beyond the African American community in reinforcing the democratic ideals on which America was founded. By means of self-representation achieved through the arts, this younger generation of African Americans could promote racial understanding by combating the myth of the "Negro" and present a more accurate picture of the African American. Locke was not so naive as to believe that racism could be successfully combated by the arts acting alone. Rather, he recognized the need for mutual understanding between the races as a basic prerequisite for furthering race relations in America. The arts could be used to promote greater knowledge among blacks and whites by contributing to a "revaluation by white and black alike of the Negro in terms of his artistic endowments and cultural contributions, past and retrospective."[35]

Still's musical poetics reflect the ideals of the Harlem Renaissance. Throughout, his writings resonated with many of the themes expressed by Du Bois and Locke and amplified them. Still also moved the ideals of the Harlem Renaissance in his music from the realm of abstract thought about the role of music to the aural realm of musical composition and performance. Though the Harlem Renaissance is considered to have ended in the early 1930s, Still continued these themes until his death, attesting to their enduring mission.

Still and his musical compositions fully realized Locke's ideals in two respects. Still created a substantial body of music, composing primarily large forms such as symphonies, operas, ballets, and choral works. Endeavoring to create both an *African American* art music and an *American* art music, Still drew on black vernacular musical traditions for his art music compositions.

Still grouped his mature musical output into three broad stylistic periods. The first spans the early to mid-twenties prior to his studies with the avant-garde composer Edgard Varèse and his modernist period during which he explored modernistic techniques; this period ends in 1925. During the second, 1925 to 1932, Still adopted what he described as the "racial idiom."

These dates correspond to the appearance of Locke's book and the accepted end of the Harlem Renaissance. The third began in 1932 when he turned from the specifically racial idiom toward the "universal idiom."

Still's earliest pre-Varèse compositions can be counted among the earliest works of the Negro Renaissance. Orchestral music and opera greatly appealed to Still. He first attempted to combine popular musics such as jazz and blues with modernistic techniques in these idioms when he arrived in New York and participated in jazz and popular music ensembles. The work *Three Negro Songs* for orchestra has movements entitled "Negro Love Song," "Death Song," and "Song of the Backwoods," all three composed in 1921 in New York. An early work, it nonetheless shows Still incorporating African American melodic idioms in an orchestral work that predates the publication of *The New Negro*. Still had an interest from the beginning of his career in composing art music on Negro themes.[36]

THE ULTRAMODERN IDIOM

During his study with Varèse, Still composed several "ultramodern" works in which he attempted to assimilate experimental techniques of the New Music into his own musical language.[37] He sought to combine traditional African American music with the atonal harmonies of modern music. *Darker America* [is] a work for orchestra composed in 1924 and one of the few surviving works from Still's study with Varèse. . . . Still used melodic types found in African American music such as the descending melodic curve, the pentatonic scale of the spirituals, and the "blues scales" of the blues. The primary harmonies used were the tonic, subdominant, and dominant harmony of the spirituals. Rhythmically, the "Theme of the American Negro" features syncopation, or if viewed in another way, additive rhythm.[38] Structurally, this theme uses the call-and-response that reflects the choral tradition of the spirituals.[39] Combined with African American musical traits are the dissonant harmonies of modern music, which Still used to dramatic end.

Though in his Varèse period works Still found ways of integrating modernist techniques with traditional African American music, he decided to limit the use of what he referred to as the ultramodern style: "Experiments proved to me that the Negroid idiom tends to lose its identity when subjected to such treatment. I wanted to employ an idiom that was unmistakenly Negroid because I wished to do my part in demonstrating to the world that the American Negro is capable of making a valuable contribution in the field of symphonic music, and I wanted to write a Negroid idiom, music that would help build more harmonious race relations."[40] The two musical idioms were not always compatible and when used together produced what he saw as incongruous results. Still felt limited by the dissonant style of Varèse and after ending his studies, began to change his style. He desired to show the beauty of black music and realize its possibilities in the concert hall by example. Dissonant modern music met with great resistance from audiences. If he was to show the beauty and worth of black music, he would have to turn away from dissonant music and compose in an idiom to which audiences would be more receptive. Furthermore, though he had leaped at the chance to study with Varèse, Still was not very comfortable assimilating this style. Still's musical aesthetic placed an emphasis on melody and music that an audience could find easily accessible.

Following his study with Varèse, Still sought a style that would reflect his racial background. He moved away from overt attempts to be modern and concentrated on realizing in an art music context the potential inherent in African American traditional music. By his own account, Still committed himself to black music during the mid-twenties: "After this period,

I felt for a while that I wanted to devote myself to writing racial music."[41] In his first efforts at writing "racial music," Still turned to jazz. He had experimented with jazz earlier but had destroyed many of those works. His first mature jazz work was *Levee Land*, a suite for chamber orchestra and soprano soloist in three movements, composed in 1925 in New York City on texts by Still. "This was one of the very first efforts toward a symphonic treatment of jazz motifs."[42] Still used instrumentation suggestive of a jazz or popular music orchestra of the twenties. Melodically, harmonically, and rhythmically, the style of the work resembles various types of popular jazz from the twenties. Carol Oja has identified the manner in which Still combined modern dissonant harmonies with standard blues harmony and vocal and instrumental techniques.[43] *Levee Land* has additional experimental features, particularly the text and the way in which Still uses the voice. The voice is used not in a narrative fashion but instrumentally, repeating a text consisting mostly of short phrases such as "hey" and "baby" that were inflected to express different emotions ranging from sadness to humor and surprise. (This is in contrast to the use of three untexted voices in *From the Land of Dreams*, another work from the same period.)

Aside from the limited use of modernistic techniques, *Levee Land* can be considered modern in the context of African American music and culture; it was a departure from Du Bois's and Locke's concept of "traditional music." Both Du Bois and Locke felt that African American folk materials of the spirituals and other "sorrow songs" could be used to build a great African American and American art music. Other proponents of the movement differed in their views on the use of folklore. Writers such as Sterling Brown, Langston Hughes, and Zora Neale Hurston held the view that the "folk" materials of jazz and blues, the vernacular of African Americans, were the substance of African American art. Their creative efforts used the expressions of African American speech, folktales, and the lyric forms of the blues. Forms such as the spirituals were rooted in pre-twentieth-century, rural African American history. The musical forms of jazz and blues, when Still began using these, were associated primarily with urban centers such as Memphis, New Orleans, Chicago, and New York and with the "city blues," or singers such as Ma Rainey and Bessie Smith, respectively. Just as Locke had documented the New Negro as urban, Still was expressing the contemporary African American, the urban black, of the mid-twenties, not the Negro of the slave or rural past. Still was also attempting in *Levee Land* to show the beauty of jazz and its usefulness as a basis for modern art music by integrating it within an experimental work.

THE RACIAL IDIOM

In the early 1930s Still, desiring to demonstrate the worth of an African American music that was denigrated by both whites and middle-class blacks, expressed his views in a typescript that may have been an early version of his earliest published essay, "An Afro-American Composer's Point of View."

> I feel that it is best for me to confine myself to composition of a racial nature. The music of my people is the music I understand best. It offers the medium through which I can express myself with greater clarity and ease. Then too, I am convinced that the time has arrived when the Negro composer must turn from the recording of Spirituals to the development of the contributions of his race, and to the work of elevating them to higher artistic planes.[44]

Still thus shifted his musical aesthetic from an objective modernistic one toward a proactive one that aligned more directly with Locke's aesthetic of redemptive culture but differed from it in one important respect.

The change in aesthetic resulted in a change in Still's musical style. He curtailed the use of dissonance but continued to create new forms, frequently drawing on folk forms and modifying them. Among his early compositions in his "racial" idiom were songs such as "Winter's Approach" and "Breath of a Rose" (composed in New York City in 1926–1927), settings of poems by Paul Laurence Dunbar and Langston Hughes, respectively. Analysis of both these songs reveals that Still combined African American vernacular musical forms such as the eight-bar blues with suggestions of modern dissonant harmony. Although Still continued to compose art songs, he was never completely drawn to the genre. He wrote, "Frankly, this art form has never appealed to me sufficiently for me to devote much thought to it."[45]

Still also turned to sources other than jazz or the spirituals. In the *Afro-American Symphony*, composed in New York City in 1930, Still turned to the blues, explaining, "I wanted to prove conclusively that the Negro musical idiom is an important part of the world's musical culture. That was the reason I decided to create a musical theme in the Blues idiom and develop it into the highest of musical forms—the Symphony."[46] Still had extensive experience with the blues during his tenure with W. C. Handy in Memphis. He assimilated elements of the idiom into his personal style. The first theme of the *Afro-American Symphony* displays essential features such as the "blues scale" of the lowered third and seventh scale degree, a falling melodic contour, and the call-and-response structure. He integrated African American musical elements into the formal aspects of the piece, basing parts of the first movement's internal sections on the twelve-bar blues form. These internal divisions were incorporated into a modified sonata form, a conventional form used in the Western European art music genres of symphony and sonata. Thus Still embedded a local form within a global form. By composing original music in an African American idiom, Still began to realize Locke's vision. By example, Still demonstrated that folk music could migrate from the dance hall to the concert hall. African American folk and vernacular music could be transformed into high art.

Still reified the Harlem Renaissance ideals not only aurally but also philosophically and historically. Many of his works bear programs. Considered by themselves, several of his works present a slice of African American life in music; considered as a group, they present a varied picture of the history, culture, and psychology of blacks in America. *Darker America* operates on multiple levels as Still's representation of his own culture and history. The themes taken in sequence depict the history of the American Negro, or the triumph over sorrow through prayer and hope.[47] At the end of the piece, Still constructed a musical profile of the psychology of the American Negro by presenting the three principal themes in counterpoint, using the dense texture of interwoven melodic lines to represent a complex psyche, or racial Self. The complex inner life of the American Negro is further expressed through Still's use of dissonance. Introduced after the first statement of the "Theme of the American Negro," the modern dissonances following the consonant "spiritual" melody illustrate irony—or double-consciousness, after Du Bois—the irony of being an American Negro in the United States, or a member of Darker America. The *Afro-American Symphony* was also meant to be a psychological or emotional portrait of the Negro. . . .[48]

Pairing the *Afro-American Symphony* and the *Symphony in G Minor* further reveals the nature of Still's historicism. *The Symphony in G Minor* was subtitled "Song of a New Race" by Leopold Stokowski, who suggested Still add subtitles that expressed what feeling or thought had inspired him to each movement in order to "help [the] public to enter more intimately [the] mood of each movement."[49] Still considered this symphony, composed in 1937 in Los Angeles, an extension of and companion piece to the *Afro-American Symphony*.[50] "The principal theme of the first movement of the G Minor is allied, indeed derived from, the thematic material in the final movement of the 'Afro-American.'"[51] Still described his intentions in composing the symphony: "It may be said that the purpose of the Symphony in G Minor is to point musically to changes wrought in a people through the progressive and transmuting spirit of America."[52] The two works are analogous to the *Souls of Black Folk–New Negro* pair that documents the progress of blacks from the nineteenth-century rural "Old Negro" to the urban, educated New Negro of the twentieth century. As a pair, Still's symphonies reflect this race progress, documenting the life and culture of blacks, in musical terms, in much the same way that both Du Bois and Locke set about to describe the condition of the Negro in letters. Outlining the program, Still wrote that "the *Afro-American Symphony* represented the Negro of the days not far removed from the Civil War."[53] He described the *Symphony in G Minor* as "represent[ing] the American colored man of today."[54] The first symphony expressed emotional longing, sorrow, humor, and aspirations; the second symphony expressed more immediate optimism and the self-empowerment of a people who could now take action.[55] Still continued to write a history of African Americans in music, tracing various stages from origins in Africa through slavery to the twentieth century. In composing his history in music, Still drew largely on musical styles of the urban New Negro and was actively expanding the range and scope of African American art music.

Still's output was not limited to musical composition. He also spoke and wrote extensively on music. In his earliest published articles, such as "An Afro-American Composer's Point of View" in Henry Cowell's *American Composers on American Music* (1932), Still wrote as a representative of the race.[56] Subsequent articles written by Still, and those on which he collaborated with Verna Arvey, addressed various subjects ranging from music to interracial marriage and politics. Still also gave numerous addresses before various groups: professional and student music organizations, college audiences and faculty, church groups, and schools. Since his days in New York, Still had spoken on music. On May 5 of the same year his first article was published, Still delivered the address "Modernism in Music." He spoke during the session "Modern Trends in Music," one of the events held during the Ninth Annual Music Week in Harlem, sponsored by the New York branch of the National Association of Negro Musicians and the West 135th Street branch of the YMCA.[57]

Throughout his writings and speeches on music, Still revealed his personal musical aesthetics, addressing modern music, American musical nationalism, African American music, and the African American musician. While his writings expressed his own ideas, within them resonate the philosophies of the Harlem Renaissance. After the public success of his *Afro-American Symphony*, Still began to occupy a prominent position from which he could speak with authority on African American music. He addressed musicological questions such as the history and stylistic features of African American vernacular music and aesthetic questions such as their value and position in African American culture and American music at a time when American art music was seeking to define itself. His writings and speeches served a twofold purpose: (1) they articulated the voice of the black composer on his own music, and (2) they educated others, black and white, about black music.

In his articles and speeches on the spirituals, jazz, and blues, Still sought to do in words what he had done in music. Since most of his writings appeared in the mainstream press, Still was addressing primarily a white audience. He dissociated black vernacular music from its negative stereotypes by explaining its style and history. Expounding on its beauty and virtues, he defended its importance and place in American art music and culture.

The promoters of the Harlem Renaissance, James Weldon Johnson and Alain Locke, had an uneasy position on jazz. They thought it could be useful in building a great art music, but by itself, it was not art.[58] Sterling Brown and Langston Hughes maintained a more amiable position toward the vernacular, basing many of their poems on the blues. Many middle-class blacks disapproved of jazz and blues, associating them with nightclubs and brothels. Still often pointed out that during his younger days, the blues were considered immoral. This he attributed to their association with barrooms and brothels and to the belief that they expressed only, in his own words, "sexual cravings." The nightlife origins of these musical forms went against black middle-class propriety and also reinforced negative white stereotypes of black sexuality. Still attempted to free both jazz and blues from their negative associations by emphasizing their beauty, their unique musical qualities, and their overall value to American music.

Still departed from Locke in recognizing the inherent value in jazz and blues. His experience touring with Handy and his blues band as a performer and arranger during 1916 and 1919 created a lasting impression on him: "I learned, for example, to appreciate the beauty of the blues, and to consider this the musical expression of the yearnings of a lowly people, instead of accepting it superficially as being immoral and sexy, as so many other people did."[59] He sought to educate others about the music, distinguishing between two distinct types of blues—rural or country blues and urban or city blues. The first was the "traditional blues," or rural folk blues, which he "associated with emotional expression." The second type was the "sophisticated blues," or city blues, which was usually associated with dancing.[60] For Still, the primary value of both types lay in their unique musical features. Assuming the role of music theorist, he noted that the blues used both a special scale and a unique form, the twelve-bar blues, neither of which was found in any other type of music.

The second redeeming feature of the blues was their emotional expressiveness. Still believed that the "emotional content of Blues springs from a deeper and worthier source than mere sexual desire." "I refer specifically," he wrote, "to the traditional type of Blues which seems to me to express a yearning for unattainable happiness."[61] Du Bois considered the spirituals to be expressive of the emotions or the inner life and strivings of the Negro during slavery. As a type of syncretic music in which African melody, rhythm, and musical structure were combined with Western musical elements such as functional harmony, they embodied the twoness of the Negro in that they were both African and American. Still's ideas on the blues as expressive of blacks' longings and desires and their unique African American features parallel those of Du Bois. The emotional content of the blues expressed the history and consciousness of African Americans in the United States as they fought slavery and racial discrimination.

Still held a similar position on jazz, which represented to him an important development in American music: "It appears to me that any form of expression which has spread over America and from there all over the world, which has (after many decades of public recognition) retained the power to interest intelligent thinkers like Mr. [Winthrop] Sargeant and which has found its way, in some form, into serious American music of all types, is a vital force that cannot be pushed aside lightly."[62] Like blues, jazz was rich in emotional expressiveness: "Negro music has given to those who create it, who interpret it and who merely enjoy it a sincerity and an emotional freedom that provides a release for pent-up feelings. The sensuous jazz as well as Negro folk music and the serious, sophisticated music created by Negroes, partake of this sincerity."[63] Still recognized the contributions that jazz musicians had made to American music, particularly in the areas of instrumental technique, orchestration, and rhythm.[64] In addition to its musical value as a vernacular art form, Still held the view that jazz should also be used in creating art music and believed further that all American composers should familiarize themselves with the idiom and use it as one of many musical resources.

Still also sought to dispel myths about jazz. The great misconception was that jazz was the African American's sole contribution to music. Having begun his career performing popular jazz, Still greatly valued this type of music; however, he sought to counter any judgments of black musicians that limited them to jazz or popular music and to bring attention to the endeavors of black composers of art music. Still did not seek to denigrate vernacular music but to clarify the public's understanding of the range of African American musical activity. He also valued the spirituals highly, considering them perhaps the African American's single most important contribution to the music of the nation. Addressing the controversy over the origins of the spirituals—whether they were of black origin or merely paraphrases of white Protestant hymn—he staunchly defended their African American origin. He addressed more than their history. The spirituals were greatly esteemed because of their history and redemptive power: "Long before the advent of jazz, Negro Spirituals had made a large dent in the public consciousness on more than one continent, and their wide dissemination also was a contribution to good race relations."[65] The spirituals were also valuable for the composer. This repertory presented the musician, in Still's estimation, with "a large amount of new and untouched musical material—material that will, in fact, always be new and untouched because it is constantly being re-born, just as the folk music in other lands."[66] African American vernacular music, sacred and secular, rural and urban, could be used by American composers, black and white, as a musical resource for art music.

Although Still consistently and strongly advocated positioning African American vernacular music within the American musical heritage, he believed that African American music should not be limited to vernacular music. In effect, he was a Talented Tenth Race leader, demonstrating that it was possible for a black man to be active as a composer of art music and encouraging young, aspiring black musicians. Still believed that art music was a new field open to African Americans. That black art music was welcomed in the concert hall was, for Still, proof of "America's basically democratic spirit" and emblematic of an improvement in race relations.[67]

Still was quite aware of the dilemma faced by the black composer. Aware that Americans patronized popular music more than they did serious music, Still advised the black composer to go into popular music if his or her goal was to become wealthy, but to resist being arbitrarily shunted into popular music. As he pointed out, "Another reason [black composers could become wealthy in popular music] is that a Negro in this field conforms to many people's idea of where a Negro ought to stay."[68] But Still encouraged other African Americans who were interested and possessed the talent to enter art music. Although not as financially remunerative as popular music or jazz, art music had greater social value for the Race. "In serious music, a Negro can be a pioneer and thus contribute to racial advancement and to inter-racial understanding, and he can have the satisfaction of doing something eminently worthwhile."[69] In the philosophy of redemptive culture, an African American working in art music served the Race both as a leader and role model and as a cultural ambassador to whites. These individuals were not merely artists but cultural activists—promoters of race relations. In the aesthetics of redemptive culture, works created by these composers were not merely artistic products but rungs in the ladder of racial uplift and racial progress.

Still directly addressed racism and race relations in his writings. Aware of racism from his own painful experiences, Still knew that though he was an accomplished man, there were obstacles facing him in society. Publicly, he tended to downplay racism, frequently stating that racial prejudice had not greatly hindered his progress and career as a composer. In his diary and in personal correspondence, however, Still frequently expressed sentiments to the contrary. For example, in a letter to Irving Schwerké, his friend and Paris-based American music critic, Still confided his frustration: "It is unfortunate for a man of color who is ambitious to live in America." At a moment when he had been unemployed for some months, he spoke of those "who are opposed to placing a colored man in any position of prominence."[70] Still expressed these sentiments in 1931, within a month after completing the *Afro-American Symphony*.

Views presented in "Are Negro Composers Handicapped?" in the November 1937 issue of the *Baton* are representative of his public statements. There, Still addressed whether the African American art music composer was denied opportunity and success because of his or her race. Though Still admitted that he had experienced racial prejudice and segregation, he did not believe that race presented a problem to the black composer. In music a composer could not succeed solely by virtue of his or her race; talent was the great determining factor. "Thus musically, the colored man is handicapped solely by the extent of his own capacity—or his lack thereof—of advancement."[71] Still did concede that African Americans faced difficulties, but these were not specific to any particular field: "No, the handicap of the Negro composer has nothing to do with music; it is one that must be faced not only by the composer but also by every person of color in America."[72] Despite incidents of racism, Still remained optimistic, believing relations between the races were improving and prejudice was being gradually replaced by racial understanding: "These and other handicaps of similar nature would probably grieve me greatly were it not that I find them gradually but steadily being displaced by better understanding and more harmonious relationships."[73] He believed that it was ignorant, "ill-bred" people who were racially prejudiced and that "cultured people in the country are those who are free from racial antipathy."[74] Through education and culture, people could overcome racism.

Music could play an active role in Still's vision of racial understanding and progress in race relations. Black art music could redeem the nation and aid in fulfilling the promise of democracy in America. A profound believer in American democracy, Still accorded the African American artist in the United States special significance: "The Negro artist is important in American society because he demonstrates that achievement is possible in our democracy."[75] The black artist was the Talented Tenth Race leader who, through the arts, dissolved the Du Boisian irony of being both black and American by merging the two selves and fulfilling the longing of being a "co-worker in the kingdom of culture." The African American artist promoted good public relations. African American composers and African American art music were powerful embodiments of the Lockeian vision of redemptive culture: "Negro music is also important to the *world* as well as to the nation, for as we place emphasis on our worthy cultural products, we also further the cause of better human relations, as well as better race relations. In a concrete way, we are helping to negate the bad effects of the actions of delinquents and others who are publicized in such a way as to give the Race a bad name. *Everything* we can do to help propagandize our *good* points should be done at this time, and also in the future."[76]

THE UNIVERSAL IDIOM

Though Still spoke specifically as a "Race Man," articulating the Harlem Renaissance/New Negro themes of racial progress and racial understanding, his vision was not limited to African Americans. He believed that each ethnic group had something to contribute musically, and therefore culturally and socially, to the fabric of the United States. The contribution of various groups to the artistic culture of the nation would unite the nation across racial boundaries. He expressed himself in what he referred to as the Negro idiom because of his desire to show the beauty of the music. However, his style was not limited to the racial idiom. During the early 1930s, he turned to what he later called his universal idiom. In addition to black vernacular music, he also drew on other American and New World folk music sources, such as cowboy songs, Latin American and Caribbean traditions, music suggestive of Native Americans, and Hispanic missionary music from pre-statehood California. The race issue was not limited to just blacks and whites but encompassed all racial and ethnic groups. Still believed that "when we all awaken to the fact that each group has something important and worthwhile to contribute to the culture of the entire country, then we will have a society that is well integrated—in which all of us will be working for the common good."[77]

Yet Still was not a political activist; he was a composer. Though his compositions bear racial titles, such as the *Afro-American Symphony* and *Darker America,* for the most part these works were not overtly political. They depict abstractions of the history or the psychology of blacks. As he put it, "Some people have tried to work through legal or political means, but I have sought to work through friendship and music, expressed in my own way and according to my personal beliefs."[78] In this respect, two works stand out in that they directly addressed racial violence and racial injustice. The composition *And They Lynched Him on a Tree* (1940), a setting of the poem by Katharine Garrison Chapin, confronted the issue of racial violence. Still employed two choruses as personae in the lynching drama: the white chorus assumed the role of an angry, unruly, hate-filled mob; the black chorus assumed the role of the victims and opposers of racial hatred. The soloist sang the role of the mother.[79] At the end of the work the choruses joined together to plead for racial tolerance and the brotherhood of man. Wayne Shirley has established that Still was composing the piece as an antilynching bill was passed by the House of Representatives and was being argued before the Senate.[80] Once again, Alain Locke played a major role in the genesis of a Still composition, sending Still a copy of the poem and recruiting him to compose the music. Locke described the poem as "really an epic indictment but by way of pure poetry not propaganda."[81] Following its first performance, Locke applauded its success in a review in the pages of *Opportunity*. The review read, in part, "[It] universalizes its particular theme and expands a Negro tragedy into a purging and inspiring plea for justice and a fuller democracy." A work such as this was a prime example of Locke's aesthetic of redemptive art: "When, on occasion, art rises to this level, it fuses truth with beauty, and in addition to being a sword for the times it is likely to remain, as a thing of beauty, a joy forever."[82]

During World War II, Still, like many other composers, turned to patriotic themes. His music, however, took on dual significance. *In Memoriam: The Colored Soldiers Who Died for Democracy* carried an ironic subtext. The work was dedicated to black soldiers who were facing discrimination both in the segregated units in the armed forces and at home yet were fighting "to make the world safe for democracy." It signified both the double-consciousness of the Negro and the incongruousness of democracy, racism, and war. It, like *And They Lynched Him on a Tree,* served a social end through artistic means.

The writings and music of William Grant Still are suffused with the ideals and spirit of the Harlem Renaissance. Resonating with Still's writings and music are central themes raised by Locke, Du Bois, and Hughes (with whom he later worked): the creation, preservation, and cultivation of African American music—art music primarily but also vernacular music; progress of the race from slavery to the early twentieth century; and redemptive culture, or the aesthetic that the arts could serve to combat racial discrimination by promoting racial understanding. Still believed that the African American composer should not be limited only to black musical idioms—to expressing only his or her racial background. All styles were open to the African American who could compose in any genre, form, or style of music he or she chose. Still himself eventually chose to move beyond a racial idiom, turning to what he described as the "universal idiom" in the 1930s. In his writings and works that specifically address issues of race relations and racism, one can hear the philosophies of Du Bois and Locke and their ideas on how art could be redemptive and serve as one tool to bring about progress in race relations and racial understanding. Although committed to using his efforts in the field of art music to serve this purpose of promoting better race relations, Still saw his work as not just serving America and African Americans. He approached his compositions with great spirituality and believed that his music should serve all of humanity and promote universal brotherhood. Despite Still's move toward the universal idiom, he remained a strong advocate for African American music. The Harlem Renaissance came to an end in the early thirties, but for Still, who came to artistic maturity at about this time, the spirit and visions of the Renaissance endured.

Still's work in African American and American art music should be reassessed at least partly on the basis of his participation as a modernist and his participation in the Harlem Renaissance. He should be seen not as the "Dean of Afro-American Composers" but more suitably as a "Harlem Renaissance Man." Like Du Bois and Locke and his other contemporaries, he was a Race Man, advocating progress of the Race and progress in race relations so as to fully realize the democratic ideals of the nation. Indeed, his ideas about the rise of modernism and twentieth-century American musical nationalism were dominated by his position as a Race man.

Still left a substantial body of music—nearly two hundred works. In many of these, just as he sought to realize the aesthetics of the Harlem Renaissance, he also sought to create a style of music that was expressive of America. Perhaps the years following the 1995 centennial of Still's birth will bring about a renaissance of Still studies and result in a deeper understanding of Still as a man of letters and as a man of music. Perhaps he will be seen, more properly, as "Still, American Composer of American Music."

Abbreviations

Du Bois — Du Bois, W. E. B. *The Souls of Black Folk.* Originally published Chicago: McClurg, 1903.

IOL — Arvey, Verna. *In One Lifetime.* Fayetteville: University of Arkansas Press, 1984.

Still-Arvey Papers — William Grant Still and Verna Arvey Papers, Special Collections Division, University of Arkansas Libraries, Fayetteville

Notes

1. See Carol J. Oja, "'New Music' and the 'New Negro': The Background of William Grant Still's *Afro-American Symphony*," BMRJ 12, no. 2 (Fall 1992): 145–169, for a study of Still's involvement in modernist music circles in New York during the mid-twenties.

2. See Nathan Irvin Huggins, *Harlem Renaissance* (London: Oxford University Press, 1971); David Levering Lewis, *When Harlem Was in Vogue* (New York: Oxford University Press, 1979); Cary D. Wintz, *Black Culture and the Harlem Renaissance* (Houston: Rice University

Press, 1988); and George Hutchinson, *The Harlem Renaissance in Black and White* (Cambridge, Mass.: Belknap Press of Harvard University Press, 1996).
3. Alain Locke, *The New Negro* (1925; reprint New York: Atheneum, 1968), 7.
4. Ibid., xvii.
5. Huggins, *Harlem Renaissance*, 291.
6. Samuel A. Floyd, Jr., ed., *Black Music in the Harlem Renaissance* (New York: Greenwood Press, 1990), 173.
7. Lewis, *When Harlem Was in Vogue,* 163.
8. Eileen Southern, "William Grant Still—Trailblazer," in Claire Detels, ed., *William Grant Still Studies at the University of Arkansas: A 1984 Congress Report* (Fayetteville: University of Arkansas–Fulbright College of Arts and Sciences, 1985), 2.
9. The Clef Club functioned as a booking agency or business organization active in securing employment for black musicians, sometimes fielding several orchestras simultaneously.
10. Arvey, *IOL,* 60.
11. Letter, William Grant Still to Ralph McCombs, March 30, 1949; William Grant Still, "Highway 1, U.S.A.," typescript of speech, p. 3, Still-Arvey Papers.
12. Still, "Highway 1, U.S.A.," 2.
13. Donald Dorr, "Chosen Image: The Afro-American Vision in the Operas of William Grant Still," *Opera Quarterly* 4, no. 2 (Summer 1986): 1–23, reprinted in *Fusion* 2, 144–161.
14. Moss was one of the organizers and one of three African American men named to direct the Negro Theater Unit of the WPA Federal Theater Project in New York City. The others were Harry Edwards and Augustus Smith. "Three Colored Men Are Named to Direct the Negro WPA Theater," unidentified clipping, Scrapbook, 1935–1936, n.p., Still-Arvey Papers. *Blue Steel* has never been performed.
15. Alain Locke to William Grant Still, July 8, 1927, Still-Arvey Papers.
16. Locke to Still, July 8, 1927, Still-Arvey Papers.
17. Dorr, "Chosen Image." Dorr erroneously interprets Locke's "Bruce" as Harold Bruce Forsythe. In his correspondence, Locke regularly referred to other males by their last names; he wrote to "Dear Still" and signed himself "Locke." Neither Richard Bruce, who eventually dropped his family name (Nugent), nor Forsythe, who was almost certainly unknown to Locke, is an exception.
18. Locke to Still, December 20, 1937, Still-Arvey Papers.
19. Locke, *The New Negro,* xv.
20. Du Bois, 44.
21. Ibid., 45.
22. Ibid., 136.
23. Ibid., 138.
24. Ibid., 47.
25. Ibid., 270.
26. Ibid., 265.
27. Ibid. Still turned beyond the spiritual to the blues as having absorbed less Caucasian influence than the spiritual, however. See "The *Afro-American Symphony* and Its Scherzo," below.
28. The preferred term to refer to persons of African descent dwelling in the United States is "African American," though "black" is also currently used. Throughout this article, the term "Negro" is employed as a metaphor, either as Locke used the term in *The New Negro*, to refer to an ideal, or as an abstraction of myths or stereotypes.
29. Locke, *The New Negro,* 5.
30. Ibid., 4
31. Ibid., 200.
32. Ibid., 210.
33. Ibid., 15.
34. Ibid., 4.
35. Ibid., 15.
36. The manuscript for this work resurfaced in 1995, since the original publication of this article, and is in the possession of WGSM. Future study of this work promises to illuminate Still's style prior to study with Varèse. I am grateful to Catherine Parsons Smith for allowing me to examine a copy of this manuscript.
37. For further discussion of Still's "ultramodernism" during his Varèse period, see Oja, "Still." . . . Still expressed his admiration for Varèse several times. A letter from Varèse to Dane Rudhyar, listing his best students and describing them, gives his teacher's view of Still:

7 March 1928
. . .
William G. Still—A Negro, my student since 1922, lyrical nature, typical of his race. I handle him with care, not wishing that he should lose these qualities, but not

wishing that he should keep the banalities of the whites that was inculcated through the course he followed at the New England Conservatory. . . . These [i.e., Edouardo Fabini, Adolf Weiss, Colin McPhee, Sam Reichmann, and Still] are the students who do themselves credit and for whom we await with confidence and hope what the future will allow them to achieve.

William G. Still nègre—mon élève depuis 1922—nature lyrique—et typique de sa race. Je le pendle avec précaution—ne voulant pas qu'il perde ses qualités—mais ne voulant pas non plus qu'il garde les poncifes "des blancs" qui lui ont été inculquè par les cours qu'il a suivi au New England Conservatory. Ceci. . . . Faites lui crèdit et attendez avec confiance et espère ce que le futur leur permettre de réaliser.

Rudhyar Collection, Department of Special Collections, Stanford University Library, Stanford University.

38. For the musical themes in *Darker America*, see "William Grant Still and Irving Schwerké," below.
39. Call-and-response is a structural pattern in which a melodic phrase or call, sung by a leader, is answered by another phrase or response, sung by another voice or by a group.
40. William Grant Still, "American Art and Culture: The Negro's Contribution," October 24–27, 1966, typescript of speech, p. 5, Still-Arvey Papers. [Editor's note: Another of his "ultramodern" works, *From the Land of Dreams*, . . . certainly helped to precipitate this decision, since it is even more dissonant than *Darker America*, and its use of blues much less obvious. *From the Land of Dreams*, however, was neither published nor given a second performance, and was unknown to critics and commentators on Still's music until the rediscovery of its score in 1997 by Carolyn L. Quin.]
41. William Grant Still, "The Contemporary Composer and His Audience," June 15, 1964, typescript, p. 6, Still-Arvey Papers. Still's move away from modernism was probably more difficult because he admired Varèse as a musician and a man.
42. William Grant Still Thematic Catalog, n.d., p. 7, Still-Arvey Papers.
43. Oja, "Still," 157.
44. William Grant Still, untitled essay, [Ladies and Gentlemen], n.d., typescript, p. 4, Still-Arvey Papers.
45. Letter, William Grant Still to William Treat Upton, n.d. [ca. 1925], Upton Collection, LC.
46. William Grant Still, untitled speech, delivered February 2., 1968, at Honors Luncheon, Association of the Presentation and Preservation of the Arts, 1968, typescript, p. 1, Still-Arvey Papers. See "The *Afro-American Symphony* and Its Scherzo," for two other statements by Still, both much closer to the time of the symphony's composition, that strongly reinforce this view.
47. Throughout this paragraph, the term "Negro" is used metaphorically.
48. Still, untitled speech on the *Afro-American Symphony*, n.d., typescript, p. 1, Still-Arvey Papers.
49. Leopold Stokowski telegram to Still, December 2, 1937, Still-Arvey Papers.
50. William Grant Still Thematic Catalog, 27.
51. Letter, Still to Rudolph Dunbar, December 1, 1945, Still-Arvey Papers. . . .
52. Letter, Still to Irving Schwerké, December 20, 1937, Still-Arvey Papers.
53. Ibid.
54. Ibid.
55. Ibid.
56. William Grant Still, "An Afro-American Composer's Point of View," in Henry Cowell, ed., *American Composers on American Music* (Stanford: Stanford University Press, 1932), 182–183.
57. Program for the Ninth Annual Music Week in Harlem, May 2–7, 1932, Still-Arvey Papers.
58. Huggins, *Harlem Renaissance*, 198.
59. William Grant Still, "A Composer's Viewpoint," *Fusion* 2, 64.
60. Still, speech, "The Composer's Creed," May 29, 1963, and January 22, 1964, for Dr. Karl With's class, University of California, Los Angeles, typescript, p. 5, Still-Arvey Papers.
61. Ibid., 6.
62. Letter, Still to Joseph W. Ferman, September 23, 1943, Still-Arvey Papers.

63. William Grant Still, "The Music of My Race" (English translation of "La Musica de Mi Raza"), p. 2, Still-Arvey Papers.
64. Ibid.
65. Still, speech, "Negro Music," July 22, 1969, typescript, p. 6, Still-Arvey Papers.
66. William Grant Still and Verna Arvey, "Negro Music in the Americas," *Revue Internationale de Musique* (Brussels) 1 (May–June): 283. In his early written remarks about the *Afro-American Symphony*, however, he argued in favor of using the blues in preference to the spirituals because the blues was the black music least influenced by the European tradition. See "The *Afro-American Symphony* and Its Scherzo," below.
67. William Grant Still, "Serious Music: New Field for the Negro," *Variety* 197 (January 5, 1955): 227.
68. William Grant Still, "Can Music Make a Career?" *Negro Digest* 7 (December 1948): 82.
69. Ibid., 82.
70. Letter, Still to Schwerké, January 9, 1931. . . .
71. Still, "Are Negro Composers Handicapped?" *Baton* (November 1937): n.p.
72. Ibid.
73. Ibid.
74. Ibid.
75. Still, interview, ed. Edward Kamarck, *Arts in Society, Special Issue: The Arts and the Black Revolution* (n.p.: Research Studies and Developments in the Arts, University Extension, University of Wisconsin, 1968): 222.
76. Still, speech for the installation of new officers of the Los Angeles Chapter of National Association of Negro Musicians, 1963, p. 2, Still-Arvey Papers.
77. Letter, Still to Richard Bardolph, October 15, 1955.
78. Still, speech, "The Composer's Creed," p. 4, Still-Arvey Papers. This becomes particularly important given Still's opposition to communism, for the Communist party took the position that music was indeed a political expression. He obviously wanted it to serve the cause of racial equality, however.
79. William Grant Still Thematic Catalog, 32.
80. Wayne D. Shirley, "William Grant Still's Choral Ballad *And They Lynched Him on a Tree*," *AM* 12 (Winter 1994): 425–461.
81. Letter, Locke to Still, August 9, 1939, Still-Arvey Papers.
82. As quoted in Dorr, "Chosen Image," 9.

19 Easter Sunday
MARIAN ANDERSON

Marian Anderson, one of the best-known and important sacred and classical vocalists to emerge in the twentieth century, spent much of her life breaking new ground. She grew up singing in her Philadelphia church and began more formal training in classical singing while in high school. Her interest in both genres continued throughout her life. Anderson emerged as a featured vocalist at the 1919 National Baptist Convention, gained fame on European stages some ten years later, and in the 1950s appeared in venues as varied as The Ed Sullivan Show and stages throughout Asia as part of a lengthy U.S. State Department tour. In 1955 Anderson debuted as the first black American to ever sing at the Met.

This piece, first published as a chapter in her 1956 autobiography My Lord, What a Morning *(currently in print by the University of Illinois Press), narrates the historical and controversial events around her scheduled appearance at Constitution Hall in 1939. Although she had appeared on the grand stages of Europe and was represented by impresario Sol Hurok, the Daughters of the American Revolution refused to allow her to take the stage. The wave of public protests that followed—led by Eleanor Roosevelt and Secretary of the Interior Harold Ickes—led to an invitation to sing at the Lincoln Memorial on Easter Sunday before a crowd of an estimated 75,000 fans. This unprecedented chain of events not only foreshadowed the Civil Rights Movement, it also stands out as one of the most significant concerts in our musical history.*

The division between time spent in Europe and in the United States changed gradually. In my second season under Mr. Hurok's management there was already more to do at home, and less time was devoted to Europe. Soon there were so many concerts to do in the cities of the United States that a trip abroad for concerts had to be squeezed in. There is no doubt that my work was drawing the attention of larger circles of people in wider areas of our country. Fees went up, and I hope that I was making a return in greater service.

Mr. Hurok's aim was to have me accepted as an artist worthy to stand with the finest serious ones, and he sought appearances for me in all the places where the best performers were expected and taken for granted. The nation's capital was such a place. I had sung in Washington years before–in schools and churches. It was time to appear on the city's foremost concert platform—Constitution Hall.

As it turned out, the decision to arrange an appearance in Constitution Hall proved to be momentous. I left bookings entirely to the management. When this one was being made I did not give it much thought. Negotiations for the renting of the hall were begun while I was touring, and I recall that the first intimation I had that there were difficulties came by accident. Even then I did not find out exactly what was going on; all I knew was that something was amiss. It was only a few weeks before the scheduled date for Washington that I discovered the full truth—that the Daughters of the American Revolution, owners of the hall, had decreed that it could not be used by one of my race. I was saddened, but as it is my belief that right will win I assumed that a way would be found. I had no inkling that the thing would become a *cause célèbre*.

I was in San Francisco, I recall, when I passed a newsstand, and my eye caught a headline: MRS. ROOSEVELT TAKES STAND. Under this was another line, in bold print just a bit smaller: RESIGNS FROM D. A. R., etc. I was on my way to the concert hall for my performance and could not stop to buy a paper. I did not get one until after the concert, and I honestly could not conceive that things had gone so far.

As we worked our way back East, continuing with our regular schedule, newspaper people made efforts to obtain some comment from me, but I had nothing to say. I really did not know precisely what the Hurok office was doing about the situation and, since I had no useful opinions to offer, did not discuss it. I trusted the management. I knew it must be working on every possible angle, and somehow I felt I would sing in Washington.

Kosti [Vehanen, Ms. Anderson's long-time piano accompanist] became ill in St. Louis and could not continue on tour. Here was a crisis of immediate concern to me. I was worried about Kosti's well-being and we had to find a substitute in a hurry. Kosti had had symptoms of this illness some time before and had gone to see a physician in Washington, who had recommended special treatment. It was decided now that Kosti should be taken to Washington and hospitalized there.

Franz Rupp, a young man I had never met before, was rushed out to St. Louis by the management to be the accompanist. I had a piano in my hotel room, and as soon as Franz, who is now my accompanist, arrived, we went over the program. I was impressed by the ease with which he handled the situation. He could transpose a song at sight, and he could play many of my numbers entirely from memory. I found out later that he had had a huge backlog of experience playing for instrumentalists and singers. He assured me that I had seen and heard him in Philadelphia when I had attended a concert by Sigrid Onegin years before, as he had been her accompanist.

Mr. Rupp and I gave the St. Louis concert, and then we filled two other engagements as we headed East. Our objective was Washington. We knew by this time that the date in Constitution Hall would not be filled, but we planned to stop in Washington to visit Kosti. I did not realize that my arrival in Washington would in itself be a cause for a commotion, but I was prepared in advance when Gerald Goode, the public-relations man on Mr. Hurok's staff, came down to Annapolis to board our train and ride into the capital with us.

Mr. Goode is another person who made a contribution to my career the value of which I can scarcely estimate. He was with Mr. Hurok when I joined the roster, and I am sure that he labored devotedly and effectively from the moment of my return from Europe for that first Hurok season in America. His publicity efforts were always constructive, and they took account of my aversion to things flamboyant. Everything he did was tasteful and helpful. And in the Washington affair he was a tower of strength.

Mr. Goode filled me in on developments as we rode into Washington, and he tried to prepare me for what he knew would happen—a barrage of questions from the newspaper people. They were waiting for us in the Washington station. Questions flew at me, and some of them I could not answer because they involved things I did not know about. I tried to get away; I wanted to go straight to the hospital to see Kosti. There was a car waiting for me, and the reporters followed us in another car. I had some difficulty getting into the hospital without several reporters following me. They waited until I had finished my visit, and they questioned me again—about Kosti's progress and his opinion of the Washington situation. Finally we got away and traveled on to New York.

The excitement over the denial of Constitution Hall to me did not die down. It seemed to increase and to follow me wherever I went. I felt about the affair as about an election campaign; whatever the outcome, there is bound to be unpleasantness and embarrassment. I could not escape it, of course. My friends wanted to discuss it, and even strangers went out of their way to express their strong feelings of sympathy and support.

What were my own feelings? I was saddened and ashamed. I was sorry for the people who had precipitated the affair. I felt that their behavior stemmed from a lack of understanding. They were not persecuting me personally or as a representative of my people so much as they were doing something that was neither sensible nor good. Could I have erased the bitterness, I would have done so gladly. I do not mean that I would have been prepared to say that I was not entitled to appear in Constitution Hall as might any other performer. But the unpleasantness disturbed me, and if it had been up to me alone I would have sought a way to wipe it out. I cannot say that such a way out suggested itself to me at the time, or that I thought of one after the event. But I have been in this world long enough to know that there are all kinds of people, all suited by their own natures for different tasks. It would be fooling myself to think that I was meant to be a fearless fighter; I was not, just as I was not meant to be a soprano instead of a contralto.

Then the time came when it was decided that I would sing in Washington on Easter Sunday. The invitation to appear in the open, singing from the Lincoln Memorial before as many people as would care to come, without charge, was made formally by Harold L. Ickes, Secretary of the Interior. It was duly reported, and the weight of the Washington affair bore in on me.

Easter Sunday in 1939 was April 9, and I had other concert dates to fill before it came. Wherever we went I was met by reporters and photographers. The inevitable question was, "What about Washington?" My answer was that I knew too little to tell an intelligent story about it. There were occasions, of course, when I knew more than I said. I did not want to talk, and I particularly did not want to say anything about the D. A. R. As I have made clear, I did not feel that I was designed for hand-to-hand combat, and I did not wish to make statements that I would later regret. The management was taking action. That was enough.

It was comforting to have concrete expressions of support for an essential principle. It was touching to hear from a local manager in a Texas city that a block of two hundred tickets had been purchased by the community's D. A. R. people. It was also heartening; it confirmed my conviction that a whole group should not be condemned because an individual or section of the group does a thing that is not right.

I was informed of the plan for the outdoor concert before the news was published. Indeed, I was asked whether I approved. I said yes but the yes did not come easily or quickly. I don't like a lot of show, and one could not tell in advance what direction the affair would take. I studied my conscience. In principle the idea was sound, but it could not be comfortable to me as an individual. As I thought further, I could see that my significance as an individual was small in this affair. I had become, whether I liked it or not, a symbol, representing my people. I had to appear.

I discussed the problem with Mother, of course. Her comment was characteristic: "It is an important decision to make. You are in this work. You intend to stay in it. You know what your aspirations are. I think you should make your own decision."

Mother knew what the decision would be. In my heart I also knew. I could not run away from this situation. If I had anything to offer, I would have to do so now. It would be misleading, however, to say that once the decision was made I was without doubts.

We reached Washington early that Easter morning and went to the home of Gifford Pinchot, who had been Governor of Pennsylvania. The Pinchots had been kind enough to offer their hospitality, and it was needed because the hotels would not take us. Then we drove over to the Lincoln Memorial. Kosti was well enough to play, and we tried out the piano and examined the public-address system, which had six microphones, meant not only for the people who were present but also for a radio audience.

When we returned that afternoon I had sensations unlike any I had experienced before. The only comparable emotion I could recall was the feeling I had had when Maestro Toscanini had appeared in the artist's room in Salzburg. My heart leaped wildly, and I could not talk. I even wondered whether I would be able to sing.

The murmur of the vast assemblage quickened my pulse beat. There were policemen waiting at the car, and they led us through a passageway that other officers kept open in the throng. We entered the monument and were taken to a small room. We were introduced to Mr. Ickes, whom we had not met before. He outlined the program. Then came the signal to go out before the public.

If I did not consult contemporary reports I could not recall who was there. My head and heart were in such turmoil that I looked and hardly saw, I listened and hardly heard. I was led to the platform by Representative Caroline O'Day of New York, who had been born in Georgia, and Oscar Chapman, Assistant Secretary of the Interior, who was a Virginian. On the platform behind me sat Secretary Ickes, Secretary of the Treasury Morgenthau, Supreme Court Justice Black, Senators Wagner, Mead, Barkley, Clark, Guffey, and Capper, and many Representatives, including Representative Arthur W. Mitchell of Illinois, a Negro. Mother was there, as were people from Howard University and from churches in Washington and other cities. So was Walter White, then secretary of the National Association for the Advancement of Colored People. It was Mr. White who at one point stepped to the microphone and appealed to the crowd, probably averting serious accidents when my own people tried to reach me.

I report these things now because I have looked them up. All I knew then as I stepped forward was the overwhelming impact of that vast multitude. There seemed to be people as far as the eye could see. The crowd stretched in a great semicircle from the Lincoln Memorial around the reflecting pool on to the shaft of the Washington Monument. I had a feeling that a great wave of good will poured out from these people, almost engulfing me. And when I stood up to sing our National Anthem I felt for a moment as though I were choking. For a desperate second I thought that the words, well as I know them, would not come.

I sang, I don't know how. There must have been the help of professionalism I had accumulated over the years. Without it I could not have gone through the program. I sang—and again I know because I consulted a newspaper clipping—"America," the aria "O mio Fernando," Schubert's "Ave Maria," and three spirituals—"Gospel Train," "Trampin'," and "My Soul Is Anchored in the Lord."

I regret that a fixed rule was broken, another thing about which I found out later. Photographs were taken from within the Memorial, where the great statue of Lincoln stands, although there was a tradition that no pictures could be taken from within the sanctum.

It seems also that at the end, when the tumult of the crowd's shouting would not die down, I spoke a few words. I read the clipping now and cannot believe that I could have uttered another sound after I had finished singing. "I am overwhelmed," I said. "I just can't talk.

I can't tell you what you have done for me today. I thank you from the bottom of my heart again and again."

It was the simple truth. But did I really say it?

There were many in the gathering who were stirred by their own emotions. Perhaps I did not grasp all that was happening, but at the end great numbers of people bore down on me. They were friendly; all they wished to do was to offer their congratulations and good wishes. The police felt that such a concentration of people was a danger, and they escorted me back into the Memorial. Finally we returned to the Pinchot home.

I cannot forget that demonstration of public emotion or my own strong feelings. In the years that have passed I have had constant reminders of that Easter Sunday. It is not at all uncommon to have people come backstage after a concert even now and remark, "You know, I was at that Easter concert." In my travels abroad I have met countless people who heard and remembered about that Easter Sunday.

In time the policy at Constitution Hall changed. I appeared there first in a concert for the benefit of China Relief. The second appearance in the hall, I believe, was also under charitable auspices. Then, at last, I appeared in the hall as does any other musical performer, presented by a concert manager, and I have been appearing in it regularly. The hall is open to other performers of my group. There is no longer an issue, and that is good.

It may be said that my concerts at Constitution Hall are usually sold out. I hope that people come because they expect to hear a fine program in a first-class performance. If they came for any other reason I would be disappointed. The essential point about wanting to appear in the hall was that I wanted to do so because I felt I had that right as an artist.

I wish I could have thanked personally all the people who stood beside me then. There were musicians who canceled their own scheduled appearances at Constitution Hall out of conviction and principle. Some of these people I did not know personally. I appreciate the stand they took.

May I say that when I finally walked into Constitution Hall and sang from its stage I had no feeling different from what I have in other halls. There was no sense of triumph. I felt that it was a beautiful concert hall, and I was happy to sing in it.

The story of that Easter Sunday had several sequels. A mural was painted in the Department of Interior Building in Washington, commemorating the event, and I was invited down for the unveiling. I met Mr. Ickes again, and as we talked and as I studied the immense mural the impact of it all was unmistakable. More recently I was in Kansas City for a concert, and a young man phoned me and asked whether he could come to see me. He had competed as a painter in the mural contest, and had won second prize. The purpose of his visit was to offer me the painting for the mural that he submitted in the contest. It was a huge picture and, like the prize-winning work, contained a message. I could not find space for so large a painting in my home, and I sent it to the Countee Cullen Foundation in Atlanta. Countee Cullen was a gifted American Negro poet who died prematurely.

I do not recall meeting Mrs. Franklin D. Roosevelt on that Easter Sunday. Some weeks later in 1939 I had the high privilege of making her acquaintance. It was on the occasion of the visit to this country of King George VI and his Queen, and I was one of those honored with an invitation to perform for the royal guests.

While waiting to sing I was in Mrs. Roosevelt's room in the White House. There was a traveling bag on a chair, and the tab on it indicated that she would soon be off again. I can still see it plainly.

Knowing that I would be introduced to the President, I tried to prepare a little speech suitable for such an occasion. When I met him, he spoke first. "You look just like your photographs, don't you?" he said, and my pretty speech flew right out of my head. All I could say was, "Good evening, Mr. President."

After the concert for the visitors was over, we were told that we would be presented to the King and Queen. I had returned to Mrs. Roosevelt's room to prepare myself. It occurred to me that it might be the right thing to curtsy. I had seen people curtsy in the movies, and it looked like the simplest thing in the world. I practiced a few curtsies in Mrs. Roosevelt's room. An aide came to call me, and I happened to be the first woman in line to meet Their Majesties. I remember that I was looking into the queen's eyes as I started my curtsy, and when I had completed it and was upright again I had turned a quarter- or half-circle and no longer faced the queen. I don't know how I managed it so inelegantly, but I never tried one again, not even for the king.

As I approached the center of the receiving line, there stood Mrs. Roosevelt, and at her right His Majesty the King. Mrs. Roosevelt put out her hand and said, "How do you do?"

I met Mrs. Roosevelt a number of times in the ensuing years, in New York, at Hyde Park, in Tokyo, and in Tel-Aviv. When I was in Japan several years ago I heard that Mrs. Roosevelt was about to arrive. I knew from my own experience with the Japanese that an extensive program would be arranged for her and that there would be an abundance of flowers waiting for her everywhere. I thought that an orchid might be the thing to get for her, so I went down to the lobby of the Imperial Hotel, intent on obtaining the orchid. But Mrs. Roosevelt arrived ahead of schedule, entered the hotel, and walked up several steps to where I had been caught standing before I could complete my errand. She stared at me. "Well, how long have you been here?" she asked.

I told her, adding that I was making a tour in Japan. "When are you singing in Tokyo?" she asked. "Tonight," I replied.

She turned to the people who were escorting her. "May I hear Marian Anderson tonight?"

I hesitate to think how her hosts had to rearrange their plans for her that evening, but she was at the concert. I know how crowded her schedule must have been, and I am sure that she did not have many minutes to herself. I shall never forget that she took the time to come and listen again.

When I was in Israel, more recently, Mrs. Roosevelt was there too. She was staying at the same hotel in Tel-Aviv, and she had left word at the desk that when I arrived she would like to be informed. We managed to have a brief visit, and soon she was on her way again.

She is one of the most admirable human beings I have ever met. She likes to have first-hand information about the things she talks about and deals with. Her bags seem to be ready for travel at any moment. Wherever she goes there is praise for her and what she stands for. I suspect that she has done a great deal for people that has never been divulged publicly. I know what she did for me.

Once when I was occupying the artist's room of a hall the stage manager told me with great enthusiasm that Mrs. Roosevelt would occupy the same room two days later. And so on the large mirror I left a greeting, written with soap.

20 Caldonia

JOHN CHILTON

*L*ouis Jordan is one of the more underappreciated and influential black popular musicians of the twentieth century. Jordan's jive, jumping-blues-based music bridged the gap between big band style swing and the rock 'n' roll of Chuck Berry, Elvis Presley, and Little Richard. Jordan influenced many artists such as Ray Charles, Etta James, and B. B. King as well as a whole range of rock and rollers like Joe Jackson. This chapter, from John Chilton's biography, Let The Good Times Roll: The Story of Louis Jordan and His Music, focuses on 1944 to 1945 when Jordan's recording of "Caldonia" became a national phenomenon—quickly selling hundreds of thousands of copies, spawning many covers, and gaining Jordan an even bigger audience than he had already earned.

Born July 8, 1908, in Brinkley, Arkansas, Jordan was the son of a musician. He left eastern Arkansas in the late 1920s to play first with Charlie Gaines and then with drummer-bandleader Chick Webb, whose band featured the then unknown Ella Fitzgerald. Shortly after Webb's sudden death, Jordan built on his own musical talents to create a more accessible version of blues-oriented-style jazz. Within a few years he was reaping the rewards with a stream of seminal and successful performances with his own band.

Jordan's first record for Decca, "Honey in the Bee Ball" (1938), billed his combo as the Elks Rendezvous Band (after the Harlem nightclub where he frequently played). From 1939 on, however, Jordan fronted the Tympany Five, which featured many talented musicians such as pianists Wild Bill Davis and Bill Doggett, guitarists Carl Hogan and Bill Jennings, as well as bassist Dallas Bartley and drummer Chris Columbus.

During World War II, the wildly popular bandleader recorded prolifically for the Armed Forces Radio Service and the V-disc program, but between 1942 to 1951, Jordan scored an unprecedented fifty-seven R & B chart hits (all on Decca), including "Let the Good Times Roll," "Buzz Me," "Choo Choo Ch' Boogie," "Ain't That Just like a Woman," "Ain't Nobody Here but Us Chickens," "What's the Use of Getting Sober," and "Saturday Night Fish Fry." Although they sound like nothing more than good-time party records, a surprising number of these songs contained subtly disguised social commentary about racial conflict, racism, poverty, and other social problems of the day. Jordan also filmed a series of short musicals during the late 1940s that were decidedly short on plot, but long on visual versions of his hits ("Caldonia," "Reet Petite and Gone," and "Look Out Sister" among others) that appeared on the short-lived video jukeboxes that were dubbed "soundies."

In the 1950s, even though his singles (now issued on the Aladdin label) were still musically solid, they did not sell as well as before. Nonetheless a fine 1956 Quincy Jones-arranged date for Mercury, which featured Micky Baker's stinging lead guitar and Sam Taylor's tenor sax, nicely updated Jordan's classics for the newly emerging rock and roll crowd. Throughout the 1960s and early 1970s, Jordan worked only sporadically as his health deteriorated and made performing regularly an impossibility. He died in Los Angeles, on February 4, 1975, overlooked by most of the popular music press. More recently, however, there has been a well-deserved look at his work, most of which is now available on compact disc. Perhaps most important is Clarke Peters's 1990 musical review Five Guys Named Moe, based on Jordan's engaging personality and his best-known songs.

Louis began the year at Fay's Theatre in Philadelphia, then played the Royal Baltimore before returning in triumph to the Apollo, New York. The run of theatre bookings spun on and on and it was something of a relief for the band to play a club date at the Bali, in Washington, DC, before they again worked at the Regal Theatre, in the city that Louis now thought of as home, Chicago.

By 1944, managing Louis Jordan was a full-time occupation, so Berle Adams decided to quit the GAC agency and set up his own offices on La Salle in Chicago. When Louis was out on tour he rarely saw Adams, but during this period the two met regularly, as Adams recalls:

Louis wasn't a typical musician, he didn't smoke and he didn't drink. In those days he had a weakness for ice cream, which he said gave him energy for the show. I don't recall that he was a gambler, and he never went crazy over any particular hobby, though he spent a lot of money on shoes—he couldn't resist them and if he saw some that were only slightly different from any he owned he'd have to buy them.[1]

Louis's bassist, Jesse 'Po' Simpkins, had been called up for service in the US Navy and his place was taken by an ex-Cab Calloway star, Al Morgan, a lively showman originally from New Orleans. Shadow Wilson had also moved on and his place at the drums was taken by the ex-Fats Waller percussionist Wilmore 'Slick' Jones. By now Louis was paying his musicians top money, so he had no difficulties in filling any vacancies that occurred, but any newcomer had to be both a fine musician and an enthusiastic showman. Eddie Roane (trumpet) and Arnold Thomas (piano) were with the band, but a new addition to the troupe was the Trinidad-born singer, Peggy Hart Thomas. Pianist Arnold Thomas's life was made easier when Louis agreed that it was no longer vital that he stood up to play.

This line-up played Flint, Michigan and Louisville, Kentucky before moving west to take up a month's residency at the swish Trocadero Club, in Hollywood, California, from 9 May to 5 June. During this period Louis and the band took part in a movie entitled *Meet Miss Bobby Sax* (which starred Bob Crosby); for the two days' work at the studio Louis received $2,700.[2] The group also recorded various items for the World Transcription Service, and appeared on the 'Command Performance' radio shows; in between all this activity they also found time to appear in some new Soundies, and to make some new sides for Decca, including one of Louis's biggest hits, 'GI Jive'. This had been written and recorded by Johnny Mercer who, seeing the prospect of harvesting more royalties, sent the song to Louis Jordan who took up the suggestion that he should record it.

Louis put his own inimitable stamp on Mercer's song, relaxedly delivering the slick lyrics over a slow shuffle rhythm, and contributing a scorching twelve-bar alto sax solo,

Arguably the most popular black musician in the decade following the close of World War II, Louis Jordan and his Tympany Five toured across the United States performing their hits at clubs large and small.

Credit: Poster from the collection of Kip Lornell.

which he resolves with a series of daringly conceived notes; Eddie Roane's cup-muted answers are perfect. The topical nature of the song, dealing with army jargon, caught the attention of many disc jockeys, so with lots of radio plays (and a Soundie to back it up) Louis's recording became a mega-hit and reached the number one spot in the *Billboard* chart (and stayed in the listing for twenty-five weeks).

Another big recording event that summer was the duet session that Louis Jordan and Bing Crosby shared (backed by the Tympany Five) in July 1944. The idea of recording a duet by two of Decca's bestselling singers (one long-established and the other a recent addition) was hastily planned, both artists having heavy work schedules, but luckily a chance telephone call to Crosby paid off. Louis Jordan recalled the circumstances: 'Bing was with Dixie [Dixie Lee Crosby, his wife] at home having a party, but was told, "We have Louis Jordan here." He said, "I'll come in tonight" and he just came down. Nothing was pre-planned and when Bing walked in they said, "Here's the music."'[3]

The resultant two sides are charming without being sensational. Bing sings an out-of-tempo verse on 'My Baby Said Yes', then Louis (on tenor sax) lays down the tempo of the bouncy chorus which the singers share, with Eddie Roane providing a dainty obbligato. Louis sounds slightly pedestrian in his eight-bar tenor sax solo, but Roane blows confidently to usher in the two singers for the final chorus, and then joins them vocally to make up a three-part harmony team. Bing Crosby apparently cut a solo vocal of the same number which was never issued.[4] On a second take of the duet version Bing offers encouragement by singing 'Come On Lou' and is answered by some fine, robust tenor sax phrases.

'Your Sox Don't Match' is the better side, featuring as it does a series of jocular exchanges between Louis and Bing (again accompanied by Roane's cup-muted trumpet). Louis plays alto on this track and takes an effective sixteen-bar solo before he and Bing relaxedly share the light-hearted lyrics, taking alternate lines then combining for a harmonized vocal ending. The two never recorded together again, but this one coupling gained an enormous amount of air plays over the years and helped broaden Louis's appeal even further. The record was released on Decca's 'Popular' label, whereas Louis's previous issues had been issued on the less well-distributed 'Sepia' series. This move also helped to bring Louis's sound to new listeners. *Down Beat*, reporting on the session, said, 'It took Bing and Louis Jordan only three hours from 6 to 9 p.m. to record "Is You is or is You ain't", "Don't Fence Me In", "My Baby Said Yes" and "Your Sox Don't Match"'.[5] Neither of the first two of these titles was issued, but Bing scored heavily by recording both of them with the Andrews Sisters.

July saw Louis add another city to his run of successes; this time the 'sold out' notices applied to his stay at the Golden Gate Theatre in San Francisco. By now Louis's popularity had spread all over the country; there were no blank regions and his appeal continued to fall evenly between black and white audiences. Echoes of the previous summer's racial friction caused promoters in many states to hesitate about booking black groups for mixed dances, but *Down Beat* outlined a compromise that was adopted:

> Due to the Louis Jordan band's popularity with both white and colored audiences, promoters in larger cities are booking the quintet for two evenings, one to play a white dance and the other a colored dance. The initial experiment came in Oakland, California where Jordan's Tympany Five drew 4,200 at a colored dance and pulled 2,700 through the turnstiles at an ofay function. Jordan begins his two-nighter tour in September and will play Oklahoma City, Chicago, New Orleans and Kansas City.[6]

Louis was now considered to be a top-of-the-bill attraction, so a package show was formed around him and the Tympany Five, consisting of comedians, dancers and George Hudson's sixteen-piece band. Hudson (a former Jeter-Pillars band trumpet player) led a St Louis-based unit which had impressed Louis when they worked with him at the Plantation Club in that city. Jordan decided to sign them up for his forthcoming 'around the world' theatre tour, commencing at the Apollo Theatre in October 1944. Hudson believed in employing promising youngsters and during the coming years he featured many future stars, including Clark Terry, Ernie Wilkins and Tommy Turrentine.

While playing the familiar theatre circuit, Arnold 'Tommy' Thomas (Louis's long-time pianist) was taken ill in Baltimore with ptomaine poisoning, and he died shortly afterwards on 26 October 1944, aged twenty-eight. Louis and the band had to fulfil existing contracts, so a replacement for Thomas was soon found. The new man was William 'Bill' Austin (not the composer), who joined the band in New York and played dates with them in Boston and Newark before moving on with them to Fort Wayne, Indiana, Columbus, Ohio, Detroit, Michigan and Chicago. It was a time of upheaval for the band; Slick Jones had left to be replaced by the former Savoy Sultans' drummer Alex 'Razz' Mitchell. A serious problem manifested itself in late 1944 when it was found that trumpeter Eddie Roane had tuberculosis. Louis offered a life-line to Roane by promising to keep his job open in the hope that rest, fresh air and a healthy diet might defeat the disease. Arkansas trumpeter Lee Trammell worked with the band briefly, as did Leonard Graham (later known as Idrees Sulieman). Another important change in the band's line-up then came when Louis decided to augment the group by adding a tenor sax player. The newcomer was Freddie Simon, a twenty-five year old ex-Alabama State Collegian, and although his presence made the unit into a sextet, it continued to be billed as The Tympany Five.

In January 1945 the new line-up recorded three highly successful numbers, two of which became huge sellers: 'Caldonia Boogie' and 'Buzz Me'. The third title, 'Somebody Done Changed the Lock on My Door', was a Bill Weldon number which the band had attempted to record before, but here the version is entirely successful with Louis underlining his admiration for Weldon's original version by making a close copy of it. The words of 'Buzz Me' were written by the ex-*Down Beat* journalist Dave Dexter, using the pseudonym of Danny Baxter, because he was then working for Capitol Records, a rival to Decca. Dexter, an old friend of Berle Adams, mailed the blues lyrics to Adams in Chicago from his home in Hollywood, more in hope than expectation. He heard nothing from Adams for several months, then he received a note saying, 'Jordan recorded your "Buzz Me" and it's a winner.'

Adams's prognosis proved all too true; the record was soon a smash hit with jukebox fans (Dexter estimated it went into 400,000 machines) and rose high in the charts. Dexter did not look a gift horse in the mouth, but he was slightly bemused to discover that he had gained a co-composer, namely Fleecie Moore—the maiden name of the woman who was by now Louis's wife. Dexter did not know of this connection and so assumed that the name Moore was a pseudonym for Louis Jordan. He therefore readily agreed to the deal, commenting philosophically, 'Half of something is better than all of nothing'.[7] But the time would soon come when Louis himself bitterly rued the day he ever agreed to allow Fleecie's name on this song, and the all-important tune from the same session, 'Caldonia Boogie'.

Louis's subsequent bitterness over his decision to 'donate' the rights and royalties of several songs to his then loving companion, Fleecie Moore, was not the only powerful source of ill feeling springing from these compositions. The founder of Leeds Music, Lou Levy, who had published several of Louis Jordan's successes, told Arnold Shaw,

> Louis Jordan was controlled in those early days by Berle Adams and a fellow called Lou Levy. I told Berle that if he would quit his job at GAC I would give him my piece of Jordan. When I got out I said, 'I'll publish the songs and you manage him.' Then Mr Adams forgot to remember. They put Louis Jordan's wife's name on the song and gave it to another publisher.[8]

Forty-six years after the initial release of 'Caldonia', Lou Levy remained decidedly vexed over the whole affair. In 1991 he said he still felt too angry about the matter to discuss it in detail, but said firmly, 'I set the whole Louis Jordan deal up, and I blame Berle Adams and Louis Jordan equally for what happened.'[9]

In later years Louis accepted his part in the strategy: 'I didn't write under my own name because I was signed with another publishing company, so I put her name on it, Fleecie Moore. Ha, she didn't know anything about music.'[10] There is no doubt that Adams and Jordan felt it to be in their best interests to register the song 'Caldonia' in Fleecie Moore's name, since they could then negotiate deals not subject to the various ongoing restrictions and limiting clauses that would have automatically been part of Louis's existing contracts with music publishers. They were able to make 'Caldonia' the title piece of a new short film, knowing that Fleecie Moore would raise no objection, and they were also able, via Fleecie's name, to make a deal with Broadcast Music Incorporated, which meant that BMI subsidized the making of the film in the certain knowledge that it would be able to recoup revenue from music-licence earnings when the short was shown in cinemas.

Berle Adams and Bill Crouch, a Soundies executive, organized the making of the band film, then took it to Robert Savini, head of Astor Films, for him to arrange distribution. Astor

Films, with twenty-six offices in various regions, then enticed various cinema operators to show the film as a short second feature a few days before Louis Jordan played in their locale (for a low rental fee of about forty dollars a week). In so doing they went against the usual practice of the major distributors by hiring the films out to individual cinemas rather than to chains. The 'Caldonia' movie proved to be a huge success with both white and black audiences, causing *Billboard* to comment, '"Caldonia" has been one of the very few all-Negro productions to get bookings in Southern white theaters.'[11] It was, they added, better to be featured in a well-produced short film than to perform one number that was buried in a poor full-length movie. Jordan links with Astor continued and resulted in several further films, the showing of which added to Louis's in-person drawing power and lifted record sales even further. Louis and Berle Adams also gained because their company Preview Music published many songs featured in the Astor films.

Louis Jordan's gramophone record of 'Caldonia' was not the first version to be released; it was preceded by a highly successful issue from the white bandleader, Woody Herman. The intriguing background was explained by Berle Adams:

> Decca seemed to be slow about releasing 'Caldonia'. Woody Herman was an old friend of mine and one night I met him in Lindy's restaurant and he said, 'You've got all that good junky material, get me something hot to record', so I suggested that Woody catch Louis's show at the Paramount. He did and flipped over 'Caldonia', so much so he went and recorded it as soon as he could, I say within hours, but certainly very quickly. [Herman recorded it for Columbia on 26 February 1945.] Then Erskine Hawkins followed up with a version for RCA Victor, and then Decca decided to issue Louis's record and that was a hit too.[12]

'Caldonia' became one of Woody Herman's most popular recordings. His treatment of the blues theme, and his emphatic stressing of the song's line 'Caldonia, Caldonia, what makes your big head so hard?' proved to be a powerful hook for the public, and the trumpet section's boldly phrased unison figures (devised quickly and without music in the recording studio) delighted all those interested in new jazz developments. Herman's version of the song was quite different from Louis Jordan's. Louis summed this up by saying: 'He did it up, real fast; mine was medium-tempo.'[13] He could afford to be nonchalant, because royalties from both versions were being paid into his publishing interest.

The actual origins of 'Caldonia' are elusive, as Milt Gabler pointed out:

> The basis of 'Caldonia' came from a Hot Lips Page record, 'Old Man Ben', from back in 1938. On that, Lips sings, 'Caldonia, Caldonia, what makes your head so hard?', but pinning down the source of blues lines can be tricky. One thing's for certain, 'Caldonia' wasn't a 'cotton-field' blues, it was a 'bar-room' blues. Louis Jordan was thrilled to think that a big bandleader had recorded his material, but I was mad as hell. It's bullshit to say Decca held up Jordan's version; it was just that Woody Herman deliberately moved so quickly.[14]

A recording by the Spirits of Rhythm in 1941 also used the 'Caldonia, Caldonia what makes your head so hard' line, but Hot Lips Page's part in the origins of the song was specially mentioned by Louis Jordan:

> 'Caldonia' started a long time before I came to New York. There used to be a long, lean, lanky girl in Memphis, Tennessee, where Jim Cannon used to have a gambling

place where people used to come to shoot a bale of cotton because they didn't have too much money to gamble. This long, lean, lanky gal used to hang out in this place and she wouldn't do anything you asked her to do. That's why they said, 'Your head was so hard,' and, God bless the dead, Hot Lips Page was very young then and I met him and he said, 'You should make a tune out of that, just a plain old blues.'[15]

Years later, a dancer, Marie Reynolds, claimed that Louis Jordan had written 'Caldonia' about her. In 1945, soon after the song had been issued, blues singer Sippie Wallace claimed that the song was based on her 1924 recording 'Caldonia Blues' (composed by George Thomas). Many years after this initial complaint, Sippie explained that she had started to take legal action over the song but her lawyer died and the complaint subsided. To an impartial ear the only obvious similarity between the two works seems to rest on the use of the word 'Caldonia', but Sippie went through life feeling she had been plagiarized.

During the spring of 1945, another hugely successful theatre tour took the Louis Jordan Show around the Baltimore, Washington, Detroit and Chicago circuit, but despite all the admiration and revenue Louis was becoming increasingly disenchanted with his band's performances. He was also again suffering from a persistent sore throat, so after completing a two-week booking in Chicago on 17 May 1945, he decided to enter hospital for a tonsilectomy. This gap in the band's working life presented him with an ideal opportunity to carry out a complete reorganization of his group: he fired everyone in the Tympany Five and began recruiting new personnel.

Louis gave, as his reason for the dismissals: 'I was dissatisfied because the band didn't jump in its usual style', adding that it 'lacked co-operation'.[16] One of the reasons he did not cite was that this edition of the Tympany Five did not take too kindly to his dictatorial ways. As a result, some of the musicians questioned his right to govern their lives by calling extra rehearsals and insisting on having first call on their spare time. They were also keen to play solos and felt disgruntled at their subsidiary roles now that Louis was featuring himself on practically every number. When a reviewer pointed out that the group's leader was excessively to the fore, his sentiments were endorsed, although not publicly, by Louis's sidemen. Louis's high rates of pay had a soothing effect on this discontent, but word was out in the profession that he was reluctant to let the spotlight linger on any individual sidemen. Indeed, when Clyde Bernhardt formed his band, he told the musicians, 'Just because my name is up front it doesn't mean I'm taking all the solos like Louis Jordan.'[17]

Louis's drastic revamping of his sextet was a result of the weed of discontent seeded in his psyche; once in a while it broke ground in random places, at random times. It was this broody side of his nature that caused him, every so often, almost dispassionately to carry out changes both in his musical and his personal life. Not long before he decided to disband in 1945, he seriously considered forming a big band, at the very time his group was being hailed as the most popular small band ever. Fortunately, Berle Adams was able to talk him out of the idea.

In forming his new outfit, Louis employed his former drummer Eddie Byrd, who had been leading his own band. Louis also asked his former bassist Dallas Bartley to rejoin, but by then Dallas was a successful bandleader and making records under his own name so he declined, but he recommended a young tenor saxist, Joshua Jackson, who had recently worked for him. Louis approached Jackson (then working with pianist Sonny Thompson in Chicago) and found that the young musician jumped at his offer. Louis heard that another of his former bassists, Jesse Simpkins, was about to be medically discharged from the US Navy, so he offered him a job, but Simpkins could not give the exact date of his release from the service, so Louis employed a temporary bassist, Carl Hogan, who had formerly been a member of the Jeter–Pillars band. Simpkins duly obtained his release from the navy and took over bass duties, but in the intervening time Jordan had heard Hogan practising the electric guitar and realized that he would be a great asset to the band on that instrument. Accordingly, Louis stretched the group to a seven-piece unit, but still retained the Tympany Five billing.

Louis's choice as his new pianist was William Davis, who had studied music, first at Tuskegee then at Wiley College, Texas. Davis, who later gained the nickname 'Wild Bill', was a fine all-round musician and a skilful arranger. This last attribute was to prove particularly useful to Louis, who felt that the recent erosion of his disciplinary powers had been partly due to the fact that a miscreant musician felt secure in his job knowing that it would take any replacement weeks to learn the repertoire since few of the new numbers had been written down. Jordan knew that the public usually liked to hear a faithful reproduction of a hit record on an in-person appearance, so he had, at times, to bite the bullet and appear more lenient than he wanted to be when a sideman became unruly. With Davis's arrival, Jordan had on hand a staff arranger who was eminently capable of writing new arrangements, and of transcribing all of Louis's previous recorded successes, thus making it relatively simple for a new musician (or a temporary substitute) to familiarize himself with the band's repertoire.

Bill Davis recalls those early days:

I first met Louis Jordan in Chicago. He was in the process of making a complete change-over, so he asked me if I would write out some of his previous hits from the recordings so that the new men would be able to just read them off. This led on to me arranging new material for the band, and as he also needed a new pianist I took the job. 'Caldonia' had just happened by the time I joined, so everyone was trying to book the group. After rehearsals we started out in Detroit then moved into the Paramount Theatre in New York. As far as the new arrangements, our working scheme was that I sat at the piano and Louis played through his ideas on alto sax; this was a regular occurrence because Louis was all the time searching for new material. He was always listening, wherever he was, for the next idea for a new recording. He never sat at the keyboard and demonstrated any ideas that way, he played what he wanted on sax; he was a good alto player, not too good on tenor. I never knew of him having any hobbies; his life was music, and finding new material. As far as I know, he didn't have any close buddies. I don't remember him hanging out with anyone, either in the music business or out. He might go out to hear someone perform, but only to check them out. When we got to a town, we were likely to go to our own individual hotels, and meet up later either to work or to rehearse. He could be jovial, but he never let that affect the business relationship he had with the musicians in his band.[18]

Louis's choice of trumpeter was Aaron Izenhall, who was to remain a mainstay of the band for the next six and a half years. He recalls the background to his joining:

Louis knew of my work with Ernie Fields so he called me here in Detroit and asked if I wanted to join the band. I said 'Yes!' because I knew most of the Jordan records and was very familiar with Eddie Roane's playing on them. Louis explained that when Eddie Roane was fit again the job was his, and as long as I understood that, everything was OK. So I went down to Chicago and we got the new band into shape at rehearsals somewhere downtown. Bill Davis wrote out some new stuff and the group started to sound fine. I hadn't been in the band long before news came that Eddie Roane had died, so I stayed with the band for years.

Louis was an excellent reader, but somehow he couldn't arrange, he couldn't write out musical ideas, even if he'd thought of them. He'd spend hours sitting backstage in his robe, and when an idea came to him he'd pick up his sax and call for Bill Davis. So many of Louis's hits were born just like that. He was a genius at thinking up these things. I didn't realize it at the time, but I know it now.

Louis couldn't stand any monkey business or sloppy playing, and if anyone smoked pot or took drugs they were fired on the spot. He was a very strict bandleader. Everyone had to behave like gentlemen, be clean, be smart and behave themselves. He didn't drink or smoke in those days; maybe he'd have a single glass of champagne if we'd finished making a movie, or at the end of a big show. But you couldn't fool him; if you'd been up all night at a party or had too much to drink, he'd know it. If nothing went wrong he'd let it go, but if it messed up the music—look out! He'd holler out loud, saying how embarrassed he'd been on stage having to listen to all the wrong notes. He was temperamental like that, highly strung. Some guys couldn't take it, but it was nothing personal and I always remained pals with Louis.[19]

The new band's first dates were in Detroit, then they moved into New York City for a three-week season at the Paramount Theatre (commencing 4 July 1945). With a schedule that involved several shows a day at the Paramount, appearances on the popular 'Chesterfield Music Shop' radio show, transcription recordings and sessions at Decca, the new group became a highly polished outfit. At the Paramount, the band shared billing with Stan Kenton's Orchestra; Kenton made the tactical mistake of trying to meet Jordan's music halfway by singing a semi-cod version of 'St James Infirmary Blues', which *Down Beat* reviewer Frank Stacy found disappointing. But Stacy was full of praise for Jordan's band: 'The music of this clever group is really delightful, though with its extra emphasis on cuteness it doesn't play as much jazz as it once did on records. It's Jordan himself who's the whole show, with his irrepressible wit and good jazz singing. "Caldonia" brought down the house.'[20]

The same issue of *Down Beat* contained another reference to 'Caldonia', but this made less satisfactory reading for Jordan because it contained details of the $100,000 law suit that Lou Levy was bringing against him, Berle Adams and publisher Buddy Morris. Levy claimed publishing rights on 'Caldonia' through prior agreements. Jordan countered by saying that 'songwriter' Fleecie Moore had penned the song and had placed it with the joint Louis Jordan-Berle Adams publishing company Preview Music. Berle Adams tried to laugh the matter off by saying, 'My mother is very proud of me. Now that I'm being sued for a hundred thousand dollars I *must* be a big man.'[21]

Neither Adams nor Jordan allowed the law suit to interfere with existing plans and the band travelled to California, where they spent two days (30 and 31 July) filming for a Monogram picture entitled *Swing Parade of 1946* (featuring Connee Boswell and Will Osborne's Orchestra). On the following day they began a week's booking at the Golden Gate Theatre in San Francisco and played that city's Plantation Club until 22 August. The band had already recorded 'Don't Worry 'bout that Mule' (written by Louis Jordan and Bill Davis) at one of their July Decca sessions, and its sales were to be considerably boosted by the release of the film. Another popular item from these same sessions was 'Salt Pork, West Virginia', composed by William Tennyson, a twenty-two-year-old from New Orleans who was just beginning his song-writing career.

In October 1945, after the band had returned to New York, they took part in another celebrated duet session for Decca, this time with Louis's old friend, Ella Fitzgerald. Milt Gabler reminisced about the date:

> This was an era when teaming acts was becoming very popular, so I thought of the idea of pairing Ella with Louis Jordan. It was simply a question of finding the right songs, because there was no jealousy at all between Ella and Louis. Then Ella came to me and told me about a song that her hairdresser had sung to her. It was 'Stone Cold Dead in the Market'.* That was easy to trace because I had recorded the composer Wilmouth Houdini's version some while before. Ella wanted to do the song and Louis could do that West Indian dialect perfectly so it paid off.[22]

The flip side of 'Stone Cold Dead' was 'Petootie Pie' (which had also started life under a different name: 'Miss Sally Sue'). The Ella-Louis recording of it got a rave review from an unlikely source, bandleader Benny Goodman who, while being interviewed by George T. Simon, suddenly said, 'You know what I like? That record Ella and Louis Jordan made of "Petootie Pie". To me that's the best jazz record of the last ten years. And it's relaxed, too. I've been playing it every morning now for about six weeks, almost as soon as I get up, and I still think it's great.'[23]

The coupling became a hit, and Ella wowed her audiences by impersonating Louis and singing both roles on stage. A week after the recording with Ella, Louis's band tried making its own version of 'Petootie Pie', but it remains unissued. However, that session produced a minor hit in the shape of 'Reconversion Blues', a topical number that had been well received by all of Louis's audiences during the preceding months. In his heyday, Louis Jordan tried out almost everything he recorded on a variety of audiences to help him establish the song's potential. If the response was consistently indifferent that number was eliminated from the repertoire; if it was enthusiastically applauded it went on a short list of material to be recorded, but even then it was not a certainty, since Louis often readjusted the arrangement and sometimes the lyrics, just to see which version the public preferred. Berle Adams and Louis were in total agreement about this method of judging reaction. Adams said, 'We did our market research by trying out material on the road. I might send Louis twelve songs and they'd all be tried out on different audiences.'[24] Small wonder that Louis did not spend much time enjoying the local nightlife; he never used written cues on stage, which meant he had the task of learning hundreds of new songs each year, knowing full well that only a small percentage of them would become fixtures in his repertoire. Louis continued to be a demanding bandleader, and Fleecie observed, 'Louis rehearsed an awful lot. You talk with anyone who played with him and they will tell you. He was really rough on the band.'[25]

The most prestigious booking of this period for Louis Jordan's Tympany Five was a residency at the Zanzibar Club in New York, playing opposite Duke Ellington's Orchestra, in a show that featured (among others) Louis's old favourite Mantan Moreland. Duke Ellington opened on 11 September and Louis was due to begin sharing the engagement on the 12th, but a last-minute dispute surfaced that almost caused a row between the managers of the two bandleaders. It had not been clearly established with the Zanzibar's managers, Carle Erbe and

---

*Frederick Wilmoth Hendricks (1991–73) originally recorded the song in 1939 as 'He Had It Coming'; Wilmouth Houdini was a stage name.

Joe Howard, who was to receive top billing, Ellington or Jordan, and for a time neither of the managers seemed willing to take second place. Berle Adams, shrewd as ever, saw publicity possibilities in the situation and had an 'open letter' from Louis Jordan printed and distributed to music-magazine editors, disc jockeys and band bookers. It read:

> Dear Duke,
>   You probably know that old saying: Heaven protect me from my friends, my enemies I can take care of myself!
>   Ain't it the truth. Imagine my surprise when I got in from Chicago last week, just in time to open at the Zanzibar with you, and found out I was feuding with you about our respective billings, or so they told me....

Louis's letter went on to say how proud he was to appear with Duke, who he called 'the master of modern music', adding:

> I'm still young enough to play second fiddle to the Duke. I don't mind admitting that your accomplishment as a musician and composer have always been an inspiration to me in my own bid for success. You understand Duke, I'm not claiming I'm a shrinking violet; with the help of all the other great performers in the Zanzibar's New Revue we'll keep giving the customers the greatest show on the main stem. You dig me, Duke?[26]

Years later, Berle Adams commented on the misunderstanding:

> The row over the billing at the Zanzibar worked out like this. Cress Courtney, who was Duke's manager at the time, was a good friend of mine, but billing hadn't been agreed so he said, 'We've got to have Duke at the top.' Eventually I agreed, saying, 'Sure, Duke is absolutely great, but Louis Jordan has got to be billed as an EXTRA ADDED ATTRACTION in the same-size type, but to make a contrast his name has to be in white letters on a black background.' Cress agreed with the idea, but (as I surmised) when the ads came out, Louis's name jumped off the page and this caught everyone's eye, more than the name Duke Ellington. Duke was greatly amused by this; he came up to me chuckling and said, 'Berle, you did it. You did it again.'[27]

During Louis's stay at the Zanzibar he gave an interview in which he had some pertinent things to say about showmanship: 'A showman must "intrigue" the customers. He must hold their interest from one minute to the next to keep them guessing as to what's coming.'[28]

One of the band's big successes at that club was 'Beware', a number that allowed Louis to banter with his audience, warning unmarried men to avoid being rushed into matrimony. One of his set pieces within the song went: 'Hey, you there. You there in the front with the lovely blonde. I'm trying to save you brother, and you're laughing. Don't laugh too long boy, or it'll be too late.'[29]

The Zanzibar booking turned out to be enjoyable for all concerned. It enabled Aaron Izenhall to achieve his ambition of sitting in with Duke Ellington, which he did a few times when a regular member of Duke's trumpet section was absent. It was also the venue at which Duke Ellington became aware of Wild Bill Davis's various skills, eventually leading to Duke commissioning arrangements from Davis. But for Louis Jordan, the most significant event at the Zanzibar was romantic rather than musical. It was there that he first met Florence Hayes, who danced in the show's chorus. Though still married to Fleecie, Louis began dating Florence (who preferred to be called Vicky); it was a move that almost cost him his life.

Notes

1. Conversation with the author, March 1991.
2. *Metronome,* June 1944.
3. Louis Jordan interviewed by Scott Ellsworth, Radio KFI, 26 April 1971.
4. Matrix 3478, according to discographer Ralph Harding.
5. *Down Beat,* 1 September 1944.
6. *Down Beat,* 1 August 1944.
7. Liner notes by Dave Dexter, MCA CD 4079.
8. Shaw: *Honkers and Shouters,* p. 71.
9. Conversation with the author, 5 September 1991.
10. *Ramparts,* January 1974.
11. *Billboard,* 8 June 1946.
12. Shaw, op. cit., p. 80.
13. Ibid., p. 69.
14. Conversation with the author, 19 March 1991.
15. Louis Jordan interviewed by Scott Ellsworth, Radio KFI, 26 April 1971.
16. *Down Beat,* 1 July 1945.
17. Bernhardt: *I Remember,* p. 177.
18. Conversation with the author, 14 March 1991.
19. Conversation with the author, 5 March 1991.
20. *Down Beat,* 1 August 1945.
21. Ibid.
22. Conversation with the author, 19 March 1991.
23. *Metronome,* July 1946.
24. Conversation with the author, 12 March 1991.
25. Conversation taped by Carl Arnold and John Byrd, 1989.
26. *Metronome,* November 1945.
27. Conversation with the author, 12 March 1991.
28. *Bandleaders,* March 1946.
29. Ibid.

21

Elder Beck's Temple

WILLIAM RUSSELL

William Russell is best known as a scholar of early jazz (New Orleans in particular) and "Oh Mr. Jelly": A Jelly Roll Morton Scrapbook (Copenhagen: JazzMedia, 1999) is considered to be his life's work. But Russell's interests were actually more wide-ranging. He also founded a small record label (American Music) at the close of World War II and explored the local black American vernacular music scene whereever he lived. Before relocating to New Orleans, Russell lived in the North, most notably in Chicago and Pittsburgh (in 1946–1947).

While living in Pittsburgh, he was attracted to the music of Elder Beck's Church of God in Christ, whose Sunday evening services were broadcast locally. He knew of Beck through his commercial recordings on Bluebird and Decca and his more recent (ca. early 1946) Eagle recordings, which were issued as "Elder Charles Beck, His Trumpet and Radio Chorus." The always adventurous Russell attended services at Beck's Pentecostal Temple and this brief article is an interesting account of his experiences.

The church itself was located on Centre Avenue in the Hill District, "one of the least desirable sections of a city notorious for bad living conditions." Russell clearly felt the power of the sanctified worship service and its exuberant music. He also noted not only the spontaneity of Beck's service and the music, but also its connections with other forms of black American music (mostly jazz, of course) and the attraction of the sanctified church to "the common man." It is significant that he felt compelled to suggest to his Record Changer *audience, which was oriented toward jazz, that they may wish to "look it up, if you enjoy hearing good music more than looking at record labels."*

The most stirring music I heard during my stay in Pittsburgh was at Elder Beck's Church of God In Christ, one of many hundred Sanctified Churches scattered throughout America. To anyone who has had to suffer or sleep through an ordinary church service, an evening in a Sanctified Church can be a revelation of the power of music to make things go. Everything is done rhythmically, with a beat—the preaching and praying as well as the singing. Their theme song, *I Sing Because I'm Happy*, also seems to work in reverse, and the people are happy because they sing.

For several years the Sunday midnight meetings have been broadcast, and recently Eagle Records has released eight sides by Elder Beck, his trumpet and radio chorus in some of his favorite songs, such as *Blow, Gabriel, Delilah,* and *Closer Walk.*

Elder Beck's Temple is located in Pittsburgh's Hill District, one of the least desirable sections of a city notorious for bad living conditions. The Hill is usually clouded with smoke from the Pennsylvania Railroad yards below, or if the wind changes, it is swept by poisonous fumes from the J and L Steel Works. The church itself is not very attractive. Originally it was a theatre, then for a while it served as the Savoy Ballroom. Today the interior is quite dilapidated, with some of the old theatre seats broken down, floor boards' missing, and the walls defaced. The old stage, stripped of scenery and theatrical lighting, is bare except for the pulpit, a few chairs, and an out of tune upright piano. However, these drab surroundings are forgotten once services get under way. Doubtless the people today have a better time, produce and hear better music than in the old days when the building housed supposedly gayer activities. The fact that these people have really learned to work, play, and sing *together* may explain why their music is so much better than that found in most dance halls and night clubs.

Elder Beck, who styles his services "Songs of the Deep South," possesses a voice of fine quality and a personality that has attracted a large following. He can also play some pretty good trumpet, when he isn't imitating Louie's "high ones." There's no telling what other instruments you'll hear up at the Centre Avenue church—everything from the tambourines several women carry to church, to banjos and saxes. Then there was the stretch two years ago when an Ike Rodgers-like trombonist was featured. Not the least of Elder Beck's musical assets are the *Saints*, the group of two dozen white and black robed girls who form the famous radio choir. They know how to enliven the already spirited proceedings with their jubilees and spirituals, and they can get off some fast rhythmic precision numbers that would startle the Andrews Sisters.

However no radio mike can capture the full enthusiasm of the congregation, and Elder Beck will announce—"The shout is coming on after the broadcast. We're going to have a big time here. Brother Hornsby's here tonight; come on and shout with us." Anyone the spirit moves can get up and start a song, and once the jubilee gets rolling the entire place can be in an uproar within two minutes. The aisles and platform fill up with a joyful, singing and shouting multitude. The singers and instruments are soon drowned out by clapping hands and stomping feet, and all that remains is the tremendous, irresistible beat.

> "You got to move, you got to move,
> For when the Lord gets ready you got to move."

I have seen nothing like the exhilarant "dancing" during such outbursts since I visited Haiti many years ago. Incidentally, the Church of God In Christ, like Voodoo, is officially banned in Haiti, though not for any connection with the Voodoo cult.

Over a year ago, when a new pianist appeared at the 'Temple things began to jump even more. He was George Hornsby, born 35 years ago in Mobile on the Gulf Coast, but raised and educated in Pittsburgh. After several years in dance bands, he decided to devote his life to religious work. Since 1939 Elder Hornsby has played only spirituals, taught piano, and toured with vocal groups.

Sister Berry, an exceptional woman, is the assistant pastor. She is a splendid soloist, frequently leads the singing, and when Elder Beck is on tour she preaches sermons that make plenty of sense. The church also sponsors many special musical programs with such distinguished guests as Sister Rosetta Thorpe and Mme. Ernestine Washington.

Elder Beck may not be the world's greatest musician, but he's smart enough to know the tremendous power of music, and how to use it to make a happier world. Music, one of the most powerful forces in the world, hasn't the destructive ability of the atom, but it has greater power to benefit man, and we have not begun to realize its potentialities. Industry has made a start in using music, after its ability to increase production and profits was proven. It is reassuring to see Elder Beck, in a capital city of science and technology—"our arsenal of military imperialism"—bring to the people something of the beauties and benefits of music. These people are not just a few intellectuals, purists—cultists, and hot club members; nor are they international jazz authorities, eminent anthropologists, and museum of art critics. Elder Beck's congregation is the common man. They dig ditches, work in factories and laundries (that's a good business in Pittsburgh). These people have learned not only that music can make hard work easier, but that they can gain happiness and relaxation as well as strength and inspiration from the right kind of music. No one can call this a "New Orleans revival" or a "classic survival," but it's the same kind of music that Bunk Johnson plays and Ann Cook sings. It's a natural and logical kind of music—simply a way of playing or singing a *melody with a beat.*

Elder Beck's flock sings, plays, and likes this music today because it gives them something they need today. As long as a thousand churches full of people like Elder Beck's jump every Sunday night, and oftener, we don't have to worry about survivals, revivals, or the future of music. If there is a Sanctified Church in your town, it might pay you to look it up, if you enjoy hearing good music more than looking at record labels.

22

T-Bone Blues

T-Bone Walker's Story in His Own Words

T-BONE WALKER

Aaron Thibeaux Walker, born in northeast Texas in 1910 to Rance and Movelia Walker, was among the first bluesmen to record on electric guitar. However, he started out as more of a down-home blues player, cutting his teeth playing rural country dance music, migrating to Dallas in the mid-1920s. Before making his first recording (as Oak-Cliff T-Bone) for Columbia Records in 1929, he had already performed with Ida Cox, a famous vaudeville blues singer. This oral history includes some fascinating recollections of touring with Cox as well as with other stage and medicine shows throughout the South.

His single-string guitar work, which was influenced by Lonnie Johnson in particular, formed the basis for the postwar stylings of B. B. King, Albert King (no relation), Buddy Guy, Otis Rush, and countless others. Walker's sophisticated approach to chords attracted the attention of the jazz media in the 1940s (there was no magazine devoted to blues until the 1960s) and his 1946–1947 recording sessions for Comet were supervised by A & R man Ralph Bass, who had already worked with modern jazz artists such as Dizzy Gillespie, Wardell Gray, and Dexter Gordon.

This interview, published originally in The Record Changer *(October 1947), does not tell all of Walker's life story for he enjoyed a performing and recording career that lasted for another twenty-seven years during which he toured not only the United States, but Europe as well. He continued to record for a variety of labels, including Imperial, Atlantic, and Polydor, with which he won a 1972 Grammy. His later, now mostly white, audience came out to hear his hits, most notably "T-Bone Shuffle" and "Call it Stormy Monday." Despite a series of health issues, Walker continued to tour until New Year's Eve 1974, when he suffered a stroke, which led to his death on March 15, 1975.*

Everybody in the South has a nickname or initial. I was called "T-Bow" but the people got it mixed up with "T-Bone." My name is Aaron Walker but "T-Bone" is catchy, people remember it. My auntie gave it to me when I was a kid. Mother's mother was a Cherokee Indian, full blooded. There were sixteen girls and two boys in my mother's family, all dead but two.

Beginning with Capitol Records in 1942, T-Bone Walker recorded for over a dozen labels (including Comet in 1947) before his death in 1975.

Credit: Record label from the collection of Kip Lornell.

I just naturally started to play music. My whole family played—my daddy played, my mother played. My daddy played bass, my cousin played banjo, guitar and mandolin. We played at root beer stands, like the drive-ins they have now, making $2.50 a night, and we had a cigar box for the kitty that we passed around, sometimes making fifty or sixty dollars a night. Of course we didn't get none of it, we kids. I and my first cousin were the only kids in the band. Before I came to California, Charlie Christian and I did the same thing in root beer stands. I'd play banjo a while, then dance a while.

I was born in a little town called Linden, near Texarkana, then moved to Dallas. Ida Cox picked me up in Dallas where I was working at Eddie's Drive-In. I was working there singing like Cab Calloway, making a lot of noise, and a hotel about two blocks away complained and they sent the wagon to take us to jail. We'd start work at seven and by nine every night for two weeks the wagon would come—the whole band would be in jail every night. I said, "I quit, I'm tired of going to jail."

Ida Cox—since I was a kid she was one of my favorite blues singers. I went on the road with her on a tour of the South. Twelve girls in the chorus, two principals, two comedians. I used to play thirty-five or forty choruses of "Tiger Rag" with a table in my teeth and the banjo on the back of my neck. Never had a toothache in my life, and I used to carry tables in my teeth and tap dance at the same time. I started that in Fort Worth at the Jim Hotel. When I was with Ida Cox and we were broke we used to eat syrup and bread, without even any butter with it. We did "Coming Around the Mountain," and the old numbers, mostly comical, and the blues and tried to be funny. One of the comedians had a bazooka and played a tin Prince Albert can with his fingers. Then I had to go home and go to school. I didn't drink or smoke then, but I did play penny dice. I was just learning to shoot then.

I also worked in a medicine show, selling Big B Tonic, with Josephus Cook and Dr. Breeding. I used to get five dollars and he sent my mother ten. I used to make the medicine, too, made it in a tub with black draught. It was called BB—double B and they were willing to pay a dollar for it because it was two dollars at the drug store. He got rich on that—it cost thirty-five cents to mix. We had movies, a stage show, a trailer and a Model T Ford. We played at small towns where people didn't have no sense and we really sold it.

LeRoy Carr gave me the inspiration for singing the blues. He was a terrific blues singer and he played with a fellow named Scrappin Iron or Scrapper Blackwell, something like that. I play in almost the same style they do. I'll take Floyd Smith for blues playing today and I'm crazy about Alvino Ray for his style. He uses a Hawaiian guitar, but you can't make it sing the blues. I can't play the Hawaiian guitar, can't make a note on one of those things. But I like his tone and his style.

I used to hear all the singers, but LeRoy Carr was my favorite and still is. If there was music, I was right there. LeRoy used to sing "When the Sun Goes Down" and "Monte Carlo Blues" and "Night Time Is the Right Time." I still sing those numbers. I used to lead Blind Lemon Jefferson around playing and passing the cup, take him from one beer joint to another; I liked to hear him play. He could sing like nobody's business. He was a friend of my father's. People used to crowd around so you couldn't see him. Blind Lemon was from Galveston. He was dark yellow and weighed around 175 or 180, kind of reminds you of Art Tatum the way he looked.

Bessie Smith is my favorite girl blues singer. Ma Rainey could sing the blues, but she couldn't sing the blues like Bessie. They had different styles. Bessie was the QUEEN for everybody, better than Ethel Waters. She was REALLY great, she could sing ANYTHING. Billie Holiday doesn't sing the blues. People will like the blues as long as they are in the world. Blind Lemon, LeRoy Carr, sang the real blues—and Lonnie Johnson—old man now, still working. Wonderful blues singer. Don't ever leave him out. Sharpest cat in the world, wore a silk shirt blowing in the wind in the winter, nice head of hair, and a twenty-dollar goldpiece made into a stickpin.

I never took a music lesson in my life, but I can read and write music and play seven different instruments. I used to think I was a terrific piano player, played boogie woogie all the time. Once I played with a band for two years without knowing what a note was. From different kids in the band if I got a wrong chord they told me how it should be.

In 1933 I left Dallas with a white band that I led and danced with, the only colored man in the show, all dressed up in white tails. I even danced with a white girl for a partner. Everybody asked me questions about California, because the band was from California. They asked me about movie stars but I couldn't tell them anything because I'd never been in California at that time.

I met Bessie Smith at Fort Worth at the Fat Stock Show in 1933–34 with Ma Rainey. Ma Rainey was a heavy set dark lady, mean as hell but she sang nice blues and she never cussed ME out. She had a show with the Haines Carnival at the Stock Show and I played for her.

I left the South in 1934 and in 1935 I began playing an electric guitar.

Well, I decided to make music my career since 1941. Before that, if I was playing, if I made money, OK. If I didn't, OK, I'd get me another kind of job. At that time I was playing at Little Harlem in the south part of Los Angeles, and a girl used to come to hear me every night. Finally she got tired of coming so far to hear me so she arranged for me to get a job with real good pay in Hollywood, and then I started to get my name. I played at Billy Berg's Capri Club and the Trocadero and lots of other Hollywood spots after that.

I started making records again too. The first time I ever made a record I was only sixteen years old. It was for Columbia and I made "Wichita Falls Blues" and "Trinity River Blues" with banjo and guitar accompaniment, under the name of Oak-Cliff T-Bone. Oak-Cliff was where I lived then. Columbia had people out scouting for talent and they picked me up. Later I made

"T-Bone Blues." Commodore bought the master and now Blue Note has it. I never made a penny out of that, but Les Hite and Louis Jordan made a million on it. I make records so fast now I don't even have time to learn the words. I read it right through and make a rehearsal one day and a record the next day. Then I take the records home and study them to learn the lyrics. People can't believe I don't know how to sing my own records. Lately I've made "Bobby Socks Baby" and "Mean Old World." I've got a year's option with Black & White and Phil Moore is my director. The other day I got a check for two thousand dollars for royalties.

I like piano, bass, guitar for blues accompaniment, the winds in between. The old time blues beat . . . one . . . two . . . has been the blues beat for years . . . since back in the days of—Zutty Singleton! I bet Zutty will laugh when he reads that. . . . I mean the old New Orleans days. The Ory band know how to play it. Somebody like Zutty or Kid Ory are just right. Singing hasn't changed but the accompaniment has changed. I use a mike so I can sing soft, you can sing better. I train myself to sing soft, you can get a better tone.

My favorite band today is Basie. I like his piano—we've been friends for twenty years, and I like Tatum's piano too. The Three Blazes is my favorite trio. Trumpet? POPS! It's GOT to be Pops all my life. Pops is my Daddy. EVERYBODY loves Louie.

You got to know what you're doing to play bebop. The young generation are different. They are mad over it. Maybe they'll grow out of it. Charlie Parker and Dizzie I could sit all night and listen, but most of them don't know what they're doing. People are crazy about it in New York and Chicago. They don't like it in California and Texas.

The city I like best is Chicago, but the state of Texas is best. People give you a room, feed you, won't let you pay for nothing. Other places everybody has their hands out. But I'd rather live in California than anywhere. You can see my tonsils smiling every time I cross that line. Only after you work in Los Angeles and San Francisco you're through and there are so many places to play in the South. Whenever they hear my guitar offstage they start screaming for me to come out. I always go over with all the kids. When I was on tour this spring I played for a lot of kids and one little girl three years old said, "Have him come over to my table, Daddy, I love him" and she brought me a five-dollar bill on the stage.

I like golf and horses. I have my own horses. A great big black one and a roan. I'll ride anything you give me to ride. My black horse jumps three feet in a Western saddle. My agent is afraid I might get hurt and cut off his living. I've played golf with Joe Louis. He's a good golfer. I'm also interested in a fighter, Rusty Paine. He fought in San Diego the other day, fights heavyweight. I haven't had a chance to be with him like I'd like to be, give him a chance and not let them beat him to death. He's got nerve and power and can take it.

I belong to the Baptist church—Hardshell—I love church songs. I'd walk ten miles to hear Sister Rosetta Tharpe sing church songs, but not two blocks to hear her sing the blues. I'd walk TWENTY miles to hear her sing my favorite number. "When I Reach the End of My Journey." Two kids made a record of that and every beer tavern and gambling place in the South has it on the juke box. In the South they can't make enough records of it. Gamblers and hustlers bought them, everybody around with me bought it. I got five copies. It's my very favorite piece. These days it isn't church like it's supposed to be. They charge a dollar ten to come to church to hear Sister Tharpe. I don't like the way Josh White is going over big with church songs. I don't think that's right. I don't sing in church because I'm no hypocrite. I don't think a fellow ought to go out cussing and drinking and gambling all week long and then come and sing in church on Sunday.

23 The Impact of Gospel Music on the Secular Music Industry

PORTIA K. MAULTSBY

During the twentieth century the complex relationships between black secular and sacred music were addressed by a wide variety of writers ranging from Peter Guralnick to Paul Oliver. These articles, record notes, and essays have noted that these relationships are more complicated than simply a divide between the devil (secular music, often the blues) and god (sacred music, often gospel). In this article, Portia Maultsby, a professor of ethnomusicology and folklore at Indiana University–Bloomington, focuses on an extremely interesting and important topic: the transformation of gospel music into popular styles during the years following the close of World War II.

This story actually began at the turn of the twentieth century with the rise of Pentecostalism, but it really began to flower in the 1930s when the Rev. Thomas A. Dorsey first infused gospel music with secular music sensibilities. The gradual commercialization of African American gospel music became more acute during the late 1940s when quartets such as the Spirit of Memphis, the Five Blind Boys of Mississippi, and the Pilgrim Jubilees attracted large crowds to their live programs. Black gospel music also began to be heard more often on the radio and via commercial record companies to an ever-expanding audience. In the minds of some conservative Christians, gospel music was veering too close to popular music—a very disturbing trend for those who believe that the religious and profane styles (like blues or soul) should never mix.

Maultsby suggests that it is important to understand that it is not only the crossover from the sacred realm to the secular world by individual artists such as Lou Rawls or Aretha Franklin, but also the wholesale incorporation of gospel's musical values into the secular music world of soul, funk, and hip hop. Artists as diverse as James Brown and M. C. Hammer acknowledged the influence of the church on their music. This inspires the author to close her essay with the question posed in 1979 by musicologist/performer Horace Boyer: "Is it possible that one day gospel music will no longer belong to the church?"

I've had a lot of offers to stop singing gospel and take up singing jazz and blues, but blues and jazz just aren't me. —ALBERTINA WALKER

Many of the past gospel hits of the [Staple Singers] crossed over into the pop charts, which is just another indication of the common roofs from which black music sprang. —"SPECIAL EDITION"

> Crossing over from gospel to pop wasn't hard because it was just a matter of changing words. —LOU RAWLS

Since the 1930s, Black gospel music has loomed from its status as the exclusive property of storefront African American churches to become a dynamic and viable force in the commercial music industry. It became an economic commodity in secular contexts when its performers were broadcast over network and independent radio stations; recorded by independent record companies; and showcased in large concert halls, coliseums, theaters, jazz festivals, and nightclubs. The exposure and acceptance of gospel music outside the sanctuaries of Black churches simultaneously expanded its consumer market and led to its appropriation by purveyors of secular idioms. The infectious rhythms, melismatic melodies, complex harmonies, call–response structures, and compelling character of this music permeate the vinyl of various popular music styles. Even the gospel message could not be contained within the walls of the Black church as former gospel singers rerecorded gospel songs under rhythm and blues, soul, and pop labels. While serving as a catalyst for new popular music styles, gospel music propelled the growth of a post–World War II, multibillion-dollar secular music industry. This essay will examine the commercialization of gospel music and its transformation into popular song.

THE COMMERCIALIZATION OF GOSPEL MUSIC

In a 1979 article on contemporary gospel music, scholar-performer Horace Clarence Boyer posed a question that continues to be debated among African American church congregations: "Is it possible that one day gospel music will no longer belong to the church?" (Boyer 1979a, 6). Eight years later, *Billboard* published a report on the status of gospel music that indirectly addressed the issue: "Perhaps the biggest news in gospel music this year [1987] is the stunning growth and wider acceptance of black gospel music. No longer an esoteric cultural phenomenon, it is now presented in many styles and is quickly becoming another popular form of black music without losing any of its message" ("Black Gospel: Rocketing to Higher Prominence" 1987, G–6). While this commentary accurately assesses the growth of a non-Christian and cross-cultural consumer market for Black gospel music, it totally misinterprets the continued existence of gospel as both a religious and a cultural phenomenon.

Over the last seventy years, gospel music has evolved from the improvised singing of congregations and from the traditional styles of Thomas A. Dorsey, William Herbert Brewster, Lucie Campbell, and Roberta Martin to the contemporary sounds of quartets, choirs, small groups, and ensembles. The coexistence and popularity of these diverse gospel styles among African American Christians and non-Christians suggest that gospel continues to be a vital form of expression in the African American community. In a study on gospel music, ethnomusicologist Mellonee Burnim concluded that "Gospel is not just a musical exercise; it is a process of esoteric sharing and affirmation. It is more than the beat; it is more than the movement; it even embodies much more than text, harmonies or instrumental accompaniment. All of these factors and others intertwine to produce a genre which represents a uniquely Black perspective, one which manifests itself in a cogent, dynamic cultural philosophy or world view" (Burnim 1988, 112). Gospel music therefore is a complex form that embodies the religious, cultural, historical, and social dimensions of Black life in America. The current misinterpretation about the religious and cultural significance of this tradition emanates from the exploitation of gospel music as an economic commodity.

From 1940 to 1993 Chicago-based Morris and Martin Music Studio published dozens of books that helped disseminate gospel songs to congregations throughout the country.

Credit: Song book from the collection of Kip Lornell.

Gospel music has been expropriated and used by the music industry to generate new consumer markets, giving rise to new functions and performing contexts. Repackaged and promoted as entertainment to a cross-cultural and non-Christian audience in nontraditional arenas, the spiritual message and cultural aesthetic of gospel were subordinated to the money-making interest of the music industry.

From the 1930s through the 1960s, performances of gospel music were held primarily at religious events in churches and in public venues for African American audiences. During this time, media exposure ranged from fifteen- and twenty-minute broadcasts on general-market radio to one to three hours of daily programs on Black-formatted radio stations. Over the last two decades, gospel music experienced an explosion on many levels. Its audiences have become multiracial in composition. It is broadcast on full-time gospel-formatted stations and on religious television programs. Its performers are featured in music festivals, with symphony orchestras, and on recordings of popular music; major concerts are jointly sponsored by record companies and national advertisers. Additionally, gospel recordings, once available only in African American "mom and pop" record shops and at performance sites, are now found in mainstream retail outlets.

Many of these trends were precipitated by the crossover appeal of the gospel song "Oh Happy Day," recorded in 1968 by the Edwin Hawkins Singers. When Hawkins recorded his gospel arrangement of the hymn "Oh Happy Day," he unwittingly opened the doors for the commercial exploitation of gospel music. The song, laced with elements from contemporary Black popular styles, was programmed as gospel and soul music on Black-oriented radio and as pop on Top 40 stations. A graduate student at the time, I remember hearing the remarks of an African American DJ when he introduced the song on WVON, a soul music radio station in Chicago: "Here's a new song climbing the charts. I don't know what to call it. It sounds like gospel and it sounds like soul. Whatever it is, the beat has a groove. I like it and I'm gonna play it." The message, aesthetic, danceable beat, and contemporary sound of "Oh Happy Day" made it accessible to a diverse audience.

Through mass-media exposure, gospel music slowly penetrated every artery of American life, linking the sacred and secular domains of the African American community, breathing life into new secular forms, and bringing flair and distinction to the American stage of entertainment.

GOSPEL MUSIC IN SECULAR CONTEXTS

Local Communities and Public Venues

The seeds for the commercialization of gospel music were planted in the 1930s when its performers were showcased in a variety of nonreligious settings. Gospel quartets were the first to garner a secular following by performing at local community events, on radio broadcasts, and on commercial records. Evolving out of jubilee quartets in the 1930s, they expanded their repertoire of Negro spirituals to include secular songs and a new body of religious music known as gospel. By the 1940s, the songs of pioneering gospel composers Thomas A. Dorsey, Theodore Frye, William Herbert Brewster, Kenneth Morris, Lucie E. Campbell, and Roberta Martin had become standard repertoire in jubilee-gospel quartet performances. Members of quartets occupied a unique position in African American community life, functioning as both evangelists and entertainers for activities sponsored by Black churches, schools, and social clubs, and by white businesses (Seroff 1980). Kerill Rubman, in his study of gospel music, comments on the widespread popularity of these quartets: "Factory and construction workers, porters, and other employees sang in company or union-affiliated quartets, performing at picnics, parties, dances, and other business or community events. Family members formed quartets. Negro colleges continued to sponsor such groups, and Baptist and Methodist churches often formed male quartets to sing sacred music at worship services and evening programs" (Lornell 1988, 18). Some local quartets developed regional and national reputations that led to a change in their status. As regional "stars" in the 1930s, they toured while maintaining full-time jobs, but by the mid-1940s, several were touring the country as full-time professional musicians (Lornell 1988, 64–78).

Gospel quartets initially performed for Black audiences. But as the gospel sound spread through radio broadcasts in the 1920s, gospel music found its way into public venues traditionally reserved for America's white bourgeoisie. Jazz critic and record producer John Hammond organized a musical extravaganza, "From Spirituals to Swing," that featured performances of blues, jazz, spirituals, and gospel music. Staged in 1938 in Carnegie Hall, Hammond selected Mitchell's Christian Singers and Sister Rosetta Tharpe to render spirituals and gospel songs, respectively. According to Hammond, "Except for one fleeting appearance at the Cotton Club, she [Tharpe] had never sung anywhere except in Negro churches. She was a surprise smash; knocked the people out. Her singing showed an affinity between gospel and jazz that all fans could recognize and appreciate" (Hammond and Townsend 1981, 203). The success of this concert and favorable reviews by music critics resulted in the staging of a second "Spirituals to Swing" concert in 1939 that featured the Golden Gate Jubilee Quartet (Hammond and Townsend 1981, 231).

During the 1950s, Hammond seized other opportunities to expose gospel singing to white America. Serving on the board of the Newport Jazz Festival, he was determined to obliterate musical and racial segregation from the nation's social fabric. To this end, Mahalia Jackson was invited to perform at the Festival. According to Hammond, "[Mahalia] gave the Festival a great boost of respectability in 1956 by her unprecedented appearance and glorious singing at a Sunday morning service in Newport's unassailably white Trinity Episcopal Church" (Hammond and Townsend 1981, 339). One year later, Clara Ward and the Ward Singers appeared on the stage of the Newport Jazz Festival, and, in 1958, Mahalia Jackson was featured again.

The cross-cultural appeal of gospel and its growing popularity across religious and social boundaries in African American communities were observed by enterprising individuals who quickly seized the opportunity to cash in on its message, musical sound, and cultural aesthetic. Facilitated by promotional strategies of the secular music industry, gospel music emerged as big business. In the 1950s, many singers became full-time performers, appearing in major concert halls, large theaters, auditoriums, and stadiums before audiences averaging twenty-five thousand or more throughout the United States and in Europe. Some performers witnessed their income rise from church free-will offerings of unpredictable amounts to actual performance fees of two to five thousand dollars. Music critic Richard Gehman noted in 1958 that "gospel singers have forged their art into a business now grossing, in the estimate of New York promoter Joe Bostic, around $15 million annually" (Gehman 1958, 113). These performances, supported by radio broadcasts and record sales, firmly entrenched gospel music in the secular fabric of Black community life. Succinctly stated by Horace Clarence Boyer, "The Black American who had never discovered gospel music, or who had simply decided to deny it for whatever reason, began to support it—not in the church, but in places outside the church" (Boyer 1979a, 9). Walter Grady, promoter for Malaco Records, which specializes in gospel and blues, further elaborates, "Most [Black] non-church goers and non-Christians can be responsive [to gospel] because of their upbringing. Once, all of us were kids and you heard gospel in the home every Sunday and maybe blues two days a week [on the radio].... When you were brought up on gospel it's very hard to get away from it" (Maultsby 1990a).

For whatever reason—its spiritual message, musical sound, or cultural aesthetic—gospel music had a magnetic effect on people, especially Black people. The music industry, in recognizing the power of this music, explored various strategies to market gospel as an entertainment commodity. One approach was to showcase gospel singers in nightclubs and theaters traditionally reserved for performances of jazz, blues, and rhythm and blues music. Sister Rosetta Tharpe appears to be the first gospel singer to sing in such nontraditional public arenas. Singing and playing the electric guitar with Lucky Millinder's band in the late 1930s and 1940s, she performed Thomas Dorsey's "Hide Me in Thy Bosom" under the title "Rock Me," which she recorded in 1939 with Millinder's band (MCA 1357).

Prompted by John Hammond, during the early 1940s, the Golden Gate Jubilee Quartet and the Dixie Hummingbirds joined Tharpe as singers of gospel music performing in nightclubs (Tallmadge 1974, 14; Salvo and Salvo 1974, 62). Such performances, however, were rare among gospel performers, since the Black church considered this activity blasphemous and, therefore, inappropriate (Hentoff 1963, 46). Even so, gospel music resurfaced in nightclubs during the following decades.

In the mid-1950s and early 1960s, Clara Ward and Della Reese, who performed at various times with Mahalia Jackson, the Clara Ward Singers, and the Roberta Martin Singers, were among the few gospel singers (including Bessie Griffin, the Dixie Hummingbirds, the Nathaniel Lewis Singers, and Howard Saunders) who accepted offers to perform in nightclubs and theaters. Surrounded by criticism from gospel performers, ministers, and the Black community, both Ward and Reese defended their position. Ward maintained that her mission was to evangelize rather than entertain: "Although perhaps there are many people who would not share my feelings on the subject, I now feel that God intended for his message to be heard in song not solely by those who attend churches, but also by the outsiders who in many cases never attend a house of worship. For that reason the Ward Singers and I have taken our gospel singing into the Apollo Theater in New York . . . [and into clubs in Las Vegas]" (Ward 1956, 16). Della Reese, to the contrary, declared that her performances with the Meditation Singers at New York's Copacabana served only an entertainment purpose: "We are not presented as holy singers; we are there to show that gospel is interesting music. We don't perform in night clubs to save souls." She also acknowledged that financial considerations played a role in her decision to perform gospel in nightclubs: "I like a comfortable apartment, a healthy bank account and some good solid real estate" ("Gospel to Pop to Gospel" 1962, 107, 110).

Despite lucrative offers for nightclub appearances, many gospel singers refused. Mahalia Jackson declared, "It's not the place for my kind of singing" (Gehman 1958, 114), and James Cleveland, in agreement, revealed, "I don't feel I can do much good in a club. I don't feel that the atmosphere is conducive, and I don't feel that the reason for bringing me there is the reason for which I am singing" (Lucas 1972, 21). Rejections from established gospel singers and the objections of African American ministers and members of the African American community, however, did not dissuade enterprising club owners from exploring alternative marketing strategies. A new twist to an old concept was the establishment of "gospel nightclubs." The May 18, 1963 and May 24, 1963 issues of *Billboard* and *Time*, respectively, reported that one such club called Sweet Chariot opened in Manhattan. Although the targeted clientele was America's white teenagers, marketing techniques proved insulting, demeaning, and contradictory to the mores of Black people. Restrooms were labeled *Brothers* and *Sisters,* and waitresses dressed as angels served alcoholic beverages during performances of gospel music. Curious patrons nevertheless filled the club to capacity, prompting the owner to announce plans to open similar clubs in Chicago, San Francisco, and Los Angeles (Hentoff 1963, 46).

Within two years, declining clientele and continued criticism from the African American community influenced the closing of some of these clubs, but not before Columbia Records recorded and repackaged gospel as a "popular" music genre. Convinced that this "new" music would rebound sagging record sales, a Columbia executive proclaimed, "It's the greatest new groove since rock 'n' roll. In a month or two, it'll be all over the charts" ("Gospel Singers: Pop up, Sweet Chariot" 1963, 48). Although Columbia's recordings did not make the charts (see Williams 1963 for a review of the recordings), its executive accurately assessed the future impact of gospel music on the pop music field. Aided by radio, gospel redefined the sound, beat, and stylings of popular music.

Gospel Music on Radio

Radio became the major source of entertainment in the 1920s. Even though its programming was targeted at middle-class white America, the gospel singing of Sanctified and Baptist storefront congregations traveled the airwaves through the Sunday morning broadcast of church services. By the late 1930s, live performances of gospel quartets, including the Southernaires, the Golden Gate Jubilee Quartet, Mitchell's Christian Singers, the Fairfield Four, the Swan Silvertones, and the Selah Jubilee Singers, had become integral to many formats. These fifteen- and twenty-minute daily or weekly broadcasts proliferated during the 1940s and 1950s in response to the growth of postwar urban African American populations (Lornell 1988, 22–26; Spaulding 1981, 101–8).

Controlling a multibillion-dollar economy, African Americans became a major consumer group at a time when the white radio audience was declining. The advent and growing popularity of television redefined the position of radio as the primary entertainment medium. Struggling to survive, radio stations experimented with programming in search of new audiences. Many expanded their Black programming, while others revamped their formats to become full-time Black-oriented stations. For example, in 1943 "only four stations throughout the country were programming specifically for blacks, [but] ten years later, 260 stations were attracting national and local sponsors to their broadcasts" (MacDonald 1979, 366). By 1961, over 310 stations "devoted some portion of their programming to black interests, about 70 of which geared at least 10 hours of air time, each week, in this area. Slightly more than half of those 70 aimed all their programming at the black [sic] community. [At the close of the decade], at least 65 outlets were geared entirely to black [sic] audiences" (Garnett 1970).

The proliferation of Black programming formats increased the exposure of gospel music. Jack Gibson, a DJ on Chicago's WJJD (a general-market station) from 1947 to 1949, recalled that gospel programs aired daily "for about an hour, 9:00–10:00 A.M. Everybody's gone to work and the woman left at home wants to settle down before she starts into housework. So she would listen to the gospel music" (Maultsby 1979).

As gospel music's audience grew by leaps and bounds during the 1950s, so did its programming on stations with an all-Black format. Birmingham's WEDR and Houston's KYOK, for example, featured two gospel music programs daily for two and three hours, respectively. On Sundays, both stations broadcast Black church services and live performances of gospel music (Maultsby 1990b, 1990c). This programming format also characterized gospel music broadcasts throughout the 1960s. The April 1962 programming schedule of Atlanta's WERD, the nation's first Black-owned and -operated radio station, for example, lists two daily gospel music programs. The first one, "Gospel Gems," aired from 6:15 to 7:30 A.M., and "The Gospel Train" from 3:05 to 4:05 P.M., the latter replaced by "Old Ship of Zion" on Saturdays and broadcast from 4:30 P.M. until the station went off the air at sunset. Sunday's format was entirely religious—church services and a variety of religious music programs.

Most radio stations targeted at African American communities were low powered (two hundred fifty to ten thousand watts) and licensed to broadcast from sunrise to sunset. Nashville's WLAC was an exception. It was a fifty-thousand-watt CBS affiliate station whose power catapulted its evening Black music programs to several regions in the United States, Canada, the Caribbean islands, and, via shortwave radio, to New Zealand, Europe, and North Africa. Before these programs were launched in 1946, the station served as the radio home from 1939 to 1951 for the gospel quartet the Fairfield Four. This group enjoyed wide exposure through their fifteen-minute morning broadcast, which was recorded and syndicated to other stations (Landes 1987, 68). When WLAC instituted its evening programs of Black music, gospel was included only in the advertising of "record specials" offered through mail-order outlets that sponsored the programs. This arrangement juxtaposed gospel with rhythm and blues and blues records, blurring the lines between sacred and secular and making gospel music available to both religious and nonreligious audiences.

Black-formatted stations began competing with general-market radio for national advertisers in the late 1960s and early 1970s. Scrambling to increase market ratings by diversifying their listening audience, these stations either rescheduled their daily broadcast of gospel music to 5:00–7:00 A.M. or discontinued the programs altogether. Black religious services and gospel music nevertheless continued to dominate Sunday programming (Maultsby 1990c). When most Black-oriented stations abated their gospel music programs, WLAC ironically instituted its first gospel show since 1951, when the Fairfield. Four went off the air. WLAC's DJ William "Hoss" Allen launched and hosted a four-hour gospel program in 1971, known as

"Early Morning Gospel Time," that aired 1:00–5:00 A.M. daily. Recalling the show's rise from its humble beginnings, Allen commented, "I knew so many record companies that had gospel and didn't know what to do with it. They had no exposure. So I called four record companies and sold them two hours and forty-five minutes [of advertising time]. That's how the gospel [program] started. It got bigger, bigger and bigger until it was as big as the blues had been, because nobody was playing gospel for four hours at a time anywhere, every night, five hours on the weekend. Well, it became the biggest gospel show in the country" (Maultsby 1984a). Allen's listening audience was diverse, including night-shift employees, truck drivers, "dyed-in-the-wool gospel fans, . . . a lot of shut-ins and people who have trouble sleeping and are just laying in bed all day and they lay awake all night" (Landes 1987, 75).

Radio was instrumental in expanding the listening audience for both gospel and rhythm and blues. The early practice of juxtaposing the two forms exposed their affinity. Among the churchgoing gospel fans who once distanced themselves from "sinful" music, some demonstrated tolerance, while others became consumers of rhythm and blues without relinquishing their loyalty to gospel music. Similarly, many "sinners" came to appreciate gospel music, identifying with its aesthetic and even its spiritual message. The experiences of Walter Grady, a record promoter and former record retailer, graphically illustrate this point: "I've even seen situations when I owned a record store where 'winos' would come in with a six-pack of beer under one arm and a bottle of wine in one hand, buy two blues records and two gospel records which means they were going to party but they still were going to give a few minutes of listening to God's music which was gospel music" (Maultsby 1990a).

Throughout the 1970s, gospel music took a back seat to the hegemonic programming of Black popular music. During this decade, Black-formatted radio stations concentrated on improving market ratings, attracting crossover audiences, and courting national advertisers. But in the 1980s, gospel music resurfaced as a viable commercial product, giving rise to several full-time gospel-formatted stations. The expanding consumer market for gospel music generated by radio and live performances created a demand for gospel records.

Gospel Music on Record

During the developing years (late 1940s–50s) of full-time, Black-oriented radio stations, DJs were challenged with the task of finding records to play. The unprecedented demand for Black music exceeded the supply. Mail-order record shops that sponsored Black music radio programs frequently ran out of stock. Retailers, in an effort to replenish their supply, went "all over the country trying to buy Black records and there weren't a whole lot" (Maultsby 1984a). This shortage was triggered by government restrictions on the use of shellac during the second World War, the 1942–44 ban on recording stemming from a musicians' strike, and the small number of record companies specializing in Black music.

The first recordings of Black religious music were issued during the first decade of the twentieth century. Beginning in the 1920s, major and independent companies marketed the music of African American preachers and their congregations and jubilee quartets under the label of "race music" (Oliver 1984). Religious music represented one-third of the five hundred race records issued in 1927 and about one-fourth of those released during each of the next three years (Dixon and Godrich 1970, 57). The Depression years severely curtailed the recording of race music. Many companies folded, and the few that remained in business limited their involvement in gospel music to reissuing previously recorded material and recording jubilee-gospel quartets and such established performers as Mahalia Jackson and Rosetta Tharpe.

The recording industry resumed full-scale production after the war years, but many of the companies that once specialized in race music chose to abandon this field. The demand for Black music nevertheless persisted. Responding to this demand, local entrepreneurs formed independent record companies and became the primary producers of postwar Black music. Some of these companies, including Savoy, Apollo, Specialty, Peacock, Nashboro, and Vee-Jay, developed an impressive catalogue of gospel music that supported the programming efforts of radio. Although major companies largely ignored gospel music during the first four decades after the war, they joined the gospel bandwagon in the 1980s. Aware of the cross-cultural popularity of this music and its pervasive influence on popular styles, they teamed up with independent companies to record and distribute gospel music. Radio, in turn, became a promotional tool for these companies and the growing number of gospel music promoters. Forming a national network, record companies, radio stations, retail outlets, and promoters brought unprecedented exposure to gospel music. The demand for the gospel sound and its beat led to the appropriation of this music by purveyors of popular styles.

The Transformation of Gospel into Popular Song

Paralleling the rise of gospel music was the growth of a teenage consumer market for popular music. African American teenagers, who served their musical apprenticeship performing in church choirs and in professional gospel groups, were lured into the more lucrative field of popular music. Gospel singer Albertina Walker contends that even though gospel music became "big business," it was "a good money-making business for everybody except the singer" (Banks 1974a, 74). Gospel singer-minister Reverend Cleophus Robinson noted that crooked managers, promoters, and record companies exploited "the art and its artists for the money, then put very little money back into the art to strengthen it and make it more popular" (Banks 1974b, 65). Rather than reinvest in the form, the industry capitalized on the popularity of the gospel sound, offering gospel singers money and other perks to switch to blues, jazz, and rhythm and blues. Savoy Records, for example, offered Clara Ward ten thousand dollars to become a blues singer ("Clara Ward . . . Gospel Singer" 1953, 38). She and others declined such offers, but some defected and transformed gospel into various popular music styles—rhythm and blues, soul, funk, and other contemporary forms. Beginning in 1949, *Billboard* used the term *rhythm and blues* to identify all post–World War II forms of Black popular music. In 1969, this term was changed to *soul*. Through the 1970s, soul music was transformed into funk and disco.

Among the first gospel singers to establish successful careers as rhythm and blues artists were soloists Sister Rosetta Tharpe and Dinah Washington and quartets including the Delta Rhythm Boys (formerly the Hampton Institute Quartet); the Larks (formerly the Selah Jubilee Singers); a gospel group led by Billy Ward and renamed the Dominoes; and the Isley Brothers. They and others found the transition from gospel to rhythm and blues to be "just a matter of changing the words," as Lou Rawls notes (Shearer 1983). All of the components—sound construct, interpretative devices, and performance style—that define the gospel tradition are found in its secular counterparts.

Rhythm and blues vocal groups had a religious sound, according to Diz Russell, a vocalist with the Orioles, because they imitated instruments in a manner popularized by gospel-jubilee quartets, and they duplicated the "straight-up" harmonies heard in church. This harmonic structure places the bass on the bottom to accentuate the chord. Russell adds, "A floating tenor, which comes in and out, carries the chord up and down. The baritone remains in the middle of the chord and sings a straight part" (Maultsby 1984b). Through their immersion in African American church culture at a very young age, emerging musicians not only learn fundamental musical concepts but also master aesthetic principles essential to Black music performance.

Soul-disco performer Candi Staton, for example, recalls her first performance at a Baptist church at age five and the responses of the congregation: "I sang and those people started shouting, really getting involved in what I was doing and that frightened me more than my singing because I didn't know why they were shouting. I didn't understand the feelings that they felt" (Shearer 1981). Having a similar experience singing a solo in an AME church choir at age eight, disco performer Donna Summer reminisces, "the people started crying and it scared me that I could touch people and they were moved by something that I had that was intangible. It gave me an incredible sense of power" (Shearer 1982).

Staton and Summer were too young to comprehend why people "shouted" and "cried," but a review of a concert by soul singer Aretha Franklin provides an explanation while revealing the affinity between performances of gospel and Black popular styles:

> At every show I wondered what it was—that very special thing she was always able to get going with an audience. Sometimes there were 16,000 people in a sports arena and Aretha would be working on stage, doing *Dr. Feelgood* [sic] and then *Spirit in the Dark* [sic], and it seemed that all 16,000 people would become involved in a kind of spiritual thing with her, sort of like what must have happened on the Day of Pentecost, and those people—all kinds: dudes, sisters in Afros and those in blonde wigs, even church-looking people—would start moving with the music, and as Aretha took them higher and higher some of them would scream and jump up on their seats, and even men like 50 and 60 years old would run down to the stage and try to touch her. (Sanders 1971, 126)

Aretha's performance transformed the concert hall into a type of spiritual celebration—one similar to that of an African American worship service in which the preacher and gospel singers engage in verbal and physical exchanges with the congregation. Gospel music scholar and performer Pearl Williams-Jones accurately observes that "in seeking to communicate the gospel message, there is little difference between the gospel singer and the gospel preacher in the approach to his subject. The same techniques are used by the preacher and the singer—the singer perhaps being considered the lyrical extension of the rhythmically rhetorical style of the preacher" (Williams-Jones 1975, 381).

Aretha revealed to music critic Phyl Garland that her vocal style was influenced by the preaching techniques employed by her father (Garland 1969, 199). This singer–preacher link is described by Aretha's brother, the Reverend Cecil Franklin:

> You listen to her and it's just like being in church. She does with her voice exactly what a preacher does with his when he *moans* to a congregation. That moan strikes a responsive chord in the congregation and somebody answers you back with their own moan, which means I know what you're moaning about because I feel the same way. So you have something sort of like a thread spinning out and touching and tieing [sic] everybody together in a shared experience just like the getting happy and shouting together in church. (Sanders 1971, 126)

As Aretha moans a meaningful message to her audience,

> She leans her head back, forehead gleaming with perspiration, features twisted by her intensity, and her voice—plangent and supple—pierces the hall:
>
> Oh baby, what you done to me . . .
> You make me feel, you make me feel,
> You make me feel like a natural woman.
>
> "Tell it like it is," her listeners exhort, on their feet, clapping and cheering. ("Lady Soul: Singing It Like It Is" 1968, 62)

Aretha's masterful display of vocal dexterity and her down-home, foot-stomping, intense and demonstrative performance style continue a tradition popularized in the 1950s by Big Maybelle, Big Mama Thornton, James Brown, Little Richard, Jackie Wilson, and the Dominoes. In the 1960s, this style defined performances of the Isley Brothers, Wilson Pickett, Gene Chandler, Otis Redding, and Sam and Dave. While this performance style prevails in rhythm and blues and its derivative forms, it represents only one dimension of the gospel sound in Black popular music.

The gospel sound encompasses many vocal styles and timbres. It ranges from the lyrical, semiclassical, and tempered style of Roberta Martin, Alex Bradford, Inez Andrews, and Sara Jordan Powell to the percussive and shouting approach of Sallie Martin, Archie Brownlee, Albertina Walker, Clara Ward, and Norsalus McKissick. Many singers, including Mahalia Jackson, Marion Williams, and the Barrett Sisters, employ components from both styles in their performances. This range of stylistic possibilities has brought variety to the Black popular tradition.

The vocal style of many rhythm and blues and soul singers, for example, is more lyrical and tempered than that of Aretha. Among the exponents of this style are the Orioles, Little Anthony and the Imperials, the Impressions, Roy Hamilton, Sam Cooke, Jerry Butler, Brook Benton, Smokey Robinson, O. C. Smith, Isaac Hayes, Dinah Washington, Dionne Warwick, the Jones Girls, and Deniece Williams. The church roots of their lyrical and tempered style and the way it differs from the percussive and foot-stomping approach of Aretha Franklin and others are explained by Shirley Jones of the Jones Girls: "Our sound was developed primarily by singing in church with our mother. Even though we are [former] gospel singers, we are not the foot-stomping, down-home gospel type singers. We are more the subdued side of it. Very soft voices . . ." (Maultsby 1983a). Deniece Williams also acknowledges that, despite her upbringing in the Church of God in Christ, her style is not "the same deliverance as Aretha or Mahalia Jackson, [but] you feel it. I've had a lot of people say [when] you sing it, I feel it. I think that feeling comes from those experiences of church and gospel music and spirituality which play a big role in my life" (Maultsby 1983b).

That "feeling" experienced by Williams's audiences results from her subtle use of aesthetic principles associated with gospel music. Regardless of vocal style employed, singers of popular idioms use a wide range of aesthetic devices in interpreting songs: melismas, slides, bends, moans, shouts, grunts, hollers, screams, melodic and textual repetition, extreme registers, call–response structures, and so on. Dinah Washington, a protégée of Roberta Martin, was a master in the subtle manipulation of timbre, shading, time, pitch, and text. Her trademark sound echoes the vocal control, timing ("lagging behind the beat"), and phrasing of Roberta Martin. Dinah's style was imitated by a host of singers, including Lavern Baker, Etta James, Nancy Wilson, Dionne Warwick, and Diana Ross.

Vocal techniques, timbres, and delivery style were not the only components of gospel appropriated by rhythm and blues. Gospel rhythms and instrumental stylings, which originated in secular contexts, became integral to this sound. David "Panama" Francis, studio drummer for many Black artists, brought a rhythmic excitement to post–World War II popular forms when he incorporated the rhythms of the Holiness church into several rhythm and blues recordings. In Screaming Jay Hawkins's "I Put a Spell on You" (1956) and Lavern Baker's "See See Rider" (1962), for example, he employed the 12/8 meter (known as common meter in the Church of God in Christ) and the triplet note pattern associated with this meter (Maultsby 1983c). These structures as well as the rhythms that accompany the "shout" (religious dance) provide the rhythmic foundation for many contemporary popular songs.

Ray Charles was another performer who drew from his church roots for musical inspiration. His performances employ every cultural aesthetic known to the Black folk church, including the movements of its congregants. Francis, who played drums on Charles's "Drown in My Own Tears" (1956), explains how he used brushes rather than sticks to capture the nuances of these movements in this song:

> Ray was the one who told me to play with brushes like in the church and with a gospel feeling. All I played was straight quarter notes with brushes. If you remember, in the church, that was the way the mothers used to keep the babies quiet on their knees when they were singing; all they did was lift their foot and then drop it—just a straight.... And they'd be patting the baby and it would go right back to sleep. And that's what I was playing on the drums in "Drown in My Own Tears." Ray Charles suggested it and showed me how to do it, too. (Maultsby 1983c)

Ray Charles also incorporated the structures and instrumental stylings of gospel music in his songs. When he repackaged the well-known gospel version of the spiritual "This Little Light of Mine" as "This Little Girl of Mine," in 1955, he retained the underlying repeated eight-bar structure. In doing so, Charles broadened the musical parameters of rhythm and blues beyond its traditional twelve-bar blues structure.

In subsequent recordings, including "Drown in My Own Tears" (1956), "Right Right Time" (1959), and "What'd I Say" (1959), Charles employed the gospel piano style of Roberta Martin in conjunction with his gospel-rooted vocals. Martin, in developing a distinctive performance style, elevated the role of the piano from that of background for vocals to one of "an integral and integrating force in the performance, supplying accompaniment, rhythm, and effects. Her style is characterized by improvisatory fills, a rhythmic bass line and colorful and complex chord structures" (Williams-Jones 1982, 15). In the 1960s, the Roberta Martin piano style, the rhythms of the Black folk church, and the harmonic structures and vocal stylings of gospel music transformed rhythm and blues into a new popular idiom known as soul music.

The spirit and energy of soul music were so powerful that this style penetrated all arteries of the African American community and spilled over into those of mainstream America. In 1969, James Brown, a pioneer with Ray Charles in the development of soul music, "became the first black man in the 30-year history of *Cash Box* to be cited as the male vocalist on single pop records. For the uninitiated, 'pop' means sales to the whole record-buying public, not simply in the predominantly Negro rhythm 'n' blues market" (Barry 1969, 56). Brown's influence was so great that many white singers, including the Righteous Brothers, Joe Cocker, Tom Jones, and Elvis Presley, imitated his style, giving rise to the concept of "blue-eyed soul singers."

James Brown, proclaimed the "godfather of soul," along with his female counterpart, Aretha Franklin, the "queen of soul," made gospel music and its delivery style a permanent fixture in American popular music. Horace Clarence Boyer, quoted in *U.S. News & World Report*, observed that "gospel became a style of performance into which you could put any message" ("Gospel Music Rolls out of the Church, onto the Charts" 1986, 56). In other words, gospel music became more than a musical genre; it was an idiomatic style that wielded tremendous influence not only on Black popular idioms but on the entire American popular tradition. The musical trends of the 1970s and 1980s support this axiom.

When funk and other urban forms evolved from soul music during the mid-1970s and 1980s, they retained the energy, rhythms, textures, and stylings of gospel music. The funk style developed by Larry Graham of Graham Central Station, for example, employs many of the features associated with the 1950s gospel sound. In the 1977 song "Release Yourself" (Warner Bros. BS 2814), the texture produced by mixed voices, the high-energy and percussive vocal style, the instrumental stylings of the organ and piano, and the beat of the tambourine recreate the fervor of the Roberta Martin Singers and the singing of Black folk churches.

Many components of gospel music have been incorporated into popular music, where they have intermingled with new techniques and expressions and then recycled back into gospel. This cyclical process has expanded the foundation of gospel and popular forms, generating new styles in both traditions. It therefore calls into question the artificial boundaries that historically have separated religious and secular styles, their performers, and their audiences. Whereas many singers once were compelled to choose between gospel and popular, they now freely move between and juxtapose both traditions on a single album. Deniece Williams, Ashford & Simpson, Al Green, and Candi Staton are singers who consistently include gospel songs on their albums of popular music. Williams explains her commitment to gospel: "I'd grown up singing in the choir and I'd always wanted to record a gospel song. . . . I told CBS I wanted to record a gospel album someday. They said, 'Yeah, sure, sure,' but never thought I was serious. I don't think CBS thought I'd go on to record a gospel song on every album after that [1976], either, but I did" (Gospel music column 1987). In 1986, when Williams's contract was up for renewal at CBS, she was granted permission to record a gospel album for Sparrow Records. The album, *So Glad I Know* (Sparrow SP 61121), not only received two Grammys but also appeared on four music charts: inspirational, gospel, pop, and Black music. Following Williams's lead, many singers in the popular idiom have begun to include gospel songs on their albums. The rap song "Pray" by M. C. Hammer (Capitol CDP 7928572) is an example of this trend among the 1990s generation of Black performers.

The 1980s witnessed the move of gospel music into the pop and rock corners of the music industry as its performers were featured as background singers on popular recordings. In 1984, the British group Foreigner recorded its "I Want to Know What Love Is" on *Agent Provocateur* (Atlantic A281999) using a gospel choir. When Foreigner toured America, it employed the services of local gospel choirs in every major city. The Winans have proven to be on the cutting edge of gospel music, pioneering new but controversial trends with each album (Gospel music column 1988). Perhaps the most controversial has been the use of established vocalists, instrumentalists, and producers from various popular idioms. For example, the 1987 album *Decisions* (Qwest 925510–1) features Anita Baker in the crossover hit "Ain't No Need to Worry." The Winans' first single, "It's Time" from *Return* (Qwest 261612), is a gospel rap produced by Teddy Riley, the force behind the success of Bobby Brown, Keith Sweat, and David Peaston. Other nongospel musicians included on the album are Stevie Wonder and Kenny G.

If other artists follow the direction of the Winans and Deniece Williams, the 1990s indeed will witness a continued wedging together of the sacred and secular spheres of Black community life. As contemporary gospel groups attempt to reach the youth and non-Christian market, and as religious record labels adopt "secular" promotion methods, the question posed in 1979—"Is it possible that one day gospel music will no longer belong to the church?"—will continue to be pondered.

References Cited

Banks, Lacy. 1974a. "Albertina the Mirror." *Black Stars* (Aug.): 68–74.

———. 1974b. "The Double-Barreled Gospel of Rev. Cleophus Robinson." *Black Stars* (Apr.): 64–69.

Barry, Thomas. 1969. "The Importance of Being Mr. James Brown." *Look* (Feb. 18): 56–62.

"Black Gospel: Rocketing to Higher Prominence." 1987. *Billboard* (Oct. 10): G–6.

Boyer, Horace Clarence. 1979a. "Contemporary Gospel." *The Black Perspective in Music* 7 (Spring): 5–11, 22–58.

Burnim, Mellonee. 1988. "Functional Dimensions of Gospel Music Performance." *Western Journal of Black Studies* (Summer): 112–20.

"Clara Ward . . . Gospel Singer." 1953. *Our World* (Dec.): 38–41.

Dixon, Robert M. W., and John Godrich. 1970. *Recording the Blues*. New York: Stein and Day.

Franklin, Aretha "You Make Me Feel Like A Natural Woman" Words and Music by Gerry Goffin, Carole King & Jerry Wexler©1968, Reproduced by permission of EMI Music Publishing Limited, London W1F9LD

Garland, Phyl. 1969. *The Sound of Soul*. Chicago: Henry Regnery Company.

Garnett, Bernard E. 1970. "How Soulful Is 'Soul' Radio?" Unpublished paper produced for Race Relations Information Center, Nashville.

Gehman, Richard. 1958. "God's Singing Messengers." *Coronet* (Jul.): 113–16.

Gospel music column. 1987. *Billboard* (Aug.).

Gospel music column. 1988. *Billboard* (Jul.).

"Gospel Music Rolls out of the Church, onto the Charts." 1986. *U.S. News & World Report* (Aug.): 56.

Gospel Pearls. 1921. Nashville: Sunday School Publishing Board, National Baptist Convention, U.S.A.

"Gospel to Pop to Gospel." 1962. *Ebony* (Jul.): 107–12. Courtesy Johnson Publishing Company, LLC. All rights reserved.

"Gospel Singers: Pop up, Sweet Chariot." 1963. *Time* (May): 48.

Hammond, John, and Irving Townsend. 1981. *John Hammond on Record*. New York: Penguin Books.

Hentoff, Nat. 1963. "Gospel Gimmick." *The Reporter* (Aug.): 46–47.

"Lady Soul: Singing It Like It Is." 1968. *Time* (June): 62–66.

Landes, John. 1987. "WLAC, the Hossman, and Their Influence on Black Gospel." *Black Music Research Journal* 7:67–81.

Levine, Lawrence W. 1977. *Black Culture and Black Consciousness: Afro-American Folk Thought from Slavery to Freedom*. New York: Oxford University Press.

Lift Every Voice and Sing. 1981. New York: The Church Hymnal Corporation.

Lornell, Kip. 1988. *"Happy in the Service of the Lord": Afro-American Gospel Quartets in Memphis*. Urbana: University of Illinois Press.

Lucas, Bob. 1972. "Gospel Superstar." *Sepia* (May): 21–26.

Maultsby, Portia. 1979. Interview with Jack Gibson, Orlando, Feb. 28.

———. 1983a. Interview with Shirley Jones, Los Angeles, Mar. 9.

———. 1983b. Interview with Deniece Williams, Los Angeles, Apr. 22.

———. 1983c. Interview with David "Panama" Francis, Orlando, Dec. 31.

———. 1984a. Interview with Hoss Allen, Nashville, Sept. 7.

———. 1984b. Interview with Albert "Diz" Russell, Washington, DC, Sept. 27.

———. 1990a. Interview with Walter Grady, Atlanta, Aug. 17.

———. 1990b. Interview with Eddie Castleberry, Atlanta, Aug. 17.

———. 1990c. Interview with George Nelson, Atlanta, Aug. 17.

Oliver, Paul. 1984. *Songsters and Saints: Vocal Traditions on Race Records.* New York: Cambridge University Press.

Patterson, J. O., German R. Ross, and Julia Atkins Mason. 1969. *History and Formative Years of the Church of God in Christ with Excerpts from the Life and Works of Its Founder—Bishop C. H. Mason.* Memphis: Church of God in Christ Publishers.

Salvo, Patrick, and Barbara Salvo. 1974. "45 Years of Gospel Music." *Sepia* (Apr.): 60–64.

Sanders, Charles. 1971. "Aretha." *Ebony* (Dec.): 124–34.

Seroff, Doug. 1980. Record album notes for *Birmingham Quartet Anthology* (Clanka Lanka Records CL 144, 001–14, 002).

Shearer, Karen. 1981. Interview with Candi Staton on radio program "Special Edition," Westwood One, Culver City, CA, Oct. 10.

———. 1982. Interview with Donna Summer, Westwood One, Culver City, CA, June 21.

———. 1983. Interview with Lou Rawls, Westwood One, Culver City, CA, Apr. 12.

Tallmadge, William H. 1974. Record album notes for *Jubilee to Gospel: A Selection of Commercially Recorded Black Religious Music,* 1921–1953 (JEMF-108).

Ward, Clara. 1956. "How a Visit to the Holy Land Changed My Life." *Color* (May): 15–17.

Williams, Martin. 1963. "Gospel at the Box Office." *Saturday Review* (Aug.): 41.

Williams-Jones, Pearl. 1975. "Afro-American Gospel: A Crystallization of the Black Aesthetic." *Ethnomusicology* 19 (Sept.): 373–84.

———. 1982. "Roberta Martin: Spirit of an Era." In *Roberta Martin and the Roberta Martin Singers: The Legacy and the Music,* ed. Bernice Johnson Reagon and Linn Shapiro, 12–21. Washington, DC: Smithsonian Institution, National Museum of American History, Program in African American Culture.

Woodson, Carter G. [1921] 1945. *The History of the Negro Church.* 2nd ed. Washington, DC: The Associated Publishers.

Work, John. 1915. *Folk Songs of the American Negro.* Reprint. New York: Negro Universities Press, 1969.

Yes, Lord! 1982. Memphis: COGIC Publishing Board; Nashville: Benson Company.

24 Singing in the Streets of Raleigh, 1963
Some Recollections
CLYDE R. APPLETON

This article, which initially appeared in Black Perspectives on Music *a dozen years after these events took place, is based on the first-hand experiences of the author and is perhaps the most personally heartfelt piece in this collection. Appleton lived in Raleigh, North Carolina, in the early 1960s while a student at Shaw College (now Shaw University). He became involved with the Civil Rights Movement and writes about the importance and uses of these songs that he and his friends used to challenge the solidly entrenched white power structure during this tumultuous period.*

Neither Appleton nor the others who marched in Raleigh were unique in their use of this music and these songs as part of the movement. Many writers, from Guy and Candy Carawan to Bernice Johnson Reagan, have detailed the importance of singing spirituals such as "We Shall Overcome" or "I Shall Not Be Moved" or newly composed songs, such as "Blowing in the Wind," which promoted solidarity during this tumultuous period of social protest and legal change. Appleton's article remains one of the most direct and focused accounts of music and the Civil Rights Movement, based on his experiences that occurred in a small southern city during the same year that Martin Luther King, Jr. delivered his iconic "I Have a Dream" speech.

The songs of the Civil Rights Movement of the early 1960s that burst from the mouths of hundreds of thousands of black Americans and echoed throughout this land are rarely sung today, just a dozen years later. Singing these songs that helped so much to bind together a generation of young black Americans in their quest for justice now sometimes generates a vague disquiet, even for some of us who would want to evoke "militant nostalgia" through their singing. The song "We Shall Overcome," a symbol of hope for the freedom movement in 1963, became a symbol of *unfulfilled* hopes just a few years later. "Someday" wasn't soon enough.

The somewhat negative "political" reputation of the freedom songs notwithstanding, the exceedingly important role of these songs in the course of the Civil Rights Movement of the early 1960s should not be so soon forgotten. That the Civil Rights Movement was a *singing* movement cannot be denied, and the central importance of song to the movement is probably unprecedented in the history of major social movements in the United States.[1] Singing was *integral* to the movement, perhaps in an even more pervasive and basic way than even demonstrations and rallies and sit-ins and jail-ins, because singing was a vital component of each of these aspects of the freedom movement.

The fact that this phenomenon—song as a central component of a mass social movement involving, in many ways and in many degrees, millions of people—occurred so recently gives impetus to the hope that scholars in many disciplines will investigate this utilization of song in the freedom movement of the 1960s. Viewing music as not only a phenomenon of sound but also as an aspect of human behavior/a component of culture, social scientists might look to that generation of black students in the southern states in the early 1960s as an exceedingly rich storehouse of data about the function of the arts in a mass social movement. Folklorists and ethnomusicologists might search out the untold hours of freedom songs that must surely be included in the files of video tape in the morgues of the national television networks and local TV and radio stations throughout the south. What are the melodic, harmonic, and rhythmic characteristics of the freedom songs? What are their musical roots? Was the repertory of freedom songs essentially the same everywhere? Did the singing *sound* the same in the "deep South" as it did in the "upper South"?[2] Did the degree of participation by whites have any effect on the sound of freedom songs? These are but a few of the questions that might be investigated.

We are fortunate that there are some valuable points of departure available to us in our studies of the freedom songs. One must be particularly grateful for the work of Guy and Candie Carawan, two freedom-movement activists who were also careful scholarly observers of the events that unfolded around them. The Carawan collections[3] stand virtually alone as significant attempts to chronicle the freedom songs of the 1960s. A few phonograph records should also be cited,[4] as well as the attention that the magazines *Sing Out!*[5] and *Broadside*[6] gave to the songs of the freedom movement.

SINGING IN THE STREETS OF RALEIGH

This paper is primarily about the songs that were sung in Raleigh, North Carolina, in the spring of 1963 during the marches, rallies, picketing, sit-ins, and jail-ins, which focused on a single demand: that every person be granted access to all places of public accommodation in that city. My principal sources are three: (1) a little mimeographed songbook that contains the words of twenty-one of the songs that were sung most frequently in the Raleigh movement,[7] (2) a tape of a program of freedom songs presented by the present writer and Teena Toombs in Tucson, Arizona, in July 1963,[8] and (3) the words and music for several of the songs which the writer transcribed from singing he heard during the period of the demonstrations in Raleigh in 1963.[9]

Except for stories in the files of the local news media, the following is perhaps the only recorded account of a demonstration in Raleigh during that spring of 1963.

> ... I remember one evening I was in the State Capitol working when I heard a heavy-beated pulsating song sung by a large group of men and women. I was alone in the building, yet the music was coming from all around me, it seemed, and was drawing closer. ... Then, through a window, I saw them, hundreds of them, almost all of them Negro young people. They carried torches. Their cadence was the beat of threatening men and women, of natives in the streets.[10]

John Ehle's words ring true for the writer, and they generate many memories of that spring of 1963 in Raleigh, North Carolina. Most of all, I remember the singing which was, for want of more expressive terminology, the most compelling and soul-stirring singing that I have ever heard.

At a typical demonstration, the marchers were primarily students from Shaw University, St. Augustine's College, and J. W. Ligon High School—along with a few older blacks and an even smaller number of whites. The "heavy-beated pulsating song" that gripped the attention of John Ehle and sent him running after the marchers with his camera was probably "We Are Soldiers." . . .

The importance of the song "We Are Soldiers" in the Raleigh movement was a consequence of certain characteristics of that local freedom movement. One can cite characteristics of the movement that were common to the "styles" of local freedom movements throughout the south. Yet in each local movement there evolved subtle variations on the overall freedom-movement framework that made each local movement unique. Ehle expresses this fact very succinctly when he compares the first demonstration in Chapel Hill in 1963 with the earlier marches he had witnessed in Raleigh.

> In Raleigh there was the attitude: "We will die for our cause." In Chapel Hill there was the attitude: "We would like you to join us so that we can improve our community."[11]

It should be remembered that the distance between Raleigh and Chapel Hill is only about forty miles.

In addition to being a *singing* movement, the Raleigh freedom movement was a *marching* movement. The characteristic action that occurred almost nightly during the course of the demonstrations was a march through the streets of downtown Raleigh, with stops (for singing) at the Court House (which housed the jail) and at selected segregated business establishments, followed by a spirited rally on the marchers return to Greenleaf Auditorium on the Shaw University campus, adjacent to downtown Raleigh. The preeminent marching song was "We Are Soldiers," adapted from the like-named spiritual; the only change in text was the substitution of "freedom banner" for "blood-stained banner."

It is of interest to compare the writer's transcription of "We are Soldiers" as he heard it with the version that appears in the Carawan collection.[12] . . . There are several differences. First, the marchers in Raleigh sang only the chorus, repeating it over and over as they marched; the verses were never sung. The writer heard and notated the song as a 6/8 (compound duple) march, characterized by a strong and steady underlying one-two marching cadence (rhythm of the beat) maintained by the left-right marching feet and the handclapping which was always *on* the beat. The Carawan version is written in 4/4 meter and characterized by the recurring triplet figure. The difference in concept is subtle but real. Over the strong marching beat was the song (the rhythm of the melody): a mixture of harmony and polyphony, the singers rarely "staying with a part" but improvising and moving here and there melodically as the spirit moved them. Of the four melodic lines I delineated in the version shown herein, the lines designated as A and B predominated. A' is merely a harmonization of A at the interval of a third higher; B' is obviously a variation on B with these two lines often converging. This musical texture was further enriched by the fact that both male and female voices sang each of the four lines—and others! African musical roots are there to see (and to *hear*): the polyphonic texture; the syncopated melodic lines; and the absence of a "church bass" part that is so characteristic of Protestant hymns solidly rooted in the tradition of western diatonic harmony.

If the song Ehle heard was not "We Are Soldiers," it was surely "I'm Pressin' On" . . . , the other marching song of the Raleigh movement. "Woke Up This Morning" was also used (and effectively) sometimes, and it is recalled that "Battle Hymn of the Republic" was used on one occasion, but the marchers abandoned it and reverted to "We Are Soldiers" and "I'm Pressin' On" after a few blocks. The beat was there, but I believe that the students must have sensed that the "four-part harmony" of "Battle Hymn" above the beat was not appropriate to the "style" of the Raleigh marches. The rich and varied texture of "We Are Soldiers" and "I'm Pressin' On" was not just a vibrant complement to the basic beat; it *got into* the beat and that became, in John Ehle's perceptive words, "the beat of threatening men and women."[13] Three well-defined parts are recorded which were, of course, elaborated upon and varied throughout the singing of the song. The variation of the text of the spiritual from whence it came was again, as in "We Are Soldiers," a very simple one: the substitution of the word "freedom" for "heaven." The words "shed" and "share" were used interchangeably. It is of interest to the present writer that "I'm Pressin' On" is not included in either of the two Caravan collections, and this suggests that the song may not have been sung in locales other than Raleigh.

A few comments should be made about the place of the song "We Shall Overcome" in the Raleigh freedom movement in 1963. I believe that there may be a mystique in the minds of many people about "We Shall Overcome"—a bit of folklore that pictures the freedom movement of the 1960s in terms of masses of reverent black folks, arms crossed to their neighbors on either side, quietly singing "We Shall Overcome." That portrayal may mirror the reality of certain times in certain places, but I do not believe the picture captures much of what was the essence of the movement. "We Shall Overcome" was sung often in Raleigh, but it is my recollection that it did not enjoy the special status of a song of more influence or deeper meaning to the freedom-movement activists than many other freedom songs. Another example of the different demonstration "styles" that evolved in different cities and towns across the south may be noted in Ehle's description of a march in Chapel Hill: "They started down the street singing: 'We shall overcome.' . . ."[14] It is possible that my memory is faulty, but I don't recall that this *ever* happened in Raleigh. It was the intent of Raleigh marches that they be demonstrations of discipline, strength, courage—and power. "We Shall Overcome" would not have been in consonance with the style of the freedom marches in Raleigh.

Most of the freedom songs are adaptations of older songs: spirituals, gospel songs, popular songs, etc. The melodies are retained well-intact, while the words are changed to a greater or lesser degree. Participants in every local freedom movement must have added their own verses to old songs, the new verses relating to specific circumstances in the local community. A popular example in Raleigh was an adaptation of the spiritual "I'm Gonna Sit at the Welcome Table." In Raleigh it was called "I'm Gonna Tell God How You Treat Me," and the words of the song title were sung as the first verse instead of the second as in the Caravan book.[15] . . .

"I'm Gonna Tell God How You Treat Me" was an excellent song for cataloging the principal targets (segregated business establishments) of the demonstrators. The verse "I'm gonna dance at the governor's mansion" deserves special comment. I vividly recall the event that gave birth to that verse. One evening the marchers proceeded to the lawn of the Governor's Mansion, and it happened that the mansion that night was the site of the annual Symphony Ball, a most significant occasion of the social season for North Carolina white society. Would that recording equipment had been there to capture the intermingling of sounds of the freedom songs from the lawn and the sounds of the orchestra playing inside the mansion! This intermingling of sounds became almost unreal when, over the singing of "We Shall Overcome" could be heard the announcement that the next dance would be the "last waltz of the evening."

Later, Governor Sanford came out on the balcony of the mansion and said to the hundreds of demonstrators gathered on the lawn below: "I enjoyed your singing." A voice from the darkness replied: "Governor, we didn't come here to entertain you." The verse about eating the twenty-eight flavors refers, of course, to Howard Johnson's Restaurant. The song "I'm Gonna Tell God How You Treat Me" was also a vehicle for proclaiming some successes of the Raleigh movement. After Gino's Restaurant did indeed begin serving blacks, the verse became: "I just ate some pizza at Gino's." Musically, the version collected in Raleigh is quite similar to the version of the song that appears in the Carawan collection, but there are melodic and rhythmic variations. As with the other fast-tempo freedom songs, handclapping was ever-present.[16] The pentatonic nature of the melody is evident, and it is of some interest that the song was always sung in unison in spite of the fact that it would lend itself readily to standard harmonization.

The writer is not aware that the spiritual "Go Down, Moses" was the source of many adaptations among the freedom singers of the early 1960s. It was an exceedingly important song in the Raleigh movement. Just before (perhaps only a night or two before) the advent of the series of mass marches in Raleigh in the spring of 1963, "Go Down, Citizens" was introduced by its author (a student at St. Augustine's College) at a meeting in an auditorium on the St. Augustine's campus. My attempts to search out the identity of this student have not been successful. Inasmuch as Raleigh's Mayor W. G. Enloe was also the owner of the Ambassador Theatre in Raleigh,[17] the song had immediate relevance for the local freedom movement. It was sung at every demonstration that spring. It was always sung in unison and, as was the case with other songs that moved at a relatively slow tempo, there was no handclapping. The effect of the singing (especially the bass voices) of the accented words "Let my people in the show" was powerful. . . .

A PERSONAL AND SUBJECTIVE POSTSCRIPT

The movement that gave birth to the freedom songs didn't bring about the dream of an integrated America free from prejudice and discrimination. But to say that "the movement didn't accomplish anything" is, I believe, inaccurate at best and slanderous at worst. I can only honor those students from Shaw University, St. Augustine's College, and Ligon High School in Raleigh, North Carolina, who did indeed force some changes, with freedom songs on their lips, in the modes of thought and behavior of the power structure of that city. The same is true of their counterparts in almost every city and town in every one of the southern states. I'll go along with the proposition that, when everything is said (or sung) and done, it's "no big thang" that a black student in Raleigh can now eat those twenty-eight flavors at Howard Johnson's. But I'm going to bring this piece to the conclusion with an affirmation that I'm glad they can.

Notes

1. Music, especially singing, has been a part of every people's movement. Singing played a role in the recent Anti-War movement, in the organizing activities of the CIO in the 1930s, in the earlier struggles for suffrage for women, etc. The writer believes that in none of these movements was the role of music so central as it was in the Civil Rights Movement of the early 1960s. Perhaps the role of singing in the "revivalism" that swept the American frontier in the early 19th century is most analogous.

2. When the late Ruby Doris Robinson from the SNCC office in Atlanta arrived on the Shaw University campus in Raleigh, North Carolina

when a freedom rally was in progress, she remarked that she had thought the singing never sounded so good outside of the *deep South*!
3. Guy and Candie Carawan, *We Shall Overcome! Songs of the Southern Freedom Movement* (New York: Oak Publications, 1963); Guy and Candle Carawan, *Freedom is a Constant Struggle* (New York: Oak Publications, 1967).
4. *The Nashville Sit-in Story* (Folkways 5590); *The Story of Greenwood, Mississippi* (Folkways 5593): *Freedom Songs: Selma, Alabama* (Folkways 5594); two beautiful recordings by the SNCC Freedom Singers *We Shall Overcome* (Mercury MG 20879) and *The Freedom Singers Sing of Freedom Now* (Mercury MG 20924): *Sit In Songs: Songs of the Freedom Riders* (Dauntless DM 4301); and especially that remarkable record, *Movement Soul* (ESP-Disk ESP 1056), a moving documentary from the freedom movement of 1963 and 1964.
5. See especially Robert Shelton. "Singing for Freedom: Music in the Integration Movement," *Sing Out!* 12 (December–January 1962): 4–17; Len H. Chandler, "Selma: A Folksinger's Report," *Sing Out!* 15 (July 1965): 7–18.
6. See especially songs and articles in *Broadside* #17 (December 1962), *Broadside* #30 (August 1963), *Broadside* #46 (30 May 1964), *Broadside* #51 (20 October 1964), and *Broadside* #57 (10 April 1965).
7. Songs included in this collection are "We Shall Overcome," "I'm Pressin' On," "We Are Soldiers," "Go Down, Citizens," "I'm Gonna Tell God How You Treat Me," "Only Believe," "Hammer Song," "Oh Freedom," "Hallelujah I'm a Traveling," "We Shall Not Be Moved," "I Know We'll Meet Again," "We Are Climbing Freedom's Ladder," "Come Out the Wilderness," "Hold On," "Certainly Lord," "This Train," "Give Me That Old Freedom Spirit," "Turn Me Round," "This Little Light of Mine, Woke Up This Morning," and "Over My Head."
8. These programs were presented on the nights of 28, 29 July at Ash Alley 241, the first of several clubs managed by Dave Graham in Tucson that featured folk music. Teena Toombs was a Shaw University student who participated in many of the demonstrations in Raleigh during the spring of 1963.
9. The present writer taught in the Music Department at Shaw University during the years 1962–1966. He was also a participant in many of the demonstrations in Raleigh that occurred in the spring of 1963.
10. John Ehle, *The Free Men* (New York: Harper and Row, 1965), pp. 48–49. Ehle's account of the demonstrations in Raleigh is very brief, but it is also very perceptive. *The Free Men* focuses on the freedom movement in Chapel Hill, North Carolina.
11. Ibid., p. 49.
12. Carawan, *We Shall Overcome*, pp. 12–13.
13. Ehle, *Free Men*, p. 49.
14. Ibid.
15. Carawan, *We Shall Overcome*, p. 14.
16. Of the twenty-one songs cited in Note 7, handclapping was characteristically present in the performance of fifteen of them. There was no handclapping with the songs sung at a relatively slow tempo: "We Shall Overcome," "Go Down, Citizens," "Only Believe," "I Know We'll Meet Again," "We Are Climbing Freedom's Ladder," and "Over My Head."
17. Mayor Enloe was also the owner of the Carolina Theatre in Chapel Hill. The writer is not aware that "Go Down, Citizens" was picked up by demonstrators in Chapel Hill.

25 Motown Calls "The Rock & Roll Kid"

DENNIS COFFEY

The Motown phenomenon marked the first time that black popular music truly crossed over into white homes across the United States. This sea change in the appreciation and consumption of black American popular music has been the subject of several well-written books by scholars and journalists as well as thousands of articles in newspapers, journals, and fan magazines. Most of these writers recount the now-familiar story of the vision of Barry Gordy, who left a job at a Ford assembly plant in the late 1950s to found what became the largest black-owned entertainment corporation in the United States. Under Gordy's forceful leadership, Motown eventually left (some might suggest abandoned) Detroit in favor of Los Angeles before he sold the corporation to MCA in 1988. Still others profile the important Motown artists, such as the Four Tops, the Supremes, Little Stevie Wonder, Marvin Gaye, and the Temptations, whose music remains both iconic and staples on "oldies" radio stations throughout the United States.

Only since the early 2000s have the inner workings of Motown—especially the song writing and studio work—been documented and disseminated. Inspired by the Allan Slutsky and James Jamerson book Standing in the Shadows of Motown: The Life and Music of Legendary Bassist James Jamerson *(1989), Slutsky's compelling 2002 film* Standing in the Shadows of Motown: The Story of the Funk Brothers *brought much deserved and widespread attention to how Motown records were actually crafted in the studio and by whom. His film documented not only how the brilliant, though wildly eccentric, bassist James Jamerson helped to craft the "Motown sound," it also illuminated the importance of other studio musicians, such as Eddie "Bongo" Brown, Richard "Pistol" Allen, Joe Hunter, and so many others in shaping these recordings through a largely informal collaborative process.*

The importance of white studio musicians, including members of the Detroit Symphony, is also part of this story. Guitarist Joe Messina was perhaps the most prolific of the white studio musicians, but Dennis Coffey also paid his dues. In this chapter from his book Guitars, Bars, and Motown Stars, *Detroit-bred rock and studio guitarist Coffey provides an informal and insightful account of the inner workings of the Motown Studio in the late 1960s. He recounts how he began working from 7–9 P.M. Monday through Thursday as part of the "Producer's Workshop" at a salary of $138 a week and ended up playing the now-famous fuzz and wah-wah pedal drenched guitar figure on the Temptations' 1969 hit "Cloud Nine."*

The brogue I heard on the other end of the line was unmistakable. "Wake up laddie, it's me, Jamerson. How ya doing?" The caller was Motown's legendary bass player, James Jamerson. I paused as I wondered why Jamerson was suddenly calling me. I had met him for the first time in a session we had recorded together a few months earlier.

"Fine, man, how you doing?" I answered. "What's going on?"

"I'd like to introduce you to someone. This is Hank Cosby."

The name Hank Cosby woke me right up. Hank was Stevie Wonder's producer and cowriter, and he was also one of Berry Gordy's right-hand men. As the music contractor who hired musicians to play on all of the recording sessions, Hank Cosby was a very powerful man at Motown.

"Coffey, how ya doing?" said Hank. "The reason we're calling is Motown's putting together a producer's workshop and we wonder if you'd be interested in playing guitar for us. It's going to be four nights a week upstairs at Motown Studio B, which is the old Golden World Studio on Davison."

"Sure, I'd be interested. Give me some more of the details?"

"We'll pay you $138.00 a week to work from seven to nine each night—Monday through Thursday—and Jamerson will be in charge. What do ya think?"

By now, I could hardly contain my excitement!

"It's next Monday," said Hank. "Let me put Jamerson back on the line. He'll fill you in."

Jamerson came back on the telephone.

"Hey, Coffey, since Motown put me in charge of this producer's workshop, there'll be me and you, Eddie Willis, Bongo, and some of the other Cats. It'll be cool, so come on down man."

I sat back down on the bed still wondering if I had heard what I thought I had. Just like that, without any warning, I had got a call from one of the most successful record companies in the world, and they had offered me a job. I had practiced eight hours a day since I was a kid for this moment, and now it was here! When you wait a long time for something to happen, and it finally happens, you still find it hard to believe.

My mind then flashed back to those live gigs I'd played with some of Motown's acts, such as the Velvelettes, the Marvelettes, and Edwin Starr. I was always trying to play my best to impress anyone from Motown, just so I'd be noticed.

I remembered an incident while playing with the Lyman Woodard Trio at the Frolic Show bar on the Lodge Service Drive.

One night, we were really kicking out the music in the middle of a set, and I looked up and saw David Ruffin, the lead singer from the Temptations, and Motown songstress Tammi Terrell walk into the bar together.

David was one of tallest people I'd ever seen. He looked like he was about six foot eight. They walked in and sat down at a table right in front of me. David, dressed in a brilliant white suit, was wearing an expensive gold watch and bracelet and those famous black, horn-rimmed glasses. Tammi was wearing a shimmering, white outfit and looked absolutely gorgeous.

The entire night, David and Tammi huddled together and seemed totally lost in each other. I was so impressed to see them in the club that I really tried to get them to notice my guitar playing. I knew a good word from David or Tammi would certainly help my chances of getting in at Motown. Melvin Davis, our drummer, was David's cousin. During the break, he introduced Lyman and me to Tammi and David.

Afterward I walked though the front door of the bar into the street to smoke a cigarette. Once I got outside, I couldn't believe my eyes. Parked right in the middle of the street was a shiny, brand spanking new Rolls Royce! You didn't see many of them in Detroit, at least not back then. The Rolls looked so rich and shiny, I halfway expected to see a chauffeur open the door and the Queen of England step out. I didn't see a driver or anyone else around. I wondered who was minding the store, because this neighborhood wasn't exactly Disneyland. Here I was, in the inner city after the '67 riots, playing in a bar for twenty dollars a night, and David Ruffin leaves a hundred thousand dollar car in the middle of the street unattended and goes into a bar with Tammi Terrell for a little music and entertainment. What a contrast in the lives of the "haves" and the "have nots." Suddenly I was face to face with the benefits of having really big money! I walked over and stared at the car in wonder. This was the first Rolls Royce I had ever seen up close. I peeked in the window. The interior was real varnished wood with seats of rich, polished leather, and I decided right then and there that I was going to work my ass off to get my part of the action. This was the effect Motown had on me. I knew Hitsville was the place to make money and play with one of the best recording bands in the world.

Monday finally rolled around, and at six o'clock I loaded up my car and drove down the Lodge Expressway. I got off at Livernois and continued down to Davison Street. I turned left on Davison, made a U-turn, and parked on the street in front of Motown's Studio B, a gray, two-story, cinder block building that used to be Golden World Studios. It was located about ten miles from Motown's Studio A.

Motown created the Producer's Workshop at Golden World to help evaluate their stable of in-house producers and to give them a chance to develop their ideas before going into the recording studio. I always felt that for some producers it was their last chance to come up with an idea for a hit record.

As I entered the building at Golden World to play guitar in the workshop, a uniformed guard behind a desk looked up and asked me to sign in. I wrote my name in the book and climbed the stairs on my right. At the top of the stairs, I entered a well-lit room and saw that James Jamerson was there and already set up.

Jamerson was an original character, with an attitude to match. He was about my height and weight, 5'10, 175 pounds, and sported a wicked Fu Manchu mustache. He could quite simply play the hell out of a bass. Jamerson and drummer Benny Benjamin really were the funky foundation of the Motown Sound. Jamerson played his fat, funky bass lines, and Benny pounded out the tight grooves and shuffles on his snare and high hat.

Jamerson usually wore black T-shirts, a black beret, Levis, and a brown leather belt with a small western buckle. Not only was Jamerson's bass playing extremely innovative, but his vocabulary had an interesting sound as well. As I walked in, Jamerson looked up at me and spoke in his Scottish-like brogue.

"Aye, me lad. What be-ith with you today?"

"Hey, man. Everything's all right. How's it going?"

"We ready to play the funk tonight Coff. You bring all your stuff?"

"You know me," I said. "I always come prepared." I got my wah-wah pedal and fuzz tone out.

Jamerson introduced me to the other workshop members: Ted Sheely on keyboards, Eddie Willis on guitar, Bongo Eddie on congas, and a new drummer called Spider. Ted Sheely was a quiet guy, a real gentleman, and very easy to work with. He just sat at the piano or electric keyboard, read the music, and played what he was asked to play. I never saw him much on the sessions at Hitsville, but I thought he could play very well. Of course, Motown already had Earl Van Dyke and Johnny Griffith, who were killer keyboard players.

Motown guitarist Eddie Willis was one of the funkiest guitar players out there. He always came up with real tasty ideas for every song. Most of the time he was given the freedom to play whatever he felt like because there were always other Motown guitarists on the session to read the music lines and guitar parts.

Eddie played a Gibson 335 hollow body guitar in the studio because the original Gibson Firebird he used at the workshop and on a lot of Motown sessions was broken. A Gibson Firebird was a thin, solid body guitar with a weird, obtuse shape. It had a sharp-edged sound that cut through an entire orchestra. (I knew this firsthand because I also owned a Firebird. Later, the nineties, I would lend it to the Henry Ford Museum for their Motown exhibit.)

Eddie "Bongo" Brown was the funky groovemeister at the workshop and played percussion on most of the recording sessions I did at Motown. Eddie also played the fantastic conga solo during the percussion break on "Scorpio." Eddie originally hailed from Memphis, and he could really play those congas and bongos. Bongo didn't believe in reading music. I used to wonder why he was always grinning to himself while we were running down our parts in the song until one day I looked at his music stand during a session, and saw that he was reading a girlie magazine.

I remember a time in 1969 when I invited Bongo to a party at my house in the Detroit suburb of Farmington Hills. Although I was born and raised in Detroit, at the time I lived in the suburbs. My house was a two-story brick and aluminum home on a pie-shaped lot at the end of a cul-de-sac in a well-manicured subdivision.

I was standing in my living room having a drink with a few of the guests when I happened to glance out of my front picture window and saw a light green Volkswagen Bug go by. Five minutes later, l saw it go by again, and it finally dawned on me who it was: Bongo driving by my house for the second time. I ran out into the street, shouted at him, and tried to wave him in. He just kept right on going like he didn't even know I was there. I waited until he went by again, but this time I ran after him, waving and shouting even louder. Shit! I said to myself. I couldn't believe this guy was still driving right by me.

On the fourth time around, he finally saw me. He stopped in front of my house, and I ran over to his car.

"Man, what's wrong with you?" I shouted. "Didn't you see me waving?"

He leaned out of his car window and grinned sheepishly.

"Shit! Coffey, is that you? Damn, I thought you was some crazy white guy trying to run me out of his neighborhood."

It occurred to me that he probably felt as nervous in my neighborhood as I sometimes did when I went to see him in his. At Motown, we were all colorblind, but other people in those days didn't see things that way.

Spider was the young drummer at the workshop. I don't know where he came from originally because he was quiet and never mentioned it. He played on a few sessions at Hitsville, notably the double-time drum cymbal part on "Cloud Nine." After that, he disappeared from the scene, and I really never heard where he went.

In the beginning, some of the producers came down to the workshop to try out their ideas. R. Dean Taylor was one producer who brought a few tunes to work on. He had one big hit with a song called "Indiana Wants Me," but after a few sessions he just faded from the scene. It may be that he left Motown. As a pop singer, he always had trouble getting Motown to promote him successfully.

The only successful pop R&B act Motown had was Rare Earth. They assigned ace producer Norman Whitfield to produce them and then broke them first on the R&B charts. I don't know why they had so much trouble promoting mainstream pop acts because most of their R&B acts crossed over to the pop charts anyway.

My biggest career opportunity began when Temptations' producer Norman Whitfield showed up. He used to come into the Twenty Grand in Detroit when I played there. Norman always wore expensive V-neck sweaters and fashionable dress slacks in the studio. He was very animated and explosive when he conducted the rhythm section. When Norman counted off each song, he would set both the tempo and the feel. Norman was a master of dynamics and built up each song to match what both he and cowriter Barrett Strong had in mind when they wrote it.

Once the Funk Brothers, Motown's studio band, got a good hold of a song in the studio, they played the hell out of it and added hot grooves and musical hooks galore. Like most Motown producers, Norman picked out which musical ideas he liked the best and recorded them in the song. A lot of producers at Motown, as well as producers at other major record companies, relied on the musicians to come up with good ideas to make hit records. But when the record became a hit everyone shared in the royalties except the musicians. In this, Motown was no different from anyone else.

Norman usually started the song off with the bass drum and percussion. Then he'd start adding instruments on each verse until the song built up to a crescendo of sweaty, raunchy funk! . . . and sweat we did. What I liked best about Norman was he always gave me the freedom to solo and experiment with my special guitar effects.

One day Norman came to the workshop with a song called "Cloud Nine." He wanted to experiment with the groove. Spider came up with a double-time cymbal part that resulted in a kick-ass groove, and I came up with the wah-wah pedal guitar effect in the introduction and throughout the song. When the pedal was pressed down and up, it produced a "wah-wah" sound on my guitar. The pedal had been used in pop rock by guitarists such as Jimi Hendrix and Eric Clapton, but no one had used it or even heard of it in mainstream R&B.

Even though some producers made use of the producer's workshop, activity there eventually slowed down. The producers lost interest and stopped showing up. Having nothing else to do, we just drank beer and watched stag movies every night. Well, what the hell—that was show business! Although the only big hit that came out of the workshop was "Cloud Nine," it happened to be the song that got me in the door at Motown.

A few days after we rehearsed "Cloud Nine," I got a call from Hank Cosby's office. They wanted me down at Hitsville the next morning.

The day of the session I was on pins and needles. I felt like I was getting ready for a concert appearance at the Philharmonic in New York. I could remember learning all the Motown records and playing them with the Royaltones in the local bars early on in my career.

As I drove up to the house on Grand Boulevard in Detroit and saw the sign, Hitsville, on the front, I suddenly realized that I too could become a part of the Motown Sound. I'd been packing them in at jazz and R&B clubs for the last two years, and I knew once they heard me play I'd be in like Flynn. Since I was fourteen, I'd been answering ads in the paper and auditioning to beat out other guitarists for jobs, and I had already played on hits with artists such as J. J. Barnes, Del Shannon, and Edwin Starr, so I was as ready as I'd ever be. I was a little nervous, but I was young and thought I could do anything. It never dawned on me just how many musicians got one chance at Motown and were never called back.

The actual recording studio was in the back of the house, but the main entrance was in the front. I walked up the steps and entered through the front door. A guard in uniform was sitting behind a desk. He asked me to sign in, so I wrote my name in the book and moved through the hall, past the control room, and went downstairs to the studio . . . the infamous "Snake Pit."

The room was well lit, and most of the musicians were already there. I could feel the energy and creative vibes flowing throughout the room, and for a brief minute I shook my head and thought to myself that this was the actual place where all the early Motown hits were recorded. I couldn't believe I was there. The place was awesome!

Growing up in Detroit as a musician, I had heard all sorts of Motown stories. A pop singer named Tommy Good signed a contract with Motown, and when his record wasn't released he actually had to picket Hitsville in front of local reporters to get his contract back. The industry standard contract in those days was a total of five years, with one-year options for renewal at the discretion of the record company. It was well known that Motown extended its contacts to seven years.

As I got ready for my first session at Motown, I looked around the Hitsville studio. It consisted of one long main room and two small overdub rooms with the guitarists all sitting together against the wall under the control room window. Jamerson was sitting on his stool next to the guitars, and both drummers were sitting behind sound baffles, or separators, against the far back wall. Later, in Los Angeles at MoWest, I would see the same sound baffles. Maybe Motown shipped them out from Detroit for luck, who knows? Bongo sat on the other side of the control room stairs, opposite the guitars. The electric keyboards and the tambourine were on the other side of him, with the acoustic piano and vibes located in the overdub rooms. The acoustic piano was sometimes placed in one of the overdub rooms to prevent the sound of the other instruments from leaking through the piano microphone and getting on tape.

The first person I spoke to was Jamerson, who was sitting on his stool smoking a cigarette. When he saw me, he looked over and grinned.

"Coffey, me lad, how be it with you? What's going on?"

I grinned back with my guitar in one hand and my special effects bag in the other. "Hey, man. I'm fine. Just tell me where I can set up."

Jamerson showed me how to plug my guitar into the direct box, which was connected to the big speaker they used for guitars. The guitars and his bass were routed directly into the recording console in the control room because there were no amplifiers. Motown gave us earphones and one big playback speaker so we could hear ourselves play. Jamerson took me around the room and introduced me to the musicians I didn't know. Everyone was smiling and real friendly, so I felt right at home.

My guitar was a Gibson Firebird that had I bought after hearing Eddie Willis use one on a recording session we did together. I really liked the sound of it—a good, tight, funky sound. I had also brought the leather bag that contained my special guitar effects. The only effects I had at the time were a fuzz tone (a distortion device) and the wah-wah pedal.

Once I got my gear set up, I looked at the music chart sitting on the stand in front of me. I saw that the notes were written on a double staff just like piano sheet music. The guitar figure and bass figure were written in sixteenth notes.

I soon learned that we were expected to record one song per hour—no small feat. We had to sight read a new chart every hour, improvise guitar fills or a solo, and try to make a hit record all at the same time. Each session lasted about three hours. On most days, we did double sessions with an hour off for lunch. We usually went to lunch at the Howard Johnson's restaurant on Grand Boulevard just down the street.

Later, I would discover that we'd been recording six songs a day, five days a week. The number of hits we made was astonishing! They didn't call Motown the hit factory for nothing. I used to collect all the records I played on, but after a while there were just so many that I couldn't keep track of them. I played on at least one hundred million sellers for Motown and the other companies that used me. At one point, I was on three of the Top 10 and ten of the Top 100 singles on the *Billboard* chart every month for an entire year.

That day on the session we had two drummers. Spider played high hat and cymbals, and Pistol Allen played snare drum and foot pedal. Most people didn't realize it, but the concept of using two drummers was born on that session. We used two drummers on almost every session after that. That was how the drum cymbal parts on Motown records became so rhythmically complicated. I was sure that a lot of drummers working in bars and clubs were going crazy trying to duplicate the drum sound of Motown by attempting to play both drum parts at once.

The rhythm section I usually played with at Motown consisted of Earl Van Dyke and Johnny Griffith on keyboards, Eddie "Bongo" Brown on congas and bongos, and James Jamerson on bass. There was also Jack Ashford on tambourine, Jack Brokenshaw on vibes, Richard "Pistol" Allen and Uriel Jones on drums, and Joe Messina, Eddie Willis, or Robert White on guitars. Usually there were three of us playing guitars at each session, but some sessions had as many as four guitars. All of the guitar players at Motown, including me, cooperated with each other to make things easier. No one tried to hog the best guitar parts or tried to take over, like I later saw in L.A. and New York.

At Motown, we all worked together to make the best records we could. I played with other musicians at Motown, including bassist Bob Babbitt and drummer Andrew Smith, but I worked with these musicians the most. The arrangers I worked with the most were Paul Riser, Johnny Allen, Dave Van Depitte, and Wade Marcus.

I learned that the song we were to record on my first day at Motown was "Cloud Nine." Now I knew why they'd called me for the session. Norman had obviously liked what I'd done at the workshop and finally wanted to use me on a record date. Sometimes all it takes in the music business is one big break. This was the break I'd been waiting for.

Norman counted off the tempo, and everyone started playing. I ad-libbed a fast wah-wah effect in the introduction and played the written figure on the guitar through the wah-wah pedal. It immediately became very clear to me that I was playing with the finest rhythm section I'd ever heard.

Once I learned the song, I began to listen more closely to what the other musicians were playing and to the interaction going on between them. Each musician complemented what the other musicians were doing. When one guy locked into a musical idea, the others supported it and built new ideas on it. Music is one of the truest expressions in the human experience. It comes from deep within the soul and communicates feelings and passion to the listener and can also stimulate the imagination to recall meaningful past relationships and events.

On the last verse of the song, the groove we were playing was so hot that I just had to jump in and play a solo. I cranked my volume up a bit, closed my eyes, and let 'er rip. It didn't get much better than this. I was finally playing at Motown's Hitsville studios with the finest damn band in the world and getting paid good money for it too. The rhythm section was so funky and exciting that I couldn't help but play a great solo. I gave Mr. Wah Wah Pedal a hell of a work out that day!

The sound of Motown on the radio was always fantastic, but to be playing guitar right in the middle of it in the studio was unbelievable! I never forgot the excitement I felt the first time I played for Motown, which to me was like a baseball player getting his first shot in the major leagues. I hit a home run my first time at bat with "Cloud Nine," which went on to become an international hit for the Temptations. The success assured me a regular slot on the home team. I was now a guitarist, and the effects specialist, at Motown.

26 Respect: 1964–1965

ROB BOWMAN

The mid-1960s were pivotal years not only for the evolution and success of Stax Records but also for black American popular music. Flush with successful artists such as the Supremes, the Temptations, and Stevie Wonder, Motown was at the zenith of its artistic and commercial success. Motown artists were staples of the Top-40 charts and you couldn't turn on a radio in the United States without encountering the sounds of young America.

Stax, on the other hand, was just about to flower. They released records by Booker T. and the MG's, Otis Redding, and Rufus & Carla Thomas that gained substantial airplay and sold pretty well. But these solid and respected Stax artists did not command as much popular attention their Detroit counterparts, even in local mom-and-pop stores that sold so many "black" records. But the sound that helped Stax to sell large quantities of records in the late 1960s was coming together in the studio. As Rob Bowman (a professor of music at York University and the author of Soulsville, U.S.A., which is where this chapter originally appeared) notes, the studio sound was just beginning to reflect the aesthetics of keyboardist and producer Isaac Hayes as well as the judgment of Stax musical guru Jim Stewart, one of the label's founders in the late 1950s.

In the middle of 1965 Stax released Otis Redding's masterful "I've Been Loving You Too Long," which Redding co-authored with Jerry Butler. This song and many others recorded by the likes of Wilson Pickett during this year epitomized all that was right with Stax during this period: the studio collaborations of writer David Porter, the tight rhythm section (often anchored by Duck Dunn's bass and Al Jackson's drums), and the improvisatory nature of the sessions. By late 1965, the "Memphis Sound" that propelled out of the Stax Studios was beginning to rival the success of Motown. Wilson Pickett scored a smash hit with "In the Midnight Hour," which only paved the road to greater success over the next few years.

In the middle of a wildly successful 1965 during which it became clear that better distribution was needed, Jim Stewart signed a contract with Atlantic that would ultimately help to bring about the dissolution of Stax. The Atlantic deal resulted in the wider distribution of Stax 45s and albums; however, a clause buried deep on page 11 gave Atlantic the rights of ownership of Stax material that they had distributed prior to May 17, 1965. Essentially Stax lost the rights to their entire back catalog, a financial blow from which the company would never recover.

All told, 1964 was a fairly quiet year at Stax. Although thirty-two 45s were issued by the company on Atlantic, Volt, and Stax, twelve of these were by the label's proven artists: Rufus and Carla Thomas, Booker T. and the MG's, and Otis Redding. Surprisingly, no one at the company was able to achieve anything remotely close to a substantial hit on the level of "Gee Whiz," "Green Onions," or "These Arms of Mine." While the lack of a mega-hit obviously disappointed Stax's brain trust, the company remained in relatively good health. With the exception of the MG's, virtually every release by each of its main artists charted.[1] The bottom line is that sales were steady but unspectacular, the majority of records being sold to a black clientele through inner-city America's numerous mom-and-pop record outlets.

While Stax was struggling, its northern counterpart, Motown Records, was in its ascendancy, with the Supremes, Mary Wells, the Miracles, the Temptations, and Stevie Wonder all regularly tearing up the pop charts. The sign outside Motown proudly proclaimed the company "Hitsville U.S.A."; the marquee outside the Stax studio, on the other hand, was adorned with the words "Soulsville U.S.A." These slogans perfectly sum up the diametrically opposed aesthetic and operating philosophies of the two companies.

Motown president Berry Gordy, Jr., was a product of the urban industrial North. Relentlessly driven, ruthlessly ambitious, and autocratic to the bone, Gordy ran his operation very much from a master plan. Utilizing sound business practices such as vertical integration, Gordy maximized both his control and ultimate profitability by operating a management company, booking agency, and record company under one roof. Jim Stewart, on the other hand, was a product of the rural, fraternal South. Although he wanted to make money, he could easily be content with what might seem to be a modicum of success, not caring a whit about making further profits via management or booking activities. In what has to be one of the great ironies of the Stax story, Stewart was always loudly championing keeping the company's sound as "black" as possible. While various black writers and later co-owner Al Bell were interested in crossover success, Stewart seemingly wasn't the least bit interested if crossing over meant compromising what he was gradually coming to understand as the "Stax sound."

"We could never grab that little thing Motown had," shrugs Stewart. "Of course, they couldn't [grab] ours either. We envied them being able to cross over to the pop market back then when we couldn't, but it just wasn't us. When we tried to do something like that, we would fall flat on our butt. We had to do what we knew best." In general, Stewart was much less authoritarian and much more egalitarian than Gordy. Within a few years, Stax would effectively engage in profit sharing, an unthinkable occurrence at Motown. Finally, Stewart certainly did not operate from a master blueprint; at Stax, things tended to occur by happenstance.

A key contributor to Stax's secure financial position was Estelle Axton's activities at the Satellite Record Shop. By now Lady A had developed into what Jim described as "the damnest salesman I ever saw." Shortly after commencing operation, she had instituted a program whereby, with every ten records purchased, customers would get one free. This little gimmick allowed Estelle to keep a file card on each customer; she not only kept track of the number of records purchased, she also wrote down the titles. The minute a customer would ask for a record, Estelle would pull his or her card and at a glance could see what they had been buying.

"I could see what type of music he'd like," Estelle chortles. "If I'd gotten any records since he'd [last] been in, I played everything that was in that vein and I got nineteen of his twenty dollars. Don't ever let a customer show me twenty dollars 'cause I'll get nineteen of it. I'll leave him money to get home 'cause I'll sell him more records [when he returns]. They wouldn't go anywhere else to buy their records. They'd say, 'If Satellite don't have it, it's not in town.'" Employee William Brown proudly asserts, "We got so good in that shop till you could hum the line and we could go get the record!"

Located in Memphis, the Stax Museum of American Soul Music opened in 2003 and sells a wide range of products, including this bumper sticker.
Credit: Bumper sticker from the collection of Kip Lornell.

If Estelle ran low on a popular record over the weekend, she would simply go across town to her major competition, Pop Tunes. She would then hit on an unwitting employee and buy, at a wholesale rate, Pop Tunes' complete stock of the title. Of course, that would mean that Pop Tunes wouldn't have the record anymore, and both their customers and Satellite's would have to come over to East McLemore to get their sonic fix.

While sales of Stax and Volt product were less than spectacular in 1964, the company did issue a number of superb singles. One was an instrumental recorded and released under baritone saxophonist Floyd Newman's name that slipped out of the gate just before the first of the year. According to Floyd his lone solo 45, "Frog Stomp" backed with "Sassy," came about directly as a result of intensive lobbying by Estelle. As was the case with most of the Stax session musicians, Newman earned a substantial part of his living playing gigs in and around Memphis. When he got the opportunity to record his own record, he elected to use his own band, including Joe Woods on guitar, Howard Grimes on bass, and Isaac Hayes on piano. Hayes had cowritten "Frog Stomp" with Newman, although he was not credited when the original record came out.

The Newman session was not the first time that Isaac Hayes had headed down to Stax. A couple of years earlier he had auditioned for the company as part of a doo-wop ensemble that went by the name of the Ambassadors, and he had also auditioned as a member of the blues band Calvin and the Swing Cats. To his disappointment, both groups were turned down.

Hayes's story is one of epic proportions. Beginning in 1969, with the release of *Hot Buttered Soul*, he would become the biggest artist Stax ever produced and one of the most important artists in the history of rhythm and blues. In the first few years of the 1970s he single-handedly redefined the sonic possibilities for black music, in the process opening up the album market as a commercially viable medium for black artists such as Marvin Gaye, Stevie Wonder, Funkadelic, and Curtis Mayfield. Earlier, Hayes, alongside partner David Porter, helped shape the sound of soul music in the 1960s with such definitive compositions as "Hold On! I'm Comin'," "Soul Man," "When Something Is Wrong with My Baby," "B-A-B-Y," and "I Thank You." The fact that one artist could be responsible for such disparate but equally great and influential music as Hayes produced in the 1960s and 1970s simply boggles the imagination.

Born August 20, 1942, in Covington, Tennessee, by the time Hayes was eighteen months old his mother had passed away in a mental institution; because his father had disappeared sometime before her death, Isaac was subsequently raised by his grandparents. To sharecroppers such as Hayes's grandparents, radio was their major contact with the rest of the world. For the first several years of Isaac's life this meant a steady diet of what was then called "hillbilly music," with Saturday night's "Grand Ole Opry" broadcast being of particular importance.[2] Hayes's musical imagination was also fired by the gospel music he heard on the radio performed by the Golden Gate Quartet (singing on the "Amos and Andy Show") and the Wings Over Jordan Choir, and he fondly remembers touring gospel groups such as the Spirit of Memphis Quartet putting on programs at the local churches in Covington.

A pivotal moment in Isaac's life occurred in June 1949, when he caught Nat D. Williams's "Sepia Swing" show for the first time on Memphis's WDIA. "That was the first black person I heard as a radio announcer," relates Hayes. "I listened to it and said, 'Wow, a black man on radio!'" That same month Isaac's grandparents moved into Memphis. Urban living was a bit of a shock for the seven-year-old Hayes. Out in the country all of the sharecroppers were equally impoverished but, because they grew their own food and there was relatively little to buy, the burden of poverty was light when compared with being poor in the city. In Memphis, you had to buy your food, and there were plenty of other products that were alluring but only attainable if you had the requisite income. A young Isaac Hayes started to understand that all men are not created equal.

"I used to dream," recalled Isaac, speaking with Phyl Garland in 1970, "just dream about being able to have a warm bed to sleep in and a nice square meal and some decent clothes to wear. But what really tore me up was when we had to split up. We didn't have a place to go, so my grandparents moved in with an uncle, my sister had to go live with an aunt, and I had to go live with a guy who was a friend of the family."

After his grandfather died, when he was eleven, Isaac, his sister and grandmother, together and separately, lived all over North Memphis. At one point the three of them were on welfare living in one room over a storefront church. When they were cut off of welfare, they could no longer afford to pay the gas bill, so they used the wood from their outhouse to burn for heat. Consequently, they had no bathroom. Then the family's utilities were cut off so they had no lights and had to borrow water from a neighbor. The next year, the family ran out of food and Isaac's grandmother and sister got sick from hunger.

"I lived in so many different places," Isaac told me many years later. "You can't imagine, man. We lived in the back of appliance stores, lived in people's backyards. One time I moved in with this guy who was an alcoholic. He got arrested and I didn't have anywhere to stay, so I slept in junk cars at a garage."

To help make ends meet, Isaac worked at the Savoy Theatre, distributed flyers, delivered groceries in a borrowed wagon, hauled wood, and shined shoes down on Beale Street. Despite his efforts, Isaac remained as poor as they came. By the time he reached the ninth grade, he became conscious of both the opposite sex and how ragged his clothes were. Putting two and two together, Isaac noticed that the guys with fine clothes did much better in terms of making time with the girls. Embarrassed by the holes in his shoes and the general state of disrepair of his wardrobe, Isaac dropped out of school.

Forced to return by his grandmother, Isaac attended Manassas High School (at the time, it covered grades one through twelve), where he took vocal music, and began fooling around every chance he got with the school piano. Although he liked music, his stated ambition was to become a doctor.

On many a school day, right after his grandmother walked him to the front doors at Manassas, Isaac bolted out the side entrance. Much of the time he would go to the fields and pick cotton for a black farmer named Armstrong. Buses would come into town early in the morning to take black field hands out to the country. If they missed the bus, they had to try to make it over the Arkansas River bridge and hitch a ride out to the fields. Over time Isaac developed a heavy-duty crush on Armstrong's daughter. Attempting to impress her, he decided to enter the school talent contest, where he sang Nat King Cole's 1958 hit "Looking Back."

Several years earlier, while still in grade four, he and his sister, Willette, had performed in another talent contest, working over Perry Como and Tony Bennett songs. At that time, his voice was light and airy, so his schoolmates nicknamed him the "Swoon Crooner" while teasing him about sounding like a girl. His grade-nine performance was a little bit different, because Isaac's voice had already dropped a couple of octaves. "I was scared to death," Hayes remembers, wincing. "They got an auditorium full of people [but] I sang the song and I fell on my knees and the girls just screamed and everything. I got to the bridge of the song, the climax, and that's when I went down to my knees and they just freaked. I mean the whole house came down. After that I was an instant celebrity on campus and I lost my passion for medicine. I found a new thing. Here's a poor kid, dressed in rags, holes in his shoes. All of a sudden beautiful girls in the twelfth grade are asking, 'Ooh, give me your autograph.' I wanted to make a career of music then because of all the attention and everything."

By the time Isaac was fifteen, he was singing in the Morning Stars, a gospel quartet that performed weekly at Pleasant Green Baptist Church on Sunday morning. The church's services were broadcast on radio station WHHN every Sunday night. A short while later, Isaac began singing doo-wop with the Teen Tones, who were proudly decked out in sweaters emblazoned with the letter *T*, emulating Frankie Lymon and the Teenagers' sense of fashion. For a short period Isaac sang with both groups.

The Teen Tones worked out stage routines that they'd use at their infrequent performances at high-school functions and at amateur night at the Palace Theatre on Beale. The emcee at these amateur nights was none other than future Stax star Rufus Thomas, working alongside his comic partner, Bones, and radio announcer Nat D. Williams. The Teen Tones were often in competition with William Bell's Del-Rios and David Porter's Marquettes, their repertoire consisting of material such as the Five Royales' "Tell the Truth" and "Dedicated to the One I Love," Hank Ballard and the Midnighters' "Let's Go, Let's Go, Let's Go," and the Spaniels' "You're Gonna Cry." "We'd get five or six dollars when we'd win and then we'd go buy doughnuts or a hot dog at the Harlem House on Beale and walk back home," Hayes says, smiling as he warmly cherishes the memory.

The Teen Tones made it into a recording studio where they sang backup in ersatz Jordinaires style for a white artist named Jimmy McCracklin, who recorded under the pseudonym Johnny Rebel.[3] While all of this was going down, Isaac also sang for a short while with schoolmate Sidney Kirk in another doo-wop group dubbed the Ambassadors; this group auditioned for Stax, perhaps Isaac's first trip to the East McLemore studio, but they were turned down.

Back at school in the wake of the talent contest, Isaac was singing in the church choir and took a year of band. He had wanted to play alto saxophone but, because school instruments were limited, he ended up playing the baritone. Alto saxophonist Lucian Coleman, brother of jazz great George Coleman, lived in the neighborhood and in 1959 took Isaac under his wing, teaching him about jazz greats such as Charlie Parker, Dizzy Gillespie, Art Pepper, and Memphis luminaries Frank Strozier and Booker Little. Soon thereafter, Isaac moved in with Coleman. The older musician was kind enough to lend Isaac his alto sax so that Isaac could play alto instead of baritone in the school band.

Getting hooked further by the music bug, Isaac started hanging outside Mitchell's Hotel on Beale Street and Curry's Club Tropicana on Thomas Street. Too young to get in, he would stand on garbage cans, peeking in the windows, and pressing his ear to the walls, trying to take in as much as he possibly could. Every Sunday afternoon, Curry's hosted a jazz jam. On one Sunday in 1961, James Moody was booked to play that evening and stopped by early to take part in the jam. When Isaac finally built up the nerve to say he wanted to come in and sing, Memphis sax great Fred Ford, a.k.a. Daddy Goodlow, smoothed the way for Isaac with the doorman. Isaac eventually summoned up the nerve to get onstage, where he sang Arthur Prysock's "The Very Thought of You" backed by the house band led by Ben Branch. "When I finished," Isaac recalls, "Mrs. Curry came over to me and said, 'Young man, do you want a job?'"

Elated, for the next two years Isaac enjoyed his first professional job, singing one or two songs every Monday, Saturday, and Sunday night with Ben Branch. At the time Branch's band included Floyd Newman, Herbert Thomas on trumpet, Clarence Nelson on guitar, Big Bell James on drums, and Larry Brown on bass. Brown, along with future Stax producer Allen Jones and Lewie Steinberg, was one of the first electric bass players in Memphis. He was to have an inordinate influence on MG bassist Duck Dunn, and, in an interesting twist of fate, Dunn would eventually replace Brown in Ben Branch's band.

A short while after Isaac began working with Branch, Lucian Coleman started playing with Calvin and the Swing Cats, a blues band that included Willie Chase on drums, Sidney Kirk on piano, Mickey Gregory on trumpet, and leader Calvin Valentine on guitar.[4] Through Coleman's intercession, Isaac began singing with the group, often working out-of-town gigs, taking the vocal lead on tunes such as "One Room Country Shack" and "Baby, Please Don't Go." Some of the gigs out in the country apparently got pretty rough; Isaac recalls many a night diving behind the piano to avoid flying bullets. Isaac's second trip to Stax was as a member of Calvin and the Swing Cats; unfortunately, for all concerned, they failed their audition.

During Isaac's senior year in high school, he briefly formed one other combo, the Missiles, giving him the chance to play sax. The Missiles included one Elmo Harris who, as Eddie Harrison, would sing in the Premiers and record one Stax 45 in September 1965, the haunting "Make It Me," which coincidentally was one of Hayes and David Porter's earliest compositions and production efforts. Harrison would later lead the Short Kuts, who recorded a series of 45s for Pepper Records, some cuts of which were written and/or produced by Hayes and Porter.[5]

While all this professional gigging was occurring, Isaac was finally finishing high school, starring in the Manassas annual show three years in a row Upon graduating in 1962, he was offered seven different vocal scholarships by the likes of Jackson State, Tennessee State, Florida A & M, Lane College, and Rust College. Unfortunately he was now married and an expectant father, so college was out of the question. Prophetically, a number of Manassas students wrote in his high school yearbook sayings like, "See you on television when you're famous." Isaac initially supported his wife and child by working at a meat-packing plant. When gigs were getting scarce in late 1962, Sidney Kirk happened to mention that a new studio had opened at Chelsea and Thomas. Hayes and Kirk walked down to American Sound Studios, met Chips Moman, and asked to audition. Moman was suitably impressed, and Isaac Hayes ended up recording one of the very first releases for Moman and Seymour Rosenberg's Youngstown label. The A-side, "Laura, We're on Our Last Go-Round," was written by a local writer named Patty Ferguson, while the B-side was a cover of Merle Travis and Cliffie Stone's "Sweet Temptations."[6] Future Stax head engineer Ronnie Capone played drums, Tommy Cogbill played bass, and Sidney Kirk took care of the piano chores. Isaac strictly sang, double-tracking his own harmony part.

According to Moman, for quite a while Isaac came by American just about every day after working at the slaughterhouse, hanging out, writing, and learning about the recording studio. Meanwhile, when the record flopped, Sidney Kirk went into the air force, which, ironically, turned Isaac into a piano player. As Isaac tells it, one day Kirk's sister, Fanny, called him up saying that Jeb Stuart had just telephoned, desperately in need of a piano player for a New Year's Eve gig at the Southern Club. She wondered if Isaac wanted to try to fit the bill. Desperate for money, he said yes. The only problem was he hardly knew how to play piano.

"After I accepted it, I broke into a cold sweat," laughs Isaac. "I was scared to death. I said, 'What am I doing? I don't know how to play piano. They're gonna kill me.' But, I needed the money. I got there before anybody, just trying to practice on little things that I did know. I started off playing with two fingers and then I added a few more fingers. Being New Year's Eve the crowd was full of spirits. Had we played 'Three Blind Mice' nobody would have given a shit! The club owner came up and said, 'You know you boys sound pretty good. Y'all want a regular job?' What put me at ease [was that] none of the other guys could play worth a shit, either. So, I was in good company. That's how I got started messing around with piano. We took that gig, built a crowd and got a hell of a following."[7]

Becoming more proficient on keyboards with each gig, Isaac next joined Floyd Newman's band at the Plantation Inn, staying onboard as the group's pianist for some five or six months. He also began writing songs under the pseudonyms Ed Lee and Anthony Mitchell, and played on a couple of Goldwax sessions in Muscle Shoals with Bowlegs Miller behind Spencer Wiggins and James Carr. All of which brings the story back to his playing piano on and cowriting the A-side of Floyd Newman's "Frog Stomp." Newman picks up the story. "That's the first time that Jim Stewart had ever heard him [play piano]. Isaac had an unbelievable ear. He was playing things that he didn't even know he was playing. But, he heard them and he would play them." With Booker T. Jones off at college, Isaac Hayes slowly became a regular Stax session musician. As he gained confidence, he slowly began to make suggestions about the arrangements of material. Eventually, he started writing songs with David Porter, inalterably changing the face of Stax Records forever.

Another important addition to the Stax family, Andrew Love, replaced Gilbert Caple at around the same time Newman cut "Frog Stomp." A graduate of Booker T. Washington, Love had been playing in Memphis night-clubs with the likes of Bowlegs Miller since he was in the tenth grade. Awarded a band scholarship, Love spent two years at Langston University in Oklahoma before heading back to Memphis to make his living as a player. He immediately was hired for sessions at Hi, playing on hit records such as Willie Mitchell's "20-75" and Gene Simmons's "Haunted House." Unable to afford a phone, he eventually moved right across the street from the studio so Willie Mitchell could simply knock on his door whenever he needed him for a session. Al Jackson recommended Love for work at Stax when Gilbert Caple said he was headed to Houston to work in the house band at Duke-Peacock Records.[8]

Isaac Hayes' first paid session as a piano player was for Otis Redding. "I was frightened," relates Hayes, some twenty-two years after the fact. "Here I am in this place I've always wanted to be and all these giants have been through there." At this late date it is impossible to ascertain which of Otis's 1964 releases featured Hayes for the first time.[9] My best guess would be February's "Come to Me" or April's "Security."

"Come to Me" was the top side of Otis's fourth Volt single. Cowritten by Phil Walden it's in Otis's patented 6/8 ballad mode featuring the ubiquitous piano triplets, this time with the addition of church-derived organ. Curiously, it's one of only two tracks recorded and released after Redding's debut Volt session not to feature horns. Peaking at number 69 pop, it undoubtedly would have been a Top 30 R&B hit if *Billboard* had published an R&B chart that year. The lively self-penned "Security," unjustly, had next to no chart action. Today, it is regarded as a watershed release in Otis's early career, featuring for the first time his trademark offbeat horn punctuations dueling with both Cropper's metallic guitar responses and Otis's voice following the horn break. The net result is absolutely sublime.

Otis closed the year with "Chained and Bound" in September and "Mr. Pitiful" in December. The latter, in many ways, was a turning point for Otis and Stax. It was the first record to include another of Otis's distinctive horn patterns, a series of eighths with the offbeats accented. It was also Otis's first full collaboration as a writer with MG guitarist Steve Cropper, and his first Top 10 R&B and Top 50 pop chart entry. Cropper recalls, "There was a disc jockey here named Moohah [WDIA's A. C. Williams]. He started calling Otis 'Mr. Pitiful' 'cause he sounded so pitiful singing his ballads. So I said, 'Great idea for a song!' I got the idea for writing about it in the shower. I was on my way down to pick up Otis. I got down there and I was humming it in the car. I said, 'Hey, what do you think about this?' We just wrote the song on the way to the studio, just slapping our hands on our legs. We wrote it in about ten minutes, went in, showed it to the guys, he hummed a horn line, boom—we had it. When Jim Stewart walked in we had it all worked up. Two or three cuts later, there it was."

By the time "Mr. Pitiful" was recorded Jim Stewart finally felt secure enough that he left First National Bank and began to devote his energies full-time to Stax. Shortly thereafter, Tom Dowd convinced him and Steve to let Dowd install a two-track recorder. "They said, 'You're not gonna lose our sound?'" laughs Dowd. "I said, 'I'll tell you what I'll do. We'll put in the two-track machine and we'll put the mono in the end of it so you can do both at the same time. If you like the mono better fine, but just don't erase the two-track.'" Each track was fed by one of the four-input Ampex mixers that Jim had been using since the studio in Brunswick. This meant that any given instrument would be either in one channel or the other, leading to the bizarre situation where the vocals and echo would be in one channel only. This, of course, only affected LP releases. The majority of the company's business was still conducted in singles which, at the time, were still issued exclusively in mono.

The B-side of "Mr. Pitiful," Roosevelt Jamison's and Steve Cropper's "That's How Strong My Love Is," is one of the pluperfect R&B ballads of all time. Jamison had originally taken it to a Stax Saturday morning audition, where Cropper had helped to refashion the lyrics. Nothing happened immediately though, and Jamison took it to another Memphis R&B label, Goldwax Records, where he cut it with O. V. Wright. In the meantime, Cropper recorded the song with Otis. Wright's and Redding's versions were released within days of each other and the Rolling Stones recorded it shortly thereafter, the combined impact of their versions making it an instant soul classic.

Both tracks were recorded as fall turned to winter. At Stax that meant coats and gloves for the horn players. The studio was equipped with a single heater that was positioned right next to Al Jackson's drum booth. "That one heater was going," laughs Wayne Jackson, "and Al Jackson would be in a T-shirt sweating. We'd be across the room in our overcoats and gloves it was so cold in there!"

By year's end, Otis had cut his second LP, most of the tracks featuring Isaac Hayes on piano or organ. *The Great Otis Redding Sings Soul Ballads* (Volt 711) was issued in March 1965, and has the distinction of being the first album to be released on Volt.[10] As *Soul Ballads* was beginning its run up the charts, Stax was readying the release of Otis's seventh Volt single, "I've Been Loving You Too Long." Cowritten with Jerry Butler in a Buffalo hotel room, it represented Redding's greatest commercial success until "(Sittin' On) The Dock of the Bay." Its success was very nearly duplicated in August by "Respect," one of Otis's finest up-tempo romps. Fueled by Duck Dunn's imaginative pulsing bass figure and Al Jackson's flat-sounding four-on-the-floor snare pattern (replete with machine-gun blasts), the track is transcendent. The second voice on the "hey hey hey" hook is that of label compadre William Bell.

Both singles were recut in stereo during the July 1965 sessions for the *Otis Blue* album. The only noticeable difference on "Respect" was that Otis's longtime friend and road manager Earl "Speedo" Sims sings the "hey hey hey" line. "I've Been Loving You Too Long," on the other hand, underwent substantial change. Otis had performed it regularly onstage and had gained a much better feel for the song. With a slowed-down tempo, doubly dramatic stop-time pauses, increased use of dynamics, much more potent horns, and an achingly impassioned vocal, it's one of the finest Otis Redding recordings ever.

For Wayne Jackson, the horn lines served the function of background vocals. "The horn is like a voice," explains the trumpeter, "but you're limited as to what you can do. You don't have syllables so you have to use dynamics tastefully. That's the one way you have of getting across your breath without having a syllable to say. 'I've Been Loving You Too Long' has great horn parts. You can almost hear the horns saying the words in that record. They're also used like a rhythm instrument on the stop line—definite punctuation."

Otis worked extremely quickly. *Otis Blue* was recorded in one amazing adrenaline-charged twenty-four-hour period. With Tom Dowd coming down from New York Thursday night to work the board, the session began at ten the next morning. Around eight o'clock that night the festivities came to a halt as several of the session musicians had to head off to their nightly gigs. Everyone reconvened at two in the morning after the dubs closed and went straight through the night until ten the next morning, and then Otis flew out for a gig the next day.[11]

The story of how the Rolling Stones' "Satisfaction" came to be included on this album provides fascinating insight into the creative process at Stax. Apparently Otis took a brief break from the sessions to have a physical for insurance purposes. Scrounging for material to round out the album, Steve Cropper had a brainstorm: "It was my idea to do it. I went up to the front of the record shop, got a copy of the [Stones] record, played it for the band and wrote down the lyrics. You notice on 'Satisfaction' that Otis said 'fashion,' not 'faction.' I love it. That's what made him so unique. He'd just barrel right through that stuff unaware of anything. He just didn't know the song. He hadn't heard it as far as I know." Phil Walden concurs: "Otis kind of read the lyrics through about once or twice and then just really jumped right into the thing. That was a real spontaneous record. He had never heard the Rolling Stones version."

Released in September 1965, *Otis Blue* represented a quantum leap for both Otis Redding and the Stax house band of Booker T. and the MG's, Isaac Hayes, and the Mar-Key horns (at this point consisting of Wayne Jackson, Andrew Love, and Floyd Newman, with Bowlegs Miller guesting on second trumpet). Whereas on many of Otis's earlier recordings he sounded tentative, feeling his way through a song, on *Otis Blue* he roars like a locomotive. From this point on in Otis's career, extremes become more apparent: tempos become either faster or slower and the parts hit harder or are treated in a gentler fashion.

A good example is provided by Otis's cover of Sam Cooke's swansong, "A Change Is Gonna Come." It's hard to imagine anyone cutting Cooke on his own song, but Otis and the Stax house band do just that. The triplet and two eighths rhythmic interjection is merely a whisper in Cooke's original; on *Otis Blue* it sounds like a sledgehammer. Otis is at his elliptical best with words, sometimes syllables, bursting from his vocal chords one moment, being swallowed and garbled the next. Emotion is the governing aesthetic throughout.

"I think he was more sophisticated and aware of who he was," suggests manager Phil Walden. "He was successful and he liked that lifestyle, being a star and having people like him.

He was into being Otis Redding and I think it reflects in his music. He was a real star finally, not something we tried to fabricate. We could turn to album sales, which was fairly unique for black artists in those days." Wayne Jackson agrees with Walden: "As he gained in stature as an artist with worldwide fame, his confidence level went up. He didn't change as a performer, I think he just got better."

Walden had just returned from a two-year hitch in the army and was both ecstatic and astonished by the session. "Everything was so up. He was finally feeling like a star. You could sense it. Everything happened right, just knocking out songs like this [snaps fingers]. Of course, I didn't know that everybody didn't do it this way, and Tom Dowd's going, 'Phew, this damn guy is a genius.' I said, 'Really?' I knew Dowd had worked with everybody and he said, 'I've only been in the studio with two other people that are in this category, Bobby Darin and Ray Charles.' I said, 'You're kidding me, my Otis?'" Dowd remembers the conversation well. "I said, 'Man, this guy's in charge like Bobby Darin was. He knows what the hell he wants. Otis was a very strong individual. He did not have the acumen or the experience musically to be able to say, 'More like this or more like that.' He'd just say, 'That ain't right' and he'd sing a part to you."

Upon its release in September 1965, *Otis Blue* stayed on the pop LP charts for thirty-four weeks, peaking at number 75, and reached the number 1 spot on the Top R&B LP chart. In addition to achieving these peaks, the album stayed on the charts for several months. Redding had become what is known as a "catalogue" artist. His records tended to sell steadily over long periods of time, reaching sales ranging anywhere from 200,000 to 250,000 copies, rather than selling in massive numbers immediately upon release and then cooling off equally quickly.

Shortly after *Otis Blue* was recorded, Otis, in partnership with Joe Galkin and Phil and Alan Walden, formed a production company, Jotis Records (the name being derived by putting the J from Joe Galkin's name in front of *Otis*), and a publishing arm, Redwal Music (*Red*ding and *Wal*den). Jotis lasted for only four releases, two by Arthur Conley, and one each by Billy Young (an army acquaintance of Phil Walden's) and Loretta Williams (a singer with Otis's road band). In 1966, Otis produced two further singles by Conley on Fame, before switching him over to Atco and hitting it big with "Sweet Soul Music" in the spring of 1967. Based on Sam Cooke's "Yeah Man," and with a horn intro variously attributed to a riff taken from either a Maxwell House coffee or a Marlboro cigarettes commercial, "Sweet Soul Music" soared to number 2 on both the pop and R&B charts.

Several months earlier, in May 1965, just after "I've Been Loving You Too Long" entered the *Billboard* charts, Stax and Atlantic finally formalized their distribution agreement, setting down in a legal contract what had existed for years as a handshake deal. Atlantic's owners had begun discussing the possibility of selling the company, and Jerry Wexler suggested to Jim Stewart that a written contract could protect Stewart. Stewart was worried that Atlantic could possibly be sold to a corporation that was not interested in or did not understand Stax's recordings or its market. He insisted on a clause in the thirteen-page document that would allow him to sever the distribution deal with Atlantic immediately should the company ever be sold and Jerry Wexler not remain a stockholder or employee, and within 180 days if the company should be sold and Wexler remained an employee but not a stockholder.

The contract gave Atlantic the exclusive right, but not obligation, to "distribute" any master Stax produced or otherwise acquired. Until Atlantic exercised that right on a given record, Stax could release "such master recordings in your local market, in order to test the salability thereof." Stax had to produce and offer a minimum of six master recordings (e.g., three singles) during a given year.[12] In return, Stax was to be paid by Atlantic fifteen cents for single records and 10 percent of the retail list price of LPs, less taxes, duties, and costs of packaging, for 90 percent of all items sold and paid for in the United States.[13] Stax was to receive 50 percent of these amounts for records sold through record clubs, and 50 percent of whatever Atlantic received for records sold outside the United States. Stax was obligated to pay mechanical royalties for all singles sold, while Atlantic assumed this obligation for LPs. Stax was also obligated to pay all moneys owed to recording artists.

While it wasn't overly generous, there was nothing particularly onerous or untoward about this agreement, with one very major exception. From the beginning of the contract, it spoke of Atlantic's right "to purchase master recordings" from Stax. Paragraph 6C, page 7, was even more specific:

> You hereby sell, assign and transfer to us, our successors or assigns, absolutely and forever and without any limitations or restrictions whatever, not specifically set forth herein, the entire right, title and interest in and to each of such masters and to each of the performances embodied thereon.

Jerry Wexler has always maintained that Atlantic's lawyers slipped this clause in, and that he was entirely unaware of it. However, if Wexler had perused the contract, it would have been clear that this was a legal instrument that gave Atlantic full ownership of Stax productions. In other words, this was not a master *lease* or distribution contract as understood by Jim Stewart, it was a master *purchase* contract.[14] Even more devastating, paragraph 12 on page 11 gave Atlantic the same rights to all Stax productions they had distributed *prior* to May 17, 1965. In one stroke of the pen, for one dollar, Jim Stewart and Estelle Axton lost the rights to their entire catalogue.

It is easy to think that, if Jim Stewart signed it, that's his problem. But it is important to understand that Jim Stewart was every inch a product of the fraternal, personalized South: a person's handshake and word were more important than any contract. Stewart trusted Wexler implicitly; he didn't read the contract or consult a lawyer, or feel the need to do so. His friend, and to some degree mentor and trusted adviser, Wexler had assured him that the contract was a mere formality that would protect him, as he had desired, if Atlantic should ever be sold.

By the summer of 1965, the notion of "The Memphis Sound" was being discussed in the industry's trade magazines. In the June 12th issue of *Billboard*, Elton Whisenhunt wrote a piece headlined "Memphis Sound: A Southern View." Whisenhunt conducted brief interviews with Memphis record label owners Joe Cuoghi, Sam Phillips, Stan Kesler, and Jim Stewart. Stewart described "the Memphis Sound" this way:

> It goes back to the colored influence in the early blues and folk lore [*sic*] music of the South. Our music is still influenced by that.
>
> All our artists at Stax are Negroes. Naturally, our sound is directly oriented in that direction. The sound is hard to describe. It has a heavy back beat. We accent the beat and rhythm in our recordings. It is very dominant. New York recordings wouldn't bring out the drums or beat as we do.
>
> But that beat—a hard rhythm section—is an integral part of our sound. The combination of horns, instead of a smooth sound, produces a rough, growly, rasping sound, which carries into the melody. To add flavor and color there is topping with the piano and fills with the guitar or vocal group.[15]

Stewart told me in 1986: "That title ['the Memphis sound'] came from outside. We didn't give it to ourselves. It sort of drifted back to us that there was a sound. We really weren't thinking about it. We came to work every day, we did what we had to do, and we went our separate ways. It was a job, but it was fun. It was just an identification thing simply because the same people were doing it day after day—seven people that were doing God knows how many releases a year." "You're going to obviously have an identifiable sound, especially if it's coming out of the same studio," affirms Booker.

Deanie Parker remembers that once the company became cognizant of the outside world's perception, Stax actively promoted "the Memphis Sound." "We were promoting the Memphis sound as a whole and trying to give a definition of a Stax sound. We focused on that to a large degree. I think that partially that happened because the question was asked so often, 'What is [the Memphis Sound]?' So we were given an opportunity to tag what it was that we felt we were creating." When Al Bell came to the company later that year, he insisted that "The Memphis Sound" be inscribed on virtually every piece of paper that emanated from the company.

Five days before the new Stax-Atlantic distribution agreement was signed, Jerry Wexler brought Wilson Pickett down to Memphis. Born in Prattville, Alabama, in 1941, Pickett was possessed of one of the harshest voices in soul music. Moving to Detroit in his early teens, he started out singing gospel with Chess recording artists the Violinaires. When he was eighteen he elected to go the secular route and signed on with the Falcons, whose membership included future Stax songwriters and vocalists Eddie Floyd and Mack Rice. With the Falcons, Pickett sang lead on the hit "I Found a Love." Egos being what they are, he quickly became a solo artist, signing on with Double L. Three chart singles later, Wexler wooed him to Atlantic. His first Atlantic single was recorded in New York at the company's studios but, when no one was happy with the results, Wexler hit on the bright idea of taking him down to Stax.

"I couldn't get over [the way they recorded in Memphis]," explains Wexler. "Coming to Stax literally changed my life. I took Wilson Pickett down there because entropy was setting in in New York . . . I lost interest in recording with the same arrangers who were out of ideas. The musicians were out of licks [and] the songwriters didn't have any songs. It got so I dreaded to go into the studio to make a record with the foreboding that I was gonna come out with the same dreadful piece of crap that we did last time with no fire in it, no originality and, worst of all, no hit potential. . . . When I went down to Stax and saw how they made records, it was really inspirational. The idea of coming to a place [like Stax] where four guys come to work like four cabinetmakers or four plumbers and hang up their coats and start playing music in the morning, and then the beautifully crafted records that came out of this! God, can I get some of this, 'cause this is the way to go. I've never changed since then. That was it. That was the way to make records."

Wexler and Pickett made three trips down to Memphis in May, September, and December 1965. Altogether nine songs were recorded, the first session producing "In the Midnight Hour" and "Don't Fight It," the last giving birth to "634-5789 (Soulsville U.S.A.)" and "Ninety-Nine and a Half (Won't Do)." Booker was away attending university during all three sessions, so Joe Hall played piano in May, and Isaac Hayes in September and December. Pickett was so happy with the success of the first session that he personally sent a $100 bonus to each member of the Stax house band, a virtually unheard-of gesture.

It was during the May sessions that the Stax rhythmic conception of a minutely delayed beat two and four was developed, inspired by Wexler's dancing of the then-new northern fad, the Jerk. This rhythm can be heard on all subsequent 1960s up-tempo Stax recordings, including "Hold On! I'm Comin'," "Respect," "Knock on Wood," and "Soul Man," and remains one of the essential defining features of the Stax sound. To some degree, the Stax rhythm section had always slightly delayed the beat, but with "Midnight Hour" it was to become that much more pronounced. "I credit it to the fact that we didn't play with headphones and we were in a big room," reasons Steve Cropper. "There was a lot of delay between the singer and us. When you put headphones on, everybody just sort of tightens up. We learned to overcome [not wearing headphones]. I had to learn basically to play watching Al [Jackson]'s left hand rather than by going by what I heard in my head. I started anticipating. When he was coming down, I'd come down with him. Rather than wait for the sound to get over to me, I'd go with his hands. . . . Obviously, everything would have fallen apart if we had just followed the delay time, but we learned how to catch up and get the downbeat on.

"The Jerk was a delayed backbeat thing. The first time that Al [Jackson] and I became aware of it, we found it in Detroit. It was the way the kids were dancing. When Jerry Wexler was down there helping to produce 'Midnight Hour,' he made a whole thing about this move, this delayed backbeat thing. We started being more conscious of putting the kick drumbeat dead on and delaying the 'two, four,' which became an actual physical thing, not room delay at that point. We worked on that. That was not something that was accidental. So, we started overemphasizing that and made it a whole way of life because it seemed to work all the time. It was never behind the beat, it's just delayed. It's like if you put it in a little time cube and you turned the switch and then you only play the delay part, rather than the accent. That's what came out."

Cropper takes great pains to point out that after a drum fill at the end of a section, they would very deliberately play the second beat dead on to synchronize the groove again before resuming delaying the backbeat on each subsequent bar.

Vocalists at Stax also tended to phrase in a slightly delayed manner. This was a natural result of standing some fifteen feet from the drummer behind a tall baffle, without wearing headphones. "They had to hear what came over the top, and bounced off the ceiling," explains Steve, "so there was definitely a delay in the room which always kept the singer just a little back so it never ran away. That's why I think the Stax stuff always felt so good."

"In the Midnight Hour," cowritten by Pickett and Steve Cropper, became a massive radio hit, topping the R&B charts at number 1 while also scaling the pop charts to number 21. Surprisingly, according to Jim Stewart, it only sold about 300,000 copies. "634-5789 (Soulsville U.S.A.)," written by Cropper and Eddie Floyd, did a little better, resting at the top of the R&B charts for a full seven weeks while peaking at number 13 on the pop charts. "Don't Fight It" and "Ninety-Nine and a Half (Won't Do)," both coauthored by Pickett and Cropper, also charted.[16]

Buoyed by the success of the first Pickett session, at the end of June Atlantic brought Don Covay down to Memphis to record with the MG's and to avail himself of the Stax songwriters. Four songs, "See-Saw," "I Never Get Enough of Your Love," "Sookie Sookie," and "Iron Out the Rough Spots," were recorded; the first three were cowritten by Covay and Steve Cropper, while Cropper, Booker T. Jones, and David Porter cowrote the last. "See-Saw" was the only hit, reaching number 5 on the R&B charts and number 44 on the pop charts. "Sookie Sookie" was later covered by the rock group Steppenwolf.

According to Steve Cropper, the Covay sessions at times got a little rocky. "I remember that Jim Stewart called Jerry Wexler and said, 'Get Don Covay out of here. He's driving us nuts.' Don Covay was a little bit on the weird side. I loved Don to death. We get along great but I don't think Jim and them understood Don. He thinks in different areas and he was kind of driving people bananas. . . . He's kind of frantic when he makes decisions. He jumps from this place to that. You never know what he's gonna do next." Covay's high energy level and extreme unpredictability were the antithesis of Jim Stewart's banker personality.

In exchange for the use of the Stax studio and musicians, Stax split with Atlantic the publishing and received an override from all sales of Atlantic product recorded at Stax. Given the success of the Pickett and Covay sessions, one would have expected Atlantic to bring a host of artists down to Memphis to record with the MG's at Stax's 926 E. McLemore studio. According to Jim Stewart, such a possibility was unfortunately precluded by Wilson Pickett's irascible personality. "It got to the point," explains Stewart, "where the guys felt they were being used, so I stopped it. They weren't getting much money for that stuff. Another thing was a personal relationship. Pickett got to be an asshole. They told me, 'Forget it, man, get his ass out of here.' The guys didn't want to work with him, and I wouldn't ask them to do it."

Both Steve and Duck deny any ill feelings toward Pickett. While both agree the singer could be difficult, Cropper stresses that that was only when he drank, and at Stax in the mid-sixties, no one, including Pickett, drank or did drugs at daytime sessions. "I don't know if there was a joint ever lit up in that place," Steve recalls, laughing. "Pretty weird, isn't it? Mainly daytime recording, mainly everybody was sober. There was a thing in those days: you drink at night and you sobered up in the morning. Guys didn't drink during the daytime. [If you did] you were considered a bum and an alcoholic."[17]

Cropper also takes pains to point out that he was making a lot of money off the songwriting on the Pickett sessions, and would have loved that situation to continue. Duck, while not sharing in the songwriting, stresses that Pickett was one of the greatest singers he ever worked with and, consequently, he loved those sessions. Jim simply told Wexler and Atlantic that the Stax studio was too busy to accommodate outside sessions and consequently would no longer be able to do them. Steve, Duck, and Jerry Wexler felt that the real reason why Stax closed its doors to outside sessions was that Jim Stewart was not happy "giving away" the Stax sound.

"[Jim] was vague," recalls Wexler. "I knew that Pickett had irritated him. Pickett was always bum-rapping Steve Cropper, claiming that Steve had stolen the song ['In the Midnight Hour'], but I never could get any exact reason. I got a feeling after a while that the real reason was that Jim had some feeling about hits coming out of the studio that were not on Stax [yet were recorded] with his band and his facilities. They really didn't want anybody else there 'cause they didn't want hits coming out of there with their imprimatur that they didn't get the full benefit of."

Al Bell, who arrived at the company just a few months before the final Pickett session, echoes Wexler's suspicions: "We had that policy to preserve the sound that we had developed. That was our identity, our trademark, our trade secret, and we preserved it in that fashion. The other thing was there really wasn't that much time, because the studio was constantly being used. When it wasn't being used, it was supposed to be available for in-house producers and writers, because what made Stax tick was that freedom, the ability to go in that studio whenever a guy had an idea and get it with no restrictions, no clock to watch, none of that. Just to be able to record and record until you got it. If it took all day or it took all week, we had that freedom to do it."[18]

A couple of months prior to the first Pickett session, Atlantic had made a rather unique arrangement with Stax. Wexler offered to loan Sam and Dave to Stax for as long as Atlantic distributed the Memphis company. Sam and Dave, in essence, would be full-fledged Stax artists, with Stax being paid the same money for every Sam and Dave record sold as they were for records by their other artists (minus Sam and Dave's royalty and an override to Henry Stone). The only difference was that Wexler insisted that Stax split the publishing with Atlantic on any songs written by Stax staff songwriters for Sam and Dave. This latter proviso would turn out to be a wise move on Wexler's part.

Born in 1935 in Miami, Florida, Sam Moore was the son of a church deacon; his mother sang in the church choir, and his grandfather was a minister. In addition, the Moore family was related to the gospel legends Albertina Walker and Ruth Davis and the Davis Sisters. Singing his first solo in church at the age of nine ("I wasn't nervous. I was a big show-off"), Sam did not develop an interest in secular music, initially doo-wop, until a little bit later, and somewhat against his parents' wishes. "Oh yes, they didn't like to hear the Chuck Berrys, the Fats Dominos, and James Browns," Sam recalls. "So, I would sneak out if I wanted to stand on the street corners and sing with the guys. Never could I bring a rock 'n' roll record in the house."[19]

One aggregation of Sam's street-corner pals that centered around his high school eventually coalesced as a quartet called the Majestics. They were together for two-and-a-half years, working with a similar repertoire as the Royal Spades in Memphis, covering tunes by R&B stars of the day such as Hank Ballard and the Midnighters, the Five Royales, and the Coasters. Playing high-school hops, they eventually became good enough to attract the attention of Henry Stone, the godfather of the Miami record scene, who owned and operated a distributorship (Tone), a studio (Federal), and several labels (Marlin, Alston, and Shot). The group recorded one single for Marlin, a prototypical talking doo-wop, "Nitey Nite" (sic) backed with "Cave Man Rock." Released in late 1954, the record generated a little local notoriety but not much else. By 1957, the Majestics had changed their name to the Gales (after the nationally popular Sensational Nightingales), left the secular world behind, and embarked upon a gospel career.

When the Gales folded two years later, Sam joined another local quartet, the Melionaires. One hot night the Melionaires found themselves opening up for Sam Cooke and the Soul Stirrers. This coincidence eventually led to Sam Moore being offered the almost impossible job of replacing Cooke when the latter decided to leave the gospel world. At the last moment Sam backed out, deciding the gospel life was not for him. "I got chicken," demurs Sam. "The night before I was to go with the Soul Stirrers I went to a show to see Jackie Wilson. I saw the electrification, the excitement. Oh God, he was a hell of a showman. I said, 'That's what I want to do.' [The next day the Soul Stirrers] looked for me. I just disappeared." Ironically, Sam's later Stax-mate, Johnnie Taylor, then of the Highway QCs, ended up taking the job.

Realizing his true calling belonged in the world of secular ecstasy, Sam left the Melionaires soon after and took to the amateur circuit, imitating his heroes. "When I started out I knew nothing about the business," confesses Sam. "The only thing I knew was to stand behind a microphone and sing. I enjoyed singing songs by Jackie Wilson, Little Willie John, and Sam Cooke. I'm a gospel man." The latter comment is telling. Even more than these three role models, Sam was never able to shake his gospel background, always incorporating the melismas, playful voicedness, and sheer intensity that has forever been the essence of black church singing. In the spring of 1961, it was dropping tentatively to his knees—a trick he learned from mentor Jackie Wilson—while singing tunes such as "Danny Boy" that won Moore first prize in a local amateur show, twenty-five dollars, and a job as amateur-night emcee of a local bastion of Miami black nightlife, the King of Hearts club. Sam worked Monday, Wednesday, Friday, and Saturday and when he wasn't emceeing, in his own words, he fulfilled the role of a lounge singer.

On one of those amateur nights in December 1961, who should walk in but Dave Prater, Jr. Prater originally hailed from the tiny town of Ocilla, Georgia (pop. c. 3,000), about five hundred miles north of Miami. Born May 9, 1937, Dave waited twenty-two years before heading to the city, wooed by his brother, bass singer J.T. Prater, to join J.T.'s gospel group, the Sensational Hummingbirds, as lead singer. The Hummingbirds pounded the gospel circuit and recorded one 45 over a period of two years while Dave worked in the daytime, first as a cashier and later as a short-order cook. Dave had known Sam through their respective gospel quartets, and now Dave also intended to test the secular waters via the traditional route of the amateur show. He had planned to sing Sam Cooke's "Wonderful World," but the house band at the King of Hearts did not know the song. The band suggested Jackie Wilson's "Doggin' Around" as an alternative, but Dave didn't know all the words. "But I knew the words," remembers Sam. "So I said to him, 'Look, if you start singing I'll pipe the words to you from the back 'cause I'm going to be up onstage.' So he started, and when he got to the verse part I would just say [the words] and he would sing them.

"When it got to the part where Jackie Wilson would drop to his knees, Dave tripped. I was responsible for all the instruments and microphones that got broken and I didn't want to pay for something that I didn't do, so he and I both went down together and I caught the mike. The audience thought that was the act. It wasn't, but they went crazy." What Sam fails to mentions is that, not only did he catch the mike, he also came up singing, something that would also become a hallmark of Sam and Dave shows for years to come. That night, with the glowing approval of owner John Lomello, Sam and Dave started working the club as a duo.

At this point Henry Stone reentered the picture, recording Sam and Dave locally for both his Alston and Marlin labels. Two singles appeared, "Never Never" b/w "Lotta Lovin'" and "My Love Belongs to You" b/w "No More Pain,"[20] both produced by Steve Alaimo (of "Everyday I Have to Cry" fame) and distributed only in southern Florida by Stone's Tone Distributors. Stone next engineered a deal for the duo with Morris Levy's Roulette label. Five 45s appeared sporadically on Roulette through 1962–63.[21]

Produced by either Roulette A&R man Henry Glover or Steve Alaimo, the records echo the sounds of Sam Cooke, the Soul Stirrers, Ray Charles, and Jackie Wilson. One of the songs, "She's Alright," was actually written by Wilson, and the astute listener can pick out Jackie singing background harmony. Another side, the sweet ballad "It Was So Nice While It Lasted," was written by Johnny Nash under the name "Billy Nash." Sam and Dave themselves cowrote two songs, "My Love Belongs to You" and "I Need Love." The Roulette records are radically different from the better-known Stax recordings.[22] At Stax, Sam assumed the role of lead dynamo with Dave functioning as his foil. At Roulette, Dave was featured much more. Even more pertinent, the writing and playing on the Roulette recordings is largely imitative with some songs, such as Steve Alaimo's "No More Pain," being literal cops of other recordings (in this case the Soul Stirrers' "I'll Build a Fence").

The Roulette singles and Sam and Dave's local notoriety at the King of Hearts served to spread their name nationally to those in the know, including Atlantic Records co-owner Jerry Wexler. In town for a disc jockey convention in Miami Beach in late summer 1964, after a hectic day of glad-handing, Wexler stopped by the King of Hearts. "It was 165 degrees in the middle of summer," recalls Wexler. "It was unbelievable. It was hot and they were hot. Henry Stone was the one who steered me there. It was wall-to-wall people. We were the only Caucasians in there. Ahmet [Ertegun, Wexler's partner at Atlantic] and I are out there boogalooing like fools, sweating and just having a ball. It was so exciting. I don't know if we were trying to impress Sam and Dave, Henry Stone, or just knock our own selves out, but we really got into the spirit of things. When I heard them there that night, that's all she wrote. I signed them up immediately.

"I thought it would be great to have Stax produce them. So I went to Jim Stewart and said, 'I want you to produce these guys and in consideration it can be released on Stax and we'll pay you the regular Stax royalty. You pay them just as though they're your artists but always with the understanding that this is on loan from us. We have the master contract.'"

It was an ingenious and inspired move on Wexler's part. Ironically, the reaction at Stax to the arrival of Sam and Dave was largely one of indifference. "There was no one interested in Sam and Dave," remarks songwriter David Porter. "It was like a throwaway kind of situation [to] see if anything could happen with them . . . so I developed a relationship with Sam Moore and Dave Prater which involved me trying to come up with material for them. No one else at the time was even thinking about it."

A native Memphian, Porter had been trying to work his way into a music career for quite some time. While in high school at Booker T. Washington, Porter had formed a quartet he dubbed the Marquettes that regularly competed in the Wednesday evening talent shows at Beale Street's Palace Theatre. Under the watchful eye of MC Rufus Thomas, the Marquettes often competed with Isaac Hayes's group, the Teen Tones, the Marquettes' specialty being a version of the Dell-Vikings' "Come Go with Me." "When I first met Isaac during that time," laughs Porter, "I wasn't too fond of him because he was beating me out of the five dollars [prize money]. He felt likewise. We knew each other but we were not running buddies."

When not entering talent shows, the Marquettes were busy auditioning for every record label in town that would listen to them. Jim Stewart was impressed enough to attempt to record a single. At Stewart's suggestion they worked on "The Old Grey Mare," but were never able to cut a version that was deemed releasable. After the initial attempts, Porter, commonly referred to as the local Sam Cooke, opted to record the song without the Marquettes, eventually bringing in the Del-Rios to sing background. But, alas, success was still not forthcoming.

Undaunted, Porter, while working across the street at Jones' Big D Grocery and selling insurance to support his wife and child, struck up a songwriting relationship with Chips Moman. Moman and Porter penned a number of songs with such unpromising titles as "Treasured Moments" and "Woe Is Me" before Moman's acrimonious split with Stewart and Axton curtailed their activity. Porter next started writing with Rufus Thomas's son, Marvell. The pair's debut effort, "The Life I Live," was waxed by Barbara Stephens and released on Satellite in October 1961.

It would be a few years before Porter's name would next appear on a Stax-related release. "They were trying to get me to stop hanging around there," Porter exclaims. "Jim Stewart didn't think I had any talent." Fortunately for David, Estelle Axton thought differently, "She believed in me all the time," continues Porter. "He was trying to get rid of me. She was trying to keep me around. There was a great amount of discussion about me because I was a pest! I wanted to be in the music business. I had no idea how to contact anybody exterior of Memphis. I'm a poor kid. I don't know anything about calling anybody in New York.

"Jim was not a great motivator for me, but his sister was. She was saying, 'Study these records.' I would go in the Satellite Record Shop and play records and scratch them up. She was such a beautiful lady. She would say, 'Well, okay Just go and study that and see what they're doing. You've got to see what everybody else is doing so you'll know what to do.'"

Not one to give up, Porter kept working on his writing skills while continuing to make the rounds to see if anyone was interested in recording him as an artist. In mid-1962 he recorded a Clyde McPhatter–influenced outing for the Golden Eagle label, "Farewell" b/w

"Chivalry." Despite being a bit of a regional breakout, "Farewell" ultimately made few waves. Later that year Porter recorded another 45, this time for Hi Records, under the name Kenny Cain. Hi co-owner Ray Harris told Porter that he wanted to develop a black artist who sounded white. Produced by Willie Mitchell, "Practice Makes Perfect" b/w "Words Can Never Say" was released just before the close of 1962. Porter also made a session for Savoy Records under the auspices of Fred Mendelsohn, "So Long" b/w "Home Is Where You Come," which was released under the nom de disque of Little David, because Porter assumed he was still under contract to Golden Eagle. None of these records achieved significant radio play or sales and, consequently, Porter continued to plug away at Stax, hoping to record and/or write songs. For a short time he dabbled in writing with Steve Cropper, "but our chemistry just wasn't quite right for it." He did, though, serve as the vocalist with the MG's on many of their weekend gigs that required a singer.

Sometime in 1964, not too long after Isaac Hayes began playing sessions at Stax, Porter suggested they write songs together. Hayes, who had gradually begun to contribute arrangement ideas on Stax sessions and had been harboring ambitions as a writer, was more than interested. Hayes and Porter's first efforts to be released on Stax were Porter's lone Stax solo single in the 1960s, "Can't See You When I Want To" (Stax 163) and Carla Thomas's "How Do You Quit (Someone You Love)" (Atlantic 2272), released in January and February 1965, respectively. The Thomas release attained a modicum of success, rising to number 39 on the pop charts. On both 45s, Hayes wrote under the pseudonym Ed Lee to avoid breaking a previous publishing commitment.

At some point, most likely in the summer or fall of 1965, Hayes and Porter, frustrated with their progress at Stax, visited their old friend Chips Moman at American Sound Studio. They formed the Genie label, jointly owned by Hayes, Porter, Moman, and Harold Atkins. The sole release on Genie was a single by future Stax songwriter Homer Banks. Porter knew Banks from Booker T. Washington High School and, with Hayes, wrote both sides of the single, "Little Lady of Stone" b/w "Sweetie Pie." The record failed to create any waves, few of the five hundred copies pressed actually being purchased. When Jim Stewart finally offered Porter a songwriting contract with a weekly draw, Genie was laid to rest.[23] As was the case with Steve Cropper, it was Estelle Axton who forced Jim to put David Porter on salary. "Jim Stewart gave me six months to make it or get out," rues Porter a quarter-century later. "Estelle Axton believed in me and he didn't. But, he was nice enough to give me the chance. Estelle had mortgaged the house so he couldn't refuse her and she was my biggest supporter."

Estelle vividly recalls the day Porter came into the record shop with the lyrics for "Can't See You When I Want To." "He had about three sheets of lyrics. So I sat down and I read his song. I saw he had a good idea but then I began to work on him. I said, 'David, there is no way possible that you could put this many lyrics in a song. You'd run ten minutes.'" Estelle had a happy knack for simultaneously critiquing and encouraging. Buoyed by her comments, David would go away, rewrite the song, and then bring it back. Estelle would then discuss the changes David had made, play some more records for him by way of illustration, and send him off again. She continued to work with David in this fashion for several months. Porter's weekly draw amounted to fifty dollars a week, which he shared with Isaac Hayes, who was still working in the meat-packing plant. Nonetheless, his foot was finally in the door. Sam and Dave would be the vehicle by which Porter and Hayes would get the key to the castle.

Sam and Dave's first single for Stax, "Goodnight Baby" b/w "A Place Nobody Can Find," coupled a Porter-Cropper composition with a rare example of a David Porter solo composition.[24] Released in March 1965, both sides of the single featured Dave Prater singing lead, in marked contrast to Sam and Dave's later Stax recordings. On "Goodnight Baby" David Porter lovingly juxtaposed organ and vibes, the latter being a direct influence of Holland-Dozier-Holland's work at Motown with the Supremes. "Part of what eventually evolved into the magic of Hayes and Porter's writing was my study of the Motown catalogue and what Holland-Dozier-Holland were doing," Porter emphasizes. "That was an ongoing process. I was a novice. To be quite honest I was learning. So [the vibes] was a thought and we tried it." On top of the arrangement, Sam and Dave are singing in glorious harmony, wringing Porter's lyric for all it's worth. One can readily hear how close their three-and-a-half years together had brought them. They answer, echo, and finish each other's lines, join in and drop out of the arrangement, individually and together, with a grace and ease that is mesmerizing. The whole is brought to a climax with an ad-lib ending that is pure ecstasy, both singers emoting in overdrive against the horns and rhythm section.

Despite the obvious strength of this initial effort, the single's success was somewhat underwhelming, and four months passed before Sam and Dave reentered the Stax studio to cut a followup. For the duo's second Stax release, Hayes and Porter wrote and produced both "I Take What I Want" and "Sweet Home." Future Hi session guitarist Teenie Hodges shares in the credit on the A-side. According to Porter, Teenie was like a little brother who often hung around the Stax studio. On this particular day Porter hummed the guitar line to Teenie, who then played it on the record. To encourage him to write, Porter and Hayes also gave him a songwriting credit. "I Take What I Want" is an up-tempo romp that, although it didn't chart, set the tone for the majority of Sam and Dave's Stax singles. Next time out, Sam, Dave, Hayes, Porter, and everyone else at Stax would be celebrating.

Notes

1. However, in a year in which *Billboard* suspended publication of its R&B charts, it's hard to precisely measure each record's impact. Suffice it to say that none of the company's releases that year managed to dent the pop Top 40.
2. This is a familiar trope in the lives of many of the first-period Stax artists. Due to the relative lack of black programming available on American airwaves until the late 1940s, a couple of generations of black musicians grew up imbued with the sounds of country music.
3. According to Isaac, one side of Johnny Rebel's 45 was called "What Can You Give in Return," and it was released on Pepper Records. Unfortunately, I have been unable to find any trace of it.
4. Kirk and Gregory would later spend time with the Isaac Hayes Movement.
5. The Hayes-Porter productions were credited to U. G. Lee.
6. Many years later the record was rereleased with "C.C. Rider" substituted for "Sweet Temptations" as the B-side.
7. Jeb Stuart was a journeyman R&B singer who over time would record for a host of Memphis labels including Phillips, Bingo, and Youngstown. He kept this particular band together for quite a while, working the Southern Club for three or four months before moving over to the Continental Club and then to the TG Club. Hayes played on and helped arrange one of Stuart's Phillips singles.
8. Over the next few years, Caple was in and out of Memphis and, on a number of occasions, played on additional Stax sessions.
9. Unfortunately, the Memphis Musicians Union has virtually no sessions sheets for sessions held before 1966. Curiously enough, Fantasy Records, which bought Stax in 1977, also has no sessions sheets pre-1966.
10. Including "Come to Me," "Chained and Bound," "Your One and Only Man," "Mr. Pitiful," and "That's How Strong My Love Is," a handful of newly recorded originals, and covers, *Soul Ballads* did not do as well as *Pain in My Heart* on the Top LP charts, only reaching the number 147 position. It did, though, make

an appearance on *Billboard*'s new R&B LP chart, first appearing April 10 and seven weeks later peaking at number 3, staying on the chart for a total of fourteen weeks.

11. To the best of Duck Dunn's recollection, "I've Been Loving You Too Long," Sam Cooke's "A Change Is Gonna Come," a cover of William Bell's "You Don't Miss Your Water," and Otis's searing version of B. B. King's "Rock Me Baby" were cut during the second shift while Cooke's "Shake" and "Wonderful World," Solomon Burke's "Down in the Valley," the Temptations' "My Girl," the Rolling Stones' "Satisfaction," and Redding's own "Ole Man Trouble" and "Respect" were out in the daytime.
12. In actuality Stax delivered 29 singles in 1965, 35 in 1966, and 49 in 1967, plus several dozen LP tracks.
13. As was, and still is among some companies, standard practice in the record industry. See note 22 for more details.
14. The inscription on Stax Records that read "Distributed by Atlantic Recording Company" was, in essence, fraudulent.
15. Elton Whisenhunt, "Memphis Sound: A Southern View," *Billboard* (June 12, 1965): 6.
16. "Don't Fight It" reached the number 4 and number 53 spots on the R&B and pop charts, while "Ninety-Nine and a Half (Won't Do)," based on a gospel song by Dorothy Love Coates and the Gospel Harmonettes, reached the number 13 and number 53 spots respectively.
17. Jerry Wexler also stresses that Stax was an anomaly in that he never saw drugs or alcohol being consumed on the premises at daytime sessions. It was simply understood that Jim Stewart forbade such activity. Various musicians point out that when Jim Stewart wasn't at the studio late at night, it was a different story, and before Jim quit his day job at the bank, it wasn't that uncommon for a quart or two of beer to be consumed in the studio. In general, though, in the 1960s, Stax was a pretty sober environment and consequently Pickett didn't get out of hand.
18. In many ways, it is a shame that this policy was ever instituted. With Atlantic barred from the Stax studio, it turned to both Muscle Shoals and Chips Moman's American Sound Studio. While undeniably great records were cut by Atlantic at both locations, it boggles the mind to imagine the MG's working with Atlantic artists such as Aretha Franklin, King Curtis, and Clarence Carter.
19. Sam sang second tenor in most of these street-corner groups. Quite surprisingly, he didn't sing lead until his late twenties, just a little before he met Dave Prater.
20. "Never Never" appeared on the ultra-rare Alston 777 while "My Love Belongs to You" was released on Marlin 6104.
21. All five plus the Marlin single were later issued by Roulette on LP to capitalize on the duo's success at Stax.
22. It seems odd that the dynamic duo did not continue writing. According to Sam, at Roulette, Stax, and Atlantic, "We were just pawns. They knew what was good for us. The only thing we were allowed to do was sing. There was no sense in telling them that I could write 'cause who would have listened? We didn't have no power or clout."
23. The above account of "Little Lady Stone" was pieced together via interviews with Chips Moman, Isaac Hayes, David Porter, and Homer Banks. Although 1965 appears to be an accurate date for the record's issue, the song itself was not registered with BMI until 1967.
24. In this period Hayes, as Ed Lee, also wrote by himself the A-side of a Mar-Keys single, "Banana Juice" (Stax 166).

27 Clifton Chenier

"They Call Me the King"

BEN SANDMEL

New Orleans-based musician, historian, and journalist Ben Sandmel suggests that "[More] than a dozen years after his death, Clifton Chenier is still regarded as zydeco's best known and most influential musician." Sandmel's bold topic sentence is no less true today than it was in 1999. As the awareness of zydeco as one of the most interesting forms of regionalized, folk-based genres of black American music expands, Clifton Chenier's place in its development and history has only grown.

Zydeco blends musical and cultural elements of cajun music and the musics that developed among black Americans in southwestern Louisiana and the southeast corner of Texas in the late nineteenth and early twentieth centuries. The word zydeco *(or zarico, zodico, zordico, or zologo) apparently derives from the French expression* les haricots, *meaning "beans." Oral tradition suggests that the genre derived its name from the well-known Creole expression "Les haricots sont pas salés" ("The beans aren't salty"). This phrase has appeared in many Creole songs and serves as the title of a popular zydeco song (called "Zydeco est pas salé") that initially emerged in the early twentieth century.*

Modern zydeco is actually the most recent form of Creolized music to emerge from Acadiana and it first appeared shortly after World War II, when pioneers of the genre like Clifton Chenier and BooZoo Chavis combined more traditional sounds with new rhythm and blues elements. In fact, the first zydeco-like recording was Clarence Garlow's hit "Bon Ton Roula," issued in 1949 by Macys, which was based in Houston, Texas, where many of the modern zydeco pioneers lived.

Zydeco has evolved considerably over the decades and now incorporates pop music influences as diverse as soul, disco, and hip hop. Pioneering zydeco artists often used fiddles and washboards, but these have now largely been replaced by the accordion, electric guitar, horns, and a more conventional rhythm section of bass and drums. As zydeco becomes more popular outside of Louisiana, it is also increasingly performed in English, instead of in its original Creole dialect.

Twenty-two years after his death in 1987, Clifton Chenier is still regarded as zydeco's best-known and most influential musician. Even though many talented figures have emerged since then, such stature is unlikely to change. An agile, inventive accordionist and a passionate singer, Chenier pioneered contemporary zydeco, opened the door to global

Older-style zydeco such as Canray Fontenot (fiddle) and Alphonse "Bois Sec" Ardoin (accordion) paved the way for the modern, more commercial music of Clifton Chenier.

Credit: Yellin photo: Photo by Robert Yellin, courtesy of the Ralph Rinzler Folklife Archives and Collections, Smithsonian Institution

recognition for his protégés, and left a legacy of recordings that have set the standard for all who follow. He is reverently referred to as "the king" by his colleagues and disciples.

Clifton Chenier's most immediately noticeable trait was keen intelligence. He emanated a shrewd and vehement vigilance reminiscent of the renowned defense attorney F. Lee Bailey. Vivid though this first impression was, it took a good while to gather, because setting up a meeting with Clifton Chenier was no simple matter. In March of 1983 the magazine *Louisiana Life* sent me to Lafayette to interview Chenier and research a feature article about him. It would be my first interview with a zydeco musician and my first writing assignment from a local publication after arriving in New Orleans from Chicago several months before.

Despite his renown, Clifton Chenier did not have an office, a secretary, or an answering service. He handled all of his own business, in classic old-school fashion, and he was very difficult to reach by phone. For a month or so I tried to catch him every couple of days, always unsuccessfully, and Chenier's wife kept suggesting, "Why you don't call back." This south Louisiana syntax was jarring to a recent emigré, and I wondered whether she was actually asking me a question.

I finally talked to Chenier in person at Tipitina's in New Orleans, and we agreed that I would come see him on the following Monday. At the appointed hour I went to his house in Lafayette, on Magnolia Street, only to have his wife crack open the door and say, "Cliff ain't here"—even though he was standing right behind her. Repeat performances of these machinations were followed by a formal postponement so that Chenier could get his hair done for the photos that would accompany the article. It was Friday afternoon before we finally sat down to talk in his living room.

Then came the question of money. Chenier wanted five hundred dollars to do the interview—not an unreasonable request, really, since the chances were slim that yet another magazine article would bring him any indirect income or enable him to raise his fees. I told him that I simply didn't have it, and that *Louisiana Life* would not reimburse me. Chenier asked if I was getting paid to write the story, and I said yes. He paused, sizing me up, and then said, "Okay, go ahead. I just don't like bullshit. People come here from all over the world, and they try to tell me they ain't making no money." "The king" proceeded to give me an articulate, expansive interview. His life story illuminated zydeco's roots and its bright future. But when the cassette reached the end of side one, he wouldn't let me flip it. "C'est tout," he said. "That's all. You got what you came for."

"I'm born and raised in Opelousas in 1925," Chenier began. "Outside of Opelousas. I come from out a hole, man, I mean out the mud, they had to dig me out the mud to bring me into town. You know, a lot of people don't like to say where they come from. But it ain't where you come from, man, it's what you is. The average fella now that's big stars, that's where they come from, out in the country."

Chenier never claimed zydeco as a personal invention, but he was well aware of his vital contributions. "The old generation had it," he explained, "but it died out. I brought zydeco back." What "the old generation had" was a blend of blues, French and Acadian material, and possible traces of Native American music, galvanized by Afro-Caribbean rhythms. This combination was expressed most dramatically in a tradition known as *juré* singing. *Juré* comes from the French *jurer*—to testify or swear—and is closely related to such archaic folk traditions as the African-American ring-shout and the Acadian danse-ronde. As with these styles, there was no instrumental accompaniment in *juré*. Hands and feet pounded out an urgent, primal beat—not unlike a fast rhumba or mambo, with added polyrhythms—while vocalists sang both secular and sacred lyrics.

There is no documentation as to just when *juré* emerged. But it has strong similarities to the antebellum music that was played at slave gatherings at Congo Square in New Orleans and described in detail by nineteenth-century journalists. It's quite possible that the two traditions are contemporaneous. Some stunning *jurés* were recorded by folklorist Alan Lomax for the Library of Congress in 1934; besides containing riveting performances, these recordings mark the first documentation of the exclamation "*les haricots sont pas salés*."

Lomax called *juré* "the most African sound I found in America," and many first-time listeners are surprised to learn that these exotic recordings were really made on this continent. At the same time, some *juré* songs had distinct Acadian roots, and used melodies from popular Cajun songs that in turn drew on Anglo-American country music. One example is "*Je fait tout le tour du pays*" ("I Went All 'Round the Land,") the most striking *juré* in Lomax's collection. The title and theme come from an Acadian folk song, while parts of the melody resemble the Cajun favorite "*J'étais au bal hier soir*" ("I Went to the Dance Last Night"). "*J'étais au bal . . .*" is based on the country song "Get Along, Cindy," and some bands play the two together as a French-English medley. Today, *juré* has all but vanished from oral tradition within the Creole community, but it is occasionally performed by musicians who have usually absorbed it from the Lomax recordings. A case in point is the Cajun band BeauSoleil, while a notable exception is accordionist Lynn August, a zydeco modernist who learned *juré* from his grandparents.

The Creole countryside where Clifton Chenier was raised was also permeated by European traditions. "We used to have two-steps, one-steps, waltzes, jigs, contredanses,"

Alphonse "Bois-sec" Ardoin told fellow accordionist Marc Savoy, in an interview conducted in French. Ardoin, one of Creole music's most important cultural ambassadors, was born in 1914, and raised in the far-flung region between Eunice and Basile. ("Bois-sec" is a nickname that literally means "dry wood.") This environment was very similar to the rural neighborhood on the fringes of Opelousas that Chenier had described as "out the mud." "The violin played all that," Ardoin continued. "That's what the people wanted. It's all forgotten now." These forms all contributed to the styles that would eventually come to be known as zydeco and Cajun music.

A crucial factor in their emergence was the accordion, which was brought to America from Germany and Austria. Peddlers sold the instrument in south Louisiana after the Civil War, and it caught on quickly. As folklorist Barry Ancelet observed, the accordion arrived "without instructions," giving the Creoles and Cajuns free reign to develop their own musical ideas. The accordion was durable, could be heard over noisy crowds, and worked well with a wide variety of styles. Continuing west, itinerant vendors also introduced the accordion into Texas, where it was welcomed in German and Czech communities and then adapted by Mexican-Americans to create the sound now known as *norteño* or *conjunto*.

One of south Louisiana's first great accordionists and recording artists was a black Creole named Amédé Ardoin. Ardoin made a series of seminal commercial recordings in the 1920s and 1930s, and there is strong debate today over whether they are appropriately classified as Cajun music or zydeco. Since both terms were coined later, the argument is academic. It is clear that Ardoin's inspired musicianship—expressed in a seamless, soulful blend of two-steps, blues, and waltzes—played a crucial role in forging both nascent schools. Ardoin's legacy still resonates today, in terms of style and repertoire, and also through the fourth-generation activity of his descendants. These include his nephew, Bois-sec, his sons Lawrence and Morris, and Bois-sec's grandson, Chris Ardoin. . . . Chris Ardoin's full, electrified band bursts with youthful enthusiasm but does not surpass the power of Amédé Ardoin's recordings, which jump across the decades with their passion and urgency.

Amédé Ardoin's records influenced young Clifton Chenier, as did the hit 78s of such acoustic blues artists as pianist and guitarist William Bunch, who recorded under the macho moniker "Peetie Wheatstraw, the Devil's Son-in-Law." Chenier was equally inspired by live performances. His father, Joseph, occasionally played a single-row accordion at house parties—until Clifton's mother slashed its bellows with a razor, disabling the instrument and presumably achieving the goal of ending her husband's career. Another family musician was Clifton's uncle, Morris Chenier, who played fiddle and guitar, and would later appear on some of his nephew's early records. But Clifton's best opportunities to learn came by watching and listening to such friends of the family as accordionists Claude Faulk, Jesse and ZoZo Reynolds, and Sidney Babineaux.

"I listened to Claude and the Reynolds a lot," Chenier told guitarist and researcher Ann Allen Savoy. "They had an old Model A Ford with a rumble seat in the back. So when they'd pass by my daddy's house to go play a dance I'd jump in that back seat, that little rumble seat. And when they'd get where they'd gone to play I'd get out the car. They couldn't do nothing, it was too far for me to walk back. I'd stay with 'em and listen to 'em. I was about eight or nine."

The young stowaway listened to music that was known in the 1930s by such names as "la-la," "pic-nic," and "bazar." "Zydeco" was still just a phrase heard in various songs, and not yet applied to the entire genre. Like zydeco in years to come, la-la incorporated elements of Afro-Caribbean juré, blues, Cajun music, and the European forms described by Bois-sec Ardoin. It was played for private gatherings more than at public dances. Creoles and Cajuns alike had a tradition of "house parties," where several extended families would take turns gathering at someone's home. Furniture would be moved aside to create a dance floor, and a weekend of fun would begin. La-la did not entail the full bands that perform zydeco today; it might be played by a lone accordion, an accordion and a washboard (the corrugated metal vest known as the *frottoir* as such had yet to emerge), and perhaps a fiddle or a harmonica.

Sadly there are few recordings, either commercial or folkloric, that can document the contemporaneous development of la-la, although Cajun music has been recorded prolifically since the late 1920s. Those tracks that do exist can be heard on *Early Zydeco,* on Arhoolie Records, a Bay Area label with an extensive catalogue of south Louisiana music. But there are some great sessions from the 1960s and 1970s, by Bois-sec Ardoin and fiddler Canray Fontenot, which harken back to this era. They appear on Arhoolie and on two anthologies of field recordings produced by Nick Spitzer for the Rounder and Maison de Soul labels. Spitzer's recordings also feature additional members of the Ardoin family, the old-time fiddlers BéBé and Eraste Carrière, and Delton Broussard, the patriarch of another important musical family.

The limits of musical terminology are evident . . . in the insistence of both Fontenot and Ardoin that their rural style should be called *"la musique créole."* They refused to identify with the term "zydeco," and had doubts that anyone else should, either. As Fontenot told radio producer Jerry Embree:

"They never had no such thing as zydeco music. No such thing as zydeco music. That's bullcorn. If you was black, you played Creole, if you was white, you played Cajun. They had a thing they called *juré*. The old people would sing for the young people, and clap their hands and make up a song. And they had a song about "zaricots," "zydeco," that's snap beans. Singin' about *"zaricots est pas salés,"* that's "snap beans with no salt in it." But I never saw one of them *juré* things.

"I met Clifton Chenier once and he asked me, "Canray, you ever went to one of them *juré?*" and I said, "No, did you?" He said, "No, I never went to one, but my daddy used to go. My daddy played the *'zaricots est pas salés'* on his accordion, but he didn't play it the right speed, he played it like *a juré*. I thought it should go faster."

Clifton told me, "I think I'm gonna make that *'zaricots est pas salés'* on a record, but I'm going to put some speed to it." He went and made that record, and after people found out that our type of music was moving, everyone wanted to have an accordion, and everyone wanted to play Clifton's stuff. But they don't know what they talkin' about when they talkin' about zydeco music, 'cause there's no such thing as that."

Having made this pronouncement, Fontenot then modified it slightly with a broader interpretation. "Zydeco mean another thing, too. If we had a dance in our neighborhood, maybe we couldn't invite some people from the other neighborhoods, 'cause then there'd be too many people to fit in the house. So we couldn't let everybody know. But they had to have some girls there, or then maybe nobody wouldn't come at all. So what they would do when they were going to have a dance, first thing, two guys would go out on horseback and start inviting people where they had some girls, to make sure some girls would come. But they would invite them to a "zydeco" so the other people from the neighborhood wouldn't know what they was talkin' about. It was like a secret word, 'cause they didn't want all them people showing up. But they never had no such thing as zydeco music. Not as far as I know. If you was black, you played Creole."

In 1947 Clifton Chenier's music was still known as la-la. He moved from Opelousas to Lake Charles, Louisiana, a bustling petrochemical town just thirty miles east of the Texas border, and took a day job at the Gulf Oil refinery. Chenier's passion for music led to impromptu performances during his lunch break; at closing time he played for tips by the front gate, while his coworkers left for the day. Young, ambitious, and attracted to new ideas, Chenier began performing in public. He expanded the parameters of la-la by adding varying combinations of drums, bass, electric guitar, saxophone, and the *frottoir*, which was played by his brother, Cleveland.

Chenier also played a dramatically broadened repertoire that drew on a then-fledgling genre known as rhythm and blues. From jukeboxes and radio, Chenier learned the infectious hits of artists including Fats Domino, Louis Jordan and His Tympani Five, Big Joe Turner, and B. B. King. With natural grace, he seamlessly adapted them to Creole French vocals and the piano accordion. It was a logical extension of his bursting talent and a quantum leap for Creole dance music. And just as this music began acquiring a new identity, thanks in large part to Clifton Chenier's efforts, its new name also was being formalized.

The phrase *"zaricots sont pas salés"* had been floating around for decades by this point—at least since 1934, and probably well before then—in a wide variety of songs such as *"Je fait tout le tour du pays."* Then, in 1949, blues guitarist Clarence Garlow recorded *"Bon Ton Roula."* Garlow lived in Beaumont, Texas, near the Louisiana border and well within the sphere of Creole culture. *"Bon Ton Roula"* was an R&B gem that combined an insistent, swirling rhumba rhythm with sensual horn arrangements and an eloquent guitar solo. But its most distinctive feature was the lyrics, which revealed the presence of an unknown subculture that functioned beneath the radar of mainstream America. By not bothering to contextualize the song for outsiders, Garlow made the implicit statement that most of his listeners were active participants in a thriving scene. The record was directed at people who would understand all of the references:

> "You see me there, well, I ain't no fool,
> I'm one smart Frenchmen never been to school.
> Want to go somewhere in a Creole town,
> You stop and let me show you your way 'round
> And let the bon ton roula . . .
> At the church bazaar or the baseball game,
> At the French la-la, it's all the same
> You want to have fun now you got go
> Way out in the country to the zydeco."

Garlow sang the line about "zydeco" in dramatic a capella fashion, following a momentary break by the band.

The song's title came from the French *"bons temps rouler."* (Different spellings such as *"Bon Ton Roulet"* have been used by various record companies, and it appears on government copyright papers as *"Bon Ton Rouleau."*) The phrase *"laissez les bons temps rouler"* ("let the good times roll") appears often in zydeco and Cajun music. During the 1980s it was co-opted by the tourism industry as a symbol of Louisiana's *joie de vivre*, and eventually became quite clichéd. "Let the Good Times Roll" is also the title of several different rhythm and blues songs, one of which, by Louis Jordan, remains extemely popular both in zydeco and blues.

In this first public reference to "zydeco" as a separate entity, independent of the words *"sont pas salés,"* Garlow used it as a general term of celebration, with music as one key component. But soon zydeco came to refer specifically to music. It appeared with a wide variety of spellings that, like *"Bon Ton Roula,"* were all phonetic attempts to spell French words in English. These efforts were complicated by the fact that Creole and Cajun French are primarily oral and aural traditions. Few French publications ever existed in southwestern

Louisiana, as opposed to the many that once flourished in New Orleans, and formal frames of reference were limited. In addition, decades of isolation had left a legacy of low literacy. Thus while *"les haricots"* had become a popular term, its multiple spellings during the 1950s included "zordico," "zologo," "zotticoe," and others. Some of these variants still appear occasionally.

The path to standardization was unintentionally blazed in Houston, Texas, where plentiful jobs have always attracted a lot of expatriate Creoles and Cajuns. They settled in ethnic enclaves such as the Fifth Ward neighborhood called Frenchtown. "That was a rough area," recalled progressive country artist Rodney Crowell, a Houston native. "I lived nearby, and I thought we were poor 'til I got a paper route over there when I was eleven." Frenchtown was a cohesive community, however, with plenty of places to go dancing, from Catholic church halls to nightclubs such as the Continental Zydeco Ballroom, Pe-Te's Cajun Barbecue, and the Silver Slipper. In addition, Frenchtown residents could easily commute to Louisiana for a weekend's infusion of fresh musical ideas. Clifton Chenier maintained a house in Houston, as well as one in Lafayette, and he proudly called both cities home.

Throughout the 1950s a Houston folklorist named Mack McCormick combed the city's streets, taping and interviewing a diverse assortment of folk musicians. His collection was released in 1960 on a two-LP anthology entitled *A Treasury of Field Recordings*. The liner notes included McCormick's transcriptions of the lyrics to all of the songs. When he came to a bilingual version of the blues classic *"Baby Please Don't Go"* with the French phrase for snap beans, McCormick pondered awhile and then wrote it down as "zydeco."

"I agonized," McCormick told journalist Michael Tisserand years later. "My objective was to get as close to the sound of the thing as possible." Considering the pronunciation heard on most recordings from the 1930s on, McCormick did just that. To his surprise, "zydeco" soon became the norm on posters for Creole dances in Houston. In 1965, there was another pivotal moment when Clifton Chenier began a long relationship with Arhoolie Records. Its founder, Chris Strachwitz, went with McCormick's spelling, and since no one else in the record business was remotely interested in Creole music at the time, Arhoolie's zydeco albums set the global standard. The frugal Strachwitz did not promote his product with expensive ad campaigns or other trappings associated with major record labels. But through a network of aficionados he did get his albums distributed, broadcast, and reviewed around the world—and the world thought that "zydeco" worked just fine.

Most of the world did, anyway. Clifton Chenier recorded prolifically for Arhoolie and made his first trip to Europe in 1969, on an all-star package show called the American Folk and Blues Tour. This led to return engagements overseas and considerable acclaim among a devoted cult audience. The early-sixties blues revival, spurred by such British bands as the Rolling Stones and the Yardbirds, had created an adoring if somewhat naive atmosphere in Europe, where African-American blues musicians received far more respect, recognition, and money than they usually got at home.

As a unique stylist playing in peak form, Clifton Chenier quickly attained "living legend" status in Europe, and as such he was sought out by rock stars. According to one often-told story, perhaps a tall tale, Mick Jagger sent an intercessor to beg Chenier for a chance to sit in. Chenier had never heard of Jagger, much less of the Rolling Stones, and he sent back the contemptuous rebuff: "Nick? That punk!" Chenier was also puzzled by the Europeans who often responded to his music with intense concentration but no dancing. "They just sat there like they was in a trance!" he recalled, shaking his head. Still, Chenier savored the memory of his audiences' obvious if immobile enjoyment.

Notoriously ornery in the business arena, Chenier did not have a savvy manager to put him on a career plane with such peers as B. B. King and Muddy Waters. But he did well for himself, and it is safe to assume that a debate on the correct spelling of "zydeco" would not have interested him in the least. Chenier was too busy creating the music, defining its modern sound, and winning new converts.

But others did debate it, in a dialogue that reflects the era's cultural upheaval. During the 1970s, southwest Louisiana was ablaze with linguistic activism fueled by fear that Cajun and Creole French were poised on the brink of extinction. Newly founded organizations such as CODOFIL, the Council for the Development of French in Louisiana, set up educational exchange programs with French-speaking nations around the world. In addition to its obvious resonance in France, this movement elicited an especially strong response in Quebec, where there was serious thought of secession from English-speaking Canada. Secession was never a real consideration in Louisiana, although Cajun rocker Zachary Richard, a pioneer in the cultural renaissance, refused for a time to answer anyone who addressed him in English.

More typically, many young people began an impassioned campaign on behalf of the region's language and heritage. This movement's leaders included Barry Ancelet, historian and linguist Ulysses Ricard, Jr., poet Debbie Clifton, musician and author Austin Sonnier, Michael Doucet, who went on to form the eclectic Cajun band BeauSoleil, and Nick Spitzer, Louisiana's first official state folklorist. They made contact with other French communities and treated zydeco and Cajun musicians with long-overdue respect.

One seminal event that embodied this new sentiment was the *Tribute to Cajun Music*, held in Lafayette in 1974. For the first time in Louisiana, zydeco and Cajun bands played in a formal concert setting with no dance floor, so that local people would focus on the cultural message of their music. The University of Southwestern Louisiana supported the event and donated the use of the venue, an eight-thousand-seat arena. Folklorist Ralph Rinzler came down from the Smithsonian Institution to assist with production, lending the official imprimatur of his prestigious Washington employer. A legion of French journalists, brought to Louisiana by CODOFIL, was honored as the evening's special guests. Clifton Chenier graced the stellar lineup, which also included Bois-sec Ardoin and Canray Fontenot, Creole ballad singer Inez Catalon, Cajun fiddler and activist Dewey Balfa, twin fiddlers Dennis McGee and Sady Courville, and the bluesy Cajun accordionist Nathan Abshire, among others. The concert was a great success, and has become a highlight of the annual Festivals Acadien, held in Lafayette in mid-September.

Such official validation represented a radical change for Louisiana, where legislation passed in 1916 had forbidden children to speak French in the public schools. As a means of forcing assimilation, this law reinforced a worldview of disdain towards expressions of regional culture such as zydeco and Cajun music. The legislators thought that it would be best for Louisiana's French-speaking citizens to become ordinary, English-speaking Americans.

Zydeco and Cajun music had finally earned respect, but the debate over terminology continued. In 1984 the noted Québecois filmmaker André Gladu released a documentary on Creole dance music that was pointedly entitled *Zarico*, in recognition of the term's French roots. Gladu insisted that accuracy and cultural sensitivity made this the only acceptable spelling. Chris Strachwitz countered with the pragmatic observation that changing the name would confuse the public at the expense of working musicians and record sales. Meanwhile, Barry Ancelet made an intriguing connection that added substance to the discussion beyond intellectual turf wars.

While listening to some field recordings from the island of Rodrigue in the Indian Ocean, Ancelet heard the term *"zarico"* used in songs that were quite similar to juré. A closer look revealed many similarities between Rodrigue and south Louisiana. Both were agricultural enclaves where a black labor force descended from West African slaves had worked for a French ruling class. Both maintained a French-based dialect and a dance-music tradition centered around the accordion. On Rodrigue, *"zarico"* was used much as the phrase *"les haricots sont pas salés"* was used in Louisiana—as a term of general exclamation, without any specific context.

Such exuberance and *joie de vivre* in the context of dance music is always implicitly sexual, if not overtly so, as is dancing itself. Some *"zarico"* references on the Rodrigue recordings were far more blatant. One song, *"Cari zarico,"* translates loosely as:

> "I'm thinking what you're thinking, pretty girl.
> Hot bean soup.
> When the moon dances the sega, we'll harvest.
> Hot bean soup."

"When the moon dances the sega" refers to *"sega zarico,"* a tradition which unfolds on Rodrigue and several other islands nearby. This dance step mimics the planting of beans, as women move backwards, digging imaginary holes with their heels, closely followed by men who fill the holes with imaginary seed. In this setting, the beans—*"zarico"*—function as obvious symbols of courtship, sexuality, and fertility.

Ancelet suggested that the phrase's prevalence in Louisiana occurred for all of the same reasons. He supported this theory with sound research in linguistics and ethnomusicology. He observed that some uses in Louisiana—such as the popular refrain "let's zydeco all night long"—referred to courtship and sex, in addition to dancing. As a grassroots activist and a staunch supporter of working musicians, Ancelet did not insist that *"zarico"* should replace "zydeco" in common parlance. He also put linguistic preservation in perspective by recognizing that French had once been imposed upon much of Louisiana's black labor force, as had English.

Nick Spitzer conducted significant research as well, beginning in 1976 with extensive community-based fieldwork among rural Creole musicians. Spitzer uncovered another set of potential roots for the term "zydeco" in various West African languages. In the Yula tongue, spoken north of the Ivory Coast, the words for "I dance" are *"a zaré."* In Ashanti, "I dance" is pronounced as either *"meré sa"* and *"meré go,"* while its Gurma equivalent is *"me dseré."* Spitzer also suggested that *"les haricots sont pas salés"* might be a deliberate pun created by Creole musicians who were aware of such West African phrases. The idea was not far-fetched, Spitzer argued, pointing out that the word "juke"—as in "juke joint" and "jukebox"—is generally believed to have derived from the pan-African word *"ndzugu,"* meaning "noise." As an active champion of working musicians, Spitzer, like Ancelet, did not support the implementation of *"zarico."*

Clifton Chenier stayed out of the theoretical arena but was a staunch linguistic supporter, nonetheless:

"All my people speak French, and I learned it from them. A lot of people, they was kind of 'shamed of French, but one thing they didn't know was how important French is to 'em. You understand? You be around here, you meet a lot of people, they don't even know how to talk French, right here in Louisiana, but now, if they're in a city like Paris, they need it.

"There's a lot of people holding back on French, you know, but me, I never was ashamed of French, and I never will be, because it go like this: if I can talk more than one language, I'm smarter than you! You can't speak but one language, and I got two or three of them I can talk, so who's the smartest?

"If you go to Europe and you want to eat, the lady bring you the menu and now what you gonna tell her? You can't talk to her, you don't know what to order. Now I'm goin' to tell you this story. They had me, Earl Hooker, Magic Sam, Whistlin' Alex Moore, we all got on a plane in New York, and it took us nine hours to cross the ocean and get to Europe. [These musicians were brought together for the American Folk & Blues Tour, in 1969.]

"We got there, those boys from Chicago, Magic Sam and Earl Hooker, they laughed at me, said, 'Oh, where y'all get that French from, can't you talk? You ain't nothin' but an old Frenchman.' I ain't said nothin' to 'em.

"So we got to France, we walk in a café. The lady asks me in French, 'Can I help you, mister?' I told her, '*Oui, madame,* yes, ma'am," you know. She said, 'What do you want to eat?' I say, '*Les oeufs, des grits, et du pain,*' that's grits, eggs, and toast bread. Okay, now, she got to them fellas, she asked them in French, they couldn't order nothin'. So I told her, I said, 'Don't worry about them,' I said, 'I'm ordering their food.' I told her in French. You know what I ordered them? A whole platter of raw fish! They eat that over there. I ordered Earl Hooker and them a whole platter of raw fish, and some pepper, and some salt, and some hard bread, hard as this brick here."

Chenier burst out laughing as he recalled his moment of sweet revenge. "I said, 'Now eat that, all y'all so smart, now y'all eat that.' They said, 'No, man, we want what you got,' and I said, 'Well, then order it!' See, they couldn't do it, they had to eat some raw fish and, man, they wanted to kill me. And from that day on, all our tour in Europe, they never would tease me no more, 'cause they knew I had 'em there. Anything they wanted to drink, they had to ask in French, wanted some wine they had to order it in French. They had to depend on me, they followed me everywhere I go, man. I said, "Y'all gonna eat what I want y'all to eat.""

There's probably some artistic license in Chenier's anecdote; few Parisian restaurants serve grits, except perhaps in Paris, Texas. But the story does reflect Chenier's pride in his heritage, years before such a stance became trendy. Nevertheless, Chenier was equally willing to sing in English or French and to adapt his repertoire to suit his audience. He explained, "We might go out tonight, and people don't want to hear nothin' but the blues. Go out tomorrow night, they don't want to hear nothin' but French music. Go somewhere else, they want to hear some hillbilly." (He pronounced this last word with emphasis on the second syllable.)

"We do all that," Chenier continued. "I like it all. It don't make me no difference. Whatever they ask for, if I know it, that's it, we play it. It makes me feel good if I make them feel good. That's what you're there for, not to satisfy you, satisfy the people."

In an effort to satisfy the people—and to score a lucrative hit in the process—Chenier approached recording in a similarly eclectic way. In 1954 he started out on a small, black-owned label called Elko Records, cutting seven songs at a radio station in Lake Charles. . . . This was a common practice at the time, when recording studios as such were less prevalent than they are today. Some of this debut material was slow blues, sung in English, while songs such as *"Louisiana Stomp"* were up-tempo romps that captured Chenier's fresh approach to zydeco and his command of the piano accordion. None of the material was wildly original—Chenier would never be known as a prolific songwriter—but all of it was spirited. The Elko material was leased to Imperial Records, a major label that featured such rhythm and blues stars as Fats Domino, and Chenier's name began to circulate nationally.

The next move by Elko's owner, J. R. Fulbright, was to unselfishly introduce his young artist to another prominent national company, Specialty Records. At the time, musicians on Specialty's successful R&B roster ranged from the frantic Little Richard to the suave crooner

Percy Mayfield. In 1955 Chenier went to Specialty's studio in Los Angeles to work with famed producer Bumps Blackwell.

"Clifton's band was traveling around in an old station wagon," Blackwell told journalist Greg Drust. "When I got them in the studio I pulled half of the guys out. I didn't let that many of them play. It kind of upset them, because they had their own little thing going, but me, I knew what was going to work on the record. I wanted to get that accordion out front."

As befits a producer whose credits included Little Richard's *"Tutti Frutti"* and Sam Cooke's *"You Send Me,"* Blackwell's instincts were on target. The Specialty sessions yielded some great material, including a raucous shuffle with a French vocal entitled *"Ay-tete-fee."* This was Specialty's attempt at a phonetic spelling of *"eh, petite fille"*—"hey, little girl"; on reissue albums, years later, they finally got it right. Other notable songs included the zydeco instrumentals *"Boppin' the Rock"* and *"Squeeze Box Boogie."* The latter became a jukebox favorite in Jamaica.

None of these records were successful in America, however, and neither were Chenier's efforts at mainstream rhythm and blues, sung in English. They did sell well enough to put Chenier and his band on the national touring circuit of R&B clubs and concert halls, including a cameo appearance at New York's famed Apollo Theater. For several years during the late 1950s, Clifton Chenier traveled around the nation, playing rhythm and blues and zydeco on his accordion and singing in both French and English. He crossed the paths of such stars as Ray Charles, Little Richard, and Chuck Berry, and worked alongside a virtual "who's who" of blues, R&B, and rock artists, including singers Bobby "Blue" Bland, Junior Parker, and Jimmy McCracklin, guitarists T-Bone Walker and Pee Wee Crayton, and organist Bill Doggett, of *"Honky Tonk"* fame. Singer Etta James toured with Chenier, and since she was still under age, Chenier became her chaperon—no easy job, because she had eyes for one of his musicians. A close call with a different type of trouble came when police in Mississippi thought that the light-skinned minor James was white. Fortunately James had legal documents that proved otherwise.

To help Chenier polish his act and improve his English stage patter, booking agent Howard Lewis hooked him up with blues guitarist Lowell Fulson. Fulson's 1950s hits included *"Reconsider, Baby"* and *"Black Nights,"* and the 1967 classic *"Tramp."* He toured with Chenier as the band's special guest, and coached him on how to dress, speak, and act like a pro. "Cliff was a country boy," Fulson told Michael Tisserand, "so you could always find something for him to tidy up a little bit . . . I showed him about all he needed, and then after about a year I got hung up with another band. But I hated to leave them old boys." Chenier, for his part, was always quick to acknowledge Fulson's help. "He'd talk to me and I'd listen," he told Ann Allen Savoy.

Fulson's *"Reconsider, Baby"* had appeared on Chess Records, and in 1956 the prestigious Chicago label signed Chenier to its Checker subsidiary. This made him a colleague of such blues titans as Muddy Waters, Howlin' Wolf, and Little Walter, but Chenier's most notable recording for Checker was a slice of contemporary R&B entitled *"My Soul."* It was the most commercially conscious song that Chenier ever cut, replete with backup vocalists who sang doo-wop harmony triplets. Although it was a powerful number that remained a staple on Chenier's live shows, *"My Soul"* did not catch on, and Chenier's tenure with Checker was short-lived.

Chenier continued touring, hiring a succession of young guitarists who would later lead their own successful blues bands. Lonnie Brooks, Philip Walker, and Lonesome Sundown all speak highly of Chenier as a bandleader and teacher, though they are quick to add that he was strict. During the seventies such prominent players as accordionist Stanley "Buckwheat" Dural and guitarist Sonny Landreth also benefitted from Chenier's tutelage, and then went on to successful solo careers. But by the late fifties, Chenier's own career was dead slow. His next move was several notches down, in the form of three sessions for Zynn Records, one of the many small labels run by Jay Miller in Crowley, Louisiana.

Miller was a paradoxical figure, even by the generous standards of the south Louisiana music milieu. Reviled for a vicious series of white-supremacist "party" records such as *"Nigger Hating Me,"* Miller showed a completely contradictory side in his flair for producing soulful and evocative blues records by black artists. Miller would produce a huge hit in 1966 with *"Baby, Scratch My Back"* by Baton Rouge harmonicist Slim Harpo. Improbably, this swamp-blues classic went way past the logical confines of southern black radio, and climbed the national charts at white Top 40 stations. Jay Miller did a typically good job of producing Clifton Chenier on sessions in 1958, 1959, and 1960. He brought in Katie Webster, the great south Louisiana session pianist, who added a complementary keyboard texture behind Chenier's accordion. Saxophonist Lionel Prevost wailed in wild sympathetic abandon. But once again, these records went nowhere.

The early 1960s found Clifton Chenier working the Gulf Coast "crawfish circuit" between New Orleans and Houston and languishing without a record deal. Fortunately, he had an ally and advocate in his cousin by marriage, the great Texas blues guitarist Lightnin' Hopkins. One night in 1964 Hopkins brought Chris Strachwitz to hear Chenier at a little beer joint near the Houston Ship Channel. Strachwitz recalled the evening in an interview with Ted Fox, a music journalist who went on to manage Chenier protégé Stanley "Buckwheat" Dural.

"Lightnin' asked me, 'Chris, do you want to go see my cuz?' I said, 'Who's your cousin?' He said, 'Cliff, Clifton Chenier.' The name rang a bell because I think I had a Specialty record by him, and maybe a Checker. To me that was rhythm and blues. I wasn't all that enthusiastic, but if Lightnin' wanted to go there—I was just like his little dog. I said, 'Sure, let's go over and see him.' So we went over to Frenchtown in Houston. I'll never forget. We walked into one of those little beer joints—hardly anybody in it, there was two couples dancing. There was this man with this accordion, and just a drummer. He didn't have no band at all. He was playing these really low-down blues. Mostly in French, but some in English, too. Clifton came up to me afterwards and said, 'Oh, you making records? Come on, make me one!'"

The two hit it off. They struck a deal, arranged a recording session for the very next day, and converged at Houston's Gold Star studio. Over the years, numerous record companies had used this facility for sessions by such important regional stylists as Cajun/western swing fiddler Harry Choates and country singer George Jones.

Strachwitz was dismayed when Chenier arrived at Gold Star with a full band. As Bumps Blackwell had done ten years before, Strachwitz wanted to emphasize Chenier's impressive accordion work. Quite unlike Blackwell, however, Strachwitz was motivated by a purist aesthetic, and he recoiled at making any concessions in order to craft a hit. He wanted Chenier to record traditional Creole music, in French, with minimal instrumentation. Chenier was convinced that his best shot at success was something in a Ray Charles vein—rhythm and blues, with a full band, sung in English. Equally opinionated and adamant, Strachwitz and Chenier eventually found middle ground by recording songs in both styles, with a wide variety in between.

From the first session at Gold Star, Strachwitz released a single entitled *"Ay Ai Ai."* It inspired some hometown sales and spins on local jukeboxes, and helped Chenier get better bookings in Texas and Louisiana. But Arhoolie was not equipped for the aggressive promotion required to turn a single into a national hit. Besides the legitimate costs involved, such campaigns could include a hefty budget for payola. Strachwitz had no desire to compete in that arena. His vision, rather, was to document the music—old-fashioned, folkloric, or downright strange—that hit-oriented labels wouldn't touch. "I never looked at it as a business," Strachwitz told Ted Fox. "I only recorded something because I liked it. If I even thought it had commercial potential, I'd probably reject it."

Strachwitz released more singles by Clifton Chenier during the next few years, but they were mainly manufactured for jukeboxes and radio stations on the Gulf Coast circuit. When these songs were packaged on LPs in the late 1960s their sales were much better, thanks to an overlapping following among the hippie counterculture and hardcore blues fans, in both America and Europe. Despite Strachwitz's stated aversion to commercial potential, Chenier was Arhoolie's highest-selling artist, and it was for Arhoolie that he recorded his finest work, on albums considered among the best in all of zydeco. These include *Louisiana Blues and Zydeco*, *Live at Montreux*, and *Bogalusa Boogie*. By the time they appeared, Chenier had named his group the Red Hot Louisiana Band.

Chenier's success encouraged Strachwitz to pursue zydeco and Cajun music in greater depth. Arhoolie has an extensive and eclectic catalogue, but it is in south Louisiana that Strachwitz has made his most important and lasting mark, by documenting the scene and bringing national exposure to the music community. The cultural renaissance that began in the late 1970s owes much to his work from the previous decade. That renaissance was also presaged by Clifton Chenier's performances at white venues in the late 1960s. At the time this was a groundbreaking occurrence. One of the most popular spots informally integrated by Chenier was Jay's Lounge and Cockpit in the small town of Cankton, near Lafayette. Chenier was also one of the first French-singing, Creole or Cajun musicians to cross over to a young, educated, urban audience—not that Jay's was a swanky bistro. The crowd was evenly divided between people wearing sandals and those sporting cowboy boots, and the "Cockpit" part of the name referred to a staging area for cockfights, which are still legal in Louisiana. "The rooster who didn't survive was usually served to the band in a 'loser's gumbo,'" Michael Doucet recalled.

"Lots of great musicians played at Jay's," Barry Ancelet said. "Asleep at the Wheel, the Fabulous Thunderbirds, Marcia Ball, Edgar Winter and White Trash. But Clifton Chenier was the first zydeco bandleader to work there. His music was incredible. He would pack the place and play for hours on end, and we would all dance 'til we were exhausted." Michael Doucet observed that "Clifton opened the doors for all the young, Cajun counterculture groups that followed. A lot of us played at Jay's and we loved it—bands like Rufus Jagneaux, Red Beans and Rice, and two bands of mine—Coteau, and then BeauSoleil."

When Jay's closed down around 1980, some of these groups began playing at a zydeco dance hall called Hamilton's. Situated on what was then the outskirts of Lafayette, Hamilton's was an atmospheric anachronism in the midst of suburban sprawl. The occasional evenings when zydeco bands were not featured were informally referred to as "white night."

By the 1980s, hard living and constant travel had ravaged Clifton Chenier's health. He laid low for a few years, and underwent major surgery. Doctors and family members advised Chenier to quit touring; he was in his mid-fifties, and needed to slow down. But Chenier's determined response was "die over here or die on the bandstand," as his guitarist Paul "Little Buck" Senegal told Michael Tisserand. Chenier set up a complicated and arduous schedule of national travel and on-the-road dialysis treatments. The twice-weekly intravenous procedure kept Chenier alive but weakened his arms, so he began playing a specially designed lightweight accordion and squeezing rubber balls to tone his muscles. I was lucky enough to see Chenier often in those days, at the Blue Angel and the Grant Street Dance Hall in Lafayette, the Casino Club in St. Martinville, and various clubs in New Orleans. Some nights he was vibrant, while at other times he seemed to be at death's door—all depending, the band told me, on how much time had passed since his last dialysis session.

Either way, Chenier insisted on playing a single set of three or four hours' length, with no breaks:

"People ask me how I can get up on the bandstand and play four hours without stopping. It's because I've always been a hard worker, always. When I get up there, I'm up there, no half-steppin'. And when I tell you 'goodnight' you can hand me a thousand dollars and I ain't gonna play no more. Not when I say 'goodnight,' that's it.

We give the people they money's worth, and a lot of people they enjoying themself. Man, I enjoy that. A lot of old people come to my dance, they be havin' a stick, and when they leave the dance they can't find the stick no more. I say, *'Quoi qu'arrivait avec ton baton?'* ('What happened to your stick?'), and they say, *'Oh, j'ai pas de baton, je l'ai jeté dehors!'* In other words, they ain't got no more stick, they throwed it outside 'cause they didn't need it no more!"

In 1984 Clifton Chenier received one of his highest career honors—a Grammy award for *I'm Here!*, as the best traditional or ethnic recording released in 1983. Although Chenier remained on good terms with Chris Strachwitz, the album appeared on Alligator Records, a Chicago label that took a far more aggressive approach to promotion and marketing than Arhoolie. "When I got with the right record company, they pushed it," Chenier told Barry Ancelet. *I'm Here!* was not Chenier's best album, but, as he observed, "That award is for a whole career, partner. You got to earn it. I figure that French music suit me, and I stuck with it. That's what got me that Grammy. And I'll tell you something, when you go to the Grammys, you see more diamonds than you ever saw in your life." Appropriately, Chenier acknowledged his royal status on the album's opening track, *"Let's Do the Zydeco"*: "They call me the king, the king of zydeco...."

The award gave Chenier an emotional boost during his last years, and issued a defiant response to people who had written him off. Sadly, this group included several of his zydeco-accordionist colleagues. As Chenier's strength dwindled, they hovered none too subtly, waiting for the king to expire. After ending a northeastern tour at New York's Lone Star Cafe, Chenier returned to Lafayette and passed away days later, on December 12, 1987. Many former bandmembers attended Chenier's wake in Opelousas, including several whom he had fired en masse amidst the stress of the decline that he had fought so tenaciously. Chenier's funeral was held the next day, in Lafayette. As is often the case at such rites for prominent musicians, Chenier's brilliant career was barely mentioned, and the generic eulogy focused instead on his chances for redemption. In a more personalized and respectful vein, his on C. J. played *"I'm Coming Home,"* a secular song that Clifton had written for his mother. The poignant number also works well as a spiritual, and it certainly did so that day, in a church packed well past capacity.

Just three weeks later, the zydeco pretenders began vying for Chenier's crown. The crown was a tangible object, as well as an abstract concept; since 1971 Chenier had sported an elaborate piece of regal headwear that, he told me, he had won at an accordion contest in Europe. Like the story about the grits in Paris, this anecdote had an apocryphal edge. Chenier might well have been inspired by the penchant for "monarchy merchandising" in the Lafayette business community, as demonstrated by "the king of seafood" and "the king of mobile homes," who appeared on local television with their crowns prominently displayed. Perhaps this trend was a literal interpretation of Huey Long's egalitarian pronouncement "Every man a king." One fact was indisputable, however. "I'll tell you what," Chenier said, "to take that crown away they'd have to roll me." But Chenier had the confidence and ability to look natural in this getup, as opposed to the "clown princes" who donned crowns at their own self-appointed coronations.

Rockin' Dopsie, in particular, tarnished his long-standing good name with one evening's ill-conceived decision to stage his own investiture in Lafayette, in January of 1988. Dopsie then made matters worse with a ludicrous story about Chenier passing him both the crown and zydeco's torch from his death bed. Unfortunately this tale was picked up by the media, is still repeated, and has acquired some credibility. But Dopsie was more naive than malevolent, and he never understood why so many people were offended. Stanley "Buckwheat" Dural dismissed the coronation as "crude," while Chenier's trumpeter, Warren Ceasar, said, "Dopsie could have waited. This looks like he was just waiting for Clifton to pass on." Although Dopsie was roasted in the local press as an opportunist, Barry Ancelet offered a different view: "Lots of people took that the wrong way, and Dopsie was shocked and hurt. He was a decent man. I believe that his intention was to provide some stability and healing for a musical community that was in mourning."

Rockin' Dopsie (pronounced DOOP-see) had emerged on the zydeco scene not long after Chenier, and then spent the next quarter-century in his shadow. Perhaps he felt that this was his time, after years of paying dues and playing second accordion, as it were. With Chenier gone, Dopsie was zydeco's best-known bandleader for the moment, although others would soon surge past him. To fuel this regal fantasy, Dopsie had already hired several of Chenier's ex-musicians to join his band, the Cajun Twisters. (The band featured Rockin' Dopsie, Jr., on *frottoir* and vocals; after Rockin' Dopsie's death in 1993, Jr. took over the group and now bills himself as "Rockin' Dopsie," creating some confusion.)

Beyond making his own prolific recordings, Rockin' Dopsie, Sr., played an important role in popularizing zydeco when he appeared on Paul Simon's *Graceland*. Dopsie and the Cajun Twisters backed the singer-songwriter on *"That Was Your Mother,"* an up-tempo tune that paired Simon's lyrics with zydeco accompaniment based on the traditional song *"Josephine est pas ma femme."* The critically acclaimed *Graceland* was Paul Simon's best-selling album, and received the prestigious Album of the Year Award at the 1987 Grammys. Rockin' Dopsie responded by threatening to sue Simon for the publishing and broadcast revenues from *"That Was Your Mother,"* which Simon had registered as an original composition. When the archaic folk roots of its melody could not be traced to any specific songwriter, Dopsie abandoned the case.

Graceland did bring Rockin' Dopsie recognition, as well as a short-lived contract with corporate giant Atlantic Records. But Paul Simon had hired Dopsie only because Clifton Chenier was unavailable due to illness, and it was Chenier whom Simon mentioned in the lyrics of *"That Was Your Mother."* Only Clifton Chenier could wear zydeco's crown with regal grace, back it up with regal talent, and look like a natural-born king.

Chenier's legacy resonates in many ways. Most obviously, his son C. J. maintains the family tradition with prolific touring and recording. Stanley "Buckwheat" Dural, who gave up mainstream R&B to work with Chenier, has emerged as the genre's most successful and influential artist, performing under the stage name Buckwheat Zydeco. Younger players such as Nathan Williams and Geno Delafose have embraced Chenier's ideas and the piano accordion while developing their own styles and original material. Accordionists Jude Taylor, Hiram Sampy, Leon Sam, T. Black, Al Rapone, Fernest Arceneaux, Sunpie Barnes, Zydeco Joe, and Roy Carrier, some of whom have since passed on, based their music more directly on Chenier's repertoire. Carrier owns a zydeco dance hall, the Offshore Lounge, in Lawtell, Louisiana, where he encourages young, entry-level players to hone their skills at weekly jam sessions. Successful graduates of this informal school include Roy's son Chubby, a sophisticated modernist. And Roy Carrier is a zydeco torch bearer himself, as a student and cousin of such la-la artists as Bébé, Eraste, and Calvin Carrière. As Chenier observed, "Lotta youngsters don't want to hear about zydeco music, but they got to remember one thing: their daddy been born and raised on that. All them youngsters should follow their daddy's footsteps sometime."

Chenier's influence also persists on broader levels. The emergence and growth of the New Orleans Jazz & Heritage Festival and the Southwest Louisiana Zydeco Festival were immeasurably enhanced by his participation. Both events have helped bring zydeco to its current level of popularity. There are many important figures on the contemporary zydeco scene that Clifton Chenier bequeathed to the world in such promising condition. . . .

28 The Art of the Muscle

Miles Davis as American Knight and American Knave

GERALD EARLY

Like so many other important figures in postmodern black American vernacular music, such as Jimmy Hendrix or James Brown, Miles Davis had a career swirled in controversy. Davis altered the sound of jazz from the bebop era of the mid-1940s through the late 1960s and early 1970s when he fused jazz and rock together. Although he died in 1991, Miles Davis had an impact on jazz, much like that of John Coltrane, Duke Ellington, and Louis Armstrong, that remains vital and holds great fascination for music historians and students of American cultural history.

Gerald Early, the Merle Kling Professor of Modern Letters at Washington University and a keen observer who has published many essays about African American culture, probes the life of Miles Davis from many perspectives. He argues that Davis was not only an innovative jazz musician but also a handsome—though often fragile—man with a serious interest in boxing, who possessed not only a volatile temper and gruff exterior but a grand ego as well. Always the restless pioneer, late in his life Davis surprisingly returned to reinterpret the Gil Evans charts that he first explored over a ten-year period beginning in the late 1940s. This unexpected reprise is perhaps not so startling when you consider that Davis spent his life confounding and challenging those who admired and loved him and his music.

When East St. Louis–born jazz trumpeter Miles Davis is remembered, it is usually recalled that he was a great innovator, that he had several distinct creative periods like Picasso, that he was a prickly, often unpleasant, personality. Davis is talked about often as a product of Cold War America and the "containment" culture it produced. (Was cool or Davis's reformulation of "free" jazz with his 1960s quintet versions of "containment" music?) He is contextualized within the civil rights movement of the 1960s and the height of jazz-rock fusion in the 1970s. He crossed several genres in his return to performing in the 1980s: hip hop, pop, smooth jazz rock, world beat, probably none of them to the satisfaction of critics or even to hard-core fans of those genres themselves, although he was accorded an enormous respect and, of course, a sort of indulgence, by the last audiences he had before his death in 1991. He also made a great deal of money in the 1980s, more than he had ever made in his life. Curiously, his last project before his death was a new performance of some of his Gil Evans charts from the late 1950s under the leadership of longtime friend Quincy Jones. This might signal to some that he was ready to go back and revisit his past, and thus he had come full circle in some respect; but this is not likely. It was a project that he enjoyed but that he did with some reluctance, and it was not his idea to do it. For those who like to be especially antiquarian and source-oriented, Davis is contextualized as a St. Louisan, a man who emerged with a particular attitude and sound from a particular regional culture.

These various contexts and views of Davis are important—and, in explaining the man, of course, undeniably true. But the major, overarching context that, I think, explains him better than most is that he came of age when jazz music ceased to be a popular commercial music. Thus, he was faced with the dilemma of trying to make a living, of being something of a personality, in a music that had a dwindling audience and lacked the cultural and artistic presence it once had. He was enormously inventive, snappishly opportunistic, yet surprisingly principled in the simple act of making a living in a dying art, that is, dying as an art form with a large audience.

Jazz was searching for a role in the culture after World War II, and it tried several possibilities: as mood music (that combined pseudo, middle-brow intellectualism with its function as background noise for mating—from Jackie Gleason to Don Shirley to Davis's *Kind of Blue*); as soundtrack for gritty, neorealistic crime cinema and television (from Ellington's *Anatomy of a Murder* to Davis's own soundtrack *Escalator to the Gallows*, from TV's *Peter Gunn* to *77 Sunset Strip* to *Ironside*); as experimental neoclassical music (from Stan Kenton's neophonic orchestras to John Lewis's Modern Jazz Quartet to Keith Jarrett's solo concerts); as politics in the form agitprop-aesthetics (the black revolutionary "new thing" to the regressive New Age-ism of the holistic Paul Winter). There might be other roles we can think of as well, and jazz certainly fulfilled these functions, more or less well, though to some degree with increasing frustration for the men and women who wanted to play this music. But no music can be played, realistically, in the United States and expect to withstand the pressures of the marketplace. No music can eschew its own commercial dimension, and if it does, as jazz sometimes has during this era of lacking commercial viability, it only winds up, paradoxically, trying to sell itself on the basis that it is noncommercial and somehow purer and less tainted than other music being sold. This is elitism, not necessarily or a priori a bad thing, but jazz certainly succumbed to this during the era that Davis was a star. What is interesting about Davis was that he clearly and cleverly made use of this elitism while always eyeing how he could maintain himself in the popular realm, walking a fine line between art and commerce. So the secret of Davis's success, his importance to us today as we remember, is not that he was a questing musician. He was hardly unique in that regard in the field of jazz after 1945: was he any more searching than Stan Kenton or Ornette Coleman or John Coltrane or Charles Mingus or Eric Dolphy or Lee Morgan or Jackie McLean or Bud Powell or Herbie Hancock or a dozen others? How Davis succeeded was being able to "sell," as an image, the iconoclastic romance of the searching jazz musician as a representation of the "committed" artist that a sizable portion of the American public wanted to buy, enough to make it possible to support himself in style as a jazz musician. He was able to do this, in part, because of his race, because of the instrument he played, because of his looks (he was thin and smolderingly handsome), and because he had considerable talent. Timing helped immensely and, of course, he was lucky. Young audiences were very open to highly experimental pop music in the late 1960s and to a kind of jazz-rock sound or a sound that expanded the idea of the typical popular song, in part because of groups like Cream; Traffic; Blood, Sweat, and Tears; and, of course, the Beatles.

I think it also helped him that he had an analogue and antithesis of sorts in pianist Thelonious Monk, a fellow bopper, who never really played bop (or he played the slowest bop in the world), who was never the technical wonderman that Parker and Gillespie were. (Neither was Davis.) Monk, who recorded for Columbia in the 1960s, as did Davis, and who was on the cover of *Time* magazine in 1964, essentially never changed his style of music from the 1940s (it was so terrifically unusual at the time that it took the public a number of years to catch on to it), although he continued to write new compositions and reconfigure his music by playing it in different settings (from solo to trio to quartet to septet to big band). But Monk was able to remain the conservative revolutionary for his breakthrough in the 1950s to the end of the 1960s, when Columbia allegedly fired him for refusing to do an album of Beatles covers. Davis, in his own way, mirrored this kind of conservative revolutionary stance until the end of the 1960s—both Davis and Monk shared important sideman John Coltrane, a story in itself—when he went in an entirely different direction than Monk, doing albums like *In a Silent Way* and *Bitches Brew*. Both men, part of a revolutionary movement in bebop, expressed contempt for the avant-garde of the 1960s. Monk continued in the path that he always had and Davis decided to embrace the avant-garde, on his terms, through rock, Indian ragas, and the like in a surprisingly daring way. Despite the criticism he endured, this change in direction did not destroy him or marginalize him, as Monk was marginalized at the end of his life. It put him at the center of everything, and remarkably, he absorbed it and remained identifiably himself, the questing, restless artist forever, like the American pioneer, seeking new frontiers. In a sense, what Davis wanted to do was transcend jazz and simply embody modern musical innovation. More than any other jazz musician, he virtually succeeded at this, and that story, of the complexity of that success, is one worth knowing and telling. Miles Davis, the American bad boy of jazz, our Huckleberry Finn, the adventurous capitalist artist, our great American picaro, who "lit out for the territories" and survived. It is one of the great tales of "manhood" and morality in modern American culture.

In 1953, at the age of twenty-seven, Miles Davis was a drug addict and his musical career was uncertain. It had seemed a long time ago when he was the rising star on the jazz scene with *The Birth of the Cool* sessions that he had done, with a racially integrated set of musicians, in 1949 and 1950. Most of his records since were not good. His stage performances were poor. He looked shot. His appearance was sloppy. His clothes were dirty and unkempt. He was nodding out. He smelled bad. He had kicked his habit once by going back to East St. Louis and living on his father's farm in Millstadt, Illinois. But he went back to narcotics as soon as he left his father's house and went to Detroit, where he also became a pimp. While in Detroit, though, he threw off the habit again. As Davis tells the story in his 1989 autobiography:

> Anyway, I really kicked my habit because of the example of Sugar Ray Robinson; I figured if he could be as disciplined as he was, then I could do it, too. I always loved boxing, but I really loved and respected Sugar Ray, because he was a great fighter with a lot of class and cleaner than a motherfucker. He was handsome and a ladies' man; he had a lot going for him. In fact, Sugar Ray was one of the few idols that I ever had. Sugar Ray looked like a socialite when you would see him in the papers getting out of limousines with fine women on his arms, sharp as a tack. But when he was training for a fight, he didn't have no women around that anybody knew of, and when he got into the ring with someone to fight, he never smiled like he did in those pictures everybody saw of him. When he was in the ring, he was serious, all business.

I decided that that was the way I was going to be, serious about taking care of my business and disciplined. I decided that it was time for me to go back to New York to start all over again. Sugar Ray was the hero-image that I carried in my mind. It was him that made me think that I was strong enough to deal with New York City again. And it was his example that pulled me through some real tough days.[1]

There are several observations to make about what I call the mythology of black masculinity that Davis constructs here. First, Detroit is a significant location because Sugar Ray Robinson was born there, as Walker Smith. He became Ray Robinson when he embarked on his amateur boxing career in Harlem. Detroit was also where Joe Louis, the great black boxing champion of Davis's boyhood, grew up and started his career. (Louis was born in Alabama.) Detroit, therefore, is the symbol of an assertive, disciplined, stylized black manhood as it is connected with the two most accomplished black boxers and, indeed, two of the most publicized black male public figures of the first half of the twentieth century. The Midwest, the center of the United States, its "heartland," takes on a complex set of mythologized meanings in Davis's book and holds a particular relationship with New York City, the center of jazz life. I shall speak more about Davis's views of his midwestern origins later.

Second, Robinson was six years older than Davis. They were close enough in age to have much in common in taste and style and to be considered of the same generation. They were far enough apart in age so that the younger man could admire the older one. They were also close in size. Robinson fought professionally as a welterweight (maximum weight: 147 pounds) and a middleweight (maximum weight: 160 pounds). He was a bigger man than Davis, but on the whole, as a fighter, he was smaller than the average man. He was clearly smaller and younger than heavyweight Joe Louis, and this almost certainly made Robinson a more accessible hero-figure for Davis than Louis would have been. The fact that Robinson was a very dark-skinned man, like Davis himself, and that Louis was light-skinned, also may have intensified Davis's identification with Robinson.

Robinson would have appealed to Davis not simply because of his age and his size but also because of the way he fought. As Davis writes in his autobiography, "Boxing's got style like music's got style.... But you've got to have style in whatever you do—writing, music, painting, fashion, boxing, anything. Some styles are slick and creative and imaginative and innovative and others aren't. Sugar Ray Robinson's style was all of that, and he was the most precise fighter that I ever saw."[2] Robinson was, without question, the most stylish, beautiful-looking fighter ever to enter the ring (with the possible exception Muhammad Ali, who admitted that he modeled himself after Robinson, who was his hero, too, when the future heavyweight champ was a teenager growing up in Louisville in the 1950s). With his mop of processed hair (the sign of ultimate cool for black men before the 1960s) flopping across his head, Robinson used his lightning-quick hands and dancing feet to pound and dazzle opponents into submission. Nearly every official boxing body has voted Robinson, not Ali, the best pound-for-pound boxer in the history of the sport. The disciplined beauty of Robinson's art was something Davis wanted to emulate in his own life and in his art. In a sense, there was something Oscar Wildean about Davis's obsession with Robinson, as if the major lesson he derived from Robinson was learning to make all life a form of aesthetics or, more precisely, a series of aesthetic postures, poses, and propositions.

Third, boxers and jazz musicians historically have occupied the same world, at least black boxers and black musicians have. It was a world referred to by the turn-of-the-century phrase, "the Sporting Life." (One of the most noted characters in Dubose Heyward's 1925 novel, *Porgy*, is called Sportin' Life, and he represents exactly all the virtues and vices of this underground class: urbanity and city life, stylish dress and figure, and drug addiction.[3]) This is the netherworld of nightclubs, gambling, prostitutes, pimps, hustlers, the world of black entertainers, including athletes, musicians, actors, and the like. It was a world of interracial sex, drug addiction and alcoholism, atheism and agnosticism. But it was also a world of wit and spontaneity, of hatred of hypocrisy and pretence, and a kind of expressive fluidity that many found comforting and some even found inspiring. It was a subversive setting, undermining all the assumptions of respectable society, including self-repression, false morality, and racism (though, unfortunately, not sexism), but it was a vicious, often criminal, almost Darwinian world as well that had little pity for losers. The denizens of this world were outcasts from the bourgeois black world of striving middle-class respectability and the work-a-day world of ordinary black Christians, such as those depicted in James Baldwin's 1953 novel, *Go Tell It On the Mountain*. So, Davis and Robinson shared a milieu, an ethos, a way of life, and more profoundly, a history that went back well into the nineteenth century and the beginnings of modern popular culture. Since he came from a black bourgeois background, Davis would have been drawn, as many bourgeois people are, particularly to this type of world. He became a jazz musician, to be sure, for many reasons, and this, the type of world the jazz musician inhabited and the type of people he associated with, was probably one of the rebelliously striking attractions. Robinson was an athlete who had to maintain a Spartan regimen, and thus possessed a kind of physical virtue, but he was also a sybarite who enjoyed the sensual experience, was indeed a connoisseur of it. Embodying this type of contradiction as a style, a measure of trying to be true to both aspects of being a man—monkish abstinence and satyr-like but highly aesthetic indulgence—became an important aspect of Davis's immensely appealing form of 1950s and 1960s cool, a kind of black male existentialism that forged a moral code from the imperatives of the male body as it alternately functioned as a symbol of engagement and detachment, of punishing discipline and plush pleasure that operated cooperatively, not in conflict, if rightly understood. Beyond that, there was no reality. Nothing transcended the senses. What was right was what was instinctively felt to be right. The body was the cosmos, the root of all self-consciousness that mattered, and if it could not explain itself, the body could, on some levels, realize and actualize itself. The Hemingway code meets the priapic poetics of Henry Miller. Davis is describing this change in his life, his defeat of his drug habit, this great admiration of Robinson, in 1954, the year Hugh Hefner starts *Playboy* magazine, which espoused a similar code of masculine cool for the white corporate bourgeoisie. Three years later, Norman Mailer offered a further elaboration of this idea in his famous (or infamous) essay "The White Negro," and Jack Kerouac offered a view of life rather like this in his famous novel, *On the Road* (1957). The striking irony is that Davis, who believed so much in the discipline of the body, suffered so much from ill-health nearly all of his life—calcium deposits, an auto accident from which he never fully recovered, which spurred bouts of drug-addiction particularly from the 1960s on. And he so mistreated his body with jags of dissipation. Perhaps that was also in keeping with his admiration of boxers: theirs is not a healthy sport, and ultimately they suffered severe physical, and in many cases mental, deterioration. But Davis went further than merely admiring the great boxer and wishing to apply, in a figurative way, the athlete's discipline to his art. He became a boxer:

> I had convinced Bobby McQuillen that I was clean enough for him to take me on as a boxing student. I was going to the gym every chance I could, and Bobby was teaching me about boxing. He trained me hard. We got to be friends, but he was mostly my trainer because I wanted to learn how to box like him.

> Bobby and I would go to the fights together and train at Gleason's Gym in midtown or at Silverman's Gym, which was up in Harlem on 116th Street and Eighth Avenue . . . on the fourth or fifth floor in this corner building. Sugar Ray used to train there, and when he came in to train, everybody would stop what they were doing and check him out. . . .
>
> A lot of people tell me I have the mind of a boxer, that I think like a boxer, and I probably do. I guess that I am an aggressive person about things that are important to me, like when it comes to playing music or doing what I want to do. I'll fight, physically, at the drop of a hat if I think someone has wronged me. I have always been like that.[4]

There are several important aspects to Miles Davis's mind here, his mythmaking, if you will. It was risky, even foolish, for a trumpeter to become a fighter, even as an avocation. One punch in the mouth and Davis would be out of work for months. Severe punishment could have ended his career. I suspect, therefore, that neither McQuillen nor anyone else ever pushed Davis seriously in the ring or even took this boxing venture as much more than a lark, a way for Davis to keep physically fit. For Davis, considering the risks, boxing had to be a form of brinkmanship, living on the edge. And that is important in understanding Davis's approach to his art. As others did with Davis, so Davis did with Robinson and fighters generally: he shamelessly romanticized their profession and their craft to find a black masculine analogue for his own life. Jazz musicians were like fighters in the sense that they were an itinerant breed; they worked in an arena that spotlighted their individualism and that was a merciless meritocracy; and they were largely an enclosed cult that outsiders found difficult to penetrate. It was the closest thing—being a boxer or a jazz musician—to being a knight, an urban paladin. Added to this was Davis's own needs to be an assertive black man at a time when a few assertive black men were becoming major figures in American culture: Jackie Robinson, in 1954, was not the nonviolent martyr he was in 1947 when he broke the color line in Major League Baseball. He was argumentative, outspoken, overly sensitive to slights, intensely competitive, and aggressive. He had gone from being beloved by the white press to being disliked, even hated in some quarters. There was Paul Robeson, who refused to back down from being a Stalinist in a repressive Cold War America, virtually daring his country to silence him. James Baldwin had published Go *Tell It On the Mountain* and was to become a new assertive voice for black America in the 1950s and arguably, along with Amiri Baraka, among the most politically engaged writers of his generation, although he was never an avowed leftist. (Baldwin modeled his writing not only after other writers, but also jazz musicians, principally Miles Davis. Other black writers of the post–World War II period were deeply affected by jazz as well, especially poets like Ted Joans, Michael Harper, Yusef Komunyakaa, Sonia Sanchez, Carolyn Rodgers, and prose writer Nathaniel Mackey. John A. Williams, Toni Morrison, and William Melvin Kelley are among several black writers who have written fiction about jazz. Baldwin's "Sonny's Blues" is considered the best jazz short story ever written and, without question, the most anthologized. Indeed, Davis's impact, as well as that of post–World War II jazz in general, can be felt among white writers as well, from the Beats to DeLillo and Pynchon.)

Black men generally had become more assertive as a result of two war experiences that occurred within a span of ten years: World War II and the Korean War, the last being particularly important as it was the first military conflict where American troops were racially integrated. So Davis fashioned himself the fighter as well and made a literal identification with this psychological mode by actually becoming one. Fashioning himself as a fighting black man made Davis an outsider. But he was more than that. Davis, for most of his career, as James Lincoln Collier once noted, was also an insider. After all, Sugar Ray Robinson, by the way he handled himself and the way he appeared, "like a socialite," according to Davis, was something of an insider, and so was Jackie Robinson by virtue of being a success in America's pastime. He also had testified reluctantly before the House Un-American Activities Committee, countering statements that Robeson had made just a few years earlier about African American unwillingness to fight in a war against the Soviet Union. Robinson would not have been called to do so if he had not been considered "loyal." Both Jackie and Sugar Ray Robinson asserted themselves but neither challenged the validity of the systems under which they worked. Davis came along at the right historical moment when he could use his outsider status as a way to be attractive to the bourgeoisie, both white and black. Davis may have abhorred the "Uncle Tom" image of smiling and shuffling, but so did a good portion of the hip, nonconformist black and white audience of the 1950s and 1960s to whom he wished to appeal, especially the young. Moreover, despite being black, Davis's rude, surly image of uncompromising artistic involvement satisfied the romantic yearnings of his white audience, which had come to accept this sort of thing from a black, partly as a refreshing novelty, to be sure, just as they had accepted it from white artists for more than one hundred years. Whites were quite willing, even thrilled, to let Davis be as Byronic as he wished. Columbia Records, for whom Davis recorded for most of his career, from the mid-1950s to the 1980s, found that the image could be marketed, and thus, the Prince of Darkness was born: the black American knave as American Heroic.

Davis used his boxing connection in a vivid and complicated way some years later when in 1970 he recorded the soundtrack to a documentary about the boxer Jack Johnson. Johnson, born in Galveston, Texas, or thereabouts in 1878, right after Reconstruction, and thus, something of a New Negro, that is, according to Southern mores, a black who did not know slavery, was the first black to become heavyweight champion when he beat Tommy Burns for the title in 1908. Before this, from the reign of John L. Sullivan to that of Jim Jeffries, no white heavyweight champion would consent to fight a black. (Blacks, during the late-nineteenth and early twentieth centuries, held boxing titles in lighter weight divisions—Joe Gans, Joe Walcott, George Dixon—but the heavyweight title was considered one of the grand titles in all of sports. It was felt to be symbolically troublesome for an inferior black—and blacks at this time were considered to be, by scientific evidence, not only intellectually inferior to whites but physically inferior to them as well—to compete and win this honor.) But Johnson came of age as a boxer ironically during the era of Jim Crow segregation that culminated in the *Plessy v. Ferguson* decision of 1896 and during the age of social reformism called Progressivism. It was this reformist urge that got him a shot at the title in 1908. And Johnson was undone by the very reformism that led him to the title. He had a penchant for white women, most, but not all of whom, were prostitutes. He tried in no way to conceal this and was eventually convicted under the 1910 Mann Act, which prohibited taking women across state lines for "immoral purposes," a federal measure meant to stem the rising tide of prostitution among working-class women. (The famous Leo Frank case of 1913, in which a Jewish factory owner was convicted, and eventually lynched, for killing a fourteen-year-old girl who worked for him, dramatically demonstrates, whether Frank actually committed the crime, the sexually exploitative atmosphere that most, working-class women and girls had to endure. For many, it was easier to become a prostitute.)

Howard Sackler wrote a play about Johnson in 1969 entitled *The Great White Hope* that became a Broadway hit and a successful film. What inspired Sackler was the saga of Muhammad Ali, the young boxer who won the championship in 1964, converted to the

Nation of Islam immediately after, a group little understood by whites at the time (or many blacks, either), known mostly for its fiery minister, Malcolm X. A few years later, an outspoken Ali refused to be drafted into the armed services during the unpopular Vietnam War, making him a hero to many nonconformist liberals, although a villain to many others, especially those, including many athletes, who had served in World War II and the Korean War. Ali was convicted of violating the Selective Service Act and sentenced to five years in prison, which he never served. Ali was banned from boxing for more than three years while he appealed his case, an act that generated a great deal of debate and made Ali a martyr for his beliefs, something that endeared him to a certain section of the public as a man of principle. Sackler wrote his play during Ali's exile years, 1967 to 1970. He saw a parallel between Ali and Johnson, and so did many during this period, including Ali himself. There was not nearly as much similarity between the two boxers as many at the time thought, but what was there was important.

Davis himself, by 1970, had radically changed directions in his music. This had started with such late 1960s albums as *Filles de Killimanjaro* and *In a Silent Way*, which made use of electric pianos, electric bass, electric guitar, and the like and used rock rhythms. The big breakthrough album for Davis was *Bitches Brew*, made from several August 1969 sessions. As drummer Tony Williams put it, "[Miles Davis]'s trying to get further out (more abstract) and yet more basic (funkier) at the some time." *Bitches Brew* was Davis's most commercially successful record and, along with the 1959 *Kind of Blue*, his most legendary. In 1970, he recorded *Jack Johnson*, possibly his most successful fusion of jazz with hard rock. In his autobiography, he writes:

> When I wrote these tunes [for "Jack Johnson"] I was going up to Gleason's Gym to train with Bobby McQuillen, who was now calling himself Robert Allah (he had become a Muslim). Anyway, I had that boxer's movement in mind, that shuffling movement boxers use. almost like dance steps, or sound of a train. . . .
>
> Then the question in my mind after I got to this was, well, is the music black enough, does it have a black rhythm, can you make the rhythm of the train a black thing, would Jack Johnson dance to that? Because Jack Johnson liked to party, liked to have a good time and dance. . . .[5]

Davis thought of a record, of music, about a black boxer as being connected with his own boxing, and the record had a certain political resonance not only because it was about Johnson, a black rebel figure, but also because Johnson, in the cultural view of those living in the 1960s, adumbrated Muhammad Ali. Davis, who abhorred liner notes, wrote the notes, succinct but telling, for this album. He opened with: "The rise of Jack Johnson to world heavyweight supremacy in 1908 was a signal for white envy to erupt. Can you get to that? And of course being born Black in America . . . we all know how that goes." But this fear and loathing of black masculinity that Davis saw in the America of Jack Johnson was part of a larger, ongoing drama that, in many ways, Davis saw as explaining himself and his music in mythical terms of assertion and resistance to "white envy." So *Jack Johnson* was a record about black male heroism that spanned and collapsed two distinct historical eras. The fact that the music was so contemporary-sounding intensified Davis's own claims as a rebel through his rebel-sounding jazz—a music that tried to be both abstract and funky, both black and white—which, in turn, intensified his identification with the rebel boxers—Johnson and, indirectly, Ali. In a most profound sense, Davis saw himself as operating within a black male heroic tradition, and black male heroes were men like Jack Johnson, not typical black leaders like W. E. B. Du Bois or Martin Luther King and certainly not someone like Booker T. Washington, whom even Johnson himself disliked.

Davis thought *Jack Johnson* his most danceable record and he thought Columbia did a terrible job promoting it. However, I remember the record well when it was released, as I was a college student then. It was a popular record but hardly considered by anyone a dance record or a party record in the sense that music by James Brown or Sly Stone was. One can sense overwhelmingly the influence of guitarist Jimi Hendrix (Buddy Miles, a drummer who had worked with Hendrix's last band, Band of Gypsies, was supposed to be the drummer for the session), but Hendrix, however much his music might be considered "black" (and it certainly had little appeal to black people at the time), did not make dance music in any conventional understanding of the term. *Jack Johnson* was toe-tapping but still fairly abstract for many people. The record was, nonetheless, commercially successful and probably Davis's most "liked" record of his early 1970s period because it was less cluttered and more simplified than *Bitches Brew* or *Big Fun* or *Get Up With It* or *On the Corner* and more coherent and structured than his live albums. The documentary itself has the virtue of showing extensive good footage of Johnson, reminding the world that he clearly was the most photographed black man of the early 1900s and that boxing was essential to the rise of the film industry, but little else. (Brock Peters's speeches throughout are simply the wrong characterizations of Johnson; one has only to read Johnson's 1927 unghosted autobiography to realize that Johnson did not express himself in the way the filmmakers have Peters speaking.[6]) Oddly, in watching the documentary today, one is struck by how jarring and out of place the music seems, how much better the documentary would have been had it used period music. In looking back, the Davis music seems rather quaint and dated, reflecting more its own time than anything about Johnson. It is just this time-bound quality of the music that Davis made during these years, its broad reach that seems both so courageous and so quixotic, that makes it difficult to access, to tease the art from the conceited, youth-obsessed artifice. The music of *Jack Johnson* has the virtues of being well-played and even brilliantly conceived, without being very good soundtrack music or very good "popular" music. But jazz, in its modernist conceit, was supposed to express the modernist, urban energy of Johnson's age. The more modern the jazz, the more powerfully wrought would be Johnson's own modernism, his own startling revolt as a "New Negro," so the filmmakers probably thought. The greatest irony of all perhaps is that Johnson, by the time he wrote his autobiography, was not a fan of jazz: "I am not a jazz enthusiast, but I will admit that this age, which has come to be known as the jazz age is better than the preceding. . . ."

> The radio and the player pianos, to say nothing of phonographs, are grinding out with ceaseless energy the latest jazz, which, while it amuses and is quite in keeping with the rapid movement of life and the lure of dance halls, nevertheless, is not of lasting substance, and its inspiration is only for the moment. For my own part, I find my delight, as for as music is concerned, in the splendid compositions of the old masters, who not only wrote music in its highest forms, but who made it live with the reality of life, transferring into it such depth of feeling and such height of expression that it arouses the best qualities of human nature.[7]

But in 1954, when Miles Davis was inspired by the heroism of Sugar Ray Robinson to change his life and rededicate himself to his craft, it was the moment that truly began the public life of Davis, the moment that made the man. Of course, Davis had been a professional musician for more than a decade, had played with Eddie Randle, Billy Eckstine, and Charlie Parker. But if he had died in 1954, Davis almost certainly would have been, at best, a minor footnote in jazz and possibly forgotten altogether, just as Freddie Webster, Gil Coggins, and Dodo Mamarosa are. That summer of 1954, when the Supreme Court, in *Brown v. Board of*

Education, declared Jim Crow unconstitutional and integrated America's public schools, Davis recorded *Walkin'*, one of his classic works that signaled his return not only as serious musician, but as one of the best jazzmen of his generation. Despite the ups and downs of his later life, no one ever considered him, from that moment on, to be anything less than a major presence and a major myth in twentieth-century American music. And he knew it, too.

Arguably, the three jazz musicians who were young men, virtually teenagers, when the bebop revolution of the 1940s took shape, and who had the biggest influence on or exerted the greatest presence in American popular music after 1945 were Miles Davis, Quincy Jones, and John Coltrane. Each man, so different in personality and geographical origin—Coltrane was from the South; Jones, by way of Chicago, grew up in Seattle; and Davis was from East St. Louis—exercised his force in distinctly different ways.

Jones became a noted arranger, record and film producer, film scorer, and popular music mogul, astute in the ways of the business practices of the industry, and open to a number of musical styles from bebop jazz to hip hop, from avant-garde film score to teenaged pop. He produced Sinatra and Basie, Dinah Washington and Ray Charles, and the biggest-selling album in the history of American popular music—Michael Jackson's *Thriller* (1982). His music is ubiquitous, although many people may not recognize it immediately as his, and he has had more commercial success than any jazz musician of his generation, perhaps of any jazz musician in history. But he did not become a major instrumentalist, nor did he develop an identifiable sound as a bandleader, although he fronted very good bands during his heyday as an active, touring musician. He was charming, handsome, talented, dependable, and willing to work extraordinarily hard. But unlike the other two men we are considering here, he did not develop a personality cult or a stylized personality or public persona that attracted people to him for reasons other than his music.

Coltrane became perhaps the greatest technical master of the saxophone in the history of modern music. He recorded a number of albums in the early 1960s that enjoyed some considerable commercial success, despite the fact that they were undiluted, uncompromising modern jazz, in other words, highly stylized art music. Records such as *My Favorite Things, Giant Steps, John Coltrane and Johnny Hartman*, and, notably, *A Love Supreme*, did well in the marketplace, attracting, particularly, young people and those possessing a genuine or pseudointellectual interest in music. The civil rights generation of young people, iconoclastic, nonconformist, and romantically inclined about both politics and art, were particular fans of this music. Coltrane's later, more radical records of the period—*Ascension, Meditation, Kulu Se Mama*, and the like—did not sell as well but nonetheless had a worshipful audience. (So worshipful, in fact, that a church has spawned in San Francisco dedicated to John Coltrane.) Indeed, listening to and owning these records became a sign of being a member of the jazz and cultural cognoscenti, in a decade when spontaneity and emancipation became virtual political and psychological obsessions. Coltrane, in important ways, signified the inchoate yearnings for change and self-improvement of his age: for blacks, his highly spiritualized racial consciousness seemed almost an aesthetic and a political aspiration; for whites, this same spiritualized racial consciousness seemed the romanticized ideal of a counterculture impulse that rebelled against a hypocritical, racist, materialist America. Coltrane, previously a sloppy drunk and drug addict, cleaned himself up and found redemption in the purity of art or the quest for pure artistic expression. He became essentially the anti–Charlie Parker, not a man who was a slave to his appetites but a man who seemingly had mastered them or, in effect, transcended them for a higher consciousness. The 1960s might be seen as the age of two gentle black male radicals who ironically were responsible for a great deal of gut-wrenching disruption: Coltrane and Martin Luther King. After his death, no one had a greater influence on aspects of 1970s popular music than Trane. No jazz musician was ever so honored by tribute songs as Coltrane was in both jazz and pop circles, and no jazz musician ever so overtly influenced how musicians wanted to live since the drug-days of Charlie Parker. Doug and Jean Corn, Carlos Santana, John McLaughlin, Billy Gault, Joe Lee Wilson, Chick Corea, McCoy Tyner, Elvin Jones, Terry Collier, the Rascals, the Last Poets, Archie Shepp, and Gil-Scott Heron were some of the many jazz and pop artists who reverently honored Coltrane, either before he died or after or both. And tributes continued to flow later from such musicians as Vanessa Daou, Sonny Fortune, Kenny Garrett, Benny Golson, Dave Liebman, and Suzanne Pittson. Coltrane is mentioned more in socially conscious rap music than any other jazz musician. Coltrane single-handedly made the soprano saxophone, a technically difficult and often unruly instrument, which Sidney Bechet once played with vibrato and abandon back in the 1920s and 1930s, one of the most popular reed instruments of the last quarter of the twentieth century in popular music and jazz. But he was not a mogul, like Jones; not a noted composer or arranger of music; not someone very open to anything other than a certain sort of jazz that emerged after 1945. He was a genius player, period, and this intensified his myth and etherealized his achievements. He also died at the relatively young age of thirty-nine, when his work as an artist hardly had come to its full maturity.

Perhaps of the three men, Miles Davis is the most complex figure. Like Coltrane, Davis was a genius player, but not the same type of genius. Coltrane was one of the most technically accomplished saxophonists ever; but no one would say that Davis was one of the most technically accomplished trumpeters ever to emerge in jazz. Almost certainly Louis Armstrong, Roy Eldridge, Fats Navarro, Clifford Brown, and Dizzy Gillespie were better players technically. Many, I am sure, feel that Clark Terry, the late Lee Morgan, and possibly Wynton Marsalis are better players in their ability to get around the horn. But few players in jazz or in modern music ever matched Davis's ability to convey deep emotion, a poetic lyricism with an instrument. And very few jazzmen ever have been able to construct better solos, use space and silence so well, and make a few notes sound so telling. Kenneth Tynan called Davis "a musical lonely hearts club."[8] Davis was more than *that*, but the fact that the public could understand him as being *that* was important to his success: he was a high-level musician whose playing was accessible, romantic. His haunted, touching sound, so moving, particularly on ballads, that seemed so much like an abstraction, distillation, and improvement of Freddie Webster, an early influence, and his uncanny ability to swing at any tempo, like Armstrong, made him a formidable musician. (Davis was capable of playing fiery enough when he wanted, and one can hear him to good effect in this vein on some live albums he made in the 1950s and 1960s, particularly some live sets he made with Coltrane: *Live at the Blackhawk* and *"Four" and More*. He could produce this effect in the studio as well, on tunes like "Gingerbread Boy," "Salt Peanuts," and "Freedom Jazz Dance." Although he purposefully limited his range on the instrument—to take advantage of his strengths—technically he was more accomplished than some were willing to give him credit for.) Davis was probably not only one of the half-dozen or so greatest soloists in jazz in the last half of the twentieth century, but he was probably one of the finest conceptualists of music in American history; arguably, only Ellington, Armstrong, Thelonious Monk, Charles Mingus, Billie Holiday, and Parker matched or exceeded him in this realm.

If anything, Davis was able to generate a greater mystique about his playing than Coltrane did with his; and Davis, never in his life, affected any sort of religious or spiritual persona that would tend to romanticize himself or his music as something transcendent. He was a die-hard sensualist and secularist his entire life. Davis became one of modern American music's extraordinary personas much to his benefit and sometimes to his detriment. Davis could be inspiringly prideful, incisive, determined, principled, and wondrously knowledgeable about music and people. He also could be remarkably crude and cruel, vain and foolish, and unnecessarily, childishly obscene in speech. Great flows and great contradictions are often the marks of great people.

Like Jones, Davis was able to maintain himself in music, as an important voice in popular culture, far beyond the years of his youth. Indeed, at middle age, Davis reached an entirely new audience of young people in the 1970s with a kind of swaggering hipness and unbridled audacity virtually unmatched anywhere in American popular music, just as Jones, during those years, reached college-aged audiences with albums like *Smackwater Jack, Body Heat,* and *Gula Matari*. Davis changed his sound radically over the years, but unlike Jones, he unmistakably stamped the sound he became associated with. No matter what he was playing, whether tightly stated cool or wild-angled fusion, everyone instantly recognized a Miles Davis record, even if everyone did not like it instantly or eventually. Davis was not a mogul or a producer like Jones; nor was he an arranger or a composer of note. (Davis has been accused of taking credit for tunes he did not write, although the few tunes he is credited for having composed have become standards in jazz: "Milestones," "Nardis," "All Blues," "So What," "Blue in Green.") Yet on the strength of his ability and reputation as a player and particularly the image and reputation he cultivated as an innovator, an explorer, he kept himself more current and he managed to keep himself vital longer than most jazz musicians ever do.

Miles Davis, the musician and the man, is largely the result of certain cultural crosscurrents that emerged after World War II. If there was a New Negro that philosophy professor and Harlem Renaissance broker Alain Locke could describe in his seminal 1925 essay, "The New Negro," which appeared in his famous anthology of the same name, it is very possible to talk about an even Newer Negro after World War II, more militant, more worldly, more urban, more alive to a changing world that was overthrowing European colonialism. Miles Davis's biggest years were between 1954 and 1975, the age of "colored" self-determination around the world. Both his music and his attitude reflected this. Davis also emerged during the age of the drug revolution, where people experimented with consciousness-alteration, with looking at what had been forbidden before (only people like jazz musicians took drugs) and to find out for themselves what these things were like. ("Better living through chemistry," as one wag of the 1960s put it.) Davis came into his own during the age of the sexual revolution. From the Kinsey Report and *Playboy* magazine to the birth-control pill, legalized abortion, the gay rights movement, and the rise of the hard-core porn industry, Davis saw not only changes in the public attitude about and cultural depiction of sex, but he saw a change in the role of women in society. His own attitudes may not have changed much, and he still may have had, until the very end of his life, the old hustler's view of women as "bitches" who occasionally needed a man "to put his foot up their asses," but the attitude of the women in the world around him changed. And this has affected very deeply how he has been interpreted since the 1980s and particularly since his death in 1991. In the jazz world, of course, as in the sporting life itself, since the nineteenth century, a great deal of casual sex and interracial sex occurred. What Davis saw happen over the years of his prominence was that the sex of the jazz world became the sex of the mainstream world. What had once been considered criminal or bohemian became rather standard by the 1960s and 1970s, particularly. Davis was at his height during the years of protest and dissent in America about Vietnam and civil rights. And in some subtle ways, there was much protest in his music, and in some blatant ways, much protest in his attitude and self-presentation. Davis chose very much to be a jazz musician on his own terms, defining this music as he felt it necessary. But Davis clearly benefited by coming of age as an artist in an age of personal experimentation that touched the core of mind and body and challenged established authority, the state, the school, the church, the family. This gave Davis's own restless quest for experimentation not only a cultural and social context but an incredibly sympathetic ambience.

Davis's most ardent admirers claim that he changed the direction of modern music four times or more in his career. First, he single-handedly created cool—when bebop grew stale and clichéd—when he did the sessions that became *The Birth of the Cool* in 1949 and 1950 and set the jazz world on its ear. He invented hard bop with *Walkin'* and his sessions for Prestige in the mid-1950s. Then, he was credited with reinvigorating orchestral jazz with the Gil Evans sessions of the late 1950s; he invented modal jazz with the seminal *Kind of Blue* album in 1959, the single most influential jazz album since World War II; he walked a line between freedom and tradition with his 1960s quintet that has become the basis of virtually all small-group jazz being played now; and he invented jazz-rock or fusion in 1970 with *Bitches Brew*. There is truth in this, but these claims rather miss the truly complex nature of Davis's genius; it is certainly always the case that admirers suspect the genius to be auteur of all he or she ever touched. This is far from accurate.

Davis had a knack for being around very talented young musicians—he saw jazz as a young musician's art—who not only understood and appreciated him but whom he understood, and in some sense, liberated. In other words, musicians who played with Davis were able to develop their own ideas and many went on to fruitful careers. When Chick Corea, Dave Holland, and Jack DeJohnette played as Davis's rhythm section in the early 1970s, they often would drop out of the music and play material that sounded very much like Corea's avant-garde group of the time, Circle. Davis permitted this, just as he did Coltrane's long solos when the latter was in his 1950s band. When Herbie Hancock was in Davis's band in the 1960s, he sounded very much like Hancock with his own band. And Keith Jarrett's solos with Davis in the 1970s sounded very much like the sort of thing Jarrett would play in his own band on an acoustic piano. In short, Davis provided his musicians with a context where they played something clearly identifiable as his music or his sound, but in that context they not only remained themselves, they very often found themselves. This is why nearly all the musicians who played with Davis during his career speak so highly of the experience.

The character of Davis's music changed significantly, depending on who was in his band. Davis became interested in modal music when pianist Bill Evans was in the band, and much of the music on *Kind of Blue* sounds like the sort of thing Evans would write (and some say, indeed, that Evans did write it, particularly "Blue in Green," "All Blues," and "Flamenco Sketches"). Yet, and this is the sign of Davis's genius, no one would ever mistake *Kind of Blue* for an Evans album. Gil Evans was the architect for Davis's orchestral sound and had much to do with the success of *The Birth of the Cool* sessions (along with saxophonist Gerry Mulligan). Wayne Shorter was the main composer for the sound of Davis's 1960s band. Davis was far from being the inventor of jazz-rock. Drummer Chico Hamilton's band, which had members like guitarists Gabor Szabo and Larry Coryell, bassist Al Stinson, and saxophonist Charles Lloyd, did far more innovative things in that direction in the mid-1960s than Davis during the same time. So did vibes player Gary Burton, saxophonist Eddie Harris, and Lloyd himself. Davis caught the wave at a certain height with the right musicians to move fusion ahead in a way that no one had quite envisioned. Timing was a significant factor in his success; for instance, the *Sketches of Spain* album had much to do with a craze for Spanish—not Latin

American—culture in the United States in the late 1950s. Garcia Lorca's poetry was hot; flamenco music was big; Henry King made his film version of *The Sun Also Rises* in 1957, and bullfighting was the rage with the American intelligentsia. (*The Brave Bulls* and *The Bullfighter and the Lady*, two other bullfighting pictures made in 1951, had been successful as well and reflected the strong interest in this subject expressed throughout the decade.) Disney's *Zorro*, set in Spanish California—with constant references to the mother country, Spain—was a popular television program. It was a good time to make a Spanish—not an Afro-Cuban—record, and part of *Sketches of Spain*'s appeal is that it makes use of what Jelly Roll Morton called "the Spanish tinge" in a remarkably fresh way. The timing for *In a Silent Way* and *Bitches Brew* could not have been better. Jazz was losing its audience; there were few venues left to play it. If one were going to make a living as a jazz musician, it was necessary to find a way for this music to be played in rock venues. Davis discovered a way to do that. Some thought of it as selling out, but Davis's music remained incredibly abstract and strikingly noncommercial despite being gussied up and marketed as youth music (Sometimes I think critics of Davis's music during this period mistake the marketing of the music for the music itself.)

In short, there was much about what Davis did in his career that was sui generis. The Gil Evans sessions were remarkable, but Ellington and Basie were still the best big jazz bands of the period and Stan Kenton was far more experimental. The Prestige small group sessions with Coltrane, Red Garland, Paul Chambers, and Philly Joe Jones—a more unpromising group of mismatched musicians could hardly be imagined, yet Davis made it work brilliantly and those men never sounded better—were influential hard bop records, among the best ever. But the hard bop records from the period that are considered quintessential are Art Blakey's, Horace Silver's, Hank Mobley's, and organist Jimmy Smith's. Davis operated in a separate sphere, in part, because the quality of his music was so high, yet he never seemed imprisoned by any of the periods or styles he recorded in. Davis had the three instincts necessary for genius: he was an opportunist; he was not afraid of talented people, even if, in some particular area, they were more talented than he; and he had supreme confidence in his ability to make anything he'd try work. Moreover, Davis understood his limitations: he wrote music, but he was not a composer in the way that Ellington or Mingus or Monk were. He was not an arranger in the way that Gil Evans was or Billy Strayhorn or Quincy Jones or Gerald Wilson were. He was not a producer like Quincy Jones or Teo Macero. Indeed, he had a rather careless attitude about his music and needed a producer in the way that a writer like Thomas Wolfe needed an editor. He had no real sense of business, although he fronted bands for many years. He discovered talent, but he was not a cultivator of it in the way Stan Kenton was. If he had had a greater entrepreneurial impulse, he probably would have made a great deal more money than he did. (As it was, he was enormously successful financially for a musician who made, for the most part, music with meager commercial appeal.) Yet it all came together for him and worked amazingly well for a number of years. His biggest gift was that he was neither afraid of his audience nor of himself.

This lack of fear is apparent in Davis's autobiography, for the book generated much controversy, not only for what was in it but how it was expressed. Stanley Crouch and Jack Chambers have said the book is largely plagiarized. Others are displeased with the crude language and the mistakes. Still others are annoyed with Davis's treatment of women. Yet, despite its shortcomings, it is one of the most fascinating jazz autobiographies ever written. Davis talks insightfully and incisively about music and music-making, about his bands and the life of a working musician. What drives a musician to make music is not at all the same as what drives an audience to listen to it. What a musician gets from making music is entirely different from what an audience gets from listening to it. This is true despite the fact that a musician understands precisely what sort of effect his or her music likely will have on an audience, because the emotional response to certain tones and keys is well established and almost never varies. Davis conveys very well the sense of music to a musician but does so in a way that a reader who is not a musician can fully understand. It is important that Davis was able to explain his craft on his own terms. After all, jazz is the most persistently explained music ever invented in America and may be the most explicated popular music in the world, despite that most of its major artists dislike critics. With his autobiography, Davis, who hated critics while in some sense he artfully courted them, became his own critic.

To appreciate better Davis's book, one might do well to compare it with *Hamp*, Lionel Hampton's autobiography published the same year. *Miles* and *Hamp* give us two distinct views of black musical innovators: drummer and vibes player Hampton, who sees himself transparently as an entertainer willing to give the people what they want; and Davis, who sees himself egotistically as the rebel who is almost opaque, impenetrable, misunderstood, and mistreated because he is black. Hampton smiles incessantly when he performs; Davis never smiled, and, indeed, for a good portion of his career, he never even spoke to or acknowledged his audience. Both attitudes symbolize the intense, inescapable racial consciousness. of the two men and the unrelenting anxiety of playing for the white establishment, which, frankly, as both books make clear, made them possible by creating and sustaining their fame. There is a sense with both men, Hampton's accommodation and Davis's resentment largely becoming reflections of the same sensibility, that jazz has only a white audience and that the poses, after all, are the only possible ones available to them. Of course, any historian of this music is well aware that Davis and Hampton, for most of their careers, had sizable black followings. Because there were so few black movie and television stars before the 1960s, black musicians and black athletes were the pop-culture aristocracy of the national black community. Yet both Hampton and Davis always must have felt that the real powers in jazz—from the concert promoters to the nightclub owners to the record company executives, from the large portion of the record-buying public to the critical and reviewing establishment—were exclusively white. How they responded to this says much about their careers and the kind of books they wrote about themselves.

Nothing demonstrates this aura of whiteness and the difference in how both men handled it more compellingly than their view of the white political establishment. Hampton writes with pride of his long friendship with Richard Nixon and his association with conservative Republican politics, of the number of Republican presidential balls he played: "I walk within the Republican party and do what I have to do, as long as Republicans are in it. . . . I believe in a lot of principles of Republicanism, like not being wasteful."[9] Later, in discussing the 1988 campaign of George Bush, Hampton says:

> I had high hopes for a Republican victory in November. I believe that the country was better off after eight years of Reagan. The country had gone more conservative, and in my opinion there was no other way for it to go. Things were really getting out of hand. They talk about getting our teenagers tuned to a better way of life and good citizenship, and then they let all this filth in. There was a time when divorce was a damnable sin. Now a couple of movie stars can shack up and have a kid out of wedlock, and they're heroes.[10]

One, of course, cannot be sure who "they" are. Perhaps Hampton means Democrats or liberals generally. It is noteworthy that his condemnation of liberalism, on the ground of corrupting the innocent, is precisely the ground upon which jazz as an art form was condemned in the 1920s and even, to a lesser extent, the 1930s, the era when Hampton emerged first as an apprentice, later as a major musical presence. Jazz, at one time in this country, when Hampton was a young man playing it in Los Angeles and later with Benny Goodman, represented a kind of liberalism and artistic dissent. It was an attack on the status quo until the late 1940s, when a certain kind of jazz had become the status quo. Later, Hampton became associated with rock and roll, another rebel music for the young that threatened the status quo. His post–World War II band was largely a rhythm and blues, jump band. He was, for instance, featured prominently in Alan Freed's 1957 film, *Mr. Rock and Roll.* (Indeed, if the film is read right, Hampton is Mr. Rock and Roll.) It is not strange, in the end, that Hampton defends the establishment and the status quo; he sees it as the culmination of his career, arriving at a level of respectability and recognition, not from critics, not from fellow musicians, not even from the general public, but from an elitist group of conservative social climbers. Finally, when he writes about how the Republican White House paid homage to him, his exchange of honorifics with President Reagan seem hollow:

> The following September the Reagans paid me just about the greatest honor I've ever had when they gave me a special reception at the White House. George Bush had a lot to do with that. It was his way of thanking me [for campaigning for the Reagan-Bush ticket in 1984]. About eight hundred people gathered on the south lawn of the White House, and President and Mrs. Reagan greeted everyone. Then we did a concert. . . . After the concert, the president called me a great American, and I called him the greatest star in the world. I was deeply honored.[11]

Miles Davis, on the other hand, never talked about politics, never indicated that he had ever voted in an election, saying only that he has "never liked that kind of political shit." (This attitude explains why he steered clear of the civil rights movement and comes very close to the view of Ralph Ellison: the artist must focus on his art, not politics, although Davis's feeling borders on utter cynicism and contempt, not simply detachment and indifference. He does not find politics distracting but outrageously immoral.) Davis writes of attending a 1987 presidential reception and ceremony for Ray Charles, who was getting a Lifetime Achievement Award:

> When I met the President I wished him good luck in trying to do what he was doing, and he said, "Thanks, Miles, because I'm going to need it." He's a nice enough guy when you meet him in person. I guess he was doing the best he could. He's a politician, man, who happens to lean to the right. Others lean to the left. Most of them politicians are stealing the country blind. It don't matter whether they are Republicans or Democrats; they are all in it for what they can take. The politicians don't care anymore about the American people. All they think about is how they're going to get rich just like everybody else who is greedy.[12]

The affair was painful for Davis, as he was insulted several times by whites who were ignorant of his art: "That was some of the sorriest shit I've ever been around. That was a hell of a feeling I had down there in Washington, feeling embarrassed because those white people down there who are running the country don't understand nothing about black people and don't want to know!"[13]

What explains the difference beyond merely pointing out that both men are of different generations? Both were midwesterners, but Hampton came up from the Deep South, whereas Davis was born in Illinois. Davis makes a considerable point of his background on at least three occasions in his autobiography. First, in assessing why he, Coleman Hawkins, and Charlie Parker got along as artists, he explains, "We—Bird, me, and Bean—were all from the Midwest. I think that had a lot to do with us hitting it off musically, and sometimes—at least with Bird—socially; we kind of thought and saw things alike."[14] Second, Davis uses his background to explain the difference between himself and the two "clown" princes of jazz trumpet, Dizzy Gillespie and Louis Armstrong: "I come from a different social and class background than both of them, and I'm from the Midwest, while both of them are from the South. So we look at white people a little differently."[15] Finally, he speaks of region in explaining why he and his second wife, Frances, were attracted to each other: "Frances was from Chicago and I was also from the Midwest, so that might have had something to do with us hitting it off so quick, because we never did have to explain a lot of shit."[16]

Unlike Hampton, who from his youth when his family ran a bootlegging operation to his early days as a musician when he played in clubs owned by the likes of Al Capone, tended to see strong white men in authority—whether gangsters or Republican politicians—as protectors, Davis was unimpressed by white men in authority. Indeed, Davis saw himself as something of an outlaw: a dope addict, a pimp, a jazzman, a boxer. He had adopted many of the fearful guises of the black man who rebels against white male authority in the United States. In this way, we must understand everything about Davis as artifice and masculine stylization. It is also a book about being at war with white masculinity and the white male presumption of power. This is perhaps in the end why Davis's book, where the language is itself so stylized after the masculine rituals of context insulting—a performance feature of both boxing and the street-corner hustler—and the authoritative, sexist denigrations of the pimp, is, by far, one of the most morally obsessed jazz autobiographies ever written. For Davis, jazz history is the allegorical battle for the black man's body and his ethical and aesthetic principles, which explains why Davis's book has richer assessments of the musicians he played with, the creative processes that constitute the making of jazz, and the artistic workings of a jazz band than any extant jazz autobiography. What Davis condemns consistently throughout the book is greed, selfishness, and people's unwillingness to pay the price for what they do. He calls not only white politicians greedy, but also the greatest musician he ever played with and possibly one of the finest musicians America ever produced, Charlie Parker. Davis suggests that not even great art can save one morally, and that it is presumptuous, as in the case of Parker, to believe that it should or that it confers a kind of preemptive grace. This is a profoundly remarkable and moving idea, because there is no self-pity in it, nor sentimentality, nor any attempt to escape the immediateness of this life and its necessity that we answer for who we are with what we are by appealing to something transcendent, not even art itself, no matter how impressive that art is. . . .

Notes

1. Reprint with the permission of Simon & Schuster, Inc. from MILES: THE AUTOBIOGRAPHY by Miles Davis with Quincy Troupe. Copyright ©1989 by Miles Davis. All rights reserved 174

2. *Miles: The Autobiography*, 181.

3. The novel became a successful play that Heyward coauthored with his wife, Dorothy. In 1935, in collaboration with the Gershwin brothers, the play became the folk opera, "Porgy and Bess."

4. *Miles: The Autobiography*, 180–81.
5. *Miles: The Autobiography*, 314–15.
6. This description of Johnson, from James Weldon Johnson's autobiography, *Along This Way* (1933), is pertinent in this regard: 'I think the most interesting person I met was Jack Johnson, who was to be, three years later, the champion prize fighter of the world. I saw him first at the theater, where he had come to see Bob [Cole, one of Johnson's songwriting partners] and Rosamond [Johnson, James's brother and another song-writing partner]. He came frequently to our apartment, and his visits were generally as long as our time permitted, for he was not training. These visits put the idea in my head of improving myself in 'the manly art of self-defense'—the manner in which gentlemen used to speak about taking boxing lessons. Jack often boxed with me playfully, like a good-natured big dog warding off the earnest attacks of a small one, but I could never get him to give me any serious instruction. Occasionally, he would bare his stomach to me as a mark and urge me to hit him with all my might. I found it an impossible thing to do; I always involuntarily pulled my punch. It was easy to like Jack Johnson; he is so likable a man, and I liked him particularly well. I was, of course, impressed by his huge but perfect form, his terrible strength, and the supreme ease and grace of his every muscular movement; however, watching his face, sad until he smiled, listening to his soft Southern speech and laughter, and hearing him talk so wistfully about his big chance, yet to come, I found it difficult to think of him as a prize fighter. I had not yet seen a prize fight, but I conceived of the game as a brutal, bloody one, demanding of its exponents courage, stamina, and brute force, as well as skill and quick intelligence, and I could hardly figure gentle Jack Johnson in the role. . . .' —James Weldon Johnson, *Along This Way: The Autobiography of James Weldon Johnson* (New York, Viking Press, 1938) 208. Johnson's books, *The Autobiography of an Ex-Colored Man* (1912), *Black Manhattan* (1930) and *Along This Way*, provide excellent accounts of the black sporting life of which Johnson, as a popular songwriter in the 1890s, was a part. For more on Jack Johnson and how he challenged the reformist era with his prize-fighting and his ownership of a nightclub (where his white wife committed suicide), see Kevin J. Mumford, *Interzones: Black/White Sex Districts in Chicago and New York City in the Early Twentieth Century* (New York: Columbia University Press, 1997), 3–18, especially. Also see, Gerald Early, "Jack Johnson: A Man Out of Time," in Michael MacCambridge, ed., *ESPN SportsCentury* (New York: Hyperion Books, 1999), 34–49.
7. Jack Johnson, *Jack Johnson—In the Ring—and Out* (Chicago: National Sports Publishing Company, 1927), 217, 221.
8. Quoted in Dan Wakefield, *New York in the Fifties* (New York: Houghton Mifflin, 1992), 300.
9. Lionel Hampton, with James Haskins, *Hamp: An Autobiography* (New York: Warner Books, 1989), 167.
10. Ibid., 174.
11. Ibid., 168.
12. *Miles: The Autobiography*, 378.
13. Ibid., 381.
14. Ibid., 77.
15. Ibid., 83.
16. Ibid., 227.

29 Evaluating Ellington

MARK TUCKER

Edward Kennedy "Duke" Ellington is now recognized as one of the most important and influential composers of the twentieth century. Born in Washington D.C., in 1899, Ellington spent his youth in our nation's capital. He moved to New York City in the mid-1920s in search of broader musical horizons and a larger, more appreciative audience. The composer of more than 1,500 orchestral works, including standards such as "It Don't Mean a Thing (If It Ain't Got That Swing)," "Satin Doll," and "Mood Indigo," Ellington operated his jazz orchestra continuously until his death in 1974. Many musicians stayed in the Ellington Orchestra for many years, most notably alto saxophonist Johnny Hodges, who played with Duke for forty years.

"Evaluating Ellington," which initially appeared as one of Mark Tucker's "Behind the Beat" columns in Brooklyn College's Institute for Studies in American Music newsletter, is Tucker's assessment of Ellington's place in jazz and American music as of the late 1980s. Tucker, who both wrote a biography of Ellington's early years in Washington D.C., and edited a reader of material devoted to Duke Ellington, suggests that there are several ways to approach Ellington's musical legacy. He writes about the recent renaissance of interest in Duke Ellington that began in the early 1980s with the Broadway production of Sophisticated Ladies *and continued later in the decade with performances of* Les Trois Rois Noirs, *an uncompleted work from the late 1960s that was finished by Ellington's son Mercer.*

*Tucker offers another approach, which is to look at "his most important contributions." Many critics, such as Martin Williams and Gunther Schuller, point to a period in the early 1940s when Ellington's mind was particularly fecund. But others, most notably Stanley Crouch and Gary Giddens, look to his later, longer, works and suites (*Black, Brown, and Beige *and* Such Sweet Thunder*) for their inspiration. He suggests that these opinions, along with the books and discographical studies of Ellington's work, help to provide scholars and listeners with a greater appreciation for Ellington. Mark Tucker, who was teaching at the College of William & Mary before his untimely death in December 2000, closes by challenging future scholars to not only compare the impact of Ellington with Beethovan but also to learn more about the important figures of early twentieth-century black American music—Bert Williams, Florance Mills, and Will Marion Cook to name but three.*

Listening to the New York Philharmonic on a radio broadcast last summer, I was troubled. Zubin Mehta had just led a stirring performance of Tchaikovsky's Fifth Symphony, and the audience at the Teatro Colón in Buenos Aires responded warmly. It was time for an encore. "'The Giggling Rapids,'" Maestro Mehta announced, "by Duke Ellington." Wild applause—but was it for the piece, a movement from *The River*, Ellington's 1970 suite commissioned by the American Ballet Theatre? Doubtful. It was probably for Ellington himself, or for the fact that an American orchestra was honoring one of its own.

Now, *The River* has its moments, and I imagine it must have been an effective vehicle for Alvin Ailey's choreography. But the score is one Ellington's lesser efforts—representative for him in the way, say, that *Wellington's Victory* is for Beethoven. On the heels of Tchaikovsky's Fifth "The Giggling Rapids" sounded like the work of an amateur. Beyond the cruel juxtaposition was the Philharmonic's unsatisfying performance: swoopy strings and overbearing brass bore little relation to Ellington's special sound world, with its subtle blend of timbres and richly dissonant voicings. And the Philharmonic's stiff, Teutonic phrasing insured a minimum of swing. This was music by the great American composer Duke Ellington? It sounded more like Leroy Anderson on a bad day.

Ellington's status is on the rise, to be sure, and audiences are hearing more of his music all the time. The current wave of interest started, I believe, around 1981 with *Sophisticated Ladies*, the Broadway musical that presented familiar Ellington pieces in glossy new arrangements. (This past fall the show traveled to Moscow to begin a two-year world tour.) Symphonic adaptations by Luther Henderson and Maurice Peress of six Ellington works, available through G. Schirmer, Inc., are turning up more often on concert programs. Recently both the American Composers

The sheet music for "Mood Indigo," one of Duke Ellington's early (1930) and most often performed compositions.

Credit: Sheet music from the collection of Kip Lornell.

Orchestra and the Northwest Indiana Symphony performed *Les Trois Rois Noirs*, an unfinished late work completed by Duke's son Mercer, and last summer at Carnegie Hall the ACO under Peress played (and recorded) its first all-Ellington program. Another late, unfinished work—the opera *Queenie Pie*—was stitched together posthumously and produced in several East Coast cities; soon it will be on Broadway, starring Patti LaBelle. Then there are the repertory ensembles that attempt to recreate the sound, style, and spirit of Ellington's band, among them the American Jazz Orchestra (New York), Red Wolfe's Echoes of Ellington (Minneapolis), Gordon Grinnell and the Mellotones (San Diego), Doug Richards's Virginia Commonwealth University Jazz Orchestra (Richmond), and Andrew Homzy's L'Orchestre de Jazz (Montréal).

These developments spring from a common conviction that Ellington's music should not just be preserved on recordings but heard live in concert halls and theaters. They also illustrate a growing regard for Ellington as a serious composer—something he did not enjoy during his lifetime, when the public viewed him as a famous bandleader and critics often typecast him as a jazz musician. In 1965 he was nominated for a Pulitzer Prize in music but was turned down by the committee. (Ellington's reaction was typically classy: "Fate doesn't want me to be too famous too young." He was sixty-six at the time.) Since his death in 1974, however, Ellington's stock has risen. Gunther Schuller, in *AmeriGrove*, offers a typical assessment, calling him "the most important composer in jazz history." Others go further, pronouncing him "one of America's greatest composers, regardless of idiom,"[1] or simply "our greatest composer."[2]

Such statements raise questions about both Ellington and our ways of viewing him. What makes Ellington a great composer? Which are his best compositions? What kind of critical framework do we have for evaluating his work?

Ellington's greatness might be measured by standards applied to European composers. In fact, writing in 1974, Gunther Schuller argued for Ellington's honorary membership in the club of European immortals:

> If I dare to include Ellington in the pantheon of musical greats—the Beethovens, the Monteverdis, the Schoenbergs, the prime movers, the inspired innovators—it is precisely because Ellington had in common with them not only musical genius and talent, but an unquenchable thirst, an unrequitable passion for translating the raw materials of musical sounds into his own splendid visions.[3]

Not quite satisfied with this rationale, Schuller continued: "What distinguishes Ellington's best creations from those of other composers, jazz and otherwise, are their moments of total uniqueness and originality. . . . Ellington's imagination was most fertile in the realm of harmony and timbre, usually in combination." Schuller then cited some of these moments: the opening of *Subtle Lament* (1939), the second chorus of *Blue Light* (1939), the first bridge of *Jack the Bear* (1940), the harmonies of *Clothed Woman* (1947).

Schuller's attempt to define Ellington's greatness reveals some difficulties in the endeavor. If Ellington's most original contributions lay in the realm of "harmony and timbre, usually in combination," how can his music survive in the repertory once the distinctive tone colors (of his original orchestra members) have disappeared? Moreover, while Beethoven, Monteverdi, and Schoenberg all have their "moments of total uniqueness," their high reputation also rests on well-defined aspects of compositional craft and their ability to control large-scale structures. Does Ellington measure up here? Schuller doesn't say. He does, however, draw an analogy between Ellington and another composer who showed an uncanny understanding of harmony and timbre: "What Chopin's nocturnes and ballades are to mid-nineteenth-century European music, Ellington's *Mood Indigo* and *Cotton Tail* are to mid-twentieth-century Afro-American music."

Another approach to evaluating Ellington might be to decide which are his most important compositions. After all, if Ellington is to live on in the concert hall, he should be represented by his best work. Ellington did write some symphonic pieces—*The River* is one, *Night Creature* and *The Golden Broom and the Green Apple* two others. Judging from recent performance trends, these are works that future audiences have a good chance of hearing. Yet they have not often been singled out for acclaim. Instead, critical opinion has tended to cluster in two camps. One includes writers like Schuller and Martin Williams, who praise the three-minute "miniatures" composed by Ellington for 78-r.p.m. recordings, especially during 1939–1942. The other includes such younger writers as Stanley Crouch and Gary Giddins, who, while acknowledging the achievements of the "miniatures," defend the extended compositions and suites from the 1940s and after—works like *Black, Brown, and Beige, Such Sweet Thunder,* and *The Latin American Suite*. In his notes for an all-Ellington concert at Lincoln Center last August, Crouch stated that the program (featuring such rarely heard works as *Suite from Anatomy of a Murder* and *Suite Thursday*) countered what he called "the longest reigning misconception in jazz criticism"—that

> Ellington's greatest period was the four year streak of three-minute masterpieces he and his orchestra produced between the years 1939 and 1942.... Between 1942 and ... 1974, Ellington went on to deepen the clarity and conception of his craft, very nearly creating something every decade that was superior to all high points in his previous work.

By contrast, in his forthcoming book *The Swing Era*, Schuller apparently takes a stern view of certain works championed by Giddins and Crouch.

Suppose we step aside from the critical lines of fire and pose another question: What information is needed to undertake a thorough evaluation of Ellington? Certainly we need a *catalogue raisonné*, and we need access to the music either in recorded or written form. We also must learn more about Ellington's compositional method, since by all accounts it was unusual. Here's the rub: except for a few dedicated collectors, most of us lack this basic information.

There is still no complete list of works for Ellington; the estimates for his output range from fifteen hundred to three thousand pieces. Erik Wiedemann, a musicologist at the University of Copenhagen, has been compiling an Ellington catalogue for some years now, but until he finishes, probably the best list is at the back of Ellington's autobiography, *Music Is My Mistress* (Doubleday, 1973).

As for discographical control over Ellington, major work has been done by researchers outside the United States, most notably Benny Aasland in Sweden (*The Wax Works of Duke Ellington*), Dick Bakker in Holland (*Duke Ellington on Microgroove*), and the Italian team of Luciano Massagli, Liborio Pusateri, and Giovanni M. Volonté (*Duke Ellington's Story on Records*).[4] Nevertheless, each month brings newly discovered Ellington radio broadcasts and live recordings—also previously unissued studio material. And new pieces keep turning up, too. For example, on the recent *Duke Ellington: The Private Collection* (LMR CD 83000–83004), there appears *Do Not Disturb*, a work recorded in 1956 but formerly known in a different version as *Le Sucrier Velour*, a movement of the 1959 *Queen's Suite*.

A good guide to the complex maze of Ellington's recording activity is W. E. Timner's *Ellingtonia: The Recorded Music of Duke Ellington and His Sidemen*, 3rd ed. (Metuchen, NJ, and

London: The Institute of Jazz Studies and the Scarecrow Press, Inc., 1988). This 534-page volume tells what Ellington recorded, with whom, and when, but provides no information about reissues. Its index, which tallies the number of recordings per title, can be interesting. The most frequently represented "Ellington" piece on disc is Billy Strayhorn's *Take the "A" Train,* for which Timner has 1,017 entries!

Musicologists do not live, however, by discs alone. Schuller acknowledged this at the end of his *AmeriGrove* entry for Ellington: "Serious study of Ellington's oeuvre has also been hampered by an almost total absence to date of his orchestral music in published form." While the statement still stands, help may be on the way. The most significant event in recent Ellington history was the Smithsonian Institution's acquisition of his personal library, including hundreds of original manuscripts, thousands of orchestral parts, and many sketches. These materials had been inaccessible, locked in a New York warehouse and a bank vault. Now through an appropriation from Congress and the persistent efforts of John Fleckner, head of the Smithsonian's Archives Center, and John Hasse, curator in its Division of Musical History, Ellington's music has come "home"—to the city of his birth. It may be years before all the materials are catalogued and available to scholars. But eventually it will be possible, through comparing what Ellington wrote in scores with what was changed in parts and played on recordings, to learn much more about his compositional process, and to carefully assess his personal contribution, as well as that of Billy Strayhorn and individual orchestra members.

How did Ellington see himself? That is hard to know, since he rarely let his guard down in public. But he once offered a revealing statement that might stand as his artistic credo:

> We are children of the sun and our race has a definite tradition of beauty and glory and vitality that is as rich and powerful as the sun itself. These traditions are ours to express, and will enrich our careers in proportion to the sincerity and faithfulness with which we interpret them.[5]

Ellington here, in 1938, was speaking of a pantheon that consisted not of Bach and Beethoven but of "Bert Williams, Florence Mills and other immortals of the entertainment field." The challenge for historians of American music, it seems to me, is not to determine whether a figure like Ellington measures up to Beethoven, but to learn more about Bert Williams and Florence Mills, and to understand why Ellington would be proud to be viewed in their company. The investigation will direct us not to Lincoln Center but to Harlem's Lincoln Theater; not to Chopin nocturnes but to the songs of Will Marion Cook; not to nineteenth-century European aesthetic principles but to the Afro-American sources which inspired Duke Ellington and which continue to enrich and redefine our culture.

Notes

1. Francis Davis, "Large-Scale Jazz," *Atlantic Monthly* (August 1987), 76.
2. Ralph Ellison, *Going to the Territory* (New York: Vintage Books, 1987), 217.
3. Gunther Schuller, "Ellington in the Pantheon," reprinted in his *Musings* (New York: Oxford University Press, 1986), 47.
4. To determine the availability of these discographies, contact Oak Lawn Books, Box 2663, Providence, RI 02907.
5. Duke Ellington, "From Where I Lie," *The Negro Actor* 1/1 (15 July 1938), 4.

30

The P-Funk Empire
Tear the Roof Off the Sucker
RICKEY VINCENT

"*Make my funk the P-Funk,*" *echoed out of radios and thumped the bass speakers of sound systems across the United States in the summer of 1976. A mere decade after the largely white "Summer of Love," a truly crazed crew of African American freakazoids invaded America's musical mainstream with songs such as "Give Up the Funk (Tear the Roof Off the Sucker)," "Supergroovalisticprosifunkstication," and "Night of the Thumpasorus Peoples." Although the P-Funk album entitled* Mothership Connection *was released in 1975, it fullest impact was felt the following year when "Funk (Wants to Get Funked Up)" and "Give Up the Funk" were issued as singles and enjoyed Top-40 and R&B airplay throughout much of the spring and summer.*

Led by the visionary, and often mind-altered, George Clinton, P-Funk evolved from a vocal group (Parliament) and a funk band (Funkadelic) into a unique organization that blended theater, music, with an otherworldly perspective of life on Planet Earth. Clinton rounded up a crew of talented musicians into this unorthodox troupe, most notably a rhythm section featuring keyboardist Bernie Worrell, Eddie Hazel (guitar), and the frequently diaper-clad bass-thumping Bootsy Collins. Significantly, P-Funk's vibrant, hard-pushing horn section was led by James Brown alumni Maceo Parker and Fred Wesley who, freed from Brown's notoriously short rein, willingly climbed on board the Mothership and helped to steer it in new musical directions.

This (hard)core mob of dedicated funkateers arrived at their large arena shows in a huge Mothership that descended to the stage and then, amid a cacophony of cheers, fat-backed funk, and enormous energy and anticipation, George Clinton stepped out. Often wearing a shoulder-length blond wig, a full-length cape, feathers, and very large sun glasses, the funkmaster worked the crowd like a Baptist preacher. P-Funk shows (circa 1975–1979) were nonstop musical theater, three or four hours of unbridled funk, fun, and freakiness, which can be characterized as James Brown meets Frank Zappa while under the influence of Sun Ra. For many it was new-age gospel music for the soul and mind. Bay-area journalist Rickey Vincent documents this very distinctive and interesting period in a chapter that come from his book Funk—The Music, the People, and the Rhythm of the One.

"Make my funk the P-Funk
I Wants to Get Funked Up!"

Parliament

THE PARLIAMENTS

This fifty-plus member aggregation of geniuses, lunatics, has-beens, wanna-bes, architects, saboteurs, and hangers-on was the epitome of the loose ensemble that by sheer will and musical mastery became a collective creation greater than the sum of its many parts. The Parliament-Funkadelics, or P-Funk (short for "Pure Funk") Mob elevated funk into an ideology. Their grandiose concepts, which preached the redemptive powers of funk, their vast informal enterprise, and their powerful affirmation of common black folks, created a small-scale movement and large-scale following, that, despite their lack of prime-time exposure, P-Funk remains the strongest influence on black music since their popular zenith in 1978.

The P-Funk shockwave hit black music like an earthquake. Among their fundamental ingredients that still reign in black pop today are the electronic "clap" sound, a synthesizer-bass (a bass track played by a keyboard), a shrewdly displayed image of political (and sexual) awareness, and a penchant for elaborately layered horn and vocal lines, often creating a synthesis of European chord structure and African rhythm grooves into a large, ensemble sound. P-Funk introduced these effects along with an eminently subversive lyrical/thematic direction that challenged the apolitical pop music status quo. George Clinton, the troupe's leader, kept the forty- to one-hundred-odd musicians and creative artists focused on one grand concept after another, milking the talents of a variety of people that have yet to reach similar heights away from The Mob. Beginning in 1976 Clinton and P-Funk began producing spinoff acts on different labels, with generally the same personnel, developing what can rightly be labeled a musical empire. Clinton's mastery of the business was taken up by other artists in the 1980s such as Rick James and Prince, who also went on to produce a number of protégés. Perhaps most importantly, Clinton and his merry band of crazies staked out new conceptual territory and asserted a postmodern black aesthetic at a time when sociologists, politicians, and writers were mired in integrationist dialectics.

With inauspicious beginnings as a doo-wop group called the Parliaments in 1956, George Clinton's Mob developed multiple identities and eventually worked their way to black pop superstardom. Born in Kannapolis, North Carolina, July 22, 1941—in an outhouse—George Clinton was well-traveled as a youth and settled in Newark, New Jersey, with his mother and eight younger siblings. He solidified his vocal group in the back room of a barbershop on West 3rd Street in Plainfield, New Jersey, with Calvin Simon and Grady Thomas, recruiting Clarence "Fuzzy" Haskins and most of the backup band through the business at the shop.

In October 1979, Parliament Funkadelic, featuring the lovely Brides of Funkenstein, completed a ten-day run at the Apollo Theater at the close of their "Motor Booty Tour."

Credit: Advertisement from the collection of Kip Lornell.

After some missed opportunities in Newark, Clinton took the band to Detroit to audition for Berry Gordy's Motown Records, often hanging around outside of the offices, singing for anyone who would listen. In typical doo-wop fairy-tale fashion, Martha Reeves, of Martha and the Vandellas, noticed the heartfelt harmonies of the ragged group hanging outside the studios, and the quintet was given an audition. But the Parliaments were only moderately received and only managed a few singles on the small Detroit-based Revilot Records. The group did score a Top 5 R&B hit with "I Wanna Testify" in August 1967, which gave the small-time outfit their first gig at the Apollo in New York. But with the demise of the Revilot label (some say due to "squeezing" from Motown), Clinton lost the group's name and a chance to play a larger role in the Motown family. Some of Clinton's irreverent songwriting made it into Motown, such as "Something I Can't Shake a Loose" to Diana Ross and "I'll Bet You" to the Jackson 5, but the Parliaments appeared done for.

The group didn't sell, but the band was *cool*. Clinton's hair conking was the hippest thang in town ("conking" was a process of melting kinky hair into a smooth, straight look, using dangerous chemicals) and only the heartiest of youngbloods frequented Clinton's barbershop after hours. Younger members of the band were often prohibited from hanging out with the cats at the shop, and word has it that when the bloods put the torch to Plainfield Avenue during the 1967 riots, George Clinton's barbershop was the only thang left standing.

Clinton's resilience would not let him quit. The genius of desperation was one of his trademarks, and facing the imminent demise of his singing group, he gave his rowdy backup band a chance, let loose on a Jimi Hendrix–style black rock image, borrowed the loudest amps they could find—something not done at R&B clubs—and let everyone loose to do their thang. The wild new band was now a mishmash of doo-woppers and rockers—now called Funkadelic (a name bassist Billy Nelson insists he coined on the road with the group), and with the help of Armen Boladian of the Detroit-based Westbound Records, Clinton signed the band.

FUNKADELIC

Funkadelic began with wide-eyed Plainfield youngster Billy Nelson strumming the guitar behind the Parliaments at gigs. After "I Wanna Testify," the group had some clout, and Nelson recruited a local session player, a childhood friend named Eddie Hazel, to play guitar. Aware of Eddie's phenomenal talents, Billy moved aside to let Eddie play lead guitar. Billy grew as a bassist and was given strong support from Motown's bass giant James Jamerson, who encouraged him to develop his own sound. The original Funkadelics consisted of drummer Tiki Fulwood, guitarists Tawl Ross and Eddie Hazel, bandleader Nelson on bass, and Mickey Atkins on organ. The band's grungy sound was accentuated by their efforts to record spacey, cosmic effects with a lack of quality recording techniques.

Funkadelic was a tough sell. Their competition on the original "heavy metal/grunge rock" circuit was the likes of MC5, the Stooges and Iggy Pop, and Grand Funk Railroad. Unlike the well-rehearsed moves of the older Parliaments crew, the band had no training, discipline, or interest in the suited-down look, and it was the youngsters in the Parliafunkadelicment Thang who influenced the psychedelic look of the act. Billy Nelson was frank about it to Rob Bowman:

> To tell you the truth, Eddie and Tiki were two trifling motherfuckers so they didn't want to be clean at all. The three of us just plain out did not want to wear them suits no more. It was all based on the theory, "Well hey, we ain't Parliaments, we're Funkadelic, we don't have to wear that. . . ." We just wore whatever we wanted to wear.

The rest of the act gradually slipped, as George was consistently raggedy from the start, and the slick look began to unravel, as each singer gave up on the suit and developed his own image: Grady had the look of a genie, Fuzzy was in long johns, Calvin donned a wizard's pointed hat, and George resorted to ripping holes in hotel sheets, poking his head through, and heading onstage. Visually, the band appeared like a group of ghetto circus clowns, with an overamped rock sound that never seemed to end. Priding themselves on playing until the crowd would leave, Funkadelics (and their Parliament vocalists) became local legends, and their first album, *Funkadelic*, was just as badly mixed, endless, and *unforgettable* as one of their concerts.

Actually, *Funkadelic* is a blues-rock classic that serves to introduce the Funkadelic concept with perfect clarity—despite the distortion. "If you will suck my soul, I will lick your funky emotions" is the intro to the first cut, "Mommy, What's a Funkadelic?", and the resulting slow throb on that jam, as well as "I'll Bet You" and "Music for My Mother" captured the gritty realism and urban blight of black rock in 1970. On side two, the eight-minute blues rock of "Good Ole Funky Music" was actually placed as a single, and the intro-beat is now a classic Hip Hop beat sample, first made famous by the D.O.C. on "The D.O.C. & the Doctor." On "What is Soul?" Clinton explains the earliest incarnations of his mission, revealing a portent of things to come:

> Behold, I Am Funkadelic
> I Am not of your world
> But fear me not, I will do you no harm
> Loan me your funky mind
> So I can play with it,
> for nothing is good unless you play with it
> And all that is good, is Nasty!
>
> *Funkadelic, "What Is Soul?" (1970)*

BERNIE WORRELL

For the group's second album recording, *Free Your Mind and Your Ass Will Follow,* the band featured keyboardist Bernie Worrell, a child prodigy and occasional teenage patron of Clinton's barbershop who was trained in classical music at New England Conservatory of Music in Boston, and Juilliard in New York City. Worrell was familiar with the antics at Clinton's barbershop and visited as often as he could without his mother finding out. Worrell's strict upbringing and formal training in music provided an eerie landscape of melodic sophistication and complexity that opened the doors for a fantastic form of fusion to occur.

In perhaps the most powerfully symbolic union of the Funk Era, Worrell's competence in classical European musical forms collided and combined with the band's twisted black urban sensibilities to generate a bizarre dichotomy of perspectives—as if Shakespeare and Stagger Lee were dropping acid together in da hood. As new keyboard technologies were made available to musicians in the 1970s, Worrell mastered a vast array of effects, almost single-handedly producing the late-seventies sound of Parliament. His talents were observed worldwide, and in 1981 he recorded with the Tom Tom Club and toured with the Talking Heads. His solo LPs, beginning with his 1978 P-Funk extravaganza *All the Woo in the World,* are all musical adventures worth taking.

With the help of Worrell and other members, P-Funk claimed the most prized elements of the European musical tradition for its own twisted use. Clinton's operatic, layered, chanting vocals and Worrell's gothic, mystical string ensemble tones connected with the band's trashy blues and James Brownish percussive rhythms to generate the archetypical African-American aesthetic in music. More important, P-Funk confiscated European musical aesthetics as a way of symbolizing just how much of Western civilization had been internalized by African-Americans, while the streetwise sensibilities of P-Funk continued to affirm the untenable bond on black/African consciousness within the group.

Playing as two bands, Funkadelic (playing "rock," which is associated with whites) and Parliaments (soul for black radio), the notion of "double consciousness" introduced by W. E. B. Du Bois in 1903 was exposed. What appeared as two acts was actually one entity with many dimensions, as most African-Americans inevitably experience as a result of their struggle in a white country. Du Bois's reference to "two warring ideals in one dark body" has dogged the racial experience in America, as racial minorities are constantly labeled as "sellouts" when status, education, or success is realized. Yet P-Funk transcended this conundrum, as the notions of intellect, education, or sophistication were totally removed from any association with white status. Thus, P-Funk became the *ultimate* in African-American liberation.

THE MAGGOT BRAIN

By the time of the recording of *Maggot Brain* in mid-1971, the Funkadelic lineup consisted of Worrell, Tawl Ross, Billy Nelson, Eddie Hazel, and Tiki Fulwood. Later that year rhythm guitarist Tawl Ross overdosed on LSD, and was abandoned by the ragged group. The resulting focus on lead guitar Eddie Hazel helped the band develop its balance and eventually its legendary lineup.

In one of rock and roll's legendary performances, George Clinton wrote a song so melancholy and compelling, he urged his lead guitarist "to play like your mother just died," and let Eddie Hazel loose in the studio. Hazel's nine-minute solo was a tour de force, challenging the late Jimi Hendrix (one of the few recordings ever to do so) as one of the great guitar solos of all time. A frightening concept had developed surrounding the song: While he denies it, some say Clinton was the one to find his brother's decomposed dead body, skull cracked, in a Chicago apartment—thus the Maggot Brain. "Maggot Brain," like most of Clinton's work, had to do with transcendence, in this case, the need to rise above the "Maggots in the Mind of the Universe," certainly the grimmest of realities from which to escape:

> Mother Earth is pregnant for the third time
> For y'all have knocked her up
>
> I have tasted the Maggots in the mind of the Universe
> and I was not offended
>
> For I knew I had to rise above it all,
> Or drown in my own SHIT!
>
> *Funkadelic, "Maggot Brain" (1971)*

In addition to Clinton's parable on record, he printed in the liner notes a polemic on the crux of fear, written by an obscure religious cult, the Process Church of Final Judgment, which proclaimed, "As long as human beings fail to see THEIR fear reflected in these and a hundred other manifestations of fear, then they will fail to see their part in the relentless tide of hatred, violence, destruction, and devastation, that sweeps the earth." The foreboding musical themes, the screaming black woman's head coming out of the earth on the album cover, and the similarity of the Process Church to mass-murderer Charles Manson's Church of the Final Process left Funkadelic out on their own with the image of a death-worshiping black rock band.

Emboldened by their success with *Maggot Brain*, the band produced the double album *America Eats Its Young*, which again featured liner notes from the Process Church, and an absurd dollar-bill cartoon that featured the Statue of Liberty eating babies (à la the censored version of the Beatles *Yesterday and Today* album). A wild, uneven splatter of rock noise and gospel feel, *America Eats Its Young* only increased the legend of the band.

By this time childhood barbershop homie Garry Shider came of age and joined the act. Shider's presence was integral to Funkadelic's identity, for his strong throat (his father was a preacher), versatile guitar chops, unmistakable diaper garb, and hysterics onstage made his vibe central to the Funkadelic experience. Shider's influence can be heard on the uncharacteristically optimistic ballad "Everybody's Gonna Make It This Time," and he is featured singing the dangerous high range of vocals for the title song of the band's fifth album, 1973's *Cosmic Slop*.

Cosmic Slop was distinctive for two reasons: As an album, no song was longer than five minutes (a first for a Funkadelic LP) and, as a result of pressure from the record label, Clinton pursued new album graphics and hired Chicago artist Pedro Bell, whose scatological landscapes are smeared over all of Funkadelic's album covers through 1981, as well as the four George Clinton solo LPs from 1982 to 1986. Bell's scandalous contributions . . . were by no means a capitulation to the censors. By 1974 the band was already aware of its ability to blast the competition, and Bell captured this sentiment on the album cover to *Standing on the Verge of Gettin' It On* with the claim: "There is nothing harder to stop than an idea whose time has come to pass. Funkadelic is wot time it is!"

By 1974 Eddie Hazel was having troubles and was arrested after a plane flight for allegedly slapping a stewardess while in flight and punching a sky marshal afterward, and landed in jail for nearly a year. Clinton used white Detroit area guitarist Ron Brykowski for the spaced-out guitar chores on *Standing on the Verge of Gettin' It On*, the band's anthem of wanna-be rock stardom anticipation. While the classic "Red Hot Mama" was already in the can featuring Hazel, Brykowski can be heard on the Grateful Dead—sounding "Good Thoughts, Bad Thoughts" and the very trashy "No Head, No Backstage Pass" from the group's next release, *Let's Take It to the Stage*. ("No Head" was sampled in 1990 by platinum rappers Eric B & Rakim on "Lyrics of Fury.")

Album artist Bell captured the psychedelic irreverence of the act, calling Ron Brykowski the band's "polyester, soul-powered token white devil." Bell labeled the young bassist Cordell "Boogie" Mosson "the world's only black leprechaun" and exalted George Clinton as "the nasty and complete minister of all Funkadelia. A scrupled Heathen growth possessing the ultimate creative blasphemies, and undisputed beholder of cosmic crankrot mechanics!" For what it's worth, George managed to live up to the image, and Bell's mutant portraits of the players became part of the Funkadelic experience.

The band continued to record its own raunchy, disconcerting black rock through 1976 on Westbound Records, gaining a reputation as an outrageous live act (that nobody wanted to follow onstage) and musical iconoclasts who never sold many records. *The Rolling Stone Record Guide* (1978) put it like this: "The music of Funkadelic is an urban soundscape—not always pretty or appealing but perhaps the truest representation of urban life offered in black music."

PARLIAMENT

Making use of his contacts with many other veterans of Motown in 1970, Clinton managed to re-sign his vocal act as Parliament for the Invictus label, the label created when Motown Records expatriates Eddie Holland and Lamont Dozier broke from Berry Gordy's stable of songwriters in 1970. The first Parliament album, *Osmium*, is a compilation of recordings performed by the entire group that combined gospel-rock, an absurd affection for country and western hooks, twisted folk-rock, and sleazy, greasy funk. The record, a masterpiece, enjoyed only a small run and was nearly forgotten, until a CD reissue in 1990.

The true success of Parliament began in 1972, when Bootsy and George Clinton finally met. While staying with family friend and show promoter Mallia Franklin in Detroit in 1972, Clinton went to see members of the band known as the Houseguests, playing at one of Franklin's locally promoted club gigs. The Houseguests featured William "Bootsy" Collins on bass and brother "Catfish" on guitar. The Cincinnati-bred brothers had played with James Brown on his hits "Sex Machine," "Superbad," and "Soul Power," but had moved on to enjoy their own brand of creative freedom.

The meeting with Clinton was a success. Both artists had fantastic imaginations, single-parent upbringings (raised by their mothers), and years of drug-induced psychedelic soul music behind them. Clinton and Bootsy quickly became an interlinked creative songwriting duo, a partnership that flourished with the social insight of Lennon and McCartney, the folksy warmth of Simon and Garfunkel, and the strength of Chuck D and Flavor Flav. Clinton has remarked of working with Bootsy, "Bootsy had a perfect personality, he had magnetism no matter what he was doing, whether it was serious funk or silly love songs." Bootsy and Phelps fell into the band so readily, they found themselves *leading* the Funkadelic band after just a couple of gigs, and left shortly afterward, but they would return only a couple of years later.

When Clinton finally signed with Casablanca president Neil Bogart in 1973, things began to change for everyone. Bogart's eye for a gimmick matched Clinton's gift of hype, and the two got things rolling for Parliament in 1974. Bogart knew Clinton in the 1960s and kept George in mind as he worked his way up through the industry at Cameo Parkway and Buddha Records until he took charge of Casablanca in 1973.

Casablanca Records was George Clinton's greatest industry ally and would be the primary reason the P-Funk was able to soar to the top. With money to back him up, Clinton began to expand, recruited Bootsy and Catfish back into the studio, and put the notion in Bootsy's head that *he* could front a band down the road. The pop success began with the Parliament single "Up for the Down Stroke" in the summer of 1974, featuring the return of Bootsy Collins's wicked bass-crunching, some absurd time changes, and a nastayness not heard on black radio since "Sex Machine." The record went to No. 10 R&B. The stirring, political *Chocolate City* hit the streets in the spring of 1975, as Clinton ranted about "Chocolate Cities and Vanilla Suburbs," warning the people that "when they come to march on ya, tell 'em to make sure they have they James Brown pass!" Clinton's absurd brand of black consciousness threw the standard gospel-soul formulas (such as "We Shall Overcome") on their heads, and made Parliament a band to reckon with. While their first two LPs were not received well at the time, *Down Stroke* is rightly becoming recognized as a classic, with *Chocolate City* not far behind.

P-FUNK

In 1975 things really got hot for the P-Funk players. Clinton had been searching for a strong horn section, and by selling Bootsy on the idea of fronting Bootsy's Rubber Band, the pair recruited ex-JBs horn players Fred Wesley, Maceo Parker, and Richard "Kush" Griffith to join the Mob, and an entire rhythmic element of sound (from Wesley's arrangements) completed the Parliament flavor. Based in the four-part harmonies as a vocal doo-wop group, and with the band inspired by Jimi Hendrix as a black rock band, the "Parliafunkadelicment Thang" was already representing a fusion of African-American musical and social values well beyond the range of most black acts. With the gothic, ethereal European classical chords and spacey keyboard riffs from Bernie Worrell; the preposterous gladiator-games horn arrangements from Wesley; the light-saber-sharp guitar chops of Shider, Hazel, and young Michael Hampton all stewed on top of gurgling, dinosaur stomp grooves championed by Bootsy and Mosson; and the stable of drummers, Tiki Fulwood, Tyrone Lampkin, and soon Jerome Brailey, a *monster sound* developed. With Clinton's devious direction, the P-Funk sound would come alive and deliver an all-encompassing musical experience—with its sensibilities straight from the hood. Rhythmically deep, strong, and seasoned, the P-Funk ensemble stretched the musical experience further and further outward.

THE MOTHERSHIP CONNECTION

The Year of the Mothership Connection (1975) began the era of P-Funk as a truly spiritual form of black music in the tradition of jazz, soul, reggae, or gospel. There is much lighthearted significance made about the night in 1975 when Clinton and Bootsy were driving home from Toronto and were "visited." As Clinton told the story to Abe Peck:

> We saw this light bouncing from one side of the street to the other. It happened a few times and I made a comment that "the Mothership was angry with us for giving up the funk without permission." Just then the light hit the car. All the street lights went out, and there weren't any cars around . . . I said, "Bootsy, you think you can step on it."

While nothing was said about the incident between Bootsy and George at the time, things blew up for the band shortly thereafter. Clinton had come up with the *Mothership Connection* concept and sprung it on their label executives Cecil Holmes and Neil Bogart, who gave them the green light—and the greenbacks—without reservations. While Eddie Hazel languished in jail, the phenomenal seventeen-year-old guitarist Michael Hampton joined the group on tour that summer in Cleveland. The brilliantly gifted guitarist and gospel-trained vocalist Glen Goins was picked up back in Plainfield, and when drummer Tiki Fulwood was starting to slip into drug and health problems, former Chambers Brothers drummer Jerome Brailey was recruited just in time for the *Mothership Connection* recording sessions. Jerome Brailey; bassist Cordell "Boogie" Mosson; guitarists Garry Shider, Glen Goins, and Mike Hampton; keyboardist Bernie Worrell; and Bootsy regularly went into the United Sound studios in Detroit and jammed, as George recorded *everything*, adding horns, vocals, and concepts later. In September the band recorded a series of tracks that ultimately became Funkadelic's *Let's Take It to the Stage* LP, Bootsy's Rubber Band's *Stretchin' Out* LP, and Parliament's *Mothership Connection*.

The *Mothership Connection* LP was a motherlode of concepts and rhythm on a level never witnessed before. Lyrics spoke of "returning to claim the pyramids" and "Supergroovalistic-prosifunkstication." For what seemed like the first time ever, a popular black album succeeded with no ballads. Even James Brown's album fillers contained at least *one* down-tempo song, but *Mothership* was an entire funk record—the prototype of the Hip Hop album of the 1990s, in which *every* beat is a funk beat. Parliament had pioneered this. The P-Funk beat, characterized by Jerome "Bigfoot" Brailey's intricate patterns surrounding his throbbing bass-drum kicks, and Bootsy's now legendary rhythmic-melodic complexities, Fred Wesley's meticulous horn arrangements, Bernie Worrell's gothic, sinister keyboard work, the many guitarists, and Clinton's brand of operatic vocal hooks made P-Funk the untouchable thang it is today.

Hip Hoppers discovered the P-Funk gold mine around 1987, but an even more interesting parallel occurred in 1993. In the same fashion that P-Funk went over the top with the *Mothership*, rap star Dr. Dre became a household name with a Hip Hop interpretation of the very same ship. Dr. Dre's three-million-selling LP *The Chronic* was the rap record of the year for 1993 and his tour de force, as well as the introduction of the now infamous Snoop Doggy Dogg. Yet *The Chronic* was the most explicit sampling tribute to the P-Funk at the time, and the *Mothership Connection* was the basis. The title song of *The Chronic* uses the lines from "P-Funk: Make My Funk the P-Funk," replacing "funk" with "shit," and "P-Funk" with "chronic." Even deeper, the melodic breakdown from the title song, "Mothership Connection (Star Child)," was taken and revamped into the Grammy-winning Dr. Dre hit, "Let Me Ride."

Moreover, Parliament had pioneered the idea that The Funk was something that one cannot get enough of. "The funk is its own reward" was the chant, as the *Mothership* concept played on the black church themes of worship to claim that the more you feel The Funk, the closer you get to a transcendent level. As Star Child made clear on "P-Funk (Wants to Get Funked Up)," "The desired effect is what you get when you improve your interplanetary funksmanship." Speaking directly to black teenagers, P-Funk was in tune with the *infinite*, and brought their followers up with them.

To top it off, the band could scorch the dance floor. Before anyone knew what hit them, "Give Up the Funk (Tear the Roof Off the Sucker)" was the No. 1 soul single in the country in June 1976. While the jam was an intricate, highly complex rhythm arrangement (high school bands had an awful time playing *that* one at local dances), the vocals amounted to a wild mix of scorching screams and sinister whispers—"We're Gonna TURN—THIS MUTHA—OUT!!" was followed in a whisper by "let us in—we'll turn this mother out." "Tear the Roof Off" had so much rhythm to it that the original title, "Give Up the Funk," was just not potent enough for the jam, and very quickly after its release, the record became (and is still) known primarily by its longer name, the more appropriately rhythmic "Tear the Roof Off the Sucker." (The record also provided the basis for the breakthrough of M. C. Hammer in 1989, who sampled the jam for his first national hit "Turn This Mutha Out.")

The year 1976 was a real mutha, as P-Funk delivered five now-classic albums under four different names for three different labels. A preposterous follow-up album for Parliament, *Clones of Dr. Funkenstein*, became the vehicle for George (now known as "Dr. Funkenstein") Clinton to express his ultimate ego trips. With lyrics like "kiss me on my ego," Clinton had begun to toy with the incredible underground celebrity he was attaining, and on "Children of Production," Clinton was bold enough to give the band so much juice it was frightening: "we are deeper than abortion/deeper than the notion/that the world was flat when it was round/we're gonna blow the cobwebs out your mind!" Still with the legendary lineup of musicians, the alter-ego hard-rock band Funkadelic continued to record, and released two albums in 1976, one for their old label Westbound *(Tales of Kidd Funkadelic)* and one for Warner Brothers *(Hardcore Jollies)*. "Kidd Funkadelic" was actually the newly acquired guitarist Michael Hampton, but the thirteen-minute keyboard groove instrumental title cut featured *no* guitars. The record is so strong, as was the entire album (liner artist Pedro Bell at his Daliesque best on this disc as well) that Hampton's tracks were not needed. The band made up for it on *Hardcore Jollies*, featuring Hampton and the return of Eddie Hazel on a number of ballistic rock thrashers, "Good to Your Earhole," "Hardcore Jollies," and a live rendition of "Cosmic Slop" for good measure. *Hardcore Jollies* indeed. Bootsy's Rubber Band hit the streets as well that year, delivering a sexy, silly style of rapping above a liquid bass, serving up a monster hit single "Stretchin' Out," a song so rhythmic, chord-heavy, noisy, and stylish that it raised one's funk expectations to a new attention.

BOOTSY'S RUBBER BAND

The Rubber Band began in the studio, when the original "Stretchin' Out" groove finally began to cook, as Bootsy, Mike Hampton, and Garry Shider were churning out the licks. The groove moved Bootsy to say, "Man, we're stretchin' out on that one," and as usual, George Clinton heard it, snapping back, "That's it, stretchin' out *in a Rubber Band*!" The rest became the nastayest and most liberated form of P-Funk, symbolically the *exposed genitals* of the P-Funk vibe. Bootsy Collins made a name for himself quickly, releasing the *Stretchin' Out* album in early 1976 and *Aaah the Name Is Bootsy, Baby*! in the spring of 1977. With a giddy, childlike geepiness as a stage showman (listen to "Psychoticbumpschool," or "Rubber Duckie") and an erotic troubador with a "verbal rappability" and orgiastic bass effects ("Munchies for Your Love," "What's a Telephone Bill"), Bootsy's Rubber Band was the complete erotic funk experience. Supported by the amazingly soulful falsetto vocal chops of Gary "Mudbone" Cooper, who brought glee club energy to the vocals; Fred Wesley and Maceo Parker's amazing decision to leave James Brown and join the Rubber Band; and Cincinnati buddies Frankie "Kash" Waddy on drums and Joel "Razor Sharp" Johnson on keys, the Rubber Band soon took on a life of its own.

Bootsy's 1977 release featured an excellent example of P-Funk's appropriation of Western cultural references for their own use: "The Pinocchio Theory" was taken to mean: "If you fake the funk, your nose gots to grow!" The record also featured a mock-live recording introducing Casper, the bass-playing ghost, as well as a ten-minute psychedelic ballad titled "Munchies for Your Love" which set Bootsy apart from all other bass performers, with a Jimi Hendrix–style rock solo that was drenched in erotic intensity. Bootsy took his popularity to new heights in 1978, with *Player of the Year*, an album that featured the funk classics "Bootzilla" and "Hollywood Squares." He called himself "The Star," years before Prince would claim that moniker, and (under the influence of his managers) created a mystique that kept Bootsy from the public, yet kept the public buying his mysteriously funky, sexy music.

Spinoff acts were popping up everywhere. Female vocalists Jeannette Washington and Sheila Horne were packaged as the Brides of Funkenstein and sang over two LPs worth of now classic material on *Funk or Walk* and *Never Buy Texas from a Cowboy*. Guitarist Eddie Hazel recorded *Games, Dames and Guitar Thangs* for Warner Brothers in 1978—easily one of the best P-Funk albums ever. Bernie Worrell delivered *All the Woo in the World* for Arista, Fred Wesley and the Horny Horns worked out two albums of groove tracks for Atlantic, and a bevy of females were lined up for Parlet, dropping three LPs for Casablanca.

Something happened along the way to the P-Funk circus. In the midst of all of the chaos and clutter, P-Funk bands managed to affect black music in at least two phenomenal ways: creative genius and financial disaster. Musically, the band introduced the electronic age into modern black music, by incorporating the most modern forms of technology while remaining identified with the James Brown groove and the bro on the street. Keyboardist Bernie Worrell was crucial to the technologization of black popular music—but had he raised the standards impossibly high? As one funkateer put it, "The world can either credit him or blame him for the synthesizer bass." P-Funk's fantastic science fiction created a series of spectacular "otherworlds" that Africans could inhabit freely, in which one could be loving, caring, sensual, psychedelic, and nasty without fear of cosmic retribution, and whites simply did not exist. The symbolic connections of P-Funk concepts to one's earthly struggles for freedom were felt by many listeners, particularly black teenagers. Furthermore, the assertion of a black worldview that incorporates modern technology, the demographics of the seventies, and a black aesthetic was a profound theoretical breakthrough, despite the silliness. Such grand visions of black people were not found in black film, black literature, or black politics in the late 1970s.

Yet the organized mayhem led to an equally awesome magnitude of confusion, as players came and went, the money was hard to locate, and people rarely knew who was in charge. Manager and producer Robert Middleman recalled his early role in the P-Funk Mob: "It was my job to tell the musicians why they weren't getting paid." Indeed, the story of "who owns the P-Funk" is deserving of a book in itself. Nevertheless, at the time, the P-Funk Earth Tour was a thing to behold.

THE EARTH TOUR

P-Funk was challenging the established giants in the industry. While the Ohio Players, Commodores, and Earth, Wind & Fire were enormously popular, their appeal crossed racial lines, while the P-Funk Mob appeared to outsiders as some sort of disco-voodoo cult. Undaunted, and with the help of Casablanca Record executives Neil Bogart and Cecil Holmes, Clinton secured the services of Jules Fischer, the set designer who had produced the stage sets for the rock bands Kiss and the Rolling Stones. With a $275,000 budget—the largest ever for any black act—Parliament took the Mothership Connection to the people, and *landed* the Mothership on stage. Meticulously rehearsed in an airport hangar in Upstate New York (one of the few times P-Funk was deliberately rehearsed to be tight live), Clinton had a wild plan for everything, from his polyester pimpmobile entrance—a stage-prop tribute to the badass gangstas and hustlers that made up life in da hood—through Garry Shider's flight through the rafters with the Bop Gun, and the endless animated props and costumes, to the thunderous descent of the Mothership. Equal parts tribal dance ("gaa gaa goo gaa!"), church revival ("swing down, sweet chariot/stop and let me ride"), and call-and-response nightclub hype ("we love to funk you Funkenstein/your funk is the best!"), the P-Funk act drew from the ribald, uncensored entirety of the black tradition in mind-blowing ways no one had yet even attempted.

Inaugurated in New Orleans in October 1976 (voodoo cult indeed?), the P-Funk Earth Tour headed westward, and recorded their seminal P-Funk Earth Tour on January 19, 1977, at the Forum in Los Angeles and on January 21, 1977, at the Oakland Coliseum. Many of the West Coast rap stars that are so well known for incorporating P-Funk music were cloned by The Funk at these Earth Tour concerts.

The Earth Tour was the culmination of the entire musical movement of the decade toward larger shows, larger venues, and larger profits. Subsequent theme-oriented "funk operas" told the story of "Sir Nose D'Voidoffunk," "Mr. Wiggles," and "Gloryhallastupid." Interestingly, in the midst of the high-profile success in 1978, Clinton deliberately took the band on an "anti-tour," performing in small clubs, without props or costumes, avoiding the ego trips of stardom, and just *jamming*. The success continued through 1980, although there were signs of wear and tear on the group. While there were other acts in competition for dominance in black music, the release of *Parliament Live: The P-Funk Earth Tour* live recording in May 1977 set to rest any illusions that "color-blind" music could substitute for the dark realities of black funk.

FLASHLIGHT AND ONE NATION

At the peak of the band's popularity as a far-out, ghoulish band of funk freaks in late 1977, Parliament released the first of five megahits that would take them over the top. While they were already well known to dance music fans for "Tear the Roof Off the Sucker," their follow-up hits "Do That Stuff" and "Bop Gun" appeared to sound like extra helpings for the funk clones only. "Flashlight" changed all that. Sneaking up on funk fans as the last song on the *Funkentelechy vs. the Placebo Syndrome* LP, the record obliterated the standards of dance music when it hit the radio in early 1978. It slithered along with layers of shrill, atmospheric string synthesizers, absurd vocal vamps ("Now I lay me down to sleep . . ."), a scorching, liquified guitar track (played by Phelps "Catfish" Collins, according to brother Bootsy), and an astoundingly loud clap track on the beat that drove listeners crazy when "Flashlight" hit the AM radio.

But what took the record over the top was the bass. *The* Bass. *The BASS!* Keyboardist Bernie Worrell had mastered the keyboard bass, and played with the subtle accents and walking bass line that any accomplished bass player might use—yet this bass sounded like nothing ever played before. The Moog synthesizer was capable not only of playing low notes, but of stacking a number of bass tones onto one key—creating the fullest bass sound ever played. Worrell's bass tones sounded louder than any other bass track heard on the radio because of this stacking effect, and his wizardry with freakish note-bending effects created a mind-scraping, Thumpasaurus gribble grind that forever changed the bottom groove in popular music. By the time the record faded and the chant "Everybody's got a little bit of light, under the sun" wound down, a new realm of The Funk had been discovered. Bands everywhere began playing stacked bass lines on their keyboards, often with disappointing results. Bernie Worrell was a child prodigy—a master of any keyboard—who had commanded the ultimate funk effect.

The record soared to No. 1 R&B (three weeks there), and made it to No. 16 on the pop charts in the spring of 1978. Parliament had made it big. Yet right on the heels of Parliament, riding the spastic funk explosion, was Bootsy's Rubber Band's most guttural and expressive hit, "Bootzilla"—another classic funk dinosaur that followed "Flashlight" at No. 1 soul. (Bootsy was apparently way too freaky for the pop charts, and "Bootzilla" never came close.)

Yet just as the glow of the "Flashlight" was fading from the radio in the summer of 1978, a strangely grooving, fast-paced percussive scorcher hit the radio. The record featured eerily sweet harmonies, a strange vocal tone from (their latest recruit, Ohio Players veteran keyboardist) Junie Morrison, an unrelenting splatter of percussion, and that fat, liquid bass synthesizer once again—Funkadelic had assaulted the dance floor with a monster that ripped apart the formulas for disco dance tracks. "One Nation Under a Groove" pulsed and throbbed, oozed with rhythm, slipped in subtle lyrical statements, and stood at No. 1 R&B for six weeks—the biggest seller of the year (even *Jet* magazine named "One Nation" the song of the year for 1978). For a minute, P-Funk was a pop phenomenon. Even Top 40 countdown deejay Kasey Casem delivered the P-Funk saga as one of his many trivia tales ("Can you name the act with two songs in the Top 40 this year, recorded under different names? The answer in a minute . . .").

Later in 1978, Parliament dared to follow up "Flashlight" with the preposterous "Aqua-Boogie," yet another No. 1 soul hit, and when the multilayered Funkadelic dance masterpiece "(Not just) Knee Deep" went No. 1 the following summer, P-Funk's dominance over the dance floor was assured.

Even the average music fan was beginning to wonder about the Parliament and Funkadelic thing. Who *were* these guys? Which one was George Clinton? What's a Funkadelic? By 1977 the Casablanca Records promotions people had taken an interest in Clinton's ideas and released the *Earth Tour* album in May 1977 with a two-by-three-foot poster *and* an iron-on T-shirt transfer in each record. The next LP, *Funkentelechy vs. the Placebo Syndrome*, offered a bright pink poster of Sir Nose D'Voidoffunk and a twelve-page full color comic book describing the escapades of the "funky superheroes." The 1978 *Motor Booty Affair* LP featured a pop-up cartoon rendition of Atlantis when the album was opened, and stand-up cut-outs of even more P-Funk characters were featured. Mattel toys entered into negotiations with the group to feature a set of *toy dolls* of the main characters in the group (a Dr. Funkenstein doll, a Bootsy doll, and a Star-Child doll!). The project was nixed because of disagreements over rights and royalties for the images. But any way you look at it, P-Funk was hot stuff. Even the often stingy Warner Brothers allowed Clinton to release an extra seven-inch single (containing a live version of "Maggot Brain" targeted at rock radio) inside the *One Nation Under a Groove* Funkadelic LP in 1978.

With Clinton's P-Funk, The Funk was elevated from a style to a way of life, but the lifestyle was only an ideal, a reality only on the stage. Before the phenomenal success, the band existed as a family, traveling, smoking, loving, creating, performing, and living together. With the success came hangers-on, stronger drugs, and lawyers. The massive entourage of the P-Funk tours ran into trouble as the industry declined, and by 1981 forces of corruption from within and without drastically reduced the group's ability to make strong music and remain on the radio. Band members who were recruited simply on the strength of the band's reputation wound up on tours or in strange towns without getting paid. Tensions were high and morale was low when Clinton "retired" in 1980, just as the band was scheduled to play a week at the Apollo Theater in Harlem—and the band played without George for the most part, although he made a few cameos.

As early as 1978 band members left the group and recorded their own music with lyrics openly critical of George Clinton. Jerome Brailey was the most vehement expatriate, leaving to produce his own band, Mutiny, whose awesome first album, *Mutiny on the Mamaship*, was wrought full of jibes at Clinton's ego, though the group's fonk was clearly in the mold of the P. The supremely talented vocalist Glen Goins left at the same time as Brailey, and recorded with Brailey the only album of the band, *Quazar*, before dying of Hodgkin's disease on July 30, 1978. Three original members of the Parliaments, Clarence "Fuzzy" Haskins, Calvin Simon, and Grady Thomas, also set out on their own in 1981 calling themselves Funkadelic, and appearing on *Soul Train*, also ripping Clinton on choice cuts of their mildly funky anachronism of an album *Connections and Disconnections*. Nevertheless the myth lived on, and Clinton persevered with a constantly changing lineup to field a band throughout the 1980s (all of these P-Funk spinoffs are delectable collector's items).

The demise of Casablanca Records and the death of Neil Bogart from cancer in 1982 eliminated one of Clinton's strongest and most generous allies. Meanwhile, Warner Brothers gave Clinton constant trouble and had his 1981 Funkadelic album *The Electric Spanking of War Babies* reduced from a two-record set to one disc and had Pedro Bell's phallic cover art censored, despite the fact that the band was following up two consecutive million-selling records. Meanwhile, Bootsy's Rubber Band found itself in a lawsuit over the "Rubber Band" name, apparently used by a country rock group in 1971. Bootsy's people incredibly lost the lawsuit, and Bootsy found himself over $275,000 in debt to his label, forced to give profits from later albums (such as the *Sweat Band* and Bootsy's *The One Giveth*) directly to Warner Brothers. It would be five years before Bootsy released himself from the contract and put out another record under his name, *What's Bootsy Doin'*, on Columbia Records in 1988.

Losing Parliament and Funkadelic almost overnight (and going out of style just as quickly) the P-Funk took a nosedive underground. While his creative input was invaluable, Clinton often brought complete legalistic and financial chaos to his projects. (Roger Troutman and his band Zapp saw the writing on the wall, and after Bootsy and George helped to bring about the first Zapp album, Roger and Zapp jumped ship, to record their own brand of monster funk . . . without the financial risks of The P.)

By the mid-1980s it appeared that anyone collaborating with George Clinton gave the impression that they were at the end of the line. Sly Stone's career never really "recovered" during his years with the P-Funk, while the band's recording with James Brown was done during one of Brown's lowest points of popularity in 1980. British rocker Thomas Dolby followed his 1983 megahit "She Blinded Me with Science" with funky duets with Clinton, "The Cube" and "Hot Sauce," and then proceeded to vanish into obscurity. Even the dethroned Miss America Vanessa Williams wound up—in the pit of her public scorn in 1988—recording with George Clinton (check out "Hey Good Lookin'" on the *R&B Skeletons* album). Clinton's collaboration with "the artist formerly known as Prince" that began in 1989 appears to have only brought him down to Clinton's underground level, and after Michael Jackson's problems with child molestation charges, his 1995 collaboration with Dr. Funkenstein seemed inevitable.

ATOMIC DOG

Despite being literally blacklisted from radio airplay, Clinton was able to continue the P-Funk magic show for four more years and four albums on the strength of his best hit of the 1980s—the dance-music classic "Atomic Dog." Clinton was able to sell himself to Capitol Records in 1982 with the help of Ted Currier, a funkateer at Capitol, and the fact that Clinton had hundreds of hours of music already produced and waiting for release. No record in modern black music history has had a more storied history than "Atomic Dog." The song is now a classic of black popular music, and perhaps the most sampled rhythm hook of all time.

An almost forgotten second single from Clinton's *Computer Games* LP for Capitol Records ("Loopzilla" was the first), the record was held back from the major R&B stations, and only after incredibly strong sales did stations begin to pick it up. In many cases across the country, "Atomic Dog" was the No. 1 R&B record, but was not on the playlist of R&B stations. Clinton's bad reputation with the industry, his political consciousness (as seen on his previous Funkadelic records), and a general move toward more youthful-looking acts kept him out of the loop. Lurking for six weeks at No. 2 behind Michael Jackson's "Billie Jean," "Atomic Dog" finally went to No. 1, lasted for four weeks, and in the most inexplicable turn of events, the record never made the pop Top 100—which was supposed to be automatic for No. 1 soul hits!

Meanwhile, the record became an instant classic, ripping dance floors with its backward-swinging synthesizer hooks, Clinton's characteristically absurd vocalizing ("Why must I feel like that/why must I chase the cat!"), and hilariously accurate expressions of the doglike nature of horny men (and women). The record captured the irreverent essence of the sexual drive in the electronic age. The black fraternity Omega Psi Phi (known as the "Q" dogs) claimed "Atomic Dog" as its theme song, and a slew of artists copied the hook note-for-note on their sexiest sides, from Karyn White's "Walkin' the Dog" to Teddy Riley's "Do the D.O.G.G." and Ice Cube's "The Nigga You Love to Hate," "My Summer Vacation," and "Ghetto Bird." Clinton himself recycled the hook on his 1983 rap version of "Dog Talk," his 1990 "Why Should I Dog U Out?," and his 1993 "Martial Law." "Atomic Dog" continues to thrive today as perhaps the *jam* of the 1980s.

After label difficulties, once again with Capitol, Clinton signed with the Paisley Park label, created by the black pop-rock superstar once known as Prince. The resulting collaborations ("Bob George" in 1988, "We Can Funk" in 1989, and "Tweakin'" remix in 1990) have produced only moderately stanky results, although the music of then-Prince has shown an even deeper appreciation of R&B and funk roots.

With little or no black radio airplay, Clinton found allies in the predominantly white hard rock scene (just as he did in 1970 with Armen Boladian and Westbound Records), and produced the second album for the upstart rock quartet the Red Hot Chili Peppers in 1985. Clinton appeared on and coproduced projects with British new-waver Thomas Dolby while producing a dance version of Warren Zevon's perplexing "Leave My Monkey Alone" in 1987. Clinton's band, while only a prototype for his nineties act, appeared on *Saturday Night Live* in 1986, and with the support of *Late Night* bandleader and devoted funkateer Paul Shaffer, Clinton appeared for the first of many times on David Letterman's show in 1986. The entire group performed in a chaotic bash on national television with the Red Hot Chili Peppers at the 1993 Grammy Awards, and toured with the "Lollapalooza" art-pop tour in the summer of 1994.

By 1988, when hard-core rap invaded the mainstream of music on the strength of Public Enemy's phenomenal recording *It Takes a Nation of Millions to Hold Us Back,* Clinton began to get some respect in the black music industry. The first single from the album, "Bring the Noise," was driven by the sampled loop from the 1975 Funkadelic tune "Get Off Your Ass and Jam." The militancy of rap music in 1988 was a marked turnaround from the somewhat adolescent raps of LL Cool J, Doug E. Fresh, and Run-D.M.C., who had dominated pop rap until then. The seriousness of the inner city, and the directness which Public Enemy (and other hard-core rappers such as KRS-One of Boogie Down Productions, Melle Mel, and Afrika Bambaataa) addressed the problems of their communities, recalled images of old-school funk, including Parliament's "Chocolate City," Stevie Wonder's "Living for the City," and James Brown's "Say It Loud (I'm Black and I'm Proud)."

For rap producers, the music of James Brown was the sample of the day back in 1988, but as rap music became more thematic, conceptual, and serious, straightforward braggadocio and the generic "Power to the People" chant needed more support. It was at this point that the Clinton/P-Funk loop surpassed James Brown as the jingle of choice (just as P-Funk surpassed the JBs fonk as the groove of choice in the 1970s). With the range of black rap music opening up to wider realms, the P-Funk catalog became the staple, and the standard by which stylistic breadth was conceptualized in Hip Hop sampling. Other known rap acts like Schooly D ("Saturday Nite"), EPMD ("Who's Booty," "So Whatcha Sayin'"), and De La Soul ("Me Myself and I") began to incorporate obvious and not-so-obvious P-Funk loops into their music.

The Oakland-based rap group Digital Underground went literally overboard with their allegiance to P-Funk, by first signifying on the underwater theme of the 1978 "Aqua Boogie" Parliament hit, recording a song on their platinum 1989 album *Sex Packets* entitled "Underwater Rimes." The group's third album was titled *Sons of the P* and claimed allegiance to Clinton, identifying the group as children of the "Father of Funk." The rappers also borrowed the P-Funk style of creating cartoon characters to enhance their image, and featured Dr. Funkenstein himself, George Clinton, on the title song, "Sons of the P," in 1991. Greg Jacobs, a.k.a. "Humpty Hump," recalls the "mind-shattering experience" of working with the Doctor:

> I don't know whether it is good or bad, but George blew our minds wide open when we was working with him in terms of how to hear things and how to play things and how to just kind of just let it happen, rather than to control and try to make it a certain way, just let it flow out of us. . . . He led me onto a theory that we're just conveyors, we're just, you might say, the people that are directing the energy in the funk, but he seems to feel like it's a collective spirit that comes from the whole rhythm of the world, the rhythm of people. Brothers seem to have a rhythm with everything they do. One of the things George was about, was capturing that in the studio.

The Rhythm of the One was and is an operating principle of P-Funk, and it has seeped into even the most mechanical of musical forms, Hip Hop.

As the P-Funk mythology continued to grow at the dawn of the nineties, the band continued to tour. While Clinton continues to find recording difficulties, the group is gaining a new generation of followers as a result of the reissues of P-Funk material by various publishers, and recording after recording of rap music is maintained by the rhythmic, melodic, and conceptual explication of the "Parliafunkadelicment Thang."

Sources and Notes

PAGE

260 "P-Funk Wants to Get Funked Up" written by George Worrell Jr, William Collins and George Jr. Clinton©Published by Bridgeport Music Inc. Administered by Kobalt Music Publishing Limited

262 "George Clinton's barbershop was the only thang left standing." "George Clinton: Ultimate Liberator of Constipated Notions," W. A. Brower, *Downbeat,* April 5, 1979, p. 17.

262 "Eddie and Tiki were two trifling motherfuckers" Billy Nelson quoted in Rob Bowman, liner notes to *Music for Your Mother,* Westbound Records, 1993.

263 "Behold, I Am Funkadelic" Funkadelic, "What is Soul?" George Clinton, Jr./William "Billy" Nelson/Eddie Hazel. Copyright © 1970 by Bridgeport Music Inc. (BMI) and Southfield Music Inc. (ASCAP) All rights reserved. Used by permission.

264 "Maggot Brain" Funkadelic. George Clinton, Jr./Eddie Hazel. Copyright © 1971 by Bridgeport Music Inc. (BMI) and Southfield Music Inc. (ASCAP) All rights reserved. Used by permission.

264 "As long as human beings fail to see THEIR fear" "Process Church of Final Judgement" liner notes to *Maggot Brain.* LP, Westbound Records, 1971.

265 "Funkadelic is wot time it is!" Pedro Bell liner art. Funkadelic LP, *Standing on the Verge of Gettin' It On,* Westbound Records, 1974.

265 "the truest representation of urban life offered in black music," *The Rolling Stone Record Guide,* 1977 ed.

266 "Bootsy had a perfect personality" George Clinton quoted in *Terminal Zone.* July, 1988, issue no. 1.

267 "We saw this light bouncing from one side... to the other." "A Funky view of the universe, courtesy of a band of weirdos," Abe Peck, *Oakland Tribune,* December 26, 1976, 13-E.

268 "P-Funk Wants to Get Funked Up" written by George Worrell Jr, William Collins and George Jr. Clinton©Published by Bridgeport Music Inc. Administered by Kobalt Music Publishing Limited

268 "Children of Productions" written by George, Worrell Jr and George Jr. Clinton©Published by Bridgeport Music Inc. Administered by Kobalt Music Publishing Limited
Tercer-Mundo, Inc. Used by permission.

269 "The world can either credit him or blame him for the synthesizer bass." Interview with Teo Barry Vincent in June, 1994.

271 "Flashlight" written by George Worrell Jr Clinton Published by Bridgeport Music Inc. Administered by Kobalt Music Publishing Limited.

272 "Rubber Band" name lawsuit info courtesy of Pedro Bell and *Jet.* April 17, 1980.

274 "George blew our minds wide open" Telephone interview with Greg "Shock G" Jacobs in October, 1993.

31

Hip-Hop, Puerto Ricans, and Ethnoracial Identities in New York

RAQUEL Z. RIVERA

In the twenty-first century, hip hop is almost always identified as African American expressive culture. That black Americans are at the artistic core of hip hop is beyond dispute. Because hip hop emerged from New York City's complex urban melting pot in the mid-1970s, its racial and ethnic origins are quite complicated. The truth is that in New York City, and the Bronx in particular, Latinos contributed greatly to hip hop's early development. Puerto Ricans, specifically, have played the largest role among Latinos in helping to define hop hop culture.

In this detailed article, Rivera argues that Puerto Ricans have more in common with the historical experiences of African Americans than Dominicans, Chicanos, or any other Lantino groups. She further argues that Puerto Ricans in New York have played a critical, underappreciated, and misunderstood, role as participants, consumers, and creators of hip hop since the mid-1970s "Hip-Hop, Puerto Ricans, and Ethnoracial Identities in New York" doesn't attempt to recast nearly three decades of hip hop history. Rather, Rivera explores several key "moments" (each of which lasted up to several years) over the past thirty years during which Puerto Rican contributions to hip hop are both identifiable and important.

The first moment occurred in the early- to mid-1970s in the south Bronx, where Puerto Ricans constituted the majority of residents. Many of the early elements of hip hop, such as break dancing and graffiti, are more closely linked to Puerto Ricans than other forms of expressive culture—most notably rhyming and DJing—that are more clearly associated with African Americans. In 1979, "Rapper's Delight" was released by the Sugarhill Gang, but during the nascent days of hip hop many local Puerto Rican rappers such as Devasating Tito of the Fearless Four, the Fat Boy's Markie Dee Morales, and the Real Roxanne emerged as important figures in commercial black music.

Some twenty years later, as the twentieth century was closing, hip hop had become a worldwide phenomenon. Rivera identifies several other important moments in the last two decades of the twentieth century but ends her essay with a meditation on "break-out" interest in Latin music in general and specifically with Puerto Ricans' continued involvement with hip hop culture. In closing she argues that hip hop has actually splintered New York's younger Puerto Ricans into two broad camps: One group identifies more readily with the Caribbean aspects of their culture. The other, however, continues to identify more closely with the experiences of African Americans in establishing an "Afro-diasporic Caribbean" culture that is not wholly subsumed but is closely associated with black American culture. Hip hop, the author suggests, provides perhaps the most vibrant form of cultural expression for more recent crews of younger Puerto Ricans.

Word Up magazine did an article where they mentioned me and it was called "The Latinos in Hip-Hop." What's wack about that is that they have to separate us [Latinos] [from blacks]. And I hated that. I was in the same article as Kid Frost, you know, [who did the song] "La Raza." And I was like, come on, man, what do I have to do with Kid Frost? It's just totally different things and they're trying to funnel us all together. You never hear an article called "The Blacks in Hip-Hop."

The above is a fragment of a conversation I had in 1995 with Q-Unique, a skilled and feisty MC who is a member of the Arsonists (a popular New York underground rap group that released its debut album, *As the World Burns*, in August 1999 with Matador Records) and the Rock Steady Crew (the legendary hip-hop organization better known for its contributions to the dance form known as breaking). A self-described hip-hop[1] activist committed to nourishing a socially responsible, historically grounded, holistic hip-hop creativity, Q. deeply resents being segregated, as a Puerto Rican, from a hip-hop cultural core that is assumed to be African American.

The problem that Q. describes is two-fold. First, hip-hop is ahistorically taken to be an African American expressive culture. Latinos (Puerto Ricans included) are thus excised from the hip-hop core on the basis of a racialized panethnicity. Second, as Latino population numbers and visibility increase in the United States, a variety of national-origin groups (Puerto Ricans, Chicanos, Dominicans, and so on) with different experiences of colonization, annexation, and/or immigration to the United States, as well as different histories of structural incorporation and racialization, are lumped under the Latino panethnic banner (Flores 1996a; Oboler 1995). This wider social phenomenon manifests itself within the hip-hop realm when Latinos are grouped together on the hip-hop margins under the presumed commonalties shared by Latino hip-hoppers.

What does a New York Puerto Rican MC like Q. have in common with a West Coast Chicano artist like Kid Frost? According to Q., the answer is, not necessarily more than what he shares with an African American MC from New York City. The ethnic funneling that he criticizes relies on prescribed experiential and artistic commonalties based on a panethnic label. Facile and questionable panethnic connections are thus drawn—in this case, between Puerto Ricans and Chicanos on opposite coasts—which may actually serve to erase other more concrete, historically-based, transethnic connections—as those between Puerto Ricans and African Americans in New York.

Puerto Ricans in the United States are commonly thought of as being part of the U.S. Hispanic or Latino population. But Puerto Ricans are also considered an exception among Latinos. Their exceptionality is based on a history that diverges from what has been construed as the Latino norm and happens to share much in common with the experience of African Americans (Chávez 1991; Flores 1996a; Smith 1994).

This essay explores the ways in which New York Puerto Ricans have navigated the murky waters of ethnoracial[2] identification within the hip-hop realm. My main contention here is that those Puerto Ricans who take part in New York's hip-hop culture construct their identities, participate, and create through a process of negotiation with the dominant notions of blackness[3] and Latinidad. Puerto Ricans fit in both categories and yet in neither.

What follows is an exploration of several moments in hip-hop's two decades and a half of history. Through it, I aim to discuss how constructions and experiences of class, ethnicity, and race have had bearing on the creative participation of Puerto Ricans in hip-hop culture. I maintain that certain articulations of class and ethnoracial identities have resulted in the construction of Puerto Ricans as virtual Blacks,[4] made them seem an exception for dominant definitions of Latino panethnicity, and facilitated their construction as part of a hip-hop Afro-diasporic "ghetto-ethnicity" (McLaren 1995:9).[5] On the other hand, understandings of Puerto Rican identity that privilege a Latinidad constructed in opposition to Blackness have landed Puerto Ricans participating in hip-hop culture in the precarious position of defending their Afro-diasporic ghetto-ethnicity and their history and creative role in hip-hop. The privileging of this kind of Latinidad leaves Puerto Ricans who participate in hip-hop explaining why they take part in a culture (mis)understood to be African American cultural property.

Hip-hop is one of the most vibrant products of late-twentieth-century youth culture. New York Puerto Ricans have been key participants, as producers and consumers of culture, in hip-hop art forms since hip-hop's very beginnings during the early 1970s in the South Bronx (Cross 1993; Flores 1988; Rose 1994; Toop 1991). This essay is meant as a contribution to the history of Puerto Rican hip-hop heads in New York as well as a necessary angle from which the Latinization of New York must be explored.[6] Useful insights can be obtained through studying how the younger generations of the Latino group with the longest, most visible presence in New York—namely, Boricuas—have grappled with and been affected by said Latinization. So here we go.

THE 1970s: IT'S JUST BEGUN

The South Bronx is widely recognized as the place where the art forms that make up the expressive foundation of hip-hop—MCing, or rhyming; DJing; breaking (b-boying/b-girling); and graffiti writing—first came together under very specific terms during the first half of the 1970s. African Americans, Puerto Ricans, and West Indians were the groups most heavily involved in the development of these expressive forms (Rose 1994; Thompson 1996).

Puerto Ricans made up the majority of the population in the South Bronx at the time (Rodríguez 1991:109). Together with African Americans and other Caribbean people, they accounted for an overwhelming proportion of the population in this impoverished Bronx area in 1970. Consistent with these groups' class standing, hip-hop was created by poor and working-class youth. In the words of Q-Unique and b-boy Ken Swift, among countless others, it began as a ghetto phenomenon (Q-Unique 1995a; Verán 1991).

Hip-hop was an ethnoracially inclusive sphere of cultural production. During hip-hop's formative years, "the strongest move was unity" (as Sekou Sundiata [1998:4] says of the previous decade), but ethnoracial distinctions and tensions still manifested themselves. These distinctions and tensions varied depending on various factors, among them neighborhood and art form.

The participation and perceived entitlement of Puerto Ricans with respect to hip-hop art forms were contingent upon locality. The South Bronx and East Harlem evidenced relatively subtle ethnoracial rifts and more transethnic cultural interaction; these rifts seemed to be greater and transethnic interaction less pronounced in other neighborhoods, particularly those with greater ethnic residential segregation.

The perceived entitlement to hip-hop of Puerto Ricans also depended on the art form. Whereas graffiti and breaking were largely taken to be multi-ethnic inner-city forms, MCing and DJing—though widely practiced by various Afro-diasporic ethnic groups—were identified more with one group, namely, African Americans.

Puerto Ricans were, for the most part, welcome and active participants in hip-hop. But even during these early times, Puerto Ricans had to step lightly on hip-hop's cultural ground—particularly when it came to MCing and DJing. They were largely considered partners in creative production, although at times the bond was reduced to a junior partnership (Flores 1992–1993, 1996b).

The perception of Puerto Rican full entitlement to graffiti and breaking versus their perceived limited entitlement to MCing and DJing could be traced to the overwhelming. Participation of Puerto Ricans in the first two. However, these different rates of participation may not have been the cause of these notions of entitlement but rather an effect. Most probably, rhyming and DJing were from the beginning more ethnoracially identified with African Americans and closed to perceived outsiders by virtue of their relying on dexterity in the English language, being most easily traceable to a U.S. Black oral tradition, and primarily employing records of music considered to be Black.

Hip-hop's musical side seems to have been premised upon an Afro-diasporic urbanity in which, though the participation of Caribbeans was pivotal (Flores 1988; Hebdige 1987; Rose 1994; Toop 1991), it was often narrowly identified with an ethnoracial Blackness (Flores 1996b; Rivera 1996). A distinction must be made, however, between the experiences within the hip-hop realm of West Indian Caribbeans (primarily Jamaicans and Barbadians) and Latino Caribbeans (primarily Puerto Ricans). West Indians are commonly thought to stand comparatively closer to Blackness than Latino Caribbeans. That is the case even for black Latinos. Though West Indians may be perceived as not ethnically Black (i.e., African American), they are, as a group, thought of as racially black (Foner 1987; Kasinitz 1992; Waters 1996). Given their relative proximity to an ethnoracial Blackness, West Indian entitlement to hip-hop as a Black-identified musical expression has not been as much of an issue as it has been for Puerto Ricans.

The position of Puerto Ricans within hip-hop must be understood within the historical context of Puerto Rican migration to New York City, their placement within the city's racial and socioeconomic hierarchies, and their relationship with African Americans.

Puerto Ricans and African Americans, though having had a presence in the city since the previous century, became thought of as the new wave of immigrants during the 1920s. Both groups were incorporated into the lowest rungs of the labor structure under similar circumstances and since then have lived parallel experiences of racialization, marginalization, and class exclusion (Grosfoguel and Georas 1996; Rodríguez-Morazzani 1996; Torres 1995). Their histories of unemployment and underemployment, subjection to police brutality and racial violence, negative portrayals in academic literature and media (Pérez 1990; Rodríguez 1997), and housing and employment discrimination have been not only similar but also linked. Puerto Ricans have come to be considered a native minority that shares the bottom of the socioeconomic structure with African Americans (Ogbu 1978; Gans 1992; Smith 1994). The histories of Puerto Ricans and African Americans in New York may not be identical, but they are certainly analogous, related, and at times even overlapping (Flores 1996a; Urciuoli 1996).

Puerto Ricans were initially a confusing lot because being even more visibly multiracial than African Americans, they could not be easily cast as black or white. Eventually, Puerto Ricans became a new racialized subject, different from both but sharing with African Americans a common subordination to whites (Grosfoguel and Georas 1996). Puerto Ricans came to be racialized as dark, dangerous others who, though different from African Americans, share with them a multitude of social spaces, conditions, and dispositions. Points of contention and separation might arise between the two groups, but there is a fundamental shared exclusion from the white, middle-class world.

Hip-hop's ethnoracial inclusiveness must be contextualized not only within this common structural history of African Americans and Puerto Ricans but also within a long-standing history of political alliances (Rodríguez-Morazzani 1996; Torres 1995) as well as joint cultural production (Boggs 1992; Flores 1988; Toop 1991).

Youth culture is one of the sites where cultural interaction and hybridization between African Americans and Puerto Ricans have been most intense. Urciuoli uses Bourdieu's concept of *habitus*[7] to illustrate how the experiences and actions of Puerto Ricans and African Americans are congruent given that their lives are structured by similar conditions and result in similar understandings of themselves and the world. She points out that the degree of congruence varies depending on other mediating factors such as gender, age, family role, and generation. Adolescent boys exhibit the highest levels of congruence (Urciuoli 1996:66). Hip-hop, as a youth cultural manifestation dominated by young males (Guevara 1987; Rose 1994), is the quintessential expression of this structural and cultural congruence.

Congruence, however, does not translate into an absence of rifts, tensions, and exclusions. The marginalizations experienced by Puerto Ricans in the hip-hop realm have not been fortuitous or circumstantial but are related to the historical relations between both groups and the particular position that each occupies in the city's racial and socioeconomic hierarchies. Cultural identity, production, and entitlement have most often been invested with the notion that Puerto Ricans are *like* blacks but *not* black. In Flores's words, "cultural baggage and black-white racial antinomies in the U.S. thus conspire to perpetuate a construction of Puerto Rican identity as non-black" (1992–1993:28). Part of this cultural baggage is a very eurocentric notion of Latinidad (Flores 1996a; Fox 1996; Pabón 1995; Thomas 1967). Puerto Rican Latinidad is constructed in such a way that precludes its coexistence with Puerto Rican Afro-diasporicity.

Furthermore, understandings of cultural identity and practice are frequently decidedly un-Afro-diasporic so that the connections between those who populate what Gilroy (1993) has termed "The Black Atlantic" are camouflaged. Hip-hop, as a site of internal movement and contentions, includes challenges as well as abidances to these un-Afro-diasporic understandings of history and culture. If, given these un-Afro-diasporic assumptions, the connections between African Americans and West Indians are disregarded, the ruptures become even more intense in the case of Latino Caribbeans such as Puerto Ricans.

These un-Afro-diasporic visions have had direct bearing on hip-hop. Despite the fact that, in practice, hip-hop has been an Afro-diasporic form, it has still been marred by narrow understandings of blackness.

FROM 1979 TO THE EARLY 1980s: THE DAWN OF THE RAP GAME

During Spring 1979, a funk group called Fatback released what can be considered the first commercial rap record, entitled "King Tim III (Personality Jock)." But that record's popularity was no match for the wide commercial acclaim with which "Rappers' Delight" was greeted a few months later. "Rappers' Delight," released on Sugarhill Records by an unknown group that called itself the Sugarhill Gang, was undoubtedly the record that signaled the commercial rise of rap, reaching number 36 on the U.S. charts and becoming the biggest-selling twelve-inch record ever (Toop 1991:81). MCing and DJing thus began their steep rise in mass-mediated popularity with the release of "Rappers' Delight."

Though most of the artists popular during rap's first five years as a mass-mediated consumer product (1979–1983) were African Americans (some of them West Indian, such as Grandmaster Flash and Kool Herc), Puerto Ricans were far from absent in this scene. DJ Charlie Chase of the Cold Crush Brothers, The Fearless Four's Devastating Tito and DJ Master O.C., The Fantastic Five's Prince Whipper Whip and Rubio Dee, Prince Markie Dee Morales of the Fat Boys, and The Real Roxanne were popular figures in commercial rap's early times.

Given rap's identification as a Black (i.e., African American) musical form, Puerto Ricans participated within a perceived Black matrix. This had been the case since hip-hop's beginnings in the early 1970s. But rap's mass-mediated commodification in the late 1970s led to an even more intense ethnoracialization of rap. Furthermore, if the cultural entitlement of Puerto Ricans to rap was sometimes ambivalent in the New York context, this ambivalence was magnified in other locations, most often landing them on the outsider side of the fence. The Afro-diasporic New York context in which Blacks and Puerto Ricans are neighbors, friends, and allies is a precious exception and hard to conceive of in most other U.S. locations. Hip-hop's initial Afro-diasporic ghetto base was hard to translate into highly segregated contexts with no corresponding histories of transethnic, Afro-diasporic cultural production. Audiences unfamiliar with New York life for the most part did not (and could not) distinguish between Blacks and Puerto Ricans. After its commercialization, rap remained class identified, but its ethnoracial scope shrunk.

THE LATE 1980s: BLACK NOISE

After breaking and graffiti crash-landed in terms of mass-mediated popularity around 1985 following their brief but intense media-propelled flight,[8] hip-hop became synonymous with the one art form that had from its inception been most intensely Black-identified, namely, rap. Subsequent creative developments and mass-marketing strategies (which did not operate independently of each other) further intensified this identification.

The explicit voicing of ethnoracial (African American) concerns by popular rap artists through rhymes, statements, and samples was one of the factors that further contributed to the ethnoracialization of hip-hop as African American (Henderson 1996; Rodríguez-Morazzani 1996). In other words, the voicing of Black-identified perspectives and concerns led to the increasingly narrow identification of hip-hop with this specific group.

Throughout its history, rap music has manifested different approaches to and articulations of Blackness. Explicit references to Blackness in the early 1980s, though elaborated and displayed, were not omnipresent. The late 1980s and early 1990s, however, saw an explosion of Black nationalist sentiment (Allen 1996).

The ideological and aesthetic reverberations of this period are still being felt, for it set the stage for creations and transformations to follow. The Pro-Black, Afrocentric, or Black Nationalist school of rap had a lasting impact on the hip-hop collective imagination—its faddish qualities notwithstanding. These formulations of an explicit ethnoracial agenda cloaked hip-hop with garb that seemed several sizes too big (or small, depending on how one looks at it) for Puerto Ricans—among plenty of others.

Louis, a Puerto Rican teenage rap fan during rap's Black Nationalist phase, recalls that when he first heard Public Enemy, it was like a revelation. He went straight to the library to look up this Huey Newton they were talking about. That's when it really hit him that they were talking about important Black historical figures and events. His first reaction to the information to which he was being exposed was pride in "us Black people." But then it started dawning on him that he was not exactly Black, given the way Blackness was being formulated. It was a Blackness whose referents were not inclusive of his side of the Caribbean because they did not fully acknowledge the cultural hybridity and fluidity of the Black Atlantic. Louis realized that he and "his people" were not quite part of the history about which Public Enemy was talking and rhyming. This point was driven home by his close friends—many of whom were African Americans—who teased him with the question, "Why can't *your* people make good hip-hop?"

Louis's experience illustrates the ambivalent position that Puerto Ricans (and other New York Caribbean Latinos) held given hip-hop's growing identification with a musical expression increasingly perceived as exclusively Black. Boricuas could be included or excluded, depending on the situation.

I mentioned earlier that both creative developments and marketing decisions worked together in the ethnoracialization of hip-hop as African American. So the issue was not as simple as Run DMC, Public Enemy, X-Clan, and others deciding to write African American–centric lyrics. The identification of hip-hop as Black must be contextualized in hip-hop's growing mass-mediation and popularity and, thus, its expansion outside territory where Puerto Ricans are a familiar presence—whether as neighbors, family, playmates, or artists. As hip-hop's scope of consumption and production grew, new players integrated themselves into the field of participation—players decidedly unfamiliar with Puerto Rican hip-hoppers. The imagined links between what was variably referred to as the hip-hop community or hip-hop nation were increasingly premised upon African Americanness so that hip-hop's Afro-diasporicity became increasingly obscured, even in its New York breeding grounds (which remained a fertile and influential spot of hip-hop creativity).

Hip-hop's Black identification must also be contextualized in the vilification/romanticization of African Americans in U.S. popular culture (Allinson 1994; Ross 1989) and the profitability of its commercial packaging. One of the hottest selling points of hip-hop has been its association with a raw, outlaw, ghetto-based, Black-identified (and particularly male) experience and image (Allinson 1994; Rose 1994; Samuels 1995). Allinson argues the relationship between rap's appeal and "a long-established romanticization of the Black urban male as a temple of authentic cool, at home with risk, with sex, with struggle" (1994:449).

Puerto Ricans, though considered virtual Blacks for some purposes, are considered nonblacks for others. Within the U.S. context, they have always had their ghetto nonwhite credentials up to date; their blackness, however, has been a different issue. So if hip-hop's mass-mediated popularity is closely connected to a romanticization/exoticization of blackness, why risk investing in a tepid/lighter/unstable version of blackness—in the form of a Puerto Rican—when you can have the real thing (Báez 1998)?

Puerto Ricanness in rap was (and still is, but less so) deemed a potential liability. Numerous Puerto Rican MCs recount being explicitly told by artists and repertory executives (A&Rs) and other industry people that they were talented but that their ethnicity worked against them.

Puerto Rican marginalization in rap has also been related to purist and narrow definitions regarding what is Black expressivity and what is Latino expressivity. Rap has been viewed as a new expression among a Black-music continuum and deemed as a breaking away from Latino music.

Rap presented similar problems for the perceived boundaries of Latino musical expression, as those that the Latin soul (which included bugalú) of the 1960s and early 1970s had presented (Flores 2000; Roberts 1979; Salazar, 1992). Though many of the critiques of Latin soul emphasized the musical inexperience of its musicians and its faddish qualities, much of the discomfort with this genre harked back to a deviation from tradition. Unflatteringly described by bandleader Willie Rosario as "American music played with Latin percussion" (Roberts 1979:167), bugalú violated the bounds that kept distinct what was Black and what was Latino/Puerto Rican.

Hip-hop's African Americanization to the exclusion of Puerto Ricans was not a product of circumstance. Neither can it be explained away by invoking only African American creative volition. The increasing Black identification of hip-hop must be understood within the steadfastness of ethnoracial categories in this country. These categories translate into a perceived limited potential for transethnic cultural production, solidarity, and political organizing. Cultural hybrids such as hip-hop threaten those categories and the comforting, simplifying myths built around them.

THE LATE 1980s: WHAT IS THIS "LATIN" IN LATIN HIP-HOP?

A twist in the story of Puerto Ricans in hip-hop came with the commercialization and popularity of two Latino-identified genres: freestyle in the late 1980s and Latin rap in the early 1990s. Terminology here provides a bit of confusion, because both were also often referred to as Latin hip-hop. But this apparent terminological confusion actually proves to be illuminating. The term *Latin hip-hop* points to the fact that both genres were somehow related to, yet distinct from, hip-hop; and key in their difference from hip-hop was a shared Latin element.

Toop describes freestyle as "faithful to the old electro sound of 'Planet Roc' adding Latin percussion elements and an overlay of teenage romance" (1991:174). Others describe it in starkly unflattering terms as the "synth-heavy bubble-salsa of Lisa Lisa and her big-haired descendants" (Morales 1991:91) and "bubble-gum ballads over drum-machine beats" (del Barco 1996:84). Groups such as Cover Girls, Exposé, TKA, and Latin Raskals and artists such as George LaMond, Sapphire, and Brenda K. Starr were among the best-known freestyle artists. The overwhelming majority of these were New York Puerto Ricans. Freestyle's audience was also primarily Puerto Rican.

In terms of vocal style, lyrics, and sound, freestyle was very different from the rap music of the time. Freestyle vocalists sang (not rapped) sticky-sweet (at times bittersweet) lyrics centered on the vagaries of love, whereas hip-hop MCs broached topics more concerned with ghetto life, racial strife, and personal/artistic prowess. Freestyle's sound was electropop, while hip-hop was usually backed by harsh funk with booming bass lines.

Toop talks of a division arising between African American and Hispanic audiences in 1987, which he attributes to "Hispanics stay[ing] faithful to the old electro sound of 'Planet Roc'" in the form of freestyle while African Americans followed the increasingly Black-identified rap music of the time (1991:174). But he offers no possible explanations and leaves one wondering, why did that separation happen?

Popular taste and cultural production can hardly ever be fully or accurately explained in cause-effect fashion. However, influential factors can be identified with relative certainty. One of the factors at play in the late 1980s schism along ethnoracial lines between hip-hop and freestyle audiences had to do with notions of cultural property and entitlement.

The growing African Americanization of hip-hop during the 1980s—largely media-driven, premised upon a reductive notion of blackness, and suffering from severe cultural-historical amnesia—prefaced the increasing alienation of Puerto Ricans (and other New York Caribbean Latinos) from hip-hop. Cultural entitlement to hip-hop was explained as a non-Latino-inclusive "Black thing" (Allinson 1994; Hochman 1990).

Freestyle, as a new genre, was in great part young Latinos' response to media marginalization—which included marginalization in rap (Rodríguez 1995; Panda 1995; Q-Unique 1995a). Discussions of the emergence, popularity, and cultural significance of freestyle must take into account this desire of Puerto Ricans and other Latinos to see "their own" in the limelight, to have a music that was theirs.

George LaMond, a popular freestyle singer during the 1980s, recalls: "I felt like I was representing my hometown and my Puerto Rican people. It made me that much more proud of being a Latino" (Parris 1996:31). Andy Panda, a key song writer, producer, and media personality of what he terms "the freestyle movement," adds: "I think it gave kids a sense of identity because finally we had something that was ours. We didn't have much of a cultural identity in the music industry other than Spanish-language music" (Parris 1996:30).

Such desires must be contextualized within Latino invisibility in mass media (E. Morales 1996; Rodríguez 1997), in general and the prevailing notion that hip-hop was Black cultural property in particular. They must also be understood with respect to the will of second- and third-generation Puerto Rican (and other Latino) youth to expand the bounds of collective expression outside of Spanish-language Latin music.

What was perceived as culturally theirs by these youths exceeded the bounds of Latinidad orthodoxy, which considered Spanish language and Latin American–originated sounds as a necessary component of music worthy of the label *Latin*. Latinos and so-called American music seemed disparate partners in terms of cultural legitimacy. In that sense, the participation of Puerto Ricans and other Latinos in Latin soul (in the 1960s), hip-hop (in the late 1970s and 1980s), and freestyle (in the 1980s) all shared an element of challenge to the dominant notions of Latinidad.

Resistance to this challenge to Latinidad took many forms: Willie Rosario's insistence on identifying bugalú as "American" music (Roberts 1979:167), Puerto Rican parents complaining of their children's fascination with so-called nigger music (i.e., hip-hop), A&Rs refusing to sign Puerto Rican MCs because "Puerto Ricans don't sell," George García being persuaded by his label to launch his freestyle career as George LaMond because his last name was considered a commercial drawback (Parris 1996).

Though grassroots perceptions are often more responsive to innovations and changing conditions than market-oriented ones, both coincided in their difficulty to grapple with the younger generation's will to embrace their New York–based, English-dominant, Afro-diasporic, lived cultural experiences. Freestyle was, in this sense, an artistic liberation from stifling (in terms of creativity and cultural identity) parameters of conformity with the reigning notions of Latinidad.

At the same time, though, that freestyle pushed the envelope with respect to second- and third-generation identity and artistic production, it also reproduced other reductive notions of identity, experience, and solidarity. It reinforced the myth of pan-Latino commonality and the drawing of puertorriqueñidad and Latinidad as identity categories in great part defined through nonblackness.

Orsi proposes that the fissures and conflicts between racialized groups have much to do with anxieties regarding group definition. "Strategies of alterity" have served to define "self-constitution through the exclusion of the dark-skinned other" (1992:336). His study of East Harlem reveals how Italians struggled to separate themselves from the "dark" African Americans, Puerto Ricans, and other Caribbean immigrants. "Proximity—actual and imagined—to the dark-skinned other was pivotal to the emergence of the identity 'Italian American'" (1992:318). Similarly, Puerto Ricanness and Latinidad have been informed by a desire to distinguish these groups from the darker African Americans.

These anxieties regarding ethnic and racial identity affect understandings of artistic production in peculiar ways. Not only can a certain mode of expression, such as freestyle, be said to be Latino because New York Puerto Ricans are the most distinguished, popular, or numerous participants, but a certain genre can also be said to be Latino because it is informed by specific modes of speech or experiences that are identified with Latinos living in the United States. But also certain myths based on a stereotypical ethnoracial ethos come to define what may or may not be Latino. Panda directed the following comment at George LaMond during an interview: "George, you never sounded black and yet everyone respected your talent as a vocalist because what you did was uniquely Latino. Black artists traditionally sing with soul. We sing with passion. We sing with sex. We sing with emotion" (Parris 1996:31).

Panda's belief in a self-evident soulful black sound distinct from a Latino sex-heavy sound is by no means peculiar to him, freestyle, or those of his generation. Similar essentialized and naturalized identity markings are often thrown around in the media, street corner cyphers, and domestic conversations.[9] These essentializing myths serve to cement difference as further strategies of alterity.

The list of areas in which difference is believed to be patently clear thus grows. Ethos, aesthetics, themes, ideas, language, and musical references and sources can all be pointed to as examples of group difference. What is African American can thus be pretended to be easily discernible from what is Puerto Rican or Latino.

Whereas certain audience segments and critics celebrated the dawn of Latin hip-hop, there was a strong feeling of suspicion and betrayal among those who felt themselves part of an urban Afro-diasporic, Black-matrixed hip-hop culture. Edward Rodríguez (1995), a Puerto Rican hip-hop journalist, bitterly explains the appearance and popularity of freestyle as a denial of Latino Afro-diasporicity.

Freestyle began as an artistic outlet within a context of Latino media marginalization and a prescribed Latinidad orthodoxy. Ironically, it also had ghettoizing and stifling consequences in terms of media perception as well as popular cultural identity. Many Puerto Ricans divested themselves from hip-hop to pursue something that was truly their own. The fickleness of mass-mediated taste did away with the basket in which many Puerto Ricans had placed their eggs. The commercial popularity of freestyle ended up taking a nosedive that affected not only its artists but also Puerto Rican MCs. Freestyle, as Latin hip-hop, cemented the idea that Puerto Ricans were marginal to the hip-hop core.

Freestyle was only one side of Latin hip-hop. Latin rap fell under the same rubric. Compared to freestyle, Latin rap stood a lot closer to hip-hop in terms of form and style. Vocal flows were rapped, and topics were ghettocentric. It was basically rap music done by Latinos, often code-switching, with topics and references particular to inner-city Latino communities.

Contrary to freestyle, whose artists were overwhelmingly New York Puerto Ricans, Latin rap was largely coming out of the West Coast and had few Puerto Rican exponents. Kid Frost (nowadays known simply as Frost), a Los Angeles Chicano who released his first album, *Hispanic Causing Panic*, in 1990, was one of the first Latino rappers to receive wide media recognition. Other artists that came out under the Latin rap rubric were Mellow Man Ace (a Cuban, also from Los Angeles), Latin Alliance (headed by Frost), and the infamous Gerardo (an Ecuadorean, aka Rico Suave).

New York Puerto Ricans never ceased being active in the local underground hip-hop scene. But in terms of Latin rap's mass-mediated exposure, they were nearly invisible. Latin Alliance had two New York Puerto Rican members, Rayski and Markski. A Nuyorican duo by the name of Latin Empire had garnered some local exposure earlier in the 1980s and even landed a deal with Atlantic Records; however, they never achieved the popularity of later Latin rap artists.

Though most commonly treated as such, Latin rap is neither a self-explanatory nor unproblematic label. Is it simply rap done by Latinos, regardless of style or content? Is it rap done by Latinos that is also necessarily related to Latino life or a Latino aesthetic? How could that reality or that aesthetic possibly be defined? Whose definition do we use? Can non-Latinos who use Spanish in their rhymes or other elements of that hypothetical Latino aesthetic also make Latin rap?

The Latin rap label has been used to categorize artists such as Kid Frost, Mellow Man Ace, Gerardo, Latin Alliance, and Latin Empire—all U.S.-based Latino artists whose music, rhymes, and themes include elements commonsensically identifiable as Latino. It has also been used to describe Latin America–based artists such as Vico C., Lisa M., and El General (Manuel 1995) whose rhymes are in Spanish (though sometimes incorporating words in English here and there). For my present purposes, the most difficult questions regarding definition and inclusion within the Latin rap category have to be asked when U.S.-based Latino artists create music that doesn't conform to the most commonly accepted bounds of Latino identity, experience, or creativity.

Cypress Hill, for example, was criticized for being too Anglocentric (Morales 1991). This Los Angeles-based trio is made up of Sen Dog (a Cuban—and incidentally, Mellow Man Ace's brother), B-Real (a Chicano), and DJ Muggs (an Italian American who spent his early childhood in Queens, New York). The assumption seems to have been that because two of its three members were Latinos, Cypress Hill had to conform to a certain mold of Latinidad. They, however, never claimed to be doing Latin rap. In fact, they scoffed at the thought and explicitly resented being boxed into the category to which others presumed they belonged (Cross 1993).

Sen Dog and B-Real were actually the first Latino artists to be deemed part of the hip-hop core—as opposed to the fringes that Latin rap artists occupied. These discussions of how Latino or Anglocentric their artistic production is or is not completely lose sight of other aspects of their music, which are more directly relevant to the social milieu in which rap is produced and consumed.

Morales has defined Latin hip-hop as "the polyphonic outburst of recent rap-oriented records" such as *Latin Alliance* (Virgin), *Dancehall Reggaespañol* (Columbia), and *Cypress Hill* (Columbia), which is "in step with the world-wide Afrocentric cultural revolution that will carry us into the next century." One of its virtues, according to Morales, is its "development of a nationwide Latino/Americano hip-hop aesthetic" that permits artists from both coasts who were once strangers to "become one nation kicking Latin lingo on top of a scratchin', samplin' substrate." He argues for an inclusive notion of this aesthetic so that Cypress Hill doesn't have to be dismissed as "de-Latinized, stoned-out Beastie Boys." Though their rhymes are mostly English, they still kick some bilingualism and their "relative Anglocentrism" doesn't necessarily "mean they're not reaching *vatos* in the hood" (1991:91).

Instead of questioning the stifling assumptions regarding ethnoracial identity and artistic expression that underpin this charge of Anglocentrism,[10] Morales explains what he sees as Cypress Hill's redeeming qualities. After all, they do inject some Spanish into their rhymes, plus they are probably reaching a vato audience. Seeking redemption through these means seems less pertinent than asking why Latino artists are, in the first place, expected to adhere to a certain orthodox Latino aesthetic (in terms of language, topics, and/or music) or to cater to a Latino audience.

This issue becomes particularly relevant in the case of Puerto Ricans in New York, whose cultural production and identity have been so tightly linked with that of African Americans that it begs the question, Why assume the naturalness or necessity of a Latino aesthetic and cultural product (myopically defined, to boot) over and against Afro-diasporic ones?

The Hispanocentric bent of the dominant definitions of Latinidad (Fox 1996; Pabón 1995) has (at times) led to Puerto Ricans placing themselves and (often) being placed by others outside the bounds of Latinidad. A cornerstone aspect of the Latin rap aesthetic was the use of bilingualism or only Spanish. However, many of those Puerto Rican participants who rejected what they perceived as the Latin rap pigeonholing sought to emphasize a U.S.-based Afro-diasporic identity. Edward Rodríguez (1995, personal communication) explains why some MCs refused to go the Latin rap route: "MC's don't wanna come out as exclusively Spanish 'cause they don't wanna exclude people. Black people are their people."

Then there's also the issue of second- and third-generation Puerto Ricans (and other Latinos) expressing themselves more comfortably in English than in Spanish. As the South Bronx's Fat Joe (Joseph Cartagena) says, even though—by virtue of being Puerto Rican— promoters expected him to rhyme in Spanish, "I can't really kick it in Spanish, I couldn't really feel the vibe, so I'm not even gonna try and make myself look stupid." Prince PowerRule (Oscar Alfonso) has the following comment to add: "There's so many Latino people in the United States that don't speak Spanish, so they don't wanna hear that bilingual rap. They're just like us; they're Americans." (del Barco 1996:82)

Similarly to the case of freestyle, the appearance of Latin rap as a Latino-specific realm within rap music on the one hand expanded the bounds of participation and expression of Latinos in hip-hop but on the other hand also ended up making the existing divides between Puerto Ricans and African Americans even deeper. The nonblack Latinidad on which Latin rap was based further put into question the Afro-diasporicity of Puerto Ricans and their position within hip-hop as a Black-matrixed culture.

THE 1990s: GHETTOCENTRICITY, BLACKNESS, AND LATINIDAD

The Afrocentric emphasis in rap of the late 1980s started shifting toward a more ghettocentric (Kelley 1996; McLaren 1995) approach in the early 1990s (Boyd 1997; Smith 1997). Blackness did not cease being a crucial identity marker within rap's discourse; it just became more narrowly identified as a *ghetto* blackness. According to Smith, "in rap's dominant market paradigm, blackness has become contingent, while the ghetto has become necessary" (1997:346).

As rap's discursive and performative focus shifted from a blackness primarily defined through (a narrow, nondiasporic take on) African American history and ancestry to one more based upon contemporary socioeconomic conditions and lived culture (as opposed to traditional, inherited, or ancestral culture), a slight relaxing of blackness's ethnoracial scope occurred. The blackness formerly restricted by the bounds of an ethnoracialized African Americanness began expanding to accommodate certain Latino groups—most notably, Puerto Ricans—as a population whose experiences of class and ethnoracial marginalization are virtually indistinguishable from the ghettocentric African American experience.

Hip-hop, during the late 1980s and early 1990s, used to be frequently described by participants as "a Black thing, you wouldn't understand"; since the mid-1990s it has become increasingly common to hear hip-hop explained in everyday conversation, as well as in mass-mediated and academic forums, as a Black and Latino phenomenon (Dennis 1992; Jiménez 1997; Lascaibar 1997; McLaren 1995; Smith 1997). Today's near-dominant convention of describing hip-hop culture (and within it, rap) as Black and Latino and the increased mass-mediated visibility of Latinos/Latinas within hip-hop would not have come about had it not been for this shifting conception of blackness that emphasizes the ghetto experience.

Rap is a central part of mainstream U.S. pop culture, has multiracial audiences all over the globe, and is immersed in the politics of the transnational music industry. Still, hip-hop authenticity—signified through the tropes of a class-identified blackness/nigganess—is contentious ethnoracial territory, and its borders are zealously policed by its participants. The ethnoracial scope of authenticity has been expanded somewhat but only to incorporate (though not always smoothly) the Latino experience.

Authenticity has been broadened to accommodate a group that is perceived to be quite close to Blackness to begin with. Latino blackness, or virtual Blackness, is thought of as a product of social, political, and economic circumstances that have led to shared lived and historical experiences in the ghetto with African Americans. But Latino authenticity is not only conceived within hip-hop in terms of socioeconomic structures; it is also constructed as related to Afro-diasporic ethnoracial identities, cultural history, and cultural formations.

But hold up! Wait a minute. To talk about a shared Afro-diasporicity between African Americans and Latinos entails that we must be talking about only a sector of Latinos, namely, Afro-diasporic Latinos. To talk about shared experiences in the ghetto means we must distinguish the intense experiential similarities between Blacks and Caribbean Latinos in New York from the comparatively more distinct experiences of Chicanos and Blacks in Los Angeles or Chicago and from the completely divergent experiences of African Americans and Cubans in Miami. This may seem all too obvious, yet it is another example of the specificities that are smothered under the seductive weight of the pan-Latino discourse.

The acknowledgment of hip-hop in both the academic and journalistic literature as an urban Black *and* Latino cultural expression has suffered from the perils of panethnic abstraction. In the haste to rescue Latinos from the hip-hop historical invisibility in which they were submerged for a period and to acknowledge the present role played by Latinos within core hip-hop, essentialized connections are drawn and crucial differences among groups within the Latino panethnic conglomerate are slighted.[11] The historical and present connections between Afro-diasporic Latinos and African Americans in New York are, at times, muted or even drowned out by the naturalizing call of panlatinidad.

THE LATE 1990s: LATINAS GET HOT

As I explained in the previous section, the rise of rap's ghettocentricity as a selling point in the latter half of the 1990s has played a part in Latinos' relegitimization as core participants of hip-hop. This legitimization is manifested in various ways: the greater media visibility of Latino hip-hop artists; the rise in the use of Spanish words and phrases in songs by the most popular African American rap artists; and widespread references to and images of Latinos and Latinas in rhymes, videos, and articles. A whole slew of artists dedicated lines or even whole songs to the *mamis*. Latina mamis actually became one of the latest faddish hip-hop fetishes. Tropicalized[12] (Aparicio and Chávez-Silverman 1997), exoticized, eroticized, and romanticized, Latinos in hip-hop have, as of late, most often been portrayed as virtual Blacks with the ghetto nigga stamp of approval and, particularly in the case of females, a sexualized flair.

New York's Afro-diasporic multi-ethnic hip-hop culture and the integral role of Caribbean Latinos—particularly Puerto Ricans—within it has set the tone for transregional, mass-mediated Latino hip-hop images. But this is a subtlety that largely remains unspoken. Therefore, oftentimes the pan-Latino aggregate is awarded a blackness really meant for Caribbean Latinos.

Let's take the example of the recent Latin mami fetish. Though most often generically referred to as Latinas, when the mamis populating rappers' wet dreams are referred to by specific national origin, it is almost invariably Boricua (and increasingly, Dominican) females that are invoked. And even when their Puerto Ricanness is not stated explicitly, subtle and not-so-subtle clues reveal these mamis as Puerto Ricans.

Puerto Rican women had had a presence in rap lyrics (almost invariably as objects of desire) before salivating after mamis became a commercial gimmick. "I like 'em yellow, brown, Puerto Rican and Haitian," A Tribe Called Quest's Phife had said of his taste in women in 1993's "Electric Relaxation." A member of the Wu-Tang Clan, using the metaphor of ice cream flavors in 1995's "Ice Cream," lusted after Chocolate Deluxes, French Vanillas, and Butta Pecan Ricans (Raekwon 1995).

The difference between then and now is that a theme that used to be occasionally touched upon—namely, the hot Latin mami—has nowadays become a market cliché. Another difference is that as New York becomes more Dominicanized, the local long-standing interchangeability of Spanish/Hispanic/Latino for Puerto Rican (Flores 1996a) has come to be expanded to include Dominicans next to Puerto Ricans.[13] Puerto Ricans used to be the prototype of the exotic/erotic New York mami; now Dominicans also inform the prototype.

Latinas are certainly not the only females that get hypersexualized through rap images and rhymes. Far from it. As Irving accurately states, the role of Black women in rap has "more often than not, been limited to those voiceless images projected unto the extended wet dream of music videos" (1998:34).[14] Within rap's heterocentric discourse, where African American male subjectivities reign supreme, Black women are the norm, the ethnoracial self—othered and hypersexualized for gender reasons—but in ethnoracial terms they are the familiar and familial. Puerto Rican women, on the other hand, are familiar yet still exotic. At times they may even be considered part of the family—but always one step removed. Black women are the "sistas"; Puerto Rican women are the othered, tropicalized, and exoticized mamis.[15]

Asian women have also had the questionable honor of occasionally populating rap's wet dreams. Similarly to Latinas, Asian women are viewed as erotic/exotic creatures. Unlike Latinas, however, their exoticism is not stamped by the U.S. ghetto experience and spliced with images of south-of-the-border tropicalism. Mamis are inner-city exotics, tropicalized ghetto creatures. They are brash, loud, hot, hard, street savvy, and bold—in terms of movies, think Rosie Perez's characters in *Do the Right Thing* and *White Men Can't Jump* and Rosario Dawson's Lala Bonilla in *He Got Game;* in terms of rap music, think Puff Daddy's "Spanish Girl" in the interlude right before his 1997 song "Señorita" from the CD *No Way Out* or Lissette and Joanne in the late Big Punisher's 1998 interlude "Taster's Choice."[16] This ghetto tropical spitfire exoticism greatly differs from the common exoticization of Asian women based on an imputed silence and subservience.[17]

The commercial hip-hop image of the Latina mami is most often based on a tropicalized virtual Blackness. The mami is typically taken to be an exotic (and lighter) variation on black womanhood. How? Lets see.

An ad[18] for the Cocoa Brovas[19] album *The Rude Awakening* features a cardboard cup full of steaming cocoa. Six chocolate-drenched young women are partially immersed in the liquid. On the right-hand side of the cup appear the erroneously accented words *Chocolaté Calienté*.

The words in Spanish seem to be indicating that these women (or at least some of them) swirling in hot chocolate and sexily awaiting ingestion are Latinas. They are all various shades of caramel—unquestionably black by this country's standards but still light skinned. Their relative lightness and the fact that all but one have straight or slightly wavy hair go with the Butta Pecan Rican Myth, i.e., the popular perception of Puerto Ricans as golden-skinned and "good-haired" [sic!].[20] But butta pecan is somehow still imagined to be a variation on chocolate. Butta Pecans are, after all, a crucial ingredient in the Cocoa Brovas recipe for chocolaté calienté. The bottom line is that these hot cocoa girls' Latinidad does not take away from their blackness. What their Latinidad does do is add an element of exoticism—signified through the ad's use of Spanish—to their blackness.

The accentuation of words that, according to Spanish orthographic rules, should not be accented serves to further intensify a sense of exoticism. Accents are deemed exotic characteristics of an exotic language. Whether this erroneous accentuation was a mistake or was done on purpose does not change the fact that the accents in *chocolaté* and *calienté* serve as tropicalizing markers of difference.

Let's move on to another example. "Set Trippin," a review of ten popular rap videos in *Blaze*'s premier issue, includes Big Punisher's "Still Not a Player." The reviews consist of short blurbs under specific headings such as Plot, Ghetto Fabulous, Estimated Budget, and Black Erotica. The following comments under Black Erotica regarding "Still Not a Player" caught my eye: "Dozens of scantily clad, lighter-than-a-paper-bag sistas and mamis end up dancing outside. Sounds like a red-light district" (Carasco 1998:207).

It is significant that the Black Erotica category includes mention of both sistas and mamis. These may be two ethnically distinct female populations, but both are included in the realm of eroticized blackness. The fact that their light-skinnedness makes the set seem like a red-light district is a commentary on gendered color-chaste hierarchies (hooks 1994) that equate lightness with sexual desirability as well as an acknowledgment of the figure of the prostitute as the embodiment of male sexual fantasy. Considering the common coding of Puerto Ricanness as butta pecanness, it is evident that their attributed phenotypic lightness plays a part in the collective eroticization of Puerto Rican females.[21]

The text of "Still Not a Player" itself poses Puerto Rican and African American women as two distinct groups. Its sing-song chorus, which consists of multiple repetitions of "boricua, morena/boricua, morena," differentiates these two groups of women through the use of Puerto Rican ethnoracializing terminology. The video adds a visual dimension to the distinction as the camera alternates between a group of lighter-skinned women when the word *boricua* is being uttered and a group of comparatively darker-skinned women when the chorus mentions *morena*. The tiny chihuahua that one of the Boricuas is holding serves as yet another mark of difference. Chihuahuas are a dog breed considered in New York ghetto lore to be popular among Puerto Ricans, but they also invoke the tropicalized pan-latinidad of Dinky, the infamous chihuahua of the late-1990s Taco Bell commercial campaign. However, though distinct, these two groups come together by virtue of Big Pun's sexual desire:

> I love 'em butter pecan
> The black, brown molass
> I don't discriminate
> I regulate every shade of that ass
> [spanking sound followed by a woman's moan] . . .
> I want a ghetto brunette
> With unforgettable sex . . .
> Since I found Joe
> Every pretty round brown ho
> Wanna go down low (Big Punisher 1998)

Pun boasts of not discriminating because he sexually engages "every shade of that ass." But the shades that he regulates are specifically three: butter pecan, black molasses, and brown molasses. Using the language of "gastronomic sexuality" (Aparicio 1998:147) that also informs the aforementioned Cocoa Brovas ad, Pun focuses his desire on African American and Puerto Rican "ghetto brunette[s]." Boricuas and morenas may be distinct but, as Pun constructs them, they are both sweet, thick, pretty, round, and various shades of brown. And, evidently, that is how he likes his hos.

The Cocoa Brovas ad as well as Pun's pronouncements are only two examples among many of rap's dominant masculinist ghetto nigga discourse, in which African American and Caribbean Latino men construct a landscape of desire where sistas and mamis take center stage as "their" women.

THE LATE 1990s: PUERTO RICANS' TROPICALIZED AFRO-DIASPORICITY

Rap music's late-1990s commercialized ghettocentricity and fetishization of mamis have helped legitimize and even trendify Puerto Ricans—and by extension, Latinos as a whole. This renewed embracing of Puerto Ricans as entitled hip-hop participants invested with cultural authenticity is also connected to the wider social context of the United States, where the rising population numbers, political clout, and media visibility of Latinos highlight their desirability as consumers and/or objects of mass-mediated exoticization.

Hip-hop's late-1990s "Latino Renaissance" (R. Morales 1996) has signaled an era of greater legitimacy and visibility for Puerto Rican (and other Latino) participants and expanded their opportunities for participation and expression. At the same time, the potential for a wider range of creative expression often fails to be fulfilled given the constraints placed on artists through flavor-of-the-month fetishization and tropicalization.

This redrawing of the realm of creative expression is reminiscent of freestyle music in the late 1980s, which pushed the bounds of New York Puerto Rican creativity through the inclusion of second-generation perspectives but reproduced other essentialist myths regarding Latino cultural production. As I explained earlier, one of its central myths was the construction of a Latino aesthetic that was imagined as excised from the Afro-diasporic history and present context of Caribbean Latino cultural expression in New York.

Despite the similarities—in terms of redrawing essentialist ethnoracialized boundaries—among freestyle in the late 1980s, Latin rap in the late 1980s/early 1990s, and Latino hip-hop participation in the late 1990s, a crucial distinction must be made. Although freestyle and Latin rap were defined as Latino cultural realms, core hip hop is a Black-matrixed cultural sphere shared by African American and Latino youth. Caribbean Latinos may tropicalize themselves and be tropicalized by others, thus being readily distinguishable from African Americans. However, their participation in hip-hop is grounded in and celebrated as part of an Afro-diasporic cultural realm.

CONCLUSION

The 1980s were dubbed the Decade of the Hispanics in the media and saw an acknowledgment of the diversification and growing numbers of the Latino population—a belated recognition, because this phenomenon had actually begun more than a decade earlier (García

1988). Puerto Ricans made up 80 percent of the Latino population of New York in 1960; by the 1990s, this number had dropped to 50 percent (Flores 1996a:173).

With the growing plurality of Latino groups, numbers, experiences, and voices began the perception of the exceptional character of Puerto Ricans with respect to other Latino groups. It also became apparent that the same factors that made Puerto Ricans a distinct case among Latinos were the same ones that they shared with African Americans.

Certain factors pull Puerto Ricans into the Latino narrative (Spanish language; other historical and cultural factors related to Spanish colonization; and later, U.S. imperialism), but others pull them closer to African Americans and toward a virtual Blackness (English language among the second and third generations, residential segregation, labor marginality, poverty, and negative symbolic capital and public image).

Young New York Puerto Ricans have often either found themselves excluded or have excluded themselves from the generally accepted bounds of Latinidad, given the constitutional urban Afro-diasporicity of their cultural identity. Puerto Ricans who participate in hip-hop culture have, for the most part, sought to acknowledge their Afro-diasporic Caribbean Latinidad without wholly submerging themselves under the reigning definition of Latinidad or merely passing as virtual Blacks.

Despite the growing appeals to an increasingly abstracted panlatinidad, Puerto Rican hip-hoppers still privilege their New York Afro-diasporic lived experience. As Q-Unique (1995b) says in his song "Rice and Beans":

> no, not Latino
> drop that "o"
> Latin's just a language, yo

Notes

1. Hip-hop is most commonly described by its participants as an Afro-diasporic urban youth culture with origins in the 1970s South Bronx. Among its primary venues of creative expression are MCing (rapping), DJing, writing (graffiti), and breaking (dancing). See Flores (1988), Norfleet (1997), and Rose (1994).
2. I use the term *ethnoracial* to acknowledge the constitutional racialization of ethnic categories.
3. In my writing, I will be using *black* and *Black* to refer to two distinct concepts: *black* as the racial or sociocultural category that refers to people of the African diaspora and *Black* as the U.S.-based ethnoracial category that refers specifically to the population known as African American. In this manner, I am seeking to distinguish between the perceived blackness but non-Blackness of Puerto Ricans (and others from the Spanish-speaking Caribbean) and the double blackness/Blackness of African Americans.
4. Thanks to Philip Kasinitz for the concept of Puerto Rican virtual Blackness.
5. Peter McLaren places rap ("gangsta rap" [sic]) within an Afro-diasporic context and a history that features economic exploitation. His case for rap's "ghetto-ethnicity" relies on the centrality of the ghetto within the rap discourse and the shared experience of African Americans and Puerto Ricans.
6. Flores (1996a) argues that the history of Puerto Ricans in New York, rather than being posited and dismissed as an exception among Latinos, can serve to illuminate and guide efforts to understand and further the position and prospects of other Latino groups.
7. Bourdieu explains *habitus* as a "system of structured, structuring dispositions" (1993:482). Urciuoli (1996) applies it in the case of African Americans and Puerto Ricans to indicate that their experiences, perceptions, and actions are shaped by common historical circumstances or "conditions of existence,"

thus leading to similar understandings of and approaches to the world around them. This is not to say, however, that experience and action are strictly determined by these two groups' shared conditions of existence.

8. See Hazzard-Donald (1996), Tompkins (1996), and Verán (1996).
9. See Menéndez (1988) and Aparicio (1998:147).
10. If Latino rappers use English in their rhymes, it is because rap is an Afro-diasporic oral/musical form of expression that originated in the United States among English-dominant Afro-diasporic youth. The assumption that the use of English by Latino rappers equals Anglocentrism whereas the use of Spanish or bilingualism signals some kind of adherence to Latinidad points to severe conceptual problems. Equating the use of English with Anglocentrism negates the appropriation and transformation of the colonizers' language by Afro-diasporic people (which includes certain Latino populations). Furthermore, not only are Latinos following rap's Afro-diasporic English-based orality, but their use of English also derives from their most immediate communicative experience as young people raised in the United States. Another problem with these charges of Anglocentrism is that they assume that a language equals a culture. Flores, Attinasi, and Pedraza (Flores 1993) challenge the notion that the use of English or Spanish indicates how much assimilation has occurred. Puerto Ricans, as well as other Latinos, assert their cultural identity through their particular way of speaking English (Urciuoli 1996; Zentella 1997).
11. For journalistic examples, see Baxter (1999) and Weisberg (1998). For examples in the academic literature, see McLaren (1995) and Smith (1997).
12. Aparicio and Chávez-Silverman forward the notion of a tropicalized Latinidad, drawing from Fernando Ortiz's concept of transculturation, Pratt's contact zones, and Said's orientalism: "To tropicalize, as we define it, means to trope, to imbue a particular space, geography, group, or nation with a set of traits, images, and values" (1997:12).
13. On the initial Puerto Ricanization of Dominicans in New York, see Grosfoguel and Georas (1996).
14. See also Morgan (1996) and Rose (1994).
15. Rap's Puerto Rican (as well as other Latino) male subjects also eroticize mamis. The difference is that, in these cases, mamis are eroticized not as a tropical (ethnoracial) Other but as a tropical self.
16. Big Punisher, a Puerto Rican rapper from the Bronx and member of the Terror Squad, was the first Latino solo act to reach platinum sales with his 1998 debut album *Capital Punishment* (Loud Records, 1998).
17. The Latina spitfire stereotype is by no means a recent phenomenon. It has populated mass-mediated images in the United States since this century's early decades (Rodríguez 1997). Lupe Vélez and the "Carmelita" character she played in various highly successful movies of the 1930s represents an early example. Rita Moreno, tellingly nicknamed "Rita the Cheetah" by the press, had a hard time breaking out of the spitfire mold in the 1950s. These early portrayals of the spitfire, as is the case with today's mami, were typically grounded within a gendered lower-class identity.
18. See *The Source* 101 (February 1998):36.
19. The Cocoa Brovas are a rap duo of African American MCs.
20. On the aesthetic and representational marginalization of black Puerto Ricans, see Jorge (1986), Gregory (1995–1996), Thomas (1967), and Tate (1995). On skin tone and Puerto Ricans, see Jenkins and Wilson (1998).
21. Samara, a dark-skinned African American twenty-six-year-old "veteran of live sex shows in New York City," says of her experience looking for work in strip clubs: "Some clubs did not want to hire me because I was black. . . . Some like black girls, but black girls who have either big tits or light skin, who tend to look more like Puerto Ricans" (Samara 1987:37).

References

Allen, Ernest, Jr. 1996. "Making the Strong Survive: The Contours and Contradictions of Message Rap." In *Droppin' Science: Critical Essays on Rap Music and Hip Hop Culture*, ed. William Eric Perkins, 159–91. Philadelphia: Temple University Press.

Allinson, E. 1994. "It's a Black Thing: Hearing How Whites Can't." *Cultural Studies* 8(3): 438–56.

Aparicio, Frances. 1998. *Listening to Salsa: Gender, Latin Popular Music, and Puerto Rican Cultures.* Hanover: Wesleyan University Press.

Aparicio, Frances, and Susana Chávez-Silverman. 1997. Introduction to *Tropicalizations: Transcultural Representations of Latinidad,* ed. Frances R. Aparicio and Susana Chávez-Silverman, 1–17. Hanover, N.H.: University Press of New England.

Arsonists. 1999. *As the World Burns.* Matador OLE 343-2. Compact disc.

Báez, Alano, vocalist for Ricanstruction. 1998. Interview by author. East Harlem, Manhattan, New York, June 15.

del Barco, Mandalit. 1996. "Rap's Latino Sabor." In *Droppin' Science: Critical Essays on Rap Music and Hip Hop Culture,* ed. William Eric Perkins, 63–84. Philadelphia: Temple University Press.

Baxter, Kevin. 1999. "Spanish Fly: Latinos Take Over." *The Source* 113 (February): 136–41.

Big Pun. 1998. *Capital Punishment.* Loud/RCA 07863 67512-2. Compact disc.

Boggs, Vernon. 1992. *Salsiology: Afro-Cuban Music and the Evolution of Salsa in New York City.* New York: Greenwood Press.

Bourdieu, Pierre. 1993. "Structures, Habitus, Practices." In *Social Theory: The Multicultural & Classic Readings,* ed. Charles Lemert, 479–84. Boulder, Colo.: Westview Press.

Boyd, Todd. 1997. *Am I Black Enough for You?: Popular Culture from the 'Hood and Beyond.* Bloomington and Indianapolis: Indiana University Press.

Carasco, Rubin Keyser. 1998. "Set Trippin'." *Blaze* (Fall): 206–7.

Chávez, Linda. 1991. *Out of the Barrio: Towards a New Politics of Hispanic Assimilation.* New York: Basic Books.

Cross, Brian. 1993. *It's Not About a Salary: Rap, Race and Resistance in Los Angeles.* New York: Verso Books.

Dennis, Reginald. 1992. Liner notes in *Street Jams: Hip Hop from the Top, Part 2.* Rhino R4 70578. Cassette.

Flores, Juan. 1988. "Rappin', Writin' & Breakin'." *CENTRO* 2, no. 3 (Spring): 34–41.

——— 1992–1993. "Puerto Rican and Proud, Boyee!: Rap, Roots and Amnesia." *CENTRO* 5, no. 1 (Winter): 22–32.

——— 1993. *Divided Borders: Essays on Puerto Rican Identity.* Houston: Arte Público Press.

——— 1996a. "Pan-Latino/Trans-Latino: Puerto Ricans in the 'New Nueva York.'" *CENTRO* 8, nos. 1 and 2 (Spring): 171–86.

——— 1996b. "Puerto Rocks: New York Ricans Stake Their Claim." In *Droppin' Science: Critical Essays on Rap Music and Hip Hop Culture,* ed. William Eric Perkins, 85–105. Philadelphia: Temple University Press.

——— 2000. "Cha Cha with a Backbeat: Songs and Stories of Latin Boogaloo." In *From Bomba to Hip Hop: Puerto Rican Culture and Latino Identity,* ed. Juan Flores, 79–112. New York: Columbia University Press.

Foner, Nancy. 1987. "The Jamaicans: Race and Ethnicity Among Migrants in New York City." In *New Immigrants in New York,* ed. Nancy Foner, 195–217. New York: Columbia University Press.

Fox, Geoffrey. 1996. *Hispanic Nation: Culture, Politics, and the Constructing of Identity.* Tucson: University of Arizona Press.

Gans, Herbert. 1992. "Second-Generation Decline: Scenarios for the Economic and Ethnic Futures of the Post-1965 American Immigrants." *Ethnic and Racial Studies* 15(2): 173–92.

Garcia, F. Chris. 1988. Introduction to *Latinos and the Political System.* Notre Dame: University of Notre Dame Press.

Gilroy, Paul. 1993. *The Black Atlantic: Modernity and Double Consciousness.* Cambridge, Mass.: Harvard University Press.

Gregory, Deborah. 1995–1996. "Lauren Vélez." *Vibe* 3, no. 10 (December/January): 129.

Grosfoguel, Ramón and Chloé Georas. 1996. "The Racialization of Latino Caribbean Migrants in the New York Metropolitan Area." *CENTRO* 8, nos. 1 and 2 (Spring): 190–201.

Guevara, Nancy. 1987. "Women Writin', Rappin', Breakin'." In *The Year Left,* ed. Mike Davis, 160–75. London: Verso Books.

Hazzard-Donald, Katrina. 1996. "Dance in Hip Hop Culture." In *Droppin' Science: Critical Essays on Rap Music and Hip Hop Culture,* ed. William Eric Perkins, 220–35. Philadelphia: Temple University Press.

Hebdige, Dick. 1987. *Cut 'N' Mix: Culture, Identity and Caribbean Music.* New York: Methuen.

Henderson, Errol A. 1996. "Black Nationalism and Rap Music." *Journal of Black Studies* 26, no. 3 (January): 308–39.

Hochman, Steven. 1990. "Hispanic Rappers Stake Out New Turf." *Rolling Stone,* November 15, 36–37.

hooks, bell. 1994. "Back to Black: Ending Internalized Racism." In *Outlaw Culture: Resisting Representations.* New York: Routledge.

Irving, Antonette K. 1998. "Pussy Power: The Onerous Road to Sexual Liberation in Hip-Hop." *The Source* 101 (February): 34.

Jenkins, "Satchmo" and "Belafonte" Wilson. 1998. "Shades of Mandingo: Watermelon Men of Different Hues Exchange Views." *Ego Trip* 4(1): 24–26.

Jiménez, Roberto "Cuba" II. 1997. "Vanishing Latino Acts." *The Source* 95 (August): 22.

Jorge, Angela. 1986. "The Black Puerto Rican Woman in Contemporary Society." In *The Puerto Rican Woman: Perspectives on Culture History and Society,* ed. Edna Acosta-Belén, 180–87. New York: Praeger.

Kasinitz, Philip. 1992. *Caribbean New York: Black Immigrants and the Politics of Race.* Ithaca, New York: Cornell University Press.

Kelley, Robin D. G. 1996. "Kickin' Reality, Kickin' Ballistics: Gangsta Rap and Postindustrial Los Angeles." In *Droppin' Science: Critical Essays on Rap Music and Hip Hop Culture,* ed. William Eric Perkins, 117–58. Philadelphia: Temple University Press.

Lascaibar, Juice (TC-5). 1997. "Hip-Hop 101: Respect the Architects of Your History." *The Source* 95 (August): 47–48.

Manuel, Peter. 1995. *Caribbean Currents: Caribbean Music from Rumba to Reggae.* Philadelphia: Temple University Press.

McLaren, Peter. 1995. "Gangsta Pedagogy and Ghettoethnicity: The Hip Hop Nation as Counterpublic Sphere." *Socialist Review* 25(2): 9–55.

Menéndez, Marilú. 1988. "How to Spot a Jaguar in the Jungle." *The Village Voice,* August 9, pp. 20–21.

Morales, Ed. 1991. "How Ya Like Nosotros Now?" *The Village Voice,* November 26, p. 91.

——— 1996. "The Last Blackface: The Lamentable Image of Latinos in Film." *Sí* (Summer): 44–47.

Morales, Robert. 1996. "Fat Joe: Heart of Bronxness." *Vibe* 4, no. 2 (March): 84.

Morgan, Joan. 1996. "Fly-Girls, Bitches and Hoes: Notes of a Hip Hop Feminist." *Elementary* 1 (Summer): 16–20.

Norfleet, Dawn Michaelle. 1997. " 'Hip Hop Culture' in New York City: The Role of Verbal Musical Performance in Defining a Community." Ph.D. diss., Columbia University, New York.

Oboler, Suzanne. 1995. *Ethnic Labels, Latino Lives: Identity and the Politics of (Re)Presentation in the United States.* Minneapolis: University of Minnesota Press.

Ogbu, John U. 1978. *Minority Education and Caste: The American System in Cross-Cultural Perspective.* New York: Academic Press.

Orsi, Robert. 1992. "The Religious Boundaries of an Inbetween People: Street *Feste* and the Problem of the Dark-Skinned Other in Italian Harlem, 1920–1990." *American Quarterly* 44(3): 313–47.

Pabón, Carlos. 1995. "De Albizu a Madonna: Para armar y desarmar la nacionalidad." *bordes* no. 2: 22–40.

Panda, Andy. 1995. Talk given at Muévete!: The Boricua Youth Conference, Hunter College, New York City, November 11.

Parris, Jennifer. 1996. "Freestyle Forum." *Urban* 2(1): 30–31.

Pérez, Richie. 1990. "From Assimilation to Annihilation: Puerto Rican Images in U.S. Films." *CENTRO* 2, no. 8 (Spring): 8–27.

Puff Daddy & The Family. 1997. *No Wag Out.* Bad Boy 78612-73012-4. Cassette. Q-Unique (Anthony Quiles), rapper and member of the Arsonists. 1995a. Interview by author. Tape recording. Lower East Side, Manhattan, New York, October 12.

——— 1995b. *Rice and Beans.* Unreleased cassette.

Raekwon. 1995. *Only Built for Cuban Linx.* RCA 66663-4 07863. Cassette.

Rivera, Raquel. 1996. "Boricuas from the Hip Hop Zone: Notes on Race and Ethnic Relations in New York City." *CENTRO* 8, nos. 1 and 2 (Spring): 202–15.

Roberts, John Storm. 1979. *The Latin Tinge: The Impact of Latin American Music on the United States.* Oxford: Oxford University Press.

Rodríguez, Clara E. 1991. *Puerto Ricans: Born in the U.S.A.* Boulder: Westview Press.

——— 1997. "The Silver Screen: Stories and Stereotypes." In *Latin Looks: Images of Latinas and Latinos in the U.S. Media,* ed. Clara E. Rodríguez, 73–79. Boulder, Colo.: Westview Press.

Rodríguez, Edward. 1995. Hip Hop Culture: The Myths and Misconceptions of This Urban Counterculture. Tms. unpublished manuscript.

Rodríguez-Morazzani, Roberto P. 1996. "Beyond the Rainbow: Mapping the Discourse on Puerto Ricans and 'Race.'" *CENTRO* 8, nos. 1 and 2 (Spring): 151–69.

Rose, Tricia. 1994. *Black Noise: Rap Music and Black Culture in Contemporary America.* Hanover, N.H.: Wesleyan University Press.

Ross, Andrew. 1989. *No Respect: Intellectuals and Popular Culture.* New York: Routledge.

Salazar, Max. 1992. "Latinized Afro-American Rhythms." In *Salsiology: Afro-Cuban Music and the Evolution of Salsa in New York City,* ed. Vernon Boggs, 237–48. New York: Greenwood Press.

Samara. 1987. In *Sex Work: Writings by Women in the Sex Industry,* ed. Frédérique Delacoste and Priscilla Alexander, 37. Pittsburgh: Cleis Press.

Samuels, David. 1995. "The Rap on Rap: The 'Black Music' That Isn't Either." In *Rap on Rap: Straight-Up Talk on Hip-Hop Culture,* ed. Adam Sexton, 241–52. New York: Dell Publishing.

Smith, Christopher Holmes. 1997. "Method in the Madness: Exploring the Boundaries of Identity in Hip-Hop Performativity." *Social Identities* (3): 345–74.

Smith, Robert. 1994. "'Doubly Bounded' Solidarity: Race and Social Location in the Incorporation of Mexicans Into New York City." Paper presented at the Conference of Fellows: Program of Research on the Urban Underclass, Social Science Research Council, University of Michigan, June.

Sundiata, Sekou. 1998. "The Latin Connection." Essay in playbill for the Black Rock Coalition's music performance *The Latin Connection,* BAM Majestic Theater, Brooklyn, New York, June 27.

Tate, Greg. 1995. "Bronx Banshee." *Vibe* 3, no. 9 (November): 44.

Thomas, Piri. 1967. *Down These Mean Streets.* New York: Vintage Books.

Thompson, Robert Farris. 1996. "Hip Hop 101." In *Droppin' Science: Critical Essays on Rap Music and Hip Hop Culture,* ed. William Eric Perkins, 211–19. Philadelphia: Temple University Press.

Tompkins, Dave. 1996. "Hollywood Shuffle." *Rap Pages* 5, no. 8 (September): 16–17.

Toop, David. 1991. *Rap Attack 2: African Rap to Global Hip Hop.* London: Serpent's Tail.

Torres, Andrés. 1995. *Between Melting Pot and Mosaic: African Americans and Puerto Ricans in the New York Political Economy.* Philadelphia: Temple University Press.

A Tribe Called Quest. 1993. *Midnight Marauders.* Jive Records 41490. Compact disc.

Urciuoli, Bonnie. 1996. *Exposing Prejudice: Puerto Rican Experiences of Language, Race and Class.* Boulder, Colo.: Westview Press.

Verán, Cristina. 1991. "Many Shades of Our Culture: A History of Latinos in Hip Hop." *Word Up!,* 24–26.

——— 1996. "That's the Breaks." *Rap Pages* 5, no. 8 (September): 6.

Waters, Mary. 1996. "Ethnic and Racial Identities of Second-Generation Black Immigrants in New York City." In *The New Second Generation,* ed. Alejandro Portes, 171–96. New York: Russell Sage Foundation.

Weisberg, Chang. 1998. "Hip Hop's Minority?: The Past, Present, and Future of Latinos in Hip Hop." *Industry Insider* 15: 50–57, 96–97.

Zentella, Ana Celia. 1997. *Growing Up Bilingual: Puerto Rican Children in New York.* Malden, Mass.: Blackwell Publishers.

32

Daughters of the Blues

Women, Race, and Class Representation in Rap Music Performance

CHERYL L. KEYES

In a chapter taken from her book Rap Music and Street Consciousness, *Cheryl Keyes (a professor of ethnomusicology at UCLA) looks at the roles played by women in hip hop through interviews with "African American women performers and audience members—and from the comments of black female critics and scholars. . . ." Keyes analyzes these interviews and suggests that black American female rappers can be placed in four basic categories: "Queen Mother," "Fly Girl," "Sista with Attitude," and "The Lesbian." Careful not to fall into the trap of stereotyping herself, the author suggests that female rappers are making steady inroads into a creative arena that has largely been dominated by males through the use of several important strategies. Perhaps the most important and commercially viable means by which they have excelled is by combining rapping and singing. Keyes cites Lauryn Hill and TLC's Left Eye as prime examples of this phenomenon.*

Keyes also points out that rap—one of hip hop's initial creative expressions—allows females to "convey their views on a variety of issues concerning identity, sociohistory, and esoteric beliefs shared by young African American women." Furthermore, rap permits women to speak more freely, thus helping other (black) women to "create spaces for themselves and other sistas." In short, this aspect of hip hop's expressive culture can, and increasingly does, serve to empower women. Whether these trends will allow black women to make strong, significant inroads into the increasingly corporatized world of commercial radio airplay, the shrinking number of record companies with enough clout to be heard on the radio and the dominance of males in this field perhaps remain the principal challenges that face the daughters of the blues in the early twenty-first century.

Rap music has been often presented in the media as an urban male phenomenon. This assumption is more apparent when observing the disproportionate representation of female MCs featured in music video programs or on radio compared to that of male artists. Though the presence of female rap artists may seem rather small, particularly during rap's formative years, observers of this form began to notice the proliferation of successful rap female acts during the 1990s. As the rap music journalist Havelock Nelson notes, "While women have always been involved artistically with rap throughout the '80s; artists like [MC]

Lyte, [Queen] Latifah, Roxanne Shanté, and [Monie] Love have had to struggle to reach a level of success close to that of male rappers" (1993:77). Like their male counterparts, women rap about aspects of inner-city life and their desire to be "number one"; unlike male MCs, they shed light on everyday realities from a woman's perspective. In challenging the predominance of male rappers, female rap artists have not only proven that they have lyrical skillz, but in their struggle to survive and thrive within this tradition they have created spaces from which to deliver powerful messages from black female and black feminist viewpoints.

Women of rap address issues pertinent to black working-class and ghetto culture in a manner unlike other black women artists in jazz, rhythm and blues, and contemporary pop song styles. While other black women singers deal with topics that conform to the traditional or mainstream idealization of romantic love, women in rap approach love themes and other topics from a viewpoint that is meaningful to black working-class women. Women in rap are more closely allied to the women blues singers, known as classic blues singers, of the 1920s. Similar to women blues singers, female MCs perceive rap as a site from which to contest, protest, and affirm working-class ideologies of black womanhood, notes Angela Y. Davis. "Through the blues, black women were able to autonomously work out—as audiences and performers—a working-class model of womanhood" (1998:46).

Davis concurs with the blues scholar Daphne D. Harrison, who writes that classic blues singers of the 1920s, such as Ma Rainey, Bessie Smith, and Ida Cox, were

> pivotal figures in the assertion of black women's ideas and ideals from the standpoint of the working class and the poor. It reveals their dynamic role as spokespersons and interpreters of the dreams, harsh realities, and tragicomedies of the black experience in the first three decades of this century; their role in the continuation and development of black music in America; their contributions to blues poetry and performance. Further, it expands the base of knowledge about the role of black women in the creation and development of American popular culture; illustrates their modes and means for coping successfully with gender-related discrimination and exploitation; and demonstrates an emerging model for the working woman—one who is sexually independent, self-sufficient, creative, assertive, and trend-setting. (1988:10)

The title of this chapter, "Daughters of the Blues," heralds my assertion that women rappers are part of a continuum established by early female blues singers, who, like female MCs, created a distinctive voice that reflected and celebrated the ethos of working-class black womanhood. Both women's traditions establish "a discourse that articulate[s] a cultural and political struggle over sexual relations: a struggle that is directed against the objectification of female sexuality within a patriarchal order, but also tries to reclaim women's bodies" (Carby 1986:12).

While one will find topics common to several black women's song traditions, including social commentary, political protest, and violence against women, there is a preponderance of prison and ghetto love songs among women blues and rap performers. Most of these songs illustrate the plight of being black and poor under a U.S. justice system that works in favor of the white and well-to-do. Using words uncommon in mainstream romantic pop or jazz songs, women of the blues affectionately refer to their male lovers as "Papa" or "Daddy," while women of rap refer to their male competitors or lovers as "sophisticated thugs" or "niggas." Songs about lesbian relationships are "mainstream" in the blues and rap traditions. Songs celebrating women loving women circulated in the classic blues repertory, for example, Ma Rainey's "Prove It On Me Blues." Similarly, rap music broke ground with a lesbian song by the female artist Queen Pen, who will be discussed in more detail below. Finally, the classic blues singers defied mainstream attitudes about the full-figured black woman, who was often portrayed in patriarchal-controlled media as a mammy, an asexual being. Classic blues singers not only privileged the large-framed black woman, they embraced her as a sexually desirable and sexually active being. Such attitudes about being full-figured, fly, and seductive remain a fixture in hip-hop. Thus I firmly contend that the rise of female MCs in the late twentieth century represents an ongoing musical saga of black women's issues concerning male-female relationships, female sexuality, and black women's representations from a working-class point of view.

Data used in this chapter derive from interviews with "cultural readers"—African American women performers and audience members—and from the comments of black female critics and scholars, who constitute what I refer to as an "interpretive community." In *Black Women as Cultural Readers,* the film critic and scholar Jacqueline Bobo explores the concept of "interpretive community" as a movement comprised of black female cultural producers, critics, scholars, and cultural consumers (1995:22). She writes, "as a group, the women make up what I have termed an interpretive community, which is strategically placed in relation to cultural works that either are created by black women or feature them in significant ways. Working together the women utilize representations of black women that they deem valuable, in productive and politically useful ways" (22). Because much of the criticism of work by black female independent filmmakers stems from male or white perspectives, Bobo finds it necessary to incorporate the views of black women involved in making or consuming these films to accurately assess the intent and effect of the films. Bobo's concept of the "interpretive community" is appropriate to this examination of women in rap because, like film, rap music is a form transmitted by recorded and video performances.

When MC Lyte was asked, for example, if she felt that there was a distinct female rap history, she separated women rappers into crews that reigned in three periods: the early 1980s, the mid-1980s through the early 1990s, and the late 1990s: "Sha-Rock, Sequence, to me, that's the first crew. Then you've got a second crew, which is Salt-N-Pepa, Roxanne Shanté, The Real Roxanne, me, Latifah, Monie [Love], and Yo-Yo. Then after that you got Da Brat, Foxy Brown, Lil' Kim, Heather B" (MC Lyte interview).[1]

In the female rap tradition, four distinct categories of women rappers emerge: "Queen Mother," "Fly Girl," "Sista with Attitude," and "The Lesbian." Black female rappers can shift between these categories, however, or belong to more than one simultaneously. Each category mirrors certain images, voices, and lifestyles of African American women in contemporary urban society.

Queried about specific categories, rap music performers and female audience members frequently used the buzz words "fly" and "attitude" (as in "girlfriend got attitude"), leading me to more clearly discern the parameters of these categories. I revised category of "Black Diva" in early interviews to "Queen Mother" after one female observer convincingly said "diva" denoted a posture of arrogance and pretentiousness as opposed to that of a regal and self-assured woman, qualities that she identified with the Queen Latifah types (Ronda R. Penrice, personal communication, 1995). Let us now examine these four categories or images of black women that female MCs and the interpretive community in general consider representative of and specific to African American female identity in contemporary urban culture.

QUEEN MOTHER

The Queen Mother category comprises female rappers who view themselves as African-centered icons, which is often evoked by their dress. The terms they use to describe themselves—"Asiatic Black Women," "Nubian Queens," "intelligent black women," or "sistas droppin' knowledge to the people"—suggest their self-constructed identity and intellectual prowess. The Queen Mother is associated with traditional African court culture. For instance, in the sixteenth-century Benin kingdom of southeastern Nigeria, she was the mother of a reigning king. Because of her maternal connection to the king, she received certain rights and privileges, including control over districts and a voice in the national affairs of the state. During her son's reign, a commemorative head made of brass, with a facial expression capturing her reposed manner, was sculpted in her honor and adorned with a beaded choker, headdress, and crown.[2]

It is certainly possible that female rap artists know of the historical significance of African queens. Women in this category adorn their bodies with royal or Kente cloth strips, African headdresses, goddess braid styles, and ankh-stylized jewelry. Their rhymes embrace black female empowerment and spirituality, making clear their self-identification as African, woman, warrior, priestess, and queen. Queen Mothers demand respect not only for their people but for black women by men. Among those women distinguished by the interpretive community as Queen Mothers are Queen Kenya, Queen Latifah, Sister Souljah, Nefertiti, Queen Mother Rage, Isis, and Yo-Yo.

Queen Kenya, a member of hip-hop's Zulu Nation, was the first female MC to use "Queen" as a stage name, but the woman of rap who became the first solo female MC to commercially record under the name "Queen" is Dana "Queen Latifah" Owens. Queen Latifah's initial singles, "Princess of the Posse" and "Wrath of My Madness" (1988), followed by her debut album *All Hail the Queen* (1989), established her regal identity. Her songs include lyrics such as, "you try to be down, / you can't take my crown from me" and "I'm on the scene, / I'm the Queen of Royal Badness." Latifah, whose Arabic name means "feminine, delicate, and kind," explains that her cousin, who is a Muslim, gave her the name Latifah when she was eight. "Well in rap, I didn't want to be MC Latifah. It didn't sound right. I didn't want to come out like old models. So Queen just popped into my head one day, and I was like 'me, Queen Latifah.' It felt good saying it, and I felt like a queen. And you know, I am a queen. And every black woman is a queen" (Queen Latifah interview).

Latifah's maternal demeanor, posture, and full figure contribute to the perception of her as a Queen Mother. Although she acknowledges that others perceive her as motherly, she tries to distance herself from this ideal: " 'I wish I wasn't seen as a mother, though. I don't really care for that. Just because I take a mature stance on certain things, it gives me a motherly feel . . . maybe because I am full-figured. I am mature, but I'm twenty-one'" (quoted in Green 1991:33).

The ambiguity of Latifah's motherly image follows what the feminist scholars Joan Radner and Susan Lanser identify as a form of coding in women's folk culture called *distraction:* a device used to "drown out or draw attention away from the subversive power of a feminist message" (1993:15). Using distraction allows the artists to deliver strong pro-woman, pro-black messages and have a better chance of being heard. Queen Latifah finds that her stature and grounded perspective cause fans to view her as a person to revere or, at times, fear. However, Latifah attempts to mute her motherly image offstage, indicating to fans that she remains modest, down-to-earth, and an ordinary person in spite of her onstage "Queen of Royal Badness" persona.

In *Black Feminist Thought*, the sociologist Patricia Hill Collins states that in the African American community, some women are viewed as "othermothers": "Black women's involvement in fostering African-American community development forms the basis for community-based power. This is the type of 'strong Black woman' they see around them in traditional African-American communities. Community othermothers work on behalf of the Black community by expressing ethics of caring and personal accountability which embrace conceptions of transformation and mutuality.... [C]ommunity othermothers become identified as power figures through furthering the community's well-being" (1990:132).

Queen Latifah's othermother posture is reflected most vividly through her lyrics, which, at times, address political and economic issues facing black women and the black community as a whole. In Latifah's song "The Evil That Men Do" (1989) from *All Hail the Queen*, she "isolates several of the difficulties commonly experienced by young black women [on welfare]" (Forman 1994:44) and depicts how the powers that be are apathetic to black women who are trying to beat the odds:

> Here is a message for my sisters and brothers
> here are some things I wanna cover.
> A woman strives for a better life
> but who the hell cares because she's living on welfare?
> The government can't come up with a decent housing plan
> so she's in no-man's-land.
> It's a sucker who tells you you're equal....
> Someone's livin' the good life tax-free
> 'cause some poor girl can't be livin' crack free
> and that's just part of the message
> I thought I had to send you about the evil that men do.

In "How Do I Love Thee," on Latifah's sophomore LP, *Nature of a Sista* (1991), she uses a seductive vocal style to suggest a young woman in love. The video shows Latifah and a man, as well as other heterosexual couples, embracing one another. The presentation of Latifah in a sexual role was problematic for some of her audience, according to the hip-hop feminist critic Joan Morgan. Morgan opined that some of Latifah's fans were restricted by Latifah's maternal persona, an image associated with nurturing but devoid of sexuality.[3] She contends that "How Do I Love Thee" not only established Latifah's sexuality but also expressed a controlled, non-promiscuous black female sexuality that defied the white patriarchal myth of the "black Jezebel" or whore (Collins 1990:77). Thus, Latifah's "How Do I Love Thee" asserts that not only can "maternal figures" be sensuous, they can comfortably enjoy eroticism on their own terms.

Latifah's role as Queen Mother of rap was etched in stone with her platinum single "Ladies First" (1989), the first political commentary rap song by a female artist. The lyrics of "Ladies First" defy stereotypes about female MCs' inability to create rhymes:

> I break into a lyrical freestyle
> Grab the mike, look at the crowd and see smiles
> 'Cause they see a woman standing up on her own two [feet]
> Sloppy slouching is something I won't do.
> Some think that we [women] can't flow
> Stereotypes they got to go.
> I'm gonna mess around and flip the scene into reverse,
> with a little touch of ladies first.

The video version is more explicitly political, containing live footage of South Africa's anti-apartheid riots overlaid with photographic stills of the black heroines Harriet Tubman, Frances Ellen Watkins Harper, Sojourner Truth, Angela Davis, Winnie Mandela, and Rosa Parks. As Queen Mother, Latifah scolds the misinformed and misogynistic and educates her listeners about the diverse and powerful matriarchs who demand respect.

Since Queen Latifah's success, she has sought out other avenues within the entertainment industry. She was an original member of the New Jersey–based MC crew known as Flavor Unit, produced by DJ Mark the 45 King. After the release of her first LP, she transformed Flavor Unit into an artist management enterprise and a record company in the early 1990s. Queen Latifah later appeared as a magazine mogul named Khadijah in the sitcom "Living Single." She has also appeared in several films alongside leading Hollywood actors. In the film *Set It Off* she plays one of the lead women gangstas with Kimberly Elise, Vivica A. Fox, and Jada Pinkett Smith. She also plays a private nurse in the thriller *The Bone Collector*, which stars Denzel Washington. Additionally, Queen Latifah began hosting her own TV talk show in September 1999. Her autobiography, *Ladies First: Revelations of a Strong Woman* (1999), became a bestseller.

Queen Latifah opened the door for other Afrocentric female MCs such as Sister Souljah. A former associate of the Black Nationalist rap group Public Enemy, Souljah launched her first LP in 1992. *360 Degrees of Power* featured the rap single "The Final Solution: Slavery's Back in Effect," in which "Souljah imagines a police state where blacks fight the reinstitution of slavery" (Leland 1992:48). With her candid yet quasi-preachy style of delivery, she earned the title "raptivist" from her followers. Souljah's fame grew after her speech at Reverend Jesse Jackson's Rainbow Coalition Leadership Summit in 1992, where she chided African Americans who murder one another for no apparent reason by figuratively suggesting, "'why not take a week and kill white people?'" (quoted in Leland 1992:48). As a consequence, Souljah was ridiculed as a propagator of hate by presidential candidate Bill Clinton. In the wake of the controversy, her record sales plummeted dramatically while her "raptivist" messages skyrocketed through her appearances on talk shows like "Donahue" and speeches on the university lecture circuit. While Sister Souljah advocates racial, social, and economic parity, she also looks within the community to relationships between black men and women in her lyrics and semiautobiographical book *No Disrespect* (1994:xiv). Sister Souljah also published *The Coldest Winter Ever: A Novel* (1999), which addresses romantic themes from a black working-class woman's perspective.

Nefertiti, Isis,[4] and Queen Mother Rage depict the Queen Mother image via their names and attire. Lauryn Hill earns the title through her lyrics and her community outreach programs like the Refugee Project. Yo-Yo, who is also regarded by the interpretive community as a Queen Mother, uses her lyrics to promote her political ideology of black feminism and female respectability, as advanced by her organization, the Intelligent Black Women's Coalition (IBWC), which she discusses on her debut CD, *Make Way for the Motherlode* (1991). But Yo-Yo's image—long blonde braids, tight-fitting shorts worn by Jamaican dancehall women performers called "batty riders," and her gyrating hips also position her in the next category, "Fly Girl."

FLY GIRL

Fly describes someone in chic clothing and fashionable hairstyles, jewelry, and cosmetics, a style that grew out of the black action films (pejoratively called blaxploitation films) of the late 1960s through the mid-1970s. These films include *Shaft* (1971), *Superfly* (1972), *The Mack* (1973), and *Foxy Brown* (1974), a film that inspired one rapper to adopt the movie's title as her moniker. The fly personae in these films influenced a wave of black contemporary youth who resurrected flyness and its continuum in hip-hip culture.

During the early 1980s, women rappers, including Sha Rock of Funky Four Plus One, the group Sequence, and the soloist Lady B, dressed in a way that was considered by their audiences to be fly. They wore miniskirts, sequined fabric, high-heeled shoes, and prominent make-up. By 1985 the commercial recording of "A Fly Girl" by the male rap group Boogie Boys and an answer rap during the same year, "A Fly Guy," by the female rapper Pebblee-Poo, launched a public dialogue of "flyness" in the hip-hop community. In "A Fly Girl," the Boogie Boys describe a fly girl as a woman who wants you to see her name and "her game" and who wears tight jeans or leather miniskirts and abundant gold jewelry and make-up. She has voluptuous curves, but contrary to other "mainstream" images of sexy, acquiescent women, the fly girl speaks what is on her mind.

By the mid-1980s, many female MCs began contesting the fly girl image because they wanted their audiences to focus more on their rapping than on their dress. Despite this changing trend, the female rap trio Salt-N-Pepa canonized the ultimate fly girl posture of rap by donning short, tight-fitting outfits, leather clothing, ripped jeans or punk clothing, glittering gold jewelry (i.e. earrings and necklaces), long sculpted nails, prominent make-up, and hairstyles ranging from braids to wraps to waves in ever-changing hair colors.

Rap's fly girl image is political because it calls attention to aspects of black women's bodies that are considered undesirable by mainstream American standards of beauty (Roberts 1998). Through their performances, Salt-N-Pepa are flippin da script (or deconstructing dominant ideology) by wearing clothes that accent their full breasts, rounded buttocks, and ample thighs, considered beauty markers of black women by black culture but ridiculed or caricatured by the mainstream (Roberts 1998).[5] Moreover, they portray the fly girl as a partygoer, an independent woman, and as an erotic subject rather than an objectified object.

Female rappers' reclamation of the fly resonates with the late Audre Lorde's theory of the erotic as power (Davis 1998:172). In Lorde's seminal essay "Uses of the Erotic" (1984), she reveals the transformative power of the erotic in black women's culture: "Our erotic knowledge empowers us, becomes a lens through which we scrutinize all aspects of our existence, forcing us to evaluate those aspects honestly in terms of their meaning within our lives" (1984:57). The cultural critic and scholar bell hooks claims that black women's erotic consciousness is textualized around issues of body esteem. "Erotic pleasure requires of us engagement with the realm of the senses . . . the capacity to be in touch with sensual reality; to accept and love [our] bodies; to work toward working self-recovery issues around body esteem; [and] to be empowered by a healing eroticism" (1993:116,121–22,124).

Black fly girls express a growing awareness of their erotic selves by sculpting their own personas and, as the folklorist Elaine J. Lawless (1998) puts it, "writing their own bodies." For example, Salt-N-Pepa describe themselves as "'women [who have] worked hard to keep our bodies in shape; we're proud to show them off. . . . We're not ashamed of our sexuality; for we're Salt-N-Pepa—sexier and more in control'" (quoted in Rogers 1994:31).

Another aspect of the fly girl persona is independence. Salt notes that "'the image we project reflects the real independent woman of the '90s'" (quoted in Chyll 1994:20). But for many women of rap, achieving a sense of independence in an entrepreneurial sense has not been easy. For instance, it is common knowledge in the rap community that during Salt-N-Pepa's early years, their lyrics and hit songs ("I'll Take Your Man," "Push It," "Tramp," and "Shake Your Thang") were written mainly by their manager/producer Hurby "Luv Bug" Azor. For the *Black's Magic* (1990) CD, Salt (Cheryl James) ventured into writing and producing with the single "Expression," which went platinum. *Black's Magic* also contained Salt-N-Pepa's "Let's Talk about Sex" (written by Azor), which Salt rewrote for a public service announcement song and video, "Let's Talk about AIDS," in 1992.

On Salt-N-Pepa's fourth LP, *Very Necessary* (1993), the group wrote and produced most of the selections. The celebratory songs "Shoop" and "Whatta Man" from that album deserve note.[6] In the video versions of both songs, the three women eyeball desirable men. The "Shoop" video presents the trio as female subjects carefully scrutinizing men they desire, from business types to ruffnecks (a fly guy associated with urban street culture), thus turning tables on the male rappers; in it ladies "'see a bunch of bare-chested, tight-bunned brothers acting like sex *objects*, servicing it up to us in our videos,'" says Salt (quoted in Rogers 1994:31). In the "Whatta Man" video, Salt-N-Pepa praise their significant others in the areas of friendship, romance, and parenting as the female rhythm and blues group En Vogue joins them in singing the chorus, "Whatta man, whatta man, whatta man, whatta mighty good man."

Other women whom the interpretive community categorizes as fly are Left Eye and Yo-Yo. Left Eye is the rapper of the hip-hop/rhythm and blues hybrid group TLC (*T-Boz, Left Eye*, and *Chili*). TLC's baggy style of dress runs counter to the revealing apparel of hip-hop's typical fly girl image, providing role models they hope will inspire their full-figured audience to do the same. TLC's T-Boz said, "'We like to wear a lot of baggy stuff because for one, it's comfortable, and two, many of our fans don't have the so-called perfect figure; we don't want them to feel like they can't wear what we're wearing'" (quoted in Horner 1993:16). Throughout the 1990s, TLC remained steadfast with the message to women of all sizes regarding mental and physical wellness and body esteem, as underscored in both music and video performances of the single "Unpretty" (1999).

Like Salt-N-Pepa, TLC has made delivering the "safe sex" message a priority. While both groups do so through lyrics, TLC underscores it visually through wearing certain accoutrements. Left Eye wears a condom in place of an eyeglass lens, while other members of the group attach colored condom packages to their clothes. TLC's warning about unprotected sex, emphasized by the condoms they wear, is conveyed powerfully in their award-winning "Waterfalls" from their second LP, *CrazySexyCool* (1994). The message is amplified in the video: a man's decision to follow his partner's wish not to use a condom leads to deadly consequences. Days after this encounter, he notices a lesion on his face, which suggests that he has contacted the virus that causes AIDS. TLC's espousal of fly, sexually independent living in their lyrics and image is firmly entwined with a message of sexual responsibility.

In "His Story," from their debut album, TLC looks beyond the supposedly superficial woman depicted by the fly image to address the real threat of violence that black women face. The unsolved case of Tawana Brawley—who was allegedly raped by white officers of the New York Police Department—becomes emblematic of the murkier intersections of race and gender politics. Race complicates the "virtue question" put to many women who have dared to speak up after being raped. In an interview, Left Eye said, "'It's already hard to be black, but we [black women] got two strikes against us.'" T-Boz added, "'We got the worse end of the stick, being black and female'" (quoted in Mayo 1992:49). While TLC's image is fly, their lyrics are serious, delving into complex social issues facing African American women in contemporary society.

Like TLC, Yo-Yo also delivers a serious message about black womanhood that earns her a place among the Queen Mothers, but her gyrating hips, stylish golden-blonde braids, tight-fitting short outfits, and pronounced makeup also categorize her as fly.[7] Yo-Yo writes about independent, empowered black women, championing African American sisterhood in "The I.B.W.C. National Anthem" and "Sisterland" from *Make Way for the Motherlode* (1991). She takes on sexuality in "You Can't Play with My Yo-Yo" and "Put a Lid on It," which, as suggested by their titles, explore sexual control and responsibility.

In 1996 Yo-Yo moved beyond the shadow of her mentor Ice Cube with her fourth CD *Total Control*, for which she served as executive producer. Following this success, Yo-Yo began a column called "Yo, Yo-Yo" in the hop-hop magazine *Vibe*, in which she addresses questions about heterosexual relationships and interpersonal growth as the representative of the IBWC.

In the late 1990s, the female MC, songwriter, and producer, Missy "Misdemeanor" Elliott joined the fly girl ranks. Mesmerizing viewers with her debut album *Supa Dupa Fly* (1997) and her single "The Rain," which was nominated for three MTV video awards, Elliott has found success with her musical partner Tim "Timbaland" Mosley. Some critics, like Hilton Als, have even called the duo a "'latter-day Ashford and Simpson'" (quoted in Weingarten 1998a:68). In addition to the reverence her creative skills engender, her fans also admire her finger-wave hairstyle, known to some as "Missy waves," and her ability to carry off the latest hip-hop fashions on her full-figured frame. Demonstrating the more typical image of a fly girl as being focused on clothes and looks, in a *Los Angeles Times* cover story Elliott revealed the source of her fashion savvy to fans: "'When I was a kid, I wanted to be like my mother. She's a very classy lady who always wore great clothes and loved to wear nice shoes'" (quoted in Weingarten 1998a:68). Elliott has occasionally appeared in television advertisements for the youth fashion store The Gap and as a spokesperson for Iman's lipstick line. She succeeds as a full-figured woman, breaking new ground in the "fly arena" that had been off-limits to all but the most slender or "correctly" proportioned women. In staking her claim to rap music's fly girl category, Elliott further reclaims sexuality and eros as healing power for all black women, regardless of size. With her single "She's a Bitch" from her sophomore LP *Da Real World* (1999), Elliott appends another image to her fly girl posture. With her face and hairstyle resembling that of the singer-actress-model Grace Jones—the femme fatale of disco—Elliott's usage of "bitch" makes a declaration about being a mover and shaker, on- and offstage, in rap's male-dominated arena, and thus she shares much in common with the artists of the next category, "Sista with Attitude."

SISTA WITH ATTITUDE

According to Geneva Smitherman, a scholar of Black English, "'tude, a diminutive form of attitude, can be defined as an aggressive, arrogant, defiant, I-know-I'm-BAD pose or air about oneself; or an oppositional or negative outlook or disposition" (1994:228). I group the prototypes of this category according to 'tude: Roxanne Shanté, Bytches with Problems (BWP), and Da Brat are known for their frankness; MC Lyte exudes a hardcore/no-nonsense approach; Boss is recognized for her gangsta bitch posture; and Eve and Mia X are first ladies with 'tude who work in the all-male crews such as Ruff Ryders and No Limit Soldiers, respectively.

In general, Sistas with Attitude comprise female MCs who value attitude as a means of empowerment and present themselves accordingly. Many of these sistas have reclaimed the word "bitch," viewing it as positive rather than negative and using the title to entertain or provide cathartic release. Other women in the interpretive community are troubled by that view. These women refused to be labeled a "bitch" because such appellations merely mar the images of young African American females (Hill 1994; "Female Rappers" 1991). Those who reclaim the term counter with the opinion that "it's not what you're called but what you answer to" (MC Lyte 1993). Some women of rap take a middle road, concurring that "bitch" can be problematic, depending on who uses the term, how it is employed, and to whom one refers. Queen

Latifah told me, "I don't really mind the term. I play around with it. I use it with my homegirls like, 'Bitch are you crazy? Bitch is a fierce girl.' Or 'That bitch is so crazy, girl.' Now, that is not harmful. But 'This stupid bitch just came down here talking...,' now that is meant in a harmful way. So it's the meaning behind the word that to me decides whether I should turn it off or listen to it" (Queen Latifah interview).

As an "aggressive woman who challenges male authority" (Ronda R. Penrice, personal communication, 1995), the Sista with Attitude revises the standard definition of "bitch" to mean an aggressive or assertive female who subverts patriarchal rule. Lyndah of BWP explains, "We use 'Bytches' [to mean] a strong, positive, aggressive woman who goes after what she wants. We take that on today and use it in a positive sense" ("Female Rappers" 1991). In a similar manner, Trina of the otherwise male crew Slip-N-Slide All-Stars, signifies on the term in her debut LP's title, *Da Baddest B***H* (2000).

Another characteristic of this category is the manner in which these sistas refer to their male competitors or suitors as "motherfuckas," "niggas," or "thug niggas." Because the element of signifying is aesthetically appealing in this style of rap, these terms may have both negative and positive meanings, depending on the context.

Roxanne Shanté is a prototype of the Sista with Attitude category. Shanté launched her rappin career at age fourteen with a female answer to UTFO/Full Force's "Roxanne, Roxanne" in 1984. The single, "Roxanne's Revenge," produced by DJ Marley Marl of Cold Chillin'/Warner Brothers, unleashed Shanté's attitude and foretold her future as a powerful sista. She grabbed her audience's attention by dissin UTFO members. Describing the UTFO member Kangol Kid as not really cute and not knowing how to operate sexually, Shanté garnered the title "The Millie Jackson of Rap" and maintained her bitch image with the follow-up LPs *Bad Sister* (1989) and *Bitch Is Back* (1992).[8] Shanté's "Big Mama," from *Bitch Is Back*, generated controversy because instead of dissin unfaithful male lovers—the standard fare of female rappers—Shanté dared to dis female rappers. She claims that she gave birth to most female MCs and that they, "all bitches," copied her style, "the capital S-H-A-N-T-E." The song "Big Mama" explicitly ridicules prominent female rappers' rhyming skills, hurling insults at Queen Latifah, Monie Love, MC Lyte, Isis, Yo-Yo, and Salt-N-Pepa. MC Lyte responded to Shanté with "Steady F—king" (from *Ain't No Other* [1993]). In this song, Lyte signifies on the male rapper KRS-One's "The Bridge Is Over" (1987), which used the words "Steady Fucking" to label Shanté as sexually promiscuous. Shanté's estrangement from female rappers as a result of "Big Mama" has not stopped her from continuing to praise herself as a "bitch." Other sistas with a bitch attitude include BWP, Conscious Daughters, and the solo rapper Boss, popularly known as the "gangsta bitch."

The male rapper Apache introduced this persona in a recording called "Gangsta Bitch" (1993). In this song, the strapped gangsta bitch packs a 9mm gun, drinks forty-ounce beers, and participates in stick-ups with her man. Although rap's first recognized female gangsta was Antoinette, Boss advanced the notion via her dress and use of expletives. Although many women of rap choose the image they feel is most aligned to their real feelings and values offstage, Boss is described by critics to be rather amiable in real life. Brought up primarily in the Midwest, she attended a Catholic college preparatory school in Detroit. On stage, Boss exchanges her middle-class origins and "the straight-up nice girl" image (Pulley 1994:A1) for that of a street gangsta. To perfect this image, she spent months being part of the street scene in Los Angeles and wearing gangsta-like attire. Boss maintains that her choice "to be real" (acquiescing to a street image) is a savvy business decision: "'I know what I'm doing, and I know how to make it in this [rap] business'" (quoted in Pulley 1994:A16).

The female rapper MC Lyte makes only moderate use of expletives and does not directly refer to herself as a "bitch" in her rap songs. Lyte's hardcore stage attitude—tough and aggressive—is intensified through the use of expletives but mostly through boisterous speech.[9] Her criticisms of men who play women for fools in the game of love are more subtle, with the predictable defeat of the male. This style is apparent in "Paper Thin," from *Lyte as a Rock* (1988), and "Lil' Paul" from *Ain't No Other* (1993). In "Paper Thin," Lyte addresses a fictitious boyfriend named Sam, who flirts with other women behind Lyte's back. Catching him in the act on the subway train (seen in the video version), Lyte proceeds to tell Sam that she is aware of his cheating, delivering her message with punch but without the malice characteristics of other Sistas with Attitude:

> when you say you love me, it doesn't matter.
> It goes into my head as just chit chatter . . .
> to look into my eyes to see what I am thinking,
> the dream is over, your yacht is sinking.
> I treat all of you like I treat all of them.
> What you say to me is still paper thin. Word!

Regardless of the topic, MC Lyte flaunts her rhyming skill in a quasi-raspy vocal timbre, which she characterizes as "quick, wicked, and buckwild" (from "Ain't No Other" [1993]). The audacity, contempt, and courage with which these Sistas with Attitude claim the microphone undoubtedly paved the way for their contemporaries, who have taken the attitude to newer, more lucrative heights. Three artists worth mentioning here are Da Brat of Chicago, Mia X of New Orleans, and Eve of Philadelphia. Da Brat is acknowledged as the first female solo rap artist to achieve platinum sales with her debut album *Funkdafied* (1994). Introduced to the Atlanta-based producer Jermaine Dupri by the rap duo Kris Kross, Da Brat has the essential traits of a Sista with Attitude. The hip-hop writer Tracii McGregor describes her as a rapper with a "foul mouth, an admitted tom-boy, [who] cusses like there's no tomorrow [but] has made that 'tude work for her" (1996:100).

The Sista with Attitude category includes Mia X and Eve, first ladies of their respective male crews. Echoing Da Brat's style is Mia X of No Limit Records, whose album *Unlady Like* (1997) garnered more than half a million dollars in sales. In an interview with Thembisa S. Mshaka, Mia X describes herself as "'hard-core, sensitive, and witty'" (quoted in Mshaka 1999:107). Unlike the other Sistas with Attitude, Mia X profiles her full-figure in fly style like Missy Elliott, but her gangsta lyrics—peppered with social commentary about southern ghetto life—temper the superficial femininity.

Eve emerged on the rap scene with the crew Ruff Ryders, led by DMX. Appearing fly with animal paw prints tattooed on her chest, "bleached-blond hair, model good looks, and rugged sound," her self-titled LP *Eve* (1999) sold more than a million copies ("Hottest Females" 2000:58). Top-selling singles from Eve's debut LP include "Love Is Blind," a domestic-violence rap featuring the vocals of Faith, and the single "Gotta Man," which sold over a million copies. Strikingly, "Gotta Man" resonates with Da Brat's "Ghetto Love" (featuring the singer T-Boz of TLC), from her second LP *Anuthatantrum* (1996). Both songs narrate the love and devotion of a woman in love with a very rowdy man. Da Brat and Eve do not present themselves as gangsta bitches; instead they view themselves as loyal, faithful, and devoted women who remain steadfast while their men do jail time. In "Ghetto Love," Da Brat boasts about her drug-dealer lover who showers her with a lavish lifestyle, whereas in "Gotta Man," Eve recalls the times when her incarcerated man draws hearts with her name on the jail cell wall. In the video version of "Gotta

Man," Eve's devotion to and support of her man is seen when she pawns her jewelry to post bail for him. Eventually, she picks him up upon his day of release, and he shows his appreciation with a rose and dinner. Eve and Da Brat affectionately refer to their male lovers as "sophisticated thug" and "motherfuckin nigga." While these songs appear to romanticize love with a "sophisticated thug," they contain a deeper message. Both songs capture the ongoing plight of some black males in the hood who, disillusioned with constant unemployment, resort to "underground" means of making a living. Furthermore, these songs reflect the devotion and adoration of some black working-class women for their men as well as the rappers' repudiation of the white patriarchal system's constant lockdown of black men and the poor.

In the late 1990s, the Sista with Attitude category was augmented with the rappers Lil' Kim and Foxy Brown, who conflate fly and hardcore attitudes in erotic lyrics and video performances, thus falling into both the Fly Girl and Sista with Attitude categories. In doing so, they are designated by some as the "'Thelma and Louise of rap'" (Brown quoted in Gonzales 1997:62) and the "bad girls of hip-hop." Foxy Brown, whose name is derived from Pam Grier's 1974 screen character, emulates the powerful and desirable yet dangerous woman: "'I think it's every girl's dream to be fly'" (Brown quoted in Gonzales 1997: 63). While Kim's debut album, *Hard Core* (1996), and Brown's *Ill Na Na* (1997) have reached platinum status, some members of the interpretive community criticize them for being "highly materialistic, violent, lewd" (Morgan 1997:77), an image exacerbated by their affiliation with male gangsta-rap style crews: Lil' Kim is associated with Junior M.A.F.I.A.; Foxy Brown is connected with The Firm. Since their debut works, Foxy Brown and Lil' Kim have released the follow-up LPs *Chyna Doll* (1998) and *Notorious K.I.M.* (2000), Kim's play on her mentor's name, Notorious B.I.G. Lil' Kim has recast herself as a daring fashion setter. At the 1999 MTV Music Awards, she generated controversy by wearing a jumpsuit that exposed her left breast, whose nipple was covered with an appliqué. She posed nude, except for boots and a hat, for a promo poster for her second album, and she characteristically dons blond wigs and blue contact lenses. Lil' Kim has also modeled clothing for top fashion designers like Versace and graced the cover of noted trade magazines including *Essence*, a magazine celebrating black women's issues and culture. Akissi Britton, a critic and research editor for *Essence*, charges that Kim is not making a fashion statement but is instead caught up in a world of make-believe, movie stardom, superficiality—sex, money, and power—the antithesis of female hip-hop figures like Queen Latifah and Sister Souljah. Britton further scolds Lil' Kim for "professing in her lyrics that the ultimate way to 'get yours' is to be a supreme bitch and make men pay for a taste" (2000:115). To some, Lil' Kim has undoubtedly become the epitome of rap's "bad girl."

The bad girl image parallels the "badman" character (e.g. John Hardy, Dolemite, and Stackolee) that is peculiar to the African American oral narrative in the toast, a long poetic narrative form that predates rap.[10] In these narratives, black badmen boast about their sexual exploits with women, wild drinking binges, and narrow brushes with "the law," symbolic of "white power" (Roberts 1989:196). The "empowered female" rendering of "the badman" includes those sistas who brag about partying and smoking blunts (marijuana) with their men; seducing, repressing, and sexually emasculating male characters; or dissin their would-be competitors (male and female)—all through figurative speech.[11]

Some female observers I queried felt that these Sistas with Attitude merely exist on the periphery of rap and are seen as just "shootin' off at the mouth." Some black female viewers viewed these sistas as misusing sex and feminism and devaluing black men. In an *Essence* magazine article, the hip-hop feminist Joan Morgan (1997) states that the new "bad girls of rap" may not have career longevity because "feminism is not simply about being able to do what the boys do—get high, talk endlessly about their wee-wees and what have you. At the end of the day, it's the power women attain by making choices that increases their range of possibilities" (1997:132).[12] Morgan argues that black women's power—on- and offstage—is sustained by "those sisters who selectively ration their erotic power" (1997:133).

Despite the controversies, Sistas with Attitude have acquired respect from their peers for their mastery of figurative language and rhyme. They simply refuse to be second best.

THE LESBIAN

While representatives of the Queen Mother, Fly Girl, and Sista with Attitude categories came into prominence during the mid- to late 1980s, The Lesbian category emerged from the closet during the late 1990s. Not only does the female heterosexual audience identify this category as "The Lesbian," but the artist who has given recognition to this division is among the first to rap about and address the lesbian lifestyle from a black woman's perspective. Though other black rap artists rumored to be gay or lesbian have chosen to remain closeted in a scene described as "'notoriously homophobic'" (Dyson quoted in Jamison 1998:AR34), Queen Pen's "Girlfriend" (1997) from her debut album *My Melody* represents a "breakthrough for queer culture" (Walters 1998:60).[13]

Although Queen Pen is recognized by her audience as the first female MC to openly discuss lesbian culture, Laura Jamison writes that ironically Queen Pen is "somewhat coy about her sexuality in personal interviews" (Jamison 1998:AR34).[14] "Girlfriend" signifies or indirectly plays on black lesbian culture with Me'Shell NdegéOcello's "If That's Your Boyfriend (He Wasn't Last Night)." NdegéOcello, who is openly lesbian, appears on "Girlfriend," performing on vocals and bass guitar.[15] In "Girlfriend," Queen Pen positions herself as the suitor in a lesbian relationship. While this song is a "breakthrough for queer culture," there remain other issues that plague black artists' willingness to openly address gay and lesbian culture in their performances.

Black lesbian culture and identity have been often problematized by issues of race and role-play, according to Lisa M. Walker (1993) and Ekua Omosupe (1991). Drawing upon the critical works of Audre Lorde (1982, 1984), Omosupe notes that lesbian identity, similar to feminism, represents white lesbian culture or white women to the exclusion of women of color. Black lesbians are at times forced to live and struggle against white male patriarchal culture on the one side and white lesbian culture, racism, and general homophobia on the other (Omosupe 1991:105). Corroborating the issue of race privilege raised by the black lesbian community, Queen Pen contends that certain licenses are afforded to openly lesbian white performers, such as Ellen DeGeneres and k. d. lang, who do not have to pay as high a price for their candidness as lesbians of color: "'But you know, Ellen [DeGeneres] can talk about any ol' thing and it's all right. With everybody, it's all right. With "Girlfriend," I'm getting all kinds of questions'" (quoted in Duvernay 1998:88).[16] She continues: "'This song is buggin' everyone out right now. [If] you got Ellen, you got k. d. [lang], why shouldn't urban lesbians go to a girl club and hear their own thing?'" (quoted in Jamison 1998:AR34).

Another aspect of Queen Pen's performance is her play on image, which suggests "role play," an issue crucial to black lesbian culture. Walker asserts that "role-play among black lesbians involves a resistance to the homophobic stereotype...lesbian as 'bulldagger,' a pejorative term within (and outside) the black community used to signal the lesbian as a woman who wants to be a man" (1993:886). On her first album cover, Queen Pen exudes a "femme" image through prominent make-up, fly clothing, lipstick, chic hairstyles, and stylish dress. However, in performance, as observed in Blackstreet's video for "No Diggity" (1996), Queen Pen "drowns out" her femme album cover image by appropriating a b-boy hand gesture and a bobbing walk commonly associated with male hip-hop culture. Regardless of issues concerning race privilege and role-play, Queen Pen concludes that "'two or three years from now, people will say I was the first female to bring the lesbian life to light [in an open way] on wax. It's reality. What's the problem?'" (quoted in Jamison 1998:AR34).

Women are achieving major strides in rap music by continuing to chisel away at stereotypes about females as artists in a male-dominated tradition and by (re)defining women's culture and identity from a black feminist perspective. Although rap continues to be predominantly male, female MCs move beyond the shadows of male rappers in diverse ways. Some have become exclusively known for their lyrical skillz, while others have used a unique blend of musical styles or a combination of singer-rapper acts, as is apparent with Grammy winners such as Left Eye of TLC and Lauryn Hill.

Women of rap still face overt sexism regarding their creative capabilities. One female MC recalls, "'Only when I led them [male producers] to believe that a man had written or produced my stuff did they show interest'" (quoted in Cooper 1989:80). The mass-media scholar Lisa Lewis notes that in the popular music arena, "the ideological division between composition and performance serves to devalue women's role in music making and cast doubt on female creativity in general" (1990:57). However, female MCs in the 1990s defied sexist repression by writing their own songs, authoring books, producing records, and even starting their own record companies.

While the majority of scholarly studies on female rappers locate black women voices in rap, they present only a partial rendering of female representation.[17] These works tend to focus on females' attitudes and responses to sexual objectification, ignoring the many roles of women and female rappers. Tricia Rose says that female MCs should not be evaluated only in relation to male rappers and misogynist lyrics "but also in response to a variety of related issues, including dominant notions of femininity, feminism, and black female sexuality. At the very least, black women rappers are in dialogue with one another, black men, black women, and dominant American culture as they struggle to define themselves" (1994:147–48). In rap music performance, a "black female-self emerges as a variation of several unique themes" (Etter-Lewis 1991:43).

More importantly, female rappers—most of whom are black—convey their views on a variety of issues concerning identity, sociohistory, and esoteric beliefs shared by young African American women. Female rappers have attained a sense of distinction through revising and reclaiming black women's history and perceived destiny. They use their performances as platforms to refute, deconstruct, and reconstruct alternative visions of their identity. With this platform, rap music becomes a vehicle by which black female rappers seek empowerment, make choices, and create spaces for themselves and other sistas.

Notes

An earlier version of this chapter appeared as "Empowering Self, Making Choices, Creating Spaces: Black Female Identity via Rap Music Performance," in *Journal of American Folklore* 113:449 (Summer 2000):255–69.

1. Other female MCs include Antoinette (Next Plateau), Bahamadia (EMI), Doggy's Angels (Degghouse), Charli Baltimore (Sony), Conscious Daughters (Priority), Finesse and Synquis (MCA), Gangsta Boo (Relativity),

Heather B (MCA), Lady of Rage (Death Row), Ladybug (Pendulum), MC Smooth (Crush Music), MC Trouble (Motown), Nikki D (Def Jam), Nonchalant (MCA), Oaktown's 3-5-7 (Capital); Solé (Dreamworks), T-Love (Down Low), and Trina (Slip-N-Slide).

2. The custom of sculpting the queen mother's head was established in Benin by King Oba Esigies during the sixteenth century. Sieber and Walker note that during Esigies's reign, he commissioned a sculpted bronze head of his mother, Idia, and placed it in his palace to commemorate her role in the Benin-Idah, thereby including queen mothers in the cult of royal ancestors for the first time (1987:93). In addition to Sieber and Walker's work, refer to Ben-Amos (1995) and Ben-Amos and Rubin (1983) for photographs and a brief discussion of queen mother heads in Benin.

3. Joan Morgan was among the women panelists at the "Sexuality in Rap Music" forum held at Tisch School of the Arts Auditorium at New York University on December 5, 1992.

4. Isis, formerly affiliated with X-Clan, records under the name of Lin Que.

5. In 1986 Salt-N-Pepa recorded "Shake Your Thang" for their second LP, *Salt with a Deadly Pepa*. In the video version, Salt-N-Pepa are seen gyrating their hips and shaking their buttocks during musical interludes. Since the 1990s, several rap songs and video performances by male artists celebrate and/or exploit black women's buttocks in bumping-and-grinding or rump-shaking dance movements. These songs include Sir Mix-A-Lot's "Baby Got Back" (1991), Wreckx-N-Effect's "Rump Shaker" (1992), Juvenile's "Back That Azz Up" (1998), and Mystikal's "Shake It Fast" (2000), to name a few. The focus on black women's buttocks in hip-hop culture is predated by Jamaican dancehall musical culture. For further discussion of this phenomenon, see Carolyn Cooper (1989).

6. "Whatta Man" is adapted from Linda Lyndell's 1968 hit "What a Man."

7. On Yo-Yo's first LP she spells her name with a hyphen; on her subsequent recordings she deletes the hyphen from her name. I will use the initial spelling of her name throughout.

8. Millie Jackson is a rhythm and blues singer who garnered the attention of listeners during the 1970s with her flair for sexually explicit songs about male/female relationships. During the musical introductions or interludes of her songs, Jackson employs sexual metaphors in a conversational manner over musical accompaniment. She is considered a role model not only by Shanté but also by other female rappers, including Lil' Kim, Foxy Brown, and Da Brat, whose third LP, *Unrestricted*, recalls Millie Jackson's 1997 album *Totally Unrestricted: The Millie Jackson Anthology*. Also see Pearlman (1988) and Saxon (1997).

9. During MC Lyte's early career, she wore no makeup, dressed in sweatsuits with sneakers, and used hardcore facial expressions (i.e. grimacing), mirroring the male hardcore image. Since her first album, *Lyte as a Rock* (1988), she has maintained her hardcore image, but, as she says, "'I've grown and I'm becoming a woman, slowly but surely. I'm finding my feminine qualities; it's okay to wear makeup and lipstick; it's something I like to do now'" (quoted in Lady G 1992:42).

10. For further information about the toast, see Abrahams (1970) and Dance (1978).

11. Sistas with Attitude accomplish this emasculation by referring to their male competitors or suitors as "motherfuckers," "niggas," and "suckers." Since the element of signifyin is aesthetically appealing in this style of rap, the former two terms may have both negative and positive meanings, depending on the context; the latter is used as an insult for men lacking in verbal or sexual skills. Examples of rap songs that portray those distinct characteristics of Sistas with Attitude include the following: "I Don't Give a Fuck" and "Mai Sista Izza Bitch" (1993), by Boss on *Born Gangstaz*; "Two Minute Brother" and "Shit Popper" (1991), by Bytches with Problems on *The Bytches*; "Da Shit Ya Can't Fuc Wit" and "Fire it Up" (1994), by Da Brat on *Funkdafied*; "Ill Na Na" and "Letter to the Firm" (1997), by Foxy Brown on *Ill Na Na*; "Big Momma Thang" and "Spend a Little Doe" (1996), by Lil' Kim on *Hard Core*; "Paper Thin" (1988) by MC Lyte on *Lyte as a Rock*; "Steady F—King" (1993), by MC Lyte on *Ain't No Other*; and "Big Mama" (1992), by Roxanne Shanté on *Bitch Is Back*.

12. Morgan speaks further about the use and abuse of sexuality by women of hip-hop in the chapter "from fly girls to bitches and hos" from her book *when chickenheads come home to roost; my life as a hip-hop feminist* (1999).
13. See Chideya (2000) for further discussion of hip-hop and homophobia.
14. While Queen Pen is a play on "kingpin," she also uses this moniker to indicate that she "pens" (or writes) her own lyrics, a skill that some have believed that female MCs lack. Although "Girlfriend" and other selections on her LP were co-written and produced by Teddy Riley, her real name (Lynise Walters) is credited on all songs. In the music industry, it is not unusual for producers to take co-writing credit on their mentees' debut works.
15. "Girlfriend" was co-written and produced by Teddy Riley, the inventor of new jack swing style (rap/rhythm and blues hybrid) and the leader of the group Black-street, in which Queen Pen performs a rap. Riley's input on "Girlfriend" is discussed by Jamison (1998).
16. When asked about "Girlfriend," Queen Pen asserts that her debut album, *My Melody,* contains nonlesbian songs, including "Get Away," which discusses domestic violence (Duvernay 1988: AR34).
17. For more on this topic see Guevara (1987), Berry (1994), Forman (1994), Goodall (1994), and Rose (1994).
18. Latifah, Queen: LADIES FIRST. Words and Music by SHANE FABER, QUEEN LATIFAH and MARK JAMES © 1989 WARNER-TAMERLANE PUBLISHING CORP., NOW & THEN MUSIC, WB MUSIC CORP., QUEEN LATIFAH MUSIC INC., FORTY FIVE KING MUSIC, FORKED TONGUE MUSIC and SIMONE JOHNSON PUB. DESIGNEE All Rights on Behalf of itself and NOW & THEN MUSIC Administered by WARNER-TAMERLANE PUBLISHING CORP. All Rights on Behalf of itself, QUEEN LATIFAH MUSIC INC, FORTY FIVE KING MUSIC, FORKED TONGUE MUSIC and SIMONE JOHNSON PUB. DESIGNEE Administered by WB MUSIC CORP. All Rights Reserved
19. Latifah, Queen: EVIL THAT MEN DO. Words and Music by QUEEN LATIFAH©1989 WB MUSIC CORP. and QUEEN LATIFAH MUSIC INC. All Rights Administered by WB MUSIC COPR. All Right Reserved.

References

Interviews

MC Lyte (MC), Irvine, Calif, August 11, 1996
Queen Latifah (MC, actress), Jersey City, July 8, 1993

Published and Other Sources

Abrahams, Roger. 1970. *Deep Down in the Jungle: Negro Narrative Folklore from the Streets of Philadelphia.* Chicago: Aldine Publishing.
Ben-Amos, Paula Girschick. 1995. *The Art of Benin.* Rev. ed. Washington, D.C.: Smithsonian Institution Press.
Ben-Amos, Paula, and Arnold Rubin, eds. 1983. *The Art of Power, the Power of Art: Studies in Benin Iconography.* Los Angeles: Museum of Cultural History.
Berry, Venise T. 1994. "Feminine or Masculine: The Conflicting Nature of Female Images in Rap Music." In *Cecilia Reclaimed: Feminist Perspectives on Gender and Music.* Ed. Susan C. Cook and Judy S. Tsou. 183–201. Urbana: University of Illinois Press.
Bobo, Jacqueline. 1995. *Black Women as Cultural Readers.* New York: Columbia University Press.
Britton, Akissi. 2000. "To Kim with Love: Deconstructing Lil' Kim." *Essence,* October, pp. 142–15, 186.
Carby, Hazel. 1986. "It Just Be's Dat Way Sometime: The Sexual Policies of Women's Blues." *Radical America* 20(4): 9–22.
Chideya, Farai. 2000. "Homophobia: Hip-Hop's Black Eye." *Step into a World: A Global Anthology of the New Black Literature.* Ed. Kevin Powell. 95–100. New York: John Wiley and Sons.
Chyll, Chuck. 1994. "Musical Reactions: Sexy Rap or Credibility Gap?" *Rap Masters* 7(7): 19–20.
Collins, Palricia Hill. 1990. *Black Feminist Thought: Knowledge, Consciousness, and the Politics of Empowerment.* Boston: Unwin Hyman.
Cooper, Carol. 1989. "Girls Ain't Nothin' but Trouble." *Essence,* April, pp. 80, 119.
Cooper, Carolyn. 1989. "Slackness Hiding from Culture. Erotic Play in the Dancehall." *Jamaican Journal* 22(4): 12–31.

Dance, Deryl C. 1978. *Shuckin' and Jivin': Folklore from Contemporary Black Americans.* Bloomington: Indiana University Press.

Davis, Angela Y. 1998. *Blues Legacies and Black Feminism: Gentrude "Ma" Rainey, Bessie Smith, and Billie Holiday.* New York: Pantheon Books.

Duvernay, Ava. 1998. "Queen Pen: Keep 'em Guessin'." *Rap Pages,* May, pp. 86–88.

Etter Lewis, Gwendolyn. 1991. "Black Women's Life Stories: Reclaiming Self in Narrative Texts." In *Women's Words: The Feminist Practice of Oral History.* Ed. Sherna Berger Gluck and Daphne Patai. 43–59. New York: Routledge.

Forman, Murray. 1994. "Movin' Closer to an Independent Funk: Black Feminist Theory, Standpoint, and Women in Rap." *Women's Studies* 23: 35–55.

Gonzales, Michael A. 1997. "Mack Divas." *The Source,* February, pp. 62–67.

Goodall, Nakati. 1994. "Depend on Myself: T.L.C. and the Evolution of Black Female Fap." *Journal of Negro History* 79(1): 85–93.

Green, Kim. 1991. "The Naked Truth." *The Source,* November, pp. 32–34, 36.

Guevara, Nancy. 1987. "Women Writin' Rappin' Breakin'." In *The Year Left.* Ed. Mike Davis et al. 160–75. New York: Verso Press.

Harrison, Daphne Duval. 1988. *Black Pearls: Blues Queens of the 1920s.* New Brunswick, N.J.: Rutgers University Press.

Hill, Lauryn. 1994. Panelist for "Hip-Hop Summit" New Music Seminar 15. Manhattan, July 20.

hooks, bell. 1993. *Sisters of the Yam: Black Women and Self-Recovery.* Boston: South End Press.

Horner, Cynthia. 1993. "TLC: The Homegirls with Style!" *Right on!* February, pp. 16–17.

Jamison, Laura. 1998. "A Feisty Female Rapper Breaks a Hip-Hop Taboo." *New York Times,* January 18, p. AR34.

Lady G. 1992. "I Want Everybody to Know." *Rap Pages,* April, pp. 40–43.

Leland, John. 1952. "Souljah on Ice." *Newsweek,* June 29, pp. 46–52.

Lewis, Lisa. 1990. *Gender Politics and MTV: Voicing the Difference.* Philadelphia: Temple University Press.

Lorde, Andre. 1982. *Zami: A New Spelling of My Name.* Trumansburg, N.Y.: Crossing Press.

———. 1984. *Sister Outsider Essays and Speeches.* Trumansburg, N.Y.: Crossing Press.

Mayo, Kierna. 1992. "Proud to Quit: Sisterhood in Baggies and Big Hats." *The Source,* June, pp. 46–49, 61.

McGregor, Tracii. 1996. "Sittin' on Top of the World." *The Source,* October, pp. 98–104.

Morgan, Joan. 1997. "The Bad Girls of Hip-Hop." *Essence,* March, pp. 76–77, 132, 134.

———. 1999. *when chickenheads come home to roost: my life as a hip-hop feminist.* New York: Simon and Schuster.

Mshaka, Thembisa S. 1999. "Marna Mia." *Blaze,* December/January, pp. 106–8.

Nelson, Havelock. 1993. "New Female Rappers Play for Keeps. *Billboard,* July 10, pp. 1, 77.

Omosupe, Ekua. 1991. "Black/Lesbian, Bulldagger." *differences: A Journal of Feminist Cultural Studies* 3(2): 101–1.

Pearlman, Jill. 1988. "Girls Rappin' Round Table," *Paper,* Summer, pp. 25–27.

Pulley, Brett. 1994. "How a 'Nice Girl' Evolved into Boss, the Gangster Rapper." *Wall Street Journal,* February 3, pp. A1, A16.

Radner, Joan Newlon, and Susan S. Lanser, 1993. "Strategies of Coding in Women's Culture." In *Feminist Messages: Coding in Women's Folk Culture.* Ed. Joan Newlon Radner. 1–29. Urbana: University of Illinois Press.

Roberts, Deborah. 1998. "Beautiful Women." *20/20 Monday.* Transcript no. 1796, March 30.

Rogers, Charles L. 1994. "The Salt-N-Pepa Interview." *Rap Masters,* July, pp. 30–31.

Rose, Tricia. 1994. *Black Noise: Rap Music and Black Culture in Contemporary America.* Hanover, N.H.: Wesleyan University Press.

Saxon, Shani. 1997. "Feelin' Bitchy," *Vibe,* February, pp. 78–79.

Sieber, Roy, and Roslyn Adele Walker. 1987. *African Art in the Cycle of Life.* Washington, D.C.: Smithsonian Institution Press.

Smithermar, Geneva. 1994. *Black Talk: Words and Phrases from the Hood to the Amen Corner.* New York: Houghton Mifflin.

Walker, Lisa M. 1993. "How to Recognize a Lesbian: The Cultura Politics of Looking Like What You Are." *Signs: Journal of Women in Culture and Society* 18(4): 866–89.

Walters, Barry. 1998. Review of Queen Pen, *My Melody. Advocate,* March 17, pp. 59–60.

Weingarten, Marc. 1998a. "All Made Up, Ready to Go." *Los Angeles Times* (Calendar Section), February 1, pp. 5, 68–69.

33 Media Interventions

MAUREEN MAHON

"Rock" is not a term very often associated with late-twentieth-century African American popular music. Aside from a handful of artists, most notably Jimi Hendrix and Lenny Kravitz as well as the D.C. punk band Bad Brains or the New York City–based Living Colour, African Americans rarely come to mind when rock music is discussed. Instead of rocking out, black American artists more typically sing soul, perform hip hop, or investigate the complex world of jazz changes.

In the middle 1980s, however, a group of black rockers based in New York City rebelled against this stereotype. Guitarist Vernon Reid, along with artist manager Konda Mason and Greg Tate (a journalist then most closely associated with the Village Voice), founded the B(lack) R(ock) C(oalition). The BRC intially sought to bring musicians and fans together to counteract the industry stereotypes against black rock music. By the late 1980s, the organization's efforts became more focused and helped Living Colour gain more national exposure.

In "Media Interventions," Maureen Mahon explores the relationships between the BRC and the mass media—particularly during the early to mid-1990s. These relationships are complex, important, and often involve more than simply conducting magazine interviews or promoting a product on an MTV station spot. For example, gaining access to shaping the band's sound in the studio as a producer is more difficult and arguably of more lasting importance than arranging to appear on BET.

Like their punk counterparts, some members of the BRC adopted a do-it-yourself mentality, releasing compilations on the BRC Records label. This gave them artistic control, but it also brought them into the problematic realm of distribution and promotion. Much of this chapter is devoted to a case study of how the BRC promoted and sold Blacker Than That (BRC Records 1993).

In terms of promotion, BRC also ventured (not surprisingly) into the realm of music videos. Once again BRC ran into the media—how to get their product on the air emerged as a more pressing issue than actually making the video. Even the production of compact discs (the cost of which plummeted in the late 1990s) was not the issue. Here, too, access to distribution and the marketplace caused the BRC (and other independent-minded artists) its most vexing problems.

We go to MTV [with our video] and they try to explain to us in their best terms that "Where do we put it? It doesn't fit our format." What? It's rock, isn't it? Yeah, but there's something, something about it. . . . So we go to BET which is black entertainment. . . . And they say, "Well, it's rock." Okay. And it's like, that's the Catch-22 that we're in.

—Bernie Kaye, Lead Singer of Total Eclipse

Long before BRC members had to grapple with the music industry's racialized dynamics as aspiring professionals, they had been influenced by the industry through its widely circulated forms. In many of our conversations and interviews, BRC members connected their exposure to music in the media to their decisions to begin playing musical instruments. In the following comment, Jesse describes his first guitar and his subsequent musical development:

> JESSE: [It] was this little cardboard Roy Rogers guitar. It had a picture of Roy Rogers on it and a horse and I turned it around and Dale was on the back. What it was was a real cheap guitar and I was stoked . . . I beat on the guitar and banged on it. Didn't know how to tune it . . . but I had that guitar. Really didn't seriously consider playing the guitar until I saw the Beatles. When I saw the Beatles I was just amazed. It changed life, you know. I said, "These guys are cool. I mean they're cool." They've got this long hair—which I had no concept of what that was like. But they had Beatle wigs, then. You could buy a Beatle wig for two dollars. So my mother bought me a Beatle wig and I had my Roy Rogers guitar . . . and this was when I was approaching fat boy days, so you have to get this image of this little fat black kid with a Beatles wig on playing an orange Roy Rogers guitar. . . . I loved that guitar and my mother said, "You know, maybe we can get you an electric guitar." She found some pawn shop somewhere where you could buy the guitar, the amps, the stand, the case, you know, the whole boxful of picks, and a wah-wah pedal for $99. You just had everything. A big guitar with strings like fenceposts on them, you know, never stayed in tune [and it] was shaped like a . . . "V." . . . But I was stoked. I said, "Now I have arrived." Of course, when that happens, the neighborhood kids get involved so you always find another kid who has a drum set or wants to get a drum set. So we had the little neighborhood band.
> MAUREEN: How old were you?
> JESSE: I must have been about 12. And it was just the thing. I think at that period in time, you're just getting into music . . . and those people who were so intrigued by it they actually want to become musicians just kind of all gravitate to each other. I remember the first song I learned was "Light My Fire" [by the Doors]. . . . I remember the first record I bought was Led Zeppelin's first album and then I discovered Jimi Hendrix and that just changed the whole situation. All of a sudden, a $99 guitar was not good enough.

Jesse's recounting of the impact of musicians like the Beatles and Jimi Hendrix on his interest in playing guitar is representative of how BRC members discussed the media encounters that informed their musical, professional, and personal development. Influenced by the images and debates they were exposed to through the media, they became increasingly interested in participating in media and making their own imprint on public culture. Media studies scholars describe the process of production, distribution, and reception of media as an ongoing circuit and analyze how various forms are produced, disseminated, and consumed (e.g., Fiske 1989; Hall 1980). Media productions that move through this circuit influence audiences and, over time, create new cohorts of producers. Jesse's comments remind us that reception is not simply the site of the creative audience interpretations and appropriations that media scholars emphasize, but also a crucial starting point for new productions. When conducting fieldwork with BRC members, I was constantly reminded that they are not only culture producers; they are also culture consumers whose productions are influenced by the media (cf. Dornfeld 1998). The countercultural scene that performers like Jimi Hendrix, the Doors, and Led Zeppelin represented were part of a broader set of social forces that together comprised the public culture that BRC members experienced as they came of age. The BRC communities formed in Los Angeles and New York were shaped in part by sounds and spectacles available in late 1960s and early 1970s media: FM radio, TV and magazine images of Black Panthers and antiwar protesters, Woodstock and Monterey Pop (the concerts and the films), *Soul Train, Midnight Special, Rolling Stone* magazine, the lunar landings of U.S. spaceships, and the arrival of the P-Funk Mothership. These media images encouraged BRC members to participate in music making, club performances, and local music scenes, activities that instilled a desire to participate in media production: to make records and to have their music played on the radio and music video programs.

When they found their access to mainstream outlets limited, many BRC members developed alternative means for producing and disseminating their music. In this chapter, I discuss two BRC projects: *Blacker Than That,* a BRC compact disc compilation produced by New York members, and *Network BRC,* the coalition's public access cable television show, produced by members of the Los Angeles BRC. Participation in these independent media productions enabled BRC members to distribute their work, although at a much more limited level than is available through mainstream outlets. In addition to these coalition-sponsored projects, individual members have worked on independent labels and also developed self-produced, self-distributed recordings and videos. Alternative music festivals, independent music distributors, noncommercial radio, public access cable television, and the Internet are components of the nonmainstream music production and distribution networks that sustain independent musicians. These venues warrant attention because they demonstrate that people can create alternatives when mainstream access is restricted. I outline the BRC's involvement in these arenas while also indicating some of the challenges associated with independent media production. Overall, the media's pervasive influence is noteworthy. It enabled BRC members to have access to music and ideas that contributed to the development of their artistic interests and activist practices. It was also the sustaining source of many of the stereotypes that, among other problematic repercussions, separated blacks from rock. Finally, it was both a target of and a channel for the BRC's cultural activism.

Consuming media forms is simple. It is easy to turn on a television, go to a movie, or buy a compact disc. Gaining sustained access to media as a producer, however, is quite a bit more difficult.[1] Although scholars talk enthusiastically about "public" culture and the "public" sphere, most of the institutions that constitute these arenas of representation are privately owned with relatively little responsibility to the public.[2] Profit orients decision making at sites of media production like record labels, television networks, and movie studios and access to these venues is far from guaranteed. This is especially true of institutions that have the widest influence at the national level. Mainstream media companies, whether black- or white-owned, have large budgets, far-reaching distribution networks, easy access to audiences, and stringent restrictions on participation. As I explained ..., it was difficult for BRC members to get airplay on black or white media outlets because their music and image did not fit the narrowly defined formats. Although black-owned, black-oriented outlets like cable's Black Entertainment Television (BET) and many black radio stations disseminated black culture, black rockers found that these networks were not interested in promoting their music. Like their white counterparts at mainstream companies, black media executives guaranteed a specific audience to advertisers and programmed certain types of music to deliver it. The economic realities of media outlets coupled with ideological assumptions about black cultural production curtailed BRC member access to the mainstream and encouraged some to turn to independent outlets like public radio, public access television, and independent record labels that make the inclusion of "alternative" voices their mission. The trade-off is that they have limited resources, making it necessary to work with shoestring production and distribution budgets. A number of BRC members accepted these constraints in order to participate at some level in production and distribution.

DO-IT-YOURSELF

The compilations *The History of Our Future* (Rykodisc 1991), *Blacker Than That* (BRC Records 1993), and *Bronze Buckeroo Rides Again* (BRC Records 2000) addressed one of the coalition's initial goals: to assist in the recording and distribution of its members' music. These compilations also challenged the limited ideas about black identity that circulated in the public sphere. In his liner notes for *The History of Our Future,* Greg Tate explains how the music industry created the need for both the BRC and an independent, BRC-produced recording. "The reason that the musicians on this record have sustained a Black Rock Coalition for six years," Tate wrote, "is because they're not interested in anyone's formulas or formats for pop success. They've got big ideas of their own, thank you, and if they've got to go around people short of vision to get them out, so be it" (Tate 1991). The BRC compilations allowed members to produce their work without repackaging themselves to fit dominant notions of black music. Indeed, one of the ways members articulated the value of the compilations was by stressing their difference from mainstream black pop.

In 1992, the BRC formed its own label, BRC Records. The promotion for its first project, *Blacker Than That,* was underway when I started my research. The shift to self-production involved the BRC in the do-it-yourself (D.I.Y.) ethic that emerged in the late 1970s when punk bands in the United States and Great Britain demonstrated that a major label deal was not the only way to spread a musical message. Like their precursors in the 1950s, these independent producers created and distributed new forms of music. Taking advantage of cheaper technology and a growing network of independent studios, labels, and distributors, musicians produced low-budget recordings, usually using personal savings and earnings from gigs to support the enterprise, instead of waiting to be discovered and financed by a major label. These recordings are unlikely to reach as large an audience as mainstream productions, but their producers can reasonably hope to receive attention in alternative music networks. These include independently owned "mom 'n' pop" record stores instead of major chains; fanzines, local press, and Web pages instead of in the mainstream music press; and small clubs and bars instead of large arenas and concert halls. In addition to challenging the mainstream, these recordings often influence it as major labels incorporate successful "outsider" styles. During the 1980s and 1990s, the majors increasingly depended on independents to identify shifts in consumer taste, locate creative energy in music, and develop the artists most able to sell the new product. Rap and grunge are two examples of independently produced music that major labels picked up and successfully sold during the 1990s. Independent labels depend on their difference from the majors and their connections to lesser-known artists for a veneer of underground credibility that sells to fans the idea that the music is authentic and uncompromised by the demands of the mainstream market. It is important, however, not to overstate the independence of independent labels. Although they have a stronger commitment to supporting untested artists and music than the majors, independent labels are frequently connected to major labels through investment, licensing, and distribution arrangements (Negus 1992, 1999).

Blacker Than That began in the spring of 1992 with a call from the Independent Music Producers Syndicate (IMPS), a New Hampshire–based publications firm that also ran a music distribution service for independent labels. IMPS president Wayne Green had read about the BRC in trade and popular press. As an advocate of independent music producers and a service provider to them, Green was interested in supporting the BRC's mission; further, since the organization was a nonprofit, working with the BRC would allow a tax write-off for his company. Ideological and business interests coincided and Green approached the BRC with an informal proposal to collaborate on a project. What followed was approximately eighteen months of planning, negotiation, and coordination. The production of the compilation was spearheaded by two longtime BRC members: Bruce Mack, the national president, whose band P.B.R. Streetgang was one of the first to join the coalition, and Jimmy Saal, director of communications, who had joined the BRC in 1987 when managing the black rock band the Good Guys. Jimmy told me that initially some of his fellow members "were kind of leery" about the project. He attributed this hesitancy to the BRC's experience with *The History of Our Future*. The BRC had anticipated a positive balance between freedom and backing from Rykodisc. Although the label financially supported the album's production, the BRC was at times frustrated with the label's promotion of the album. One of the things that made the IMPS deal attractive was the fact that the BRC would be in greater control of the marketing and distribution of its own product. "I always wanted to do a second compilation because I had been hearing so many demo tapes that sounded really good," Jimmy explained. Although members generally supported the project, Jimmy told me, "I don't think people believed that it was really going to happen and then when it did happen, people were like, 'Wow, it's here.'" Although the BRC exists to support musicians who want to challenge commonsense assumptions, they do not always escape them. Jimmy's comment indicates that the meager resources of the BRC, especially when compared to the pervasive power of mainstream labels, made it difficult for many members to imagine that the coalition would be able to produce its own record.

Bruce and Jimmy organized the production and financial arrangements to produce the compilation for a minimal amount of money. No new recording was necessary since the bands had submitted their own studio-recorded master tapes which, if selected, would be used directly. The only concern would be mastering tapes to achieve a consistent sound level across the recording. The twelve-song compilation was released on only one format, compact disc, to further cut production costs. Under the contract that each band signed, artists allowed the BRC to use their recordings on the compilation, but the artists still held all rights, meaning they could use the song again on other compilations or on their own releases. The deal worked out well for the bands and the organization. "We felt like we put something together that offered something to the bands, which was a record . . . that would be commercially available with their music on it." Jimmy recalled, "It's something we thought would be of interest to the media. . . . So we said, look, this will get you some attention, it won't cost you anything, your tapes are sitting around anyway, so why don't you work with us?" Bruce and Jimmy selected nine East Coast bands and three West Coast bands for the disc. They tried a number of titles for the compilation and finally borrowed the contribution of Greg Tate's band, Women in Love. *Blacker Than That* plays on the phrase "blacker than thou," a colloquialism that critiques those who claim to be more authentically black than others. Both the compilation's title and the music it contained were about going beyond simplistic representations of blackness.

Cover art came from BRC member and graphic artist Sid Blaize, who had also designed the cover art for *The History of Our Future*. The image represents the membership at both philosophical and physical levels. The Afrocentric colors red, gold, and green are featured throughout. They appear in the BRC logo and on the striped pullover of the image's centerpiece: a crouching, brown-skinned figure holding a black guitar. The drawing is cropped so the face is not visible; thus, he becomes an everyman BRC member. The fact that a woman is not featured is indicative of the predominantly male composition of the organization and of rock generally. The figure's right hand balances on one of the scattered black rocks glowing blue, creating a visual pun about African American music genres. Also figuring prominently are dreadlocks, black combat boots, a gold ankh hanging from a chain, bracelets, and a button of Harriet Tubman. The guitar is decorated with a variety of stickers: a silver X for Malcolm X; the cover art of the first BRC compilation; a red, black, and green flag; and the face of Muhammad Ali. The placement of images of American heroes like Harriet Tubman who led enslaved blacks north to freedom, Malcolm X who exhorted blacks to free their minds, and Muhammad Ali who refused to go to war against other people of color alongside a prototypical black rocker visually links the BRC to the tradition of African American freedom fighters. The result is a visually arresting blend of African diaspora style and politics intercut with rock 'n' roll.

The BRC leadership believed that a compilation could represent the musical breadth of the organization and provide exposure for several member bands. The twelve songs collected on *Blacker Than That* epitomize the variety of approaches taken by BRC bands. D'Tripp's "Run From the World" uses vocal harmonies and a funky bass line that echo Sly and the Family Stone. Menace, a guitarist who has worked with George Clinton and Madonna, offers "Detroit (Old School Funk Remix)," a song that delves into the P-funk; in fact, Clinton sidemen Bootsy Collins (bass) and Bernie Worrell (keyboards) are featured on the cut along with James Brown's saxophone player Maceo Parker. In "Commercialized," Faith underpins its rock guitar solos with reggae bass lines played by leader Felice Rosser in a meditation about a man consumed by consumerism. Synaestisia's "Green Balloon" features an eerie soprano by Michelle Johnson and fusion-infused guitar by David "Fuze" Fiuczynski who, in the space allotted each act to print lyrics, liner notes, and acknowledgments, lists vocalist Nina Hagen, alto saxophonist Eric Dolphy, and German expressionist painting as musical inspirations. The song "Contradictions" by Drek DuBoyz mixes hip-hop beats and hard rock guitar in a song that explores the link between frequently articulated social concerns and rarely assumed social responsibility. "Home, Home on the Range" by Suburban Dog signifies on the traditional cowboy song and depicts the suburban postwar American dream home as a fortress against real world concerns. "Blacker Than That" by Women In Love uses witty lyrics shared between vocalists Mikel Banks and Helga Davis to comment on the simplistic way blackness is constructed in the United States.

A few songs are in the tradition of heavy metal and hardcore, genres that are associated with white musicians and audiences, but that claim important African American precursors including Mother's Finest, the Los Angeles heavy metal band, and Bad Brains, the black thrash-reggae band who were central figures in the 1980s hardcore punk scene in Washington, D.C. Guitar-made sirens lead into "N.Y.D.S. (New York Death Squad)" by D-Xtreme, the self-proclaimed "Original Slam Funk Posse." Their song uses high-speed, high-volume playing and singing to convey their anger about New York City Police Department activities in communities of color. The all-female Los Angeles band P.M.S. (who insist the initials stand for Play Me Seriously) in "Man With the Power" and Bozaque in "Shadow of Shadows" incorporate the vocal and instrumental approaches of hardcore punk and metal with lyrics that address freedom, empowerment, and black unity. Navigator, the band led by ex–Bus Boys bass player and Los Angeles BRC Orchestra Director Kevin O'Neal, contributes "Stolen Child," an elegantly arranged, mid-tempo groove featuring horns, strings, scats, and lyrics about the quest for freedom. Sophia's Toy contributes "Lifetime," the compilation's only clear-cut love song, a bright, slowly building number featuring Sophia Ramos's vocal finesse.

New York City radio personality Imhotep Gary Byrd, long associated with the black-owned radio station WLIB-AM (1190) and host of news and talk show *The Global Black Experience*, contributed the compilation's liner notes. He explains the paradox black rockers face and observes that the oxymoron "black rock" must be used because it is in keeping with the divisions made by the music industry. He adds that those who know music history recognize that in addition to the white rock groups that emerged in the 1960s and 1970s,

> the evolution of the music also produced Sly Stone, The Chambers Brothers, Richie Havens, Stevie Wonder, War, Earth, Wind and Fire, Isley Brothers, Mandrill, Commodores, Graham Central Station, Parliafunkadelicment [*sic*], Rufus, Kool and the Gang, Ohio Players, Edwin Birdsong, Jimmy Castor, Mother's Finest, and a host of others who were dedicated to a form which when compared to that so called "white rock" was definitely "Blacker Than That." (Byrd 1993)

After naming, claiming, and praising black rock precursors—a common practice among BRC members—Byrd turns to the question of selling black rock, "a music marketed primarily to white audiences projected in mass media as being 'originated' by white artists 'suddenly' being played by artists who were obviously 'Blacker Than That'" (Byrd 1993). He describes the formation of the Black Rock Coalition as a response to this dilemma and an effort to bring together the "children of Hendrix and Sly" in order to "unite their collective forces to somehow continue the legacy." In this capsule description, Byrd pays tribute to BRC members as defenders of and participants in an African American musical tradition. He concludes by describing the compilation as "an assault on the senses and the stereotypes related to what is being produced in Black music today. You will hear an extremely diversified mix of music and bands which touches Folk, Funk, Blues, R & B and Rap with messages that deal with where we are in the world today without having to call anybody Bitch/Ho/Nigger etc." (Byrd 1993). Collected in one recording, these twelve songs are sonic evidence of the musical talent in the BRC and also an example of the variety of ways members reclaimed their right to rock.

PROMOTING AND SELLING *BLACKER THAN THAT*

Having finally launched its own label, the BRC wanted to reach as many potential listeners as possible. Robert Fields, the New York director of publicity, sent copies of the compilation to magazines and newspapers that had been supportive of the BRC in the past. As a result, *Blacker Than That* was reviewed in the national publications *Musician*, *Vibe*, and *Billboard* (e.g., Gardner 1993). To publicize the record, East and West Coast chapters sponsored listening parties and record release parties at local clubs, and the New York BRC executive committee arranged for members of the coalition to participate in high-profile alternative music conferences. By putting together conference showcases featuring bands from the compilation, the BRC could expose member bands to a concentrated audience of music industry people. Alternative music conferences were founded to cater to the influx of independent labels and bands whose unconventional music marked them (usually to their delight) as industry outsiders during the 1980s. Developed to support less mainstream music and identify the rising stars of rock, rap, and electronica undergrounds, the most well-known of these conferences are New York's New Music Seminar/New Music Nights Festival (NMS), which operated from 1980 to 1994; New York's College Music Journal Music Marathon (CMJ), which started in 1980; and Austin's South By Southwest Music and Media Conference (SXSW), which has run since 1986. Like hundreds of independent artists and labels, the BRC and its members have been involved with each of these conferences. In addition to promoting music and networking, the conventions offer panel discussions about the labyrinthine workings of the music industry and topical issues of interest to music professionals. As mainstream taste began to embrace the more experimental sounds promoted in these conferences, major labels turned to NMS, CMJ, and SXSW to locate commercially viable new talent. What began as networks for the underground developed into major music industry events, the place for up-and-coming bands to be heard and seen by the right people.

These music conventions allowed fans, musicians, industry executives, and a researcher like myself to hear numerous unknown bands performing sets at dozens of rock venues around the host city. At the July 1993 NMS, the BRC presented a showcase at the Manhattan Center featuring New York bands Women in Love, Drek DuBoyz, and Sophia's Toy and Los Angeles band P.M.S., all of whom appear on *Blacker Than That*. Further raising the coalition's profile during the five-day conference, BRC member acts D'Tripp, Shock Council, the Ancestors, Faith, Me'Shell NdegéOcello, Tracie Morris, and D-Xtreme played in other venues during the week. A few months later at the November CMJ Seminar, the BRC executive committee arranged for Screaming Headless Torsos, Faith, and Sophia's Toy to appear in a BRC showcase with headliner Me'Shell NdegéOcello in a show hosted by poets Tracie Morris and Samantha Coerbell. A BRC showcase at the March 1994 SXSW featured Tracie Morris from New York, Monkey Meet from Los Angeles, Follow for Now from Atlanta, Sinister Dane from St. Louis, and Brothers From Another Planet from Detroit. BRC involvement in these conventions was important not only because it gave visibility to member bands and black rock. By connecting rock with African Americans, the BRC created at least one space that disrupted the genre-dictated separation that in turn produced the racial segregation of black and white convention-goers that marked most of the non-BRC NMS, CMJ, and SXSW sets that I attended during the years I conducted research. Furthermore, the BRC's involvement ensured the onstage presence of black instrumentalists who were typically absent in contexts where rappers and vocalists comprised the overwhelming majority of black performers. BRC participation in the conferences also boosted the black presence on industry panel discussions. For example, at the 1993 CMJ, Me'Shell NdegéOcello and Tracie Morris sat on a panel called "The 'F' Word: Being a Feminist in the Music Industry"; Bruce Mack spoke on the panel "Bitches Ain't Shit But Hos and Tricks," a session exploring men's perspectives on women in music; and Beverly Jenkins moderated a panel on the image of African Americans in popular culture. Chiefly, however, these conventions are scenes for business and self-promotion. "It's about schmoozing," Jimmy Saal told me during the coalition's NMS showcase. The BRC executives and band members were working that event, talking to industry professionals—journalists, publicists, record executives, and distributors. When I asked Robert Fields about his activities during the

NMS, he told me, "I've been shaking a lot of hands." He also explained that he was making a special effort to connect with European and Japanese distributors, both for the BRC and for some of his own black rock clients.

To increase the impact of the NMS showcase and to further promote the compilation, Steve Williams broadcasted some of the proceedings on the BRC's radio show, "Strange Vibrations from the Hardcore," a few hours after the performances occurred. He recorded the bands' sets and then played highlights during the show. He interspersed these "live" cuts with tracks from *Blacker Than That* and brief, on-air interviews with band members who came by the studios. Greg Tate, Konda Mason, and Vernon Reid had started the radio program in 1986, securing a slot for it on New York's WBAI-FM. This Pacifica Radio station had a 50,000 watt signal that reached out from midtown Manhattan into the boroughs and beyond to New Jersey, Connecticut, and parts of Pennsylvania and Delaware. WBAI was a noncommercial, nonprofit, listener-supported station with news, arts, political, and cultural coverage in addition to music programming. By 1993, Steve Williams and Earl Douglas Jr. hosted and produced the show on alternate Fridays, from midnight to 3 AM, providing a regularly available radio venue for black rock.[3] In a BRC newsletter article published a few months before the showcase, Steve urged his fellow members to support the show during WBAI's pledge drive. Reiterating the service the program provided, he noted that "Strange Vibrations" had been a strong and consistent voice for alternative black,

> providing listeners with the opportunity to hear music that has been shut out of mainstream radio airwaves. I'm talking about such artists as Defunkt, Eric Gales, Eye & I, Follow for Now, the Family Stand, and Divine Styler—bands that have managed to obtain recording deals, but yet still don't enjoy the same access to commercial radio as bands like Nirvana or U2. It is through "Strange Vibrations" that we're able to play music by unsigned bands such as Miss Mary Mack, Shock Council and Drek Du Boyz, which helps strengthen their audience base for their live performances. In addition, we've also been able to bring to you music by artists like Ice-T and Bodycount, who has come under fire for his statements about police violence in the song "Cop Killer." (Williams 1993:1)

On the night of the NMS showcase and the WBAI post-showcase broadcast, Living Colour played on the *Tonight Show with Jay Leno* to promote its new album, *Stain*. Obviously, most bands—BRC or otherwise—could not reasonably hope for that kind of national exposure. Inclusion in a set of music spun by Steve Williams and Earl Douglas on WBAI offered another kind of opportunity. Member bands often sat in on "Strange Vibrations." Here, they could air newly produced recordings, promote upcoming events, play some of their favorite songs by other artists, and talk with Steve and Earl about music. This black rock presence on the radio was another way members publicized their musical vision and expanded the black public sphere.

As the BRC embarked on the *Blacker Than That* project, a member who had been involved with the first BRC compilation reminded the executive committee that "making a record is not the same as selling a record." The freedom that enabled the production and energized the launch of the CD was tempered by limited resources for distribution and promotion. The BRC could not saturate the market with their product in the fashion of major labels and, indeed, selling the compilation was an uphill battle. The modes of distribution were through IMPS's 800-number, purchase at band gigs and BRC events, and mail order directly through the BRC. Initially, *Blacker Than That* was on sale at Tower and HMV record stores in Manhattan and in two independent record stores in New Jersey. The BRC eventually had to sign a contract with a regional distributor when Tower changed its policy and stopped accepting product from independent producers, insisting instead on dealing with distributors. In a change that is typical in the independent side of the recording industry, Wayne Green sold IMPS, leaving the BRC with no contacts in the new management. This eliminated the BRC's access to a nationally distributed mail order catalogue as a sales outlet. Jimmy was philosophical when commenting to me in an e-mail message about the end of the IMPS association: "I think the whole deal was tricky to begin with," he wrote, "but with smoke and mirrors we got a CD out of the deal."

Generally speaking, compilations are easy to produce, but difficult to sell. Usually they are a way of repackaging hit songs by multiple artists that are already familiar and a "safe buy." Independent and major labels also use compilations as a tool for introducing new artists and upcoming releases; these compilations are sold cheaply or given away to targeted consumers. A compilation of unknown, unsigned bands priced at $12 was a much harder sell, especially since there was no easily identifiable single or hit to focus on. In promoting the CD, the BRC hoped that the general concept of black rock would inspire interest. One of the founding concerns of the BRC was to encourage networking, support, and collaboration among musicians. Choosing one band from among all the members and focusing the organization's limited energies on that artist's record would have meant giving one band unfair attention. Producing a compilation involved and invested a cross section of the membership, making it a BRC enterprise rather than a showcase for a single act. It was, therefore, something more members could feel comfortable supporting. The efforts to protect the interests of the BRC as an organization while also attempting to engage in the marketplace reflected a concern with internal relations, morale, and resources. The question remains whether it would have been better in the long-term to have recorded one group, followed by another (and another and another). Some members argued that there was really no point to the label if it did not release the work of individual bands. In the end, practical considerations also influenced the form the label took. Members of the BRC executive committee, already overburdened with the work of running the organization (and doing so on a voluntary basis), knew how much time and energy running a viable independent label would require.[4] The approach they chose may have limited sales, but it also protected personnel. They developed a project that could trade on the organization's reputation, gain attention in the media, and provide bands with exposure. The CD was just one instance in which the BRC had to confront the challenges of running a non-profit organization in a profit-oriented arena, negotiating the tensions between competition and community in the process.

The length of time it took the BRC to start its label is another reflection of the competing value systems with which the organization operates. The coalition's role as an artists' organization with a mission to promote alternative black music has been fairly clear, but determining how best to offer this support has been less so. Most members agreed that the BRC should preserve and advance black popular music, using any means available—independent labels and the Internet, for example. BRC Records was a way of "taking it to the next level," as many members told me, but some felt it took the BRC too long to reach this stage. One member argued, "You've got to be independent: The BRC, independent, nonprofit, finally started a label. I mean, I feel that we should have started that *way* back—even when we just had cassettes from live gigs—from jump. And we didn't do that and I think that does reflect a lot of where the BRC is at now." I suspect that the slowness to move toward the D.I.Y. model is related to the members' early interest in pursuing the mainstream. This is a focus that resulted from the musicians' assumption that if they were talented enough, they could follow in the footsteps of artists like

Jimi Hendrix, Sly Stone, and Led Zeppelin. Rock and funk acts of the late 1960s and 1970s typically had contracts with major labels which were, at that time, responsible for an outpouring of diverse music. Another member commented:

> I read an interview with Prince once where he was talking about how it used to be. [Black] music used to be artist-driven and then once it becomes a producer's medium, the stuff started getting really constricted. So in the seventies you could have a Parliament, Earth, Wind & Fire, War, Ohio Players, Isley Brothers—all these different bands, completely different sounds, and all being successful—played on the radio. Stevie Wonder, you know. And now, you listen to the radio and there are definite parameters on what you hear. So at that point, [in the mid-1980s] black musicians—at least the musicians I knew—were all trying to deal with the black music industry, you know, trying to write and get into that whole black pop thing. And getting in touch with the Black Rock Coalition was great—seeing the people dealing with original music and different stuff.

While the narrowing of mainstream channels may have convinced BRC members to develop their own distribution networks, the financial realities of undertaking such a project coupled with the time required to run a label apparently were deterrents. Instead, the BRC primarily produced shows intended to generate media interest, build a fan base for black rock, and attract the attention of deep-pocketed major labels. The signing of Living Colour and the band's success made the dream of getting a major label deal seem within reach and may have detracted from a focus on the independent route. Talking about his band's early years, Vernon Reid recalled, "At that time, the whole thing was to get a [major label] record deal. Times have really changed now. Even though a record deal is still considered to be something that's significant, its significance has changed" (Reid quoted in BRC 2001b:II). There may have been ideological factors at work, as well. Having framed its critique around issues of race and access in the mainstream music industry, it was important for the BRC to focus on entering the mainstream. Arguably, this is not an unusual perspective for beneficiaries of civil rights–era demands for equal opportunity for African Americans. Participating in the somewhat separate and unequal independent media network did not seem attractive when the coalition started. As time passed and major labels passed most black rockers up, however, going independent became a viable option. By producing *Blacker Than That*, the BRC represented the musical range and multifaceted nature of the organization. "We never expected a million seller," Jimmy told me. What they hoped for and developed was a product that would get the music of BRC bands into the marketplace while also providing a permanent document of the Black Rock Coalition in 1993.

PUTTING ON A SHOW

Producing recordings was one part of the battle; another was finding ways to disseminate them. The importance of video to music promotion and the difficulties of access to national cable music stations encouraged many musicians to seek alternative ways to show their videos. Public access cable television provided one outlet. In the 1970s when cable television was first being developed in the United States, the Federal Communications Commission established a requirement that cable systems in the nation's largest 100 television markets provide channels devoted to public, educational, and government services (Kellner 1990:188). This ruling created public access or community access programming.⁵ Public access stations inject a local focus into otherwise national cable programming and serve groups that are excluded from mainstream cable offerings. Advocates of public access television believed that it could democratize the media by creating a space for public discussions of traditional political concerns like voting, legislation, and policy that received inadequate attention in commercial outlets (182). Arguably, the push for public access was rooted in an understanding that the media played a significant role in the public sphere and that privatization curtailed accessibility. Although initially geared toward informing viewers about politics, public access stations quickly became forums through which an array of local, non-mainstream interests were able to gain a voice. In Los Angeles, BRC members were among those involved in public access programming.

Members of the Los Angeles BRC produced their program, *Network BRC*, at the San Fernando Valley studios of community access cable station United Artists Cable–Channel 25, a station serving parts of northern and western Los Angeles County. Produced and written by the husband and wife team of Rod and Melva Miller, *Network BRC* featured interviews and performances with BRC musicians. Like all BRC members, Rod, Melva, and the show's host Todd Washington worked on a strictly volunteer basis. To put together an episode, the three would hold a production meeting with the guest several weeks before the shoot to determine what issues they would cover in the interview and preview the songs the artist would perform. Based on these conversations, Melva would develop a script, working closely with Rod to outline the precise timing of the show.⁶ *Network BRC* guests had to provide a copy of the broadcast-quality videos they wanted to present. Guests without videos could lip synch to a broadcast-quality audiotape, miming a live performance in the station's studios. Because of financial, equipment, and time limitations, there were no live performances on the show, a necessary compromise that stemmed from the program's low budget. In March 1995, I attended a taping to see how the production operated and meet the producers. While setting up for the shoot, Rod explained that he had to take Channel 25's sixteen-week training course in order to earn the certification that all individuals involved in the production aspects of any program on the station had to have. The training was completely free—that was part of the station's contract with the city—but anyone interested in participating had to make the effort to get to the sessions.

"The certification itself isn't really worth much," he admitted. "It's not like any network TV station will hire you, but it does allow me to work on the show. Now, I'm the producer and all the techs on the show—the guys on the cameras and the sound board—are interns. Only the director, the one who calls the show, is on the station's staff. He was also in my training group, but he was the best in the class, so they hired him."⁷ Rod described the training program as "totally hands on." He recalled, "The first night I came to class, they told me I was on Camera 2. I'd never run a camera before, but they let me fool around with it for a little bit and I learned my way. While we were shooting."

Rod's description of United Artists Cable Television–Channel 25 delineates practices that are typical of public access stations nationwide. Their original objective was to make television production equipment and airtime available to any member of a given community. Individuals received access to the training and technology needed to produce programs on which they could say or do anything as long as they avoided obscene or libelous material (Kellner 1990:207). Training sessions, equipment, and time slots were available on a first-come, first-served basis and were usually free of charge. Through the kind of internship Rod described, community members could get working knowledge of the studio equipment, station rules, and production practices; ideally they would be prepared to produce a program on a small budget. At Channel 25, for example, the BRC's only expenditures were for the three-quarter-inch videotapes onto which each episode was recorded. Based on their resources and energy, cable access producers can program weekly, bimonthly, or monthly series as well as occasional shows; their main constraint is the number of programs already in rotation at the station (213). The titles of programs scheduled to air on Channel 25 in March 1995 reveal the mix of shows typical of public access: *Assyrian Weekly Magazine, Tinsel Town's Queer, Astrology and You, Tele Romania, Senior Scene, Chick TV, Your Democratic Party* and, of course, *Network BRC* (Cablecast 25 News 1995:2–3).

"It's funny," Rod recalled while we waited for the taping to begin. "When I was planning the show, I kept putting off actually starting it. I kept coming up with reasons why I wasn't ready or the show wasn't ready. This woman I work with noticed what I was doing because she'd hear me on the phone, plus I was talking to her about it. Finally, she said, 'Look, Rod. Just schedule the time and do it. You'll probably never be completely ready.' So I took her advice."

"So it worked out," I said.

"Yeah . . . I mean, the first show was rough. Really rough. But there was a First Show."

Network BRC was taped on two simple sets. Bands prerecorded "live" lip-synched performances on a bare soundstage using their own equipment as props. Todd interviewed guests on a talk show style set: a carpeted platform with straight-backed chairs arranged around a small table and a large, leafy plant off to the side. Each episode of the program fits in a half-hour time slot and is structured similarly. The show opens with Todd's welcome to the viewers, a short description of the BRC, and an introduction of the guest. There is an immediate cut to a public service announcement and then a return to Todd and his guest. A brief conversation ensues and is followed by the first video or performance. The show returns to the host and guest who chat again before introducing the second song. After the second video or performance, Todd and his guest make a few final comments and then Todd wraps up the show with a reiteration of the guest's name, information about any recordings available in stores or through mail order, and a pitch for the BRC. In order to give each show a longer shelf life, there is no mention of time-sensitive information like upcoming club dates. The BRC's Los Angeles address and hotline numbers are displayed, followed by production credits.

At this point, I turn to a specific *Network BRC* episode in order to illustrate how the program provides a forum for black rock and black rock musicians. It was not unusual for the host and the guests to draw attention to this aspect of the show as the following transcription of a segment demonstrates. This episode, shot in 1993, featured Bernie "BK" Kaye, lead singer of Los Angeles BRC band Total Eclipse, in an interview with Todd. I had heard about Total Eclipse soon after I arrived in Los Angeles for my three months of fieldwork. Their story was a textbook example of the difficulties black rock bands faced. Signed to a major label deal on A&M Records and able to release an album and produce a video, Total Eclipse was stymied when MTV refused to put their video into rotation. Introducing the video, Bernie described "Fire in the Rain" as "probably the most commercial song" on Total Eclipse's first album. The video is typical of MTV rock fare of the early 1990s: a slick compendium of the requisite cryptic images—a shadowy boy playing outdoors, bricks being laid, a fire burning—intercut with footage of the four band members performing amid a moodily lit studio arrangement of fog-swathed, leafless trees. The difference is that the rockers are black. After screening the video, Bernie and Todd discussed its fate on music television. The following is my transcription of a portion of their interview (BRC 1993b). I have bracketed and italicized descriptions of camera movements and speaker actions.

TODD: [*midshot of Todd smiling and nodding*] Nice video. I like that. "Fire in the Rain." That was Total Eclipse here on *Network* BRC. And this is the album [*holds up CD case*] if you can find it anywhere.

BERNIE: [*laughs*]

TODD: I would definitely try to find it [*puts CD case on table*]. Now let's talk about that video. Who directed that video?

BERNIE: [*close-up of Bernie*] That's Josh Taft out of Seattle.

TODD: Josh Taft. Okay.

BERNIE: Yeah, yeah. He's part of that Seattle scene, Pearl Jam and Alice in Chains. A real nice cat. We shot that in Seattle.

TODD: Great. Liked those images [*cut to close-up of Todd*]. I have never seen that video before—

BERNIE: [*cut to Bernie*] No one has! [*Bernie leans forward in his seat, twists as if about to stand up, grabs vest and sits back in the seat*] [*cut to midshot of Todd and Bernie seated*]

TODD: [*laughs*] Okay. Why don't we talk a little about that?

BERNIE: Oh, man [*pause*]. Okay, I'll try.

TODD: Okay, try to dig up a little of that information.

BERNIE: [*close-up of Bernie*] Here's the thing about it, as far as the BRC, people out there know this is the BRC and that stands for Black Rock Coalition and that initially started with a lot of black rockers, right. So this leads me into this video. We did this video and being black [*punctuates by hitting the side of his right hand against his open left palm*] and playing rock [*the same gesture, now with a sarcastic laugh*] are like, you know, shit (did I say that?), two evils. So here's the deal—

TODD: It hasn't always been.

BERNIE: [*camera still on Bernie*] So here's the deal. We go to MTV and they try to explain to us in their best terms that "Where do we put it? It doesn't fit our format." What? It's rock, isn't it? "Yeah, but there's something, something about it."

TODD: [*cut to reaction shot of Todd*] Something about that video ...

BK: [*close-up of Bernie*] So we go to *bet* which is black entertainment and I'm not downing anybody here, okay, but I'm just—this is the bottom line. And they say, "Well, it's rock." Okay. And it's like, that's the Catch-22 that we're in, because I think each one should have played it on its own merits.

TODD: Right.

BERNIE: Period. But there it is, as they say.

TODD: [*cut to close-up of Todd who speaks directly to camera*] Ladies and gentlemen, here you have a quality video, quality band, no airplay. We need you, you need the BRC, we need to come together. Call up the stations, call up these networks, talk to them, write letters, say, "Look, I saw this band Total Eclipse, I've never seen them on your program." Let's get the people together, let's put this stuff on the air. It's going to take some letters, it's going to take some people coming down to support these bands so people can see that these bands have something to say that needs to be heard. [*Todd turns to Bernie*] I personally would like to see an alternative to MTV so we don't have to depend—

BERNIE: True.

TODD: —on MTV.

BERNIE: That's so true.

TODD: Or BET. The beginnings of what we have here may generate some of what we need in the future, but unfortunately MTV provides a service but they don't really have any competition as far as what I can see. So when they say this is the number one video, who's going to argue with them? You know what I'm saying?

BERNIE: [*cut to Bernie*] Everyone jumps on the train.

TODD: MTV is a radio [*sic*] station that basically has no competition, so bands like you come along, put their heart and soul in the music, and they say, "Well, sorry." [*camera has been on Bernie during this statement. He smiles slightly and affirms Todd's observations with emphatic nods*]

BERNIE: True.

TODD: So where do we go [*cut to Todd*] from here? I mean—

BERNIE: We go to Europe.

TODD: [*laughs*] Let's talk about that. You guys been over there?

BERNIE: [*midshot of both of them*] No, but we sell a lot of records, a lot of records over there.

Although the existence of *Network BRC* is an implicit critique of MTV and BET, in this clip, Bernie and Todd are direct in their attack, a result of Total Eclipse's bitter encounter with the two national cable networks. Their comments about the band's experiences trying to get included on MTV and BET playlists underscore the ways race informs executive decision making and influences the production, distribution, and reception circuit. For Los Angeles BRC members, the fact that video director Josh Taft, whose videos for white rock bands Alice in Chains and Pearl Jam were put into rotation on MTV, was unable to produce an equally acceptable video for a black rock band was an indication of MTV's continued racism. While the station featured black rappers on its popular *Yo! MTV Raps*, it abandoned black rockers, even a band with a major label deal and a quality video. A&M Records had the familiar difficulties marketing Total Eclipse, and these were probably exacerbated rather than relieved by the presence of other black rock bands on the scene. Many BRC members told me that the industry seemed reluctant to sponsor more than a handful of black rock bands. Lenny Kravitz, Living Colour, Fishbone, Bad Brains, and 24-7 Spyz were already out there. The logical question for the industry was whether there was a need or market for Total Eclipse, another black rock act. Any differences in sound, style, and ethos were trumped by their most notable similarity to existing nationally known black rock bands: their blackness. In the end, A&M dropped Total Eclipse from its roster because of the failure of the record to sell—or, as BRC members saw it, after the failure of the label to sell the record.

Bernie's invocation of Europe as a viable alternative to the U.S. mainstream is a revealing response. At one level, it indicates the range of approaches musicians can take when seeking outlets for their work. At another level, it points out that the problems black rock bands encounter have been constructed in a U.S. context that constrains African American cultural production. American media outlets are structured by economic imperatives and racialized assumptions that limit the ways both producers and consumers can engage with music. As Bernie noted later in the *Network BRC* interview, Europe is an appealing alternative "because the people there, they don't need MTV to convince them." Historically, European outlets and audiences have been more willing to embrace music "on its own merits" rather than based on the image of the performers, leading a long line of African American musicians to turn to overseas markets. Black rockers found that in Europe their creativity was not stifled by U.S. racial politics. Furthermore, to the extent that image is important, black Americanness is often a positive selling point for many Europeans—at least in the realm of music. Not surprisingly, many black rock musicians—including BRC members Gene Williams, Michael Hill's Blues Mob, Screaming Headless Torsos, and Kelvyn Bell—have focused touring and distribution efforts on Europe and also in Japan. The comparative openness of European audiences also led the BRC to produce a BRC Orchestra tribute to Jimi Hendrix in Bari, Italy, in 1991 and a black rock set at the 1992 International Pori Jazz Festival in Finland.

Although offering alternatives to the music available on MTV and BET, *Network BRC* was constrained by the conditions of its production: the limited reach of its show, its low budget, and its modest production values. Still, by providing a forum where black rockers could perform and discuss their music, *Network BRC* expanded mainstream media representations of black music and black people. Other cable access programs share this mission and have featured BRC artists. In New York, Fikisha Combo dedicated several episodes of her program, *CACE International TV*, to coverage of the BRC's 1993 Jimi Hendrix Birthday Tribute. Her program was in rotation on four Manhattan and Brooklyn cable stations. In 1995, *New York New Rock*, a local music program airing on Manhattan Cable, covered the 1995 Hendrix Tribute Show and in 1994 it featured a group interview with BRC executive committee members Bruce Mack, Jimmy Saal, and Chuck Brownley. In Los Angeles, *Video Nouveau*, produced by Clarise Wilkins and Erica Bristol, dedicated an episode to screening videos by BRC artists from New York and Los Angeles in 1995. The Los Angeles-based cable program *City TV*, produced and hosted by Terry Cross, devoted a 1992 program to documenting the Los Angeles BRC's weekly Black Rock Cafe band showcase at the Gaslight in Hollywood. Both programs were played several times on Los Angeles cable access stations.

During the 1990s, cheaper and more accessible technology made it easier for artists to produce their videos and CDs independently. BRC bands like D-Xtreme, Civil Rite, and Drek DuBoyz made their own videos that could be screened on these outlets when the opportunity arose. They also used these videos when seeking performance opportunities internationally or nationally. Through networks of friends and acquaintances, bands usually had a connection to someone with inexpensive but professional video production equipment and the ability to use it effectively. D-Xtreme made its video for "N.Y.D.S." when a fan volunteered his equipment and services. A number of BRC members have home studios where they record their own work and make a little cash on the side by renting the space to other musicians. Others took advantage of special deals offered by independent studios in Los Angeles and Manhattan where, for around $50 an hour, they could get the services of an engineer and the use of a professional studio and equipment for a recording. Bands also found creative ways to subsidize professional quality recordings. Suburban Dog cut a session in January 1993 at a New York technical school where the band had volunteered to play so the class could be trained on studio recording equipment.

In spite of the high prices charged for them at stores, compact discs are relatively inexpensive to produce. In the mid-1990s, it cost less than $2,000 to press and package 1,000 discs. By going to a CD production company, bands could turn their studio recordings into compact discs in jewel boxes with artwork. Among the BRC bands who released and distributed recordings independently were Suburban Dog, Civil Rite, Gene Williams, Women in Love, and Faith. Los Angeles band Rainbows End sold cassettes of its self-produced recording *No Far Out* to underwrite the cost of compact disc production; those who supported the band by purchasing a cassette received a copy of the compact disc once it was available. Bands sold these recordings at shows and also sent them to radio stations, independent record distributors, booking agencies, and alternative music press with the hope of getting some attention. Other BRC bands signed contracts with independent labels. The greater open-mindedness, flexibility, and autonomy of the independent labels compensated for their more limited production, promotion, and distribution resources. BRC members who have released recordings on independent labels include Screaming Headless Torsos on Discovery, Queen Esther and Elliot Sharp's Hoosegow on Homestead Records, and Michael Hill's Blues Mob on Alligator. The Blues Mob, incidentally, exemplifies the ways BRC members use the organization's network to support projects. Hill started the band with his siblings, but over the years, the personnel changed, and Hill called in fellow BRC members to play in the band. In its 2003 incarnation, the Blues Mob featured Hill on guitar and vocals; Pete Cummings, formerly with Shock Council, on bass; and Bill McClellan, formerly with P.B.R. Streetgang, on drums. The 1994 album *Bloodlines* features liner notes by Greg Tate and cover art by Sid Blaize who contributed the artwork for BRC compilations. Soon after the record's release, the band opened for Me'Shell NdegéOcello's 1994 performance at Irving Plaza in New York.

Since the mid-1990s, the Internet has expanded the possibilities of independent production by giving performers access to an inexpensive and wide-reaching marketing tool that offers some professional autonomy. After being disappointed by a lack of support from his independent record label, David Fiuczynski, with the help of his wife Lian Amber, regained the rights to the first Screaming Headless Torsos album. He released it on his own Fuzelicious Morsels label and distributes it, along with his other projects, through his Web site. Like Fiuczynski, a number of BRC members set up Web pages that provide information about their bands, club dates, and merchandise as well as links to other sites of interest—these can be for other bands, online publications, and favorite rock venues. Many BRC bands also included a link to the BRC Web site, a clearinghouse for black rock information. The coalition's Web site features the BRC Manifesto, an events calendar, band names, links to the Web sites of black rock and BRC artists, information about the radio show, photographs of events, articles about and interviews with BRC members, and frequently asked questions about black rock and the BRC.[8] These independent outlets provide a space for audiences who are willing to go to the trouble of seeking nonmainstream fare through the World Wide Web, alternative publications, e-mail lists, and word of mouth.

In their struggle over representations of blackness, BRC members engage the very media that have influenced the music and identities they produce and the images they critique. Using alternative circuits to disseminate their message, they push the boundaries of race and genre that shape the U.S. popular music industry and circumscribe African Americans—in the media and beyond. This kind of cultural activism produces *Network BRC, Blacker Than That*, the BRC's radio show—which by 2002 was being streamed online—black rock-oriented Web sites, and independent videos and recordings. Together these independent productions address the exclusionary nature of the music industry and challenge the ways racism has shaped music industry practices, audience expectations, patterns of consumption, and the erasure of African Americans from the history of rock. A refusal or inability to fit the demands of mainstream media led many BRC members to turn to more accessible independent outlets. Of course, a local public access cable TV program affords different audience access and career cachet than mainstream national channels like MTV or BET. Similarly, the BRC record label is not the same as a major label or even a large independent label. Still, these grassroots outlets allow bands to have their music commercially available—if on a smaller scale. By working in independent media, BRC members develop alternatives to the mainstream. At one level, this is a compromise—members lose out on large audiences and the accompanying recognition that most artists desire. At another level, however, this is a critique of the mainstream media. Many members view independent production as a way to avoid compromising one's musical and individual integrity. Konda Mason, commenting about the importance of taking an independent approach, observed:

> We have to break outside of the box. We have to be in charge of our own destinies creatively. It won't happen inside the industry. There have been little gains. But if you're in the middle of the industry, they are going to control what you do in order to meet their bottom line. And they aren't going to touch those things that are outside the box. The Internet has changed everything. We need to redirect our focus not on how to get a record deal, but how to set up our own companies and how to make good music. Like I said, I have a love/hate relationship with the industry, but it's mostly hate. I have seen this business kill too many great artists' spirits. (Mason quoted in BRC 2000/2001:10–11)

Media, the context that led to the emergence of the BRC, became a context into which BRC members intervened as they sought to do the primary thing musicians desire: produce and share music while keeping their spirits intact.

Notes

1. By extension, it is relatively easy to identify and get access to potential research subjects who are media consumers. Indeed, most media studies by anthropologists focus on audiences and consumption rather than production. For discussion of the challenges associated with conducting fieldwork with producers, see Dornfeld 1998 and Kondo 1997.
2. For discussions of media and the public sphere, see Appadurai et al., 1994; Calhorn 1992; Cornfeld 1998; Neal 1999; Rubbins 1994; Sreberny-Mohammadi and Mohammdi 1994.
3. In April 1994. Williams and Douglas stepped down from the show. After a transition period, Gregory Amani and Lace began broadcasting the BRC's "Crosstown Traffic" in January 1995 in a Friday early morning time slot. By 2002, the coalition pretended *Radio BRC* online at www.soul.patrol.com/funk/blk.rock.htm. The show's hosts were LaRonda Davis, Earl Douglas, and Darrell McNeill, and occasional guest host Vernon Reid.
4. See Gray 1988 for a discussion of black independent record production.
5. During the 1980s, over 1,000 cable systems were launched across the United States (Kellner 1990:188). The high level of competition between different cable operators for local franchises gave cities and municipalities the leverage to demand that cable carriers provide services like public access in order to be awarded a contract.
6. To format the show for its thirty-minute time slot, Rod and Melva had to carefully schedule the minute and second point at which a public service announcement would be placed, how much time would be spent on a given segment of an interview, and how much time would be devoted to camera effects like fades and dissolves.
7. To "call the show" means to direct camera movement supervise the composition of the shots, and select which shots from the two cameras are used in the broadcast.
8. The BRC Web site address at time of publication was http://www.blackrockcoalition.org.

References

Appadurai, Arjun, Lauren Berlant, Carol A. Breckenridge, and Manthia Diawara. 1994. Special issue on the Black Public Sphere. *Public Culture* 7(1).

Black Rock Coalition (BRC). 1995b. Network BRC featuring Total Eclipse [cable television program].

———. 2000/2001. Progressive Forum: Konda Mason. BRC *Newsletter* (New York), December/January, pp. 10–12.

———. 2001a. Progressive Forum: Greg Tate. BRC *Newsletter* (New York), February, pp. 8–11.

Cablecast 25 News. 1995. *Cablecast 25 News United Artists Cable Community. Access Newsletter.* March.

Calhoun, Craig, ed. 1992. *Habermas and the Public Sphere.* Cambridge, Mass: MIT Press.

Dornfeld, Barry. 1998. *Producing Public Television, Producing Public Culture.* Princeton, N.J.: Princeton University Press.

Fiske, John. 1989. *Understanding Popular Culture.* London: Routledge.

Gardner, Elyse. 1993. The Black Rock Coalition Mission. *Musician,* November, pp. 22–24.

Gray, Herman. 1988. *Producing Jazz. The Experience of an Independent Record Company.* Philadelphia, Pa.: Temple University Press.

Hall, Stuart. 1980. Encoding/Decoding. In *Culture Media, Language.* S. Hall et al., eds., pp. 128–38. London: Hutchinson.

Kellner, Douglas. 1990. *Television and the Crisis of Democracy.* Boulder, Colo.: Westview Press.

Kordo, Dorinne. 1997. *About Face: Performing Face in Fashion and Theater.* New York: Routledge.

Neal, Mark Anthony. 1999. *What the Music Said: Black Music and Black Popular Culture.* New York: Routledge.

Negus, Keith. 1992. *Producing Pop: Culture and Conflict in the Popular Music Industry.* London. Edward Arnold.

———. 1999. *Music Genres and Corporate Cultures.* New York: Routledge.

Robbins, Bruce, ed. 1993. *The Phantom Public Sphere,* Minneapolis University of Minnesota Press.

Sreberny-Mohammadi. Annabelle, and Ali Mohammadi. 1994. *Small Media, Big Revolution Communication, Culture, and the Iranian Revolution.* Minneapolis: University of Minnesota Press.

Tate, Greg. 1991. Liner Notes. *The History of Our Future* [BRC compilation]. Ryko-disc.

Williams, Steve. 1993. Support the BRC Radio Show! BRC *Newsletter* (New York), May, p. I.

34

Black Artistic Invisibility
A Black Composer Talking 'bout Taking Care of the Souls of Black Folks While Losing Much Ground Fast

WILLIAM BANFIELD

A man with wide-ranging interests, William Banfield has written about various aspects of contemporary black American popular music, mused in print about the importance of cultural historian and singer Bernice Johnson Regan, and reported on the 2004 BET Awards Show. He holds a Ph.D. from the University of Michigan and presently teaches at the Berklee School of Music in Boston. Banfield holds two other distinctions: He's a composer and he's invisible.

In this piece, Banfield discusses the dilemma of being an academically trained composer in "this age of P. Diddy, Jay-Z, and Beyonce" in a culture where "the only music that is now accepted as defining a Black modern cultural aesthetic is 'Hip Hop.' Instead of putting down hip hop, the author suggests that we need not only to understand and embrace it, but also to look toward modern black composers as an alternative creative model. He wonders why so few educated [black] music lovers know about the work of Gary Powell Nash, who teaches at Fisk University, or Anthony Davis at UC–San Diego.

In many respects Banfield echoes the lament of earlier black composers, few of whom (William Grant Still, is perhaps the main exception) received much recognition. Many others, such as R. Nathaniel Dett and Will Marion Cook, have received more attention in death than during their lives. In this essay, which was first delivered to University of Pennsylvania students in 2002, Banfield blames the "lack of inspirational models of excellence, image, and identity" that move younger people to follow and embrace popular music. I can only image that Dett and Cook (both of whom also taught at colleges) would have applauded this statement.

The ultimate effectiveness (power) of any group of people is the degree to which they have as awareness of who they are and respect for themselves. The instruments that facilitate this development is education, cultural images and celebrations that build a shared aesthetic, role models and the projection of cultural heroes and heroines.

—Na'im Akbar[1]

> I am an invisible man. No, I am not a spook like those who haunted Edgar Allan Poe; nor am I one of your Hollywood-movie ectoplasms. I am a man of substance, of flesh and bone, fiber and liquids—and I might even be said to possess a mind. I am invisible, understand, simply because people refuse to see me.
>
> —Ralph Ellison[2]

INTRO THEME: THE BLACK COMPOSER AS INVISIBLE

Dear reader; I am a Black American composer and I am invisible. I am perceived I think like a ghost passing in a memorable melody, heard rarely and never seen. I wanted to share a composer's take and journey on defining an aspect of a Black artistic tradition, its representation and identity in twenty-first-century expression. If we examine the state of scholarship about African American culture in traditional music disciplines, we find that too often the academy consistently obscures the beauty, complexity, and variety of Black life and artistic expression. By doing this the academy misses an opportunity to have an encompassing and relevant discourse related to the study of Black music, folk, and life, in total. Basically there is sumptin' going on that allows us to ignore and thus dismiss the variety and diversity heard and taught within the whole of Black artistry. I like to think of this as the cultural politics of misrepresentation. I am as well concerned with a definition of Black musical value and our current generational divides on this issue. I want to erase the invisibility of Black composers, the men and women who are our "Black Beethovens."

In this age of P. Diddy, Jay-Z, and Beyonce, I want to introduce into the scholarly discourse, into the loop of representations, this identity and expression which has been central to Black American composers since William Grant Still wrote, in 1930, the "Afro-American Symphony" based on the Blues.

Mainstream American media has dismissed important creative, cultural/social/spiritual aspects of Black artistic expressive culture and following that lead as well are the educational, cultural institutions that arm our society with relevant and lasting impressions of what is valued and what is preserved. This devaluation leads to not only the suffocation of major portions of Black culture, but as a counterproductive ploy, investments are made into the commodification of negative cultural imagery and overblown pop teen "celebri-dom." The dark clouds of cultural chaos and the ever present potential of the invisibility of our own diversity in music is underscored in the fact that for the most part in mainstream America, the only music that is now accepted as defining a Black modern cultural aesthetic, is Hip Hop. I listen and enjoy Hip Hop music. I love the form and the forum for engaging ideas. But in our current suffocation, our current drowning as Rome is definitely on fire, too much of popular culture in this way is doing more damage than good. Unfortunately because idea inspiring messages and strong healthy doses with images of Black productivity are missing, the possibilities of empowering values inherent in contemporary expression are muted.

> Writing the book confirmed ideas that had been rolling around in my head for years ... how to measure this world in which we find ourselves, where we are not at all happy, but clearly able to understand and hopefully, one day transform. How to measure my own learning and experience and to set out a system of evaluation, weights and meaning.... This is the history ... this is your history, my history and the history of the people ... the Music, this is our history.[3]

So the question now is, how are we measuring ourselves and are the cultural forms engaged in expressing, celebrating, and critiquing culture in ways that continue to help navigate our survival as in the past and give us hope and joy in our living frames? If we are measuring our world only in terms of Hip Hop and Destiny's Children, we are in trouble. I have a friend who speaks of BET as our televised Festival of Ignorance, a sexual minstrel show where Black males are being constructed as the commodity of anger and Black females in too many videos are diminished further as an image of a slut, sex-driven, power access thirsty babe for leisure use for the crew.

No other voice or use. I'm convinced that Black people and scholars are as much of the problem as anyone else in this cultural phenomenon. Mostly because we don't speak out and educate. I respect Tricia Rose's *Black Noise*,[4] but after seeing her recently, I am convinced she is saddened by the diminished potential of what could have been a major cultural marker in our expressive evolution forward. For all of my big brother Michael Eric Dyson's powerful portrayal and advocacy for the use of Hip Hop as an aesthetic tool for young Black people, our popular music art forms need retooling. So, instead of complaining I wanted to offer a few alternative models, places, and movements in our culture, heroes, and heroines of Black music culture; Black American composers, their work and their worlds.

I am reminded of the seriousness we gave again to Black women writers after seeing the Oprah book club. As well hearing spoken word and freestyle poetry after SLAM with Saul Williams, we got "literate again." Our reconsideration of our dance forms as a cultural expression of note with Savion Glover and George Wolfe's "Bring on the Noise" helped us to see dance as an expressive historical/cultural form and narrative. We will need of course launching forums supported by Black engaged scholarship to take a serious look at the work of Black composers and other forgotten and overlooked Black art forms as a part of the packaging of our cultural rituals, intellectual artistic canon(s), our literature in poetic and musical form.

This is my goal as a Black artist in the academy. Along with a camp of colleagues representing at least three generations of artists, we are creating the spaces and making the works of a Black music canon in modern serious Black music. I don't like labeling music, but this is a movement that includes Jazz, operas, contemporary instrumental music, ballet and symphonies.

We got some Black Beethovens living up in here, and what's most sad is y'all don't even know it!

BRIDGE: THE POLITICS OF MISREPRESENTATION

> The Negro is a natural musician. He will learn to play on an instrument more quickly than a White man. They may not know one note from the other, yet their ears catch the strains of any floating air, and they represent it by imitation. Inferior to the White race in reason and intellect, they have more imagination, more lively feelings and a more expressive manner. With their imagination they clothe in rude poetry the incidents of their lowly life and set them to simple melodies. Blessed power of music. It is a beautiful gift of God to this oppressed race to lighten their sorrows in the house of their bondage.
> —"Songs of the Black," *Dwight's Journal of Music*, 1856[5]

If it were left up to academic discourse as seen in the above, we would continually be reduced by a shallow and limited analysis offered as "the fact" of our creative work. Recently, I read a

New York Times article complaining that Hip Hop singer Mary J. Blige needed to become angry again in order to reach her best as an artist. They don't want us to be doing anything but... "clothing our rude poetry in the incidents of our lowly lives."

As I see it one of the most valuable battles, movements to watch on the music/cultural front is in the field of new concert music composition. The players in this game are Black American composers and the performing/commissioning concert music venues (symphony, chamber, opera). For many Black composers our historical/cultural sensibilities are always clashing with mainstream schooling; that is, with what we want to write, how we are organizing contemporary musical materials, and the historical-cultural narrative for libretto, scripts are not rooted in the traditional formula. Black composers writing in the academy and concert performance industry is in itself the embodiment of cultural warfare. Because we use the Blues in complex forms, we use melodic, rhythmically complex formulas, disjunctive 12-pitch tone rows, but we too express our romance and rage through 100 instrumental voices.

These works are heard in 100 concert halls a year across America, but y'all ain't there. Black American composers have been synthesizing Black expression and experience in these powerful representations for at least 100 years in American music literature.

There are numerous recording labels carrying this important work: Albany, Videmus/Visionary, Tel Arc, Columbia, Koch, Collins Classics, New World, CRI.

My role models are T. J. Anderson, my teacher, who served as one of the Atlanta Symphony's first Black composers in residence. Also, my dear friends Patrice Rushen and David Baker and many others who place culture, experience, and craft in a blender and serve up works that are some of the best examples of the successful contemporary multiethnic perspective in arts culture. The embodiment of the politics of culture(s) and representation are best exemplified in the music processes and products of contemporary Black American composers. These works are extremely rich, relevant and provide multiple sources for study in music, literature, cultural studies and Black music history, which reflect a rich past and project the potentiality of a strong future in Black musical artistry, in total.

Composers of African descent from Chevalier de St. George's writing in pre-Beethovenian times to Francis Johnson in the early nineteenth century, to James Reece Europe at the top of the twentieth and Tania Leon a contemporary twenty-first century example, have been involved in one of the bloodiest battles in Western aesthetic construction and thought. They have done this by bringing the meaning of vernacular culture, ideas, and identity to bear on the meaning of being an architect of Western art form. Upon the waters of Western expression, these ethnic boats that carry vernacular music, culture, and identity hold crew, mission, and captain in place and have succeeded in "crossing over." In doing so Black composers have created one of the best examples of truly innovative Black music, rarely heard.

Two books recently published which document this work: published in 2001, the *International Encyclopedia of Black Composers,* Fitzroy Press, produced by Center for Black Music Research, CBMR (Sam Floyd). As well, my own *Landscapes in Color: Conversations with Black American Composers,* Scarecrow Press, 2003. This book explores the life and work of contemporary living Black American composers working across the United States.

Landscapes in Color is a rare collection of insights by contemporary Black musical artists and one of the most diverse with a broad view of Black music making. The composers speak from such a wide variety of backgrounds on American music and culture. These days we usually just hear about Black music from rappers, producers, and artists in R&B, Gospel, or jazz. So much of who we are has come from musical artists and so their work is extremely important as well to gauge where we are headed. The book serves several purposes related to our central question and the idea of finding the core of twenty-first-century expression and representations of Black American music culture. Sources like these:

- Serve as an important and rich commentary on American music making and its development from the perspective of Black music makers.
- Composers are talking about their musical making process and the development of their musical careers, narratives, and inside stories.
- Challenge, make certain changes to the way we teach, look at and consume music in our culture.
- Present very powerful alternative views, which are transformative to the way we have learned about American artistry. (Namely, that White artists were the only ones creating worthwhile important works.)

The writing as well contains discussion between myself and 40 of the leading Black American composers of our day. Many of these people our readers are very familiar with, for example:

Composer Ysaye Barnwell (member of Legendary and Sweet Honey in the Rock) talking about the essential functional character of music making in the world. Bobby McFerrin talking about creative responsibility. Patrice Rushen, in many ways the model for a Janet Jackson, Alicia Keys, Norah Jones and one of the most influential women in the L.A. music scene, taking a stab at the lack of personal accountability that rappers have when they speak. Anthony Davis, composer of the opera *Malcolm X,* talking about jazz redefining the direction of symphonies and operatic tradition in America. Great drummer Tony Williams talking about life as a young musician working with Miles Davis or the old great Jester Hairston, composer of "Amen," talking about how the Spirituals changed American social sensibility, seeing this happen as early as the 1920s in his long professional life.

These perspectives are far reaching insights about music making, music education, the record and performing industry, and the transformative role of art in our culture. The work of Tania Leon, Daniel Romain (New York), Donal Fox (Boston), Julius P. Williams, Jonathon Holland (Berklee School of Music, Boston), Alvin Singleton (Atlanta), Regina Harris Bioacchi (Chicago), Lettie Beckon Alston (Michigan), George Lewis, Anthony Davis (University of Southern California, San Diego), Stephen Newby (Seattle) along with Billy Childs, Patrice Rushen (Los Angeles), Jeffery Mumford (Oberlin College, Ohio), Gary Powell Nash (Fisk, Tuskegee), Roger Dickerson (New Orleans), Anthony Kelley (Duke University), William Banfield (University of St. Thomas, St. Paul, Minnesota) are examples of contemporary Black composers of this generation creating in various places all around the country.

One of the main deterrents to present-day successes for young people is the lack of inspirational models of excellence, image, and identity. When there is less of that kind of talking, which is exactly what we face in popular music culture today, our society becomes bereft of places where young people especially get nurturing. Black artists of this caliber are a real shot in the arm and their examples and music are so powerful.

DEVELOPMENT SECTION: THE PROBLEM OF A CLASH IN GENERATIONAL VALUES AND MARKETS

Every generation out of relative obscurity must discover their mission, fulfill it or betray it.

—Frantz Fanon, *Wretched of the Earth*[6]

> If this generation does nothing, they are not our future, they are our fate.
>
> —Maulana Kerenga[7]

I recently participated in a conference on the state of Black scholarship and the arts. Black studies programs that began after the Civil Rights era in the early seventies arc celebrating 25- and 30-year anniversaries. And they are asking just this question, where is Black America, the Black academy, arts institutions and communities in leadership? Just as important is the question how is Blackness represented and evolving in the global environment? This wider lens is the result of our recognition of the ways that, "African Diaspora experiences and traditions have functioned on a global scale and resonated within the spaces of a variety of international projects."

In most of these discussions the focus is on: the critical examination of the human, cultural, social, political, economic, and historical factors that have created and shaped the African American and African Diaspora experiences post-1970. The main point in agreement is the degree to which Black artists have taken up the torch to be instruments of change. It is clear that a more progressive and informed generation preceded us who were the models of this kind of activism. So how do we encourage and not just attack due to possible generational, even class differences, a new generation with seemingly stark differences of cultural values?

The Hip Hop underground is the most socially and politically active generation since the long death and silence of the Black community which fell asleep throughout the eighties. Grand Master Flash reminded us, "It's like a jungle sometimes it makes me wonder how I keep from going under."[8] The relevancy of more contemporary underground Hip Hop and Rap scores big in this discussion.

But to be honest though, this is a "teaching moment" where it is crucial that we all instill forward direction by both celebrating and critiquing contemporary culture.

I enjoyed recently exchanges I had at a similar conference in St. Louis aimed directly at the role of Black theater in addressing a lack of diverse artistic hearings in our culture. Cultural critic-historian Gerald Early, well known as cultural commentator on recent PBS specials such as Ken Burns's *Jazz*, *I'll Make Me a World* and others, commented on the fact that art always has engagement in the world. Art is politics in that anyone who does a work of art defends a certain set of values. Early reminded us of the history of Black audiences, that despite commodification and commercialism, we were an audience who could always see beyond bad politics and empty rhetoric and still be moved powerfully inwardly and externally. So, I guess there is still hope even in our current flood of suffocating popular images and music that on the current surface seem bleak with possibility.

All the playwrights and directors who attended the St. Louis gathering like the University of Pennsylvania event spoke of an eternally understood and practiced notion, that Black art has maintained many of its dynamic characteristics and still remaining intact is the power of the rhythm in speech and its soul motion the Blues aesthetic. The players in this dialogue, playwrights, director and composer, began then to speak of collaboration and the processes of envisioning new Black artistic movements that allow seeing ourselves trusting, sharing, and working in a variety of capacities attempting to reveal "truth."

RECAP: SOME HISTORY, EXTENSIONS OF THE TRADITION, AND ARGUMENTS FOR THE MUSIC OF BLACK COMPOSERS

Bohemian composer Anton Dvorak, while living here in the United States, stated in 1893: "I am satisfied that the future music of this country must be founded upon what are called the Negro melodies. They are American. They are the folk songs of America and your composers must turn to them. . . . I discover in them all that is needed for a great and noble school of music." In 1912, James Reece Europe, composer, bandleader, and conductor of New York's Clef Club Orchestra, stated, "As composers, no matter what else you might think, we [Black composers] have created an orchestral language that is unique and distinctive and lends itself to the peculiar compositions of our race."

In the discipline of composition and concert music, Black American composers have in recent years provided many examples of what I have called, "extensions of the tradition." These composers and their traditions are the result, the call and response if you will, to the prophetic words of Anton Dvorak.

Black American creative thinkers in the concert tradition are both vindicating past blocked voices and forging new musical practices. Contemporary black composers are gradually becoming a real presence on the American concert music scenes.

This is important I think because the music so wonderfully reflects much of what we already accept as our own musical culture. But we didn't come to accept all this music as American and worthy overnight. Black music innovators such as James Reece Europe (1881–1919) who experimented with the 100-plus All Black Clef Club Orchestra included five pianos, ten drum sets, mandolins, harp-guitar, banjo, cello, and brass. The band work of Francis Johnson, Scott Joplin's *Treemonisha*, or Sister Rosetta Tharpe's eclecticisms are early-twentith-century experiments which were pioneering. Fletcher Henderson's orchestrations and pathbreaking arrangements which set the pattern for the American Big Band Jazz, or as mentioned earlier, William Grant Still's evocative and innovative early fusing of rural Blues and the orchestra producing his *Afro-American Symphony* in 1930. These were all experiments as trailblazing as anything in American music by our White counterpoints such as by Ives, Cowell, Varese, and Cage, though almost never recognized.

As tradition bearers, the generations who succeeded these innovators work back and forth between a great range of traditions: African American vernacular, West African and Western European Classical/Romantic and avant-garde traditions. And all this pluralistic, boundary crossing innovation occurs within the matrix of contemporary American music.

CODA: A CLASH IN CULTURAL VALUES IN MUSIC?

When you have a Black artist who attempts to make art, that art should be an expression of one's culture, gifting, and be a product as well of the time, individual tastes, and craft. But in order to be heard, many times a Black composer's work is relegated to the Black History Month program when the work truly deserves to simply be on a concert program on any month. Many people are unaware of the whole of the process and politics of being a Black composer, and I mean hearing about the problems, process, and actually hearing the product.

I have been extremely blessed, fortunate, and have a big enough mouth to have been given a great number of opportunities to grow and develop as an actual composer. I mean I really am commissioned to write symphonies, concertos, operas, ballets and to write music for the opening of bridges, museums, and libraries. I know this must be rare. After I completed my eighth symphony, many of my friends began to get worried, as several of the European composers died after their eighth or ninth symphonies. But for a Black composer writing in the academy and concert performance industry is in itself the embodiment of cultural warfare, and certainly Black cultural representation and identity is one of the exchanges most salient points.

You may ask, what are some of the central issues that rise up in this exchange, this clash that provides us with some understanding of an embodiment of the politics of culture and representing Blackness? When a voting person decides they want to be a composer, that choice is wrought with a whole battery of restrictions, strictures, and terrain that must be navigated within traditional art venues and it's especially tricky for a Black person. My musical hero was Jimi Hendrix. My mother and father took me regularly to hear the Detroit Symphony. My mother told me, "One day that orchestra is going to play your music." So, I logically thought I would write music for Jimi Hendrix to play with the orchestra. As it turned out, some thirty years later the Detroit Symphony did play my music, but not before a long series of identity crises which I am still repairing from. Here are eight political "mine and mind fields":

- Finding the opportunity to do one's art (A Jazz player can go play somewhere where the musician can see and be seen among peers. Where does the Black composer go?)
- Liberation of Voice (In concert music you can't always have just your own voice like Ellington or Macy Gray because it must be mediated through the thick aesthetic of conventions of traditional concert music instruments, methods. This can limit what you can say, and how you say it.)
- Audience (Who's listening?)
- Acceptance and placement (I used to say, "We are choking at the neck of a big white goose who we expect to falsely hatch golden brown eggs.")
- Documentation (Who cares? Record companies . . . history books . . . curriculum writers?)
- Workplace, job (How many Black composers did you have for your theory/composition teacher? The old boys' network still exists. I was the first Black man to graduate with a doctorate in composition in 1992 from the University of Michigan. Why aren't more young Black scholars in the fields of composition, musicology, theory, and conducting encouraged and supported to pursue the academy?)
- Language dilemma: tone row or Blues scale (If you sound slightly Black, you might not be called back. Or if you don't "sound Black," you may be asked to flatten some of your thirds.)
- Disruption of the Western cultural formula (A Black composer? What and where is that? Here there is double backlash from both sides, White and Black, because of the behavioral/social/cultural codes entrenched deeply in the identity formation of both communities.)

I should mention, that being a composer, an artist is tough, tough work for anybody green, blue, or fuchsia. But the Black artists' challenges in a classical art world dwarfs our White contemporaries' issues by legions.

CADENCE

My suggestion is to ignore and fight the misrepresentation and past limited acknowledgment of Black artistry and seek out the music products of contemporary Black American composers. For educational, observation, and study, you can see the richness in the whole dynamic from performance practices to the embodiment of our cultural heritages, and the best examples of the amalgamation of western European practice and vernacular culture. It's all there in the work, processes, and product of Black American composers.

Here for cultural study and references are the politics of embodying culture and the tangles of representing and defining Black art in our contemporary culture. In all this perhaps we are trying to make the institution do something it was not meant to do? Again, I always say, "We are at the neck of a big white goose trying to make it lay a golden brown egg." And implicit in this is the reevaluation of cultural and national values. There is much to gain from this view and engagement.

The task for us here will still be the challenge in addressing how to tap into the current generation's sensibilities that are forward, but critique that which is shackles and chains. We have to have enough love and courage to roll up the sleeves and commit to educating and artucating in a way that maintains those powerful and needed foundations in arts. This must be parallel to positive, productive Black movement in the world socially, artistically, and spiritually. We must be up to this task or we perish and go down, empty. Our cultural critiques, explorations and vision(s) keep us filled and overflowing, thusly fulfilling our missions and ensuring our future.

The instruments that will facilitate a rich future will be by employing a knowledge to a full range of Black peoples' expressions, images, and ideas. This is how we take care of the Souls of Black folk in the twenty-first century.

Notes

1. Na'im Akbar, "Making Black America Better through Self Knowledge," in *How to Make Black America Better*, ed. Tavis Smiley (New York: Doubleday, 2001), 133.
2. Ralph Ellison, *Invisible Man* (New York: Vintage Books, 1980), 3.
3. Amiri Baraka, *Blues People* (New York: William Morrow, 1999), vii–viii.
4. Tricia Rose, *Black Noise: Rap Music and Black Culture in Contemporary America* (Hanover, NH: University Press of New England, 1994).
5. As quoted in Branford Marsalis, liner notes from *Bloomington* (CD), Sony, 1993.
6. As quoted in Bakari Kitwana, *The Hip-Hop Generation: Young Blacks and the Crisis in African American Culture* (New York: Basic Civitas Books, 2002), 23.
7. As quoted in Kitwana, *The Hip-Hop Generation*, xi.
8. Lyrics from Grand Master Flash's *The Message* (LP), Sugarhill, 1982.

35 Stepping Out an African Heritage

ELIZABETH FINE

Stepping is a highly organized movement that relies on improvisation, call and response, complex meters, propulsive rhythms, and a percussive attack. Because it is largely the province of sororities and fraternities, anyone who has attended a historical black college or university knows about stepping. I first encountered the tradition in 1973 as a college student in Greensboro, North Carolina, and learned about stepping through a "step show" being held at nearby North Carolina A&T University.

Modern stepping dates back to the early twentieth century when it was pioneered by black veterans of World War I enrolling in mostly southern "black" colleges like Livingstone, Hampton, and Grambling. Inspired by their military training, they brought to their dances a highly rigorous, drill-like component that was at once militaristic and refined. In the 1920s and 1930s, stepping incorporated elements from other vernacular black dances, just as twenty-first-century steppers add hip hop movements.

During the "Black Power" and related Afro-centric movements of the 1960s, stepping was renewed and revitalized by incorporation of traditional African ritual dancing and other elements like cheerleading, tap, and gymnastics that resulted in the "shout 'n foot stomp 'n tribalism" that dominated stepping formats during this era. The 1970s saw the beginning of the "Greek Weekend," at which stepping performances began to transform into more formal performances that emphasized increased competition among the steppers who wore elaborate costumes.

This article, a chapter from Elizabeth Fine's book Soulstepping: African American Step Shows, *is a social and culture history of stepping. In this essay Fine, a folkorist and cultural historian who teaches at Virginia Tech, explores the importance and renewing influence of African culture throughout the history of stepping. She notes the influence of African dance folklore on stepping, particularly during the 1960s and 1970s among sorority women whose counterclockwise pattern of stepping is associated with the African dance patterns of the ring shout and the patting juba. Fine closes this complex, fascinating journey by suggesting that the links formed by the African American founders of Step Afrika! between dancers in South Africa and the United States, in particular, offer exciting prospects for continued intercultural exchange.*

Deep in my heart
I love Africa.
I love, I love, I love,
my Africa.

—Step Afrika! USA, Kennedy Center, Washington D.C., 23 January 2000

Claims for the African roots of stepping are widespread and appear in many different contexts. In 1997, when emcee Tyrone Petty introduced the first large Christian step show in the District of Columbia area, he explained, "It was commonplace in the tribes of Africa to use dance in all of their lives. It was part of wedding ceremonies, it was part of funeral ceremonies, it was a part of religious ceremonies." Stepping was "just taking it back and putting in proper focus . . . that which was ours to begin with." In 1994 a Christian step team in Detroit, Michigan, chanted, "Africa is where stepping began, from the beat of the drums to the sound of our feet." Alphonso Ribiero, emcee of the 1993 televised S.T.O.M.P. competition, alluded to South African gumboot dancing when he said, "Others insist that stepping was started by miners in South Africa. It was a clever way to communicate while they knocked the dirt from their boots after a long day in the coal mines." In 1990, AKA sisters at the University of South Florida in Tampa also claimed that stepping originated in African dance traditions. Stepping "goes all the way back to African culture," when different tribes would show their competition through dance, maintained an AKA soror at Virginia Tech in 1986.[1]

Indeed, competitive tribal dancing in African cultures is well known. In the West African country of Benin, for example, people participate in a monthly dance called *avogan* in which young men and women from different quarters of a city take turns satirizing their rivals: "Much prestige goes to those who live in the same quarter as the composers whose songs bite deepest into the shortcomings of their rivals, and thereby become the popular hits of the city at large."[2]

Despite the many claims of stepping's African origins, not all agree. Michael Gordon, former executive director of the NPHC, pledged the Alpha Phi chapter of Kappa Alpha Psi at Virginia State University in 1955. He says that he "disappoints a lot of young brothers" when he tells them that during this period "there was no great Afrocentric movement." Indeed, Gordon recalls, "especially in the historically black colleges during that period, Africa was the last thing that people tried to identify with." Although there "were certain individual people who were a little more advanced than others who cared about or knew about African history and maybe admired W. E. B. Du Bois, . . . most young black people in the colleges in the 1950s were trying to be upwardly mobile and accepted in the mainstream of American society." Gordon acknowledges that the stepping of that period reflected African movements, such as an African American way of walking, as well as African American songs, such as the spirituals from which many fraternity and sorority songs borrowed their tunes, but maintains that steppers did not self-consciously imitate African movements. Not until the early 1970s at Howard University did Gordon encounter "Omega Psi Phi men who deliberately put on certain movements that recalled their African heritage. And I remember being thrilled at seeing that."[3]

Confirming Gordon's assessment that steppers in earlier years did not associate their activities with African influences, Darryl R. Matthews, Sr., a former executive director of Alpha Phi Alpha who pledged in the Delta Rho chapter at the University of Missouri at Kansas City in 1972, wrote in an e-mail debate with a younger brother:

> When my big brothers did it in the 60's, it was to the doo-wopping style of the r&b artist of the day. There was nothing deliberately African about that. In the 70's we modeled ourselves after the Temptations and the Dramatics. It was syncopated harmony with show business choreography, pure and simple. It was not about anything African.
>
> We did not know anything about this side of Africa. We only knew of the British imposed colonial imperialism and the revolutionaries who were trying to

free their physically and mentally enslaved countrymen. To say we were stepping to relate to Mother Africa is disingenuous and inaccurate.

No news, art, dances, nothing was getting in or out of South Africa so we did not know anything about rubber boot dancing. That is recently discovered phenomena. I guess y'all young folks had the serious hook up on the goings on inside of the formerly apartheid-ridden regime. Nobody else did, and there was no CNN in those days.[4]

The rubber boot or gumboot dancing to which Matthews refers is an excellent example of the complex relationships between African and African American music and dance. Gumboot dancing (*isicathulo*), one of the first urban working-class dances in South Africa, may have been developed in rural missions by Zulu pupils who were not allowed to perform traditional dances. The word *isicathulo*, Hugh Tracey notes, means "shoe." When the students danced, the shoes that missions required them to wear created louder sounds than did bare feet. Around the time of World War I, "rural, urban, mission, and working-class performance traditions" intermingled in *isicathulo*, which "as a step dance" was "closely related if not identical with other dance forms that had evolved earlier among farm laborers and inhabitants of the rural reserves."[5]

Erlmann suggests that *isicathulo* dancers "frequently indulge in sophisticated solo stepping, prototypes of which had been available to migrant workers from the mid-1920s through Charlie Chaplin and Fred Astaire movies as well as touring black tap dance groups." Indeed, South Africans were exposed to African American music and dance traditions as early as 1890, when Orpheus M. McAdoo and the Virginia Jubilee Singers spent almost five years touring South Africa. In subsequent years, black South Africans came to the United States. One, the famous "ragtime" composer Reuben T. Caluza, renowned "as a skilled *isicathulo* dancer," enrolled in Virginia's Hampton Institute in 1930 to earn a B.A. in music. Caluza and three other students from Africa formed the African Quartette..., performing both songs and dances along the East Coast. They even sang for Franklin D. Roosevelt. Quartette member Dwight Sumner wrote that in their summer tour of 1931 the "African Quartette sang Zulu songs, under the direction of Mr. Caluza, and also gave African folk dances." It is likely that Caluza shared his talents with students. If so, members of fraternities and sororities could have incorporated some gumboot movements into stepping. Caluza went on to earn a master's degree at Columbia University in 1935, where again he could have shared gumboot dancing with students.[6]

Malone notes that during the 1970s and 1980s gumboot dancing "was introduced in North American urban areas and showcased by many of the dance companies that performed styles of traditional African dances." Evidence from Erlmann, however, suggests the possibility of a much earlier American exposure to gumboot dancing and, conversely, the incorporation of African American influences into South African dances. Caluza's story is only one small example of the continuous interactions among Africans and African Americans that created a complex interaction between music and dance forms on both continents. The founding director of the Soweto Dance Theatre, Jackie Semela, explains that just as South Africans were influenced in their music and dance by touring performers from the United States such as Duke Ellington, so, too, did South Africans display their own dances: "And wherever South Africans travel, they would always show a gumboot dance, they would also show a Zulu dance, they would also show some tradition of South Africa in some of their songs." ... Semela agrees that there is a "likelihood" that Caluza's interactions with black people in colleges in the United States could have brought a gumboot influence to stepping.[7]

Thus, it is impossible to argue that "pure" African dances directly influenced African American stepping, because the same popular culture traditions that were influencing stepping in America might also have been influencing African dances. As James Clifford observes, identities in the twentieth century "no longer presuppose continuous cultures or traditions. Everywhere individuals and groups improvise local performances from (re)collected pasts, drawing on foreign media, symbols, and languages." The more recent work of Step Afrika! to exchange American, U.K., and African dance traditions in an annual international festival in Johannesburg has only heightened the intercultural mixture of movement traditions.... The step team of the D.C. Coalition of Alpha Phi Alpha, Inc., has used "Dun-Dun-Bah," a West African dance from Guinea, as well as Zulu dances from South Africa in their step shows, Jeff Johnson reports.[8]

Some movement patterns in stepping may have been conscious adoptions of African dance patterns, but it is more likely that movement and communicative patterns from Africa came with the first black immigrants and slaves who adapted those patterns to their new North American environment. A people who had highly developed verbal, musical, and dance traditions in their various cultures would surely find some way to continue them in new contexts, especially when they offered psychological release from the horrors of slavery. These African traditions melded with traditions from other cultures to create the distinctive African American expressive genres found in stepping.

PATTING JUBA AND RING SHOUTS

The characteristic clapping and stomping movements of stepping have their earliest counterparts in African American dances that emerged during slavery. Patting juba, perhaps the best-known of these dances, may have originated in an African dance called *guiouba* and grown in popularity after slaveholders outlawed drums among slaves for fear they would be used to communicate revolts. Solomon Northup describes the dance as "striking the hands on the knees, then striking the hands together, then striking the right shoulder with one hand, the left with the other—all the while keeping time with the feet, and singing." Lewis Paine's 1851 description comments on how patting juba was used to provide "music" by which to dance:

> Some one calls for a fiddle—but if one is not to be found some one "pats juber." This is done by placing one foot a little in advance of the other, raising the ball of the foot from the ground, and striking it in regular time, while, in connection, the hands are struck slightly together, and then upon the thighs. In this way they make the most curious noise, yet in such perfect order, it furnishes music to dance by.... It is really astonishing to witness the rapidity of their motions, their accurate time, and the precision of their music and dance. I have never see it equaled in my life.[9]

The juba step was often done in a counterclockwise circle, with "both the words and the steps" in call-and-response form. It involved improvisation, the shuffle, and clapping, all "major Afro-American traits," as Marshall and Jean Stearns have noted. "The two men in the center start the performance with the Juba step while the surrounding men clap, and then switch to whatever new step is named in the call, just before the response 'Juba! Juba!' sounds and the entire circle starts moving again." The counterclockwise circular motion is common to rituals in the Kongo culture, from which one-third of U.S. blacks derived, and symbolizes the "circle of the sun about the earth."[10]

Minstrel dancers featured patting juba. Perhaps the best of all African American minstrels, William Henry Lane ("Master Juba"), earned a reputation as "the greatest dancer of them all" by 1845. Because Lane performed in the "dance dives" of the Five Points district in Lower Manhattan, a place of tenements that housed both Irish immigrants and blacks, it was inevitable that he, like other African Americans, would blend African dance elements with Irish jigs. Gradually, people adopted the term *jigs* to describe "the general style" of African American dancing. Thus, just as stepping has incorporated African influences, it may have picked up European influences as well.[11]

Early circular stepping routines reflect the influence of patting juba as well as another early African American dance, the ring shout, which still exists in small areas of the South. A true ring shout consisted "of movement in a circle with the feet never crossed and usually not lifted from the ground, accompanied by a vocal 'band' composed of lead singer and 'basers' who sang only religious texts; it flourished in the Sea Islands and the adjoining coastal region, the area of the distinctive Gullah dialect." Baptists as well as many other evangelical Christian groups believed that dancing was sinful, but, Stearns and Stearns note, because "Baptists defined dancing as a crossing of legs, the Ring Shout was considered acceptable."[12]

Although ring shouts were part of black religious services, they also occurred in secular contexts—in schools and homes and among black soldiers—and were popular with adults as well as children. Charlotte Forten, a black teacher among the freedmen on the Sea Islands in 1862, describes the "shouts" that children performed:

> In the evening, the children frequently came in to sing and shout for us. These "shouts" are very strange,—in truth, almost indescribable. It is necessary to hear and see in order to have any clear idea of them. The children form a ring, and move around in a kind of shuffling dance, singing all the time. Four or five stand apart, and sing very energetically, clapping their hands, stamping their feet, and rocking their bodies to and fro. These are the musicians, to whose performance the shouters keep perfect time. The grown people on this plantation did not shout, but they do on some of the other plantations.[13]

Although many accounts of ring shouts describe shuffling steps, the diary of Thomas Wentworth Higginson, a colonel in the first black regiment to be called into service in the Civil War, records a variety of steps performed by soldiers of the First Regiment, South Carolina Volunteers. At dusk on 3 December 1862, for example, they gathered around fires built inside a "sort of little booth made neatly of palm leaves covered in at top, a native African hut in short." The men sang "at the top of their voices, . . . all accompanied with a regular drumming of the feet & clapping of the hands, like castenets." Then, as "the excitement [spread]":

> [Men] outside the enclosure begin to quiver & dance, others join, a circle forms, winding monotonously round some one in the centre. Some heel & toe tumultuously, others merely tremble & stagger on, others stoop & rise, others whirl, others caper sidewise all keep steadily circling like dervishes, outsiders applaud especial strokes of skill, my approach only enlivens the scene, the circle enlarges, louder grows the singing about Jesus & Heaven, & the ceaseless drumming & clapping go steadily on. At last seems to come a snap and the spell breaks amid general sighs & laughter. And this not rarely & occasionally but night after night.[14]

AN AFRICAN AESTHETIC IN STEPPING

Although stepping bears striking resemblances to the early dances of ring shouts and patting juba, it also powerfully embodies aesthetic elements widely recognized in the music and dance of Western and Central Africa. In 1966 Robert Farris Thompson identified five common features of West African music and dance: percussive dominance, multiple meter, apart playing and dancing, call and response, and songs and dances of derision. Expanding his study to include Central Africa in *African Art in Motion* (1974), Thompson compared native African aesthetic criticism with that of outside, academic observers. He identified ten "canons of fine form" in African art and dance. Many are highly visible in African American stepping.[15]

Thompson argues that both African art and dance prize youthful vitality and that "without vital aliveness we are no longer talking about African art." Applying the argument to dance, Thompson writes, "People in Africa, regardless of their actual age, return to strong, youthful patterning whenever they move within the streams of energy which flow from drums or other sources of percussion. They obey the implications of vitality with the music and its speed and drive." Three other aspects of African art and dance convey this youthful power. The first, to "swing every note and every color strong" calls for "phrasing every note and step with consummate vitality." The second, "vital aliveness" or "playing the body parts with percussive strength," not only involves powerful percussive force but also leads to multiple meter and the "interpretation of the parts of the body as independent instruments of percussive force." Thus, a stepper may throw down a sharply percussive rhythm with her feet while her hands beat out a counter rhythm and her head sharply enunciates yet another beat. Thompson's observation that "vital aliveness, high intensity, speed, drive—these are some of the facets of artful muscularity and depth of feeling that characterize the dances of this continent" could just as easily be applied to African American stepping.[16]

Indeed, youthful vitality might also be expressed as a quality of "hot," which works in opposition to the aesthetic of cool maintains Alicia J. Rouverol. She finds this "hot" quality expressed through a rapid and intense form of stepping called "hard-stepping," which is used to heighten audience response. Hard stepping works to "elevate" a routine, much as gospel singers add improvisational segments to reach a strong climax. A third trait that conveys youthfulness is "flexibility." "Dance with bended knees," the Kongo say, "lest you be taken for a corpse." A young Luba dancer in Kinshasa told Thompson that a Luba must "manifest his suppleness with bent knees, bent elbows, and suave oscillations to the music." The posture of bent knees and bent elbows is one of the most common stances that steppers use.[17]

Because steppers use several parts of their bodies as percussive instruments they can develop sophisticated, complex rhythmic patterns that embody two of Thompson's canons of an African aesthetic: simultaneous suspending and preserving of the beat and multiple meter. Just as African musicians frequently suspend the beat in order to insert accented, melodic tones, steppers often produce a syncopated rhythm as they play with the timing of the beat to create complex rhythmic patterns. One stepper alone may create multiple meter or polyrhythm. Within a group of steppers, each performer might perform different clapping and stepping patterns so that a contrapuntal rhythmic fugue emerges. Musicologists have long observed that "African music is distinguished from other world traditions by the superimposition of several lines of meter." Part of the great appeal of stepping may lie in its difference from European-based musical traditions, which have "at any one moment one rhythm in command," whereas "a piece of African music has always two or three, sometimes as many as four." As the Phi Beta Sigma chapter at Virginia Tech describe their stepping style, "Sigmas utilize virtually every part of their anatomy to produce soulful, syncopated rhythms. Sigma stepping at its best is speed, precision, and complication."[18]

To increase the complexity and audibility of percussive sounds, stepping groups often use canes or sticks to beat out rhythms. Similar use of sticks and canes is used by such African cultures as the Mbuti and Zulu and by groups from northern Zaire, Sudan, Zambia, and Mozambique, Malone asserts. Abrahams notes that African American slaves preferred to dance on wooden planks so they could better hear the polyrhythmic sounds. Clearly, an appreciation of strong, percussive beats unites stepping with earlier African American and African dance traditions.[19]

One of the most striking stances that African American steppers assume is best described as the "get-down" position. Steppers often begin and end a step by bending deeply from the waist so their torsos are at an almost forty-five-degree angle to the ground. From this stance they may swing their arms out sharply in front of them or to the side. Even in the midst of a step routine, steppers often bend their knees deeply and move low to the ground. Noting the importance of getting down, the Sigma Doves, Phi Beta Sigma's sweetheart organization, chanted "stepping real hard / and stooping real low / the Sigma Doves / are going to put on a show" during the 1985 Blue and White Weekend at the University of Florida. Many Central and West African cultures consider dancing low to the ground to be virtuosic and symbolize "a dual expression of salutation and devotion," Thompson observes. "Get-down sequences" show "honor and respect, either to a fine drummer, in response to the savor of his phrasing, or to a deity." In some cases, a get-down posture coincides with the point in the performance at which a dancer shows greatest vigor and intensity. Thus it, too, conveys youthful vitality and, as Rouverol argues, may also indicate a hot rather than a cool aesthetic quality.[20]

In contrast to the hot power of a get-down stance combined with the youthful intensity of multiple meter and hard-stepping, African American steppers exhibit the African aesthetic of the cool, an aesthetic and philosophical concept that unites all other aesthetic canons. In Africa, maintains Thompson, "coolness is an all-embracing positive attribute which combines notions of composure, silence, vitality, healing, and social purification." Five qualities contribute to the aesthetic of the cool: visibility, luminosity, smoothness, rebirth and reincarnation, and facial composure (the "mask of the cool" as Thompson observes). All these features appear, in varying degrees, in stepping. Perhaps the most noticeable is Thompson's mask of the cool, when steppers' composed, serene faces contrast with their intricate and powerful percussive movements.[21]

Steppers also strive for visibility or clarity in their motions and voices; indeed, judges of competitions often look for those attributes. Thus, bodily movements are sharp, crisp, and emphatic. Step teams often exhibit appreciation for luminosity or brilliance through the bright colors they wear as well as the ways they use spotlights and strobes to intensify their movements. Another "function of perfected clarity" is smoothness, which Thompson identifies as a "unified aesthetic impact" in which "seams do not show." Step teams pride themselves on displaying unity through synchronized, carefully rehearsed movements. In competitions, judges often deduct points for lapses in unity.[22]

A more philosophical way of invoking coolness comes through Thompson's concept of rebirth and reincarnation, which overlaps with his category of ancestorism. The categories are related, and both are particularly important in the secular stepping of Greek-letter organizations as well as the sacred stepping of religious groups. Fraternities and sororities often invoke the names or the number of their founders (e.g., Alpha Phi Alpha's "Seven Jewels"), especially when they perform retrospective steps that commemorate group history. Likewise, religious steppers often invoke biblical passages for the text of a routine. In both cases, such references connect the current moment of stepping to venerated people and words from the past. Thompson contends that pleasure derived from the "motion arts" in Africa comes "because many people see the founders of the nation or lineage returning in these styles." Through the dances, they are participating "in an alternative, ancient, far superior universe."[23]

Stepping also has the power to link both audience and performers to important images and ideas from the group's shared history. In their 1995 spring step show, for example, the Omega Psi Phi brothers at Virginia Tech performed a retrospective routine dedicated to the four founders of their fraternity. The stepmaster began each of the four verses of the routine by saying that if Oscar J. Cooper, Frank Coleman, Edgar A. Love, and Ernest E. Just were there they "would do a little step that goes like this." Each of the three other steppers then demonstrated a different step and kept performing it during subsequent verses. By the last verse, each of the four was performing a different step but in unison, demonstrating not only the variety of steps in their repertoire but also the ability to maintain their own rhythm and form. At the same time, they demonstrated virtuosity in having mastered a key feature of African dance and music tradition—multiple meter or cross rhythm.[24]

One of the most notable aspects of step shows is the concern steppers give to their appearance. Step teams pay great attention to their dress and keep their uniforms for competitive shows secret until the public appearance. "Looking smart," Thompson notes, is the African English phrase used to praise dancers who make a good impression. As Thompson defines it, looking smart involves "strikingly attractive use of style, loaded with notions of preening and the making of the person sexually attractive." Judges of the Overton R. Johnson Step Competition at Virginia Tech use the criteria of execution (precision, technique, and synchronization); appearance; vocalization; crowd appeal; and personality. Thus, it is not surprising that groups would give so much attention to looking smart, because it has great bearing on three of the five criteria for excellence. At Howard University, Malone observes, "dress is always an important part of the planning process," and sororities and fraternities pay "close attention to the types of fabrics selected and the heaviness and sound quality of the shoes."[25]

The clothes worn by a fraternity or sorority step team usually indicate the group's colors and are often metaphors for group identity. In the 1986 Overton R. Johnson Step Competition, Alpha Kappa Alpha chose green taffeta, knee-length dresses with puffy, short sleeves. They accessorized with matching green garters and high heels. The outfits were in keeping with the refined, feminine image that AKA sorors cultivate and with their routines, which in that show included a great deal of singing and dancing to music. In the same competition, Delta Sigma Theta wore white tuxedos and gloves, along with red cummerbunds, boutonnieres, bow ties, half-masks, and high heels. Not only did their outfit display the sorority's red and white colors, but it also conveyed concern for showmanship, style, and glitz and allowed freedom of movement for intricate hard stepping.[26]

While attention to dress helps make a group "look smart," so do two other African aesthetic qualities: a "correct entrance and exit" and "personal and representational balance." Teams work hard to capture the audience's attention through innovative and memorable entrances and exits. Groups that perform on stages equipped with curtains, lights, and sound systems might use special props, lighting, and sound effects. Omega Psi Phi, for example, won first place in the 1987 Overton R. Johnson Step Competition with what one brother described as "something new and different":

> Agent ooQ, briefcase in hand and clad in a tan trench coat, stands before a female spy wearing sunglasses and carrying a portable stereo. He exchanges his briefcase for the cassette player then turns it on and listens for his mission.

A voice booms over the box describing, in detail, six men known collectively as the "deadliest stepping brothers in VPI history," slide shots of the six brothers flash on a nearby projection screen as the voice lists their names and aliases, also known as "dog names."

Six men emerge from behind a black curtain to the beat of Herb Alpert's song, "Keep Your Eye on Me" while the Burruss Auditorium crowd cheers wildly. The men of Omega Psi Phi fraternity are ready to step.[27]

Groups frequently enter to popular music, often performing what black fraternities and sororities label "party walks" and what Latino Greek organizations call "strolls." Malone defines a party walk as an "organized line movement performed around the floor at a party." Party walks and strolls may or may not include the characteristic stomping and clapping of stepping, but they are performed to music.[28]

In addition to crowd-captivating entrances and exits, steppers define routines by doing what Thompson calls "cutting the dance," "killing the song," or establishing "clear boundaries" around each. Just as the Yoruba say that "dancers must prepare for the opening beat of the dance before moving—like a boxer, bracing for the punch" and the Luba and Tiv "demand that a dancer determine the position of his body, as a quasi-sculptural force with bent knees and arms held close to the trunk, before actually dancing," African American steppers launch into a stepping routine from a position of stasis. To borrow a term used in classical art criticism to describe the representation of motion, the characteristic resting pose could be called a "rhythmos" ("shape" or "pattern"). The term *rhythmos* was derived from the "momentary stops" in dancing called "eremiai," in which a body is "held for an instant in characteristic positions." One such stop was called a "rhythmos." Ancient Greeks used the term to refer to the pose of sculpture that conveys the expectation of movement. Thus, Myron's classic statue Diskobolos (the Discus Thrower) depicts an athlete, coiled tightly, a moment before he throws his discus.[29]

Similarly, except for their entrance onstage, steppers begin from some position of rest, often a position that anticipates motion. In one common stance they stand at attention, heads held high and arms bent, clenched fists resting in front of or under their chins. In another typical stance they bend forward at the waist at a forty-five-degree angle to the ground and with both arms extended to one side. In the former case, one anticipates that the arms will swing free; in the latter, that the torso will spring up. Anticipation builds as the steppers use the moment of repose to catch their breath, focus their attention, and listen for the stepmaster's cues to begin the next routine.

Just as a step routine emerges from a quiet rhythmos, it ends with another rhythmos. Thompson writes that the Akan "strike moralistic poses."[30] Frequently the final poses of a step routine are symbolic as well. Often routines end with members forming their group's hand signals. During the 1999 Latino Greek Summer Step and Stroll Show in the Bronx, a Lambda Upsilon Lambda fraternity step team ended a step with a remarkable rhythmos that called for great poise because the steppers were standing, balanced on one leg. The pose, a variation of Rodin's *The Thinker,* mimed a sitting position, one leg crossed and resting on the other knee, elbow resting on the elevated knee, and chin on folded hand. The fingers of both hands formed the fraternity's hand signal.... The steppers assumed the pose at the end of a chanted step:

> I looked to the sky
> and what did I see?
>
> I saw the thirteen knights
> looking down at me.

They took my hand
and said "understand
you're a brother
like no other.

You're a Lambda man" (*knee-elbow-chin pose*).[31]

Such a pose is certainly in keeping with the up-scale image of Lambda Upsilon Lambda fraternity, which has chapters at six of the seven Ivy League colleges. The pose is not unique to Lambda Upsilon Lambda, however. In 1986 Alpha Phi Alpha, also known for having an intellectual image, used a similar one in the Overton R. Johnson Step Competition. In 1985 at the University of Florida's Blue and White Weekend the Sigma Doves used a slight variation to illustrate "we're number one." Instead of resting their chins on their hands, they held up pointed index fingers in front of their chins.[32]

Striking a one-legged pose is unusual and crowd-pleasing because doing so deviates from the typical emphasis on what Thompson calls "personal and representational balance." Both in African art and dance, the human image "rises, in the main, from feet set flat and firm upon the earth." Thompson quotes Bessie Jones and Beth Lomax Hawes, who compared differences in the dances of mainland whites and Sea Island blacks: "All [black] dancing is done flat-footed; this is extremely difficult for [white] Americans, whose first approach to a dancing situation is to go up on their toes." While West Africans "cultivate divinity through richly stabilized traditions of personal balance," Thompson notes, the convention of balance would "doubtless soon wax boring, were it not honored so magnificently in the breach by kicks, spins, and leaps of certain of the men's dances in Africa."[33] Although most ending and beginning stances express the strong African emphasis on equilibrium, occasionally breaking the norm makes a step routine stand out.

The interrelated African canons of call and response and "apart dancing" are prominent in African American step shows. The first, call and response, embodies the important step team goal of expressing group unity. The pervasive antiphonal structure of call and response within African American expressive arts is familiar to many people. From the dynamic interactions of traditional black preachers and their congregations, to work songs, the blues, and jazz, the concept of a leader calling out and a chorus responding seems omnipresent. In stepping, too, many chants and steps have a call-and-response structure.... In sub-Saharan Africa, notes Thompson, not only words and song but also dance take on a call-and-response structure, and "solo-and-circle, or solo-and-line, or solo-and-solo forms of dancing mirror melodic call-and-response."[34]

Call and response in dance reveals another characteristic of African dance, apart dancing, in which participants maintain separate spaces rather than have the sustained body contact seen in Western couple dancing. But dancing apart does not mean there is no unity. Rather, apartness fosters a dialogue between dancers as they call and respond with both voice and body. As Thompson says, "West Africans perform music and dance apart the better to ensure a dialog between movement and sound."[35]

Beneath the aesthetic use of call and response lies a significant message: "perfected social interaction." Call and response, Thompson observes, is "a danced judgment of qualities of social integration and cohesion." In Africa, a performer who disappoints the audience will find their responses "growing progressively weaker until they ultimately reform about a man with stronger themes and better aesthetic organization." Audiences of African American step shows judge the cohesiveness and unity of a group in part by the level of enthusiasm and responsiveness demonstrated through call and response. Not only do performers call and respond to each other, but also the audience responds and calls out in dynamic interchange as the steppers play to it. For example, references to a particular fraternity or sorority will often stimulate audience members affiliated with that group to shout out a group call such as "skee wee" or "nupe, nupe." As Amy Davis attests, "Steppers are greeted either with applause and cheers of support throughout a routine, or if they lose the audience's respect and attention, murmurs and unnerving quiet."[36]

The preceding canons of good form in African art and dance have focused on stylistic features, but a final characteristic, dances of derision, deals with content rather than style and, as Thompson maintains, plays a moral function. Throughout Western, Central, and Southern Africa, people use songs of allusion and dances of derision to make moral judgments on the behavior of others. Frequently, a fraternity or sorority will perform chants that define its ethos in opposition to that of its competitors. Through cracking on rivals, groups elevate their own images, as the Alpha Phi Alpha brothers at East Tennessee State University in Johnson City did in a classic step entitled "King Tut":

> *All:* My-y-y old King Tut
> was the very first Greek,
> a-a-h, when he clapped his hands
> he had the ladies at his feet.
> A-a-h, Tut, Tut, Tut,
> a-a-h, Tut, Tut, Tut.
> *One brother:* I said
> *All:* When he saw the Sigmas,
> it made him mad.
> When he saw the Kappas,
> it made him mad.
> A-a-h, when he saw the Ques,
> it made him sick.
> When he saw the frat,
> then he had to pledge it quick.
> A-ah, Tut, Tut, Tut,
> a-a-h, Tut, Tut, Tut.
> He had a black and gold whip
> and a black and gold cane,
> then he came up
> a-a-h with this black and gold name.
> A-ha-h A Phi A,
> A Phi A,
> A Phi A.[37]

The popularity of crack steps stems from the strong emphasis on competition in both African and African American verbal art and dance. Competition pervaded such early plantation dances among slaves as the cakewalk and the chalk-line walk. At set dances and buck dances at neighborhood frolics in Georgia during the early 1900s, the best dancers were rewarded with special clothing.[38] Twentieth-century dances such as tap, the lindy, the jitterbug, and break dancing have all involved competitions. Moreover, the verbal duels of the dozens (also called sounding and snapping), rapping, and signifying encourage quick wit and oral skill, bringing elevated social prestige to those who can best their peers.[39]

CONCLUSION

The syncopated, percussive hand-slapping and foot-stomping movements in stepping reveal their descent from early African American dances such as patting juba and ring shouts. The outlawing of drums among slaves may have heightened the development of percussive slapping and stomping as substitutes for drumbeats. Stepping also exhibits the key aesthetic features found in Western and Central African cultures as delineated by Robert Farris Thompson. The first Africans who came to North America brought their dance, movement, and musical traditions with them; in North America, they blended with other cultural influences, such as Irish step dancing. Winning competitions with Irish jig dancers, the famous African American minstrel William Henry Lane combined both African and Irish step dancing. Gradually, the most popular term to describe the general style of African American dancing became *jigs*. Stepping has African roots, but it also bears European influences.

After the Civil War, cultural exchanges between musical performers from Africa and the United States created a two-way flow of African and African American influences. Traveling black American minstrel shows brought spirituals and dances such as the cakewalk to Africa. Dances in American films influenced South African gumboot dancers during the 1920s and 1930s, and traveling groups of African singers and dancers such as Reuben T. Caluzo's African Quartette may have inspired African Americans to copy some of their movement patterns. Even though steppers in the 1950s and 1960s may not have consciously adopted an African style or expressed solidarity with African cultures, they expressed elements of an African aesthetic through stepping. As Afrocentrism grew in popularity during the 1970s, steppers began to articulate the connections they saw between the art of stepping and African culture.

Understanding the attitudes of black secret societies toward African culture in the early part of the twentieth century requires more investigation. If, as Malone argues, some members of the earliest black American secret societies of the eighteenth century were "either born in Africa or were one generation removed from the continent" and shared Central and West Africa concerns for proper burials, mutual aid, and economic cooperation, then it is possible that these African values continued in the mutual aid societies in existence when the first black Greek organizations were founded.[40] Because elaborate parades and drill team competitions were important activities of these societies at the beginning of the twentieth century, it is likely that early members of the first black Greek-letter organizations may have modeled their ritual of marching on line after such traditions.

By the 1990s the African American steppers of Step Afrika! had linked forces with dancers in South Africa and the United Kingdom to use the dance traditions of Africa, the Caribbean, and the United Kingdom to foster intercultural dialogue. Such intense international dance exchanges may heighten contemporary African influences on African American stepping.

Notes

1. Transcription of videotape, *A Christian Step Show and FUN-draiser*, 29 Mar. 1997, Theodore Roosevelt High School, Washington, D.C.; transcription from videotape by Fredrick Scott of Oak Grove Steppers, *Get Rid of the Garbage*, 30 Nov. 1994; transcription of videotape of *S.T.O.M.P.* competition, 1993; Alpha Kappa Alpha interview, University of South Florida; Alpha Kappa Alpha sorority member number one, interview.
2. Herskovits and Herskovits, *Dahomean Narrative*, 61.
3. Gordon interview.

4. Matthews interview.
5. Erlmann, *African Stars*, 99, quoting Tracey, *African Dances*, 7.
6. Erlmann, *African Stars*, 100, 145–47; Sumner, "African Quartette," n.p. There were no fraternitites or sororities at Hampton Institute until 1947, but students at other colleges could have been exposed to his dancing.
7. Malone, *Steppin' on the Blues*, 247; Erlmann, *African Stars*, 100, 145–47; Semela interview.
8. Clifford, *Predicament of Culture*, 14; Johnson correspondence.
9. Northrup, *Twelve Years a Slave*, 219, quoted in Epstein, *Sinful Tunes*, 141; Paine, *Six Years in a Georgia Prison*, 179–80, quoted in Epstein, *Sinful Tunes*, 143.
10. Stearns and Stearns, *Jazz Dance*, 28; Thompson, *Four Moments*, 43, 28, 32.
11. Stearns and Stearns, *Jazz Dance*, 44–45. European influences on slave dances began earlier than the 1840s. Stearns and Stearns observe that many slaves were transported first to the West Indies, "leaving the slaves to become acclimatized before taking them to the mainland." There, "fashionable dances from the courts and elegant salons of Europe—Spanish, French, and English—became popular and were imitated by the slaves" (*Jazz Dance* 16–17).
12. Epstein, *Sinful Tunes*, 286; Stearns and Stearns, *Jazz Dance*, 30.
13. Forten, "Life on the Sea Islands," 594, quoted in Epstein, *Sinful Tunes*, 280. See also, Floyd, Jr., "Ring Shout!" 135–56.
14. Higginson, Diary, entry for 3 Dec. 1862, quoted in Epstein, *Sinful Tunes*, 280–81.
15. Thompson, "Aesthetic of the Cool," 88–96; Thompson, *African Art in Motion*, 5–45. Thompson inverviewed ninety-four individuals from the Dan in Liberia; the Popo, Fon, and Yoruba of Dahomey; the Yoruba and Abakpa of Nigeria; the Banyang and Ejagham of Cameroon; the Kongo of Zaire; and migrant workers in Cameroon and Zaire.
16. Thompson, *African Art in Motion*, 6–7, 9.
17. Rouverol, "'Hot,' 'Cool,' and 'Getting Down,'" 104–6; Hinson, "When the Words," 396–421, quoted in Rouverol (104); Thompson, *African Art in Motion*, 9–10.
18. Thompson, *African Art in Motion*, 14; Overton R. Johnson Step Competition program, spring 1989, Virginia Tech.
19. Malone, *Steppin' on the Blues*, 192; Abrahams, *Singing the Master*, 93–94.
20. Transcription of videotape of Blue and White Weekend Step Show, 1985, University of Florida; Thompson, *African Art in Motion*, 14; Rouverol, "'Hot,' 'Cool,' and 'Getting Down,'" 105.
21. Thompson, *African Art in Motion*, 43.
22. Ibid., 44.
23. Ibid., 44–45.
24. Transcription of videotabe by Teresa Torain of spring step show, 28 Apr. 1995, Dietrich Dining Hall Courtyard, Virginia Tech; Malone, *Steppin' on the Blues*, 15, 16, 189; Thompson, "An Aesthetic of the Cool," 89–90.
25. Thompson, *African Art in Motion*, 16; Malone, *Steppin' on the Blues*, 209. Reacting to the difference in the costumes worn by the two rival sororities, Brooks ("'Steppin' Out,'" A4) criticizes AKA for choosing to wear dresses rather than what "should have been worn in a step show—*pants*." Brooks also observes that "performers are supposed to 'step'—not sing or dance excessively" and criticizes other groups as well for too much singing. By the late 1980s, Malone notes (209), many sororities had begun to adopt fraternities' emphasis on fancy footwork, acrobatics, and hard stepping and so had begun stepping in pants or shorts rather than dresses. The idea that stepping should be different than singing and dancing was expressed in the Philadelphia Greek Picnic Stepshow on 24 June 1999 by AKA sisters from Old Dominion University, who proudly declared that they were not there to sing or dance but to step.
26. Videotape of Overton R. Johnson Step Competition, spring 1986, Virginia Tech.
27. Thompson, *African Art in Motion*, 18–24; Noches, "Stepping with Pride," A5, A8.
28. Malone, *Steppin' on the Blues*, 208.
29. Thompson, *African Art in Motion*, 18, 20; Pollitt, *Art and Experience*, 54–60.
30. Thompson, *African Art in Motion*, 20.
31. Transcription of videotape of Latino Greek Summer Step and Stroll Show, 1999, Roberto Clemente State Park, Bronx, N.Y.
32. Aldaño interview, 25 May 1999; transcriptions of videotapes of Overton R. Johnson Step Competition, spring 1986, Virginia Tech, and of Blue and White Weekend Step Show, 1985, University of Florida.

33. Thompson, *African Art in Motion,* 24; Jones and Hawes, *Step It Down,* 44, as quoted in Thompson, *African Art in Motion,* 24; Thompson, *African Art in Motion,* 24, 26.
34. Thompson, *African Art in Motion,* 30.
35. Thompson, "Aesthetic of the Cool," 94.
36. Thompson, *African Art in Motion,* 28; Davis, "'Deep in My Heart,'" 87.
37. Thompson, "Aesthetic of the Cool," 95–96; transcription by Jane Woodside of videotape of Dance Heritage Festival, 6 Apr. 1991, East Tennessee State University, Johnson City.
38. Davis, "'Deep in My Heart,'" 89, quoting Jones, *For the Ancestors,* 36–37.
39. Mitchell-Kernan, "Signifying, Loud-talking, and Marking"; Abrahams, "Black Talking on the Streets" and *Deep Down in the Jungle;* Jackson, "Get Your Ass in the Water."
40. Malone, *Steppin' on the Blues,* 172.

Bibliography

Abrahams, Roger. "Black Talking on the Streets." In *Explorations in the Ethnography of Speaking.* Ed. Richard Bauman and Joel Sherzer, 240–62. New York: Cambridge University Press, 1974.

———. *Deep Down in the Jungle . . . : Negro Narrative Folklore from the Streets of Philadelphia.* Rev. ed. Chicago: Aldine Publishing, 1970.

———. *Singing the Master: The Emergence of African American Culture in the Plantation South.* New York: Pantheon, 1992.

Brooks, Yvette. "'Steppin' Out to No Avail." *Collegiate Times,* 23 May 1986, Az.

Clifford, James. *The Predicament of Culture: Twentieth-Century Ethnography, Literature, and Art.* Cambridge: Harvard University Press, 1988.

Davis, Amy. "'Deep in My Heart': Competition and the Function of Stepping in an African American Sorority." *North Carolina Folklore Journal* 43 (Summer–Fall 1996): 82–95.

Epstein, Dena J. *Sinful Tunes and Spirituals: Black Folk Music to the Civil War.* Urbana: University of Illinois Press. Copyright 1981 by the Board of Trustees of the University of Illinois. Used with permission of the University of Illinois Press.

Erlmann, Veit. *African Stars: Studies in Black South African Performance.* Chicago: University of Chicago Press, 1991.

Floyd, Samuel A., Jr. "Ring Shout! Literary Studies, Historical Studies, and Black Music Inquiry." In *Signifyin(g), Sanctifyin', and Slam Dunking: A Reader in African American Expressive Culture.* Ed. Gena Dagel Caponi, 135–56. Amherst: University of Massachusetts Press, 1999.

Forten, Charlotte L. "Life on the Sea Islands," 13 May 1864, 587–96. Quoted in Dena J. Epstein, *Sinful Tunes and Spirituals: Black Folk Music to the Civil War,* 280. Urbana: University of Illinois Press, 1981.

Herskovits, Melville, and Frances Herskovits. *Dahomean Narrative: A Cross-Cultural Approach.* Evanston: Northwestern University Press, 1958.

Higginson, Thomas Wentworth. Diary entry for 3 Dec. 1862. Ms. Houghton Library, Harvard University. Quoted in Dena J. Epstein, *Sinful Tunes and Spirituals: Black Folk Music to the Civil War,* 280–81. Urbana: University of Illinois Press, 1981.

Hinson, Glenn. "When the Words Roll and the Fire Flows: Spirit, Style, and Experience in African American Gospel Performance," Ph.D. diss., University of Pennsylvania, 1989. Quoted in Alicia J. Rouverol, "'Hot,' 'Cool,' and 'Getting Down': African American Style and Aesthetics in Stepping." *North Carolina Folklore Journal* 43 (Summer–Fall 1996): 96–108.

Jackson, Bruce. *"Get Your Ass in the Water and Swim Like Me": Narrative from Black Oral Tradition.* Cambridge: Harvard University Press, 1974.

Jones, Bessie. *For the Ancestors: Autobiographical Memories.* Urbana: University of Illinois Press, 1983. Quoted in Amy Davis, "'Deep in My Heart': Competition and the Function of Stepping in an African American Sorority." *North Carolina Folklore Journal* 43 (Summer–Fall 1996): 82–95.

Malone, Jacqui. *Steppin' on the Blues: The Visible Rhythms of African American Dance.* Urbana: University of Illinois Press, 1996.

Mitchell-Kernan, Claudia. "Signifying, Loud-Talking, and Marking. In *Rappin' and Stylin' Out: Communication in Black America*. Ed. Thomas Kochman, 315–35. Urbana: University of Illinois Press, 1972.

Noches, Lucinda. "Stepping with Pride: Contest Raises Funds for Scholarship." *Collegiate Times*, 26 May 1987, A5, A8.

Northup, Solomon. *Twelve Years a Slave: The Narrative of Solomon Northup, a Citizen of New York, Kidnapped in Washington City in 1841 and Rescued in 1853, from a Cotton Plantation near the Red River in Louisiana*. Auburn, N.Y.: Derby and Miller, 1853.

Paine, Lewis W. *Six Years in a Georgia Prison, Narrative of Lewis W. Paine, Who Suffered Imprisonment Six Years in Georgia, for the Crime of Aiding the Escape of a Fellowmen from the State, after He Had Fled from Slavery. Written by Himself*. New York: Printed for the Author, 1851. Quoted in Dena J. Epstein, *Sinful Tunes and Spirituals: Black Folk Music to the Civil War*, 143. Urbana: University of Illinois Press, 1981.

Pollitt, J. J. *Art and Experience in Classical Greece*. New York: Cambridge University Press, 1972.

Rouverol, Alicia J. "'Hot,' 'Cool,' and 'Getting Down': African American Style and Aesthetics in Stepping." *North Carolina Folklore Journal* 43 (Summer–Fall 1996, 96–108).

Stearns, Marshall, and Jean Stearns. *Jazz Dance: The Story of American Vernacular Dance*. New York: Schirmer Books, 1968.

Summer, Dwight. "African Quartette on School Campaign." *Hampton Script*, 30 Sept. 1931, n.p.

Thompson, Robert Farris. "An Aesthetic of the Cool: West African Dance." *African Forum* 2 (Fall 1966): 85–102.

———. *African Art in Motion: Icon and Act*. Los Angeles: University of California Press, 1979.

———. *The Four Moments of the Sun: Kongo Art in Two Worlds*. Washington, D.C.: National Gallery of Art, 1981.

Tracey, Hugh. *African Dances of the Witswaterand Gold Mines*. Johannesburg: African Music Society, 1952. Quoted in Veit Erlmann, *African Stars: Studies in Black South African Performance*, 99. Chicago: University of Chicago Press, 1991.

36

Rhythm and Bullshit?
The Slow Decline of R&B
MARK ANTHONY NEAL

A cultural historian and Duke University professor, Mark Neal is a keen observer, commentator, and chronicler of African American popular culture, especially the musical genres that have emerged over the past thirty years. His books, essays, articles, and blogs have often focused on postsoul black popular music. This three-part essay originally appeared in the online magazine PopMatters.com in the summer of 2005 and examines the business of black popular music with a strong focus on the past thirty-five years.

Although the complicated questions related to the exploitation of black artists by major record companies can be traced back to the 1920s, Neal suggests that it is instructive to look to the early 1970s when Clive Davis was steering the fortunes of Columbia Records and a group of Harvard M.B.A. students authored "A Study of the Soul Music Environment." This report suggested that what happened (utterly coincidentally, as Neal argues in this article) is that the major record companies largely eschewed direct relationship and eventual ownership of major African American–bred record companies like Motown and Stax. Instead, a multinational conglomerate like Columbia (now owned by Sony) forged alliances with smaller, up-and-coming labels such as Philadelphia International Records, which were more able to deal with breaking artists and trends.

This trend led to a distancing of R&B from the hip-hop–driven youth culture that developed in the 1980s. As R&B continued to be marketed and differentiated from hip hop, it became more ghetterized and played less frequently on radio stations that in a world remade by the Telecommunications Reform Act of 1996 are increasingly owned by a select group led by Clear Channel Communications intent on gobbling up stations across the United States. The stakes driving the desire to produce a hit record have only increased as the ownership of the mass media has become more concentrated in the hands of a few corporations. Aside from the satellite radio options, the ability for many emerging (and established) R&B artists to make inroads into a marketplace that now respects hip hop over any other genre of black popular music will, as Neal suggests, only become increasingly problematic.

PART ONE: RHYTHM & BUSINESS, CULTURAL IMPERIALISM AND THE HARVARD REPORT

Yeah, I'm nostalgic: When Mary J. Blige first uttered the opening lines to "You Remind Me," it was about making sure that hip-hop remembered that R&B came from the same streets where crackheads roamed and the same tenement vestibules where drama went down on the regular. But as I listen to Mario's "Let Me Love You" for the 727th time, it is perhaps easy to suggest that R&B has lost its Soul, or that Clear Channel, Radio One (luv ya, Cathy!), AOL-Time Warner and Viacom—a neo-plantation cabal if ever there was one—ripped its heart out. Hip-hop may have sold out, but at least it has sold out on its own terms. R&B, on the other hand, has sold out on somebody else's, on a pop-chart paper chase. Truth be told, U(r)sher was nothing more than a soon-past-his-peak R&B singer before John Smith laced him with some crunk junk; Ray J. could have sang the hook on "Yeah" and topped the pop charts. And now, 10 million units later, we want to act like Mr. Raymond is the second coming of Michael Jackson? I ain't willing to grant him the second coming of Bobby Brown. And it is not like we even knew Mr. Legend (in his own mind) and Ms. Queen of Crunk n' B were in the room, until some hip-hop act sanctioned their presence. But what ails contemporary R&B is not just a matter of the commercial success of John Legend—and Amerie and Ciara and Mario. The current state of R&B comes not from a sudden decline, but a process more than 30 years in the making.

This story begins in 1972, when a few enterprising master's students at the Harvard Business School prepared a study, commissioned by one of Columbia's execs, detailing how the Columbia Records Group could better integrate the then largely independent black music industry into the mix. The now infamous Harvard Report—officially known as "A Study of the Soul Music Environment"—has often been referred to as a sinister blueprint aimed at arming a litany of "culture bandits" with the theoretical tools to return black culture to a neo-colonial state. There's no denying that this is exactly the situation we're staring at now, but it has nothing to do with the Harvard Report. What those MBA students articulated was a no-brainer marketing plan, informed by the commercial success of Motown and the cynical (though not mistaken) view that the Civil Rights "revolution" likely had more to do with the realities that black folk had disposable income and white folk consumed a hell of a lot of black popular culture than anything to do with real structural change in American society. In response to those expecting more sinister designs in the Harvard Report, David Sanjek rhetorically chimes, "why did [Columbia] feel the need to document what they should have already known?" (*Rhythm of Business*, 62). What Sanjek suggests is that eventually somebody in the music industry would have come up with their own version of the Harvard Report—say, Clive Davis, who incidentally was a president at Columbia at the time that the report was commissioned. The point is, with or without the Harvard Report, the takeover was well underway.

Black music has always had a complicated relationship with big business. That this relationship has typically had little to do with actual *music* perhaps explains the often unbalanced quality of this thing we've come to call R&B. This complicated relationship also partly explains what exactly R&B is. The term *R&B* is essentially a shortened version of "Rhythm & Blues", but as a novice might discern, that which is called R&B bears little resemblance to the musical landscape created by Ruth Brown, Louis Jordan, Laverne Baker, Charles Brown and the Coasters. And perhaps that was the point. Musical innovations aside, R&B was essentially a marketing ploy that finally gained a significant foothold during the late 1970s. R&B was born out of competing logics—record companies tried to negotiate the realities of black culture and identity within the history of race relations in America while trying at the same time to reach a wider audience of black consumers *and* white record buyers. As black radio needed mainstream advertisers to court the emerging black middle class (as much an ideology as a measurement of economic and social status) and mainstream record labels became fixated on crossing over black artists to white consumers, terms like *Soul* and *Rhythm and Blues* quickly became too black. The same terminology turnover occurred during the late 1970s when *urban* began to stand for radio stations that essentially programmed black music. As Nelson George explains, "Urban was supposedly a multicolored programming style tuned to the rhythms of America's crossfertilized big cities.... But more often, urban was black radio in disguise" (*The Death of Rhythm and Blues*, 159).

According to the "Harvard Report" black radio was strategically important to record companies because it provided "access to large and growing record buying public, namely, the Black consumer." The report is oblivious to the fact that the very birth of what was called "race music" in the 1930s was premised on selling goods and services to a uniquely defined audience, namely African-Americans constrained by Jim Crow segregation—an audience that might even buy a record or two, in the process of buying furniture, cleaning supplies and an insurance policy. Nevertheless, the report is cognizant of the growth of an emerging black middle class, one that would prove attractive not just to record companies but also advertisers eager to fuel black desires to consume the fetishes of a post–Civil Rights world. In the aftermath of centuries of struggle, exploitation and violence, some members of the black middle class often viewed their ability to consume widely throughout mainstream society as an emblem of the "freedoms" won during the Civil Rights struggle.

To get a sense of what this urbane blackness would look and feel like, think of the immensely popular early 1980s Colt 45 commercials featuring Billy Dee Williams. Twenty years later, no one really blinked an eye when poet Sonia Sanchez and Eric Benet used "smooth" R&B to hawk for an automobile maker. As R&B began to be viewed as the quintessence of upscale blackness, the more gritter aspects of black popular music—that which was, as Houston Baker Jr. describes it, "too blackly public" (as in embarrassing, like black folk eating watermelon in public)—began to disappear from the program list of some urban radio outlets in the late 1970s. So-called Southern Soul—the ZZ Hills, Denise LaSalles and Betty Wrights of the world—was an example of the kind of music that vanished from urban radio. Though Southern Soul didn't disappear—labels like Malaco and Ichiban continue to promote Southern Soul artists to this day—the more bluesier aspects of its sound and its references to black southern culture were the very antithesis of the post–Civil Rights worldviews of many African-Americans. The popped-over P-Funk of Rick James—one of the best selling black artists at the beginning of the post-Soul era—was emblematic of the brave new world of R&B. The challenge for record labels at this point was to come up with product to feed the R&B machine.

The Harvard Report was adamant that the Columbia Records Group should not attempt to purchase any of the prominent Soul labels (Motown, Atlantic, Stax) or poach from them any of their established artists. (CRG eventually purchased Stax, but only after the label was in serious decline.) What the report did advise was that CRG cultivate relationships with small independent labels, as was the case when CRG began a relationship with Kenny Gamble and Leon Huff. The product was Philadelphia International Records (PIR), and the impact of this groundbreaking relationship continues to reverberate 33 years later. As some critics—notably John A. Jackson in *A House on Fire: The Rise and Fall of Philadelphia Soul*—have observed, many of the Harvard Report's suggestions were already in play at Columbia, and the relationship with PIR is one such example. This brings us back to Clive Davis, the point-person on both the PIR and Stax deals. Dismissed from Columbia is 1973 for financial irregularities (some have linked his dismissal to our jumble word for the day: alopya), Davis had nonetheless instigated the distribution and creative-resource relationship with PIR that would become the defining model for relationships between large corporate labels and black music, making Davis himself arguably the most prominent figure in the story of R&B.

The language that the Harvard Report uses to describe the value of indie Soul labels is undisputable: "These small independents could provide a source of product, in the form of 'hot masters'; talent which could have national potential; experienced personnel . . . in the areas of promotion and production; and serve as a source of captive independent producers." Davis has claimed that he never read the Harvard Report, though it's clear that he would have been one of key figures that the authors of the report would have interviewed, and Davis may well have provided them with substantive info regarding the importance of indie labels. Regardless of the source, what the report details is the blueprint for the black boutique label—essentially based on a model of neo-colonialism, where an imperialist power exploits the raw materials and talents of its satellites under the pretense that such satellites are autonomous. As Norman Kelley observes, "In classic colonialism, products were produced in raw periphery and sent back to the imperial motherland to be manufactured into commodities, then sold in metropolitan centers or back to the colonies. The outcome for the colony was stunted economic growth, as it was stripped of its ability to manufacture products for its own needs" (*Rhythm of Business,* 10). Looked at within the context of artistic production, the colonial model creates a context where black artistic production is mediated by a commodity culture more interested in "moving product" than cultivating art or developing artists, and then sold back to the masses as "art", in the process stunting creative development. The irony is that which could be defined as organic artistic expression is seen as illegitimate by the masses, who have been programmed to accept corporate packaging as the real.

Clive Davis is probably less a sinister figure in the rise and fall of R&B and more the embodiment of the corporate hustler. But there's no denying that the very blueprint he outlined at Columbia became the most bankable strategy for R&B especially as he ascended to the leadership of Arista. For example, the most significant and successful black "boutique" labels of the 1990s, LaFace and Bad Boy Entertainment, were developed in Clive Davis's house. Despite the negative impact that the corporate co-opting of black culture has on black creativity, we're still left with the brilliance of the boutique model, as witnessed by the success of PIR. It all began with the production: the simple elegance of Billy Paul's "Me and Mrs. Jones" or Harold Melvin and the Bluenotes' "If You Don't Know Me By Now" or the glossy funk of The O'Jay's "I Love Music". The "Philly sound" (include Thom Bell and Mighty Three Publishing in this mix) became the soundtrack for an upscale blackness as far removed from the plantations of the South as it was from the factories of the Midwest. Kenny Gamble and Leon Huff were the real deal, and although they were not the sole innovators of this sound—think of the symphonic landscapes of Gene Page or the string arrangements of Paul Riser—the promotional and distribution muscle of Columbia allowed the duo to nationalize what was essentially a regional sound. By the end of the 1970s strains of the PIR could be heard in virtually every popular R&B song.

The boutique model was not necessarily about crossing R&B over to the mainstream, but rather positioning the larger corporate labels to better control the R&B market. As such, R&B artists were less compelled to compete with so-called pop artists. Although this meant that R&B artists had less access to resources—particularly as the record industry went through a financial slump in the late 1970s—it also created conditions where the R&B sound could develop without the additional pressure of attracting a wider audience. Very few soul artists made the transition to the R&B world. Notable examples are figures like Bobby Womack, whose *Poet* (1981) and *Poet II* (1984) represented the best work of his career and Diana Ross, whose *Diana* (1980), produced by Nile Rodgers and Bernard Edwards, represents the apex of her solo career. And then there's the case of Michael Jackson, who remade himself into an R&B artist on his groundbreaking *Off the Wall* (1979), three years after he sat at the feet of Gamble and Huff, who produced the Jackson's first CBS album after the Jackson 5's departure from Motown in 1975. Often lost in conversations about Jackson's emergence as the "King of Pop" is that he was cultivated in the R&B world—along with such other singular black pop crossovers of the 1980s as Whitney Houston and Lionel Ritchie.

If there was one figure who defined the genius of R&B it was Luther Vandross, who with the release of his eponymous debut in 1981 became the genre's dominant artist. By coyly distancing himself from the black gospel vocal tradition, which grounded so much of the soul music of the 1960s and 1970s, Vandross cemented his appeal as the quintessential R&B singer. Specifically Vandross was trying to distinguish himself from generations of "shouters" such as gospel artists Joe Ligon (lead vocalist of the Mighty Clouds of Joy) and the late Archie Brownlee (of the Five Blind Boys of Mississippi) or soul vocalists like Wilson Pickett, the late Otis Redding and James Brown. As Jason King and others have suggested, Vandross was a student of various music traditions, notably black female vocalists of the 1960s (Dionne Warwick, The Bluebelles, Aretha Franklin), the Burt Bacharach and Hal David songbook, and the background-vocal stylings of the Sweet Inspirations. In addition, the lush orchestrations that figured so prominently in Vandross ballads—he is the definitive balladeer of the last generation of popular singers—suggested that he too was a fan of Gamble and Huff and Gene Page.

Still others such as Stephanie Mills, Frankie Beverly and Maze, Jeffrey Osborne, Anita Baker, Peabo Bryson, Atlantic Starr, Kashif, Loose Ends, Alexander O'Neal, The Whispers, Kenny "Babyface" Edmonds, and Chaka Khan (post Rufus) helped give R&B a cohesive sound in the early 1980s. As R&B was about attracting upscale "urban" audiences—whether legitimate members of the black middle class or working class strivers—it was by definition a genre targeted to mature audiences. As the 1980s progressed R&B was increasingly out of touch with a generation of black youth consumers, who felt little need to distance themselves from the realities of the Jim Crow era, especially as they faced down the venomous edge of the Reagan era. In real terms the R&B world was being challenged by the embryonic sounds of hip-hop for the attention (and disposable income) of "urban" audiences. A telling sign was the success of Chaka Khan's remake of Prince's "I Feel for You" (1984), which featured an opening rap by Melle Mel (technically the first hip-hop and R&B collaboration, though in my mind Jody Whatley's "Friends", which was blessed by Rakim, is more significant). The song remains Khan's best-selling single. Khan's version of "I Feel for You" began a tenuous relationship between R&B and hip-hop, one which would finally earn hip-hop validation from the black mainstream and ultimately render R&B irrelevant.

PART TWO: NEW JACK SWING, MARY J. BLIGE AND THE HEGEMONY OF HIP-HOP

As ubiquitous as it is today, as recently as 15 years ago hip-hop faced a real battle just to be heard on urban radio. Like Soul and Rhythm and Blues before it, hip-hop was too publicly black for advertisers, and when it found its way on the playlists of big market urban radio it was often after-hours on the weekend. There were a few exceptions—Whodini, for example, doesn't get enough credit for their melding of hip-hop and R&B (courtesy of Larry Smith) on tracks like "Friends", "Funky Beat" and in particular "One Love", a strategy that Heavy D and the Boyz later exploited to become a radio-friendly favorite. The success of Jody Whatley's collaboration with Rakim, "Friends" (1989), made some R&B artists and labels more willing to rent-a-rapper for some street credibility, but at the same time, it was still common practice for labels to deliver to radio versions of R&B singles in "rap" and "no rap" mixes to maximize radio airplay. Ultimately it took the sound christened the "new jack swing" to bring record labels and urban radio on board with the changing dynamics of R&B.

Teddy Riley is generally recognized as the genius behind new jack swing, a sound that married the old-school harmonies of the black church with a hard rhythmic edge. Riley's group Guy (originally featuring Aaron Hall and Timmy Gatling) was the primary vehicle for his production, but he also produced Johnny Kemp ("Just Got Paid"), Keith Sweat ("I Want Her"), James Ingram ("I'm Real"), Boy George ("Don't Take My Mind on a Trip"), the Winans ("It's Time") and Michael Jackson ("Remember the Time"). The range of artists that Riley worked with gives some indication of new jack swing's impact on the recording industry.

Riley might have been the true innovator of the swing, but Bobby Brown gave it its public face. Bobby Brown was the first true embodiment of hip-hop in the R&B world, even daring to drop a rhyme or two himself, like a low-rent LL Cool J. Many folk looked askance a few years ago when Whitney Houston referred to her husband as the "king of R&B", but the reality is that Brown's breakthrough recording, 1988's *Don't Be Cruel*, is singularly responsible for the trajectory of R&B well into the 1990s. It is virtually impossible to imagine the careers of R. Kelly, Dave Hollister, Jaheim, Joe, Avant, Usher and Justin Timberlake without the success of *Don't Be Cruel*, which produced five bonafide R&B and pop hits, including "Every Little Step", "Rock Wit'cha" and, of course, "My Prerogative", produced by Riley.

In a 1988 *New York Times* feature on Brown, Peter Watrous was prophetic when he suggested that Brown's "success could have important implications. . . . If [his] achievement is followed by the deserved success of others, then perhaps the wall, kept sturdy by radio, press and record companies, that has historically divided black and white music worlds will begin to crumble." Behind Watrous's prescient observation was the realization among the major labels that hip-hop possessed real commercial potential beyond urban audiences. The popular view is that the majors got involved with hip-hop in the aftermath of successful crossover releases by Run-DMC (*Raising Hell*) and the Beastie Boys (*License to Ill*) and the strong response to MTV's *Yo! MTV Raps* (1988). While this view may indeed be correct, a more cynical view is that major labels adopted hip-hop once the independent labels that supported it throughout the 1980s became a threat to their hegemony in the field of black music. What was most important was maintaining complete control over the urban contemporary market. If hip-hop happened to crossover—so the thinking was in the late 1980s—it would be simply gravy.

By the mid-1990s hip-hop would of course do so much more, eventually becoming one of popular music's dominant genres. But the germ of that success came years earlier via a small boutique label distributed by MCA, the label Brown recorded for. Sean Combs gets much of the credit for carrying hip-hop over the crossover hump, but before Bad Boy Entertainment there was Uptown, the brain-child of former Dr. Jekyll and Mr. Hyde frontman Andre Harrell. In the early 1980s Jekyll and Hyde ('Genius Rap") were known for the business attire they wore on stage while rapping, a look that captured the very aesthetic that Harrell hoped to cultivate with the Uptown label, a style he would call "High Negro", which melded the upscale blackness of R&B (and the yellow-power-tie/Reagan-era generation of niggeratti strivers) with the street. Harrell was not necessarily an innovator; groups like Full Force ("Alice, I Want You

Just for Me") and The Force MDs ("Let Me Love You") were already charting this territory. But Harrell had the genius to mass market this sound. Not surprisingly, Heavy D and the Boyz were one of the label's first successes, the group's "We Got Our Own Thing", produced by Riley in 1989, became an anthem for the era of asymmetrical high-top fades, Africa medallions and pastel colors. But Uptown's two signature acts, Jodeci and Mary J. Blige, defined the Uptown sound and the possibilities of a true hip-hop and R&B hybrid.

Jodeci was comprised of two sets of brothers from North Carolina, Dalvin and Devante Degrate and K.C. and Jo Jo Hailey, who were the group's primary vocalists. In many ways Jodeci was like a quartet of Bobby Browns, though none in the group possessed Brown's charisma. Their deft command of harmonies was a throwback to the classic Soul-man era, with K.C. Hailey often doing his best imitation of Bobby Womack. Their debut, *Forever My Lady* (1991) featured popular hits such as "Stay", "Come and Talk to Me" and the title track. What caught the attention of urban audiences was their gear—thugged out in baggy jeans and Timbaland boots (courtesy of budding fashion designer Sean Combs)—which helped Jodeci pioneer a sub-genre that I like to refer to as Thug Soul (Dave Hollister and Jaheim are the most successful converts). Though the group never achieved real mainstream appeal, Jodeci became the perfect counterweight to the popfectionary R&B of Boyz II Men during most of the 1990s.

It would be Jodeci's female counterpart at Uptown, though, who would ultimately change the game, at once representing the best of R&B and facilitating its demise. Andre Harrell heard a demo of Mary J. Blige singing an Anita Baker tune, but was at a loss as to how to promote her. Blige's big opportunity came when she recorded a song for Uptown's soundtrack for the 1991 film *Strictly Business*. Though it was not released as a single, "You Remind Me" caught the attention of hip-hop DJs and soon found its way on the playlists of urban-radio programmers. With a hit record in hand, Uptown forged ahead with Blige's debut *What's the 411?* The success of the recording pivoted on the lead single, "Real Love". Built around the rhythm track of Audio Two's 1987 hip-hop classic "Top Billin'", "Real Love" was the blueprint for what Combs would dub "hip-hop soul"—essentially the marriage of R&B vocals with hip-hop beats and samples, which by the end of the decade became the standard form of R&B production.

What separated Bilge from her peers was that she tapped into the emotional core of a generation of music fans for whom loss and betrayal were always the first and foremost expectations, whether in love or public policy. Hence a song like "Real Love" resonated very powerfully, because it captured the hip-hop generation's utter fixation with delineating "the real", its existential quest for authenticity. Unlike the civil rights generation, which was often consumed with defending its legitimacy in the face of an all-too-present white gaze, the hip-hop generation rejected the significance of the white gaze, defining the real within the context of black community instead. What is at stake in this quest for the real is the very real possibility of rejection and censure from the community. It's a product of the apprehensions and ambivalences associated with coming of age in an era where you are free to be whatever. And it was Blige's vocals—ragged, displaced and aching—that summoned all of these emotions, as she struggled with the demons of betrayal and abuse in her own life. Blige quickly became known as hip-hop's Aretha Franklin, not so much for her technical proficiency but her ability to speak for a generation, much the way Franklin spoke for the civil rights generation.

What hip-hop soul did was bring the production values of hip-hop to the R&B world. Combs is notable if only because he was best positioned to exploit this marriage. By the end of the 1990s others were doing it much more consistently: Timbaland (in his work with Aaliyah and Ginuwine), Chucky Thompson, Jermaine Dupri and even Dr. Dre, who produced one of

Bilge's biggest hit singles, "Family Affair" (2001). The use of hip-hop production in R&B created a wider audience for hip-hop itself, something Combs quickly took advantage of with Craig Mack, the Notorious B.I.G. and Mase. While there were artists who had crossed over to the pop mainstream—Run-DMC, the Beasties, NWA and Hammer being the most notable—only after the success of hip-hop soul were popular hip-hop artists routinely expected to cross-over as well, as has been the case with Jay Z, Nas, DMX, Ja Rule, Eminem, Nelly, Ludacris, and the rest. Telling in this regard is the fact that R&B vocalist Ashanti's breakthrough onto the upper tier of the pop charts, "Foolish", featured a sample of the Notorious B.I.G.'s "One More Chance (remix)" (itself built on a sample of DeBarge's "Stay with Me").

Despite the success of hip-hop soul and purveyors like Bilge, Faith Evans and later Ashanti, the R&B world of the mid-1990s still allowed for the relatively old-school stylings of Gerald Levert, Brian McKnight, Keith Sweat and the so-called neo-soul movement, which was essentially R&B packaged in opposition to hip-hop soul and marketed to traditional R&B audiences tiring of hip-hop's urban-radio hegemony. Ironically many neo-soul artists also relied on the sample-based production that hip-hop initially popularized (listen to Angie Stone's "Sunshine" and D'Angelo's "Send It On", which sample Gladys Knight & the Pips and Kool & the Gang respectively). This moment in R&B would be short lived, as the massive consolidation within the music and radio industries would create the context where virtually all forms of urban music would begin the pop-chart paper-chase in pursuit of the new queen: hip-hop.

PART THREE: MEDIA CONGLOMERATION, LABEL CONSOLIDATION AND PAYOLA

On February 8, 1996, Bill Clinton signed into law the Telecommunications Reform Act of 1996. At the same time Jay Z was preparing for the late-spring release of his debut, *Reasonable Doubt*, unaware that he and many other hip-hop acts were about to benefit from the atmosphere of deregulation and capital accumulation that the new law typified. *Reasonable Doubt* was released by Roc-A-Fella Records, an independent label founded by Carter, Karreim Biggs and Damon Dash. By 1998 Roc-A-Fella would enter into a joint equity deal with Def Jam, itself a former indie label, founded in 1984 by Russell Simmons and Rick Rubin and later distributed by Sony and Polygram. When Roc-A-Fella and Def Jam agreed to partner, a 40 percent share of the latter was about to be sold to Polygram for $130 million. Shortly thereafter Polygram was bought by Seagram (yes, the liquor company), creating the Universal Music Group, which would later be acquired by the French company Vivendi. At the very moment that Vivendi/Universal (where Jay Z, 50 Cent, The Game and Eminem currently work) was unveiled, Clear Channel could claim ownership of more than 1,200 radio stations—247 of them in the top 250 national radio markets. Clear Channel's emergence as the dominant force in commercial radio was directly related to the bill that Clinton signed into law in 1996. Confusing? Of course it is, but imagine how confusing it was—and still is—for your local up-and-coming R&B artist who can't find a major label to sign her or an urban radio station that would play her music even if she did.

Arguably the most noticeable of the wide-ranging effects of the Telecommunications Act has been the Clear Channeling of America's public airwaves. Prior to 1996 companies were constrained from owning more than two radio stations in any market and could own no more than 28 nationally. The logic behind this was simple: As the Broad Artist Coalition and the Future of Music Coalition argued in their joint letter to the FCC and Congress in 2002, "radio is a public asset, not private property. . . . The quid pro quo for free use of the public bandwidth requires that broadcast stations serve the public interest in their local communities." While many radio stations do some form of public-affairs programming—usually in the early morning hours on the weekend—serving the public is broader than that. Part of the responsibility of any radio station is to support music that speaks to local tastes. This is one of the ways that local music scenes have developed and been nurtured in the past, whether it was Rhythm and Blues in the Midwest in the early 1960s (which produced Motown and Curtis Mayfield), the Philly Soul of Thom Bell and Gamble and Huff in the 1970s or hip-hop in the San Francisco Bay area in the late 1980s.

In the aftermath of the Telecommunications Reform Act, the massive consolidation in radio has left fewer people making the decisions about what music will be played. The ten largest radio conglomerates in the U.S. control more than two thirds of the national radio audience, with Clear Channel and Viacom (which, incidentally, owns both MTV and BET) controlling more than 40 percent of that. That these conditions impact what music you hear on the radio and the ability of local groups to get on their local radio station goes without saying. In the past, for example, if a particular region had 20 radio stations, 20 different program directors (PDs) would likely decided what would be played. The current environment playlist decisions are now in the hands of a smaller group of PDs, who often cede some of their decision making power to regional and national program directors. Furthermore, as the Future of Music Coalition noted in their 2002 report "Radio Deregulation: Has It Served Citizens and Musicians", in any given region, the concentration of ownership among a small number of conglomerates is even more intense. The Clear Channeling of radio has homogenized American radio. This is why urban stations in the major markets all sound the same.

The nationalizing of local radio has made it increasingly difficult for listeners in various locales to hold programmers accountable. One of the best examples of these struggles was the protest of New York City's Hot 97 (WQHT-FM), after the station's morning drive-time team performed a racially insensitive parody about the tsunami that destroyed portions of Indonesia and Africa. Though nationwide protest eventually forced the station's parent company, Emmis, to fire a producer and a host at WQHT and to pledge $1 million in tsunami relief, the fact that the drive-time hosts felt comfortable enough to perform a bit that was so insensitive to its core audience in the first place speaks to the distance between the conglomerates that manage the stations and the communities they are supposed to serve. About the people who ultimately decide what's heard on your local radio station, activist and journalist Davey D recently told Democracy Now, "we've got to know that these are 40 and 50-year-old men and women behind the scenes, calling the shots, deciding that at 7:00 at night, you can hear the Yin Yang Twins talking about 'wait until you see mi d-i-c-k' and that it's not a problem."

Along with radio consolidation has come the emergence of nationally syndicated morning drive-time programming (6:00 to 10:00 A.M. in most markets) geared toward African-American and other so-called urban audiences. Of these syndicated shows, the *Tom Joyner Morning Show* (*TJMS*) is best known. With a foothold in more than a hundred urban radio markets, the *TJMS* is potentially a formidable political force, as it can reach and unify listeners across the country. In its best moment, the *TJMS* is a digitized version of the chitlin' circuit, the network of clubs, restaurants, hotels, dance halls and the like that were crucial components of black life and culture during the era of Jim Crow segregation. As African-Americans pushed for integrated social and cultural institutions in the 1950s and 1960s, the thinking was that the chitlin' circuit would die off. But in the current era of niche marketing—which urban radio and R&B exemplify—the chitlin' circuit survives not to unite to black audiences but to deliver advertisers access to a vibrant black middle class with disposable incomes.

Musically, the *TJMS* adheres to a standard "smooth R&B and classic Soul" format with no interest in breaking new R&B acts. Instead they have made it even harder for local acts to break through. Nationally syndicated shows such as the *TJMS* or *The Doug Banks Morning Show* (on ABC Radio Networks), have made local drive-time personalities obsolete, thus denying many audiences the opportunity to have their local culture and music reflected during the drive-time hours, when listenership is at its peak. Despite being jettisoned from New York's WRKS in early 2003, the *TJMS* cemented its domination of the urban market when Tom Joyner entered into a partnership with Cathy Hughes's Radio One Corporation, the largest black-owned radio conglomerate.

Consolidation was not restricted to radio. In the late 1990s record-label consolidation also played its part in the demise of R&B. As Michael Roberts notes in his essay "Papa's Got a Brand New Bag," label consolidation began in the late 1960s when WEA (Warner Brothers, Elecktra, Atlantic) became one of the first super labels (see *Rhythm of Business*). Motown Records, which the Harvard Report urged the Columbia Record Group not to purchase in 1972, was eventually sold to Polygram in the mid-1980s. The Columbia Records Group itself was purchased by Sony in 1988, at which point much of the popular music produced in the United States was controlled by what was referred to as the "big six". With the merger of Seagram's music holdings with Polygram in 1998 and the recent annexation of Sony music by BMG (Sony BMG Music Entertainment), six has become four. With the recording industry dominated by four transnational conglomerates, fewer people make development and production decisions and fewer staff the A&R (artist and repertoire) departments responsible for signing new talent.

Because R&B had lost market share to hip-hop in the late 1990s and because new R&B was neglected due to the programming logic of "classic Soul and smooth R&B" formats, R&B became viewed as a retrograde genre. While undiscovered Soul and R&B artists suffered under consolidation, hip-hop has benefited. Forms of hip-hop thought to be regional as little as 10 years ago thrived in the new media landscape. The perception among both the record labels and radio programmers is that this older audience is unwilling to support contemporary R&B music to the extent that younger urban and crossover audiences support hip-hop (the success of "classic Soul and R&B" tours of course suggest otherwise). Even those acts perceived to have commercial potential among traditional R&B audiences—I'm thinking specifically of the Philly Neo-Soul scene that produced Musiq, India.Arie, Jill Scott, Bilal, Res, Kindred, Jaguar Wright, Amel Larrieux and Floetry—we're marketed as throwback performers, whose proclivities for so called positivity were construed as an aesthetic value. Regardless of the critical acclaim that Neo-Soul (organic R&B) received, major labels and urban radio never thought it anything but a niche market. Of course, such top-tier stars of R&B as Mary J. Blige, Usher, and Mariah Carey (no longer marketed as a pop act) held their own in the marketplace, often trading creativity for familiarity, rehashing the production styles that first made them popular or acquiescing to the allure of hip-hop-style production in an attempt to remain relevant to younger urban audiences.

One would be hard pressed to think of an R&B artist, established or otherwise, that has received the kind of promotional support that 50 Cent or The Game received for their major label debuts. One recent exception might be Alicia Keys, though a fair amount of her initial success must be chalked up to Clive Davis's bag of tricks—this *is* the man who helped established a little known teenage singer from New Jersey, Whitney Houston, as the best selling female vocalist of the last generation. And such artists as Ashanti, Clara and John Legend weren't necessarily promoted on their own merit but on the merit of their hip-hop benefactors.

Lacking strong promotional support, many established R&B acts have little incentive to push the envelope on their recordings. The career trajectories of Gerald Levert and Brian McKnight are instructive. Though these two are easily the most consistent artists in contemporary R&B, their recent recordings rarely break from the formula that helped establish them more than a decade ago (Levert's *Do I Speak for the World?* might be the exception). Their respective labels value such an approach because when peddling a known commodity McKnight and Levert can regularly move 500,000 units without any real promotional support.

Meanwhile consolidation allowed hip-hop to leverage its growing commercial power. As major labels began to seek out regional hip-hop groups to sign—much like the imperial powers of the past seeking to annex new lands (and resources) to their empires—it created the context where these groups could quickly and easily gain a national audience once they were added to the playlists of the urban stations of the major radio conglomerates (and video channels). The damn-near-hegemony of crunk in 2005 is probably the best example of this process. Crunk is not a new phenomenon—can anybody say MC Shy-D?—but the Telecommunications Reform Act of 1996 allowed for the regional Southern sound to be heard in places like Detroit, New York and other locales far-removed from the "dirty, dirty."

But aspiring R&B artists have been challenged by what the Future of Music Coalition calls the "twin bottleneck" effect. Basically, with intense consolidation in both the recording industry and commercial radio, artists are squeezed out of a hearing at both the labels and radio stations. While independent labels remain an option for artists, the reality is that the four major label conglomerates—the four industry gatekeepers—are responsible for more than 80 percent of what makes it on commercial radio play lists. As the Future of Music Coalition explains, "Major record labels have large promotional budgets. Because the promotional money is there, radio companies have an incentive to make *access to the airwaves more scarce, and thus more expensive*" (my emphasis). And of course, among the major-label conglomerates, the competition for the airwaves is fierce, as airplay directly affects sales.

What strategies can a label employ to guarantee that their artists will receive the kind of airplay that they deserve? In the early days of rock and roll, the practice of payola was critical for up-and-coming labels trying to get the attention of DJs, who at the time were primarily responsible for what was played on the radio. For example, there is a subtle scene in the recent film *Ray*, where Jerry Wexler of Atlantic Records passes cash on to a DJ to get him to play Ray Charles's breakthrough crossover hit "I Got a Woman". But paying DJs to play certain records has been illegal since the early 1960s, when Cleveland-based DJ Alan Freed was indicted on charges of bribery.

As program directors replaced DJs as the primary gatekeepers of radio playlists, forms of payola have become more elaborate and covert (See Fredric Dannen's *Hit Men*). In fact there were two notable forms of payola, that while highly suspect, were legal. One was the practice of using "independent" promoters to interact with radio programmers (thus obscured the possibility that labels are directly paying stations) and the other was that of "paid spins", where songs for a particular label are played as part of an advertisement spot. The latter is perfectly legal, as long as it's disclosed that the spot is paid for by said label. The cases of independent promoters received much of the attention in investigations of illegal payola, simply because of the huge amount of money exchanged between labels, promoters and radio stations to guarantee that certain records regular airplay. According to Eric Boehlert, in the latest of his on-going articles on commercial radio at Salon.com, the practice of paying independent promoters cost labels as a group as much as $150 million annually. In this environment, virtually everything that appears on a station's playlist has been paid for in one form or another.

Most radio programmers retreated from using independent promoters when Representative Russ Feingold and others in Congress, and most recently New York State Attorney General Eliot Spitzer, began to raise questions about the process. (The same retreat occurred in the mid-1980s when Rudy Guliani, then a U.S. Attorney, and Al Gore, then a senator from Tennessee, announced payola probes). Though Boehlert can boldly claim that payola, in its most recent incarnation, is "dead", he has also acknowledged that urban radio is the "Wild, Wild, West" of the record industry. Indeed, Cedric Muhammed of Blackelectorate.com, asserts that in the recent past DJs at Radio One, for example, have been "admonished" for playing music that is not on the station's playlist and in some cases "terminated" if a non-playlist song is played five or more times. R&B artists who don't appeal to younger urban/hip-hop audiences are already at a disadvantage at the major labels, and even those aligned with independent labels who do support them, like, say, Hidden Beach, home to Jill Scott, Lina and Kindred the Family Soul, are further disadvantaged because commercial radio is governed by how much one is willing to pay to get tunes on the air. While it's easy to suggest that audiences have the power to demand music that they would like to hear, the reality is that an audience must first know alternatives exist. And mainstream commercial radio remains the place where most listeners become aware of new music.

The current radio and label consolidation, along with the emergence of hip-hop as the dominant cross-over genre and the perceived aging of traditional R&B audiences, has created the situation where the best R&B being recorded is simply not heard by the audience that would be attracted to it. Satellite Radio has been one of the places where new R&B can be heard, but the format's overall audience is still paltry when compared to that of commercial radio. The alleged death of payola suggests that at the moment, at least, there exists the possibility for a more diverse range of music to hit the commercial airwaves, but even Boehlert laments that "tight radio playlists are unlikely to improve anytime soon", in part because programmers "will rely more and more on proven hits singles as well as older, already familiar songs, leaving less airtime for new acts." Ultimately, the current state of contemporary R&B has little to do with the mediocrity of R&B's status quo—there is great music to be heard—but unless mainstream labels create conditions in which emerging R&B artists can be nurtured, without the pressure to cross-over to urban youth audiences, and audiences themselves become more vigilant about seeking out and supporting new music, much of R&B's current greatness will fall on deaf ears.

EPILOGUE

While the slow collapse of the independent-promoter payola scheme suggests an opportunity for non-mainstream artists, the practice of legal sponsored spins (pay for play legitimized by a broadcast disclaimer) continue to put small independent labels and the innovative R&B they cultivate at a disadvantage—they simply don't have the resources to compete in that arena. Even major-label R&B artists struggle to be heard: Tweet garnered far less attention for her truly nuanced R&B than for the "scandal" of her first single "Oh My" and the rumor of a relationship with Missy Elliot. Perhaps John Legend's success signals a small shift—I'm not sure many programmers would have risked playing a singer-songwriter five years ago. But for every John Legend, there are others who never break through. For those enterprising program directors and fans looking for R&B that deserves greater recognition, here's a brief list of worthy artists still below the radar.

Lewis Taylor

That I need to begin with Lewis Taylor epitomizes the tragedy of contemporary R&B. Although Taylor is arguably the most brilliant talent to emerge in R&B in the last decade, most R&B fans in the United States are still unaware of his existence, even after six studio recordings (the last four on his own label). The reason for Taylor's invisibility are many, starting with his Britishness and his whiteness and his commitment to push the boundaries of R&B. Taylor makes R&B for folk as fluent in Marvin Gaye and Bobby Womack as they are in the Beach Boys (*Pet Sounds* specifically) and Radiohead. Taylor's eponymous 1977 debut is simply classic, and it earned him the attention of D'Angelo, who reportedly referred to Taylor as his favorite R&B artist. Even the late Aaliyah remarked that she was into Taylor, telling the *New York Daily News* in 2001, "My favorite CD right now is *Lewis Taylor*. My stylist had a mixed tape with his song 'Bittersweet' and I had to know who was singing." The influence of Taylor's "Bittersweet" can be heard on the Timbaland-produced "Come Back in One Piece," from the *Romeo Must Die* soundtrack. Taylor's obscurity has a great deal to do with his then-label's inability to grasp what he was doing musically, particularly as Taylor resisted being packaged like blue-eyed-soul hacks such as Michael Bolton. *Lewis Taylor* and *Lewis II* (2000) (which included Taylor's sweet cover of Jeff Buckley's "Everybody Here Wants You") are the best introductions to Taylor, though his independently released *Stoned, Part 1* (2003) is also a fine outing. *Stoned, Part 1*, will be released in the United States in September by Hacktone Records.

Rahsaan Patterson

In his thoughtful biography of Luther Vandross, journalist Craig Seymor suggests that one of Vandross's great talents was his ability to expand the range of emotions that could be expressed by a black male Soul or R&B artist. Of course Vandross paid a symbolic price for his expressiveness: His emotional depth was often read as evidence of a diminished masculinity, as if the two were antithetical. Journalist Ernest Hardy says it best: "Naked emotionalism renders almost any male in American culture suspect, but especially if he's of the Negro persuasion, and most especially if the emotion is not exaggeratedly countered with macho or thug signifiers." In this regard, Vandross suffered the fate of Ronnie Dyson—tragically obscured in an era marked by Teddy Pendergrass-like gruffness and hypersexuality—and foreshadowed that of Rahsaan Patterson. Though Patterson's two major label releases, *Rahsaan Patterson* (1996) and *Love in Stereo* (1999), lack the musical depth of, say, D'Angelo's *Voodoo* (2000) or the catchy riffs of Maxwell's *Urban Hang Suite* (1996), Patterson's voice is otherworldly. In a recent *Village Voice* piece, Jason King describes Patterson as the "love-child of Chaka Khan and Al Jarreau." No other contemporary vocalist, in my view, could pull off the emotional intricacies that Patterson displays on tracks like "Can't We Wait a Minute", "Joy" (backed by Take 6), and "It's All Right Now". After an amicable split with MCA, Patterson is currently touring in support of his indie-label debut *After Hours*.

Jaguar Wright

It was Jaguar Wright's misfortune that her debut, *Denials, Delusions, and Decisions* was released just as the neo-Soul gravy train was grinding to a halt. Truth be told, Wright never really fit the neo-Soul script, something that her label at the time never quite understood. Wright's vocals were ragged with the kind of emotion last heard in these parts from the likes of Betty Wright (no relation), Ann Peebles and Millie Jackson. As Wright told Philadelphia's *City Paper* back in 2002, "I make cussin' sound natural. I'm not vulgar. I make grown-folks music; I don't make music for kids. It's grown language, talking 'bout grown shit for grown people." The title of Wright's new recording on the Artemis label—*Divorcing the Neo 2 Marry Soul*—suggests she has finally made a recording that speaks to her grittier sensibilities. Tracks such as "Play the Field" and "Free" sound like they could have been recorded at Muscle Shoals (Fame Sound Studio) 25 years ago. Thus it's not surprising that Wright dares to remake Shirley Brown's "Woman to Woman"—a song that brought the drama of infidelity to Soul and R&B audiences when R. Kelly was still in kindergarten. Wright's new-found musical freedom is best expressed on "Do Your Worst"—a nearly 12-minute display of anger, betrayal and murderous rage that recalls Lonette McKee's heartbreaking rendition of Van McCoy's "Giving Up" in the film *Sparkle* (1976).

Eric Roberson

Bilal and Musiq are generally regarded as the signature male vocalists of the so-called Philly Neo-Soul movement. But Musiq is perhaps a better songwriter and arranger than he is a vocalist, and Bilal's vocal sensibility is limited somewhat to the recording studio. Arguably the most accomplished artist to emerge from the Philly scene is Eric Roberson. Roberson's songwriting credits can be found on albums by Will Downing, Musiq, Vivian Green and on Jill Scott's *Experience: Jill Scott (826 +)*, where most first heard Roberson, opposite Scott on "One Time". At that point, Roberson already had a small underground following courtesy of his now out-of-print and hard-to-find *The Esoteric Movement* (2001)—it lists for $30-plus used on Amazon. Trying to feed the needs of those clamoring for more music, Roberson emptied his drawer and independently released *Eric Roberson Presents: The Vault 1.0* (later updated as *The Vault, 1.5*). There are many standouts on Roberson's latest, including "Def Ears" and "Couldn't Hear me". Throughout, Roberson proves that sample-based R&B is not totally bankrupt. On the nostalgic "Right Back to Me" Roberson makes ample use of Isaac Hayes's version of the Carpenters' "Close to You (They Long to Be)", creating a lush musical landscape reminiscent of Hayes's own creative peak in the early 1970s on *Hot Buttered Soul* and *Black Moses*.

Frank McComb

Like the title of the song he performed on Buckshot LeFonque's (Branford Marsalis) *Music Revolution*, Frank McComb is a phoenix-Donny Hathaway reborn. After a canned Motown outing, his major label debut *Love Stories* (2000) offered him chance for wider recognition beyond those few who caught his performance with Marsalis. But that recognition never came, as McComb suffered the fate of so many decidedly mature R&B artists from the late 1990s— Will Downing, Johnny Gill, Rachelle Ferrell and Regina Belle among them—who were too "old" for contemporary R&B and arguably too soulful for the "Smoove" jazz denizens. *Truth* (2003), McCombs's follow-up, wasn't even released in the States, and that's a shame. Tracks such as "When You Call My Name", "Better Off Without You", and "Intimate Time" only reinforce McComb's furthering of Hathaway's legacy—hopefully a duet between Combs and Lalah Hathaway awaits us in the future—especially at a time when contemporary R&B could desperately use the secularized spirituality that made Hathaway so affecting in the first place.

Mint Condition

When Mint Condition, six musicians from Minneapolis, first emerged in 1991 with their debut *Meant to Be Meant*, they were quickly regarded as part of the R&B avant-garde-group that includes Meshell Ndegeocello, Jol, Van Hunt, Martin Luther, Anthony David, D'Angelo,

Erykah Badu and Res. Though Mint Condition recorded some of the best R&B of the past 15 years with recordings like *From the Mint Factory* (1993) and *Definition of a Band* (1996), and though their lead vocalist, Stokley, is on the shortlist of the best vocalists of the 1990s, the group never caught on with most R&B listeners. Six years after the largely ignored *Life's Aquarium*, Mint Condition—now a quintet since Keri Lewis (Mr. Toni Braxton) departed the group amicably—returned with *Livin' the Luxury Brown*, released on their own label, Caged Bird. Mint Condition is in regular form throughout the album, though it lacks a signature ballad on the level of "Pretty Brown Eyes" (1991), "If You Love Me" (1999), or their classic "What Kind of Man Can I Be". Highlights include "Sad Girl", the breezy "Look Whatchu Done for Me" and the lead single, "I'm Ready".

Carmen Rodgers

While so many of us profess our love for the indie world of neo-Soul, Nu-Soul or whatever label we're attaching to this music today, the reality is that many of these artists—no matter how good their music sounds while we're waiting for the open mic performance at the local Afro-Boho spot—are somewhat flawed. The major labels might not be interested in promoting R&B artists who don't have some kind of affiliation with a hip-hop crew, but give then some credit for at least being able to identify talent. That said, Carmen Rodgers might be an exception—On her indie debut *Free* (ABMG/Expansion Records), Rodgers manages to neither pander to Soul music's past nor tries to keep pace with the fleeting rhythms of contemporary R&B. There is much to like about *Free*, including "Missing You" and "Fallen", but the real gem of the disc is Rodgers's remake of the Captain and Tennille's "The Way (I Want to Touch)".

Faith Evans

In many ways Faith Evans doesn't belong on this list, but she has always been in the shadow of Mary J. Blige and her late husband Christopher Wallace and too often betrayed by material deemed appropriate by the Puffinator. Liberated from Bad Boy land, Evans released *The First Lady* (Capitol), which is simply her most accomplished recording. On the lead single, "Again", Ivan Barias and Carvin Haggins (late of A Touch of Jazz Productions) provide Evans with some Motown-era pop candy, helping her to live up to the regality of the disc's title. The duo continues their winning ways on tracks like "Stop and Go", "Get Over You" and cutesy "Jealous", which samples Los Angeles Negroes' "Esta noche la paso contigo" (1975). *The First Lady* loses much of its glow when Barias and Haggins aren't in the room—Pharrell's "Goin' Out" is easily the worst track. That the recording's quality drops when Pharrell and Jermaine Dupri are producing should be an indication to the majors that star producers don't always deliver the goods—the money could be better spent on actual promotion. The one exception here is "Mesmerized," produced by Chucky Thompson, Andre Johnson and Todd Russaw (Faith's hubby). Replete with rhythm guitar jacked from George Benson and the bassline from Lou Donaldson's version of "Who's Making Love", "Mesmerized" might be Evans's strongest track. The first lady of R&B, though? More like the second coming of Lynn Collins.

Raheem DeVaughn

Raheem DeVaughn is one of those artists that has benefited from the presence of Satellite Radio. While it's likely that the same kind of paid-spins politics is happening at XM and Sirius, satellite radio for the time being still delivers on its promise to break the monotony.

DeVaughn's *The Love Experience* (Jive) exemplifies this. The album suffers from the ongoing need of artists to use all 80 minutes the compact disc format allows, but once you strip away the filler, what's left is compelling. DeVaughn's vocals are reminiscent of Dwele's, but where the latter's music was overly restrained, DeVaughn is R&B unreconstructed—messy and ragged. The lead single, "Guess Who Loves You More", with its smart use of Earth, Wind and Fire's "Can't Hide Love", is a fine introduction to DeVaughn, but the real gems are the Prince-like "Who" and two political tracks, "Until" and "Catch 22". On the latter track DeVaughn perfects the symphonic thug soul of Dave Hollister ("Baby Mama Drama") and Blackstreet ("Hustler's Prayer").

References

Frederic Dannen. *Hit Men: Power Brokers and Fast Money Inside the Music Business*, New York: Vintage, 2001.

Nelson George. *The Death of Rhythm and Blues*, New York: Penguin, 2003.

John A. Jackson. *A House on Fire: The Rise and Fall of Philadelphia Soul*, New York: Oxford University Press, 2004.

David Rottenberg and Jeffrey C. Shuman. *The Rhythm of Business: The Key to Building and Running Successful Companies*, New York: Butterworth-Heinemann, 1998.

CREDITS

1. "Adrift on Stormy Seas," from *The Jubilee Singers; with Their Songs*, by J. B. T. Marsh (New York: Houghton Mifflin and Co., 1881), pp. 16–23.

Photo, page 3: This 1926 Columbia Record Company catalog lists the most recent recordings by the Fisk University Jubilee Singers, who began recording for Columbia in 1915. *Source:* Catalog from Kip Lornell Collection.

2. "Richards and Pringle's Original Georgia Minstrels and Billy Kersands, 1889–1895," from *Out of Sight: The Rise of African American Popular Music, 1889–1895*, by Lynn Abbott and Doug Seroff (Jackson: University Press of Mississippi, 2002), pp. 106–109.

Photo, page 9: This photograph (ca. 1936) underscores that minstrel shows toured throughout the South into the 1930s and later. *Source:* Library of Congress Photo.

3. "The Virginia Jubilee Singers in Bourke, Australia," an article printed in Australian newspaper on September 17, 1892, and reprinted in the *Indianapolis Freeman*, ca. October 1892.

4. "Conclusion," from *African Banjo Echoes in Appalachia: A Story of Folk Traditions*, by Cecelia Conway (Knoxville: University Press of Tennessee, 1995), pp. 285–296.

Photo, page 17: Joe Thompson (fiddle) and Odell Thompson (banjo), two cousins from Orange County, North Carolina, carried the African American string band tradition into the 1990s. *Source:* Kip Lornell Photo.

5. "War on Ragtime" and "Suppression of 'Ragtime,'" in *American Musician*, July 1901.

6. "Of the Sorrow Songs," from *The Souls of Black Folk*, by W. E. B. Du Bois (Chicago: A. C. McClung & co. 1903), pp. 107–114.

7. "The Nineteenth-Century Origins of Jazz," by Lawrence Gushee, which was originally published in the Black Music Research Journal 14, no. 1 (1994), 33-50. Reprinted with the permission of the Center for Black Music Research at Columbia College Chicago.

8. "Marshall Lullaby," from *The Life and Legend of Leadbelly* by Kip Lornell and Charles Wolfe (New York: DeCapo Press, 2001), pp. 14–25.

Photo, page 53: In 1982, the State of Louisiana's Department of Culture, Recreation, and Tourism placed this historical marker in Lead Belly's hometown of Mooringsport. *Source:* Kip Lornell Photo.

9. "The Scene and the Players in New York," from *Just Before Jazz: Black Musical Theater in New York, 1890–1915*, by Tom Riis (Washington, DC: Smithsonian Institution Press, 1989), pp. 78–92.

10. "Jelly Roll Blues," from *Mister Jelly Lord* by Jelly Roll Morton with Alan Lomax (Berkeley: University of California Press, 2000), pp. 147–159.

Photo, page 77: The sheet music for this widely circulated Spencer Williams and Clarence Williams song suggests why Ferdinand Morton choose the nickname "Jelly Roll." *Source:* Sheet Music from Kip Lornell Collection.

11. "William Marion Cook," by Cary B. Lewis in *The Chicago Defender*, May 1, 1915.

Photo, page 82: This rather obscure 1907 composition was introduced to the public as part of the George Walker and Bert Williams's show *Bandana Land*. *Source:* Sheet Music from Kip Lornell Collection.

12. "Ma Rainey and the Traveling Minstrels," by Charles Edward Smith in *The Record Changer*, 1953, pp. 13–14.

Photo, page 87: An artist's rendering of Ma Rainey appears on this rare and colorful Paramount Record Company release label from 1924. *Source:* Record from Kip Lornell Collection.

13. "Black Sacred Harp Singing from Southeast Alabama," record notes from the Alabama Folklife Program by Henry Willett, 1982.

Photo, page 92: For nearly 70 years Dewey Williams organized and participated in sacred harp singing near or in his Ozark, Dale County, Alabama, birthplace. *Source:* Photo courtesy of the Ralph Rinzler Folklife Archive and Collections, Smithsonian Institution.

14. "A Negro Explains 'Jazz,'" from *The Literary Digest*, April 26, 1919.

15. "Paul Robeson, Musician," from *Paul Robeson—Artist and Citizen*, by Doris McGinty and Wayne

Shirley, edited by Jeffery S. Stewart (New Brunswick, NJ: Rutgers University Press, 1998), pp. 105–122.

16. "Conflict and Resolution in the Life of Thomas Andrew Dorsey," from *We'll Understand It Better By and By*, by Michael W. Harris (Washington, DC: Smithsonian Institution Press,1992), pp. 165–182.

Photo, page 108: Between 1928 and 1932, when Thomas Dorsey turned exclusively to sacred music, Tampa Red and Georgia Tom [Dorsey] recorded dozens of blues sides for the Vocalion Record Company. Source: Advertisement from Kip Lornell Collection.

17. "Fats Waller (Comedy Tonight)," from *Visions of Jazz*, by Gary Giddins (New York: Oxford University Press, 1998), pp. 143–150.

18. "'Dean of Afro-American Composers' or 'Harlem Renaissance Man': The New Negro and the Musical Poetics of William Grant Still," from *William Grant Still: A Study in Contradictions*, by Catherine Person Smith,©2000, by Regents of the University of California. Published by the University of California Press.

19. "Easter Sunday," from *My Lord, What a Morning*, by Marian Anderson (New York: Viking Books, 1956), pp. 184–196.

20. "Caldonia" from *Let the Good Times Roll: The Life of Louis Jordan*, by John Chilton (Ann Arbor: University of Michigan Press, 1997), pp. 105–120.

Photo, page 156: Arguably the most popular black musician in the decade following the close of World War II was Louis Jordan. Jordan and his Tympany Five toured across the United States performing their hits at clubs large and small. Source: Poster from Kip Lornell Collection.

21. "Elder Beck's Temple," by William Russell, in *The Record Changer*, September 1947, p. 10.

22. "T-Bone Walker in His Own Words," by T-Bone Walker, in *The Record Changer*, October 1947, pp. 5–6, 12.

Photo, page 170: Beginning with Capitol Records in 1942, T-Bone Walker recorded for over a dozen labels (including Comet in 1947) before his death in 1975. Source: Record from Kip Lornell Collection.

23. "The Impact of Gospel Music on the Secular Music Industry," from *We'll Understand It By and By*, by Portia Maultsby (Washington, DC: Smithsonian Institution Press, 1992), pp. 19–33.

Photo, page 175: From 1940 to 1993, Chicago-based Morris and Martin Music Studio published dozens of books that helped disseminate gospel songs to congregations throughout the country. Source: Song Book from Kip Lornell Collection.

24. "Singing in the Streets of Raleigh, 1963: Some Recollections," by Clyde R. Appleton, in *The Black Perspective in Music* 3 (Fall 1975), pp. 243–252.

25. "Motown Calls 'The Rock & Roll Kid,'" from *Guitars, Bars and Motown Superstars*, by Dennis Coffey (Ann Arbor: University of Michigan Press, 2004), pp. 48–58.

26. SOULSVILLE U.S.A. THE STORY OF STAX RECORDS by Rob Bowman. Copyright 1997 by York: Schirmer Books, 1997), pp. 49–69.

Photo, page 203: Located in Memphis, the Stax Museum of American Soul Music opened in 2003 and sells a wide range of products, including this bumper sticker. Source: Bumper Sticker from Kip Lornell Collection.

27. "Clifton Chenier: 'They Call Me the King,'" from *Zydeco!* by Ben Sandmel (Jackson: University Press of Mississippi, 1999), pp. 69–90.

Photo, page 222: Older-style zydeco, here played by Canray Fontenot (fiddle) and Alphonse "Bois Sec" Ardoin (accordion), paved the way for the modern, more commercial music of Clifton Chenier. Source: Photo from Smithsonian Folkways.

28. "The Art of the Muscle: Miles Davis as American Knight and American Knave," from *Miles Davis and American Culture*, by Gerald Early (St. Louis: Missouri Historical Society, 2001), pp. 7–23.

29. "Evaluating Ellington," by Mark Tucker, "Behind the Beat" column in Institute for Studies in American Music newsletter, Brooklyn College, Brooklyn, NY, November 1988.

Photo, page 256: The sheet music for "Mood Indigo," one of Duke Ellington's early (1930) and most often performed compositions. Source: Sheet Music from Kip Lornell Collection.

30. "The P-Funk Empire: Tear the Roof Off the Sucker," from *Funk—The Music the People, and the Rhythm of the One*, by Rickey Vincent (New York: St. Martin's Press, 1996), pp. 231–252.

Photo, page 261: In October 1979, Parliament Funkadelic, featuring the lovely Brides of Funkenstein, completed a ten-day run at the Apollo Theater at the close of their "Motor Booty

Tour." *Source:* Advertisement from Kip Lornell Collection.

31. "Hip-Hop, Puerto Ricans, and Ethnoracial Identities in New York," from *Mambo Montage,* by Raquel Z. Rivera, edited by Agustin Lao-Montes and Arlene Davila (New York: Columbia University Press, 2001), pp. 235–262.

32. "Daughters of the Blues: Women, Race, and Class Representation in Rap Music Performance," from *Rap Music and Street Consciousness,* Copyright 2002 by the Board of Trustees of the University of Illinois. Used with permission of the University of Illinois Press.

33. "Media Interventions," from *Right to Rock,* by Maureen Mahon (Durham, NC: Duke University Press, 2004), pp. 176–203.

34. "Black Artistic Invisibility: A Black Composer Talking 'bout Taking Care of the Souls of Black Folks While Losing Much Ground Fast," from *Black Notes: Essays of a Musician Writing in a Post-Album Age,* by William Banfield (Lanham, MD: Scarecrow Press, 2004), pp. 121–128.

35. From Soulstepping: African American Step Shows. Copyright 2003 by the Board of Trustees of the University of Illinois. Used with permission of the University of Illinois Press.

36. "Rhythm and Bullshit? The Slow Decline of R&B," by Mark Anthony Neal, retrieved in June 2005 from PopMatters.com.

INDEX

81 Theater (Atlanta), 112

accordion, 51, 54
Adams, Berle, 158–164
African American fraternities and sororities, 342–52
Afro-American Symphony, 138–39, 334, 341
"Ain't Misbehavin'," 125–26
Ali, Mohamed, 240, 244
"All Coons Look Alike to Me," 68
All Hail the Queen, 300
American Sound Studios, 206
Ancelet, Barry, 224, 228, 232–34
Anderson, J.T., 336
Anderson, Marian, 100, 131, 148–53
Apollo Record Company, 181
Apollo Theater, 157, 178, 231, 261, 272
Ardion, Alphonse "Bois-sec," 222, 224, 228
Ardion, Amede, 224
Arhoolie Record Company, 225, 227
Armstrong, Louis, 33, 43, 79, 86, 87, 125–26, 167, 172, 247, 253
Atco Record Company, 210
Atlanta, GA, 110–114, 179, 307, 321, 336, 367
Atlantic Records, 210–19, 285, 359
authenticity (in hip hop), 288
Axton, Estelle, 202–3, 211, 217–18

Bad Brains, 314, 319, 328
Ballad for Americans, 101, 104
banjo songs, 16–21
Basie, Count, 102, 125, 172, 250
Beatles, The, 238–39
Beck, Elder, 166–68
Big Punisher, 289–91
Billboard (magazine), 156, 158, 178, 182, 209–11, 320
Birmingham, AL, 8, 179
Birth of the Cool, The, 239, 249
Bitches Brew, 239, 244–45, 249–50
Black & White Record Company, 172
Black Entertainment Television (BET), 317, 328–330, 335, 365
Black Noise, 335
Black Rock Coalition (BRC), 314–331
Black Swan Record Company, 116, 132

Blacker Than That, 316–19, 321–22
Blige, Mary J., 336, 358, 361, 363–64, 366, 371
Blue Bird Record Company, 167
BMI, 158
Bolden, Buddy "King," 34–35, 46
"Bon Ton Roula" 221, 226
Booker T. and the MGs, 201, 209
Bootsy's Rubber Band, 269–70, 272
"Bootzilla," 272
Boyer, Horace, 173–74, 177
BRC Record Company, 317–332
breakin', 276–81
Brewster, Rev. Herbert Walker, 174, 176
Broadside, 189
Brown, Eddie "Bongo" 197
Brown, James, 176, 182, 185, 215, 245, 264, 266, 270, 275, 361
Brown, Lawrence, 98–102
Brunswick Record Company, 119
"Buddy Bolden Blues," 34
Burleigh, Harry, 66–67, 81, 97, 99–100, 119

"Cake Walking Babies from Home," 88
Caldonia (Boogie), 158–60
Calloway, Cab, 124, 155, 169
Campbell, Lucie, 174, 176
Capitol Records, 158, 273
Carawan, Candie & Guy, 192
Carr, Leroy, 171
Casablanca Record Company, 266–67, 270–72
Casey, Al, 127
"Change Is Gonna Come, A," 209
Chapel Hill, NC, 190–91
Charles, Ray, 184, 232, 252, 367
Chavis, Boozoo, 221
Chenier, CJ, 234–35
Chenier, Cleveland, 226
Chenier, Clifton, 221–36
Chess Record Company, 212, 231
Chicago, IL, 2, 9–10, 19, 40, 42, 46, 75, 78, 81, 106, 113–121, 128, 137, 155, 157–58, 160–61, 172, 175, 178, 246
"Chocolate City," 267, 275
Chronic, The, 268

Cincinnati, OH, 2
Civil Rights Movement, 188–92
Clear Channel Communication, 357–58, 364–65
Clinton, George, 260–75, 319
Clones of Dr. Funkenstein, 269
Clorindy, or the Origins of the Cakewalk, 68, 70, 72
"Cloud Nine," 194, 198–200
Cocas Brovas, 289–90
Cole, Bob, 63, 65–68, 70, 82
Coleman, Bill, 127
Collins, Bootsy, 266–70, 319
Colored Sacred Harp, The, 90, 93–94
Coltrane, John, 238–39, 246–47, 250
Columbia Record Company, 3, 102–03, 116, 169, 171, 239, 243, 273, 286, 336, 357–60, 366
Comet Record Company, 169–70
Constitution Hall (Washington, D.C.), 148–53
Cook, Will Marion, 42, 63, 66–72, 80–84, 97, 102, 259, 333
Cooke, Sam, 209, 215–16, 231
Cosmic Slop, 265
Cotton Club, 176
Covay, Don, 213–14
Cox, Ida, 169, 170, 298
"Crazy Blues," 115
Cropper, Steve, 209, 213–14

Da Brat, 307–08
dance steps, early (waltz, two-step, Grizzly Bear, etc.), 36–37, 45–47, 57–59
Darker America, 136, 138
Davis, Anthony, 333, 337–38
Davis, Clive, 358–60, 366
Davis, Miles, 237–53
Decca Records, 155, 157–59, 163, 167
"Deep River," 99–100
Detroit, MI, 10, 157, 160–62, 194–200, 240, 262, 306, 321, 343
DeVaughn, Raheem, 371
Dixie to Broadway, 132
Djing, 279–81
Dr. Dre, 268, 363
Domino, Fats, 226
Dorsey, Rev. Thomas, 106–122, 173–74, 176–77
Dowd, Tom, 208–09, 216
Downbeat (magazine), 157–58, 162
Du Bois, W.E.B., 107, 111, 131, 133–37, 139, 142, 244, 264
Dunbar, Paul Lawrence, 64, 67, 80, 138
Dunham Jubilee Singers, 8

Dupsie, Rockin', 235
Dural, Stanley "Buckwheat," 235

Eagle Records, 166
Elko Record Company, 230
Ellington, Duke, 75, 125, 131, 163–64, 238, 247, 250, 255–59, 340, 344
Elliott, Missy, 305, 368
Europe, James Reese, 95–99, 339
Evans, Faith, 371
Evans, Gil, 237, 249–50

Fairfield Four, 177–79
Famous Hokum Boys, 120
field holler, 52
Fisk (University) Jubilee Singers, 1, 13, 26–27, 41, 99
Fitzgerald, Ella, 163
"Flashlight," 271–72
"Fly Girl, A," 303
Fontenot, Conray, 222, 225, 228
Foxy Brown, 308
Franklin, Aretha, 173, 182–83, 185
free jazz, 23
freestyle (rapping), 284–85, 291
frottoir, 224, 225, 235
Fulbright, J.R., 230
Fulson, Lowell, 231
Funk Brothers, 198
Funkadelic, 203
"Funkafied," 308
Future of Music Coalition, 363–64, 367

"G.I. Jive," 155
gangster rap, 23
Gaye, Marvin, 203
Gillespie, Dizzy, 124, 169, 172, 206, 247, 253
"Give Up the Funk (Tear the Roof Off the Sucker)," 268–69
"Go Down, Moses," 100
"Goin' Down Town," 20
Gold Star Record Company, 232
Golden Gate Quartet, 52, 176–78, 204
Goldwax Record Company, 207
Goodman, Benny, 87
Gordon, Michael, 344
Gordy, Barry, Jr, 202, 262
"Gospel Train," 151
Got the South in My Soul," 102
Gottschalk, Louis M., 36
Graceland, 235
graffiti, 279–82

Green, Al, 185
"Green Onions," 202
Griffith, Johnny, 196
griot, 16
gumboot dancing, 344–46

Hammer, M.C., 173, 185
Hampton, Lionel, 251–52
Hampton Institution, 13, 181
Handy, W.C., 132, 138, 140
Harlem Renaissance, 130–38, 141–44
Harpo, Slim, 232
Hawkins, Edwin Singers, 175
Hawkins, Screamin' Jay, 184
Hayes, Isaac, 203–10, 212, 217–18
Hayes, Roland, 100–101, 131
Hazel, Eddie, 263–66
Hearn, Lafcadio, 38–40, 42
Henderson, Fletcher, 126
History of Our Future, The, 317–19
Hogan, Ernest, 63, 67–69, 80
"Honeysuckle Rose," 125, 128
Hooker, Earl, 230
Hot Buttered Soul, 203
Hot Chocolate, 126
Houston, TX, 7, 51, 227
Hughes, Langston, 129–32, 137–38, 140, 143
Hurok, Sol, 148–49
Hurston, Zora Neale, 130–31, 137

"I Sing Because I'm Happy," 166
I've Been Lovin' You Too Long," 201, 211
"If You See My Savior," 120
In Dahomey, 70, 72, 83
"In the Midnight Hour," 214
"In Zanzibar," 97
Indianapolis, IN, 14
Isley Brothers, 181, 183
"It's Tight Like That," 108, 120

Jackson, "Judge," 90, 03
Jackson, Mahalia, 176–78, 180, 183
Jammerson, James, 194–96, 199
Jarrett, Keith, 238
"Jawbone," 56
Jefferson, Blind Lemon, 51, 171
"Jelly Roll Blues," 78–79
"John Henry," 20, 86
Johnson, J. Rosamond, 65–67, 82, 102
Johnson, Jack, 243–44
Johnson, James P., 123–27

Johnson, James Weldon, 65–67, 82, 130–31, 149
Jones, Quincy, 238, 250
Jordan, Louis, 155–165, 226, 358
Jotis Record Company, 210
jure, 223

Kaye, Bernie, 315, 327–28
Kid Frost, 276, 285, 286
Kind of Blue, 238, 244, 249
King, B.B., 226, 228
Kmen, Henry, 35–36

la-la, 223–25
Lamond, George, 284–85
Left Eye (TLC), 304
Levee Land, 137
Library of Congress, 51, 54, 60, 75
Lil Kim, 308
Lipscomb, Mance 56
Little Richard, 230
"Livery Stable Blues," 34
Living Color, 323, 325
Locke, Alain, 130, 132–37, 139–40, 143–44, 248
Louisiana Life, 222–23
Love Supreme, A, 246

Mack, Bruce, 318, 321
Macy's Record Company, 221
"Maggot Brain," 264–65, 272
Magic Sam, 228
Malaco Record Company, 178, 360
Malcolm X, 337
"Maple Leaf Rag," 78
Martin, Roberta (Singers), 174, 177, 183, 185
MC Lyte, 298, 299, 306–07
McAdoo, Orpheus, 13, 14, 345
McComb, Frank, 370
McCormick, Mack, 227
McGhee, Brownie, 52
McGinty, Artiebelle, 85–89
MCing, 278–80, 283, 287, 299–301
Meditation Singers, 177–78
Memphis, TN, 137–38, 159, 201–219
Metronome (magazine), 37–38
"Midnight Hour," 213
"Milestones," 248
Miller, Jay, 232
Miller, Rod & Melva, 326–27
Minstrel Shows, 6–12, 17–19, 28–29, 76, 85–89, 346
Mint Condition, 371–72
Mr. Load of Koal, 72

"Mr. Pitiful," 208–09
Mitchell's Christian Singers, 176–78
Modern Jazz Quartet, 238
"Molly Put the Kettle On," 20
Moman, Chip, 206–07, 217
Monk, Thelonious, 125, 239, 247
"Mood Indigo," 256, 258
Moore, Monette, 116
Moore, Sam, 215–19
Morris, Kenneth, 176
Morton, Jelly Roll, 33–34, 75–79, 250
Mothership Connection, 267–68
Motown, 194–200, 202, 219, 262, 359, 361, 370
MTV, 315, 327–30, 362, 365
"My Ragtime Lady," 25

Nashboro Record Company, 181
Nashville, TN, 2, 179
Negro Songs of Protest, 102
Network BRC, 317, 326–29
New Orleans, LA, 6, 7, 10–11, 33–44, 75–86–88, 96–97, 137, 163, 222
New Orleans Jazz & Heritage Festival, 236
New York City, 7, 40, 51, 63–72, 75, 79, 95, 98–100, 128, 137, 155, 157, 161–63, 172, 176, 234, 240, 257, 272, 277–92, 304, 316, 320–21, 329, 339, 357, 365–66
Newport Jazz Festival, 176–77

Off the Wall, 362
OKeh Records, 115–116, 126
"Ol' Man River," 101, 103–04
"Old Black Joe," 14, 29, 104
"Old Joe Clark," 20
Oliver, "King," 32, 86, 116
"One Nation Under a Groove," 272
Original Dixieland Jazz Band, 33–34, 47, 79
Orioles, 181
Otis Blue, 208–10

P-Funk Mob (Parliament-Funkadelic), 260–75, 316, 319–20, 324, 359
Panda, Andy, 284–85
"Paper Thing," 307
Paramount Records, 86–88, 117
Parker, Charlie, 239, 245–47, 253
Patterson, Rahsaan, 369
Peacock Record Company, 181
Perez, Manuel, 44–45
Philadelphia Internal Record Company, 359–60

Phillips, Sam, 211
Pickett, Wilson, 183, 212–14, 362
Pittsburgh, PA, 166–68
"Po' Howard," 55
Porter, David, 201, 203, 207, 217–19
"Porter's Love Song to a Chambermaid, A," 126
Powell, Bud, 125
Prater, David, 216–19
Presley, Elvis, 184
Public Enemy, 281–82

Q-Unique, 277–78
Queen Latifah, 298, 299–302, 306
Queen Pen, 309–10

ragtime, 23–24, 38, 41, 78, 81
Rainey, Gertrude "Ma," 85–89, 117, 137, 171, 298–99
Raleigh, NC, 188–92
"Rapper's Delight," 281
Rawls, Lou, 173–74, 181
Razaf, Andy, 123, 125
Real Roxanne, The, 281
"Reconsider, Baby," 231
"Reconversion Blues," 163
Record Changer, The, 166, 169
Redding, Otis, 183, 201, 204–10, 361
Reese, Della, 177–78
Reid, Vernon, 322, 324
"Respect," 208, 213
Richard, Zachary, 228
Riley, Teddy, 362
ring shout, 236–38
Roberson, Eric, 370
Roberts, Dink, 15, 16, 19–21
Roberts, Lucky, 123–24
Robeson, Paul, 98–104, 131, 242
Robinson, Smokey, 183
Robinson, Sugar Ray, 240–43
Rock Steady Crew, 277
Rodgers, Carmen, 372
"Roll, Jordan, Roll," 29
Rolling Stones, 227
Roosevelt, Mrs. Eleanor, 149, 152–53
Ross, Diana, 183
Ruffin, David, 195–96
Rufus Rastas, 68
Run DMC, 274, 282, 362–64
Russell, William, 39, 46

St. Augustine's College, 190, 192
St. Cyr, Johnny, 35

St. Louis, Ill, 149, 237, 246, 321, 338
"St. Louis Blues," 102
Sacred Harp, The, 90–91, 107
Salt-n-Pepa, 30–4, 306
"Satisfaction," 209
Saul, Jimmy, 318–19, 325
Savoy Record Company, 181–82, 218
Schuller, Gunther, 257
"See, See Rider," 86–87
Shante, Roxanne, 298, 299, 305–06
shape note singing, 90–94, 107, 109
Shaw University, 188, 190, 192
Shepard, Ella, 1, 2, 4, 5
Shoo-Fly Regiment, The, 67
Shuffle Along, 131–32
"Sign of Judgment, The," 93
Simon, Paul, 235
Sing Out, 189
Sister Souljah, 302
"Sittin' on the Dock of the Bay," 208
Smith, Bessie, 86, 116, 126, 131, 137, 171, 298
Smith, Mamie, 115–116
Smith, Willie "The Lion," 123–24, 126–27
Snipes, John, 16
"So What," 248
"Soldier's Joy," 21
"Somebody's Been Using That Thing," 120
Sony BMG, 367
sookey jump (dance), 51, 55–56
Sophisticated Ladies, 256
"Soul Man," 203, 213
Southern, Eileen, 131
southern soul music, 359
Specialty Record Company, 181, 230–31
Spitzer, Nick, 224, 228–29
"Stack O'Lee Blues," 86
Standing on the Verge of Gettin' It On, 265–66
Staton, Candi, 182, 185
Stax Records, 201–219, 369–60
Step Afrika, 342, 345, 353
step show & steppin', 342–53
Stewart, Jim, 201–202, 208, 211–14, 217
Still, William Grant, 104, 129–44, 333–34, 339
"Still Not a Player," 291
Stone, Henry, 214–16
Strackwitz, Chris, 227–28, 232–33
"Strange Vibrations from the Hardcore," 322
Strayhorn, Billy, 259
Study of the Soul Music Environment, A, 357–58

Sugarhill Gang, 279
Sugarhill Record Company, 279
Summers, Donna, 182
Supremes, The, 202
"Sweet Soul Music," 210
"Swing Low, Sweet Chariot," 29
Symphony in G, 138–39

"Take the A Train," 259
Talented Tenth, 134–35, 142
Tampa Red (Hudson Whitaker), 120
Tate, Greg, 317–19, 322, 330
Taylor, Johnnie, 215
Taylor, Lewis, 369
Teen Tones, 2–5
Telecommunications Reform Act of 1996, 364–65, 367
Temptations, The, 195
Terry, Sonny, 52
Tharpe, Sister Rosetta, 167, 172, 176–77, 179, 181, 339
Thomas, Rufus, 201, 205, 217
Thompson, Odell, 16
Thompson, Robert Farris, 347–48, 351
Thriller, 246
Tipitina's, 222
Tribe Called Quest, A, 289
Trip to Coontown, A, 66
T.O.B.A., 85
Tom Joyner Morning Show, 365–66
Total Eclipse, 315, 326–27
"Trampin'," 151
Tympany Five (Louis Jordan's), 155–65

Universal Music Group, 364
Uptown Record Company, 362–63

Van Dyke, Earl, 196
Vandross, Luther, 361, 369
Vaudeville, 6, 85–89, 95
Vee-Jay Record Company, 181
Victor Talking Machine Company (RCA Victor), 95, 126, 128, 159
Virgin Record Company, 286
Volt Record Company, 207–8

Walden, Phil, 207, 209–10
Walker, Albertina, 173, 182–83, 214
Walker, George, 63, 71–72, 82–83
Walker, T-Bone, 169–72
Waller, Fats, 123–28

Ward, Clara (Ward Singers), 177–78, 182, 183
Warner Brothers Record Company, 273
Washington, Dinah, 125, 181, 183, 246
Washington, Todd, 325–28
Washington, D.C., 51, 54, 60, 75, 81, 84, 95, 148–53, 160, 314, 319
"Water Boy," 103
Waters, Muddy, 228, 231
WBAI, 322
WDIA, 204, 208
"We Are Climbing Jacob's Ladder," 100
"We Are Soldiers," 190–91
"We Shall Overcome," 188, 191
WEA, 367
WEDR, 179
WERD, 179
Westbound Record Company, 262, 274
Wexler, Jerry, 209–14, 367
What's the 411?, 362
White, George, 1, 2, 26–27,
White, Josh, 172
Whitfield, Norman, 198–200
"Who Stole the Lock (From the Henhouse Door)," 8
Wilberforce University, 4

William Ransom Hogan Jazz Archive (Tulane University), 39, 42
Williams, Bert, 63, 65, 71–72, 82, 123, 259
Williams, Deniece, 183, 185–86
Williams, Dewey, 91
Willis, Eddie, 196–97
Winans Family, 186
WJJD, 179
WKOK, 179
WLAC, 179
WLIB, 321
Wonder, Stevie, 203, 320
Worrell, Bernie, 263–8, 319
WQHT, 365
Wright, Javon, 369–70
WRKS, 366
Wu-Tang Clan, 289
WVON, 175

Yardbirds, The, 227
Yo-Yo, 304–6
"You Can't Lose Me-Cholly," 58

zydeco, 90, 221–36
Zynn Record Company, 232